NAVAL WAR COLLEGE
NEWPORT, RHODE ISLAND

INTERNATIONAL LAW
STUDIES

THE LAW OF WAR AND NEUTRALITY AT SEA

by

Robert W. Tucker
The Johns Hopkins University
Consultant, Naval War College

1955
NAVPERS 15031
Volume XLX

THE LAWBOOK EXCHANGE, LTD.
Clark, New Jersey

ISBN 978-1-58477-582-9

Lawbook Exchange edition 2006, 2022

The quality of this reprint is equivalent to the quality of the original work.

THE LAWBOOK EXCHANGE, LTD.
33 Terminal Avenue
Clark, New Jersey 07066-1321

Please see our website for a selection of our other publications and fine facsimile reprints of classic works of legal history:
www.lawbookexchange.com

Library of Congress Cataloging-in-Publication Data

Tucker, Robert W.
The law of war and neutrality at sea / Robert W. Tucker.
p. cm.
Originally published: Washington : U.S. Govt. Print. Off., 1957. (International law studies ; v. 50).
Includes bibliographical references and index.
ISBN 1-58477-582-3 (alk. paper)
1. War, Maritime (International law) 2. Neutrality. 3. Neutral trade with belligerents. I. Title. II. Series: International law studies ; v. 50.
JX1295.U4 vol. 50a
[KZ6563]
341 s--dc22
[341.6'3]

2004030207

Printed in the United States of America on acid-free paper

NAVAL WAR COLLEGE
NEWPORT, RHODE ISLAND

INTERNATIONAL LAW
STUDIES

THE LAW OF WAR AND NEUTRALITY AT SEA

by

Robert W. Tucker

The Johns Hopkins University
Consultant, Naval War College

1955

NAVPERS 15031

Volume XLX

UNITED STATES
GOVERNMENT PRINTING OFFICE
WASHINGTON : 1957

For sale by the Superintendent of Documents, U. S. Government Printing Office
Washington 25, D. C. - Price $2.25

FOREWORD

Any inquiry into the present status of the law of war and neutrality at sea is confronted with the difficult task of seeking to evaluate the cumulative effect of two World Wars upon the so-called "traditional law." It has become abundantly clear that it is no longer possible to look upon the events that followed the outbreak of hostilities in 1914 and in 1939 as little more than one long manifestation of "lawlessness" on the part of belligerents (and, during World War II, of neutrals as well). Yet it would appear only slightly less misplaced to accept indiscriminately these same events as "law creating" in character. But where to draw the line in each concrete instance between belligerent behavior that has succeeded in replacing the traditional law and behavior that remains unlawful is a problem that frequently seems almost insoluble. It may well be asserted that the continued validity of law is dependent upon at least a minimum degree of effectiveness, and that this relationship between validity and effectiveness is particularly compelling with respect to the rules regulating the conduct of war. However, as will be seen, there is a deceptive simplicity about the test of effectiveness when stated in general terms that becomes fully apparent only when applied to concrete cases. Whatever its intrinsic utility, this test must encounter serious obstacles in the course of its application.

Nor can these obstacles be readily surmounted by an analysis which intends to lay bare the developments that have led belligerents in this century apparently to abandon so many of the restraints they had formerly accepted. It is one thing to inquire into the causes of state behavior and quite another thing to determine whether or not this behavior has actually resulted in invalidating a given rule—or rules. There is the further consideration that even as an instrument for prediction an inquiry into the determinants of belligerent behavior is not without grave pitfalls. No satisfactory method has been devised that would enable the observer to distinguish accurately between developments of a merely transient nature and developments that may rightly be regarded as irreversible. Of course, developments in technology may be considered as irreversible. However, the recurrence of total war in the twentieth century is not primarily the result of technological advance—though this advance has contributed greatly to the ease by which total war may be waged—but rather of social and political developments. The latter are the product of human interests and as such are rarely—if indeed ever—irreversible. It is for this reason that the possibility cannot be excluded that men might once again find it in their common interests to return to a form of limited warfare, to wars that are limited not only in the number of participants and in the purposes for which they are fought but also in the weapons and methods that are employed against an opponent. Admittedly, this possibility depends upon a certain optimism that men may learn something from past experience, and over this one cannot be at all certain.

It should be made quite clear, therefore, that as matters presently stand no writer can hope to speak on the law of naval warfare with the assurance and precision that readers might expect. Although this fact cannot fail to be a source of dissatisfaction, it ought not to serve as a deterrent against emphasizing those areas of the traditional law in which a substantial measure of uncertainty prevails. In the present study the attempt has been made to provide such emphasis. While the traditional law generally has been maintained as the starting point for further discussion, the attention of the reader is directed principally to the recent period and to the numerous problems which this period has raised.[1]

The broad survey that is undertaken in the following pages of this volume lays no claim to completeness even in what it does attempt to do. It is particularly limited in two respects, however, and these limitations perhaps require some explanatory remarks.

In the first instance, no effort has been directed towards providing a detailed analysis of recent prize decisions, although the rules determining both the substantive grounds for capture and the procedure of visit, search, and capture have been adequately reviewed. In defense of this omission it may be pointed out that the second World War added very little in the way of substantive developments to the law of prize. Almost all of the important—and still disputed—developments in prize law that have occurred since the nineteenth century resulted from the events of World War I, and they have received thorough treatment in a number of competent monographs. The prize cases resulting from World War II were concerned—for the most part—either with refining further the substantive grounds for capture or with developing rules of a largely procedural character. They are, therefore, quite technical in character and their exposition in a general survey of the conduct of maritime war would have little, if any, place. It is also worthy of note that World War II witnessed a clearly discernible shift away from the former emphasis upon prize court adjudication toward more flexible and less time-consuming methods of

[1] In this connection it may be noted that the contemporary challenge to the traditional system is not solely the result of persistent belligerent—and neutral—departures from rules once quite effective. In part this challenge is also a consequence of the change that has occurred in the legal position of war itself, particularly as a result of the Charter of the United Nations. For this reason it has appeared desirable to treat at some length the problem of the effects that the change in the legal position of war may have upon the operation of the law regulating war's conduct.

disposing of vessels and cargoes seized as prize. The results frequently have been to the mutual advantage of belligerent and neutral. Finally, mention must be made of the fact that the courts of the United States have made no contribution in this century to the law of prize.

The second limitation relates to the material to be found in the notes. No attempt has been made to give extensive bibliographical references in support of, or relating to, points discussed in the test. Instead, the references given are selective and have been chosen either for illustrative purposes or because they are considered to represent a point of view thought to bear some significance. Wherever possible, care has been exercised to choose the more recent materials (whether documents, general treatises or articles), though here again the careful reader may observe some omissions. It is always tempting for a writer to believe that there is a definite logic to, and a readily apparent consistency in, the materials he has chosen to cite. Unfortunately, this is only rarely the case, and what is readily apparent to the writer is seldom altogether obvious even to the sympathetic reader. What may be said of the notes in the present study is that while a good deal of license has been taken with them they have been designed to be of immediate use and interest to the reader.

There is one "source material" frequently referred to in the notes that deserves special mention. In the appendix to this volume the official United States Navy manual entitled *Law of Naval Warfare* has been reproduced. Issued in 1955 by the Chief of Naval Operations, this manual is prepared for the information and guidance of the naval service. In the preparation of this latest manual the Naval War College once again performed a task it has undertaken on several occasions over the past half century.

It is a pleasant duty to acknowledge the assistance I received in the preparation of this volume. Professor Josef L. Kunz and Professor Julius Stone were kind enough to read the manuscript and to offer helpful suggestions and needed criticism. Appreciation must also be expressed to Miss Barbara Johnson, Mr. Michael Jaworskj and Mr. Arnold Simkin for their willing performance of various essential tasks.

I am particularly indebted to Rear Admiral Thomas H. Robbins, Jr., President of the Naval War College, whose wise and understanding assistance has been of the greatest value.

PREFACE

The publication of this series was inaugurated by the Naval War College in 1894. This is the fiftieth volume in the series as numbered for index purposes. The titles have varied slightly from year to year. The preceding volume is entitled "*International Law Studies, 1954*, Collective Security under International Law," by Professor Hans Kelsen.

The Naval War College has maintained a continuing interest in the law of war and neutrality at sea. The present volume, prepared by Professor Robert W. Tucker, is the first complete study of the subject undertaken by the Naval War College since the Second World War.

The opinions expressed in this volume are not necessarily those of the U. S. Navy or the Naval War College.

THOMAS H. ROBBINS, JR.
Rear Admiral, United States Navy,
President, Naval War College.

NEWPORT, 1 DECEMBER 1956.

TABLE OF CONTENTS

PART TWO

APPENDIX: LAW OF NAVAL WARFARE

Chapter

Chapter | Page

Chapter

PART ONE

I. WAR AND THE LAW OF WAR

A. THE LEGAL POSITION OF WAR AND THE OPERATION OF THE LAW OF WAR: GENERAL CONSIDERATIONS

The problem of assessing the present state of that body of law serving to regulate the conduct of war is, in part, the result of recent changes in the international legal system, and particularly in the legal position of war itself. According to the generally accepted traditional theory the act of resorting to war was interpreted, save in exceptional circumstances, as being neither legal nor illegal, but simply a fact, situation or event which occurred periodically in the relations among states.[1] International law took cognizance of this event mainly through the provision of rules, the law of war and neutrality, designed to regulate the conduct of states once war did occur.

States actively participating in a war were therefore considered as possessing equal legal status as far as the war itself was concerned, this equality of legal status being the logical result of the purported liberty states had under customary international law to resort to war. In addition, the duties imposed and the rights conferred upon states participating in war presupposed a similar equality of legal status in the conduct of war. It also followed that the effects of war, territorial or otherwise, as registered principally through treaties of peace, created no special problems with respect to their validity. Finally, those states not choosing to participate in a war were governed, in their relations with the belligerents, by a special

[1] Not infrequently the resort to war was considered by writers to be "extra-legal," much as an event occurring in nature (e. g., an earthquake or flood) can be extra-legal. See A. D. McNair, "Collective Security," *British Yearbook of International Law* (cited throughout as *B. Y. I. L.*), 17 (1936), p. 152. The act of resorting to war can hardly be considered a natural event, however. It is, most thoroughly, a social action, and as such must be regarded as being either legal or illegal, as being either permitted or forbidden. Of course, it is not infrequent that an act may be permitted in a negative sense; though not specifically authorized by law, it is not legally forbidden since the law does not attach a sanction to the commission of the act. In the latter instance the act must be regarded as legal, and this would seem to be the correct explanation of the "extra-legal" interpretation of war. Thus Julius Stone states that: "Customary international law, indeed, does not even regulate *the occasions* on which extreme private force (i. e., war) may be resorted to by States *inter se*. Resort to war was neither legal nor illegal; international law suffered, as it were, a kind of blackout while the choice of peace or war was being made." *Legal Controls of International Conflict* (1954), p. 297. Later, however, Professor Stone speaks of the "liberty of States to resort to war under customary international law" (p. 303).

399334—57——2

set of rules, whose principal purpose was to insure the strict impartiality of the non-participants in their behavior toward the belligerents.

It is unnecessary for present purposes to discuss or to criticize in any detail this traditional interpretation of war. Despite the fact that its acceptance made very doubtful the legal character of this so-called system of law, it was by no means an inaccurate reflection of the actual practices of states. However, the developments effected principally by the Covenant of the League of Nations, the General Treaty For the Renunciation of War (Kellogg-Briand Pact), and the Charter of the United Nations have resulted in the general abandonment of this traditional interpretation of war. For all three instruments are characterized by the distinction they make between a legal and an illegal resort to war. Indeed, the Charter of the United Nations goes much further than did the Covenant and the Kellogg-Briand Pact in avoiding altogether the use of the term "war." The Charter attempts to ensure—mainly through Article 2, paragraph 4[2]—that a distinction shall henceforth be made between the lawful and the unlawful resort to armed force. In principle, then, it is now possible to assert that the place of war in the international legal order has undergone a fundamental change. The resort to war can no longer be regarded as an act which states are at liberty to take for whatever reason they may deem proper.[3]

As a result of this general transformation in the legal position of war the question has been raised as to whether it is correct to assume the continued validity of the law that traditionally has served to regulate the conduct of war. Insofar as belligerents are no longer to be regarded as legally equal with respect to the act of initiating a war, and the resort to war is no longer a matter of indifference to the international legal order, then it would appear to some as contrary to principle to continue to assume equality with respect to the duties imposed and the rights conferred upon belligerents in the actual conduct of war. The suggestion has therefore been made that in a war waged unlawfully by one side, and particularly a war that assumes the character of a United Nations' enforcement action, the traditional law regulating inter-belligerent relations must be considered as substantially modified in its operation.[4]

The contention that the rules regulating inter-belligerent relations are no longer wholly operative when one side is waging an unlawful war is frequently based upon an application of the principle—assumed to be a

[2] Article 2, paragraph 4: "All members shall refrain in their international relations from the threat or use of force against the territorial integrity or political independence of any state, or in any other manner inconsistent with the Purposes of the United Nations."

[3] For further reflections on the nature of this change in the legal position of war—particularly in relation to the present status of neutrality—see pp. 165-71.

[4] A quite different problem concerns the effects of the changed legal position of war, and the obligations incurred by states within a system of collective security, upon the institution of neutrality, especially if this institution is characterized by the principle of strict impartiality. See pp. 171-80 for an analysis of these and related problems.

principle of positive international law—*ex injuria jus non oritur*. Illegal acts cannot become a source of new legal rights beneficial to the wrongdoer. Yet if illegal acts may not serve to establish new legal rights intended by or beneficial to the wrongdoer, how then is it possible for a state, consistently with this principle, to acquire by virtue of its illegal acts those rights that have customarily accompanied belligerent status? The view that *ex injuria jus non oritur* is an inescapable principle of every legal order has led to the conclusion that a state "cannot acquire new powers under international law by illegal action; consequently a state which is illegally engaged in hostilities acquires no belligerent powers."[5]

At the same time there has been an understandable reluctance to press this argument to its logical conclusion, since it is recognized that a rigid reliance upon the principle *ex injuria jus non oritur* would have undesirable consequences. "In relation to the applicability of rules of warfare to the belligerent engaging in an unlawful war rigid reliance on that principle (i. e., *ex injuria jus non oritur*) would mean in practice that rules of war do not apply at all in a war of this nature. For, unless the aggressor has been defeated from the very outset . . . it is impossible to visualize the conduct of hostilities in which one side would be bound by rules of warfare without benefiting from them and the other side would benefit from rules of warfare without being bound by them. Accordingly, any application to the actual conduct of war of the principle *ex injuria jus non oritur* would transform the contest into a struggle which may be subject to no regulation at all. The result would be the abandonment of most rules of warfare, including those which are of a humanitarian character." [6]

---

[5] Quincy Wright, "The Outlawry of War and The Law of War," *American Journal of International Law* (cited throughout as *A. J. I. L.*), 47 (1953), pp. 370–1. Articles 2 and 3 of *Harvard Research in International Law, Draft Convention on Rights and Duties of States in Case of Aggression* (*A. J. I. L.*, 33 (1939), *Supp.* p. 828) read:

"*Article 2.* By becoming an aggressor, a state does not acquire rights or relieve itself of duties.

Article 3. (1) Subject to Article 14, an aggressor does not have any of the rights which it would have if it were a belligerent. Titles to property are not affected by an aggressor's purported exercise of such rights. (2) An aggressor has the duties which it would have if it were a belligerent."

It should be noted that whereas the preceding draft articles constitute no more than a statement *de lege ferenda*, Professor Wright offers his opinion as one representative of the existing law. And for a quite recent—and influential—view leaning toward the discriminatory character of the laws of war in an unlawful war, see "La Revision du Droit de la Guerre" (Institut de Droit International, Rapport des Trois—Francois, Coudert, Lauterpacht), *Annuaire de l'Institut de Droit International*, 45 (1954), I, p. 555.

[6] H. Lauterpacht, "The Limits of the Operation of the Law of War," *B. Y. I. L.*, 30 (1953), p. 212. Nevertheless, Sir Hersch Lauterpacht has consistently expressed the conviction that the equal application of the law of war in an unlawful war represents a deviation from principle, justified largely out of humanitarian considerations. See, for example, Oppenheim-Lauterpacht, *International Law* (7th. ed., 1952), vol. II, pp. 217–22.—In a recent survey of the problem, Professor J. L. Kunz ("The Laws of War," *A. J. I. L.*, 50 (1956), pp. 317–21) has pointed out

In fact, a strict reliance upon the principle *ex injuria jus non oritur* presumably would imply that all acts of killing and destruction performed by the armed forces of a state that has resorted unlawfully to war would be equally unlawful and would thereby render the authors of such acts liable to appropriate punishment. The well known phrase in the Charter of the International Military Tribunal at Nuremberg, defining as a crime against peace the "waging of a war of aggression," would then become literally true.[7]

Hence, for humanitarian reasons alone there has been a marked reticence to contend that the full consequences of the principle *ex injuria jus non oritur* must be drawn in the case of a state waging an unlawful war. Instead, suggestions have been made that a distinction be drawn between the rules of warfare which bear a humanitarian character, particularly the rules relating to the treatment of victims of war, and other rules relating to the actual conduct of hostilities, only the former being considered equally applicable to all belligerents despite the fact that one side has resorted to war in violation of its international obligations. But whatever the specific consequences—and concessions to principle—drawn from the application of *ex injuria jus non oritur*, it is clear that the common premise underlying these varying consequences deserves a more careful consideration. For once the "inescapable" quality of this principle is granted its application becomes largely a matter of discretion; its limitation will depend upon the concessions made by those states waging war against an aggressor, concessions made either for humanitarian reasons or for reasons of expediency.

As already noted, the meaning of the principle *ex injuria jus non oritur* is that a violation of law may not give rise to a new legal situation, to new legal rights or duties, intended by or beneficial to the wrongdoer. The

---

that the majority of writers remain opposed to the discriminatory application of the law of war—even though hostilities have been unlawfully initiated by one side. Yet the basis for this continued opposition to any discriminatory application of the law of war rests largely upon practical considerations, and particularly those considerations that emerge from the statement quoted in the text above. Among many writers, however, the feeling persists that continued equal application of the law of war as between an aggressor and his victim is somehow contrary to principle; and this uneasiness mounts in the possible case of United Nations enforcement action bearing the character of war. Hence, one of the principal purposes of the above comments is to attempt to show that the case for discrimination is open to criticism not only on practical grounds but on grounds of principle—or theory—as well.

[7] In their closing addresses before the International Military Tribunal at Nuremberg both the British and French Chief Prosecutors gave expression to this extreme view. The Chief British Prosecutor declared: "The killing of combatants in war is justifiable, both in International and in Municipal law, only where the war itself is legal. But where a war is illegal, as a war started not only in breach of the Pact of Paris but also without any sort of warning or declaration clearly is, there is nothing to justify the killing, and these murders are not to be distinguished from those of any other lawless robber bands." *Nazi Conspiracy and Aggression* (1946), *Supp.* A, pp. 85–6.

rule forbidding theft may not, according to this principle, give rise to ownership. In international law conquest as a method of acquiring territory may not be considered as giving rise to a new legal situation, that is to rights and duties which would otherwise result from the acquisition of territory when undertaken in violation of a rule of international law forbidding conquest.[8]

There are, however, serious restrictions to the operation of this principle in international law. The contention that the unrestricted operation of *ex injuria jus non oritur* constitutes a logical necessity for the very existence of a legal order cannot be maintained. The existence of law does not preclude the possible operation of the contrary principle *ex injuria jus oritur* (or, as some prefer, *ex factis jus oritur*). Illegal acts may give rise to new legal rights intended by or beneficial to the wrongdoer. Of course, within a highly centralized and consequently a very effective legal system the principle *ex injuria jus oritur* will of necessity have a severely restricted operation. The case is quite different in international law.[9] Here, decentralization—the absence of centralized judicial, executive and legislative organs—and a relatively low degree of effectiveness have led to a corresponding restriction of the principle *ex injuria jus non oritur*.[10] A state may violate a rule of either customary or conventional international law, and yet this violation may give rise to a new legal situation beneficial to the wrongdoer. The consequence of an illegal resort to war—or to armed

[8] In this connection, it is necessary to observe that *ex injuria jus non oritur* does not mean, though this has been assumed on occasion, that an illegal act ought not to give rise to a new legal situation the legislator expressly intended to prevent through a rule of positive law. To so maintain would be to impute a tautological meaning to the principle. The legislator whose intention is to prevent a certain behavior does so by attaching a sanction to such behavior. He may also stipulate, however, that certain further consequences are not to follow from this behavior. In international law the resort to force may not only be forbidden under certain circumstances, in the sense that force when resorted to under these circumstances is made the condition of a sanction, but the law may further provide that the illegal use of force ought not to give rise to specific consequences intended by or beneficial to the wrongdoer (e. g., the acquisition of territory). The principle *ex injuria jus non oritur* has no application in this latter instance; it does not forbid what a rule of law already has expressly forbidden. It is of possible application only where the legislator has not expressly stipulated that an illegal act ought not to give rise to consequences intended by or beneficial to the wrongdoer.

[9] In rejecting the argument on behalf of the discriminatory application of the laws of war Professor Kunz (*op. cit.*, p. 318) emphasizes that: "The present primitive state of international law makes any analogy with an advanced municipal law futile. Even a more advanced international law, as a law binding on great groups of men who dispose of power, will be very different from municipal law, which is essentially a law among individuals."

[10] The scope of such restriction will be almost inversely proportional to the effectiveness of a legal system. The less effective a legal system, the greater the restrictions. Up to a certain ill-defined point this condition may be considered compatible with law. Beyond that point all attempts to account for this situation bear the character of a rather strained rationalization of the impossible, that is the attempt to equate law with power. It is for this reason, altogether understandable, that many writers have been so insistent in their emphasis upon the necessity of an unrestricted operation of the principle *ex injuria jus non oritur*.

force—may be the establishment of new legal rights and duties favorable to the wrongdoer. It is quite conceivable that this type of situation may occur under the Charter of the United Nations.[11] It did occur more than once under the Covenant of the League of Nations. Its occurrence under the Covenant did not imply that that instrument had ceased to be valid law. Nor would a similar event mean that the Charter had ceased to be valid. What it does mean is that a violation of a general rule of law may in time give rise to new law—to new legal rights and duties—if the illegal act is successfully consummated. And it will be successfully consummated if, and when, it is no longer effectively contested by other interested states. To contest effectively the illegal act can only mean to deprive the act of some—if not all—of the legal consequences it would otherwise have, had it not originated in a violation of law.[12]

But even if it is assumed that the principle *ex injuria jus non oritur* is operative as against a state waging an unlawful war it does not follow that the aggressor is thereby deprived of the rights traditionally accorded to belligerents for the regulation of the conduct of war. To forbid, in principle, the resort to war—or the resort to armed force—is to prohibit a specific act. The principle *ex injuria jus non oritur* may then have the effect of preventing this illegal act from giving rise to a new legal situation beneficial to the

[11] The prohibition of the use of force under the Charter means, first and foremost, that the illegal use of force is made the condition of a sanction, which includes—though not limited to—the use of force as a lawful reaction. But although the use of force is in principle forbidden under the Charter it does not follow *from that fact alone* that the unlawful use of force may not in time give rise to a situation intended by or beneficial to the wrongdoer. The Charter does not contain a provision expressly prohibiting this possibility. According to the actual provisions of the Charter the Member states are under no obligation to refuse to "recognize" those advantages accruing to a state that has violated (and successfully so) its obligations by resorting to the use of force. It has been asserted that "non-recognition" in this instance is the only reasonable interpretation of the Charter; that we are obliged to infer that under the Charter the unlawful use of force has, in conformity with *ex injuria jus non oritur*, this effect (see, for example, Lauterpacht, *op. cit.*, pp. 208–10). But is this, in fact, the only reasonable interpretation? Do not the virtually unlimited powers accorded the Security Council under the Charter suggest that the Council may decide that the ends of peace and justice—if not law—are best served by recognizing the consequences of an illegal action? And if, which is more probable, the Security Council is unable to function as intended, there is all the more reason for believing that the resort to force—even though unlawful—may give rise to a situation beneficial to the wrongdoer.

[12] See R. W Tucker, "The Principle of Effectiveness in International Law," in *Law and Politics in the World Community* (essays in honor of Hans Kelsen, ed. by George A. Lipsky) (1953), pp. 31–48. The statements made above therefore assert the existence of a rule of effectiveness in international law restricting the operation of *ex injuria jus non oritur*, and that it is through the operation of this rule that an illegal act may, in time, give rise to new legal rights and duties beneficial to the wrongdoer. Properly conceived, there is no essential conflict between this assertion of the operation of a rule of effectiveness, as a rule of positive law, and the general admission by writers that illegal acts may be "validated" through prescription, the consent of the injured party, or by general recognition.

aggressor. More specifically, this may mean that the aggressor is not entitled, though victorious, to legitimize those gains which would otherwise follow from his illegal act. The territory he has temporarily obtained through conquest, the peace treaty he attempts to impose upon the defeated party, and in general those rights he seeks to acquire by virtue of his victory are all *prima facie* deprived of legal validity.[13] But these considerations are quite independent of the assertion, which is here considered as unwarranted, that the same principle *ex injuria jus non oritur* must be interpreted further to mean that *no* legal consequence may result from the illegal act or that *no* legal rights of the wrongdoer may come into operation as a result of the act, legal rights specifically provided by law for just this very contingency.

War—or the resort to armed force—is an action constituting a legal status defined by law. This status consists in bringing into operation certain duties and rights as between the belligerent states. The argument that the unlawful act of resorting to war cannot become the condition for the acquisition of certain rights by the aggressor, rights determined by the law of war, is in principle mistaken. From the fact that the resort to war is, under certain circumstances, illegal, it follows only that the counter-war is, as a sanction, legal. It does not of necessity follow that the duties and rights of belligerents are, as a matter of positive law, different in an unlawful war from what they have been in a lawful war. Nor is it actually the unlawful act *per se* that here becomes the source of right beneficial to the wrongdoer; it is rather a certain status as determined by law which forms the necessary condition for the exercise of certain duties and rights expressly provided for by the law.[14]

Even if it is conceded that the principle *ex injuria jus non oritur* is not necessarily applicable to the relationships between belligerents as determined by the traditional law of war, the conviction nevertheless persists that it is

---

[13] In time, however, this situation may nevertheless give rise, through the operation of the rule of effectiveness, to a new legal situation beneficial to the aggressor. Indeed, so long as the international legal order retains its decentralized and relatively weak character this latter consequence must remain a strong possibility, despite the assumed operation of *ex injuria jus non oritur*.

[14] If the argument dealt with above were really well-founded it would, again in principle, be applicable consistently to any violation of international law It is not difficult, however, to demonstrate that it is not so applicable. The case of reprisals furnishes a convenient example. It is generally agreed that the reprisals an injured state may take against a delinquent state are subject to certain restrictions. Presumably the most important of these restrictions is that reprisals "must be in proportion to the wrong done, and to the amount of compulsion necessary to get reparation." Oppenheim-Lauterpacht, *op. cit.*, p. 141. But what is this restriction if not an obligation of the state taking the reprisal? And to whom must the obligation refer? Obviously to the delinquent state who possesses the right to see that "disproportionate" reprisals are not taken against it, and to take measures of reprisal itself in the event this rule of proportionality is not observed. Yet if the argument dealt with above were correct the delinquent state could not acquire this "new power," that is a new legal right, by virtue of its illegal action.

somehow illogical or contradictory to continue to assume that the status and content of this law remains unchanged once the resort to war has been rendered, in principle, unlawful. However, there is no contradiction—at least no logical contradiction—involved in asserting the validity of a rule which prohibits in principle a certain act (the resort to war) and in asserting at the same time that should this act occur certain behavior (as determined by the rules regulating war's conduct) is to be mutually observed by the aggressor state as well as by those states resisting the aggression. The legal inequality between belligerents with respect to the war itself does not logically preclude their legal equality as concerns the applicability of the rules regulating the conduct of war.[15]

Nor does the argument appear convincing which rests upon the belief that the historic origin and justification of the traditional rules regulating belligerent relations presupposed the legal equality of the belligerents in relation to the war itself; and that in the absence of this legal equality as between belligerents there no longer remains any justification for assuming equality of rights and duties in the conduct of war. Whatever the historic origin and justification of the law of war, these considerations cannot of themselves affect the positive law. They suggest, at best, a disparity between the purposes which prompted the development of this law and the purpose behind the attempt to prohibit war in principle. It is supposed that the law of war had its primary justification in the traditional interpretation of war as an "exercise of power." Assuming the effective prohibition of this "exercise of power," and the consequent change in the interpretation of war, the conclusion is drawn that the justification for retaining that law serving to regulate war's conduct has also ceased to exist.

There is strong reason, though, for maintaining that the rules of warfare had both their origin and justification not so much in any indifference to the legal character of war but in the conviction that whatever the interpretation given to war there must be rules for the regulation, and hence the mitigation, of war's conduct. It is not without significance that Grotius, though he was by no means alone in doing so, has given a classic expres-

---

[15] In order to avoid a similar conclusion, while nevertheless seeking to retain at least a part of the law of war, a distinction has been made between war "in the legal sense" and war "in the material sense." For example, Quincy Wright, *op. cit.*, p. 365. This distinction seems both unacceptable and unnecessary. It is unacceptable because it implies that the fact or situation "war" is no longer recognized in law, though a part of the law of war may nevertheless apply to this situation. But if the law of war is at all applicable to this situation it is because this situation has been given a specific legal existence. Thus from the point of view of law there can only be war "in the legal sense." It would seem that the real reason for the distinction between war "in the legal sense" and war "in the material sense" is the desire to differentiate between a war in which parties are legally equal as regards the war itself and a war in which there is not this legal equality. See, *Harvard Research In International Law, Rights and Duties of States In Case of Aggression, op. cit.*, p. 823.

sion of this conviction.[16] Indeed, it must remain a source of some astonishment that so many writers have insisted that it is hopeless to believe violence (war) can be regulated—admittedly a paradox of no small proportion—and that the only solution is to do away with war itself. It is only a minor consideration that this opinion is not deterred by the fact that war has been regulated in the past, with varying degrees of effectiveness. More important is the dismissal of a relatively modest goal as being inherently unattainable and the ready acceptance of an ideal infinitely more difficult of realization.[17]

B. THE OPERATION OF THE LAW OF WAR DURING WORLD WAR II

The contention that the changed legal position of war must of necessity affect the operation of the law of war finds little, if any, historical support in the attitude and behavior of the belligerents during the second World War. Although the Axis Powers were regarded as having resorted to war in violation of their international commitments—especially the obligations assumed under the Kellogg-Briand Pact—there was no disposition for that reason to claim that the law regulating the conduct of hostilities did not apply equally to all belligerents. Nor has the attitude manifested toward this question by war crimes tribunals contributed in any substantial measure to the view that a state waging an unlawful war cannot enjoy those rights relating to the conduct of war that have heretofore been conceded to all belligerents. In the vast majority of war crimes trials the question simply did not arise, and the assumption that even in an unlawful war the rules regulating the conduct of war are equally applicable to all belligerents appears to have been taken for granted. It was only exceptionally that tribunals were called upon to declare otherwise legitimate acts of warfare unlawful for the reason that they had been performed on behalf of a state waging an illegal war. In these latter cases, the decisions of tribunals seem to indicate—on the whole—a refusal to deduce any consequences for

[16] In his masterful essay on "The Grotian Tradition In International Law," *B. Y. I. L.*, 23 (1946), Sir Hersch Lauterpacht, while placing emphasis upon the distinction Grotius makes between just and unjust wars, goes on to state: "At the same time, in conformity with the view which has remained unchallenged and which is in accordance with the humanitarian character of his treatise, he (Grotius) lays down that the question of the justice or injustice of the war is irrelevant for the purpose of observing the rules of warfare as between the belligerents" (p. 39).

[17] See, for example, the excellent article by J. L. Kunz, "The Chaotic Status of the Laws of War and The Urgent Necessity for Their Revision," *A. J. I. L.*, 45 (1951), pp. 37–61.

the operation of the law of war from the fact that the war itself was unlawful.[18]

The same attitude characterized the judgment of courts, other than war crimes tribunals, in applying the rules regulating the economic aspects of warfare, i. e., the rules governing the lawful acquisition by belligerents of title over enemy property. In particular, the long-established right of belligerents to capture and condemn the public and private property of an enemy found at sea was not questioned, so long as the captured enemy vessels and goods were otherwise condemned in accordance with those rules governing the international law of prize.[19]

---

[18] Thus the statement of the United States Military Tribunal in the Hostages Trial: " . . we desire to point out that International Law makes no distinction between a lawful and an unlawful occupant in dealing with the respective duties of occupant and population in occupied territory There is no reciprocal connection between the manner of the military occupation of territory and the rights and duties of the occupant and population to each other after the relationship has in fact been established. Whether the invasion was lawful or criminal is not an important factor in the consideration of this subject." (*Trial of Wilhelm List and Others*), *Law Reports of Trials of War Criminals* (cited throughout as *Law Reports* . .) 8 (1949), p. 59. In The Justice Trial another tribunal declared: "It is persuasively urged that the fact that Germany was waging a criminal war of aggression colours all of these acts with the dye of criminality. . . . If we should adopt the view that by reason of the fact that the war was a criminal war of aggression every act which would have been legal in a defensive war was illegal in this one, we would be forced to the conclusion that every soldier who marched under orders into occupied territory or who fought in the homeland was a criminal and a murderer. The rules of land warfare upon which the prosecution has relied would not be the measure of conduct and the pronouncement of guilt in any case would become a mere formality." (*Trial of Josef Altstotter and Others*), *Law Reports* . . ., 6 (1948), p. 52.—Very rarely have courts seen fit to deduce certain consequences for the operation of the law of war simply from the fact that the war itself was unlawful. In one case, the Netherlands Special Court of Cassation declared that Germany, as an occupant, had no right of reprisal against the Dutch population for acts performed by the latter which would *otherwise* have been unlawful according to the law of belligerent occupation. The apparent reason given for this opinion was the "unlawful war of aggression" initiated by Germany against the Kingdom of the Netherlands. (*Trial of Hans Alben Rauter*), *Law Reports* . ., 14 (1949), pp. 133–8.

[19] "Neither judicial authority nor, to any substantial extent, the practice of Governments support the proposition that a State waging an unlawful war does not obtain or validly transmit title with respect to property acquired in connexion with the conduct of war and in accordance with international law." Lauterpacht, "The Limits of the Operation of the Law of War," p. 239 (for a review of cases bearing upon the acquisition by the aggressor of property in the course of an illegal war, pp. 224–33).

In this connection it may be noted that Annex XVII (A) of the Treaty of Peace between the Allied and Associated Powers and Italy, Paris, 10 February 1947, provided that: "Each of the Allied and Associated Powers reserves the right to examine, according to a procedure to be established by it, all decisions and orders of the Italian Prize Courts in cases involving ownership rights of its nationals, and to recommend to the Italian Government that revision shall be undertaken of such of those decisions or orders as may not be in conformity with international law." Text in *U. S. Naval War College, International Law Documents, 1946–47*, p. 104. The "international law" referred to is the traditional law of prize.

C. COLLECTIVE SECURITY AND THE OPERATION OF THE LAW OF WAR: THE UNITED NATIONS[20]

The preceding considerations have concentrated upon pointing out that there appears to be no valid reason for assuming that the changed legal position of war must necessarily result in the alteration of the rules regulating inter-belligerent relations. To the extent that the experience of the second World War is relevant in this connection it serves to support the conclusion that a state unlawfully resorting to war cannot, for that reason alone, be deprived of established belligerent rights. It may be contended, however, that these considerations, even if accepted, can have only a limited bearing upon the present situation; that they are relevant mainly as applied to the period prior to the establishment of the United Nations. Whereas the Covenant of the League of Nations and the Kellogg-Briand Pact sought to place limitations upon the customary liberty of states to resort to war, both instruments recognized that war might nevertheless be resorted to by a state in violation of its obligations. Neither instrument provided for a procedure whereby the unlawful resort to war could be determined authoritatively, in a manner the signatory Parties were bound to accept. Although each state that was a Member of the League or a Party to the Paris Pact had the right to determine for itself when an unlawful resort to war had occurred, such determination—or interpretation—had no binding effect upon other states. Nor did either instrument provide for the establishment of an international armed force apart from the armed forces of the various states. In particular, the illegal "resort to war" under Article 16 of the Covenant presupposed the creation of a state of war between the state violating its obligations and other Member states choosing to resort to a counter-war. Despite the contemplated coordination of effort on the part of those states waging a counter-war under Article 16 there seems to have been little doubt that the rules of war would apply to such action.[21]

In brief, although the Covenant of the League of Nations and the Kellogg-Briand Pact placed limitations upon the circumstances under which war could be resorted to lawfully it was clearly assumed that war continued to enjoy a legal existence. But even more important was the fact that neither instrument overcame the normal conditions of decentralization that served

[20] It must be made clear that the following pages are concerned only with inquiring into the possible effect of recent developments in collective security upon the operation of the law of war. The reader must look to other sources should he desire a detailed and systematic analysis of these recent developments. Among a vast literature, of particular value for further reference are Hans Kelsen, *The Law of the United Nations* (1951), and Julius Stone, *op. cit.*, pp. 165–293.

[21] *Reports and Resolutions on the Subject of Article 16 of the Covenant*, Report by the Secretary-General, League of Nations Doc. A. 14. 1927 V., pp. 83–7. See also H. J. Taubenfeld, "International Armed Forces and the Rules of War," A. J. I. L., 45 (1951), pp. 671–2.

in large measure to provide the justification for the traditional interpretation of war. This decentralization not only implied the absence of a procedure which would make possible an authoritative judgment that in a given instance a state had unlawfully resorted to war; it also rendered doubtful whether a counter-war could technically serve as an enforcement measure—as a sanction—in view of the unknown outcome of almost every war.

The Charter of the United Nations, on the other hand, has been interpreted as effecting basic changes in the conditions that appeared to justify the traditional interpretation of war and that provided a favorable environment for the development of the law of war. Not only does the Charter refrain from the use of the term "war," speaking only of the illegal use of armed force (or of armed attacks) and of enforcement measures to be taken by the Organization, it also establishes a procedure whereby the unlawful resort to armed force can be determined in a manner binding upon the Member states.[22] In addition, the Charter provides for the establishment of what may appropriately be termed an international armed force, as distinguished from the armed forces of the Member states.[23] It is the assumption of the effective realization of these Charter provisions in practice that generally forms the basis of suggestions that the United Nations may select from the traditional law of war those rules considered desirable to govern the conduct of international armed forces and may determine the obligations

---

[22] This is, in principle, the result of Articles 24, 25 and 39 of the Charter. According to Article 24 the Members of the United Nations confer on the Security Council "primary responsibility for the maintenance of international peace and security" and agree that in carrying out its duties the Security Council "acts on their behalf." In Article 25, the Members agree "to accept and carry out the decisions of the Security Council in accordance with the present Charter." Article 39 declares that the Security Council "shall determine the existence of any threat to the peace, breach of the peace, or act of aggression and shall make recommendations, or decide what measures shall be taken in accordance with Articles 41 and 42, to maintain or restore international peace and security." Article 41 refers to acts not involving the use of armed force, Article 42 to acts involving the use of armed force.

[23] The statement in the text presupposes, of course, the conclusion of the agreements provided for in Article 43, whereby the Members of the United Nations "undertake to make available to the Security Council, on its call and in accordance with a special agreement or agreements, armed forces, assistance, and facilities, including rights of passage, necessary for the purpose of maintaining international peace and security." Article 47 authorizes establishment of a Military Staff Committee, and stipulates that one of the Committee's principal functions is to advise and assist the Security Council on questions relating to the "employment and command of forces placed at its [i. e., the Security Council's] disposal." In their *composition* the armed forces placed at the disposal of the Security Council would still remain units of the armed forces of the various Member states. Nevertheless, they could appropriately be designated as "international" armed forces, and, in this respect distinguished from "national" armed forces, by virtue of the fact that they would be placed at the disposal of the Security Council and would operate under its strategic direction and command. See, for example, Kelsen, *op. cit.*, pp. 762–8. To date, no agreements of the nature referred to in Article 43 have been concluded. Nor is there any real prospect of their conclusion in the foreseeable future.

and rights of the delinquent state(s) against which enforcement action is taken.[24]

In view of the present realities of international organization the assumption that the Security Council may make effective use of the powers granted it under Chapter VII of the Charter must clearly be regarded as improbable; so improbable, in fact, that the utility of a careful examination of the possible effect of this situation on the operation of the law of war appears distinctly limited. It may be observed, however, that it is by no means certain that even if this situation were realized the law of war would thereby cease to be equally applicable as between the international armed forces and the national armed forces against which action is taken. Whether or not these rules would cease to be applicable is a question that poses many difficult considerations. It is at least doubtful that these considerations can be resolved by inferential or deductive judgments which assert, in effect, that the law of the Charter may be interpreted to imply a change in the status and content of the law of war as one of its necessary effects.[25] In the absence of any reference—direct or indirect—to this matter in the Charter itself, the resulting uncertainty can be resolved only by a clear manifestation of the intention of the Member states of the United Nations. The most satisfactory methods for manifesting this intention would consist either in an amendment to the Charter or in a convention concluded by the General Assembly and ratified by all of the Member states. At the very least it would appear necessary that the intention to modify the rules of war in United Nations enforcement actions be established by a clear and effective practice to this effect.

In particular,[26] however, it is not sufficient to contend that in hostilities undertaken by *national armed forces* acting in response to a mere recommendation of the Security Council a change in the status and content of the rules of war must be assumed for the reason that the "United Nations acting on behalf of the organized community of nations against an offender, has a superior legal and moral position as compared with the other party to the

---

[24] For proposals to this effect, see Philip C. Jessup, *A Modern Law of Nations* (1948), pp. 188–221. Also Taubenfeld, *op. cit.*, pp. 672–7.

[25] It is in this sense that Lauterpacht's remarks may be understood when, in referring to the possible effect of the Charter upon the law of war, he states: " once a treaty has been adopted which is of fundamental and comprehensive character, it is difficult—and probably unscientific—to act on the view that it settles only that part of the law to which it expressly refers and nothing else. A treaty is not concluded in a legal vacuum. It is part of a legal system which, for that very reason, cannot contain rules which are contradictory Any such contradiction must be removed by a reasonable application of the principle that newly enacted law, if it is of a general and fundamental character, alters rules inconsistent therewith." *op. cit.*, p. 209.

[26] The remarks made in the immediate paragraph of the text are largely relevant to the particular circumstances attending the outbreak of hostilities in Korea—circumstances dealt with in the following paragraphs—and must be read with this consideration in mind.

conflict." [27] As already noted, there is at present almost no possibility of the United Nations as such "acting on behalf" of the community of nations, implying thereby the existence of international armed forces at the disposal of the Organization, used to defend the legitimate interests of the Member states. On the contrary, the most reasonably optimistic situation—and the situation probably referred to in the above quoted statement—is that of national forces "acting on behalf of the United Nations," that is acting in conformity with a determination taken by a competent organ (at present only the Security Council) of the United Nations.[28] It is true that the legal position of states whose armed forces are acting on behalf of the United Nations—in the sense indicated above—is superior to the position of those parties unlawfully resorting to force. But this superiority does not of itself yield a right to modify the rules regulating war's conduct.

Thus the hostilities undertaken in Korea by Member states of the United Nations were preceded by a *determination* of the Security Council that the action of North Korea constituted a breach of the peace and a *recommendation* of the Council that members of the United Nations furnish assistance—including armed forces—to repel this unlawful action and to restore international peace and security.[29] It is possible to consider those states re-

[27] Report of Committee on Study of Legal Problems of the United Nations, "Should The Law of War Apply to United Nations Enforcement Action?" *Proceedings*, American Society of International Law (1952), p. 217. The report of the Committee, which has reference primarily to the Korean action, concludes that: ". . in the present circumstances . . . the United Nations should not feel bound by all the laws of war, but should select such of the laws of war as may seem to fit its purpose (e. g., prisoners of war, belligerent occupation), adding such others as may be needed, and rejecting those which seem incompatible with its purpose. We think it beyond doubt that the United Nations, representing practically all the nations of the earth, has the right to make such decisions."

[28] But a "determination" (e. g., that a "breach of the peace" has occurred) which does not—and in the Korean Case did not—impose upon Member states the *obligation* to take measures involving the use of armed force against the party unlawfully resorting to force.

[29] In its resolution of June 25, 1950 (*U. N. Security Council, Official Records, 5th year, No. 15* (*Doc. S/1501*) p. 18.), the Security Council, after *determining* that the armed attack upon the Republic of Korea by forces from North Korea constituted a "breach of the peace," called for the immediate cessation of hostilities and for the "authorities of North Korea to withdraw forthwith their armed forces to the thirty-eighth parallel." In addition, the Council called upon all Members "to render every assistance to the United Nations in the execution of this resolution and to refrain from giving assistance to the North Korean authorities." In its resolution of June 27, 1950 (*U. N. Doc. S/1511*) the Council merely *recommended* that: "Members of the United Nations furnish such assistance to the Republic of Korea as may be necessary to repel the armed attack and to restore international peace and security within the area." On July 7, 1950, the Security Council adopted a resolution (*U. N. Doc. S/1588*) in which it welcomed the "prompt and vigorous support" given its earlier resolutions, noted the offers of assistance for the Republic of Korea on the part of Members, recommended that "all Members providing military forces and other assistance . . . make such forces and other assistance available to a unified command under the United States," requested the United States to designate the commander of such forces, authorized the use of the United Nations flag by the Unified Command, and requested the United States to provide the Council with periodic reports on the course of action taken under the Unified Command.

sponding to this recommendation as having acted "on behalf" of the United Nations.[30] There was no suggestion emanating from authoritative sources, however, that the opposing parties to this conflict were not equally bound by the existing rules of war. Neither the refusal to designate these

[30] This possibility necessarily assumes that the resolutions of the Security Council in the Korean Case—and particularly the resolution of June 25—not only were permitted by the Charter but that they imposed certain obligations and conferred certain rights upon the Member states. It will be recalled that the resolutions in question were passed in the absence of the Soviet Union. The question therefore arose as to whether valid decisions on nonprocedural matters could be made in the absence of a permanent Member (and a Member who later challenges the validity of such decisions). The opinions of writers have been sharply divided on this question. An impressive negative reply has been given by Julius Stone, *op. cit.*, pp. 207–12, and Leo Gross, "Voting in the Security Council. Abstention from Voting and Absence from Meetings," *Yale Law Journal*, 60 (1951), pp. 209–57. For an affirmative reply see Myres S. McDougal and Richard N. Gardner, "The Veto and The Charter: An Interpretation for Survival," *Yale Law Journal*, 60 (1951), pp. 258–92. And for an argument holding both answers equally possible, see Kelsen, *op. cit.*, pp. 290–4, 940–1.

If the view is taken that an affirmative reply to the above question is possible—and it is the view adopted here—the problem remains of determining the duties imposed and the rights conferred upon Member states. Although the resolution of June 25 called upon all Members to render every assistance to the United Nations in the execution of that resolution it is extremely difficult—if not impossible—to contend that Member states were under any *obligation* to take active measures in support of South Korea, and particularly measures involving the use of armed force. This view is supported by the fact that the Security Council's two later resolutions merely recommended that Member states furnish assistance—including armed forces—to the Republic of Korea. The Security Council expressly refrained from making any decision under Article 39 to order those enforcement measures provided for in Article 42. It must be further observed that the obligation of Member states to take measures of armed force provided for in Article 42 is probably dependent upon the conclusion of the special agreements provided for in Article 43. In the absence of such agreements it is entirely doubtful that the Security Council is competent to obligate Member states to take military measures against a party considered by the Council to have committed a threat to or breach of the peace. For these reasons it does not appear possible to characterize the action in Korea as a "United Nations enforcement action"—at least not in the strict legal sense—since this would imply an enforcement action *ordered* by the Security Council under Articles 39 and 42. Similar doubt must be expressed over the accuracy of references to "United Nations forces" in Korea. The Unified Command in Korea was not created by the Security Council in conformity with Article 29 of the Charter. Strictly speaking the Unified Command was not an "organ" of the United Nations and the forces serving under this command were not—again in a strict sense—"United Nations forces." See, in this respect, Kelsen, *op. cit.*, pp. 936–40 and the excellent remarks of Richard R. Baxter, "Constitutional Forms and Some Legal Problems of International Military Command," *B.Y I. L.*, 29 (1952), pp. 333–7.

On the other hand, it can be maintained that Member states were at least under the obligation "to refrain from giving assistance to the North Korean authorities." In addition, it seems clear that the effect of the Security Council's *determination* of a breach of the peace and of its later *recommendations* was to confer upon Members the right to take measures of armed force in support of the Republic of Korea. In so doing Member states acted "on behalf" of the United Nations, even though their action may not be strictly characterized as a "United Nations enforcement action." Of course, it may be contended that even in the absence of any Security Council action, under Article 51 (see p. 18) Member states could have claimed the right to assist in the collective defense of the Republic of Korea (though this requires interpreting Article

hostilities as "war" nor the questionable insistence upon considering the national contingents involved as "United Nations troops" [31] affected the application of the international law of war. On the contrary, there was on more than one occasion express affirmation that both the aggressor forces and the forces acting on behalf of the United Nations were equally obligated to conform in their actions to the law of war. It is quite true that in the Korean conflict the primary concern was to secure the observance of those rules governing the treatment by belligerents of prisoners of war. The rules governing the behavior of armed forces in actual combat received only minor consideration. But this does not detract from the conclusion that the Korean conflict saw no substantial alteration in the status and content of the rules regulating inter-belligerent relations.

The circumstances attending the outbreak of hostilities in Korea must be regarded as exceptional, however. In view of the factors which render any future decisions by the Security Council under Chapter VII extremely unlikely,[32] the most probable situation is that of armed conflict being waged under Article 51 of the Charter.[33] Each side must be expected to maintain that it is acting in self-defense—or collective defense—against an aggressor, with no subsequent decision taken either by the Security Council or by any other organ endowed with the proper competence to review—particularly while hostilities last—the competing claims of the contending parties. This situation would then resemble, in its essential features, that of World War II, and there would seem little doubt that in such a conflict the rules

---

51 as applying—despite its wording—to non-Member states as well). At the same time, it must be admitted that there is a substantial difference between the resort to armed force under Article 51, and without any authoritative determination of the party that has unlawfully resorted to an armed attack, and the resort to armed force when taken in conformity with a valid determination to that effect by the Security Council (here again, the assumption being that such determination in the Korean Case was valid.).

For a quite different point of view from that taken in the present note, see particularly the learned and stimulating analysis of the Korean affair advanced by Professor Stone, *op. cit.*, pp. 228–37.

[31] See note 30 above.

[32] I. e., the voting provisions of the Charter, requiring as they do the unanimity of the permanent Members on any *decisions*—or *determinations*—taken under Chapter VII. And while it may be argued that Article 27 does not forbid such decisions in the absence of a permanent Member, it is altogether improbable that a permanent Member will ever again absent itself from the Council during a critical period.

[33] Article 51 reads: "Nothing in the present Charter shall impair the inherent right of individual or collective self-defense if an armed attack occurs against a Member of the United Nations, until the Security Council has taken the measures necessary to maintain international peace and security. Measures taken by Members in the exercise of this right of self-defense shall be immediately reported to the Security Council and shall not in any way affect the authority and responsibility of the Security Council under the present Charter to take at any time such action as it deems necessary in order to maintain or restore international peace and security."

regulating the conduct of war would be fully applicable as between the belligerents.[34]

The above situation would not be substantially altered by the attempt, incident upon the outbreak of armed conflict, to obtain a "collective determination" of the party unlawfully resorting to armed force by a decision reached under the General Assembly Resolution "Uniting For Peace." [35] At present, such collective determinations the General Assembly may make under the Resolution "Uniting For Peace" constitute only recommendations to the Members. Although expressive of the opinion of the majority of states making up the Organization, these recommendations do not create legal obligations for the Member states.[36] Nor, for that reason, may the nature of these recommendations be compared with the decisions the Security Council is competent to render under Articles 39, 41 and 42 of the Charter. It is also necessary to distinguish between the "collective measures" that may be taken by the national armed forces of Member states acting in response to a recommendation of the General Assembly and

[34] Occasionally, the opinion has been expressed that the situation resulting from the inability of the Security Council to reach an authoritative determination (of the party unlawfully resorting to the use of force) under Chapter VII of the Charter can be overcome by other, and equally binding, procedures. Thus Professor Quincy Wright states that: "While in some cases it may be difficult to obtain a decision as to the justifiability of a particular use of force because of the veto in the Security Council, customary international law provides a procedure, that of general recognition, applicable when conventional procedures fail to function." *op. cit.*, p. 370. The same writer has suggested that a two-thirds vote of the states making up the General Assembly will suffice for such "general recognition." It is difficult to find a basis in existing law in support of this opinion.

[35] For text of Resolution, see *U. N. General Assembly, Official Records, 5th Sess. Supp. No. 20 (Doc. A/1775)*, p. 10. The heart of this resolution is to be found in two operating paragraphs which read—in part—as follows:

"The General Assembly, . . .

1. Resolves that if the Security Council, because of lack of unanimity of the permanent members, fails to exercise its primary responsibility for the maintenance of international peace and security in any case where there appears to be a threat to the peace, breach of the peace, or act of aggression, the General Assembly shall consider the matter immediately with a view to making appropriate recommendations to Members for collective measures, including in the case of a breach of the peace or act of aggression the use of armed force when necessary, to maintain or restore international peace and security. . . .

8. Recommends to the States Members of the United Nations that each Member maintain within its national armed forces elements so trained, organized, and equipped that they could promptly be made available, in accordance with its constitutional processes, for service as a United Nations unit or units, upon recommendation by the Security Council or the General Assembly, without prejudice to the use of such elements in exercise of the right of individual or collective self-defense recognized in Article 51 of the Charter."

[36] "There is no warrant in the Charter for considering the designation of the aggressor by virtue of a Resolution of the General Assembly, and the resulting illegality of war on his part, as legally binding upon States which have not voted for the Resolution." Lauterpacht, *op. cit.*, p. 207. Indeed, there is no warrant for regarding the designation of an aggressor by virtue of a General Assembly Resolution as legally binding even upon states which have voted for the resolution.

measures of a collective character taken by national armed forces acting not merely in response to a recommendation of the Security Council but also in conformity with an authoritative determination of the aggressor by that same organ.[37] Although a considerable degree of coordination may be achieved among the national armed forces of Member states acting in response to General Assembly recommendations made under the "Uniting For Peace" Resolution, the present character of such recommendations does not appear to allow the conclusion that these forces may be considered as acting "on behalf" of the United Nations. Indeed, there would seem to be no substantial reason for differentiating between the coordination of collective military measures made in response to General Assembly recommendations and the coordination of collective defense measures allowed to Member states under Article 51 of the Charter, even though the moral authority with which the former would be endowed ought not to be neglected. In any event, it is significant to observe that the reports submitted to date by the Collective Measures Committee, established under the "Uniting For Peace" Resolution,[38] contain no suggestion that the rules traditionally regulating the conduct of hostilities between belligerents ought not to apply to hostilities undertaken in response to General Assembly recommendations. To the extent that the Collective Measures Committee has dealt with the question of the applicability of the law of war there is the assumption that these rules will continue to be applicable.[39]

---

[37] Once again, the evident basis for the statement made in the text is provided by the cirtumstances attending the outbreak of the Korean hostilities. See notes 29 and 30 above.

[38] Paragraph 11 of the "Uniting For Peace" Resolution establishes "a Collective Measures Committee consisting of fourteen Members" and directs the Committee "in consultation with the Secretary-General and with Member states as the Committee finds appropriate, to study and make a report to the Security Council and the General Assembly, not later than September 1, 1951, on methods . . . which might be used to maintain and strengthen international peace and security in accordance with the Purposes and Principles of the Charter, taking account of collective self-defense and regional arrangements . . ." Since its establishment, the Collective Measures Committee has issued several reports. The first, and basic, report was completed in 1951; see *U. N. General Assembly, Official Records, 6th Sess. Supp. No. 13 (Doc. A/1891).*

[39] Paragraph 246 of the first report of the Collective Measures Committee (*U. N. Doc. A/1891,* p. 29) states that: "In any future operations, the executive military authority designated by the United Nations should follow the humanitarian principles applied and recognized by civilized nations involved in armed conflict. In particular, the special position and functions of the International Committee of the Red Cross should be recognized, and its activities assisted, by the executive military authority." The "executive military authority" is to comprise a state or a group of states. Thus the Collective Measures Committee Report states that "upon the determination to adopt measures involving the use of United Nations armed force, the Organization should authorize a State or group of States to act on its behalf as executive military authority, within the framework of its policies and objectives as expressed through such resolutions as it may adopt at any stage of the collective action" (p. 25). At present, however, the executive military authority would not act "on behalf" of the Organization, but rather on behalf of the Member states of the Organization which decide to adopt collective military measures. Throughout the report the example of Korea is used as a guide and precedent a precedent which is apt to prove misleading. Although the forces acting in Korea could properly

D. CONCLUSIONS

It may be useful, at this point, to summarize the principal conclusions that appear to emerge from the preceding examination of the possible effects of the changed legal position of war on the operation of the law of war. In addition, brief attention will be directed to those situations involving the use of armed force between states, though situations not recognized by the parties involved as war, in which the law of war—or at least a part of this law—may nevertheless be considered as operative.

(1) A clear distinction must be drawn between the legality of the act of resorting to war and the applicability of the rules regulating the conduct of war. The fact that the resort to war has been rendered, in principle, unlawful does not compel the conclusion that in a war illegally resorted to by one side the rules regulating inter-belligerent relations are either inapplicable or substantially modified in their operation.[40] The rights conferred and the duties imposed upon belligerents in the conduct of war are not dependent for their operation upon an equality of legal status as concerns the war itself. Nor does it appear correct to assume that, given the changed legal position of war, a continued equality of belligerent status with respect to the rules regulating war's conduct is contrary to the principle *ex injuria jus non oritur*. For this principle ought not to be interpreted to mean that *no* legal rights may accrue to the lawbreaker as a result of his unlawful act, particularly those legal rights that have been expressly provided by law for just that situation arising out of the unlawful act.

(2) To the extent that the applicability of the law of war is to be restricted in its operation by virtue of the changed legal position of war in international law such restriction can be brought about only through the customary practice of states or by convention. Neither the Covenant of the League of Nations nor the Kellogg-Briand Pact have been interpreted as so restricting the operation of the law of war. It also seems clear that neither

---

be considered as acting "on behalf" of the United Nations, the same phrase when used to describe the action of forces responding to a General Assembly recommendation overlooks the decisive legal difference between hostilities whose character rests upon a determination rendered by the Security Council under Article 39 of the Charter and hostilities whose character is determined by a recommendation of the General Assembly. Nor is it accurate to speak, as does the above report, of "measures involving the use of United Nations armed force," the obvious intention being to include in this term the national armed forces of Member states acting in response to General Assembly recommendations. For such forces bear to an even smaller degree the appellation of "United Nations armed forces" than did the armed forces serving in Korea—forces whose status has already been commented upon.—Once again, the general observation should be made that the decisions taken and the collective measures applied by virtue of the "Uniting for Peace" resolution do not substantially differ at present from decisions and measures of collective defense taken under Article 51. The altogether commendable desire to strengthen the present system of collective security should not serve to obscure this basic consideration.

[40] *Law of Naval Warfare* (see Appendix), Section 200.

the attitude of the belligerents during World War II nor the decisions rendered by courts in applying the law of war provide any solid basis for the opinion that the changed legal status of war has affected the applicability of the law of war.

(3) In general, it is difficult to establish any significant restriction on the operation of the rules regulating inter-belligerent relations consequent upon the avoidance of the term "war" in the Charter of the United Nations. (On the contrary, it is more than likely, as will be noted, that the Charter will have the contrary effect, i. e., of expanding the situations in which the law of war is applicable.) By forbidding to member states the use of armed force in their mutual relations, save as a measure taken in conformity with a decision of the Security Council or as a measure of individual or collective defense against an armed attack, the Charter seeks to regulate every use of armed force and not only the use of armed force which assumes the character of war. It has already been noted that the refusal on the part of certain states to designate the hostilities in Korea as "war" did not, for that reason, have any appreciable effect upon the operation of the international [41] law of war as this law applies to the mutual relations of belligerents. The same absence of effect upon the operation of the law of war will probably hold for future occasions, similar to Korea, in which states wish to avoid the use of the term war, mainly in order to give hostilities what is considered to be a higher dignity and purpose (i. e., by terming such hostilities "international police actions," "measures of collective defense") than war had according to the traditional doctrine. But it would seem a mistake to attach too great significance to verbal devices, particularly at the expense of legal reality. Insofar as the law of war is applied as between the parties to an armed conflict the legal relevance—or, rather, the lack of legal relevance—in refusing to term such a conflict war should be clearly understood.

(4) The assertion that the rules of warfare would not apply to international armed forces engaged in a United Nations enforcement action, must be very seriously questioned. Neither the principle *ex injuria jus non oritur* nor the admittedly superior legal position of the forces undertaking United Nations enforcement actions provide sufficient basis for contending against the continued applicability of the rules regulating inter-belligerent relations. Besides, given the present state of international organization these questions can possess no more than a remote hypothetical significance. At the very

[41] On the other hand, this refusal to designate the contest in Korea as war has had certain effects in relation to the decisions of municipal courts and the operation of municipal legislation intended for periods of war. It is, of course, always necessary to distinguish between the operation of municipal legislation, dependent upon a status or condition of war as defined by municipal law, and the operation of the international law of war. For some effects of this distinction in the case of Korea, see Lauterpacht, *op. cit.*, pp. 221–3. In the United States the highest military court, the United States Court of Military Appeals, considered the Korean conflict as war for the purpose of applying the provisions of the Uniform Code of Military Justice.

least, they must assume not only an authoritative determination by the Security Council of the party unlawfully resorting to armed force, but also the *actual direction* by this organ of the armed forces of Member states undertaking enforcement measures against the aggressor. National armed forces acting *under the direction* of the Security Council do so in response to a Council decision imposing a legal obligation upon the Member states. The exceptional conditions accompanying the outbreak of hostilities in Korea may be interpreted as having permitted the fulfillment of the first of these conditions, though not the second. And Korea is not likely to be repeated. The strong probability, then, is that in a future resort to armed conflict there will be no authoritative determination of the aggressor. Although it is not at all unlikely that in the event of hostilities some kind of collective determination will be made of the party considered to have unlawfully resorted to armed force, possibly under Article 51 of the Charter or according to the "Uniting For Peace" Resolution, such determination cannot be considered at present as binding—in any legally relevant sense—upon those states dissenting from it. Under these circumstances there is still less reason for asserting any restrictions upon the operation of the rules regulating war's conduct.

(5) Recent practice would appear to indicate that, if anything, the situations in which the law of war is considered applicable have expanded rather than contracted.[42] There is, in fact, a discernible tendency today to attempt to apply at least a substantial part of the rules governing the weapons and methods of war, and particularly the rules regulating the treatment of victims of war, to situations in which the parties engaged in armed conflict refrain from making a declaration of war and, at the same time, deny any intent of waging war. The evident purpose of this growing effort may be rightly described as the humanitarian one of extending as widely as possible the beneficial effects resulting from the application of the law of war.

Thus Article 2 common to the four 1949 Geneva Conventions for the Protection of the Victims of War, provides that the provisions of these Conventions are to be regarded as applicable "to all cases of declared war or of any other armed conflict which may arise between two or more of the High Contracting Parties, even if the state of war is not recognized by one of them." The apparent intent of those drafting this article was to make the Geneva Conventions applicable to all international armed conflicts, without regard to whether or not such conflicts are recognized as war by the parties involved, though the wording of the article is not altogether

[42] See *Law of Naval Warfare*, Section 110 and notes thereto. In a sense, the tendency to apply the rules of war—or, at least, a substantial part of these rules—to armed conflicts regardless of whether these conflicts are considered by the parties involved as war finds a certain parallel in the attempt made in the Charter of the United Nations to regulate the resort to armed force generally and not merely the resort to war.

adequate in meeting this purpose.[43] It is also apparent that the 1949 Geneva Conventions are fully applicable either in the case of an illegal resort to war or an illegal resort to armed force; no differentiation is made in this respect, or even suggested, as between the rights and duties of the contracting parties.

At the same time, it is difficult to determine the precise extent to which other rules regulating the conduct of war apply to situations in which states—engaged in armed conflict—neither make a declaration of war[44] nor admit the intent of waging war. Although it has been claimed that even in the absence of a formal state of war the rules regulating the mutual relations of belligerents are applicable to states immediately involved in

---

[43] See J. L. Kunz ("The Geneva Conventions of August 12, 1949," *Law and Politics in The World Community*, pp. 304–6), who asserts that since a state of war may not be recognized by any party to a conflict "such a conflict would, under the letter of Article 2, not be included." This, for the reason that Article 2 speaks only of armed conflicts not recognized as war by *one* party to the conflict. In this connection, it may be of interest to note that Article 2, paragraph 11 of the "Draft Code of Offences Against the Peace and Security of Mankind," prepared by the United Nations International Law Commission at the request of the General Assembly, refers to "acts in violation of the laws and customs of war." In the explanatory comment following this paragraph it is stated that the latter "applies to all cases of declared war or of any other armed conflict which may arise between two or more States, even, if the existence of a state of war is recognized by none of them." *U. N. General Assembly, Official Records, 6th Sess., Supp. No. 9 (Doc. A/1858)*, p. 13. In the essay quoted above Professor Kunz also criticizes Article 2 of the 1949 Geneva Conventions for failing to provide clearly for "large scale fighting in the course of an international military enforcement action, as now going on in Korea. For this is not an armed international conflict 'between two or more of the High Contracting Parties'." But this interpretation assumes that the armed forces in Korea were United Nations armed forces in the strict sense, and not the national forces of member states acting on behalf of the Organization. If the latter assumption is made, and it is submitted to be the more feasible one, then this particular difficulty does not arise.

[44] Hague Convention III (1907) Relative to the Opening of Hostilities obligates the contracting parties not to commence hostilities "without previous and explicit warning, in the form either of a reasoned declaration of war or of an ultimatum with conditional declaration of war." It is doubtful whether customary international law required a state to give "previous and explicit warning" before commencing hostilities. Be that as it may, the commencement of hostilities without previous warning or declaration nevertheless results in a state of war if this is the intention of the state commencing hostilities. Thus: ". . . States which deliberately order the commencement of hostilities without a previous declaration of war or a qualified ultimatum commit an international delinquency; but they are nevertheless engaged in war." Oppenheim-Lauterpacht, *op. cit.*, p. 299. The more difficult questions arise, however, as Professor Stone correctly points out, "where war is not openly intended by one or other parties, who insist rather on conducting their hostilities under some other name." *op. cit.*, p. 312.

armed conflict, the practice of states in this respect is still characterized by a substantial measure of uncertainty.[45]

[45] See generally on this problem, Fritz Grob, *The Relativity of War and Peace* (1949). With respect to Hague Conventions II (1899) and IV (1907) regulating the conduct of war on land Grob declares: "Whether or not military operations are accompanied by naval operations, whether they are geographically limited or not, whether they are conducted by large units or merely by minute detachments, whether they extend over a period of years or last a few minutes only, all this cannot possibly make any difference for the application of the above rules of law on war." (p. 217). Though this statement is probably correct it is doubtful whether the application of these conventions on land warfare to all international armed conflicts can be deduced—as the author contends—from the intent and purpose of those drafting the conventions. However, it is true that despite the fact that these conventions refer to "war," the recent practice of states has been to apply them to all international armed conflicts, and it is this practice rather than the strict wording of the conventions in question that may be regarded as decisive in determining their present application to armed conflicts ("military operations") generally. On the other hand, P. Guggenheim (*Traite de Droit International Public* (1954), Vol. II, p. 312) observes that while those rules having a military and humanitarian character are made increasingly applicable to all international armed conflicts, rules regulating the economic domain of war remain limited in their operation to war in the formal sense. Thus in hostilities at sea it is doubtful that the right to seize and, under appropriate circumstances, to destroy enemy private property may be extended at present to situations other than those characterized as war in the formal sense. (See pp. 102–3.) Indeed, instances of "undeclared hostilities" have been confined, by and large, to operations on land, and for this reason alone it is difficult to estimate the degree to which the rules regulating the mutual behavior of belligerents may be considered applicable to naval hostilities where the parties involved deny any intent to wage war. No doubt one reason for confining "undeclared hostilities" to operations on land is the desire to avoid raising problems concerning the position of third states or the nationals of third states. In naval hostilities it is seldom possible to avoid such problems.—Finally, distinguish clearly between the operation of the rules governing the mutual behavior of the combatants and the rules governing the mutual behavior of combatants and non-participating states. The latter rules—the law of neutrality—are clearly dependent for their operation upon recognition of a state of war, though such recognition may be effected either by the combatants or by third states acting independently of the parties directly involved in hostilities (see pp. 199–201).

II. THE SOURCES AND BINDING FORCE OF THE LAW OF NAVAL WARFARE

A. THE SOURCES OF THE LAW OF NAVAL WARFARE

The great dividing line in the historical development of the law of naval warfare must be drawn at the outbreak of the first World War in 1914, for what is generally referred to as the "traditional law" is substantially the law as it appeared at this date. In the main, the traditional law of naval warfare is customary in character, developing out of eighteenth and—particularly—nineteenth century practices. The various attempts to codify this customary law have never enjoyed the same degree of success that have attended similar efforts with respect to the codification of land warfare. There is no convention dealing with the regulation of naval hostilities that compares in scope and importance to the Regulations attached to Hague Convention IV (1907), Respecting the Laws and Customs of War on Land. The Hague Conventions of 1899 and 1907 which dealt specifically with the conduct of naval warfare are few in number and, with the exception of XIII (1907) concerning the Rights and Duties of Neutral States in Maritime War, of relatively minor significance.[1]

Historically, the most important, and certainly the most controversial, disputes arising in the course of naval hostilities related to the extent and character of the right of belligerents to interfere on the high seas with private neutral trade. In the Declaration of London of 1909 the attempt was made to produce a generally acceptable codification of nineteenth century practices in this area of the law. However, the Declaration was never ratified by any of the signatory states; and despite the occasional claims of belligerents and neutral states during the first World War that the Declaration of London set forth the valid law regulating belligerent behavior at sea, it was not binding upon the naval belligerents in either World War.[2]

---

[1] The Hague Conventions of 1907 relating to the conduct of naval warfare are: VI Status of Enemy Merchant Ships At the Outbreak of Hostilities; VII Conversion of Merchant Ships in Time of War; VIII Laying of Automatic Contact Mines; IX Bombardment by Naval Forces in Time of War; X Adaptation to Naval War of the Principles of the Geneva Convention; XI Certain Restrictions with Regard to the Rights of Capture in Naval War; and XIII Concerning the Rights and Duties of Neutral States in Maritime War. The United States ratified Conventions VIII, IX, X and XI. Convention XIII was adhered to by the United States subject to certain reservations (see pp. 218 ff.).—During the nineteenth century the most important Convention concluded for the regulation of maritime warfare was the Declaration of Paris (1856). On the present status of the rules making up the Declaration of Paris, see pp. 99–102.

[2] For further remarks dealing generally with the Declaration of London, see pp. 187–9.

In the period of over four decades that has elapsed since the outbreak of the first World War there has been only one international instrument concluded for the regulation of naval hostilities that has received general adherence, and that instrument is the London Protocol of 1936 requiring submarines to conform in their actions against merchant vessels to the rules of international law to which surface vessels are subject.[3] To the extent, then, that the traditional law has been changed, such change has come principally through the practices of two World Wars.[4]

In recent years attention has been increasingly called to the uncertainty that characterizes a substantial portion of this traditional law of naval warfare. The principal source of this uncertainty undoubtedly stems from the practices of the two World Wars. Although exaggerated accounts of the lawless behavior of the major naval belligerents frequently have been given there is no denying the fact that both wars—and particularly the second World War—witnessed the widespread violation of the traditional law. In the period following World War I it seemed plausible to contend that the circumstances of this conflict were exceptional (which, indeed, they were as judged by the circumstances of earlier wars), and that the effects of the war upon the traditional law had to be considered in the light of these exceptional circumstances. In general, this attitude led to the result that the traditional law—the law in force at the outbreak of World War I—was still considered, on the whole, to remain unimpaired.

Thus H. A. Smith has observed that:

> After the armistice of 1918 opinion in the Allied countries tended to regard the experience of the war as something both deplorable and exceptional. It was hoped that the authority of the old rules could be restored and this view found expression in the unratified treaty drawn up at the Washington Conference of 1922, which declared in effect that submarines must obey the same rules as surface ships. Almost all the writers of textbooks assumed that the rules of 1914 were still in force, and that the departures from these rules could be attributed to temporary causes not likely to be repeated. The official manuals issued in many countries for the instruction of naval officers all assumed the same point of view.[5]

The general reaction that has followed in the wake of the second World War, a war that served largely to confirm and to carry still further the prac-

[3] For the text and commentary upon the present status of the Protocol, see pp. 63–70. It may be noted that the Protocol was very largely a restatement, in conventional form, of pre-existing rules of customary law applicable to the operation of surface vessels.

[4] We are neglecting for the present the possible changes effected in the rules governing neutral-belligerent relations that result from obligations states may assume by virtue of membership in collective security organizations (see pp. 171–80).—A fairly detailed account of the historical development of the law of naval warfare up to World War II is given by Raoul Genet, *Droit Maritime Pour le Temps de Guerre* (1936–38), Vol. I, pp. 57–91.

[5] H. A. Smith, *The Law and Custom of the Sea* (2nd. ed., 1950), p. 72.

tices initiated a quarter of a century earlier, has been quite different. The argument that the circumstances of this second conflict were exceptional appears, for obvious reasons, far less plausible and has been resorted to only infrequently. If anything, there now seems to be a widespread—though by no means unanimous—conviction that the experience of World War II must be considered as the probable standard for the future conduct of war at sea rather than an exceptional event of the past whose recurrence is unlikely.[6] Occasionally, this more recent reaction has taken the form of expressing the belief that in modern war much of the traditional law is simply inapplicable given the far-reaching transformation of the nineteenth century environment in which this law developed and from which it derived its meaning and significance. From this latter point of view it is insufficient to concentrate attention only upon the actual practices of the two World Wars. In addition, an inquiry must be made into the social, political and technological developments that have led to these recent practices. The experience of the two World Wars is held—according to this view—to indicate not only the relative ineffectiveness of many of the traditional rules. Even more important is the allegation that the traditional law no longer bears a meaningful relationship to the contemporary—and, it is assumed, the future—environment. Hence, it is this ever widening gap, this growing tension, between the contemporary social, political and technological environment and the environment presupposed by the traditional law that will presumably determine the inapplicability of this law in future hostilities at sea.[7]

To a limited degree, the difficulties encountered in the endeavor to assess

---

[6] Among recent expressions to this effect, Julius Stone, *op. cit.*, pp. 402–13, 508–10, 599–607; H. A. Smith, *The Crisis in the Law of Nations* (1947), pp. 33–66; H. Lauterpacht, "The Problem of the Revision of The Law of War," *B. Y. I. L.*, 29 (1952), pp. 373–7. It is an interesting gloss on the complexity of the attempt to evaluate the effects of recent practice on the traditional law that assertions as to the future ineffectiveness of this law are frequently made by writers—including those cited above—who nevertheless insist upon the continued validity of this law.

[7] Thus the argument cited above usually places emphasis upon the fact that the traditional law developed from, and consequently presupposed for its operation, a certain type of state and a certain type of war. The conception of the state was not necessarily democratic, but it was a state with limited powers. It presupposed economic liberalism, with a clear distinction to be drawn between the activities of the state and the activities of the private individual. The nineteenth century conception of war was that of a limited war, limited not only in terms of the number of states involved in any conflict, but also limited in terms of the fraction of each belligerent's population which either actively participated in or closely identified itself with the conduct of war. Finally, this conception of war presupposed limited war aims on the part of belligerents, which in turn facilitated the introduction of effective restraints upon the methods by which these aims might be pursued. Perhaps the decisive factor in conditioning the development of the traditional law was the assumption that in any war a substantial number of states would refrain from participating in hostilities, and that the interests of these non-participants would have to be respected (see pp. 181–4). The conditions under which the two World Wars were fought, it is contended, have either placed in serious question or have swept away entirely these nineteenth century conceptions.

the impact of the two World Wars upon the traditional law may be lessened once it is recognized that the continued validity of this law is dependent upon a minimum degree of effectiveness. In a legal system characterized by a low stage of procedural development—as is the international legal system—the prolonged and marked ineffectiveness of a once valid rule would appear to result in rendering this rule no longer binding.[8] In the case of customary rules—and they form the primary concern here—the requirement that continued validity must presuppose a minimum degree of effectiveness would seem almost compelling, for the creation of customary law depends upon a well-established practice of states that is accompanied by the general conviction that the practice in question is both obligatory and right.[9] The effectiveness of the practice which serves to create customary law forms an essential prerequisite. Conversely, the invalidation of a rule of customary law may be brought about by a sustained and effective practice that is contrary to once-established custom, particularly a practice that has ceased to provoke either protest or reprisal on the part of interested states. Presumably, the same requirement of effectiveness may be considered applicable to general rules established by convention; rules that are neither obeyed nor applied by the parties to a convention over a substantial period of time may be considered as being no longer valid.

The apparent ease with which the general relationship between the binding quality of the rules of war and the effectiveness of these rules may be stated should not prove misleading, however. In practice, the difficulties occur when the descent is made from the general proposition to the concrete case, and the question is posed: has this rule of customary (or conventional) law ceased to be valid for the reason that over a defined period of time it has been ineffective in regulating belligerent behavior? Merely to formulate the problem in this manner suggests the serious obstacles in the way of a practical and useful solution.

There is, to begin with, no rule of positive international law indicating either the length of the period or the degree of ineffectiveness sufficient to invalidate established rules of custom (or convention), just as there is no rule determining the point at which established usage turns into custom. And although the development from usage to custom is a decisive one, since it is only after this development has occurred that we are entitled to speak of laws of warfare, it is frequently difficult to determine this point in time. Nor is the absence of precise criteria for the determination of these questions relieved by the presence of an international tribunal competent to render authoritative and binding judgments in doubtful cases. In the absence of international tribunals competent to render such decisions in a manner binding upon states, the latter themselves must so decide, and

[8] In this sense, the "procedural development" of a legal system refers to the process of effective centralization of the judicial, executive and legislative functions.

[9] See, *Law of Naval Warfare*, Article 211.

the evidence of such decisions will commonly be manifested in the instructions many states issue to their naval forces, in the diplomatic correspondence carried on by states, in the prize codes states enact when engaged in hostilities, and in the decisions rendered by national prize courts. Yet these "decisions," insofar as they constitute an interpretation of the law of naval warfare, are not binding upon other states; the right of each state to interpret the law is not a right to decide this law in the sense that this interpretation is obligatory for other states.[10]

It is quite true that the absence of compulsory international tribunals affects the utility of conventional rules as well, since not infrequently the provisions of conventional rules are subject to widely varying interpretations.[11] Nevertheless, in the case of customary rules this difficulty is normally magnified, since the degree of uncertainty as to the content of a customary rule is not only likely to be greater, but the very existence of the rule is in many instances the real subject of dispute. In the history of naval warfare controversies over the meaning or even the purported existence of customary rules have never been absent, and this uncertainty has had as a consequence the furnishing of belligerents with a convenient pretext for the taking of reprisals against allegedly unlawful behavior of an enemy.

In short, the obvious consequences of the far-reaching decentralization characteristic of the international legal order are perhaps even more readily apparent in time of war than in time of peace, and the uncertainty produced by this condition is more clearly evident in the case of customary rules than in the case of conventional rules. Hence, even if it is generally admitted that a necessary relationship must exist between the validity and the effectiveness of the rules regulating the conduct of war at sea, the above considerations would appear to indicate that in practice a large number of these rules must continue to lead what might be termed a "shadowy existence."

There is a further, and closely related, factor that contributes to the difficulty of rendering a satisfactory evaluation of the impact of recent practices upon the traditional law. During both World Wars the major

10 "The technical organizational insufficiency of international law may, and in fact does, make it difficult to determine whether a state acts in accordance with, or contrary to, international law. . . . It is generally recognized that the root of the unsatisfactory situation in international law and relations is the absence of an authority generally competent to declare what the law is at any given time, how it applies to a given situation or dispute, and what the appropriate sanction may be. In the absence of such an authority, and failing agreement between the states at variance on these points, each state has a right to interpret the law, the right of auto-interpretation, as it might be called. This interpretation, however, is not a 'decision' and is neither final nor binding upon the other parties." Leo Gross, "States as Organs of International Law and the Problem of Auto-Interpretation," *Law and Politics in the World Community*, pp. 76–7.

11 An example of such widely varying interpretations may be seen in the case of the provisions of Hague VIII (1907), dealing with the laying of automatic contact mines. See pp. 303–5.

naval belligerents deemed it necessary to conduct hostilities at sea largely upon the basis of measures whose legal justification—*if* the continued validity of the traditional law is assumed—could rest only upon the belligerent right of reprisal. The declaration of operational (war) zone within which neutral shipping was subject to special hazards, the indiscriminate laying of mines, the resort to unrestricted aerial and submarine warfare, the substantial alteration of the traditional law governing blockade and contraband—these and other measures were based for the most part upon the belligerent claim of reprisal. There is no need, at this point, to consider the nature and permissible extent of the belligerent right to resort to reprisals in maritime warfare, particularly when belligerent reprisals are found to operate principally against neutral shipping.[12] Nor is it necessary to examine in this connection the controversial question of ultimate responsibility for the initiation of the seemingly endless series of reprisals at sea. It is relevant to observe, however, that the resort to reprisals in both World Wars provided—in certain instances at least—a convenient method for evading the restrictions imposed by the traditional law, and, it has been contended, for effecting changes in this law that ordinarily would have been left to the explicit agreement of the interested states.[13]

At the same time, the care with which belligerents have frequently sought to base departures from the traditional law upon the right of reprisal against allegedly unlawful actions of an enemy [14] has had the result of denying the possibility of rendering an unambiguous interpretation of the measures which formed the content of these reprisals. Normally, the resort to reprisals may be interpreted as an affirmation of the continued validity of the law the violation of which forms the condition of the reprisal. A reprisal between belligerents is an act, otherwise unlawful, that is exceptionally permitted to a belligerent as a reaction against a previous violation of law by an enemy.[15] Despite the evident desire of belligerents

[12] See pp. 187–90, 253–8.

[13] "In the sphere of maritime law the operation of reprisals in both World Wars has, in practice, replaced most of the traditional rules. In a sense, reprisals have often fulfilled the function which would normally have been left to the agreement between States, namely, that of the adaptation of the law to the changed conditions of modern warfare. For this reason it is not always profitable to inquire whose original illegality opened wide the flood gates of retaliation. It is sufficient to note that the torrent swept away with devastating thoroughness many of the elaborate, though often controversial, rules." H. Lauterpacht, "The Law of Nations and the Punishment of War Crimes," *B. Y. I. L.*, 21 (1944), p. 76. See also the penetrating comments of Julius Stone (*op. cit.*, pp. 355–66, 366–7) on the "legislative function" of reprisals in naval warfare.

[14] A care which Nazi Germany did not abandon even at the height of her wartime victories. Thus the German "blockade" announcement of August 18, 1940, sought to justify the measures to be taken against enemy and neutral vessels upon the right of retaliation. For text of the German "blockade" announcement, see *U. S. Naval War College, International Law Documents, 1940*, pp. 46–50. Also, see pp. 296–305.

[15] On reprisals generally, see pp. 150–3.

in recent maritime warfare to use reprisals as a pretext for evading the traditional law, there is nevertheless considerable merit in the argument that the very care with which such departures were usually justified as reprisals indicates the continued existence of a conviction that behavior in conformity with this law is normally both obligatory and right. It has already been observed that this conviction is a necessary element—along with the criterion of effectiveness—in the creation of customary law. It would appear equally true that the retention of this conviction must be taken into consideration when attempting to determine the continued validity of the traditional law. This consideration, therefore, must form a qualification upon an uncritical use of the principle of effectiveness.

There are, of course, limits to the significance that reasonably can be given to the claim of reprisals. This is especially so when acts resorted to as reprisals threaten to become part of the permanent structure of naval hostilities rather than a temporary and limited exception. Still, the fact that belligerents have felt the necessity to use the plea of reprisals when departing from the traditional law warrants the most careful inquiry before a rule of maritime warfare can be considered, with assurance, as no longer valid.[16]

B. THE BINDING FORCE OF THE LAW OF NAVAL WARFARE

As a general rule, the binding force of conventional rules of war is limited to the contracting parties, and then only to the extent specified by the terms of the convention in question and by the conditions accompanying ratification or adherence.[17] On the other hand, the customary rules of the law of war are binding upon all states and under all circumstances. The

---

[16] The remarks made in the text above on the relationship between the validity and the effectiveness of the laws of war form a problem upon which succeeding chapters provide almost a continuous commentary. Indeed, it is surely no exaggeration to state that the effect of recent practice upon the traditional law constitutes *the critical problem* in any contemporary inquiry into the present status of the rules of naval warfare. Unfortunately, however, it is next to impossible to present a clear and satisfactory answer to this problem, largely for those reasons that have already been indicated in the preceding pages of this chapter.

[17] See *Law of Naval Warfare*, Article 213b and notes thereto. All of the Hague Conventions of 1907 contain a provision known as the "general participation" clause, to the effect that the convention in question applies only to the contracting parties, and then only if all the belligerents are parties to the convention. In strict law, therefore, these conventions are not binding unless the requirements of the general participation clause are met. During World Wars I and II some of these conventions were nevertheless applied, despite the fact that not all the belligerents were parties to the convention in question. In practice, states have looked more to the element of reciprocity than to the formal standards of this clause. In addition, some of the 1907 Hague Conventions have come to be considered as a codification of customary law, hence binding upon all belligerents irrespective of ratification or adherence—e. g., Hague IV, Respecting The Laws and Customs of War on Land. More recently, the contracting parties to multilateral conventions regulating the conduct of war have avoided the "general participation" clause. The common Article 2 paragraph 3 of the 1949 Geneva Conventions

statement is frequently made that reprisals form one clear exception to the binding force of customary rules.[18] However, this manner of formulation may easily prove misleading. The act of taking reprisals does not represent a restriction to the binding force of customary law. On the contrary, this law remains fully binding, and the act of taking reprisals is itself a clear indication of the continued binding force of the customary law the violation of which forms the condition for the act of reprisal. Reprisals do not represent—at least not in theory [19]—an abandonment of the customary law (or the conventional law for that matter), but rather the enforcement of that law; at the very least, reprisals represent an act of "self help" permitted against a previous violation of law.[20]

Apart from reprisals, the principle of military necessity has generally been considered as the most important qualification to the binding force of both the customary and conventional law of war. Indeed, the extent to which this principle may be held to restrict the operation of the rules of war has provided one of the most disputed issues among writers.[21] The core of the controversy has centered about the doctrine that interprets military necessity as serving to justify departure from any of the established rules of war when the observance of these rules either would endanger the

---

on the Protection of Victims of War provides that the contracting Parties to the conventions—in time of conflict—remain bound by the conventions, as among themselves, even though one of the belligerents is not so bound. Thus: "Although one of the Powers in conflict may not be a party to the present Convention, the Powers who are Parties thereto shall remain bound by it in their mutual relations. They shall furthermore be bound by the Convention in relation to the said Power, if the latter accepts and applies the provisions thereof."

[18] Thus Oppenheim-Lauterpacht (*op. cit,*. p. 231): "As soon as usages of warfare have by custom or treaty evolved into laws of war, they are binding upon belligerents under all circumstances and conditions, except in the case of reprisals as retaliation against a belligerent for illegitimate acts of warfare by the members of his armed forces or his other subjects."

[19] A different question, of course, concerns the practical effect of reprisals, particularly as operative in hostilities at sea.

[20] *Law of Naval Warfare, Article 213a.*

[21] It should be made clear that in this context the principle of military necessity is considered as a rule of positive law and not as an ideal (or policy) influential in the development of the law of war. However, as a rule of positive law the principle of military necessity has been used in two quite different senses, which should be distinguished clearly. In the first sense, military necessity is held to constitute a restriction—whether explicit or implicit—upon the operation of the positive rules of custom and convention. Here military necessity refers to those exceptional conditions or circumstances in which behavior otherwise prescribed by established rules of law may be disregarded. In the second sense, the principle of military necessity forms a standard (along with the principle of humanity) for determining the legality of a weapon or method of warfare not already expressly regulated by a rule of custom or convention. In the former sense, then, military necessity relates to restrictions upon the operation of existing rules; in the latter sense military necessity provides a standard for judging the legality of weapons and methods not already expressly regulated. It is the first meaning of the principle that is considered here, whereas the latter meaning is considered when dealing with the general principles governing the weapons and methods of warfare (see pp. 45–50). Article 220a of the *Law of Naval Warfare* includes both meanings within its definition of military necessity.

success of a military operation or would threaten the survival (self-preservation) of a military unit.[22] In either circumstance, the principle of military necessity is considered to be operative and to free belligerents from behaving in accordance with *otherwise valid* law.[23]

As against this interpretation of military necessity it has been argued, principally by English and American writers, that military necessity—more precisely, that the circumstances held to constitute a condition of military necessity—can justify a departure from behavior normally demanded by the law of war only when conventional or customary rules expressly provide for the exceptional operation of military necessity.[24] According to this latter interpretation—which is believed to be correct—military necessity must be interpreted "to denote those exceptional circumstances of practical necessity contemplated by express reservations to be found in several Articles of the Hague Regulations and other Conventions in regard to acts otherwise prohibited. The general principle is that conventional and customary rules of warfare are always binding upon belligerents and cannot be disregarded even in case of military necessity." [25]

[22] In its classic form this doctrine is usually identified with the German proverb—*kriegsraison geht vor kriegsmanier*—necessity in war overrules the manner of warfare. The proverb is somewhat misleading since it has not been used primarily to refer to the manner or usages of war (*kriegsmanier*)—which would raise no serious question—but rather to the established law of war (*kreigsrecht*)—which does raise a serious question. This is clear from the formulation of *kriegsraison* given by Leuder (quoted in *The Collected Papers of John Westlake on Public International Law* (1914), pp. 244-5) to the following effect: "*Kriegsraison* embraces those cases in which, by way of exception, the law of war ought to be left without observance. . . . When . . . the circumstances are such that the attainment of the object of the war and the escape from extreme danger would be hindered by observing the limitations imposed by the laws of war, and can only be accomplished by breaking through these limitations, the latter is what ought to happen."

[23] Strictly speaking, this particular interpretation of military necessity does not deny the general validity of the customary and conventional law of war. Hence, military necessity is not used to deny the binding force (validity), in the formal sense, of these rules, though this may well be the practical effect of the doctrine. It is asserted, however, that this principle must be held to constitute an implied restriction to, and therefore can in the appropriate circumstances override, any otherwise valid rule of warfare.

[24] Examples of conventional rules providing for the exceptional operation of military necessity are: in land warfare, Article 23g of the Regulations attached to Hague Convention IV (1907) forbidding belligerents to "destroy or seize the enemy's property, unless such destruction or seizure be imperatively demanded by the necessities of war"; in naval warfare, Article 16 of Hague Convention X (1907) requiring that "after every engagement the two belligerents, so far as military interests permit, shall take steps to look for the shipwrecked, sick and wounded, and to protect them, as well as the dead, against pillage and ill treatment" (Article 18 of the 1949 Geneva Convention for the Amelioration of the Condition of Wounded, Sick and Shipwrecked Members of Armed Forces at Sea substantially repeats this earlier provision, save that it uses the words "take all possible measures to search for").

[25] N. C. H. Dunbar, "Military Necessity in War Crimes Trials," *B. Y. I. L.*, 29 (1952), p. 444. To the same effect, W. G. Downey, Jr. ("The Law of War and Military Necessity," *A. J. I. L.*, 47 (1953), p. 262): ". . . military necessity cannot justify an act by a military commander which disregards a positive rule of law or which goes beyond the express limitations of a

Hence, the principle of military necessity cannot be considered as superior to, and thereby restricting the operation of, all other rules of warfare, whether customary or conventional. On the contrary, it is the principle of military necessity that may be restricted by the positive law of war, and occasionally is so restricted.[26] Not everything necessary to the purpose of war is allowed by the law of war.[27]

---

qualified rule of law. Such acts always constitute a violation of the law of war." Oppenheim-Lauterpacht (*op. cit.*, p. 232): "These conventions and customary rules cannot be overruled by necessity, unless they are framed in such a way as not to apply to a case of necessity in self-preservation." Also Erik Castren (*The Present Law of War and Neutrality*, (1954), p. 66): "This view (i. e., doctrine of *kriegsraison*) of the elasticity of the laws of war must be absolutely *rejected* as it cannot be legally justified and as its *practical consequences* are most dangerous." Section 220a of the *Law of Naval Warfare* speaks of the operation of military necessity when "not otherwise prohibited by the laws of war." (And see notes to this provision for further elaboration.)

[26] It has been pointed out by many writers that one reason why military necessity may not be invoked except when expressly provided for by rules of warfare is that in establishing these rules military necessity has already been taken into consideration. This is held to be particularly true of conventional rules. (And the preamble to Hague Convention IV (1907), furnishes some support for this opinion in declaring that: "according to the views of the High Contracting Parties, these provisions, the wording of which has been inspired by the desire to diminish the evils of war, as far as military requirements permit. . . . ") While this contention is justified in large measure, it is important to recognize, at the same time, that certain rules clearly do *not* allow for the operation of military necessity. Thus the prohibitions against killing prisoners of war—or helpless survivors at sea—are absolute, and circumstances of military necessity do not justify any departures from these prohibitions. To a certain extent, therefore, it is a fiction to maintain that the law of war has in each instance already taken into account the requirements of military necessity, since in some instances action is prohibited even though circumstances constituting military necessity may otherwise require the performance of the prohibited action. Article 1 common to the four 1949 Geneva Conventions states that: "The High Contracting Parties undertake to respect and to ensure respect for the present Convention *in all circumstances*." [italics added] Finally, for an earlier—and emphatic—statement in the German literature to the effect that military necessity can be invoked only in the case of norms specifically providing for the exceptional operation of military necessity, see J. L. Kunz, *Kriegsrecht und Neutralitätsrecht* (1935), pp. 26–8.

[27] With respect to this more restrictive interpretation of military necessity it has been recently stated that: "This reasoning . . . would forbid departure from the rules of war-law even in face of the direst needs of survival. Yet it remains ground common to British, American, French, Italian and other publicists, as well as German, that a State is privileged, in title of self-preservation, to violate its ordinary duties under international law, even towards States with which it is at peace; and may also itself determine when its self-preservation is involved. Neither practice nor the literature explain satisfactorily how the privilege based on self-preservation in times of peace can be denied to States at war." Stone, *op. cit.*, pp. 352–3. Although the principle of military necessity more commonly refers "to the plight in which armed forces may find themselves under stress of active warfare" and not to "a danger or emergency of such proportions as to threaten immediately the vital interests, and, perhaps, the very existence of the state itself" (Dunbar, *op. cit.*, p. 443), it is nevertheless true that departures from the law of war can be—and frequently have been—justified in terms of the states' "fundamental right" of self-preservation. To this extent Professor Stone is certainly correct in observing a contradiction between the latitude ascribed by writers to the states' "right of self-preservation" in time of peace and a denial of the same right in time of war. In fact, however, the criticism

It is this latter, and more restrictive, interpretation of military necessity that has recently received clear judicial endorsement. In the war crimes trials following the second World War the chief preoccupation of tribunals called upon to interpret the principle of military necessity was to determine when circumstances of military necessity could be considered as serving to justify departures from conduct normally prescribed by the rules of warfare. Although the judgments of tribunals were by no means identical on a number of points, there nevertheless was a remarkable uniformity of judicial opinion, which—taken as a whole—clearly appears to support the narrow interpretation of military necessity. The following is a brief summary of these judgments.

(1) Military necessity may serve as a defense plea against charges of committing acts normally forbidden by the law of war only when the rule in question can be interpreted as permitting such exceptional departure in circumstances constituting a condition of military necessity. Thus in the Hostages Trial the tribunal stated that the prohibitions contained in the Hague Regulations "are superior to military necessities of the most urgent nature except where the Regulations themselves specifically provide the contrary. . . ." [28] In the case of conventional law the rule in question *must provide expressly* for military necessity In particular, where the prohibition contained in a rule is absolute in character, military necessity cannot be used as a defense. Thus circumstances of military necessity have not been considered as justifying the killing of prisoners of war.[29]

Professor Stone properly raises points to the necessity of a "frank review of the meaning of the self-preservation" doctrine as it applies in time of peace. The right of self-preservation accorded to a state in time of peace must therefore be limited to a right of action against measures which are *prima facie* unlawful. Neither "necessity in self-preservation" in time of peace nor "military necessity" in time of war can be held to justify a departure from established law, if such departure is taken in response to acts admittedly lawful in character.

[28] *(Trial of Wilhelm List and Others), Law Reports. . .*, 8 (1949), p. 69. Elsewhere the Tribunal went so far as to state that "the rules of International Law must be followed even if it results in the loss of a battle or even a war. Expediency or necessity cannot warrant their violation" (p. 67). In the Krupp Trial the tribunal declared that: "It is an essence of war that one or the other side must lose and the experienced generals and statesmen knew this when they drafted the rules and customs of land warfare. In short these rules and customs of warfare are designed specifically for all phases of war." *(Trial of Alfred Felix Alwyn Krupp von Bohlen und Halbach and Eleven Others), Law Reports. . .*, 10 (1949), p. 139. Also see the *Trial of Erhard Milch, Law Reports. . .*, 7 (1948), pp. 44, 64–5.

In his excellent survey of these and other cases, Dunbar (*op. cit.*, p. 452) states that: "It seems likely that courts will be disinclined to enlarge the doctrine of military necessity beyond that countenanced by express reservations appearing in the Hague and Geneva Conventions. The general principle is that belligerents must always respect and observe customary and conventional rules of warfare."

[29] In the *Trial of Gunther Thiele and Georg Steinert* (*Law Reports . . .*, 3 (1948), pp. 56–9) a United States Military Commission tried and sentenced the accused to death by hanging for unlawfully ordering and killing prisoners of war. At the time the offense was committed the accused were "part of a German unit which was closely surrounded by United States troops, from which the Germans were hiding.

(2) In the case of rules allowing for the exceptional operation of military necessity, departure from normally prescribed behavior is justified for reasons of self-preservation or for insuring the success of a military operation. In addition, there must be an element of urgency involved that allowed—or seemed to allow—no alternative course of action. However, it does not appear that it is essential to establish that the circumstances constituting a condition of military necessity were objectively present in a given situation. It is sufficient only to establish that the individual putting forth the plea of military necessity as a defense honestly believed at the time that such circumstances were present.[30]

[30] This last point was given special emphasis in the Hostages Trial where one of the accused had been charged with the wanton destruction of property while retreating before Russian forces. The accused maintained that he acted only under circumstances he believed to constitute a condition of military necessity, and that his behavior was justified by Article 23g of Hague IV (1907). In its judgment, the Tribunal stated: "There is evidence in the record that there was no military necessity for this destruction and devastation. An examination of the facts in retrospect can well sustain this conclusion. But we are obliged to judge the situation as it appeared to the defendant at the time. If the facts were such as would justify the action by the exercise of judgment, after giving consideration to all the factors and existing possibilities, even though the conclusion reached may have been faulty, it cannot be said to be criminal." (*Trial of Wilhelm List and Others*) *Law Reports. . .*, 8 (1949), pp. 68–9. A substantially similar conclusion was reached by the Tribunal in the German High Command Trial (*Trials of Wilhelm Von Leeb and Thirteen Others*) *Law Reports . . .*, 12 (1949), pp. 93–4.

III. THE NAVAL FORCES OF BELLIGERENTS

A. THE NAVAL FORCES OF BELLIGERENTS ACCORDING TO THE TRADITIONAL LAW

In warfare at sea it is important to be able to identify clearly the naval forces of belligerents. The reason for this is that many of the rules regulating inter-belligerent and neutral-belligerent relations are dependent for their operation upon the possibility of distinguishing between combatants and non-combatants. Only the naval forces of a belligerent are permitted to conduct offensive operations against an enemy. In addition, the treatment accorded to a belligerent vessel depends, in the first place, upon whether or not the vessel forms a part of the belligerent's naval forces. Whereas the naval vessels of a belligerent are subject to attack and destruction on sight, enemy merchant vessels are normally exempt from such treatment. Whereas title to a vessel in the military service of an enemy immediately vests in the government of the captor by virtue of the fact of capture, title to an enemy merchant vessel normally depends upon adjudication by a prize court. So also may the treatment of personnel taken from enemy vessels differ, depending upon the status of the vessel. Finally, the traditional rules governing neutral-belligerent relations in naval war presuppose throughout the possibility of distinguishing between the naval forces of belligerent and belligerent merchant vessels.[1]

Although the naval forces of states comprise vessels, aircraft and personnel, the warship remains the main combatant unit in warfare at sea and therefore forms the principal object of inquiry.[2] While there is no multilateral convention that directly defines a warship, Hague Convention VII (1907), by enumerating the conditions that must be satisfied in order to convert a merchant vessel into a warship, indirectly defined the latter. In this Convention a vessel in order to qualify as a warship must be placed under the direct authority, immediate control, and the responsibility of the power whose flag it flies; it must bear the external marks distinguishing the warships of the state under whose authority it acts; the commander of the ves-

[1] See pp. 56 ff.

[2] To this extent, a discussion of lawful combatants in naval warfare differs from a similar discussion in relation to land warfare where attention is directed primarily toward determining the status of personnel. As a general rule, in naval warfare the combatant status of the vessel is sufficient to determine the combatant status of the personnel on board the vessel. This is equally true for aircraft, the combatant status of the vessel being extended to aircraft carried on board.

sel must be in the service of the state, duly commissioned, and listed among the officers of the fighting fleet; the crew must be subject to naval discipline; and the vessel must observe in its operation the laws and customs of war. In principle, these criteria may still be regarded as furnishing the distinctive features of warships.[3]

Included among the commissioned naval forces of states are many vessels that are neither heavily armed nor capable, in fact, of carrying out offensive operations against an enemy. The suggestion has occasionally been put forward that such vessels ought not to be subject to the same treatment meted out to heavily armed warships.[4] However, the practice of states has not been to consider these naval vessels as possessing a status essentially different from the status of naval vessels whose primary purpose is to conduct offensive operations.[5] It is the fact of being duly commissioned as a naval vessel, hence being *legally competent* to exercise belligerent rights at sea, that is the decisive consideration, and not the fact that many naval vessels may be only lightly armed or perhaps altogether without offensive armament.[6] A consequence of this incorporation into the naval forces of a belligerent, and the attending legal competence to exercise belligerent rights, is the liability to attack and destruction on sight.

Thus commissioned naval vessels, commanded by commissioned naval officers and flying the naval ensign, which serve either to transport the armed forces of belligerents or to perform various auxiliary services to fighting vessels (i. e., supply tenders, colliers, etc.) are subject, in principle, to the same treatment as naval vessels whose purpose is to conduct offensive operations at sea. To this extent, at least, it would appear misleading to distinguish between the "combatant" and "non-combatant" naval forces

[3] See *Law of Naval Warfare*, Section 500c. Among writers the following statement may be considered to be representative: "The essential features of a warship are that her commander holds a commission from his state, the ship flies the flag of the navy which in many countries is different from that of the merchant marine, and the officers and crew are under naval discipline." Higgins and Colombos, *The International Law of the Sea*, (2nd ed. rev. by C. John Colombos, 1951), p. 350.

[4] C. C. Hyde, for example, states that "the public belligerent ship which is impotent to fight through lack of armament should not be dealt with as though it were a dreadnought. Hence there appears to be need of a fresh classification differentiating the fighting from the non-fighting public vessels of a belligerent, in case at least it be acknowledged that both are not to be treated alike by an enemy." *International Law, Chiefly As Interpreted and Applied By The United States* (2nd. rev. ed., 1945), Vol. 3, p. 1920.

[5] A similar position is taken by Professor Guggenheim (*op. cit.*, p. 326), who points out that as long as a vessel makes up a part of the naval forces of a belligerent, in the sense described in the text above, it is immaterial whether or not the vessel is armed in the regular manner of warships.

[6] Exception must be made, of course, for naval hospital vessels and cartel vessels, which bear a special status. Although included within the naval forces of belligerents, neither of these categories of vessels is legally capable of exercising belligerent rights at sea, and the unlawful exercise of belligerent rights serves to deprive hospital and cartel vessels of the special protection otherwise guaranteed to them. See pp. 96–8, 126–8.

of belligerents.[7] Whatever differentiation in treatment is to be given to these two categories of naval vessels must instead be attributed to the rule obligating belligerents to apply only that degree of force required for the submission of the enemy.[8]

A special problem concerns the conversion of merchant vessels into warships. In both World Wars the naval belligerents freely resorted to the practice of converting merchant vessels into warships. So long as such conversion was effected within the jurisdiction of the belligerent resorting to conversion (or within the jurisdiction of Allies) and the converted vessel fulfilled the requirements stipulated in Hague Convention VII (1907), requirements which have already been summarized, there was no serious disposition to challenge the right of converting merchant vessels into warships. But neither Hague Convention VII (1907) nor subsequent practice succeeded in settling the question as to whether merchant vessels may be converted on the high seas.[9]

Although the legitimacy of converting merchant vessels into warships must be considered as well established, it has been contended that to permit conversion revives, in fact if not in law, the centuries old practice of privateering, a practice formally abolished by the Declaration of Paris of 1856. There is much to be said for this view.[10] It is quite true that the control

[7] Frequently, however, this distinction results from the fact that belligerents employ vessels in order to perform auxiliary services to combatant naval units though without formally incorporating such vessels into the naval forces. Vessels so serving belligerent forces may retain their private ownership and merely serve under charter to the belligerents for the purposes of the war. On the other hand, they may be owned by the government. In any event, unless commissioned as naval vessels they are not competent to exercise belligerent rights at sea. Thus the term "fleet auxiliaries" must be used with caution, since it may refer to vessels formally incorporated into the naval forces of a belligerent, and therefore competent to exercise belligerent rights, and those not formally incorporated. Neither the fact that both categories of vessels perform essentially similar services nor the fact that both categories are *subject to the same liabilities* if encountered by an enemy (i. e., attack and destruction) should serve to obscure this distinction.

[8] See pp. 46–50.

[9] Conversion within neutral jurisdiction being clearly prohibited. In practice, however, the question as to whether merchant vessels may be converted on the high seas did not prove to be too significant a controversy in either World War. Far more important has been the dispute over the status of vessels that have not been openly converted, but that have been "defensively" armed and subjected to a considerable measure of state control (see pp. 58 ff.). A further unsettled point concerns the legality of reconversion as well as the place where reconversion may take place, if permitted.

[10] E. g., Stone asks whether Hague Convention VII (1907) was not "an abrogation *pro tanto* of the rule of the Declaration of Paris which abolished privateering. Analytically . . . Hague Convention No. 7 contains no such abrogation. Yet it seems idle to blink the fact that functionally the Convention sanctions the use of merchantmen to fill gaps in regular navies formerly filled by the privateers." *op. cit.*, p. 576. These views echo the opinions of earlier writers. On the other hand, Oppenheim-Lauterpacht declares that: "The opinion . . . that by permitting the conversion of merchantmen into men-of-war privateering had been revived, is unfounded, for the rules of Convention VII in no way abrogated the rule of the Declaration of Paris that privateering is and remains abolished." *op. cit.*, p. 265.

belligerents now exercise over converted merchant vessels, and the disappearance of the motive of personal gain, has served to remove some of the most undesirable features that were characteristic of privateering. Yet it seems equally true that widespread resort to conversion serves to fulfill in large measure the principal function formerly accomplished through the use of privateers. Through the conversion of merchant ships a weak naval power hopes to compensate for its weakness in much the same manner that weak naval powers in the past compensated for their weakness by the use of privateers. In view of the disparity that will usually exist between a regular warship and a converted merchant vessel, the principal use of the latter must be—and in practice has been—confined to forays against enemy merchant shipping. Rather than utilize his warships for the protection of merchant shipping, the belligerent against whom such converted merchant vessels operate will resort to the defensive arming of his merchant vessels. In this manner the widespread use by belligerents of converted merchant vessels has been one factor, in addition to the submarine and aircraft, that has served to lead to the present unsettled status of the distinction between combatants and non-combatants in naval warfare.

B. THE PROBLEM TODAY

The preceding considerations have dealt with the identifying characteristics of naval forces, characteristics which are well established by the customary practices of states. Vessels possessing these characteristics are competent to exercise belligerent rights at sea, are subject to attack and destruction at sight by the military forces of an enemy, and are obligated to observe certain restrictions when in neutral territorial waters and ports.[11] Recent developments, however, have served to cast considerable doubt upon the adequacy of the characteristics established by the traditional law for identifying the naval forces of belligerents. The criticism is increasingly made that the traditional law, and the formal requirements laid down by this law, are no longer entirely appropriate given the circumstances under which the two World Wars were fought. More specifically, it has been held that the traditional law fails to include within the naval forces of belligerents many vessels which constitute at present an integral part of a belligerent's military effort at sea.

This criticism undoubtedly warrants the most serious consideration. Despite the obvious importance of being able to identify clearly the naval forces of belligerents the task has never proven easy. The traditional law attempted to resolve some of the difficulties involved in making this identification by drawing a distinction between those vessels competent to exercise belligerent rights and those vessels not so competent but whose behavior might nevertheless result in liability to the same treatment as belligerent warships. Competence to exercise belligerent rights, as already

[11] See pp. 219–45 for a discussion of such restrictions.

noted, is vested by the traditional law only in those vessels that are formally incorporated into the naval forces of a belligerent, that are commanded by a commissioned naval officer and manned by a crew submitted to naval discipline, and that fly the naval ensign. On the other hand, any merchant vessel—including the merchant vessels of neutral states—could become liable to the same treatment as belligerent warships, such liability following from the performance of certain acts. Thus a merchant vessel actively resisting visit and search or performing certain acts of direct assistance to the military operations of a belligerent has always been considered as subjecting itself to attack and possible destruction.[12] Nevertheless, this liability of merchant vessels did not warrant their being considered as bearing the same legal status as the naval forces of belligerents. In particular, the subjection of merchant vessels to treatment similar to that meted out to belligerent warships did not, for that reason, serve to confer upon such vessels the rights which belonged only to warships.

The utility of this distinction admittedly has been substantially reduced today when belligerents either own and operate directly all vessels engaged in trade or submit the activities of privately owned vessels to far reaching controls. The traditional law necessarily assumed that the occasions in which privately owned and operated vessels would become liable to the same treatment as warships would be limited in number. Perhaps equally important was the assumption that this liability of merchant vessels would follow—when it did occur—as the result of acts freely undertaken by the owners of private vessels. These assumptions are valid only to a very limited extent at present, and it is with their gradual disappearance during the two World Wars that the principal difficulty involved in identifying the naval forces of belligerents is intimately related. The "defensive" arming of belligerent merchant vessels at the direction and expense of the state, the manning of defensive armament by naval gun crews, sailing under convoy of warships, and the incorporation of merchant vessels into the intelligence system of the belligerent, have become common practices.

It may, of course, be argued that despite this ever increasing control exercised over merchant vessels, that despite this growing integration of merchant vessels with the military forces of a belligerent, the legal status of merchant vessels—whether publicly or privately owned—remains essentially unchanged so long as such vessels do not satisfy the strict requirements of warships as established by the traditional law.[13] The accuracy

[12] See pp. 56–7, 67–70, 319–22, 336–7.

[13] In one opinion of the American-German Mixed Claims Commission, established after World War I, adjudicating claims for compensation of losses suffered through the destruction of ships by Germany or her allies, the following conclusion was reached: "Neither (a) the arming for defensive purposes of a merchantman, nor (b) the manning of such armament by a naval gun crew, nor (c) her routing by the Navy Department of the United States for the purpose of avoiding the enemy, nor (d) the following by the civilian master of such merchantman of instructions given by the Navy Department for the defense of the ship when attacked by or

of this contention must be found, however, largely in the identification of "legal status" with the competence to exercise belligerent rights at sea. It cannot prejudice the possible conclusion that this lack of competence to exercise belligerent rights does not—at the same time—also serve to confer upon merchant vessels continued exemption from the liability of commissioned naval vessels to attack and possible destruction.[14] It should further be observed that if the principal purpose of restricting the legal status of naval forces to those vessels possessing the characteristics of warships as established by the traditional law is to preserve the distinction between combatants and non-combatants in naval warfare this purpose is not being well served. For the apparent effect of retaining the traditional requirements in a period when merchant vessels are increasingly integrated into the military effort of belligerents is to deprive such vessels of the immunities of non-combatants while at the same time denying them the full rights conferred upon combatants in warfare at sea.

C. AERIAL FORCES IN WARFARE AT SEA

It is hardly possible to assert that the identifying characteristics of combatant forces in aerial warfare has as yet been resolved in a definitive manner. In the absence of international convention regulating this aspect of aerial warfare such regulation as does exist must be based either upon an application to aerial warfare of the rules identifying legitimate combatants in naval or land warfare or upon the actual practices of belligerents in the conduct of aerial warfare. Both of these possibilities involve certain difficulties. The practices of belligerents during World War II were not always uniform, and even where a marked degree of uniformity was apparent doubt may remain as to whether so short a practice is to be considered as satisfying the requirements of customary law.[15] The application "by analogy" of the requirements lawful combatants must meet either in naval or land warfare is objectionable if only for the reason that aerial warfare is a distinct form of waging war, which cannot be easily assimilated to the older forms of warfare. The differences existing between land and naval warfare with respect to the identification of legitimate combatants

---

in danger of attack by the enemy, nor (e) her seeking the protection of a convoy and submitting herself to naval instructions as to route and operation for the purpose of avoiding the enemy, nor all of these combined will suffice to impress such merchantman with a military character." At the same time, however, the Commission expressly disclaimed passing judgment upon whether any of the conditions enumerated above entitled Germany, according to the existing rules of international law, to attack and destroy allied merchant vessels. *U. S. Naval War College, International Law Decisions and Notes, 1923*, pp. 189–90, 214.

[14] See pp. 55–70 for a detailed discussion of the conditions under which belligerent merchant vessels may be attacked and destroyed either with or without prior warning.

[15] See pp. 27 ff.

should constitute a warning against attempts to apply to aerial warfare rules operative to troops on land or to vessels at sea.[16]

In this study the problem of identifying legitimate combatants in aerial warfare is limited to aircraft which either make up a part of the naval forces of belligerents or which participate in operations of a naval character. In the light of this qualification and of the relevant practices of World War II the following tentative conclusions may be drawn. In principle, the characteristics considered essential to qualify a vessel to exercise belligerent rights at sea have been applied to the conduct of aerial warfare as well. During World War II there was a general disposition on the part of the belligerents to consider as entitled to exercise belligerent rights only those aircraft that were incorporated into the military forces of the state, that were commanded and manned by military personnel, and that showed such marking as would clearly indicate nationality and military character.[17]

---

16 Thus an element of uncertainty remains as to whether in naval warfare the identifying characteristics of lawful combatants should attach to the aircraft (as in naval warfare to the vessel), to the personnel manning the aircraft (as in land warfare to troops), or to both aircraft and personnel. J. M. Spaight, *Air Power and War Rights* (3rd. ed., 1947), pp. 76 ff., contends that in aerial warfare combatant identification must be primarily attached to the aircraft, that aircraft are obligated to use the military markings of their state, and that personnel are not required to wear a uniform (identity tokens being sufficient to establish combatant status). It is apparent that Spaight considers aerial warfare to resemble, in this respect at least, naval warfare. Stone (*op. cit.*, p. 612), on the other hand, questions these conclusions, and while admitting that practice to date suggests an "inchoate prohibition" against the use of false markings by aircraft, asserts that the details of any clear prohibition to this effect have yet to emerge.

17 See *Law of Naval Warfare*, Section 500d.—For a review of World War II practices regarding combatant quality in aerial warfare, see Spaight, *op. cit.*, pp. 76–107.—Articles 13 and 14 of the unratified 1923 Rules of Aerial Warfare, drafted by the Commission of Jurists at The Hague, stated that: "Belligerent aircraft are alone entitled to exercise belligerent rights . . . A military aircraft shall be under the command of a person duly commissioned or enlisted in the military service of the State; the crew must be exclusively military." The General Report on these provisions of the 1923 Rules declared that: "Belligerent rights at sea can now only be exercised by units under the direct authority, immediate control and responsibility of the State. This same principle should apply to aerial warfare. Belligerent rights should therefore only be exercised by military aircraft . . . Operations of war involve the responsibility of the State. Units of the fighting forces must, therefore, be under the direct control of persons responsible to the State. For the same reason the crew must be exclusively military in order that they may be subject to military discipline." *U. S. Naval War College, International Law Documents, 1924*, p. 114.

IV. RULES GOVERNING WEAPONS AND METHODS OF NAVAL WARFARE

A. THE GENERAL PRINCIPLES OF THE LAW OF WAR[1]

The guiding principle in a consideration of the rules governing the weapons and methods of naval warfare is that in the absence of restrictions imposed either by custom or by convention belligerents are permitted in their mutual relations to use any means in the conduct of hostilities. The essential purpose of the law of naval warfare is to define those actions that are prohibited to belligerents in warfare at sea. Indeed, this purpose is characteristic not only of the law of naval warfare but of the whole of the law of war. Historically, it is true that in the development of the means for waging hostilities it has been frequently asserted—both by governments and by writers on the law of war—that the introduction of a novel weapon or method must be regarded as unlawful until such time as expressly permitted by a specific rule of custom or convention. To the extent that such assertions have been based upon the alleged principle that what is not expressly permitted in war is thereby prohibited, they must be regarded as unfounded.

It is not uncommon, however, that claims as to the illegality of a novel weapon or method of war have been based upon the quite different premise that the weapon or method in question violates some general principle of the customary law of war; that although not expressly forbidden by a specific rule of custom or convention, the disputed means nevertheless falls within the purview of the prohibitions contained in one or more of these general principles. The validity of this latter claim has occasionally been obscured by its identification with the unwarranted assertion that what is not expressly permitted in war is thereby prohibited. In fact, what ought to be contended is that the lawfulness of the weapons and methods of war must be determined not only by the express prohibitions contained in specific rules of custom and convention but also by those prohibitions laid down in the general principles of the law of war.[2]

[1] It is to be emphasized that the following pages are concerned only with the mutual relations of belligerents and not with neutral-belligerent relations.

[2] Erik Castren correctly expresses the point made above as follows: "The idea, entertained by some writers, that everything is allowed in warfare that is not expressly prohibited cannot be accepted, as customary law alone may condemn such acts. The approbation or rejection of new arms and new methods of waging war depends on whether they conform to the general principles of warfare." *op. cit.*, p. 187. A similar view is taken by Alfred Verdross, who

The general principles of the law of war may be briefly stated. There is, to begin with, the principle distinguishing between the armed forces and the civilian population of a belligerent. In accordance with this principle individuals who form the non-combatant population of a belligerent must not be made the object of direct attack provided they refrain from the commission of all acts of hostility, and must be safeguarded from injuries not incidental to military operations directed against combatant forces and other legitimate military objectives.[3] There is, in addition, the principle of humanity which forbids the employment of any kind or degree of force that is unnecessary for the purpose(s) of war; force which needlessly or unnecessarily causes human suffering and physical destruction is prohibited.[4] Finally, there is the principle forbidding the resort to treacherous means, expedients, or conduct in the waging of hostilities.[5]

It has long been recognized that one of the primary purposes of the more specific customary and conventional rules of war has been to secure, through detailed regulations, the effective observance of these general principles. In naval warfare, for example, the specific rules governing the treatment to be accorded to enemy merchant vessels, as contrasted with the treatment accorded to warships, are based largely upon the principle distinguishing between combatants and non-combatants. In this instance, it is usual to state that the treatment of belligerent merchant vessels must be considered as the application to naval warfare of the principle distinguishing between combatants and non-combatants. Assuming this contention to be correct, it may be further stated that where the general principles of the law of war have received—through the agreement of states—detailed application in the

observes that all means which serve the purpose of defeating the enemy in war are permitted if they do not transgress *either* specific prohibitions *or* the general principles of the law of war. *Völkerrecht* (3rd. ed., 1955), p. 361. In this connection it is important to distinguish between the position taken in the text and the opinion—considered as incorrect—that any weapon necessary for the purpose of war may be employed by belligerents except a weapon designed solely to cause unnecessary suffering and injury to personnel. The military necessity of a weapon is not, of itself, a guarantee of its legality. The use of a weapon in war is legal only if it is not forbidden by the law of war. Such prohibition may result either from a specific rule of custom or convention or from the general principles of the law of war.

[3] *Law of Naval Warfare*, Article 221 and notes thereto. It may be observed that in Article 221 the terms "civilian population" and "non-combatants" are used interchangeably. The same usage is followed throughout the present text. Strictly speaking, the distinction between "combatants" and "non-combatants" is one made within the armed forces, the latter category comprising those individuals (e. g., medical and hospital personnel, chaplains) attached to or accompanying the armed forces in a special capacity. On the other hand, the term "civilian population" refers—in this strict sense—to the population of a belligerent other than those persons making up the armed forces. Most writers use the terms "civilian population" and "non-combatants" interchangeably, however, and do not use the latter term solely in its original—and restricted—sense. This is quite unobjectionable and need not give rise to any confusion.

[4] *Law of Naval Warfare*, Section 220b and notes thereto.

[5] *Law of Naval Warfare*, Section 220c and notes thereto.

form of specific rules, the question of the proper interpretation of these general principles can only be answered by an examination of the former. Hence, to the extent that the conduct of war is increasingly subjected to such regulation resort to the general principles of the law of war must become, in turn, correspondingly less frequent. The reason for this is simply that the essential function of these general principles is to provide a guide for determining the legal status of weapons and methods of war *where no more specific rule is applicable.*

In a period marked by rapid developments in the weapons and methods of war—and whose regulation by specific rules of custom or convention has not as yet been achieved—it is only natural to expect that the general principles of the law of war will assume a special significance. Unfortunately, however, considerable difficulties are encountered in the attempt to apply these general principles to means for conducting hostilities that have not as yet been made a matter of common agreement among states. In part, this may be attributed to the fact that the states themselves interpret and apply these principles, and being interested parties must be expected to act in accordance with their varying interests. However, even if it were assumed that states possess a greater degree of objectivity in their interpretation of legal rules than past experience could possibly vindicate, difficulties would still remain owing to the very nature of the general principles of the law of war and their uncertain status in an era of total war.

To a certain extent the application of the general principles of the law of war has always varied, depending upon the area of warfare to which they have been applied. This disparity in application is readily apparent when comparing the methods of warfare forbidden in hostilities on land as distinguished from naval hostilities.[6] In part, this disparity is due to differences in the conditions and circumstances attending the conduct of war on land and at sea. In part, it may be attributed simply to the peculiarities of historical development. Whatever the cause, it is hardly to be expected that these general principles will receive either a uniform or a self-evident application to novel methods of warfare in view of this past experience with respect to the traditional methods of conducting hostilities. New forms of warfare inevitably create new problems in the attempt to apply the general principles of the law of war. It may be—and is—true that the novel circumstances attending new forms of warfare do not constitute a valid reason for failing to apply these general principles. But the validity of this contention should not serve to gloss over the practical obstacles invariably encountered in all such endeavors. The meagre results to date of the attempts to apply the general principles of the law of war to the conduct of aerial warfare may serve, in this respect, as a clear warning. Elsewhere it

[6] E. g., the varying rules relating to the seizure and confiscation of enemy private property, the right of enemy merchant vessels to resort to acts of forcible resistance against a warship attempting seizure, and the disparity in the rules governing ruses in land and naval warfare.

is pointed out that when the principle distinguishing between combatants and the civilian population is applied to the particular circumstances of aerial warfare the results are likely to prove altogether different from the results of applying this same principle to land and naval warfare.[7]

To the foregoing must be added a further consideration. Recent experience has made it quite clear that the general principles of the law of war depend for their application upon standards which are themselves neither self-evident nor immutable. Hence, it is not merely the application of general principles to varying circumstances that is in question but the very meaning of the principles that are to be applied. It will be apparent, for example, that the scope of the immunity to be granted non-combatants must depend very largely upon the meaning given to the concept of military objective. But the concept of a military objective will necessarily vary as the character of war varies. And even if it were possible today to enumerate with precision those targets that could be regarded as constituting legitimate military objectives there would still remain the problem of determining the limits of the "incidental" or "indirect" injury that admittedly may be inflicted upon the civilian population in the course of attacking military objectives. The answer to this latter problem may largely depend, in turn, upon the kinds of weapons that are used to attack military objectives, including weapons whose legal status is itself a matter for determination in accordance with these same general principles.

The principle of humanity raises similar considerations. As applied to weapons and methods of war not already expressly regulated by specific rules, the principle of humanity is used to determine the lawfulness of novel weapons and methods for conducting hostilities in terms of their military necessity.[8] The necessity of a weapon must be determined by the purpose—or purposes—of war. Even assuming that the purpose of

---

[7] See pp. 146–9.

[8] Mention must be made of the widely held belief that the principles of military necessity and humanity largely contradict one another, that they serve opposing purposes, and that it is the task of the law of war to attempt to balance considerations of military necessity against the requirements of humanity. A recent expression of this view is given by W. G. Downey (*op. cit.* pp. 260–1), who, following Spaight's earlier formulation in *War Rights on Land*, asks: "The question is how best to balance these conflicting interests and the problem must be answered, each time a new weapon or new projectile is developed, under the test established by Spaight: 'Does the new weapon or the new projectile disable so many of the enemy that the military end thus gained condones the suffering it causes?' " This belief must be seriously questioned. Rather than "contradict" the principle of humanity, the principle of military necessity implies the former principle. The principle of necessity does not allow the employment of force unnecessary or superfluous to the purposes of war. Nor does the principle of humanity oppose human suffering or physical destruction as such. It is the unnecessary infliction of human suffering and the wanton destruction of property that is opposed, both by the principle of military necessity and by the principle of humanity. Although generally considered as two quite separate principles these remarks suggest the conclusion that military necessity and humanity may be regarded as merely two aspects of the same principle.

war remains constant, it has never been easy to determine whether a specific weapon or method does cause unnecessary suffering or physical destruction.[9] Nor is this difficulty alleviated by the assertion that in order to determine the proper interpretation of the principle of humanity attention must be directed to the practice of states. Undoubtedly it is true that the practice of states may determine that the resort to certain means for waging hostilities is unlawful, particularly if it is assumed that such practice is constitutive of a rule of custom. But then the source of the particular prohibition would be the very practice that is considered constitutive of a rule of custom, and it is merely superfluous to cite the general principle of humanity Thus, the contention that the use of poison gas is forbidden by the principle of humanity must be distinguished from the quite different contention that the numerous efforts by states to outlaw gas warfare is indicative of a practice that has now assumed the character of custom. Although the efforts to prohibit gas warfare may be the result, in large measure, of the conviction that gas constitutes an inhumane weapon, it would nevertheless appear that the present legal status of gas warfare must be determined by inquiry into the practice of states (specifically: by inquiring whether this practice has now become constitutive of a specific rule of custom) rather than by continued reference to the criteria contained in the principle of humanity.[10]

Still more relevant in this connection, though, is the further consideration that the purposes of war have not remained constant. A war fought for the purpose of obtaining a more defensible frontier is something quite different from a war whose purpose is the complete defeat and unconditional surrender of the enemy. But if the purposes of war may vary, then the measures necessary to achieve these purposes may be equally varied. It can hardly be expected that the principle of humanity will receive the same interpretation in a war that is total, with respect to its purposes, as it has received in wars that have been fought for limited purposes.

In summary: despite their intrinsic significance and undoubted validity,

---

[9] It is generally agreed that Article 23e of the Regulations annexed to Hague Convention IV (1907) has been without substantial effect. By forbidding belligerents "to employ arms, projectiles, or material calculated to cause unnecessary suffering," this provision merely states, in conventional form, the principle of humanity as this principle applies to weapons. Since Article 23e does not attempt to enumerate any specific weapons falling within this prohibited category it does not materially improve upon the general prohibition already laid down by the principle of humanity. And it is presumably for this reason that the newly revised U. S. Army *Rules of Land Warfare* (1956) quite correctly declare, in interpreting Article 23e of the Hague Regulations, that: "What weapons cause 'unnecessary injury' can only be determined in light of the practice of states in refraining from the use of a given weapon because it is believed to have that effect" (paragraph 34 (b)).

[10] See pp. 51–3 for an examination of this practice. In fact, the ready assumption that the use of gas constitutes an inhumane form of warfare has always been questioned. It is not at all self-evident that the suffering caused by the use of gas outweighs the military purposes achieved through its use. Yet this must be the test.

the general principles of the law of war have always suffered under certain limitations which have served to limit their potential utility. The very character of these general principles must lead to difficulties of interpretation and application. These difficulties are magnified, of course, by the fact that the principal subjects of the law normally must interpret and apply the law. The consequences of this latter condition admittedly are not without effect upon the whole of the law of war. No rule can be so specific that its interpretation and application remain unaffected by the condition of extreme decentralization characteristic of international law. Nevertheless, a measure of certainty may at least be achieved to the degree that the general principles of the law of war are given a more concrete form through the establishment of detailed rules of custom and—particularly—convention. In the absence of such detailed regulation their interpretation and application with respect to the rapidly changing weapons and methods of warfare will be—almost of necessity—a matter of endless controversy and consequent uncertainty.

B. WEAPONS IN NAVAL WARFARE

The distinction between the legality of a weapon, apart from its possible use, and the limitations placed upon the use of an otherwise lawful weapon, is frequently overlooked, despite its importance. Any weapon may be put to an unlawful use, e. g., if directed exclusively against the civilian population or if used to inflict unnecessary suffering or wanton destruction. In naval warfare there have been very few—if any—specifically naval weapons whose legality, irrespective of their possible use, has been the subject of serious dispute, though there have been numerous controversies over the uses to which weapons—legitimate in themselves—have been put.[11] However, to the extent that naval hostilities may involve the use of weapons whose principal employment is in land warfare, it is clear that the rules applicable to land forces are equally applicable to naval forces.[12]

[11] Perhaps the best illustration of this point is furnished by mines. As against the naval forces of belligerents the use of all types of mines has never been seriously questioned. The provisions of Hague Convention VIII (1907) did not purport to establish restrictions upon the employment of mines against enemy warships, but attempted—however inadequately—to insure the "security of peaceful shipping." Nor did the disputes arising from the belligerent use of mines during the two World Wars relate to the status as such of this category of weapons. These disputes did concern the possible use to which mines could be put, particularly when such use resulted in endangering the security of peaceful shipping (see pp. 303–5). A further illustration of the distinction drawn above is provided by submarines. As a weapon employed in naval warfare there has never been serious doubt over the legality of submarines. Instead, the controversy has concerned the particular uses to which submarines have been put or—more precisely—the methods that have characterized the use of submarines (see pp. 57–73).

[12] Thus, Article 23c of the Regulations annexed to Hague Convention IV (1907), although immediately directed to land warfare, is equally applicable to naval warfare. See also Article 23a of the Hague Regulations forbidding belligerents "to employ poison or poisoned weapons."

There are three categories of weapons whose possible use in naval warfare warrants their brief consideration: weapons employing fire, poisonous and asphyxiating gases, and nuclear weapons. As employed against the naval forces of a belligerent—and it is from this point of view alone that these weapons are examined here—the first and third categories may be considered as permitted, whereas the second category must probably be regarded as prohibited.

Weapons employing fire include tracer ammunition, flame-throwers, napalm, and other incendiary instruments and projectiles. Although the use of such weapons occasionally has been questioned, principally upon the ground that they inflict unnecessary suffering, the practice of states may be considered as sanctioning their employment.[13]

A measure of uncertainty still characterizes the legal status of poisonous and asphyxiating gases, when employed by a belligerent not obligated by a treaty which prohibits their use. It is true that a large number of states are now bound by the provisions of the 1925 Geneva Protocol forbidding the "use in war of asphyxiating, poisonous, or other gases, and of all analogous liquids, materials or devices," and have extended this prohibition to include bacteriological methods of warfare. However, there remain a substantial number of states, including the United States and Japan, that have never ratified the Protocol. In the absence of treaty restrictions the latter states are bound only by those obligations imposed by customary law.

Apart from treaties, it has been argued that the use of poisonous or asphyxiating gases violates at least two prohibitions of the customary law of war: the prohibition against the employment of weapons calculated to cause unnecessary suffering and the rule forbidding attack upon non-combatants.[14] In the case of poisonous gases the further contention has

---

[13] The Declaration of St. Petersburg (1868) prohibited the signatories from employing projectiles of a weight below 400 grams (14 ounces) which are "explosive or charged with fulminating or inflammable substances." It is doubtful whether the Declaration has ever been considered as applicable to aerial warfare. Article 18 of the unratified 1923 Hague Rules of Aerial Warfare stated that the "use of tracer, incendiary or explosive projectiles by or against aircraft is not prohibited," and subsequent practice has been to use such projectiles against aircraft. See Spaight, *op. cit.*, pp. 197 ff. As for flame throwers and similar weapons, a few writers still challenge their status, maintaining that they inflict unnecessary suffering. In view of present practice, this opinion is difficult to accept. The U. S. Army *Rules of Land Warfare*, paragraph 36, states: "The use of weapons which employ fire, such as tracer ammunition, flame-throwers, napalm and other incendiary agents, against targets requiring their use is not violative of international law. They should not, however, be employed in such a way as to cause unnecessary suffering to individuals." And see *Law of Naval Warfare*, Article 612a.

[14] The report of the General Board of the U. S. Navy on the question "Should Gas Warfare be Prohibited," and submitted by the American delegation to the 1922 Washington Conference On the Limitation of Armaments, stated: "The two principles of warfare, (1) that unnecessary suffering in the destruction of combatants should be avoided, (2) that innocent non-combatants should not be destroyed, have been accepted by the civilized world for more than one hundred years. The use of gases in warfare insofar as they violate these two principles is almost uni-

been made that their use violates the rule forbidding the employment of poison or poisoned weapons.

Each one of the foregoing claims is open to question, however. The rule prohibiting poison or poisoned weapons can be considered applicable to gases only by analogy or by necessary implication.[15] The rule forbidding attack against the civilian population is not relevant here, since the assumption is that the weapons under consideration will be employed only against combatant forces. Nor is there reason to believe that these weapons cannot be confined, in their use, to the combatant forces of a state. Whether such suffering as is caused by gas is "unnecessary" when judged by the military purposes thereby served, and therefore inhumane, is at least doubtful. Earlier discussion has pointed out that in view of the vague criteria forming the content of the principle of humanity, the decision as to whether a particular weapon is inhumane, hence forbidden, must depend upon the actual practice of states. The important question, then, would appear to be whether or not the practice of states may be considered as providing sufficient evidence that the use of poisonous or asphyxiating gases is now generally forbidden, quite apart from any specific obligations imposed by treaty.

It is believed that a review of state practice does support the conclusion that the use of poisonous or asphyxiating gases is to be regarded as presently forbidden in war to all states; that this practice—which consists of treaties, proposed drafts of treaties, and the pronouncements of states both in time of peace as well as in time of war—is constitutive of a customary rule forbidding the use of poisonous or asphyxiating gases.[16] It is of course

---

versally condemned today, despite its practice for a certain period during the World War." The report went on to declare that although certain gases, e. g., tear gas, could be used without violating the two basic principles cited above, "there will be great difficulty in a clear and definite demarcation between the lethal gases and those which produce unnecessary suffering as distinguished from those gases which simply disable temporarily." For this reason the General Board recommended the prohibition of gas warfare "in every form and against every objective." *U. S. Naval War College, International Law Documents, 1921*, pp. 193–4.

[15] It would appear that the rule prohibiting poisoned weapons would apply—if at all—only in the event a poisonous gas is both odorless and colorless. In the latter case, detection and prior warning might prove impossible and there would be clearer grounds for assimilation of poisonous gases under the rule prohibiting poison, since the latter is based principally upon the conviction that the use of poison constitutes a form of treachery. Presumably the same considerations would apply in considering the legality of bacteriological and biological weapons, even though such weapons are used only against combatant forces.

[16] But see *Law of Naval Warfare*, Article 612b as well as U. S. Army *Rules of Land Warfare*, paragraph 38.—For a brief review of state practice see Stone, *op. cit.*, pp. 553–7. Also Oppenheim-Lauterpacht (*op. cit.*, pp. 342–4), where it is concluded that recent drafts and pronouncements "bear witness to the tendency to universality in the prohibition of chemical warfare." The broad scope of this conclusion must be questioned. The prohibition against the resort to all forms of "chemical warfare" is binding—at best—only upon the contracting parties to the 1925 Geneva Protocol. Even here there is some doubt since the English text of the Protocol prohibits "asphyxiating, poison, or other gases," whereas the French text forbids "gaz asphyxi-

true that in the absence of a system of international inspection and control of prohibited weapons the effectiveness of the rule forbidding poisonous or asphyxiating gases must depend largely upon the expectation of states that resort to these weapons will provoke retaliation in kind from an opponent.[17] It is not easy to understand, however, why this fact should be considered as an argument against the position that resort to poisonous or asphyxiating gases is now prohibited in law.[18] The threat of retaliation, or reprisal, must provide a decisive factor in leading to the observance of the whole of the law regulating the conduct of war. Yet it has seldom been contended that to the extent that this law is dependent for its observance upon the threat of reprisal it is thereby deprived of its validity.[19]

ants, toxiques ou similaires." Under the English version all forms of gas are prohibited, by a literal interpretation. Under the French version only specific types are forbidden. In addition, certain chemical types of weapons, at times asphyxiating in nature (e. g., white phosphorus, smoke, flame throwers), were employed during World War II without raising serious question.—Greater uncertainty must be expressed, however, over the existence today of a customary rule prohibiting the use of bacteriological weapons. No doubt as between the parties to the 1925 Geneva Protocol the resort to such weapons—save as a measure of reprisal against their prior use by an enemy—is forbidden. But whereas there is in the case of gas an impressive practice of states pointing toward the unlawful character of the resort to gas warfare, a similar practice does not yet exist in the case of bacteriological weapons. It does seem reasonably clear, though, that the present tendency with respect to bacteriological warfare is moving in a direction similar to that earlier taken with respect to gas warfare.

17 Thus the 1925 Geneva Protocol was ratified by a number of states with the qualification that it would cease to be binding with respect to other ratifying states which failed to observe the provisions of the Protocol. The Protocol does not forbid the manufacture of gases and bacteria, only their use in war.

18 "Since . . . the Protocol of 1925, is subject to reciprocity, its compulsiveness as *law* seems difficult to distinguish from the *factual* compulsion arising from the mere threat of retaliation." Stone, *op. cit.*, p. 556. Precisely the same statement could be made concerning any number of the rules of war whose character as law are not questioned.

19 In this connection, it is relevant to note the reasons given by the representative of the United States in the United Nations Disarmament Commission for refusal on the part of the United States to support the proposal that the Security Council appeal to all states to accede to or ratify the 1925 Geneva Protocol. "The United States representative . . . stated that the United States did not trust the paper promises of those who bore false witness especially when the false charges provided false excuses for breaking promises—on alleged grounds of reprisals. The United States had never used bacterial warfare. It had used gas warfare only in retaliation during the First World War, when it was first used by Germany. Of the two wars in the twentieth century in which poison gas was used, it was significant that its use was inaugurated by States which had bound themselves on paper not to use it. Aggressor States which started wars in violation of their treaty obligations could not be trusted to keep their paper promises regarding the methods of waging wars, if keeping those promises stood in the way of their accomplishing their aggressive designs. If men fought to kill, it was not easy to regulate how they killed. The United States wanted to eliminate all weapons which were not expressly permitted and appropriate to support the limited number of armed forces which might be permitted to maintain public order and to meet Charter obligations. The United States, as a member of the United Nations, had committed itself, as had all other members, to refrain not only from the use of poisonous gas and bacterial warfare, but the use of force of any kind contrary to the Charter. The United States . . . would support effective

The preceding considerations relating to the legal status in war of poisonous or asphyxiating gases are not without significance in considering the legal status of nuclear weapons. In marked contrast to gas warfare there is neither any treaty expressly regulating—or prohibiting altogether—the use of nuclear weapons nor is there any evidence as yet of a practice that may be considered as constituting sufficient basis for the emergence of a customary prohibition. Whatever restriction may be applied to nuclear weapons must therefore be derived from rules already regulating war's conduct. In this connection the rules prohibiting the infliction of unnecessary suffering and requiring that a distinction be drawn between combatants and civilian population undoubtedly constitute the more general, and the more significant, grounds for questioning the legality of using nuclear weapons in war.[20]

The objection that the use of nuclear weapons must cause unnecessary suffering (and destruction) deserves only the briefest comment. As already pointed out, the question as to whether or not a particular weapon is to be considered as causing unnecessary suffering is one that can be answered only by examining the practice of states. In the case of poisonous and

proposals to eliminate all weapons adaptable to mass destruction, including atomic, chemical and biological weapons. But until such measures and safeguards had been agreed upon, it did not intend to invite aggression by committing itself not to use certain weapons to suppress aggression. To do so in exchange for mere paper promises would be to give would-be aggressors their own choice of weapons." *Disarmament Commission, Official Records, Spec. Supp; No. 1, 2nd Report of the Disarmament Commission* (1952), pp. 144–5. The resort to the unlawful use of force—aggression—does not thereby serve to justify use by the victims of aggression of weapons that are otherwise unlawful according to the law of war. If the contrary were true then it could also be argued that none of the rules regulating war's conduct bind the victims of aggression. Nor is it easy to understand the objection that the signing of "paper promises" (i. e., treaties) necessarily invites aggression, if unaccompanied by an effective system of control and inspection. Aggression is "invited" only if the treaty in question forbids the use *and the manufacture* of certain weapons without, at the same time, establishing an effective system of control. This is certainly not true of the 1925 Geneva Protocol.

[20] Of lesser importance is the rule prohibiting the use of poison or poisoned weapons and the provisions of the 1925 Protocol of Geneva forbidding the use of gases as well as "analogous liquids, materials or devices." For a detailed consideration of atomic weapons in the light of these principles—and the conclusion as to their illegality—see A. N. Sack, "ABC—Atomic, Biological, Chemical Warfare in International Law," *Lawyers Guild Review*, 10 (1950), pp. 161–80. The preponderant opinion among writers has not been to condemn nuclear weapons as being necessarily unlawful, however. Where doubt has been expressed it is concentrated principally upon the legitimacy of using such weapons against military objectives located in or near centers of population and the danger of obliterating completely the already threatened combatant-noncombatant distinction. This is, for example, the burden of Spaight's remarks, *op. cit.*, pp. 273–7. On the other hand, it has been recently concluded that "the total elimination or limitation, as a matter of law, of the use of the atomic weapon cannot be accomplished by way of a restatement of an existing rule of law. Such a restatement denying the legality of the use of the atomic weapon must, of necessity, be based on controversial deductions from supposedly fundamental principles established in conditions vastly different from those obtaining in modern—total and scientific—warfare." Lauterpacht, "The Problem of the Revision of The Law of War," p. 370.

asphyxiating gases it has been suggested that the practice of states does point to the existence of a rule of universal validity forbidding the use of such weapons as inhumane. In the case of nuclear weapons the matter is quite different. The present attitude of most of the major powers is clearly not that of considering the suffering caused by nuclear weapons as unnecessary, when judged by the military purposes these weapons are designed to serve.

It is equally difficult to accept the objection that nuclear weapons are necessarily illegal for the reason that their use must lead to the complete obliteration of the rule distinguishing between combatants and the civilian population. It is only when such weapons are used against military objectives in the proximity of the non-combatant population that this objection warrants serious consideration.[21] To the extent that nuclear weapons are used exclusively against military forces in the field or naval forces at sea, they escape this objection. Nor is there reason to believe that nuclear weapons cannot be directed exclusively against combatant forces in the strict sense of the term. To the extent that they are so limited, their use at present may be considered as permitted by the law of war.[22]

C. THE ATTACK AND DESTRUCTION OF ENEMY VESSELS

In the following pages attention is directed to the present status of the rules governing the liability of enemy vessels—and particularly of enemy merchant vessels—to attack. It is still customary in treatises on the law of naval warfare to consider the problem of the liability of enemy merchant vessels to attack as one largely incidental to, and resulting from the exercise of, the belligerent right to seize and condemn the vessels and goods of an enemy. In view of recent developments this procedure bears a distinct element of artificiality, and this would seem so even though it be asserted that the traditional rules governing the liability of enemy merchant vessels to attack retain their validity today. At the very least, the conditions in which recent hostilities at sea have been conducted no longer permit considering the liability of enemy merchant vessels to attack as an exceptional circumstance—save perhaps in the most formal sense. Indeed, as between belligerents it is the seizure of merchant vessels that

[21] There should be little doubt that, as judged by the traditional meaning given to the principle distinguishing combatants from non-combatants, the use of nuclear weapons against cities containing military objectives must be deemed illegal. However, the same judgment would probably have to be made in considering the practices of aerial bombardment followed by belligerents during World War II, though very few writers have condemned these recent practices as unlawful, and no records of war crimes trials are known in which allegations were made of illegal bombardment from the air (see pp. 146–9).

[22] See *Law of Naval Warfare*, Article 613 and notes thereto. Paragraph 35 of the U. S. Army *Rules of Land Warfare* reads: "The use of explosive 'atomic weapons,' whether by air, sea or land forces, cannot as such be regarded as violative of international law in the absence of any customary rule of international law or international convention restricting their employment."

threatens to become the exception rather than—as it once was—the normal procedure. In consequence, the once clear distinction drawn between combatants and non-combatants in naval hostilities has been placed in serious jeopardy. The events that have led to the present situation warrant careful consideration.

1. *The Traditional Rules Governing the Liability of Enemy Vessels to Attack*

In the period preceding the outbreak of war in 1914 the rules governing the liability of enemy vessels to attack and destruction appeared reasonably well settled. Enemy warships, that is to say all enemy vessels possessing the competence to exercise belligerent rights at sea,[23] could be attacked on sight and, if necessary, destroyed.[24] Privately owned and operated enemy merchant vessels were liable—with minor exceptions [25]—to seizure and subsequent condemnation in the prize courts of the capturing belligerent.[26] This belligerent right to seize and condemn the privately owned vessels of an enemy found at sea did not preclude the application in other—and more important—respects of the principle distinguishing between combatants and non-combatants. In particular, it did not serve to free a belligerent from the obligation to refrain from attacking the merchant vessels of an enemy so long as these vessels refrained from the performance of certain acts. It is true that a belligerent was permitted, under exceptional circumstances,[27] to destroy seized enemy merchant vessels rather than to conduct the latter into port for adjudication. But in those circumstances where destruction was permitted it could be carried out only after the passengers and crew had been removed to a place of safety.

At the same time, it is important to observe that belligerent merchant vessels were placed under no obligation to submit to visit and search, and seizure, by an enemy. According to well established custom, belligerent merchant vessels were at liberty to use the means at their disposal in order

---

[23] See pp. 38–41.

[24] The liability to attack of other public vessels which did not form a part of the military forces of a state (e. g., customs and police vessels), and which did not fall within the category of public vessels accorded special exemption from either capture or destruction (see pp. 96–8), remained uncertain. Some writers assume that the liability to attack of such public vessels has always been substantially the same as that of warships. For example, Hyde declares that the "absence of armament on a public vessel (not exempt from capture) has not been deemed to offer a sufficient reason why an enemy force should not attack it at sight." *op. cit.*, p. 1993. In fact, neither Hyde nor many other writers appear to distinguish sufficiently between unarmed public vessels which do not form a part of the armed forces of a state and unarmed vessels which do form a part of these forces. Whereas the latter are always liable to attack on sight, the liability of the former to attack was not free from doubt. If anything, the preponderance of opinion seemed to incline to capture, and to attack prior to capture only if resistance were offered. See *U. S. Naval War College, International Law Topics, 1914*, pp. 1–34.

[25] See pp. 86–98.

[26] A procedure not required in the case of captured public vessels since ownership in such vessels immediately vested in the government of the captor by virtue of the fact of capture.

[27] The nature of these circumstances is discussed elsewhere (see pp. 106–7).

to avoid seizure. They could refuse to stop upon being duly summoned by a warship of the enemy. They could, in addition, take measures of resistance against enemy warships attempting seizure, and for this purpose were permitted to carry defensive armament. However, in the event either of persistent refusal to stop upon being duly summoned or of active resistance to attempted seizure belligerent warships were permitted to take those measures of force necessary to compel submission. In these circumstances the rule forbidding the attack upon or destruction of enemy merchant vessels without first placing passengers and crew in a place of safety ceased to apply. Immunity from attack also ceased to apply to those merchant vessels performing acts of direct assistance at sea to the naval forces of a belligerent.

2. *The Experience of World Wars I and II.*

The rules outlined above represented the application to naval warfare of the general principle distinguishing between combatants and non-combatants. When the first World War broke out in 1914 these rules were accorded general recognition by the major naval powers. It soon became apparent, however, that not all of the belligerents were prepared to conduct hostilities in accordance with the traditional law. The most serious departures from the principle distinguishing between combatants and non-combatants in hostilities at sea must be attributed to Germany and to the latter's use of submarines. Despite these departures, the care with which Germany sought to justify her conduct of submarine warfare—primarily upon the right of reprisal[28]—is not without a certain significance. It indicated that during the first World War, at least, the conviction strongly persisted that under normal circumstances the rules distinguishing between the treatment to be accorded combatants and non-combatants ought to be respected. The widespread opinion that Germany justified her conduct of submarine warfare simply by the proposition that new weapons create new rules must therefore be seriously questioned.[29] It

[28] The principal "reprisal" measures resorted to by Germany were declared in February 1915 and January 1917. On the former occasion Germany proclaimed the intention to attack and to destroy all enemy merchant vessels found within the waters surrounding Great Britain and Ireland. On January 31, 1917 the German Government announced that henceforth it would forcibly prevent "in a zone around Great Britain, France, Italy and in the eastern Mediterranean all navigation, that of neutrals included, from and to England, and from and to France, etc. All ships met within that zone will be sunk." cited in Hackworth, *Digest of International Law* (1943), Vol. VI, pp. 465–81. For a further discussion of these measures, see pp. 296–305.

[29] It is quite true that isolated expressions to this effect may be found. Thus, in a memorandum of March 8, 1916, from the German Ambassador to the American Secretary of State, it was noted that: ". . . Germany was compelled to resort, in February 1915, to reprisals in order to fight her opponents' measures, which were absolutely contrary to international law. She chose for this purpose a new weapon the use of which had not yet been regulated by international law and, in doing so, could and did not violate any existing rules, but only took into account the peculiarity of this new weapon, the submarine boat." cited in Hackworth, *op. cit.*, Vol. VI, p. 478. It is also true that in 1916 the German Naval Staff concluded that the sub-

would appear more accurate to state that, apart from reprisals, Germany's principal argument on behalf of her conduct of submarine warfare was based upon the contention that the novel circumstances in which that conflict was being waged justified a policy of attacking enemy merchant vessels on sight and without warning. One of the principal circumstances upon which Germany came to rely was the vulnerability of the submarine in relation to armed British merchant vessels instructed to use their armament against any attempt at seizure by an enemy submarine.[30]

The central question raised by the arming of belligerent merchant vessels concerned the effect this measure could be considered to have upon the immunity from attack normally granted the latter.[31] The position consistently taken by Great Britain has been that the right of merchant vessels to carry armament to be used for defensive purposes only is one clearly recognized by customary law, and that so long as merchant vessels restrict the use of such armament to measures of self-defense they may not be deprived—simply for the reason that they are so armed—either of their non-combatant status or of their normal exemption from attack.[32] In

marine, being a novel weapon, must provide "its own lines of conduct." Nevertheless, despite these and other isolated expressions to the contrary, Germany's official position was not based upon the argument that new weapons must thereby create new rules. Nor—for that matter—was it based upon the closely related argument that "old rules" cannot automatically bind "new weapons" (i. e., the submarine).

[30] In the latter stages of World War I, and during World War II, armed merchant vessels were instructed to use their armament upon sighting an enemy submarine, the assumption being that unlawful attack by the submarine would—in any event—be forthcoming.

[31] This, at least, is the central question raised *as between belligerents*. A quite different question concerns the effect the arming of merchant vessels may have in determining the treatment to be accorded them in the ports and territorial waters of neutral states (see pp. 247-51).

[32] See Higgins and Colombos (*op. cit.*, pp. 363-9) for a statement of the British position. Substantially the same position was taken in both World Wars by France, and Article 2 of the French Naval Instructions of 1934 provided that enemy merchant vessels were not to be attacked for the sole reason ("le seul motif") that they bore defensive armament.—During World War I the position finally taken by the United States, while still neutral, was in support of the British attitude. Earlier, however, the United States had advocated that in return for a pledge that submarines would adhere strictly to the customary rules in carrying out search and seizure, merchant vessels of belligerent nationality should be prohibited from carrying any armament. In the 1939-41 period of neutrality this country refrained from raising any question as to the belligerent arming of merchant vessels. Finally, as a belligerent in both wars the United States resorted to the practice of arming its merchant vessels and of manning such armament with naval gun crews. See, generally, Hackworth, *op. cit.*, Vol. VI, pp. 489-503.

It may also be noted that frequently the discussion of the effect of arming merchant vessels suffers from the endeavor to establish that the carrying of armament does not thereby serve to confer upon a merchant vessel the status of a warship. In principle, this argument may be considered to be correct. Defensively armed merchant vessels have no competence to exercise belligerent rights at sea, and if found doing so the officers and crew may be treated—in strict law—as war criminals. However, this fact does not of itself prove that armed merchant vessels, if refraining from the exercise of belligerent rights at sea, must thereby be accorded exemption from attack without prior warning. There are two quite different questions involved here, as Hyde (*op. cit.*, p. 1997) correctly observes in stating that the fact that "an

practice, this position would require a warship to follow the procedure normally prescribed by the traditional law in attempting to seize an armed enemy merchant vessel, in the absence of other reasons providing an independent justification for attack [33] force may be resorted to—according to this view—only if the merchant vessel first makes use of its armament in order to resist.

The German view, on the other hand, has been one of refusing to accept the claim that the arming of belligerent merchant vessels does not result in rendering such vessels liable to attack on sight. Indeed, the initial German reaction to the arming of British merchant vessels was to consider the act a violation of international law on the part of Great Britain, and to threaten to treat the personnel of vessels making use of their armament—even for allegedly defensive purposes—as war criminals. But the more consistent, and more moderate, position has been to consider the carrying of armament simply as depriving enemy merchant vessels of immunity from attack without warning and without taking prior precautions for the safety of the crew.[34]

---

armed merchantman may retain its status as a private ship is not decisive of the treatment to which it may be subjected." The difficulty involved is due to the frequent use of the term "legal status" in two different senses. It may refer to the conditions necessary for the conversion of a merchant vessel into a warship. But it may refer to the fact that a merchant vessel is subject to the same liabilities as a warship although, by retaining its non-combatant character, it does not possess the competence to exercise belligerent rights at sea.

[33] The significance of this qualification ought not to be overlooked. As will presently be noted, the "other reasons" that provide independent justification for the attack on sight of enemy merchant vessels—whether armed or unarmed—have reduced substantially the importance of the question under immediate consideration. These circumstances not only include the persistent refusal to stop upon being duly summoned and any form of active resistance to seizure (e. g., the sending in of position reports upon sighting enemy warships, and particularly enemy submarines) but the integration of merchant vessels in any manner into the enemy's military effort at sea.

[34] The German position has never been altogether clear, though, and the statements made in the text therefore border on over-simplification. On a number of occasions Germany has contended that any armed resistance to the regular measures of prize law is forbidden. During World War I it appeared that this latter position would necessarily lead to treating armed resistance on the part of enemy merchant vessels as a war crime. But this position was certainly without foundation in the traditional law and—apart from the notorious trial and execution of Captain Fryatt for attempting in 1915 to ram a German submarine that had ordered him to stop—was not seriously pursued by the German Government. In addition, neither the German Prize Law Code of 1914 nor the preponderance of German writers lent any substantial weight to this extreme claim. Quite different, however, was the contention that merchant vessels engaged in unlawful behavior if they sought to destroy an enemy warship (e. g., submarine) before the latter took any steps to effect seizure. And there is no question but that the so-called "defensive-offensive" action permitted to armed British merchant vessels came very close to the exercise of forbidden offensive action. Of course, the British argument was that the persistent unlawful behavior of German submarines permitted British merchant vessels to anticipate the probability of an unlawful attack and to take "preventive measures of self-defense."

On the whole, however, it would appear that the principal German position has been that

The controversy thus occasioned during the first World War over the arming of belligerent merchant vessels continued into the inter-war period and can scarcely be considered as wholly resolved even today. When judged by the customary law the British position appears, on first consideration, as unexceptionable. The difficulty of this position, however, is that despite its apparent conformity with the customary law it was applied during World War I (and during World War II) in both a manner as well as in circumstances that bore little relation to the circumstances and manner of employment characteristic of the preceding period.

It has always appeared rather paradoxical that although enemy merchant vessels were at liberty to resist attempted seizure, and could even carry armament for this purpose, warships were normally obliged to refrain from attacking merchant vessels until the latter had first actually resorted to measures of resistance. If an enemy merchant vessel carried armament whose sole purpose was evidently to provide means of resistance against attempted seizure, then it would seem only reasonable to allow a warship—particularly if inferior in defensive power—to attack such armed vessels on sight. In part, the explanation of this seeming paradox may be attributed to the carrying over of a practice formed under quite different historical circumstances. During an earlier period the danger of attack from privateers, or from pirates, served to justify the carrying of arms not only in time of war but in time of peace as well. As the nineteenth century progressed this earlier justification for arming belligerent merchant vessels largely disappeared. At the same time, the rule exempting the merchant vessels of an enemy from attack gained ground. Indeed, it was only during

---

while arming of merchant vessels does not serve to transform the latter into warships, it does justify treating such vessels as liable to attack without warning. The German Prize Law Code of September 1939 was silent on this matter but on September 30, 1939, the *Deutsches Nachrichten Büro* stated that henceforth armed enemy merchant vessels would be treated like warships and sunk without warning. It was further declared: "Armed resistance to the regular measures of prize law is not permissible. Arming a merchant ship alone does not make of the latter a warship, but does justify the adversary in treating the merchant ship as a warship to the same extent that it is equipped for the use of armed force." cited in Hackworth, *op. cit.*, Vol. VI, p. 499. In substance, this has also been the position taken by perhaps the majority of German writers. Indeed, the view that the presence of armament on board an enemy merchant vessel served to justify attacking such vessel without warning was urged even prior to World War I. See, for example, the opinions expressed by Professor Heinrich Triepel before the Institute of International Law in 1913 (*Annuaire de l'Institut de Droit International*, 26 (1913), pp. 516 ff.). And for the inter-war period see, in particular, P. A. Martini, *Reformvorschläge zum Seekriegsrecht* (1933) and the detailed argument given by Werner Plaga, *Das bewaffnete Handelsschiff* (1939). The latter writer argued that the British position was devoid of any legal foundation even in the pre-1914 law, and that, in any event, the specific measures taken by the British in arming their merchant vessels after 1914 served to deprive the latter of immunity from attack.—And for a recent view, see Professor Verdross, *op. cit.*, p. 389. Though declaring that the carriage of armament for "mere defense" is admissible, in that it does not serve to turn enemy merchant vessels into illegitimate combatants, Professor Verdross is not altogether clear as to whether such carriage may deprive enemy merchant vessels of immunity from attack without warning.

the course of this past century that the distinction between the treatment of combatants and non-combatants in warfare at sea became firmly established. The continued retention, on the one hand, of the ancient rule allowing belligerent merchant vessels to arm in self-defense and, on the other hand, the growing immunity granted to merchant vessels if they refrained from measures of resistance, is to be explained, however, largely by the disparity in power that existed between warship and merchant vessel.

In retrospect, it is clear that one of the principal reasons for the increased measure of immunity granted enemy merchant vessels during the nineteenth century was this very disparity, and that the degree to which this immunity was observed was roughly proportionate to the difference in power between warship and merchant vessel.[35] In fact, during the century preceding the outbreak of war in 1914 the practice of arming merchant vessels was abandoned almost entirely, only to be revived by the announcement of the British Government in 1913 that in the event of war it would supply its merchant vessels with defensive armament. Although the initial purpose of this measure was to provide merchant vessels with the means to defend themselves against seizure by converted enemy warships it soon became readily apparent that the principal employment of such armament was to be directed against enemy submarines (and, during World War II, against enemy aircraft as well). But in the case of submarines this former disparity in power between warship and merchant vessel became negligible, provided that the merchant vessel was armed and the submarine required to attempt seizure before resorting to force. Under these circumstances the submarine—and any other type of warship not clearly superior in power to the armed merchant vessel—was almost certain to encounter active resistance if it attempted to conform with the traditional law. And the instructions furnished British armed merchantmen in both World Wars, stipulating that enemy submarines should be attacked on sight, made it difficult—and in many cases impossible—to draw a clear line between defensive and offensive action. In any event, it is not easy to see why belligerent merchant vessels may be armed for the sole purpose of attacking enemy submarines on sight,

---

[35] It is upon this consideration that many writers have placed greatest emphasis. Thus Hyde (*op. cit.*, p. 1997), in concluding that the carrying of armament by a merchant vessel serves to deprive the vessel so armed of the right to claim immunity from attack without warning, states that the "immunity of merchant vessels from attack at sight grew out of their impotency to endanger the safety of public armed vessels of an enemy, . . . maritime states have never acquiesced in a principle that a merchant vessel so armed as to be capable of destroying a vessel of war of any kind should enjoy immunity from attack at sight, at least when encountering an enemy cruiser of inferior defensive strength." Also, to the same general effect, G. G. Wilson, "Armed Merchant Vessels and Submarines," *A. J. I. L.*, 24 (1930), pp. 337–8; Edwin Borchard, "Armed Merchantmen," *A. J. I. L.*, 34 (1940), p. 110; and J. L. Kunz, *Kriegsrecht und Neutralitätsrecht*, pp. 118–35.

but enemy submarines considered as without a similar right to take "defensive" measures by attacking armed merchant vessels on sight.[36]

Perhaps even more important was the manner in which merchant vessels were armed and directed to use their armament. The traditional law assumed that the owner of a private vessel would decide for himself whether or not to carry arms, would arm—if at all—at his own expense, and would determine under what conditions he would choose to make use of such arms. In short, the fact that a merchant vessel was armed did not mean that it was in any way incorporated into the military effort of a belligerent, or that it was acting under the direct control of the state. In World War I, as in World War II, the manner in which merchant vessels were armed and were directed to use their armament no longer met these assumptions. The state decided upon the arming of merchant vessels, providing both guns and personnel to operate the guns, and directed merchant vessels as to the manner in which they were to employ their armament.[37]

On balance, then, the lengthy dispute relating to the position of armed merchant vessels, particularly with respect to submarines, appears inconclusive. The real strength of the British position is not to be found in the claim that the arming of merchant vessels was sanctioned by the customary law. Instead, it must be found in the contention that the effective use of the submarine was, in the vast majority of cases, incompatible with the observance of the rules distinguishing between combatants and noncombatants, that Germany had not observed these rules in conducting submarine warfare, and that the arming of merchant vessels was the only possible means to be taken against the unlawful use of submarines. Yet the fact remains that the initial British decision to arm merchant vessels was taken prior to World War I. More important were the circumstances in which merchant vessels were armed and directed to use their arms, circumstances which hardly allowed the assumption that these vessels retained a peaceful and strictly non-combatant status. It is difficult to avoid the conclusion that the immunity granted merchant vessels by the traditional law can be observed only under the conditions that merchant

---

[36] In a memorandum of March 25, 1916, prepared by the Department of State for the President, it was observed that: "A merchantman entitled to exercise the right of self-protection may do so when certain of attack by an enemy warship, otherwise the exercise of the right would be so restricted as to render it ineffectual. There is a distinct difference, however, between the exercise of the right of self-protection and the act of cruising the seas in an armed vessel for the purpose of attacking enemy naval vessels." The German Government in commenting upon this memorandum observed: "It admits . . . the merchant vessel's right to resort to self-defense as soon as it is certain of attack by an enemy warship, as otherwise the exercise of the right would be so restricted as to be made ineffectual; exactly the same grounds support the position that a warship that is entitled to exercise the right of capture may use force when certain of attack by an armed enemy merchant vessel." cited in Hackworth, *op. cit.*, Vol. VI, pp. 497–8.

[37] See H. A. Smith, *Law and Custom of the Sea*, p. 87, and *The Crisis in the Law of Nations*, pp. 60–2.

vessels do not present—in terms of their armament—a serious threat to enemy warships and that they are in no way integrated into the military effort of a belligerent. If either, or both, of these conditions do not obtain, and they were not satisfied even in World War I, warships—whether submarines or surface vessels—cannot be expected to refrain from attacking enemy merchant vessels.

In the period following the first World War the continued validity of the traditional rules regulating the attack and destruction of enemy vessels was reaffirmed on a number of occasions, and in 1930 these rules were given conventional expression at the London Naval Conference in the Treaty on the Limitation and Reduction of Armament. Article 22 of the London Naval Treaty of 1930 declared:

> The following are accepted as established rules of International Law:
>
> (1) In their action with regard to merchant ships, submarines must conform to the rules of International Law to which surface vessels are subject.
>
> (2) In particular, except in the case of persistent refusal to stop on being duly summoned, or of active resistance to visit and search, a warship, whether surface vessel or submarine, may not sink or render incapable of navigation a merchant vessel without having first placed passengers, crew, and ship's papers in a place of safety. For this purpose the ships' boats are not regarded as a place of safety unless the safety of the passengers and crew is assured, in the existing sea and weather conditions, by the proximity of land, or the presence of another vessel which is in a position to take them on board.[38]

According to the terms of the 1930 London Naval Treaty, Article 22 was to remain in force "without limit of time." Upon the expiration of the remainder of the Treaty in December 1936 this provision therefore remained

[38] It should be observed that Article 22, insofar as it attempted merely to restate in conventional form the traditional law, ought not to be interpreted as permitting attack *only* under those circumstances to which reference is expressly made. Any such interpretation clearly would not be in accord with the pre-existing law, which allowed a belligerent warship to attack enemy merchant vessels for acts in addition to refusal to stop on being duly summoned or active resistance to visit and search. The committee of jurists responsible for the formulation of Article 22 of the London Naval Treaty stated in its report on this article: "The committee wish to place on record that the expression 'merchant vessel', where it is employed in the declaration, is not to be understood as including a merchant vessel which is at the moment participating in hostilities in such a manner as to cause her to lose her right to the immunities of merchant vessels." *Proceedings*, London Naval Conference, (1930), p. 189. No reference is made to the treatment to be accorded armed merchant vessels. In fact, the Treaty left this all important question where it found it. And see *U. S. Naval War College*, *International Law Situations, 1930*, pp. 1–65, for a general review of the 1930 London Naval Treaty in its bearing upon the conduct of submarine warfare.

binding upon the contracting Parties. However, in November of the same year (1936) Article 22 of the London Naval Treaty was incorporated *verbatim* in the form of a Protocol, the purpose of this being to increase the number of states accepting the obligations contained therein. At the time of the outbreak of war in 1939 some forty odd states, including all the major naval powers, had either ratified, or had expressly acceded to, the 1936 London Protocol, and the provisions of the Protocol were given prominent place in the naval instructions issued by many governments to their naval forces.[39] Nor was there any serious question over the applicability of these rules to military aircraft when used in operations against enemy merchant shipping.[40]

Despite this reaffirmation of the traditional law in the 1936 London Protocol, the record of belligerent measures with respect to enemy merchant vessels during World War II fell far below the standards set in the preceding conflict. In the Atlantic Germany resorted to unrestricted submarine and aerial warfare against British merchant vessels almost from the very start of hostilities.[41] Once again the measures taken by Germany were justified in part as measures of reprisal and in part as resulting from the

[39] See paragraph 50 of the 1941 *Tentative Instructions For the Navy of the United States Governing Maritime and Aerial Warfare* (cited throughout as *1941 Instructions*). The earlier 1917 *Instructions For the Navy of the United States Governing Maritime Warfare* (cited throughout as *1917 Instructions*) did not contain a parallel provision, paragraph 45 providing for the resort to forcible measures against enemy merchant vessels if the latter resisted or took to flight after once being summoned. Article 22 of the London Naval Treaty also formed a part of the German Prize Law Code of 1939 (Article 74).

[40] Distinguish between the diversion of merchant vessels by aircraft and the attack of merchant vessels by aircraft. Although there was a good deal of dispute over the former question during the inter-war period there was no dispute over the applicability to aircraft of the rule—already applicable to surface warships and submarines—forbidding the attack and destruction of enemy merchant vessels without having first placed passengers and crew in a place of safety.

[41] S. W. Roskill summarizes the German resort to unrestricted submarine warfare in the following passage:

"On the 23rd of September, Hitler, on the recommendation of Admiral Raeder, approved that 'all merchant ships making use of their wireless on being stopped by U-boats should be sunk or taken in prize.' As the immediate despatch of a wireless signal in such circumstances was included in the Admiralty's instructions to merchant ships and was essential—if for no other reason—to the rescue of their crews, this German order marked a considerable step towards unrestricted warfare. . . . On the 30th of September observance of the Prize Regulations in the North Sea was withdrawn; and on the 2nd of October complete freedom was given to attack darkened ships encountered off the British and French coasts. Two days later the Prize Regulations were cancelled in waters extending as far as 15° West, and on the 17th of October the German Naval Staff gave U-boats permission 'to attack without warning all ships identified as hostile.' The zone where darkened ships could be attacked with complete freedom was extended to 20° West on the 19th of October. Practically the only restrictions now placed on U-boats concerned attacks on liners and, on the 17th of November, they too were allowed to be attacked without warning if 'clearly identifiable as hostile.' Although the enemy this time carefully avoided the expression 'unrestricted U-boat warfare,' it can therefore be said that, against British and French shipping, it was, in fact, adopted by the middle of November 1939."

circumstances in which hostilities at sea were being conducted. The obligations laid down in the 1936 London Protocol were not denied. Emphasis was placed rather upon the argument that the methods of warfare employed by Great Britain, and particularly the measures taken to integrate British merchant shipping into Britain's military effort at sea, prevented German compliance with the provisions of the 1936 London Protocol.[42]

Great Britain refrained during the initial stages of the conflict from resorting to measures of a similar nature. The British reprisals order of November 27, 1939, taken in response to alleged unlawful German mine and submarine warfare, sought instead to cut off all German exports whether carried in enemy or in neutral bottoms.[43] Indeed, for a substantial period of time British aircraft were forbidden to attack any enemy ships other than warships, troopships, and "auxiliaries in direct attendance on the enemy fleet." [44] As the war progressed certain areas were declared to be "danger-

---

Military History of the Second World War: The War at Sea, 1939–1945 (1954), Vol. I, pp. 103–4. This summary follows substantially the evidence brought forward against Admirals Raeder and Doenitz during their trial before the International Military Tribunal at Nuremberg. See *Nazi Conspiracy and Aggression* (1946), Vol. II, pp. 815–76. The German resort to unrestricted aerial attack on enemy shipping followed almost immediately upon the decision to initiate unrestricted submarine warfare. Spaight (*op. cit.*, pp. 487–8) lists the date as December 17, 1939.

[42] On September 19, 1939, the Commander in Chief of the German Navy, Grand Admiral Raeder, declared:

"Germany is conducting submarine warfare in accordance with the Prize Laws issued on August 28, 1939. These are strictly in accordance with the acknowledged rules of maritime war. The provisions of the London Submarine Protocol are taken over in full in them. The submarines have strict orders to comply with these provisions. In harmony with the rules of the Submarine Protocol they are however justified in breaking armed resistance with all means. It is obvious that ships which participate in warlike measures or travel in convoy of enemy warships place themselves in danger and cannot complain when in the course of belligerent actions they are damaged or destroyed." cited in Hackworth, *op. cit.*, Vol. VI, p. 484. Also the passage from the judgment of the Nuremberg Tribunal summarizing the testimony of Doenitz:

"Doenitz insists that at all times the Navy remained within the confines of international law and of the Protocol. He testified that when the war began, the guide to submarine warfare was the German prize ordinance taken almost literally from the Protocol, that pursuant to the German view, he ordered submarines to attack all merchant ships in convoy, and all that refused to stop or used their radio upon sighting a submarine. When his reports indicated that British merchant ships were being used to give information by wireless, were being armed, and were attacking submarines on sight, he ordered his submarines on 17 October 1939, to attack all enemy merchant ships without warning on the ground that resistance was to be expected." *U. S. Naval War College, International Law Documents, 1946–47*, p. 298.

[43] See p. 312.

[44] Roskill states that by this policy "only warships, troopships or 'auxiliaries in direct attendance on the enemy fleet' could be attacked, and then only if identified beyond doubt. Even if an enemy merchant ship opened fire with her defensive armament our craft were forbidden to retaliate . . . It will readily be understood how far this policy made air action ineffective against all types of enemy merchant ships, including, for example, disguised merchant raiders. During the whole of 1940 only sixteen enemy merchant ships, totalling 22,472 tons, were sunk by air attack and seventeen were damaged." *op. cit.*, p. 144. In March 1940

ous to shipping" and within some of them enemy vessels were liable to be attacked and sunk on sight. In the final stages of the conflict the measures taken by Great Britain against enemy shipping wherever encountered were only barely distinguishable from a policy of unrestricted warfare.[45]

In the Pacific no attempt was made by either of the major naval belligerents to observe the obligations laid down by the 1936 London Protocol. Immediately upon the outbreak of war the United States initiated a policy of unrestricted aerial and submarine warfare against Japanese merchant vessels, and consistently pursued this policy throughout the course of hostilities.[46] Japan, in turn, furnished no evidence of a willingness to abide by the provisions of the Protocol, and—in fact—Japanese submarines attacked without warning and destroyed an American merchant vessel within a few hours following the attack upon Pearl Harbor.[47]

---

these restrictions were relaxed slightly, and in May unrestricted attacks against enemy shipping were permitted "off the south coast of Norway and in the Skagerrak" (p. 145). Further relaxations were announced in June and July 1940, but it was not until March 1941 "that permission was given to attack enemy or enemy-controlled merchant shipping at any time, whether at anchor or under way, at sea or in port" (p. 337). See also Spaight, *op. cit.*, pp. 489–93. One factor in bringing on unrestricted aerial warfare was the German practice of scuttling their ships, an act which, in effect, amounted to resistance to seizure.

[45] In these latter stages the British practice was to assimilate enemy merchant vessels to the status of supply or auxiliary vessels. According to custom such vessels are considered as liable to attack without prior warning. — It is feared that the above summary does less than justice to the British record at sea, particularly in the first year or so of the conflict. It should be emphasized that during this period Great Britain clearly manifested a desire not to be drawn into unrestricted warfare against enemy shipping and, in the end, did so only reluctantly.

[46] The U. S. Navy Department despatch of December 7, 1941 to naval forces in the Pacific read: "Execute unrestricted air and submarine warfare against Japan."

In an official survey made following World War II it was estimated that United States forces sunk 2,117 Japanese merchant vessels. Of this number 1,113 were sunk by submarines. See *Japanese Naval and Merchant Shipping Losses During World War II by All Causes* (Prepared by the Joint Army-Navy Assessment Committee, NAVEXOS P-468) (1947), pp. 6–7.

[47] No apparent attempt was ever made officially by the United States to base the policy of unrestricted warfare against Japanese merchant vessels either upon the right of reprisal or upon the quasi-military character of Japanese merchant shipping. On February 2, 1946 a curious statement occurred in a Navy Department Press Release entitled *United States Submarine Contributions to Victory in the Pacific*. Referring to the despatch of December 8, 1941 to execute unrestricted air and submarine warfare the statement noted:

"It is true that Germany had for years been waging unrestricted submarine warfare in the Atlantic. It is true that Japanese submarines sank a merchant ship in the Pacific within a few hours after the attack on Pearl Harbor. It was also true that the conditions under which Japan employed her so-called merchant shipping was such that it would be impossible to distinguish between 'merchant ships' and Japanese Army and Navy auxiliaries and these conditions would sooner or later have forced us to adopt the position which we boldly assumed at the outset. However, the existing 'Instructions for the Navy of the United States Governing Maritime and Aerial Warfare' were so restrictive as to practically preclude a submarine attack on anything but an unmistakable man of war. . ."

In point of fact, neither the 1936 London Protocol—on which the 1941 *Instructions* were

3. *The Present Situation.*

In its judgment on Admiral Doenitz for charges of violations of the laws of war the International Military Tribunal at Nuremberg declared that it was "not prepared to hold Doenitz guilty for his conduct of submarine warfare against British armed merchant ships." In reaching this decision the Tribunal did not thereby imply that the rules laid down in the 1936 London Protocol were to be considered as no longer binding upon belligerent warships in their behavior toward enemy merchant vessels.[48] There was no indication that, in the Tribunal's opinion, the ineffectiveness of the Protocol in regulating belligerent conduct had served to deprive it of its character as law. Indeed, the most reasonable interpretation of this particular aspect of the judgment rendered by the Nuremberg Tribunal is that the latter clearly assumed the continued validity of the 1936 London Protocol as it relates to inter-belligerent measures.

The significance of the Tribunal's judgment must instead be found in the reasons given for its refusal to hold Doenitz guilty for his conduct of submarine warfare against British armed merchant ships. These reasons are summarized as follows:

> Shortly after the outbreak of war the British Admiralty, in accordance with its Handbook of Instructions of 1938 to the merchant navy, armed its merchant vessels, in many cases convoyed them with armed escort, gave orders to send position reports upon sighting submarines, thus integrating merchant vessels into the warning network of naval intelligence. On 1 October 1939, the British Admiralty announced that British merchant vessels had been ordered to ram U-boats if possible.[49]

---

based—nor the traditional law were as restrictive as the above quoted press release appears to assume. It is probable that the resort to unrestricted submarine warfare could have been justified in this instance either as a reprisal against similar action by the enemy or as a consequence of the nature of employment of Japanese merchant vessels.

In this connection it is also of interest to note that in testimony submitted to the International Military Tribunal at Nuremberg, Fleet Admiral Chester W. Nimitz declared that: "The unrestricted submarine and air warfare ordered by the Chief of Naval Operations on 7 December 1941 was justified by the Japanese attacks on that date on U. S. bases, and on both armed and unarmed ships and nationals, without warning or declaration of war." *Trials of The Major War Criminals* (1947–49), Vol. XL, p. 111.

48 Though it is true that a number of writers have so interpreted the Tribunal's judgment. However, for reasons noted in the text above it is believed that this interpretation has little, if any, support. It is, of course, quite another matter to ask how relevant may be the affirmation of the continued validity of the rules laid down in the 1936 London Protocol, in view of recent belligerent practices. To this latter question it is hardly possible to reply other than by stating that given those conditions characterizing the belligerent conduct of naval hostilities in World War II the traditional rules according enemy merchant vessels immunity from attack without warning, and without safeguarding the lives of passengers and crew, can have but limited relevance.

49 *U. S. Naval War College, International Law Documents, 1946–47*, p. 299.

In this brief passage the Nuremberg Tribunal took cognizance of practices that have transformed the character of naval warfare during the past half century and that have made increasingly difficult the application of the rules distinguishing between the treatment of combatant and non-combatant vessels. Although varying in both form and degree, the near universal tendency in recent maritime warfare has been for merchant vessels to become a part of the belligerents' military effort at sea.[50]

In consequence, the principal assumption on which the traditional law was based no longer obtains—or, at least, did not obtain during World War II. This assumption was that a reasonably clear distinction could be drawn between the naval forces of a belligerent and merchant vessels having no relation to the belligerent's military operations.[51] It is necessary only to recall that even under the traditional law the immunity granted merchant vessels from attack depended upon a strict abstention from all active participation in hostilities, upon refraining from rendering any kind of direct assistance at sea to the military operations of a belligerent, and upon a refusal to accept the protection of a belligerent's naval forces (e. g., in the form of a convoy). Failure to place sufficient emphasis upon these requirements of the traditional law may easily lead to the mistaken belief that the recent claims of belligerents to possess the right to attack enemy merchant vessels are invariably rooted in the theory that novel circumstances must

[50] It was this common tendency of belligerents during World War II that reduced the importance of earlier controversy over the effect of arming belligerent merchant vessels. Whether with or without armament merchant vessels were nearly always under instructions to report the position of enemy warships immediately upon sighting the latter. In effect, this practice amounted to incorporating merchant vessels into the belligerent's intelligence system, and the danger that could thereby arise for submarines attempting seizure might easily prove as great as the danger arising from the carriage of armament. In either case, seizure in accordance with the traditional methods was normally incompatible with the safety of the warship and—indeed—was no longer demanded of the latter. A number of writers—e. g., Guggenheim (*op. cit.*, pp. 400–1) and Castren (*op. cit.*, pp. 282–90)—in continuing to insist upon the validity of the traditional rules governing the attack and destruction of enemy merchant vessels, and justifiably so, nevertheless fail to place sufficient emphasis upon the significance of these recent developments, and their effect in depriving merchant vessels of that immunity formerly enjoyed.

[51] It may be noted that the immunity from attack normally granted merchant vessels need not, and probably should not, be made wholly dependent upon their public or private character. It is of course true that the distinction drawn by the traditional law between combatant and non-combatant vessels was heavily influenced by, and largely developed from, nineteenth century liberalism, with its clear separation between public and private economic activities. It is also clear that a state which exercises public ownership over all merchant vessels will most probably integrate these vessels in time of war into its military effort. Nevertheless, it is at least conceivable that a state might refrain from associating its publicly owned vessels engaged in trade with its military operations. Under these circumstances—highly improbable though they may be—there would seem to be no apparent justification for attacking such vessels on sight simply by virtue of their public ownership. To argue otherwise is to identify the combatant-non-combatant distinction with an economic system rather than with the nature of the acts performed, an identification which is considered erroneous. See *Law of Naval Warfare*, section 500b.

serve to create new rules. These novel circumstances are generally considered to be the effectiveness of the submarine and aircraft as commerce destroyers and the central importance of the economic objective in modern war; circumstances which, when taken together, are held to justify the practice that he who cannot seize (in accordance with the traditional law) may nonetheless sink.[52] The rejection of this theory, however justified, ought not to lead to a similar rejection of the quite different contention that novel circumstances may be considered as permitting the application of measures which, in an earlier period, found only the most infrequent use.[53] These novel circumstances are—from the present point of view—neither the submarine (and aircraft) nor the central importance of what has

[52] It is another matter, however, to argue that while the novel circumstances adverted to above may not be urged as a *legal justification* for departing from the traditional law (which retains its formal validity), they must provide an essential part of the explanation as to why belligerents did depart from this law and a key to any rational expectations regarding future belligerent behavior. This is, essentially, Professor Stone's position, *op cit.*, pp. 599–607. Stone starts from the proposition that naval war law must now be seen as a function of the economic objective in warfare at sea, which is to shut off completely the enemy's commerce. ". . . the future of naval war law must be envisaged in the close context of the modern objectives of the economic arm of warfare. The economic and industrial struggle is a main if not *the* main conditioning factor . . ." (p. 602). Hence the central question to Stone is "whether he who cannot seize may lawfully sink" (p. 603), a question applied not only to enemy merchant vessels but to neutral merchant vessels as well. While not denying the continued validity of the 1936 London Protocol (at least as "law on paper") Stone's conclusion is that in view of the transcendent importance of the economic objective in modern war the "immediate task is to regulate the future of naval warfare in which submarines and aircraft will join in the attack on enemy commerce; for it is regrettably clear that no rule purporting to exclude them from this role, however well grounded in humanity, will be brooked" (p. 606). With this change once made Professor Stone is confident that we may then look forward to the "growth of real rules for the mitigation of suffering under modern conditions" (p. 607), though no concrete suggestion is given as to the express character these "real rules" might assume.

[53] A clear distinction should be drawn, therefore, between the position that the virtual incorporation of merchant vessels into the belligerent's military effort precludes the application of rules presupposing the possibility of clearly separating combatant from innocent merchant vessels, and the position that recent belligerent practice in sinking without warning all enemy vessels has invalidated these same rules. Whereas the former position insists upon the continued validity of the traditional law, *under the condition that belligerents refrain from incorporating merchant vessels in any way into their military effort at sea*, the latter position insists that belligerent practice—and the "necessities" of total war—now permit belligerents to sink enemy merchant vessels on sight. Sir Hersch Lauterpacht would appear to come very close to endorsing this latter position when he observes that the London Protocol "remained a dead letter during the Second World War" and that the problem of unrestricted submarine warfare "is deeper than that raised by the arming of merchant vessels for defensive purposes and by the interplay of the operation of reprisals. It touches upon the reality of any solution grounded primarily in the distinction between combatants and non-combatants." "The Revision of The Law of War," p. 374. Elsewhere, however, the same eminent writer has observed not only that Germany's unrestricted submarine warfare was an "illegal practice," but that in acquitting Admiral Doenitz of this charge—with respect to British merchant vessels—the judgment of the International Military Tribunal by attaching "decisive importance to the circumstance that merchant vessels were armed for defensive purposes or engaged in activities and received assist-

come to be known as economic warfare, but rather the insistence of belligerents upon the resort to measures which have as their direct consequence the integration of merchant shipping into the military effort at sea.[54]

4. *Obligations of Belligerents When Attacking Enemy Vessels.*

In view of the present status of the law relating to the liability of enemy vessels to attack it would appear especially important to place the strongest possible emphasis upon those few specific rules a belligerent is obligated to comply with in the course of attacking enemy vessels and personnel. In the standard treatise on naval warfare it is not uncommon to find only the briefest reference to these rules. It is probable that most writers have deemed it superfluous to lay emphasis upon what have heretofore been regarded as almost self-evident prohibitions, as—for example—the prohibition against firing on unarmed and defenseless survivors. It is also probable that this relative inattention has been due in the past to the assumption that only in the most unusual circumstances would enemy vessels other than warships be made the object of direct attack. Unfortunately, however, the circumstances in which enemy merchant vessels are now held subject to attack are no longer unusual and the excesses committed by belligerents during World War II no longer allow the sanguine assumption that some prohibitions are too self-evident (and too deeply ingrained) to require laboring over.

---

ance of essentially defensive character . . . is not likely to command general assent." Oppenheim-Lauterpacht, *op. cit.*, pp. 491–2. On the one hand, then, the belligerent claim to discard the fundamental distinction between combatants and non-combatants is very nearly acquiesced in, and the "necessities" imposed by total war conceded. On the other hand, the belligerent claim to attack enemy merchant vessels without warning, if the latter have been integrated into the belligerent's military effort, is largely denied, so long as this integration is justified as having a "defensive character." It should be apparent that the position taken in the text above is such as to deny the validity of the former claim while at the same time arguing for the legitimacy of the latter claim.

[54] *Law of Naval Warfare*, Article 503b (3), reads as follows:

"Destruction of enemy merchant vessels prior to capture. Enemy merchant vessels may be attacked and destroyed, either with or without prior warning, in any of the following circumstances:

(1) Actively resisting visit and search or capture.

(2) Refusing to stop upon being duly summoned.

(3) Sailing under convoy of enemy warships or enemy military aircraft.

(4) If armed, and there is reason to believe that such armament has been used, or is intended for use, offensively against an enemy.

(5) If incorporated into, or assisting in any way, the intelligence system of an enemy's armed forces.

(6) If acting in any capacity as a naval or military auxiliary to an enemy's armed forces."

It is believed that this provision does not substantially depart from the requirements of the traditional law, although it does focus attention upon those recent practices of belligerents which serve, and have always served, to deprive belligerent merchant vessels of immunity from attack.

Article 23, paragraphs c and d, of the Regulations annexed to Hague Convention IV (1907) declare that it is especially forbidden to "kill or wound an enemy who, having laid down his arms, or having no longer means of defense, has surrendered at discretion" or to "declare that no quarter will be given." These rules are applicable to hostilities wherever conducted. Hence, in warfare at sea, it is forbidden to refuse quarter either to an enemy vessel that clearly indicates a desire to surrender in good faith or to fire upon the unarmed and defenseless survivors of sunken enemy vessels. A belligerent is required to use only that degree of force necessary in order to compel submission of the enemy, force in excess of this requirement being strictly prohibited. In addition, a belligerent is required, following every engagement at sea, to take all possible measures to search for and to rescue the shipwrecked and wounded survivors of an enemy and to protect the latter, as well as the dead, against pillage and ill-treatment.[55]

The rules outlined above have long been considered applicable to warships in their conduct toward the naval forces of an enemy. The same rules must be considered to be especially applicable to warships in their conduct toward enemy merchant vessels which are—in principle—liable to attack. Indeed, it is only reasonable to demand that in the case of enemy merchant vessels a special effort be made by the attacking warship to cease the attack once active resistance has come to an end and to exert the utmost endeavor to search for and rescue shipwrecked survivors.[56]

---

[55] See *Law of Naval Warfare*, Article 511b and c. The customary prohibition against the unnecessary use of force has already been discussed (see pp. 46–50). On the duty of giving quarter to enemy vessels, see note 36 to Chapter 5, *Law of Naval Warfare*. The prohibition against firing on unarmed and defenseless survivors of sunken enemy vessels forms a part of the customary law. The obligation to rescue enemy shipwrecked and wounded survivors may also be considered a rule of customary law though it has received expression first in Article 16 of Hague X (1907) and more recently in Article 18 of the 1949 Geneva Convention for the Amelioration of the Condition of the Wounded, Sick and Shipwrecked Members of Armed Forces at Sea. In both conventions the belligerent obligation to rescue shipwrecked and wounded survivors is qualified. Article 16 of Hague X uses the phrase "so far as military interests permit" whereas Article 18 of the 1949 Geneva Convention states that: "After each engagement, Parties to the conflict shall, without delay, take all possible measures to search for and collect the shipwrecked, wounded and sick, to protect them against pillage and ill treatment, to ensure their adequate care, and to search for the dead and prevent their being despoiled."

[56] These remarks are considered to apply with even greater force in the case of attacks upon merchant vessels by surface warships. In the *Trial of Helmuth von Ruchteschell*, (*Law Reports . . .* 9 (1949), pp. 82–90) the accused, a commander of a German armed raider, was charged with committing the following acts against enemy merchant vessels: continuing to fire after the enemy had indicated surrender; failure to make any provision for the safety of survivors; and firing at survivors in liferafts. The British Military Court trying the accused found him guilty of committing the first and second acts, though not the third. In the notes to this case the following statement occurs:

"Three propositions seem to emerge, either from the utterances of the Judge Advocate or from the findings of the Court: (1) no war crime is committed if an unwarned attack is made upon a merchantman who by reason of arms and wireless communication is part of the war

The position of the submarine (and, even more, of the aircraft) with respect to the fulfillment of this latter obligation is admittedly a difficult one. In normal circumstances the submarine has been unable to take on any appreciable number of survivors. In fact, even the partial attempt to fulfill the obligation to search for and rescue survivors may result in subjecting the submarine to serious danger from enemy warships and aircraft. A submarine (or aircraft) commits no violation of the law of war, however, if after attacking an enemy vessel[57] it is required by reasons of operational necessity immediately to leave the scene of the attack. The obligation to search for and rescue survivors is not an absolute one. A belligerent is required only to take all possible measures to rescue survivors consistent with his own security. On the other hand, the prohibition against firing on the defenseless survivors of sunken vessels is not similarly qualified and, it is believed, cannot be justified by pleading reasons of operational necessity.

The foregoing considerations were involved in those war crimes trials conducted after World War II which dealt with charges arising under, or as a result of, the so-called "Laconia Order." This order, issued September 17, 1942, originated from the German U-boat command and was directed to all German submarine commanders. It ran as follows:

> (1) No attempt of any kind must be made at rescuing members of ships sunk, and this includes picking up persons in the water and putting them in lifeboats, righting capsized lifeboats and handing over food and water. Rescue runs counter to the rudimentary demands of warfare for the destruction of enemy ships and crews.
>
> (2) Orders for bringing in captains and chief engineers still apply.
>
> (3) Rescue the shipwrecked only if their statements would be of importance for your boat.

---

effort of the opposing belligerent; (2) the impunity of attack without warning on a merchantman in these circumstances forms an exception to the general rules of sea warfare and imposes upon the attacking warship the duty to use only adequate force and not to kill or wound a greater number of the crew than is reasonably necessary to secure the defeat of the attacked vessel; (3) as soon as the attacked merchantman is effectively stopped and silenced, all possible steps must be taken by the raider to rescue the crew" (pp. 87–8). It was further observed that: "(1) if the raider is aware of survivors who have taken to their lifeboats, he must make reasonable efforts to rescue them; (2) it is no defense that the survivors did not draw attention to their boats if they had reasonable grounds to believe that no quarter was being given" (p. 88).

According to S. W. Roskill, with the one exception noted above, the captains of German armed merchant raiders "generally behaved with reasonable humanity towards the crews of intercepted ships, tried to avoid causing unnecessary loss of life and treated their prisoners tolerably" *op. cit.*, p. 279. Attacks upon merchant vessels by German raiders were very frequently the result of the merchant vessel's resort to the use of its defensive armament or to an insistence upon making use of its wireless in order to report the raider's presence and position. Under either of these circumstances attack upon the merchant vessel could be considered justified.

[57] It is assumed, of course, that the attack upon the enemy vessel is justified.

(4) Be harsh, having in mind that the enemy has no regard for women and children in his bombing attacks on German cities.[58]

The International Military Tribunal at Nuremberg found the Laconia Order ambiguous, and therefore refused to hold the originator of the order—Admiral Doenitz—guilty of deliberately ordering the killing of shipwrecked survivors.[59] The ambiguity of the order apparently was considered to stem from an uncertainty as to whether its intent was only to forbid submarine commanders from making any attempt to rescue survivors or was intended to enjoin them deliberately to kill survivors. The International Military Tribunal seemed to have been of the opinion that if the former interpretation was intended the order was a lawful one. But even this opinion is doubtful, since the rule in question allows only for circumstances of operational necessity. The most favorable interpretation of the Laconia Order was that it laid down a policy of no rescue, not solely—or perhaps not even primarily—for reasons of operational necessity, but because rescue was deemed to run "counter to the rudimentary demands of war for the destruction of enemy ships and crews." On this basis alone the unlawful character of the order would seem to be readily apparent. In any event, in two reported trials held before the British Military Court at Hamburg it was amply shown that in the course of interpreting and applying the Laconia Order its supposed ambiguity was resolved in favor of the killing of survivors. As such, the illegality of the order should be placed beyond question.[60]

---

58 The order was given orally, never in writing. In the *Peleus Trial* (*Law Reports* . . . 1 (1947), p. 5) and the *Trial of Karl-Heinz Moehle* (*Law Reports* . . . 9 (1949), p. 75) the accused confirmed the contents of the order, reproduced above.

59 On this point the Tribunal's judgment declared: "The Tribunal is of the opinion that the evidence does not establish with the certaintly required that Doenitz deliberately ordered the killing of shipwrecked survivors. The orders were undoubtedly ambiguous, and deserve the strongest censure." *U. S. Naval War College, International Law Documents, 1946–47*, p. 300.

60 In the *Trial of Karl-Heinz Moehle* the accused, a senior officer of the 5th U-boat Flotilla, was charged with giving orders "to commanding officers of U-boats who were due to leave on war patrols that they were to destroy ships and their crews." *Law Reports* . . . 9 (1949), p. 75. The orders were given in the form of briefings and were based upon the Laconia Order. From the sample briefings furnished as evidence at the trial it appeared clear that the Laconia Order was interpreted in practice as an order to kill survivors. The British Military Court found the accused guilty of ordering the commission of acts contrary to the law of war. In the notes on this case it is observed that: "If a submarine commander can, without danger to his boat, save or succour survivors, he is no doubt under a duty to do so. If, however, by so doing he would endanger his boat he cannot be held responsible if he does not save any such survivors since it is recognized that the safety of his own boat and its crew must be his primary consideration. It is clearly recognised, on the other hand, that the killing of defenceless survivors of a torpedoed ship is a war crime" (p. 80).

In the *Peleus Trial* the commanding officer of a German submarine was charged with having given orders to fire on the survivors of the steamship *Peleus*. In presenting his defense the accused quoted the Laconia Order, though he did not plead superior orders. The principal defense plea was that the order to fire on the rafts containing survivors was an operational necessity, and by destroying all evidence of the sinking pursuit of the submarine was made less

D. THE SEIZURE OF ENEMY VESSELS AND GOODS

Unless specially protected by a rule of customary or conventional international law all vessels and goods encountered at sea in time of war are liable to seizure and to subsequent condemnation if impressed with an enemy character. In this respect the conduct of naval warfare is to be distinguished from the methods characterizing land warfare, where the private property of the enemy population may not—as a general rule—be seized and confiscated. There is no need to deal here with the arguments both for and against this belligerent right in warfare at sea to seize the private property of an enemy. It is sufficient merely to note that despite a substantial opposition during the late nineteenth and early twentieth centuries to the retention of this right, an opposition led very largely by the United States, there has been no general disposition on the part of naval powers to relinquish a practice as old as naval warfare itself.[61] If

---

probable. In finding the accused guilty the court rejected the plea that the order was operationally necessary under the given circumstances. It is not possible to determine, however, whether the court was of the opinion that circumstances constituting a condition of operational necessity could ever serve, in law, to justify the act of killing helpless survivors. In the notes on this case it is stated that: "The case contains . . no decision on the question whether or to what extent operational necessity legalises acts of cruelty such as shooting at helpless survivors of a sunken ship because on the facts of the case this behaviour was not operationally necessary, i. e. the operational aim, the saving of ship and crew, could have been achieved more effectively without such acts of cruelty " *Law Reports* . . . 1 (1947), p. 16. However it seems clear that this latter question must be answered in the negative.

[61] A useful summary of earlier arguments for and against the retention of the belligerent right to seize and condemn the private property of enemy subjects may be found in *U. S. Naval War College, International Law Topics, 1905*, pp. 9–20. Hyde (*op. cit.*, pp. 2059–63) contains a brief review of the traditional American position, citing the proposal urged by the American delegation at the 1907 Hague Peace Conference, which declared that: "The private property of all citizens or subjects of the signatory Powers, with the exception of contraband of war shall be exempt from capture or seizure on the sea by the armed vessels or by the military forces of any of the said signatory Powers. But nothing herein contained shall extend exemption from seizure to vessels and their cargoes which may attempt to enter a port blockaded by the naval forces of any of the said Powers." And in a recent review of the inactivity since the Spanish-American War of American courts sitting in prize it has been stated that: "The history of the matter shows that the policy of the United States has tended to avoid resort to capture and prize, and to substitute for the form, if not always the whole substance of the doctrine, gentler legal devices, such as requisition for use or title upon promise or payment of just compensation. . . . Thus our country has maintained its position of endeavoring to lead the world towards a general law or rule of immunity from capture or destruction of peaceful merchantmen and cargoes not contraband." A. W. Knauth, "Prize Law Reconsidered," *Columbia Law Review*, 46 (1946), p. 86. It may be relevant to observe, however, that the conditions attending American participation in the two World Wars are not so easily interpreted as a reluctance "to abandon the great reform." The device of requisition for use or title upon promise or payment of just compensation was used almost exclusively with respect to enemy merchant vessels caught in American ports at the outbreak of hostilities—and it may still be contended that such vessels ought to be given special consideration (see pp. 86–90). With respect to enemy merchant vessels encountered at sea, any conclusions drawn must be extremely tentative. In both World Wars

anything, recent belligerent practice has moved in the contrary direction of restricting—and, in certain instances, invalidating entirely—the application of the few rules formerly granting certain enemy vessels and goods exemption from seizure. However this may be, the liability of vessels and goods to seizure in naval warfare depends, in the first instance, merely upon the fact that such vessels and goods possess an enemy character. This being so, the determination of enemy character in relation to vessels and cargoes may be taken as the starting point of an inquiry into the nature and scope of the belligerent right to seize enemy property at sea.[62]

German merchant shipping was—by the time America became a belligerent—almost nonexistent in any event. And during World War II the methods pursued in the Pacific hardly pointed toward any practice save that of unrestricted submarine and aerial warfare against Japanese merchant shipping (see pp. 66–7). It may also be noted that in both World Wars neutral shipping no longer remained a major problem by the time America entered as a belligerent. These, and other, circumstances surely render hazardous any interpretation of the possible lines of action this country might pursue in the future if involved in hostilities at sea against a major maritime Power—and given the task of controlling substantial neutral trade.

[62] In a broader sense, of course, the belligerent right of seizure in naval warfare also extends to vessels and cargoes bearing a neutral character. Normally, however, neutral commerce is exempt from belligerent interference, and liability to seizure arises only from the performance of acts—contraband carriage, blockade breach, unneutral service—belligerents have a right to prevent according to international law. In the case of enemy vessels and goods, liability to seizure and confiscation follows simply from the character of the property, and requires no further justification (except, perhaps, to establish that the property does not come within a category given special protection from seizure). The law of prize therefore encompasses the totality of the rules governing the belligerent right to seize and to condemn privately owned vessels and cargoes, whether of enemy or of neutral subjects.

Attention may once again be called to a point earlier made in the Foreword, that a detailed examination of prize law does not form one of the purposes of the present study. In the immediate section (D) of this Chapter, as well as in Chapters IX through XII, the attempt is made to indicate only in broad outline those rules which determine both the substantive grounds for capture and what are generally considered the procedural rules regulating the conduct of visit, search and seizure. No endeavor is made, however, to examine the nature and organization of belligerent prize courts, or the procedural rules applied by these courts—save perhaps where these rules have had, as in the case of contraband (see pp. 270–6), a marked impact in extending the belligerent's control over neutral trade. It will also be apparent that emphasis has been placed primarily upon British Prize Law since 1914—or rather the interpretation given the law of prize by the British prize courts during the two World Wars. The justification for this emphasis may be based not only upon the fact that the British decisions have been the most numerous and by far the most influential but also upon the conjecture that if the United States should in the future resort to prize proceedings—admittedly an unlikely contingency—American prize courts would in all probability lean heavily upon these decisions.

The principal studies of prize law developments during World War I are J. H. W. Verzijl, *Le Droit Des Prises De la Grande Guerre* (1924); J. W. Garner, *Prize Law During the World War* (1927); and C. J. Colombos, *A Treatise on the Law of Prize* (3rd. ed., 1949). The work by Colombos is particularly useful since it includes the significant decisions of the 1939 War. And on World War II see also S. W. D. Rowson, "Prize Law During The Second World War," *B. Y. I. L.*, 24 (1947), pp. 160–215 and A. Gervais (for a review of French, British, Italian and German prize decisions) in *Revue Générále de Droit International Public*, Vols. 52 (1948), pp. 82–161; 53 (1949), pp. 201–75; 54 (1950), pp. 251–316, 453–504; and 55 (1951), pp. 481–546. An

1. *Enemy Character.*

a. Vessels.

Normally, the enemy or neutral character of a vessel is determined by the flag which she has the right to fly. A vessel entitled to fly the flag of an enemy state and therefore having an enemy nationality may be regarded in every instance as bearing enemy character. But although the owners of a vessel are always bound by the flag they have chosen to adopt, belligerents are not so bound in determining the neutral or enemy character of a vessel. For the practice of states is clear that even though entitled to fly a neutral flag—and thus possessing a neutral nationality—a vessel may nevertheless be considered as impressed with an enemy character.[63] The neutral flag cannot serve as a device to protect vessels from seizure whose actual status indicates either continued ownership or control by individuals who themselves possess enemy character.[64]

---

invaluable summary of the more significant World War II prize cases may be found in the *Annual Digest and Reports of Public International Law Cases* (ed. by H. Lauterpacht), 1938–48. Finally, among general treatises on the law of war special mention should be made of the stimulating and thoroughly up to date analysis given in Stone, *op. cit.*, pp. 457 ff.

[63] It is therefore important that a clear distinction be drawn between the *neutral or enemy nationality and the neutral or enemy character of vessels*. The former—nationality—is determined by the flag a vessel has the right to fly, and the conditions of this right are directly determined by the municipal law of each maritime state. But the latter—character—is a matter solely within the province of international law, and international law may or may not make the character of a vessel coincide with its nationality. In point of fact, international law does not identify the two.

In this connection the relevant provisions of the 1909 Declaration of London deserve passing mention. Article 57 of that unratified instrument declared:

"Subject to the provisions respecting the transfer of flag, the neutral or enemy character of a vessel is determined by the flag which she has the right to fly.

"The case in which a neutral vessel is engaged in a trade which is reserved in time of peace, remains outside the scope of, and is in nowise affected by, this rule."

Article 57 thereby made the nationality of a vessel the principal test for determining its character. Three exceptions were provided for, however. The first concerned the fraudulent transfer of flag, dealt with in Articles 55 and 56. The second, mentioned in paragraph 2 of Article 57, refers to the so called "Rule of 1756," which holds that neutral merchant vessels acquire enemy character if in time of war they engage in a trade the enemy state exclusively reserves in time of peace to merchant vessels flying its own flag. According to the practice of several states the neutral vessel accepting this privilege from a belligerent thereby becomes so closely identified with the belligerent as to lose its neutral character. Finally, and not mentioned in Article 57, neutral vessels performing certain types of unneutral services for a belligerent thereby became impressed with enemy character—according to Article 46—and liable to the same treatment as enemy merchantmen.

[64] See *Law of Naval Warfare*, Article 501, which abandons entirely the "right to fly" formula, it now being clear that flying the enemy flag is conclusive evidence of enemy character regardless of whether or not a vessel has the right to do so. Of course, the principal defect of Article 57 of the Declaration of London—at least from the belligerents' viewpoint—was the exclusion of ownership as a criterion for the determination of enemy character. During World War I a number of neutral states, including the United States, nevertheless persisted in considering Article 57 as accurately reflecting the law governing enemy character of vessels. But the prac-

In addition, a merchant vessel though entitled to fly a neutral flag may nevertheless forfeit its neutral character by undertaking to perform any one of several services on behalf of a belligerent. In a later chapter these acts—generally considered under the heading of "unneutral service"—are examined in some detail.[65] Here it is sufficient to observe that the more serious forms of unneutral service may so identify merchant vessels of neutral nationality with the armed forces of an enemy as to expose such vessels to the same treatment as is meted out to enemy warships. Thus merchant vessels of neutral nationality which take a direct part in hostilities on the side of an enemy or act in any capacity as a naval or military auxiliary to an enemy's armed forces not only acquire enemy character but are liable to the same treatment as enemy warships.[66] Further, neutral merchant vessels may acquire enemy character and be made liable to the same treatment as enemy merchant vessels if found operating directly under enemy orders, employment, or direction.[67] Finally, it is customary to

---

tice of belligerents in both World Wars has made sufficiently clear that they are not prepared to refrain from the seizure and condemnation of vessels whose ownership is vested in individuals (or corporations) possessed of enemy character.—The attitude of the British Prize Court was best set forth in the following passage:

"It is a settled rule of prize law, based on the principles upon which Courts of Prize act, that they will penetrate through and beyond forms and technicalities to the facts and realities. This rule, when applied to questions of the ownership of vessels, means that the Court is not bound to determine the neutral or enemy character of a vessel according to the flag she is flying, or may be entitled to fly, at the time of capture. The owners are bound by the flag which they have chosen to adopt; but the captors as against them are not so bound." *The Hamborn* [1918], 7 *Lloyds Prize Cases*, p. 62.

The criteria for determining the enemy character of the owners of a vessel are considered in connection with the discussion of the criteria for determining the enemy character of goods generally (see pp. 81–4).

65 See Chapter XI.

66 *Law of Naval Warfare*, Article 501a. Also, see pp. 319–21, for a more detailed discussion.

67 *Law of Naval Warfare*, Article 501b. See pp. 322–3 for a more detailed discussion. Parenthetically, it may be noted here, though in later pages this point is developed more fully, that not all acts falling under the category of unneutral service result in impressing enemy character upon a vessel. There are certain acts of unneutral service which, when performed by neutral vessels, result only in a liability to seizure in the same manner as for the carriage of contraband or breach of blockade (see *Law of Naval Warfare*, Article 503d (3), (4), and also pp. 324–31). But these acts do not of themselves result in the acquisition of enemy character on the part of the vessel performing them, just as the acts of contraband carriage and blockade breach do not of themselves result in impressing an enemy character upon the vessel performing them.

Now it may be contended—and with a certain merit—that the differences required by the traditional law in the treatment of vessels bearing an enemy character (see pp. 102–8) and the treatment of vessels retaining a neutral character (see pp. 347–53) are no longer very considerable. It is true that the treatment of cargo carried on board a seized vessel differed according to whether the status of the vessel was enemy or neutral, though this difference too is no longer very significant. Even further, although the destruction of neutral prizes following seizure is a far more serious measure than is the destruction of enemy vessels, the former may admittedly be destroyed

consider a merchant vessel of neutral nationality as acquiring enemy character if it resists the exercise of the legitimate belligerent right of visit and search.[68]

(i) Transfer of Flag

The imminence of hostilities or the actual outbreak of war is generally productive of attempts on the part of the owners of vessels possessing enemy character to avoid the risk of seizure and confiscation by transferring such vessels to a neutral flag. It is universally acknowledged that although the transfer of a vessel from an enemy to a neutral flag may take place in accordance with the municipal law of the neutral state international law may nevertheless regard the transfer as fraudulent and not serving to divest the vessel of its enemy character. The general principle involved is clear: the fraudulent transfer of vessels, a matter determined by international law, cannot serve to defeat the rights of a belligerent. But the detailed application of this principle is quite another matter, and states have long disagreed upon the specific conditions that must be satisfied before vessels can be regarded as properly divested of enemy character.

It has been observed that the traditional view maintained in this matter by the United States is that "a neutral national may lawfully purchase a private ship under a belligerent flag and thereby acquire a title to be respected by the enemy of the State of the vendor, provided the transaction is a *bona fide* one, by the terms of which no right to purchase or recover the vessel is reserved to the seller, and the price paid gives evidence of a reasonable sacrifice by the purchaser. Other considerations, such as the motives impelling a sale have not been deemed to be decisive of the validity of the transaction." [69] A substantially similar view, enphasing the *bona fide*

---

in circumstances of exceptional necessity. Hence, the differences in this latter respect, while not to be lightly brushed aside, should not be exaggerated.

However, the significant and rather unexpected point is that in view of the increasing liability of enemy merchant vessels to attack (see pp. 67–70), the importance of clearly distinguishing between neutral merchant vessels acquiring and neutral vessels not acquiring enemy character becomes even more imperative than previously. For if the law may now be considered as permitting—under certain circumstances—the sinking without warning of enemy merchant vessels, special caution must be exercised in making clear precisely those vessels either possessing enemy character or acquiring such character by the performance of certain acts. The consequences of even a partial abandonment of the heretofore valid rule requiring warships (whether surface or submarine) to refrain from sinking any merchant vessels without having first placed passengers and crew in a place of safety are sufficiently grave to warrant a very careful discrimination between enemy vessels, including neutral vessels acquiring enemy character, to which this partial abandonment applies, and neutral vessels, which may perform prohibited acts (e. g., contraband carriage) but which do not acquire by these actions enemy character.

[68] Strictly speaking, the act of resisting visit and search does not fall within the category of unneutral service, though it nevertheless results in a neutral vessel acquiring enemy character.

[69] Hyde, *op. cit.*, pp. 2078–9, and sources cited therein. Paragraph 58 of the 1917 *Instructions* issued to the U. S. Navy declared:

"The transfer of a private vessel of a belligerent to a neutral flag during war is valid if in accordance with the laws of the State of the vendor and of the vendee, provided that it is made

and absolute character of the transfer of a vessel from enemy to neutral ownership, has long been endorsed by Great Britain.[70]

On the other hand, the traditional practice of certain of the continental European states, and notably France, has been to refuse to recognize the validity of any transfer made from an enemy to a neutral flag in time of war, though treating such transfers as were made prior to the outbreak of hostilities as valid merely if carried out in accordance with the laws of the state of the vendor and vendee.

In retrospect, it is clear that the provisions of the 1909 Declaration of London relating to the transfer of flag did not successfully meet the difficulties posed by these divergent practices. The relevant articles of that instrument provided for a distinction to be drawn between the transfer of an enemy vessel to a neutral flag when effected shortly before the opening of hostilities and transfer when effected after the outbreak of war. In both

---

in good faith and is accompanied by a payment sufficient in amount to leave no doubt of good faith; that it is absolute and unconditional, with a complete divestiture of title by the vendor, with no continued interest, direct or indirect, of the vendor, and with no right of repurchase by him; and that the ship does not remain in her old employment."

This provision was substantially repeated in paragraph 64 of the 1941 *Instructions*. There is no reason to believe that the above quoted provision does not still remain the position of this country, the United States having never endorsed the principles—discussed below—concerning transfer of flag provided for in the Declaration of London. As regards the transfer to a neutral flag before hostilities, both the 1917 and 1941 *Instructions* merely declared such transfer to be valid provided it was made in accordance with the laws of the state of the vendor and the state of the vendee. But this provision must be considered along with this country's endorsement—as reflected in earlier manuals—of Article 57 of the Declaration of London. Simply stated, this led to the position that so long as a belligerent vessel was transferred to a neutral flag prior to the outbreak of war, and in accordance with the municipal law of the neutral state, such vessel enjoyed a neutral character once war broke out. Thus the requirements demanded of transfer made prior to hostilities were different from, and exceedingly more liberal, than the requirements made for transfer during war. The present validity of this distinction must be doubted, however, if only for the reason that Article 57 of the Declaration of London can no longer be regarded as valid. If anything, it would appear that the test heretofore established in American practice for determining the validity of transfers made during war is equally applicable to transfers made immediately prior to the commencement of hostilities.

On October 3, 1939 the Panama meeting of the Foreign Ministers of the American Republics resolved that the latter: "Shall consider as lawful the transfer of the flag of a merchant vessel to that of any American Republic provided such transfer is made in good faith, without agreement for resale to the vendor, and that it takes place in the waters of an American Republic." *A. J. I. L.*, 34 (1940), *Supp.*, p. 11. Also see Hackworth, *op. cit.*, Vol. VI, pp. 524-41.

70 "From the British point of view, transfers of vessels during the war are not *per se* invalid, but the belligerent is entitled to inquire into the transaction in order to determine whether it was made in fraud of his rights and whether there has been an effective divestment of enemy title and an effective vesting in the neutral owner." Colombos, *op. cit.*, p. 105. In practice, this has been interpreted to mean that the seller must not retain any interest in the vessel, or any right to repurchase or recover the vessel following the termination of the war. Still further, British practice forbids transfer while in a blockaded port or while the vessel is *in transitu* (though once having reached port and taken possession of by a neutral owner the voyage has been regarded as terminated).

instances transfer from an enemy to a neutral flag was to be considered void if made "in order to evade the consequences which the enemy character of the vessel would involve." However, for transfers made immediately prior to hostilities the burden of proving such a purpose was placed upon the captors, whereas for transfers made during the period of war the claimant was obliged to displace the presumption that transfer was made in order to avoid seizure. This principal test was further supplemented by a number of related presumptions.[71]

These provisions constituted an obvious attempt to compromise differences in state practice already noted. However, the manner in which they were formulated was such as to allow a considerable latitude in interpretation, and during World War I belligerents—or at least those belligerents professing to follow the Declaration of London—did not hesitate to resort to that interpretation most nearly in accord with their traditional practice.[72]

---

[71] Thus according to Article 55 of the Declaration, an absolute presumption of a valid transfer was to be made if the transfer was effected more than thirty days before hostilities and was absolute, complete, conformed to the laws of the countries concerned, and the former owners were divested both of control and of earnings. But a rebuttable presumption that the transfer was void resulted if the bill of sale was not found on board a vessel that lost her belligerent nationality less than sixty days before the opening of hostilities.

According to Article 56 an absolute presumption that transfer—in time of war—was void followed if the transfer was made during a voyage or in a blockaded port, if the vendor retained a right of redemption or of revision, or if the requirements for a valid transfer laid down by the municipal law of the flag state were not observed.

[72] A rigorous interpretation of the stipulation that transfer was void if made in order to "evade the consequences which the enemy character of the vessel would involve" easily served to render wartime transfers practically impossible. Thus the position of France and Germany was that this injunction applied to the intentions of both the seller and the purchaser. Since the motives of the former are necessarily suspect it is at best an extremely difficult task for a claimant to establish that the transferor's motives were not to "evade the consequences" of enemy character, particularly when the acts held to constitute an evasion of the consequences of enemy character were never clarified or made the object of common agreement.—The well known case of *The Dacia*, decided by the French Prize Council in August 1915, indicated the French interpretation of Article 56 of the Declaration of London. The *Dacia*, a German merchant vessel purchased by an American citizen, and transferred to American registry while lying in an American port, was seized by a French cruiser on a voyage from Port Arthur, Texas, to Rotterdam. The cargo carried was destined for Bremen. Earlier, the French Government had notified the American Government that it would not recognize the validity of any transfer of German vessels lying in American ports to American registry. In condemning the *Dacia*, the French Prize Council asserted that the American owner had failed to establish—as required by Article 56—that the German transferor had not sold the vessel in order to "evade the consequences" of enemy character. Even further, the Prize Council declared that a transfer could be regarded as valid "only if there was reason to believe that it would have been effected just the same had the war not occurred. . . ." For translation of *The Dacia*, see *A. J. I. L.*, 9 (1915), pp. 1015–26. The French Council of State, on appeal, upheld the decision of the Prize Council and in doing so made the same point. In effect, then, this interpretation—also made by Germany—placed an impossible burden upon claimants. In the case of *The Dacia*, however, the Prize Council did lay emphasis upon the additional circumstance that the vessel was engaged in a trade "for which it had been chartered when it was under the German flag, and in view

At present, then, the disparate rules governing the transfer of vessels from an enemy to a neutral flag remain roughly what they had been prior to the Declaration of London. So far as Anglo-American practice is concerned this would appear to mean that transfers effected either immediately prior to or following the outbreak of war will be—in principle—recognized as valid if made in good faith by the purchaser and if resulting in the complete divestiture of enemy ownership and control. However, it remains to be emphasized that the very circumstances normally attending the transfer of vessels in time of war are such that belligerents and belligerent prize courts will subject such transfers to the most careful investigation. It also seems clear that in this process the burden of proving that the divestiture of enemy ownership in and control over a vessel has been complete and genuine rests largely upon the claimant.[73]

b. Goods (Cargoes)

Whereas in the case of vessels the fact of ownership serves as a supplementary criterion for determining neutral or enemy character, in the case of cargoes ownership becomes the principal test. But although it is recognized that the neutral or enemy character of goods is dependent upon the neutral or enemy character of the owners, states have differed in the tests they have established for determining the enemy character of individuals. The 1909 Declaration of London failed to resolve the traditional disparities in state practice, being limited to an endorsement of the customary rule that all goods found on board enemy merchant vessels are presumed to have an enemy character unless proof of neutral character is furnished by the owners. With respect to the central question, however, the Declaration merely provided that the enemy character of goods is determined by the enemy character of the owners, thereby selecting neither the "territorial" test, adhered to by the United States and Great Britain,

---

of which it had been transferred to a neutral flag; such transfer to a neutral flag with the object of carrying on enemy trade and protecting the ship from capture cannot be valid against belligerents." This latter point does appear to offer a clear basis for the voidance of transfer and to provide sufficient indication that transfer was not made in "good faith."—For the diplomatic correspondence on the *Dacia*, see *U. S. Naval War College, International Law Situations, 1934*, pp. 7–17.

In contrast to France and Germany, Great Britain applied a liberal interpretation to Article 56 and one that accorded with her previous practice. Thus in *The Edna*, [1919]—(9 *Lloyds Prize Cases*, p. 70) the Judicial Committee of the Privy Council declared that Article 56 was intended to prevent colorable or fictitious transfers and that the only change made by this Article was to place the burden of proving a *bona fide* transfer upon the purchaser. But the latter is under no obligation to establish the motives—innocent or otherwise—of the seller.

[73] It should be apparent that the task of ascertaining whether or not a transfer does satisfy the requirements demanded by Anglo-American practice is one suited to a court of prize and not to belligerent commanders undertaking visit and search. Save in exceptional circumstances the latter may treat the fact of transfer from an enemy to a neutral flag as sufficient cause for seizure, leaving the ultimate determination of the vessel's status to the prize court.

nor the "nationality" test, followed by France and other continental powers.[74]

It has frequently been observed that the true purpose of the belligerent right to seize enemy goods at sea is to prevent an opponent from retaining a control over any trade that will serve to augment his economy and thus enable him the more effectively to conduct war. From this point of view it is neither the possession of enemy nationality nor the subjective attachment to the cause of an enemy state that—in itself—provides sufficient reason for the confiscation of an individual's goods on the ground that they are impressed with an enemy character. Instead, it is the existence of an objective relationship between the trade of an individual—whatever his nationality or allegiance—and the territory belonging to or occupied by the enemy; a relationship the result of which is to subject the property of an individual to the control of the enemy, thereby increasing the latter's potential for waging war.

This is, at any rate, the rationale upon which Anglo-American practice may be said to have developed. The test for determining the neutral or enemy character of an individual, at least so far as the determination of the character of goods is concerned, is made dependent upon what is commonly termed the individual's "commercial (trade) domicile."[75] Even though of non-enemy nationality, an individual is regarded as having a hostile commercial domicile if he resides in territory belonging to or occupied by an enemy. In consequence, all goods belonging to the subjects of neutral states who reside and carry on trade in enemy territory bear an enemy character; and the same holds true for the goods belonging to the subjects of a belligerent, or of the belligerent's allies, resident in the territory of an enemy and remaining there following the outbreak of war. Conversely, through residence in a neutral state (or in the territory of the belligerent or of an ally) an individual of enemy nationality may so remove himself and his commercial activities from enemy territory and control as to obtain a neutral (or friendly) commercial domicile and to no longer warrant treating his property as impressed with an enemy character.

Furthermore, it may be that a neutral subject, though residing in neutral territory, has an interest in a house of trade that is established and doing business in or from an enemy state. In this event the goods he owns as a result of such commercial enterprises in the enemy country are impressed with an enemy character, the neutral owner being considered as acquiring an enemy commercial domicile with respect to—though only with respect to—his assets in the enemy house of trade. The enemy character that is imputed to goods in this instance follows from the connection held to obtain between the latter and enemy territory; a relationship that is considered

[74] And, by implication, thereby sanctioning both tests.

[75] See Article 633a, *Law of Naval Warfare*—which follows a parallel provision found in both the 1917 and 1941 *Instructions*.

to increase the enemy's resources. It is this relationship rather than the actual residence of the neutral owner that is held to be decisive here. On the other hand, the converse situation does not hold true, for the doctrine of commercial domicile does not exempt from enemy character the goods of individuals permanently resident in an enemy country though having a house of trade in a neutral state.[76] Last of all, mention should be made of the special rule relating to articles which form part of the produce of enemy soil. According to American and British practice goods which are the products of the soil of an enemy country and which are shipped therefrom after

---

[76] The above remarks constitute no more than the barest summary of the principal lines of development that the territorial test has taken in its application to cargoes owned by individual traders. To these remarks some additional observations may be appended in this note.—In British prize law a distinction is drawn between the acquisition of a neutral or friendly commercial domicile and of a hostile commercial domicile. With respect to the former, residence is an essential element, and although it is not possible to lay down a general rule covering all cases it is at least clear that the residence required must be of a fairly permanent character. But a hostile commercial domicile may be acquired either by residing and trading in an enemy state or simply by having an interest in a business established in hostile country. Thus in the *Anglo-Mexican* [1918], Lord Parker declared on behalf of the Judicial Committee of the Privy Council that "a neutral wherever resident may, if he owns or is a partner in a house of business trading in or from an enemy country, be properly deemed an enemy in respect of his property or interest in such business. He acquires by virtue of the business a commercial domicile in the country in or from which the business is carried on, and this commercial domicile, though it does not affect his property generally, will affect the assets of the business house or his interest therein with an enemy character." 5 *Lloyds Prize Cases*, pp. 113–14. However, in the case of a hostile commercial domicile acquired by residing and trading in hostile country, enemy character is imputed to an individual's goods wherever situate (i. e., whether in hostile, neutral or friendly territory). Nor have individuals acquiring a hostile commercial domicile through residing in enemy territory been allowed a period of grace, upon the outbreak of hostilities, in which to abandon their acquired domicile (though such abandonment may be taken by an unequivocal act, following which the goods of neutral individuals will not be considered as any longer impressed with enemy character and liable to capture). But in the case of neutral subjects resident in neutral territory and partners in an enemy house of trade it is *only* the assets owned as a result of the interest in the enemy house of trade that have been considered impressed with enemy character. Furthermore, in this instance practice has been to allow neutral subjects a reasonable period of time in which to break off their enemy interests. Indeed, it is only by a kind of projection of the concept of commercial domicile that it is used to cover the case of being a partner in an enemy house of trade though without being actually resident in hostile country.

Where the ownership of cargoes (and vessels) is vested in a corporate entity rather than in an individual the application of the territorial test must of necessity undergo certain modifications, and here again it is British practice that has pointed the way. It is clear, to begin with, that a corporation will be impressed with an enemy character, and its property rendered liable to seizure, if its place of incorporation is within hostile country. Nor will the imputation of enemy character to a corporation thus having an enemy nationality be affected by the fact that those who own or control the enterprise are made up largely of neutral nationals residing in neutral territory. In addition, a corporation, even though its place of incorporation is within neutral territory, may be considered as possessing an enemy character if it is substantially owned and controlled by individuals who themselves bear enemy character—this at least according to the British view.

the outbreak of war are impressed with an enemy character even though the owner of the goods may be domiciled or resident in a neutral country.

In contrast with the territorial test is the test traditionally applied by France and other continental states which emphasizes the nationality of the owner of goods as the decisive criterion for determining the neutral or enemy character of cargoes. In applying the nationality test goods belonging to the subjects of an enemy state are impressed with an enemy character, despite the fact that the owners may be permanently resident in neutral territory; and if found on board enemy merchantmen such goods are always considered liable to capture. Conversely, goods owned by the subjects of a neutral state normally do not bear enemy character—again according to the nationality test—despite the fact that the owners may be residing in enemy territory.[77]

---

[77] It is now generally recognized, however, that the experience of the two World Wars has demonstrated that the traditional divergence between the territorial and the nationality test has lost a substantial measure of its former significance. In practice, many of the belligerents refrained from a rigid adherence to either test, but sought to effect a combination of both. Nor can it be said that a belligerent acts in violation of international law by applying both tests, should the particular circumstances attending a war render such behavior expedient. See, for example, Hyde, *op. cit.*, pp. 2090–1. At the same time, the importance that may be attached to belligerent practice in this respect during the two World Wars is difficult to assess, since much of the "evidence" that belligerents are in fact abandoning an exclusive adherence to either the territorial or the nationality tests has been found in belligerent "trading with the enemy" acts. At the outbreak of war every belligerent is at liberty to prevent its subjects, as well as other individuals residing within its territory, from carrying on any intercourse—commercial or otherwise—with the enemy. Such prohibition may extend not merely to all persons residing in the enemy state but to enemy nationals residing abroad in neutral states and even to individuals—regardless of nationality and residence—found to have an association with the enemy. During World War I Great Britain's Trading With the Enemy Act authorized the Government to forbid trade not only with all persons residing in an enemy state but also with any person not resident in enemy territory whenever such prohibition appeared expedient "by reason of the enemy nationality or enemy association of such persons." In accordance with this Act so-called "black-lists" were made up containing the names of individuals, many of them residing in neutral states, with whom trading was deemed unlawful. As a neutral the United States protested against the British black-lists, though upon becoming a belligerent it resorted to similar measures. France, on the other hand, in addition to forbidding trade with enemy subjects wherever resident also prohibited trade with non-enemy subjects residing in enemy territory.—In World War II the belligerents once again resorted to similar measures in their trading with the enemy legislation. For the text of Great Britain's Trading With the Enemy Act, 1939, see *A. J. I. L.*, 36 (1942), *Supp.*, pp. 3–12. The United States' Trading with the Enemy Act, 1917, is given in *A. J. I. L.*, 12 (1918), *Supp.*, pp. 274 ff., and the World War II amendments in *A. J. I. L.*, 36 (1942), *Supp.*, pp. 56–8. In effect, then, these states adopted both the territorial and the nationality tests for determining enemy character in their trading with the enemy legislation. Nevertheless, such legislation is mainly a matter of municipal law rather than of international law; it places restraints upon the subjects of the belligerent and all other persons residing within its territory and provides appropriate penalties in the event these restrictions are broken. There is nothing to prevent a belligerent from taking such measures. Nor does there appear any solid basis in international law for neutral protests against these measures simply for the reason that the belligerent has forbidden its subjects

(i) Transfer of Goods at Sea

Although the character of goods seized at sea is normally dependent upon the character of the owners, difficulties may frequently arise in determining who are the true owners at the time of seizure.[78] It is generally acknowledged that with respect to goods sold prior to, and without anticipation of, hostilities, the question whether or not ownership in the goods has passed from seller to buyer at the time of seizure is one that may be determined either in accordance with the municipal law of the parties involved in the transaction or in accordance with the municipal law of the captor.[79]

Quite different considerations[80] govern the transfer of goods when made after the outbreak of war or in contemplation of hostilities. Were the municipal law governing the passing of property to remain applicable to these latter cases of transfer, and to determine the neutral or enemy character of goods, risk of confiscation would be rendered negligible so long as ownership in goods being shipped from neutral to enemy or from enemy to neutral could remain vested in neutral hands. In the case of goods being

---

from trading with individuals, residing in neutral territory, known to be either of enemy nationality or to have enemy associations. To this extent American protests against the British "black-lists" during World War I appear misplaced. Even further, Great Britain was well within her lawful rights as a belligerent in taking other discriminatory measures against the vessels belonging to individuals residing in neutral territory though placed on the statutory lists, e. g., in refusing to allow such vessels to be insured by British companies or in denying to them the facilities of British controlled ports. But it should be emphasized that the "enemy character" imputed to individuals in trading with the enemy legislation has been relevant only for those purposes already noted, not for the purpose of determining whether the goods of such individuals are impressed with an enemy character and therefore liable to seizure as lawful prize. In this latter sense Great Britain and the United States have yet to depart from the territorial test, though it is true that the scope of this test has been limited by virtue of other belligerent measures.

[78] And it is ownership in the goods at the time of seizure that is decisive in determining their neutral or enemy character. The right of belligerents to confiscate cargoes (and vessels) thus owned by individuals or corporations endowed with enemy character is not affected by any special rights that may be attached to the seized enemy property, and recognized by municipal law, e. g., mortgages, liens, etc. On this point the practice of prize courts is uniform, it being recognized that to allow such special claims by neutrals would doubtless render the belligerent right to seize enemy property at sea of very little value.

[79] The captor may therefore determine the question of ownership by the law of sale applicable in his own state. Generally speaking, the delivery of goods on board a vessel is normally considered as equivalent to their delivery to the consignee, the latter thereby accepting the risk and the right to dispose of the goods. But this need not be the case, and the decisions of prize courts—particularly the British, which apply the English law governing the sale of goods—are clear that ownership can be determined only by an inquiry into the intentions of the parties and the terms governing each particular contract for the sale of goods. For an enlightening commentary on some of the recent problems arising in English practice, see Stone, *op. cit.*, pp. 469–70, 475–7.

[80] Here again it is British prize decisions that provide the substantial basis for the remarks to follow, though this practice is shared in varying degrees by other states and particularly the United States.

transferred from a neutral to an enemy this result is prevented by the established practice of considering such goods as impressed with enemy character during the entire period of transit. Nor does it matter that according to the strict terms of the sale the property is not to pass into enemy hands until the time delivery has been made and actual possession of the goods has been taken.[81] In addition, there is the principle governing converse cases involving transfer of property from enemy to neutral, and according to which a belligerent may seize such goods while in transit—although title to the goods has already passed to the neutral—if the transfer is deemed to be fraudulent, i. e., entered into for the purpose of defeating the rights of the captor.[82] This is almost always considered to be the case if transfer of title to enemy goods is carried out once the goods are already at sea.[83] But quite apart from this special case the transfer of title to goods in transit from enemy to neutral, however clear, cannot operate against the captor if fraudulently made. And while it may be open to the neutral claimant to disprove any presumption of fraud against the captor the practical effect of the foregoing rule, as well as the rule governing the transfer of goods from neutral to enemy, is to regard all goods in transit—whether from neutral to enemy or from enemy to neutral—as enemy property.[84]

It should be made clear, in conclusion, that the preceding rules are always relevant to the transfer of title in goods found on enemy vessels. The extent to which they will prove applicable to the transfer of goods on neutral vessels must depend, of course, upon whether or not the rule of "free ships, free goods" is being observed by belligerents.[85]

2. *Enemy Property Exempt From Seizure*

a. Enemy Vessels at the Outbreak of War

During the course of the nineteenth century the practice gradually took root of granting belligerent merchant vessels caught in enemy ports at the

[81] Of course, if title to goods has already passed to the enemy owners then obviously no problem arises with respect to their character.

[82] Again it may be noted that no difficulty arises with respect to the passing of property from enemy to neutral if the title to the property remains in the vendor at the time of seizure—the goods evidently retain their enemy character. It is only when a neutral title has been perfected that any problem arises and when the principle that transfers of property cannot be made in order to defeat the rights of the captor becomes applicable.

[83] *Law of Naval Warfare*, Article 633b. Article 60 of the Declaration of London, the only provision concerning the transfer of goods upon which the drafters were able to agree, provided that the "enemy character of goods on board an enemy vessel continues until they reach their destination, notwithstanding an intervening transfer after the opening of hostilities while the goods are being forwarded."

[84] But once the neutral buyer has taken actual possession of the goods through their delivery the transit is complete and the belligerent cannot seize them—at least not on the basis of the rules presently considered—unless it can be shown that the enemy seller has nevertheless retained an interest in or control over the property.

[85] As to the present status of the latter rule, see pp. 99–102.

outbreak of war a period of grace in which to depart unmolested.[86] Exemption from seizure also was frequently accorded to belligerent merchant vessels which left their last port of departure before the outbreak of war and when encountered on the high seas were unaware that hostilities had broken out.[87] Hague Convention VI (1907), Relative to the Status of Enemy Merchant Ships at the Outbreak of Hostilities sought to codify this practice, and Article 1 of that Convention provided that in the event a merchant ship belonging to one belligerent is at the commencement of war in an enemy port "it is desirable that it should be allowed to depart freely, either immediately, or after a reasonable number of days of grace, and to proceed, after being furnished with a pass, direct to its port of destination or any other port indicated." A similar rule was provided for a belligerent merchant ship which, having left its last port of departure before the outbreak of war, entered a port belonging to the enemy in ignorance of the fact that hostilities had broken out. Merchant ships unable to leave an enemy port within the allotted period of grace, owing to circumstances of *force majeure*, were not to be confiscated, but could either be detained, without payment of compensation though subject to restoration at the conclusion of hostilities, or requisitioned, on payment of compensation. Belligerent merchant vessels met at sea and ignorant of the outbreak of war, having left their last port of departure before war's outbreak, could be seized by an enemy and either detained or requisitioned in the same manner as vessels unable to leave an enemy port. Confiscation was, in any event, forbidden. Finally, the Convention expressly excluded from the benefit of its provisions those merchant ships whose build indicated that they were intended for conversion into warships.[88]

A large number of states, including the United States, failed to ratify

---

86 A review of nineteenth century opinion and practice with respect to the status of enemy merchant vessels at the outbreak of war is given in *U. S. Naval War College, International Law Topics, 1906*, pp. 46–65, where it is concluded that the exemption granted enemy vessels should be conditioned upon a strict reciprocity of treatment, that it should be subject to the protection of a belligerent's military interests, and that it should not extend to private vessels suitable for warlike use.—It should be observed that prior to the middle of the last century the practice of belligerents had been to seize and confiscate enemy vessels caught in belligerent ports at the outbreak of hostilities. And there were a number of instances of states placing an embargo upon the vessels of a foreign state in anticipation of war with the latter.

87 Such vessels, if destined for an enemy port, were usually allowed to enter such port, discharge their cargo, and depart. On the other hand, if seized they were generally not subject to confiscation but instead to detention or to requisition upon compensation.

88 The foregoing is a brief summary of Articles 1, 2, 3 and 5 of Hague VI. Article 4 provided that in all instances enemy cargo was likewise liable to detention, subject to restoration after the termination of war without compensation, or to requisition, on payment of compensation. It should be observed that the exclusion of "potential auxiliary cruisers" from the protection of the Convention seriously limited its applicability from the very start. Even then, the only strict obligation laid down by the Convention was that which forbade confiscation.

the Convention, however.[89] In addition, among those states ratifying Hague VI several did so only after attaching certain reservations. During World War I observance of the Convention by the contracting parties was far from uniform and in consequence of this failure to secure "either uniformity or liberality of treatment" Great Britain denounced Hague VI in 1925.[90] Following the outbreak of hostilities in 1939 neither Great Britain nor France granted any days of grace to enemy merchant vessels caught in their ports. Instead, such vessels as were found in Allied ports—or encountered upon the high seas—were held liable to seizure and subsequent confiscation.[91]

At the present time, it must be considered very doubtful that in the absence of specific obligations imposed by treaty a belligerent is required by customary international law to accord any favorable treatment—in the form of exemption from seizure and confiscation—to enemy merchant vessels found in its ports at the commencement of hostilities. Despite the

---

[89] The failure of the United States to ratify the Convention was not due to a lack of support for its purposes. On the contrary, one of the chief complaints made by this country was that the Convention did not provide sufficient guarantee that enemy vessels would be permitted to depart from the ports of the other belligerent upon the outbreak of war.

[90] A review of World War I practice is given by A. P. Higgins, "Enemy Ships in Port at the Outbreak of War," *B. Y. I. L.*, 3 (1923–24), pp. 55–78. Of the British denunciation of Hague VI, Colombos (*op. cit.*, p. 138) writes that: "This development in the law is to be regretted. The provisions contained in the Hague Convention appear substantially just and equitable and deserve to be followed on their own merits." The British decision to denounce Hague VI was very largely a result of the decision rendered by the Judicial Committee of the Privy Council in *The Blonde and Other Vessels*, [1921]—(10 *Lloyds Prize Cases*, pp. 248 ff.), where Lord Sumner held that during the war of 1914–18 Great Britain had acted on the basis that Hague Convention VI was in effect. This being so, Article 2 of the Convention—forbidding confiscation—was regarded as obligatory even though Article 1—concerning the granting of days of grace—was considered as only optional. ("Ships which find themselves at the outbreak of war in an enemy port shall in no case be condemned if they are not allowed to leave, or if they unavoidably overstay their days of grace, but it would be better that they always be allowed to leave, with or without days of grace.") Thus the argument that the prohibition in Hague VI against confiscation was dependent upon a prior reciprocal agreement between belligerents on the days of grace to be granted enemy merchant vessels in which to depart from belligerent ports was expressly rejected. Such an agreement had not been reached between Great Britain and Germany in 1914 and consequently each state detained the merchant vessels of the other. The effect of the decision in *The Blonde* was to require the British Government either to restore the detained German vessels to their owners or to requisition the vessels on payment of compensation.

[91] France denounced Hague VI in 1939. Other allied states, e. g., Canada, followed the same pattern and seized all German ships either found in their ports or encountered upon the high seas without granting any period of grace. Nor did these states refrain from confiscating the seized vessels. However, it is true that a number of belligerents retained the provisions of Hague Convention VI in their prize codes. Thus Article 18 of the German Prize Law Code of 1939 declared that the provisions of the Convention "remain unaffected." But Article 18 was interpreted as being conditioned only upon reciprocal treatment by Germany's enemies. Italy also retained the provisions of Hague VI in her prize code of 1938 and offered to apply these provisions upon becoming a belligerent in 1940, though nothing came of the offer.

fairly widespread practice of belligerents in the years prior to World War I of granting either a period of grace or, in any event, exemption from confiscation, it is difficult to accept the occasional assertion that this practice had hardened into a rule of customary law by 1914.[92] A belligerent is, of course, at liberty to refrain from resorting to its customary right to confiscate enemy vessels found in its ports at the commencement of hostilities, and to date the United States has chosen to follow the policy of requisitioning such vessels on payment of compensation.[93] Neverthe-

[92] This was also the opinion of the British Prize Court in *The Pomona* [1942], where Lord Merriman held that in the absence of reciprocal agreement there was no rule of international law which exempts from condemnation an enemy ship found in a belligerent's port at the outbreak of war. See *Annual Digest and Reports of Public International Law Cases*, 1941–42, Case No. 159, pp. 509–14. The judgment in *The Pomona* rejected the contention put forward by the claimants that the provisions of Hague VI were merely declaratory of established customary rules of international law. This contention, shared by a number of writers, has been considered as receiving some support from the preamble to Hague VI which stated that the protection of operations undertaken in good faith and in process of being carried out before the outbreak of hostilities was "in accordance with modern practice." Hyde (*op. cit.*, pp. 2045–53), in a review of the subject declares that while there is no obligation to grant a period of grace, in the absence of treaty, "Provision for the detention or requisition on compensation, of enemy vessels in port, in lieu of confiscation, is a mark of respect for private property which should enjoy universal approval." Judicial opinion in the United States, although in general accord with this view, has nevertheless refrained from declaring that seizure and confiscation would be contrary to customary international law. In *Littlejohn v. United States*, (1926), 270 U. S. 215. p. 225, the Supreme Court stated that: "In the absence of convention every government may pursue what policy it thinks best concerning seizure and confiscation of enemy ships in its harbors when war occurs."

With respect to enemy merchant vessels which left their last port of departure before the outbreak of war, and are encountered at sea, there seems little question but that they are liable to seizure and confiscation. Even Hague Convention VI exempted them from confiscation only if "still ignorant that hostilities had broken out." Developments in communications render such ignorance highly unlikely today.

[93] The United States upon becoming a belligerent in 1917 did not grant to enemy merchant vessels any period of grace in which to depart freely from American ports. Nevertheless, this country acted in substantial accord with the injunction contained in Article 2 of Hague Convention VI by refraining from confiscation and by applying instead the principle of requisition. On May 12, 1917, Congress authorized the President to take "immediate possession and title of" any enemy vessel within ports under American jurisdiction, and "through the United States Shipping Board, or any department or agency of the Government, to operate, lease, charter, and equip such vessel in any service of the United States, or in any commerce, foreign or otherwise." A decade later Congressional provision was made, through the Settlement of War Claims Act, for compensating the owners of the requisitioned enemy merchant ships. See Hackworth, *op. cit.*, Vol. VI, pp. 572–6. Also Edwin Borchard, "The German Ship Claims," *A. J. I. L.*, 25 (1931), pp. 101–7.

During World War II a quite different situation arose owing to the fact that foreign merchant vessels—both belligerent and neutral—lying idle in American ports were forcibly acquired prior to the entrance of the United States in the hostilities. The Idle Foreign Vessels Act, signed by the President on June 6, 1941, authorized the President—until June 30, 1942—to purchase, requisition, charter, requisition the use of, or take over the title to, or the possession of, any foreign merchant vessels lying idle within the jurisdiction of the

less, a policy either of requisition or of detention, while within the discretion of each state, is not demanded by customary international law. Even clearer is the absence of any rules granting either a period of grace or exemption from confiscation to belligerent civil aircraft found in the territory of an enemy upon the outbreak of hostilities.[94]

b. Postal Correspondence

Prior to the conclusion of Hague Convention XI (1907) no general rule existed granting postal correspondence special exemption from seizure. It is true, however, that during the nineteenth century a number of treaties were concluded which provided that in the event of war between the contracting parties the mail boats as well as the postal correspondence of the belligerents were to be regarded as immune from seizure. With respect to the postal correspondence carried on board neutral vessels, there are a number of impressive precedents that can be drawn from nineteenth century practice indicating a widespread disposition toward the granting of special treatment to mails. Not infrequently belligerents exempted neutral mail bags from search; and even when neutral vessels were seized for carriage of contraband the mail on board such vessels was often forwarded unopened.[95]

At the second Hague Conference in 1907 the problem of postal corres-

---

United States, the Philippine Islands and the Canal Zone, and which were deemed to be necessary to the national defense. The Act further provided that just compensation must be paid the owners of such vessels, and specified a procedure for insuring this result. (For similar action by a number of South American states, see Hackworth, *op. cit.*, Vol. VII, pp. 545–9.)

Although at the time the Idle Foreign Vessels Act was passed the United States had openly abandoned any pretense of conforming to the duties imposed by international law upon neutral states, this country nevertheless retained the formal status of a neutral (see pp. 197–8). Hence there is little point in considering the action from the standpoint of the powers a belligerent may exercise with respect to both enemy and neutral vessels found within its ports. Instead, the measures taken may simply be regarded as the exercise of the generally acknowledged right of a state to assume control—subject to compensation—over any property found within its jurisdiction, when such control is required for a public purpose. In this particular instance the purpose was that of national defense. And in a review of the Act one writer observed: "It is generally admitted that a government has supreme sovereign right of control of all persons and property within its jurisdiction and may exercise this right whenever necessary to preserve its independence. The exercise of this right in time of peace is generally under the doctrine of eminent domain, that is, the taking of property for a public purpose upon the payment of just compensation judicially determined. It is submitted that this doctrine is applicable whether the nation is at war or at peace." L. H. Woolsey, "The Taking of Foreign Ships In American Ports," *A. J. I. L.*, 35 (1941), p. 502. Also see, pp. 348 (n).

[94] Spaight (*op. cit.*, pp. 397–8) is of this opinion, which appears correct.

[95] For a brief review of nineteenth century practice, *U. S. Naval War College, International Law Topics, 1906*, pp. 88–96. A more extensive review, carried through World War I, is given in *U. S. Naval War College, International Law Situations, 1928*, pp. 40–72. The case for exempting postal correspondence found on board neutral vessels is obviously a much stronger one—as seen from nineteenth century practice—than is the case for according special treatment to mail found on board enemy vessels. Even so, the opinion that customary law accorded no special exemption to postal correspondence, but instead regarded it in the same manner as other merchandise, is believed to be correct.

pondence was subjected to conventional regulation, Articles 1 and 2 of Hague Convention XI providing as follows:

> Article 1. The postal correspondence of neutrals or belligerents, whatever its official or private character may be, found on the high seas on board a neutral or enemy ship, is inviolable. If the ship is detained, the correspondence is forwarded by the captor with the least possible delay.
>
> The provisions of the preceding paragraph do not apply, in case of violation of blockade, to correspondence destined for or proceeding from a blockaded port.
>
> Article 2. The inviolability of postal correspondence does not exempt a neutral mail ship from the laws and customs of maritime war as to neutral merchant ships in general. The ship, however, may not be searched except when absolutely necessary, and then only with as much consideration and expedition as possible.[96]

From a formal point of view it must probably be concluded that these provisions remain binding today upon the parties to Hague Convention XI.[97] On the other hand, it is difficult to avoid the conclusion that the events of the two World Wars have reduced the significance of these provisions almost to a vanishing point. As between belligerents the Convention presupposes that enemy vessels will be seized and not sunk without warning. In both World Wars the destruction of the postal correspondence of belligerents formed only one of the incidental effects of a policy of unrestricted warfare waged against enemy merchant vessels.[98]

As between belligerent and neutral it soon became apparent during the 1914–18 War that the varying interpretations placed upon Article 1 of Hague XI were—for all practical purposes—irreconcilable. In principle,

---

[96] It is clear that the inviolability granted is to postal correspondence, not to vessels. Thus the liability of enemy mail boats to seizure remains unaffected by the Convention. Similarly, the liability of neutral mail ships to seizure for any of those acts a belligerent has a right to prevent when undertaken by neutral vessels—contraband carriage, blockade breach, unneutral service—also remains unaffected, save for the qualification that search of neutral mail ships should be undertaken only when "absolutely necessary"—a phrase that seems to have remained unclear as judged from the context in which it is used. It does appear though that Article 2 refers to *privately owned* neutral mail ships, not to mail ships of a public character.

[97] Technically the Convention was not operative in World War I since a number of the belligerents, and particularly Russia, had never ratified it. Hague XI, as the other treaties in this series, contained the general participation clause. But in neither War did the belligerents indicate that the Convention was not regarded as operative for that reason.

[98] The destruction of Allied mail boats without warning by German submarines was initiated almost at the start of World War I. In general, the German conduct of submarine warfare against enemy merchant vessels—and, for that matter, neutral ships as well—requires no further comment with respect to the German record in meeting the requirements of Articles 1 and 2 of Hague XI. As to the Allied record, there is little information regarding the disposition made of mail found on board seized enemy vessels, though it is hardly hazardous to assume that such postal correspondence was not considered "inviolable."

agreement proved wanting both as to the meaning of "postal correspondence," considered as inviolable, and the construction to be given the phrase "found on the high seas." The initial neutral position, as might be expected, was to insist that postal correspondence be understood to refer to all sealed envelopes, regardless of contents.[99] In turn, the injunction of inviolability was interpreted as forbidding the opening of sealed mails for any reason, an interpretation that would evidently exclude application of the principle of contraband to the mails. Still further, the neutrals contended that the scope of Article 1 of Hague XI extended inviolability to postal correspondence on board neutral vessels, even after such vessels had been seized and conducted into belligerent ports (and particularly if merely diverted into belligerent ports for the purpose of searching the cargo). In opposition to the foregoing, belligerents insisted that "postal correspondence" did not include contraband materials, and refused to regard letters containing such materials as "genuine" correspondence entitled to receive special protection. Thus bonds, stocks, securities, checks and money orders were considered, among other articles, as constituting contraband merchandise which, if destined to neutral territory, a belligerent had the right to seize even though contained in sealed correspondence. This claim to apply the principle of contraband to the mails was accompanied by the further assertion of the right to search neutral mail bags and the contents contained therein, whether at sea or following diversion to a neutral port.[1]

[99] It has always been understood that the inviolability granted to postal correspondence in Hague XI does not extend to parcels or packages sent by parcel post.

[1] The correspondence occasioned between neutral and belligerent—and particularly between the United States and Great Britain—over interference with mails is reviewed in Hackworth, *op. cit.*, Vol. VI, pp. 608–22. As judged by both the actual wording of Article 1 of Hague XI, and the known intention of the drafters, it is difficult to deny the force of the initial neutral position. Quite briefly, the inviolability of postal correspondence guaranteed in Article 1 meant that sealed envelopes could neither be opened nor their contents seized nor censored in any way by belligerents. It may of course be asked why prospective belligerents were prepared to grant such a substantial concession for future conflicts. In part, the answer is to be found in the fact that the attention of the drafters was concentrated largely upon the effect that new means of communication would have upon the continued importance of the mails in transmitting intelligence of value to an enemy. It was thought that the importance of mails as a means for conveying intelligence would prove small enough to warrant the concessions made in Hague XI. In part, the answer is to be found in an underestimation of the possible importance of the mails as a means for conveying contraband merchandise of value to an enemy. But despite these assumptions, which later proved to be largely misplaced, Article 1 must be seen as part of the compromise between the conflicting interests of neutral and belligerent—and the devitalization of Article 1 of Hague XI must therefore be seen as only one rather limited development in the much larger process whereby belligerents have severely restricted, if not invalidated entirely, traditional neutral rights. Thus it is, at best, misleading to argue, as did the Inter-American Neutrality Committee in its recommendation of May 31, 1940 on the inviolability of postal correspondence (*A. J. I. L.*, 34 (1940), *Supp.*, pp. 135–9), that by Article 1 of Hague XI the recognition of the inviolability of postal correspondence "was made necessary in order to give the greatest possible scope to the right of immunity and privacy of postal communications, even in time of war, and in view of the grave injuries resulting from the examination of corre-

Whatever the respective merits of these opposed positions, both World Wars provide abundant evidence that belligerents are not prepared—in any event—to exempt mails from the application of the principle of contraband. Nor, for that matter, have neutrals been either united or consistent in adhering to their initial position that the inviolability of mails must be interpreted as forbidding the opening of sealed envelopes whatever the contents of the latter.[2] But once it is admitted that the principle of contraband applies to postal correspondence it is obviously incongruous to deny belligerents the right to open and scrutinize mail whose ultimate destination may be to enemy territory; for without this right there can be no meaningful application of the principle of contraband to the mails. No less incongruous is the recognition of the belligerent right to divert neutral merchant vessels into port in order to conduct search for contraband among the cargo and the denial of the same right of diversion for the purpose of screening postal correspondence.[3]

---

spondence, which injuries are unjustly disproportionate to the military advantages derived from the seizure of any contraband found in this correspondence . . ." This may reflect the viewpoint of neutrals, but it is clear that belligerents did not consider the military advantages disproportionate to the injuries inflicted. Nor, apparently, did the Committee so believe since it went on to declare "that the principle of inviolability, by its nature and object, may be completely applied only to the protection of epistolary correspondence, properly so called, and may not be extended to protect the transmission of goods or things of value ordinarily sent by postal means . . ." Yet this concession to belligerent interests, by conferring inviolability only upon "epistolary correspondence," and thus excluding postal correspondence containing goods or things of value, has no evident foundation in the wording of Article 1.

[2] As a neutral the United States conceded in 1916 that the principle of contraband was applicable to the mails by declaring that letters containing articles of merchandise—understood to include stocks, bonds, coupons and similar securities, money orders, checks, drafts, notes and other negotiable instruments—were liable to seizure by belligerents.

[3] In reply to an American protest of December 22, 1939, that British authorities had removed from American and other neutral ships American mails addressed to neutral countries, and had opened and censored sealed letter mail sent from this country, particularly after having compelled neutral vessels to call at designated British control bases, the British Government declared (January 16, 1940) that "in the case of merchandise, His Majesty's Government are entitled to ascertain if it is contraband intended for the enemy or whether it possesses an innocent character, and it is impossible to decide whether a sealed letter does or does not contain such merchandise without opening it and ascertaining what the contents are." cited in Hackworth, *op. cit.*, Vol. VI, pp. 620–1. In commenting upon this exchange Clyde Eagleton has noted that: "If . . . the principle of contraband is to be applied to the mails, it makes little difference whether they are searched upon the high seas or in port. It is not the fact that they have come into port, willingly or unwillingly, and therefore under British jurisdiction, which gives to the British Government the claim to search mails; it is the admission that mails may have a contraband character which gives the authority to search, whether upon the high seas or in port, and to seize contraband contained found therein . . . At this point, the debate ceases to be one of inviolability of mails; it now becomes part of the controversy over visit, search, and seizure of contraband goods." "Interference With American Mails," *A. J. I. L.*, 34 (1940), pp. 317–9. Eagleton's conclusions are reflected in Hyde's (*op. cit.*, p. 1979) comment that the "real basis" of the American complaint "was the British action that caused mails on board of neutral ships, and having an immediate or direct neutral destination, to be carried

Nor has the belligerent's position been limited only to the assertion of a right to prevent contraband merchandise from being sent to an enemy through the mails. The much broader claim has been made of a right to screen all postal correspondence carried on board neutral vessels entering belligerent ports—whether voluntarily or involuntarily—with a view to the removal of any materials or information which is judged as providing some assistance to an enemy in the conduct of war.[4] Goods of enemy origin as well as of enemy destination have been seized. Information destined to an enemy and instructions sent out by the latter to its agents abroad have been censored.[5] In these circumstances, it need hardly be pointed out that the "inviolability" of postal correspondence, even though still proclaimed by belligerents, no longer retains its former meaning. In effect, postal correspondence has been made subject—at least when judged

---

into belligerent ports and there be subjected to a rigid censorship. It was the abuse of a belligerent privilege revealed in the method by which it was applied which was the chief ground for objection." On this view, the issue is no longer the "inviolability" of mails but the methods—e. g., diversion into port—a belligerent uses in preventing "letter mail that might by reason of its contents or character be fairly assimilated to contraband from reaching the enemy." On diversion of neutral vessels generally, together with related problems, see pp. 338–44.

[4] Thus in the "long distance" blockades imposed against Germany in both World Wars (see pp. 305 ff.) Great Britain and her Allies made liable to detention (and later to seizure) all goods of enemy origin. In practice, the control exercised over enemy exports was employed as a means for screening outgoing postal correspondence. During World War I the "blockade" system—whose legal basis rested upon the right of reprisal—finally required all neutral merchant vessels sailing to or from neutral ports providing access to enemy territory to call at British or Allied ports. Failure to do so resulted in a liability to seizure. Once in British ports the mail carried on board was subject to censorship. During World War II, the Order in Council of July 31, 1940 (see pp. 313–5) resulted in an even tighter control over postal correspondence carried to or from neutral ports providing access to the enemy. In consequence, many neutral vessels ceased carrying any mails, and for those vessels that continued to do so "mailcerts" were introduced as a part of the navicert system.

[5] It should be noted that the term "censorship," frequently used in diplomatic interchanges as well as in academic discussions over belligerent interference with mails, has partially confused the relevant issues due to its ambiguous use. More often than not it has been used as a general term to indicate any form of belligerent interference with mails regardless of the specific objective. But belligerent censorship of mails in order to prevent the import to, or export from, an enemy of merchandise is a quite different matter than the exercise of censorship in order to prevent the enemy transmission of information of a political or military nature. In practice, belligerents have sought to prevent the latter as well as the former, and in the British reply of January 16, 1940 to the American note of December 22, 1939, regarding interference with mails on neutral ships, it was observed: "Quite apart from transmission of contraband, the possibility must be taken into account of the use of the letter post by Germany to transmit military intelligence, to promote sabotage and to carry on other hostile acts. It is in accordance with international law for belligerents to prevent intelligence reaching the enemy which might assist them in hostile operations." Cited in Hackworth, *op. cit.*, Vol. VI, p. 621. As judged by Article 1 of Hague XI this last contention has an even more doubtful basis than the claim to apply the principle of contraband to the mails. For while the drafters of Hague XI perhaps paid insufficient attention to the possibilities of using the mails for contraband carriage, a good deal of attention was devoted to the possibility of using the ordinary mails for conveying

by recent practice—to practically the same restrictions that belligerents have imposed upon neutral commerce generally in time of war.[6]

c. Coastal Fishing Boats and Small Boats Engaged in Local Coastal Trade

Article 3 of Hague XI provides that:

> Vessels used exclusively for fishing along the coast or small boats employed in local trade are exempt from capture, as well as their appliances, rigging, tackle, and cargo.
>
> They cease to be exempt as soon as they take any part whatever in hostilities.
>
> The contracting powers agree not to take advantage of the harmless character of the said vessels in order to use them for military purposes while preserving their peaceful appearance.

The exemption from seizure accorded to coastal fishing boats is founded upon the conviction that considerations of humanity warrant the absence of belligerent interference with a class of men normally felt to be both inoffensive and of no material importance to the military effort of an enemy. Their immunity from seizure, though provided for by conventional rule, has been considered by many states—including the United States [7]—as resting upon well established custom. Whether or not a vessel falls within this exempted category depends primarily upon the use to which it is put rather than to its size or mode of propulsion. Thus it is clear that immunity from seizure does not extend to vessels engaged in deep sea fishing or to vessels which do not bring fish fresh to the market.

---

military intelligence. Despite this consideration it was decided to exempt mails from seizure, even though containing military intelligence. The British claim, therefore, cannot possibly find support in the "international law" of Hague XI. Instead, it is an open disavowal of the continued validity, in this respect, of the clear intent of Hague XI. Nevertheless, Great Britain (as well as other belligerents) sought to, and did, exercise this right of censorship over mails on neutral vessels that entered (whether voluntarily or involuntarily) British territorial waters and ports.

[6] In this general connection brief attention may be directed to another form of neutral intercourse with a belligerent—i. e., intercourse through submarine telegraph cables. The comparison frequently drawn between neutral mail boats and cables is, as Higgins and Colombos (*op. cit.*, p. 380) point out, hardly sound. The only conventional rule on the subject is that contained in Article 54 of the Regulations attached to Hague IV (1907), which reads: "Submarine cables connecting an occupied territory with a neutral territory shall not be seized or destroyed except in case of absolute necessity. They must likewise be restored and compensation fixed when peace is made." It will be readily apparent that the severance of an enemy's communications forms an essential object in the conduct of hostilities, and belligerent practice is clear that cables connecting two points in enemy territory, or connecting the territory of two enemies, may be severed. So also the cables connecting enemy and neutral territory, though only in case of necessity. On the other hand, cables connecting two points in neutral territory must be held inviolable. See *Law of Naval Warfare*, Article 520b.

[7] The Supreme Court in the *Paquete Habana* (1900), 175 U. S. 677, considered the immunity of coastal fishing boats as based upon custom—though it was made clear that the rule applied only to coastal fishing vessels and not to those engaged in deep sea fishing.

The test is that the fishing should serve a purely local need, and that it must not be deep sea fishing. On the other hand, there is no indication that coastal fishing boats must remain strictly within territorial waters or that they must refrain from fishing off the coasts of third states (the latter so permitting).

Similarly, in the case of boats engaged in coastal navigation it is local trade only that is permitted by Hague XI. Steamers engaged in general coastal trade, i. e., cabotage, are not accorded immunity from seizure. Furthermore, with respect to this latter category of boats it is not only the character of the trade that is restricted but the size of the boats as well. The Convention does not accord protection to large boats even though engaged only in local trade.

The special protection granted to coastal fishing boats and small boats engaged in local coastal trade has always been dependent upon an abstention from any kind of participation in the conduct of hostilities. In addition, it is only reasonable that belligerent naval forces operating in the vicinity of these craft should be able to insure their security by requiring such vessels and boats to conform to the regulations of the belligerent naval commander operating in the area.[8] The movements of such vessels and boats may be restricted as military operations require, and immediate identification must be provided upon demand. The necessity for emphasizing these latter points is due to the ubiquity of radio-telephonic apparatus in even the smallest of boats and the ease with which coastal craft may be integrated into the intelligence network of an enemy. Indeed, recent experience points to the increasing use by belligerents of coastal craft for intelligence purposes. It should be clear that this development can only result in an increased liability to seizure or destruction of vessels and boats formerly exempt from such treatment.

d. Vessels Engaged in Missions of a Religious, Scientific or Philanthropic Character

Article 4 of Hague XI states that exemption from capture is to be accorded "vessels charged with religious, scientific, or philanthropic missions."[9] The value of this provision has been found to be extremely limited in practice. During World War I the question arose on several occasions as to the definition of a "philanthropic mission," the conduct of which would exempt an enemy vessel from seizure.[10] In the absence of special

---

[8] See *Law of Naval Warfare*, Article 503c (6).

[9] See *Law of Naval Warfare*, Article 503c (3).

[10] So far as vessels charged with religious or scientific missions are concerned the present significance of these exemptions is practically negligible. It is difficult to conceive of a "scientific" mission belligerents would now be prepared to accept and grant immunity to—except on the basis of a specific agreement. Earlier scientific missions generally were voyages of discovery, and on several occasions such missions were granted special protection. Thus Article 13 of the U. S. Naval War Code of 1900 exempted from capture public vessels of the enemy engaged in "scientific pursuits, in voyages of discovery . . ." In the Naval War

agreement on specific voyages, and the consequent issuance of safe conduct passes, belligerents indicated that they were prepared to allow only the most narrow of interpretations.[11] This has meant, however, that the basis for the immunity granted enemy vessels performing humanitarian functions has not depended primarily upon the general rule contained in Article 4 of Hague XI but—in almost every instance—upon the express agreement of the belligerents.[12]

e. Hospital Ships, Medical Transports and Medical Aircraft

The 1949 Geneva Convention for the Amelioration of the Condition of the Wounded, Sick and Shipwrecked Members of Armed Forces At Sea provides that belligerent hospital ships, medical transports and medical aircraft are, when properly marked and duly notified to the other belligerents, immune from either attack or seizure. A more detailed analysis of the provisions of this recently concluded Convention, which replaces for the Contracting Parties Hague Convention X (1907), is presented in later pages.[13]

f. Cartel Ships

Ordinarily the term cartel is used to indicate an agreement concluded between belligerents for the purpose of regulating the exchange of prisoners

---

College commentary to Article 13 of the Code the opinion is expressed that *private vessels* engaged in religious, scientific or philanthropic missions are liable to capture: "the difficulty of responsible control is so great that these (private) vessels should be exempt only by grace of the commander in the immediate region, not by general rule." *U. S. Naval War College, International Law Discussions, 1903*, pp. 51–2. But Article 4 of Hague XI does not require that vessels so exempted be of a public character, and it is the general opinion that the immunity provided for extends either to public or to private vessels.

11 Thus the transport of women and children refugees by an enemy vessel has not been construed as a philanthropic mission which, in the absence of a safe conduct pass, may result in exemption from seizure. Nor has the carrying of supplies for the purpose of succoring starving women and children. See Hackworth, *op. cit.*, Vol. VI, pp. 543–6.

12 Of course, the source of the special agreement may be a convention to which the belligerents are contracting parties. Thus the 1949 Geneva Convention Relative to the Protection of Civilian Persons in Time of War provides in Article 59 that an occupying power shall agree to relief schemes on behalf of the population of an occupied territory that is inadequately supplied, and shall facilitate such schemes by all the means at its disposal. Accordingly, the Contracting Parties to the Convention are obligated to permit the free passage of consignments of foodstuffs, medical supplies and clothing to occupied territory and to guarantee their protection. Article 59 further declares that a state "granting free passage to consignments on their way to territory occupied by an adverse Party to the conflict shall, however, have the right to search the consignments, to regulate their passage according to prescribed times and routes, and to be reasonably satisfied through the Protecting Power that these consignments are to be used for the relief of the needy populations and are not to be used for the benefit of the Occupying Powers." It will be apparent that although the Convention on the Protection of Civilian Persons establishes a general obligation for the Contracting Parties to grant exemption to vessels carrying those supplies noted above, and for the relief of occupied populations, the immunity granted to specific voyages must rest upon prior and express agreement between the belligerents (and—in all probability—upon the issuance of safe conduct passes).

13 See pp. 123–34. The practice of belligerents during World War II, while still governed by Hague X (1907), is also discussed in these later pages.

of war. In a broader sense, however, the term has been used to refer to agreements permitting various kinds of non-hostile relations between belligerents, e. g., the exchange of official communications.[14] Vessels (and aircraft) engaged in carrying out the terms of such agreements, and particularly when engaged in the carriage of prisoners of war, must be regarded as inviolable.[15] But this inviolability is to be guaranteed only so long as cartel vessels (and aircraft) confine themselves strictly to those services for which they have been engaged. According to custom they must not carry any cargo—unless such carriage has been expressly permitted. Nor can they carry ammunition or other instruments of war. It is also customary to furnish cartel vessels with documents testifying to their character and to the missions upon which they are engaged.

In addition to cartel vessels (and aircraft) belligerents may agree to extend safe conduct passes to enemy vessels (and aircraft) in order that the latter may perform any of various services bearing a humanitarian character. Here, as elsewhere, exemption from either attack or seizure is guaranteed only so long as the vessel (or aircraft) strictly confines itself to the performance of those functions for which it has been engaged.[16]

[14] "In its narrower sense a cartel is an agreement entered into by belligerents for the exchange of prisoners of war. In its broader sense it is any convention concluded between belligerents for the purpose of arranging or regulating certain kinds of non-hostile intercourse otherwise prohibited by reason of the existence of the war. Both parties to a cartel are in honor bound to observe its provisions with the most scrupulous care, but it is voidable by either party upon definite proof that it has been intentionally violated in an important particular by the other party." U. S. Army *Rules of Land Warfare*, paragraph 469.

[15] And this inviolability extends to return voyages or flights as well as to voyages or flights to ports or airfields in which the duties of a cartel vessel or aircraft are to be taken up.

[16] *Law of Naval Warfare*, Article 503c distinguishes among the following categories of enemy vessels and aircraft exempt from destruction or capture:

"1. Cartel vessels and aircraft, i. e. vessels and aircraft designated for and engaged in the exchange of prisoners.

4. Vessels and aircraft guaranteed safe conduct by prior arrangement between the belligerents.

5. Vessels and aircraft exempt by proclamation, operation plan, order, or other directive."

Whereas the first two categories enumerated (1 and 4) depend upon the prior agreement of the belligerents, the third category (5) does not. A belligerent is, of course, at liberty to grant any exemptions he may desire to vessels or aircraft otherwise subject to either attack or seizure.—The distinction normally drawn between cartel vessels and vessels granted safe conduct passes is not entirely free from obscurity. In either case the immunity of the vessel has as its basis an agreement concluded by the belligerents. It is also true that both categories of vessels are usually provided with special documents testifying to their character and innocent employment. It would appear that the distinction has its basis partly in the fact that cartel vessels are engaged in the performance of particular kinds of missions, and especially in the carriage of exchanged prisoners of war, that they are especially commissioned as cartel ships, and that the services performed generally extend over the period of hostilities and not merely a voyage. On the other hand, vessels may be granted—by prior arrangement—safe conduct passes in order to perform any type of humanitarian service. The period during which the pass is valid may cover only one voyage and return or a number of voyages.

During World War II the incident involving the sinking of the *Awa Maru* illustrated some of the problems involved in the satisfactory execution of agreements, concluded between bellig-

g. Enemy Goods Under a Neutral Flag

At the outbreak of hostilities in 1914 the principle that free ships make free goods had been accepted by the overwhelming majority of states for well over a half a century. Article 2 of the Declaration of Paris of 1856 had provided that "the neutral flag covers enemy goods, with the exception of contraband of war." [17] The rule constituted the most important excep-

erents, providing for the safe conduct of enemy vessels. By prior agreement the Japanese vessel *Awa Maru* had been designated to carry relief supplies to Allied nationals held in Japanese custody and for this purpose had been granted Allied safe conduct. On the evening of April 1, 1945, the *Awa Maru* was torpedoed and sunk by an American submarine while returning from a voyage to Hong Kong, Singapore and other ports, on which relief supplies furnished by the Allied Governments had been carried as part of the cargo. At the time of the sinking the *Awa Maru* was carrying a large number of Japanese nationals evacuated from danger zones, and although the United States questioned the propriety of utilizing the ship for this purpose the point was not pressed since Japan had earlier notified this country that the *Awa Maru* could not be used for the sole purpose of carrying relief supplies. Japan charged that the sinking represented a deliberate violation of the agreement and demanded that the United States apologize to the Japanese Government for the sinking, punish those responsible, and indemnify the Japanese Government for the loss incurred. In reply, this Government categorically denied that the sinking had been either willful or deliberate, though it acknowledged—following an investigation—responsibility for the sinking and expressed its "deep regret." Disciplinary action was promised against the commanding officer of the submarine, and a promise of indemnification was deferred until the termination of hostilities. Later, however, the United States offered to replace the *Awa Maru*, not as indemnification but in order that there might be no impediment placed in the way of shipping and distributing relief supplies to Allied nationals. For the diplomatic correspondence on the *Awa Maru* sinking, see *U. S. Naval War College, International Law Documents, 1944–45*, pp. 125–38. The incident of the *Awa Maru* is indicative of the responsibility a belligerent must accept in guaranteeing safe conduct to enemy vessels. Although the *Awa Maru* had deviated slightly from her prescribed course and the visibility was low (though later investigation indicated she was showing the prescribed lights), it was clearly the burden of the commander of the American submarine to establish the identity of the vessel prior to attacking it. The failure to have done so placed responsibility for the incident squarely upon the United States. It may also be observed, however, that the sinking of the *Awa Maru* is suggestive of the possible consequences following upon the waging of unrestricted submarine (or aerial) warfare.

[17] The other provisions of the Declaration of Paris are dealt with elsewhere. Article 1, abolishing privateering, is considered in connection with the naval forces of belligerents, see pp. 40–3. Article 3, declaring that neutral goods—contraband excepted—are not liable to capture under the enemy's flag is referred to in earlier pages (85–6) of this chapter. Article 4, requiring that blockades must be effective in order to be binding, is discussed in Chapter X, pp. 288–9. Prior to the Declaration of Paris the principle that free ships make free goods had not enjoyed general acceptance. Great Britain, in particular, had never accepted it, maintaining instead the position that enemy goods were liable to seizure if found under a neutral flag. France, on the other hand, followed the practice of condemning neutral goods if found under an enemy flag. During the Crimean War both states abandoned their previous practices, though intending this only for the hostilities then being carried out. However, in the years immediately following the Crimean War the pressure of neutral interests became very strong and led to the Declaration of Paris. In effect, the Declaration represented a far reaching concession to neutrals, and British writers never tire in pointing out that from the viewpoint of British interests the Declaration represented a bad bargain. In surrendering the right as a belligerent to seize enemy goods even though under a neutral flag Great Britain received

tion to the principle that a belligerent may seize and condemn enemy goods found at sea.[18] Indeed, the significance once attached in many quarters to this acceptance of the principle of "free ships, free goods" was such that it was used in support of the argument that the belligerent right to seize and confiscate enemy property at sea ought to be generally abolished, the expectation being that a belligerent could—in any event—transfer his trade to neutral vessels and thereby secure immunity from seizure. Given these circumstances the advantage enjoyed by belligerents in retaining the right to seize enemy property at sea was considered to be substantially diminished.[19]

This expectation has never materialized, however. In both World Wars the Declaration of Paris, though remaining formally binding upon the belligerents, was nevertheless rendered ineffective—largely through the resort to reprisal measures.[20] But even apart from reprisals belligerents sought to reduce the possible scope of application of the principle that free ships make free goods. Thus belligerent prize courts have interpreted Article 2 of the Declaration of Paris as failing to provide protection to enemy goods when found under the flag of the captor state or of his allies. Further, immunity from seizure has been extended to enemy goods only while on board the neutral vessel; once unloaded, whether afloat or on shore, liability to seizure applies. Nor have goods transshipped from an enemy to a neutral vessel been regarded as entitled to the protection afforded by the Declaration of Paris.

Still more important inroads upon Article 2 have followed from the

---

nothing comparable in return. Article 1 of the Declaration did provide for the abolition of privateering—a practice from which Great Britain had seriously suffered during the Napoleonic Wars—but by 1856 privateering was already on its way out. Even then, the small advantage accruing to Great Britain was further reduced by Hague Convention VII (1907), allowing as it did the conversion of merchant vessels into warships though failing clearly to forbid such conversion on the high seas. The United States refused formally to adhere to the Declaration of Paris—for reasons now no longer relevant—though in practice this country followed the provisions of that instrument, and in 1914 considered them binding upon all belligerents.—See H. W Malkin, "The Inner History of the Declaration of Paris," *B. Y. I. L.*, 8 (1927), pp. 1–44; and for a brief summary of the American attitude both prior to and following the Declaration, see Hyde, *op. cit.*, pp. 2041–5.

[18] Of relatively minor significance is the practice, generally regarded as forming a part of customary law, of restoring to master and crew of seized enemy vessels their personal effects.

[19] Thus in 1905 the Naval War College concluded: "The Declaration of Paris of 1856 . . . has made possible the transfer of a large portion of the enemy sea commerce to neutral flag in time of war. The absence of risk under neutral flag will also make possible cheaper rates under neutral flags. Under ordinary economic laws commerce would thus go to neutrals in time of war." *U. S. Naval War College, International Law Topics, 1905*, p. 18. This conclusion was offered in support of the recommendation that "innocent enemy goods and ships"—i. e., goods not constituting contraband of war and ships not engaged either in contraband carriage or blockade breach—be made immune from capture.

[20] See pp. 296 ff., for a review of these reprisal measures and their effect upon Article 2 of the Declaration of Paris.

changes that have since occurred in the law of contraband. Article 2 specifically deprives enemy goods of the protection otherwise afforded by the neutral flag if such goods have the character of contraband of war. Aside from certain peripheral questions arising in the interpretation of this exception the main intent was simply to provide that the "neutral flag covers enemy's goods, with the exception of such as would, if neutral, be contraband of war." [21] In practice, the importance of this exception must be found to be proportionate to the degree to which belligerents have expanded the list of goods regarded as susceptible of use in war as well as the destination required of goods in order to justify their seizure and condemnation as contraband. Modern developments in the law of contraband are dealt with elsewhere; [22] here it is sufficient to note that these developments have operated drastically to reduce the significance formerly attributed to Article 2 of the Declaration of Paris.[23]

Formally, the Declaration of Paris may be regarded as retaining its validity even today. In neither the decisions of belligerent prize courts nor the policies expressed by belligerent governments is there to be found evidence of a formal abandonment of that instrument.[24] In practice, how-

---

[21] *U. S. Naval War College, International Law Topics, 1905*, p. 118. This is, in fact, the only plausible interpretation since, as Stone (*op. cit.*, p. 467) points out: "Strictly, the doctrine of contraband is inapplicable to enemy goods found at sea, since these are in any case confiscable *as enemy goods*. Presumably then the term refers to goods which, *if owned by a neutral or allied trader* would be contraband." The same writer further points out (p. 468) that although Article 2 expressly excepts only contraband from the immunity otherwise granted enemy goods covered by a neutral flag, "it is difficult to see why blockade-running goods should be immune when contraband is not; and the contrary seems to be generally assumed."—Belligerent prize courts have also applied the so-called doctrine of infection (see p. 276 (n)) to enemy goods carried in neutral bottoms. Thus goods otherwise immune from seizure have been held liable to condemnation if belonging to the same enemy owner of contraband goods and carried on the same neutral vessel along with the contraband cargo.

[22] See, generally, Chapter IX.

[23] At least so far as the import of goods to an enemy state under a neutral flag is affected. With respect to enemy exports under neutral flags, belligerents have sought to rely primarily upon reprisal measures (see pp. 296 ff.).—Still other questions have arisen in the interpretation of Article 2, which deserve some attention. Although it is clear that the neutral shipowner as well as the private enemy owner of goods were intended to benefit from Article 2, it is not at all clear whether this benefit is to extend to goods owned by the enemy state. The Declaration itself speaks only of enemy goods (*la marchandise ennemie*) without further qualification as to private or public ownership. Nevertheless, the purpose of the provision—and of the Declaration as a whole—was to apply to the private property of an enemy and to private transactions. It has therefore been contended that goods owned either in whole or in part by the enemy state need not be given the protection of the Declaration. See H. A. Smith, "The Declaration of Paris in Modern War," *Law Quarterly Review*, 55 (1939), pp. 237–49. In principle, this position appears sound, though the practice of states affords no sufficient indication of the attitude taken on this point. Nor is there likely to be any further development in this respect, given the other belligerent measures which have practically done away with the protection granted by Article 2.

[24] None of the prize codes issued by belligerents in the 1939–45 war denied this continued formal validity. And see Article 633c, *Law of Naval Warfare*.

ever, Article 2 of the Declaration has been deprived of material effect upon the conduct of hostilities by the interpretation given it by the belligerents, by the changes wrought in the law of contraband, and by its subordination to belligerent reprisal measures. It may of course be argued that these latter measures provide no sufficient reason for questioning the continued significance of Article 2; that, on the contrary, the fact that belligerents felt compelled to resort to reprisals in order to override the rule that free ships make free goods itself testifies to its continued validity—and significance. As already observed, the merit of this particular argument—while not to be dismissed—ought not to be overestimated. It would, in fact, be much nearer the mark to state that in departing from Article 2 of the Declaration of Paris through the device of "reprisal measures" taken against allegedly unlawful behavior of an opponent belligerents found a ready instrument for preventing what they were in any event determined to prevent—if need be by the formal denunciation of the Declaration. In a word, the present significance of the Declaration of Paris in general, and Article 2 of that instrument in particular, must be further assessed in the light of the common belligerent determination to destroy the whole of an enemy's seaborne trade, whether carried in enemy or neutral bottoms.[25]

3. *The Conduct of Seizure*

The seizure—or capture [26]—of enemy merchant vessels as prize, being a hostile operation exercisable only during the existence of a state of war,[27]

---

[25] For further reflections on this point, see pp. 284–7, 315–7.

[26] For further observations on the use of the terms "capture" and "seizure," see p. 105 (n).

[27] It remains the prevailing consensus of states, prize courts and writers on the law of war that the seizure of enemy vessels and goods as lawful prize (and, of course, the right of seizure as exercised against neutral vessels and cargoes, see pp. 332 ff.) can only be exercised during a formal state of war and not during a period of armed conflict in which the parties involved do not admit—either explicitly or implicitly—that war as such exists. To this extent the law of naval warfare—at least so far as the right of prize is concerned—must be excepted from the more recent trend, noted in an earlier chapter (see pp. 23–5), of applying the law of war to situations of armed conflict held—for varying reasons—not to constitute a state of war. (Though it may be noted that during the period of hostilities (1947–48) between certain Arab states and Israel, Egypt exercised the right of seizure and established a prize court to pass upon the validity of maritime captures. At the time Israel was not considered as constituting a state in the sense of international law.)

Even so, there is some question as to the period in which the right of prize is applicable. Its starting point may be taken as from the time a state declares war. But a declaration of war may be—and occasionally has been—made retroactive, though such retroactive declarations may prove to be only a device whereby a state resorts to an "anticipatory embargo," in substance if not in form. Still further, it is in all cases true that in the absence of express treaty provision to the contrary the seizure of enemy property after the conclusion of peace is forbidden (though the decisions of prize courts upon vessels and goods seized prior to this time are valid). Some difficulty, and uncertainty, does arise, however, with respect to the effect of a general armistice upon the right of prize. In principle, the conclusion of an armistice seems to have the effect of suspending the right of prize unless the armistice agree-

is forbidden within neutral jurisdiction.[28] But apart from the inviolability of neutral jurisdiction enemy property may—if not accorded special protection—be seized anywhere upon the high seas, within the territorial waters, harbors and ports of either the captor or the enemy state, and even upon rivers, inland seas or lakes. The subjects of the right of seizure are normally the units which comprise the naval forces (i. e., warships and military aircraft) of belligerents, although exceptionally the seizure of enemy vessels and cargoes may be undertaken by the civil authorities of a belligerent and even by private individuals.[29]

The act of seizure itself consists essentially in the taking of effective control over an enemy vessel; from the time such effective control is exercised the vessel is regarded as seized.[30] In the past, the effective control required was normally accomplished through the sending of a prize crew on board the captured enemy vessel following visit and search. In the circumstances presently characterizing the conduct of warfare at sea this procedure must frequently prove impracticable, however, and there is nothing to prevent the captor from seizing and maintaining effective control through other methods. There is no legal requirement that the act of seizure be preceded by the visit and search of the enemy merchant

---

ment itself provides to the contrary During World War I the armistice of November 11, 1918 declared that the so-called "blockade" of Germany continued in force and that German merchant vessels met at sea remained liable to seizure. See Garner, *op. cit.*, pp. 204–6. Thus the law of prize—both in its application to enemy as well as to neutral vessels—remained in effect as far as the Allies were concerned. Germany, on the other hand, was required not only to renounce the right of seizure but to release all neutral vessels already seized. World War II practice, in this respect quite varied, is reviewed by S. W. D. Rowson, *op. cit.*, pp. 172–4.

[28] See pp. 219–23, 259–60 for a discussion of the nature and scope of the prohibition against resorting to seizure—or to visit and search—within neutral jurisdiction.

[29] "The persons effecting a capture may in fact belong to the military, naval or other public service, or they may be private citizens. They may even be occupants of the ship that is seized. Thus the crew of a captured vessel, in charge of a prize crew of inferior strength, may rescue the ship from those asserting control over it, and so capture it. The work of capture, save when such action takes the form of rescue by occupants of a captured ship, or is the consequence of resistance to capture, should be confined to the public, and preferably the naval forces of a belligerent." Hyde, *op. cit.*, p. 2023.

[30] As to what constitutes capture the most frequently cited statement is that given in the judgment of the Judicial Committee of the Privy Council in *The Pellworm*:

"In principle it would seem that capture consists in compelling the vessel captured to conform to the captor's will. When that is done *deditio* is complete, even though there may be on the part of the prize an intention to seize an opportunity of escape, should it present itself. Submission must be judged by action or by abstention from action; it cannot depend on mere intention, though proof of actual intention to evade capture may be evidence that acts in themselves presenting an appearance of submission were ambiguous and did not result in a completed capture. The conduct necessary to establish the fact of capture may take many forms. No particular formality is necessary." *The Pellworm and Other Ships* [1920], 9 *Lloyds Prize Cases*, p. 175. In this instance it was decided that hauling down the flag did not result in capture unless the enemy merchant vessel actually submitted to the captor's will.

vessel, although the contrary opinion still finds frequent expression.[31] Nor is it necessary to send a prize crew on board. Instead, enemy vessels may simply be ordered to proceed under escort of a belligerent warship, or belligerent military aircraft,[32] to one of the belligerent's ports or to the port of an ally.[33]

a. Destruction of Enemy Prizes

In a general sense the act of seizure in naval warfare, and hence the effects of seizure, may be considered in relation to all the vessels and goods of an enemy, whether public or private in character. Although the warships of an enemy are always liable to attack and destruction, they may in-

[31] The statements made in the text above raise several points which deserve additional comment. The traditional procedure for effecting seizure had been the same for both enemy and neutral vessels. Visit and search preceded seizure, and the latter was normally effected through sending a prize crew on board the vessel. In the case of enemy vessels armed resistance might well be offered, but in this circumstance the vessel had to accept the consequences of its action. It will be apparent that this traditional procedure can no longer be regarded as wholly compatible with naval warfare as presently conducted, given the dangers presented by armed enemy merchant vessels, submarines and aircraft. (Of course, in the improbable case of belligerent military aircraft attempting seizure of enemy vessels it is normally absurd even to contemplate visit and search at sea, let alone to provide prize crews.)—It is entirely doubtful, though, whether this traditional procedure was ever *strictly* required. The purpose of visit and search has always been—in principle—to determine whether sufficient cause for seizure exists. In the case of enemy vessels such cause will always exist unless the vessel falls in one of the categories granted special protection. In the case of neutral vessels the matter is admittedly different since the latter are liable to seizure only if engaged in certain acts (contraband carriage and blockade breach); and the seizure of neutral vessels without sufficient cause gives rise to a liability of the captor for losses incurred by the owners of the vessel as a result of wrongful seizure. But certainly the seizure of an enemy vessel or of a neutral vessel for sufficient cause has never been questioned by prize courts simply because not preceded by visit and search. Nor have neutrals complained if seizure was not preceded by visit and search, so long as legitimate cause for the seizure of a neutral vessel could later be established in a court of prize. Besides, if belligerents wish to take the risk of illegal seizure they may clearly do so. See, generally, *U. S. Naval War College, International Law Situations, 1930*, pp. 25 ff.—From a rather abstract point of view, therefore, it may be said that visit and search forms no part of the act of seizing enemy merchant vessels, such vessels always being liable to seizure. From a practical point of view, visit and search may of course prove necessary if positive identification of enemy character cannot be made by other methods. See *Law of Naval Warfare*, Article 502a. In the main, however, visit and search may properly be regarded as a procedure relevant to the seizure of neutral merchant vessels and as such is considered in a later chapter (Chapter XII).

[32] In the case of enemy merchantmen, readily identified as such, the scope of action permitted to belligerent military aircraft is certainly no less than that granted to belligerent warships. The right of the latter to seize enemy vessels without prior visit and search must be accorded equally to belligerent military aircraft. On the quite different question of the diversion of neutral merchant vessels by belligerent military aircraft, see pp. 342–3.

[33] Still further, the belligerent may compel the enemy prize—if need be by measures of force—to accede to such orders as are given her. In the event a prize crew is sent on board the prize the master and crew may be requested to assist the captor, although they cannot be compelled to do so. The act of seizure is signified by ordering the captured enemy vessel to lower her flag, the captor's flag being flown at the usual place (peak or staff) over the enemy flag.—On the ultimate disposition of the officers and crews of captured enemy merchant vessels, see pp. 111–6.

stead be captured. Where enemy warships are captured title to such vessels immediately vests entirely in the captor state by virtue of the fact of capture.[34] In this respect, however, the consequences following upon the taking of effective control over an enemy warship differ from the consequences following upon the seizure of privately owned enemy merchant vessels. Title to the latter does not finally vest in the captor state until the vessel has been brought before a prize court and duly condemned as lawful prize.[35] In the case of cargo carried on board seized enemy merchant vessels the need for adjudication is clearer still, since part of the cargo may well be owned by neutrals.[36] For these reasons, among others, it

---

[34] *Law of Naval Warfare*, Article 503a (2).

[35] Simply stated, the function of a prize court is to pass upon or to confirm the validity of all maritime captures, and title to the privately owned vessels or goods of an enemy (or of a neutral) seized in prize does not finally pass to the captor until adjudication by a court of prize. Hence, even if an enemy vessel has been destroyed following capture, adjudication remains necessary. Occasionally, however, it has been contended that as between the belligerents title to privately owned enemy vessels normally vests in the captor state by virtue of the fact of capture. Thus Hyde (*op. cit.*, p. 2383) observes that: "As long as the law of maritime war permits a belligerent to appropriate generally enemy ships and enemy property thereon, both private and public, the State of the captor would seem to be justified in claiming that the fact of capture vests title in itself as against the enemy." (And see *Law of Naval Warfare*, Chapter 5, note 19.) At the same time Hyde goes on to declare that to establish "an indefeasible title to an enemy prize as against the legitimate claims of neutral States or persons, condemnation is regarded as necessary. This circumstance together with other practical considerations render it highly expedient that enemy prizes should always be made the subject of adjudication with a view to condemnation." This view is clearly a minority one, though, since the prevailing opinion—shared by the great majority of writers and frequently endorsed by prize courts—is that every enemy prize ought to be judged, that a valid title cannot arise simply from the military act of seizure, and that title passes only with the condemning judgment of a court of prize.

[36] This for the reason that neutral goods—contraband excepted—on enemy ships ordinarily are not liable to condemnation, at least if the neutral owner can clearly establish their innocent character.—Although the distinction drawn above in the text is an old one, and in itself raises no novel questions, there is a certain difficulty—or at least an ambiguity—involved in the terminology used to describe acts of varying legal significance and involving different legal consequences. Thus H. A. Smith (*The Law and Custom of the Sea*, p. 100) criticizes the "indiscriminate" use of the terms "capture" and "seizure," suggesting instead that capture be used "to indicate those cases in which the act of taking control immediately transfers the full legal ownership of that which is taken" (e. g., warships, enemy vessels in the public service and state owned property) and seizure to indicate "these cases in which the act of taking control does not by itself change the ownership, but is merely provisional, the final change of ownership being conditioned on what is called 'condemnation' by a court of prize" (e. g., privately owned enemy vessels and goods, neutral vessels seized for unneutral service, blockade breach and contraband carriage). It must be observed, however, that general usage has been, and will probably continue to be, to use the terms interchangeably. Nor is there any real harm in this so long as it is understood that there is a distinction to be drawn between the appropriation of state owned property— which falls to the captor as legitimate booty of war— and the appropriation of privately owned enemy property—which comes under the right of prize and is therefore governed by the law of prize, including the necessity for adjudication.—In this connection one further point should be noted. The traditional law is clearly based on the assumption that

is considered desirable that—circumstances permitting—enemy merchant vessels once seized should either be sent or conducted into port for adjudication.[37]

Occasions frequently arise, however, when the sending of an enemy prize into port proves either impossible or highly inconvenient. The condition of the prize may be such as to prevent her further navigation. The captor may be unable to spare a prize crew and unwilling to conduct the enemy prize into port if such action would thereby interfere with the military operations upon which he is engaged at the time of seizure. Rather than release the prize the practice of belligerents in these—as well as in still other—circumstances has been to resort to the destruction of the vessel and cargo; and—in principle—the belligerent license to destroy enemy prizes in certain circumstances is firmly established in law, despite continued controversy as to the precise nature of the circumstances in which belligerents may resort to destruction. Although the assertion is still made by some writers that the destruction of enemy prizes is permitted only where circumstances render any other course impossible, it now appears reasonably clear that this

warships apart (and certain other limited categories of vessels in the enemy's public service) the vessels and goods of an enemy will be privately owned. But what of publicly owned vessels engaged solely in commercial activities? Is their seizure, as well as the seizure of state owned cargoes, to be regarded as the taking of legitimate booty of war, and therefore outside the law of prize? Or is their seizure to be assimilated to the act of seizing privately owned enemy vessels and goods? Belligerent practice to date hardly furnishes a clear answer in this regard, though on principle the former alternative would appear correct. See, for example, Rowson, *op. cit.*, pp. 175–7. Even so, a clear distinction would still be warranted between the liability of state owned vessels—engaged in commercial activities—to seizure as booty of war and their liability to attack in a manner similar to warships. As already pointed out (see p. 68 (n)), there appears to be no justification for making such vessels liable to attack simply by virtue of their public ownership.—As to the quite different question of the applicability of prize law to neutral state owned vessels and cargoes, see pp. 213–4, 335–6.

[37] State practice is equally clear, however, that a belligerent may convert captured enemy merchant vessels to his immediate public use should circumstances so require. In American law the procedure to be observed when sending in enemy and neutral prizes for adjudication is set forth in the text of the Prize Statutes, *U. S. Code*, Title 34, Chapter 20, Secs. 1131–67. Prior to World War II the requirement had been that in order for a Federal District Court to obtain jurisdiction to entertain prize proceedings a seized vessel had to be brought to the United States. During World War II amendments to the prize law were made in order to allow such jurisdiction to Federal Courts if a prize "was brought into the territorial waters of a co-belligerent (the latter so consenting) or into a locality in the temporary or permanent possession or occupation of the armed forces of the United States." In addition, the World War II amendments extended prize law to aircraft. Finally, the procedure for making immediate use of captured vessels, and avoiding the necessity for applying to the Prize Court for requisition of the prize, was broadened. See, generally, the publication *Instructions For Prize Masters and Special Prize Commissioners* (NAVEXOS P-825), Office of the Judge Advocate General, Department of the Navy, (1949). Also, *Law of Naval Warfare*, Article 502b (8) and notes thereto. See also Chapter XII, pp. 344–8, for further discussion of these and related points as they apply to neutral prizes. And on the taking of prizes—whether enemy or neutral—into neutral ports, see pp. 245–7.

formula is much too restrictive. Instead, it would seem that the widespread practice followed by belligerents is indicative of the conviction that the destruction of enemy prizes is permitted whenever military necessity—a term which, in this context, must have broad application—so requires.[38]

Before resorting to the destruction of enemy prizes the captor is obliged to remove the passengers and crew, as well as the ship's papers, to a place of safety.[39] And despite the practices pursued by many of the belligerents during the two World Wars there is as yet insufficient warrant for denying the continued validity of obligations established by custom and subsequently reaffirmed by convention. No doubt it is true that in the past submarines (and aircraft) have been—in nearly every instance—incapable of

[38] Distinguish, though, between the destruction of enemy prizes and the destruction of neutral prizes. The conditions permitting the destruction of neutral prizes are considerably more restrictive and are examined in a later chapter (see pp. 349–53). (It should be made clear, however, that in referring to the destruction of enemy prizes, neutral vessels acquiring enemy character are included.) See Article 503b (2) *Law of Naval Warfare*. The formula of "military necessity" given in the initial sentence of Article 503b (2) follows earlier *Instructions* and represents the traditional policy of this country. British practice has been interpreted as permitting destruction of enemy prizes in two cases ". . . first, when the prize is in such a condition as prevents her from being sent to any port of adjudication; and, secondly, when the capturing vessel is unable to spare a prize crew to navigate the prize into such a port." Oppenheim-Lauterpacht, *op. cit.*, pp. 487–8. In effect, however, British practice has allowed destruction in other cases of "military necessity." Thus Higgins and Colombos (*op. cit.*, pp. 607–8) point out that the British Prize Court has permitted destruction of enemy prizes when "the capturing British warship was engaged in pursuing the enemy fleet and could not stop for the purpose of taking the vessel into port." Article 72 of the 1939 German Prize Law Code declared that captured enemy vessels may be destroyed "if it appears to be inexpedient or unsafe to bring them into port." In both wars German surface warships, even when first seizing enemy vessels—and not resorting to sinking without warning—nearly always resorted to destruction.

It remains disputed whether or not the captor state is obliged to render compensation to the neutral owners of goods on board an enemy vessel that has been lawfully destroyed. The opinions of writers are sharply divided on this point, and the practice of states is none too clear. German prize courts during World War I denied neutral owners any right of compensation. Before the British Prize Court the matter was never clearly adjudicated upon, though nineteenth century decisions can be cited on behalf of a right of compensation. Nor is there any clear indication as to what the position of the United States may be on the matter. Hyde (*op. cit.*, p. 2229) contends that there ought to be no right of compensation to neutral owners, that neutral cargo on board enemy vessels ought not to become a shield to protect such vessels from the lawful act (i. e., destruction) of the captors. This may well be, but it is equally true that if this opinion is accepted Article 3 of the Declaration of Paris is rendered practically worthless. For the latitude now given belligerents in destroying enemy prizes would amount to granting belligerents an equal latitude in destroying innocent neutral goods when carried on board. Nevertheless, it must be conceded that the view holding that no compensation need be accorded the neutral owners of cargo is much more in accord with the over-all recent trends of belligerent practices.

[39] An obligation which is not fulfilled merely by allowing passengers and crew to take to the ship's boats unless the safety of the latter is assured, in the existing sea and weather conditions, by the proximity of land, or the presence of another vessel which is in a position to take them on board.

satisfactorily fulfilling these obligations. But the fact that the captor may be unable to provide for the safety of passengers and crews of enemy merchant vessels cannot be regarded as a justification for non-compliance with the law.[40] Indeed, to argue otherwise must logically involve the further assertion that he who cannot seize may nonetheless sink. It has been previously urged that the law of naval warfare has still to condone the latter doctrine.[41] There is no more reason to believe that this law as presently constituted has accepted the doctrine that he who cannot provide for the safety of passengers and crew following seizure may nonetheless destroy.

E. THE SEIZURE AND DESTRUCTION OF ENEMY AIRCRAFT

It remains uncertain to what extent the rules regulating the seizure and destruction of enemy merchant vessels are applicable—by analogy—to enemy civil aircraft.[42] Quite apart from the fact that the rules governing the treatment of enemy merchant vessels are themselves in an unsettled state, the attempt to adopt rules operative in naval warfare to the seizure and destruction of aircraft presents obvious difficulties. At the same time, it is clear that in many respects belligerent practice in conducting aerial warfare is so slight at present as to provide no real guidance to that behavior belligerents may consider as both obligatory and right. Nor is it very useful—in the absence of such practice—to continue to place undue emphasis upon the 1923 Rules of Aerial Warfare, drafted by the Commission of Jurists at The Hague. Though undoubtedly a significant contribution at the time, these draft rules provide today little more than a landmark to

---

[40] Though in the circumstances presently characterizing the conduct of naval warfare it has been argued that the equities of passengers and crew may be affected by the nature and conduct of their own ship. Thus, Hyde (*op. cit.*, p. 2026) declares that in the case of an armed merchant vessel "which in consequence of resistance or otherwise has become unseaworthy, the duty to offer safe accommodation to persons on board would appear to be dependent upon the military requirements of the captors." Strictly speaking, though, there is no apparent basis for this opinion in the traditional law. Undoubtedly acts of resistance render enemy merchant vessels liable to attack and possible destruction. But once the vessel had been seized, and the captor had asserted his effective control, no discrimination was made toward crews for having offered resistance prior to capture. It may well be claimed, however, that it is no longer reasonable that captors be expected scrupulously to fulfill the obligation of ensuring the safety of crews of enemy merchant vessels when such vessels are—for all practical purposes—integrated into the enemy's military effort at sea and have offered acts of resistance prior to capture; and in these circumstances a captor unable to take officers and crews on board before resorting to the destruction of enemy prizes nevertheless fulfills his duty by permitting the latter to take to the ship's boats. Certainly, there is much force to this argument, even though it is still unrecognized in law.

[41] See pp. 67–70.

[42] On the classification of enemy aircraft, see *Law of Naval Warfare*, Section 500. The term "civil aircraft," as used in the text above, is intended to include the same aircraft as are included in Section 500b.

one phase in the historic development of juristic thought on the regulation of aerial warfare.[43]

On one central issue state practice does appear to be reasonably well settled. The liability to capture and confiscation of enemy civil aircraft, and of enemy goods on board, now enjoys general support, and it is not likely that this adaptation of the practice operative in warfare at sea rather than the practice governing seizure of property on land will be reversed.[44]

---

[43] For a general discussion and analysis of the problems dealt with in this section, see Spaight, *op. cit.*, pp. 394–418. The attempt to apply maritime practices to aerial warfare formed the basis of much earlier speculation, and the influence of the maritime analogy was apparent in the work of the Commission of Jurists. For the text of the 1923 Rules of Aerial Warfare, together with the general report of the Commission of Jurists, see *U.S. Naval War College, International Law Documents, 1924*, pp. 108–54. With respect to the seizure and destruction of enemy civil aircraft it is difficult to estimate the effect of the 1923 Rules upon later belligerent practice, if only for the reason that this later practice has been so slight. If the deference shown to the provisions of the 1923 Rules dealing with aerial bombardment are to be regarded as generally indicative of the degree to which belligerents may be expected to follow the other prescriptions of this draft code, then the 1923 Rules hardly retain more than an historic interest. However, the fate suffered by the 1923 Rules of Aerial Warfare does not justify their characterization as "examples of a high-water mark in legal fantasy" (C. P. Phillips, "Air Warfare and Law: An Analysis of the Legal Doctrines, Practices and Policies," *George Washington Law Review*, 21 (1953), p. 326), unless the excesses of modern—and total—war are to be regarded as an entirely normal state of affairs. The mistake—though hardly a fantasy—of the Commission of Jurists was in assuming that belligerents would not look upon the practices of World War I as a desirable standard for the conduct of future wars. On this assumption—however sanguine it may now appear with the advantage of hindsight—the 1923 Rules were quite realistic.

In the absence either of conventional regulation or of belligerent practice constitutive of customary rules it has been contended that the general principles of the law of war place restrictions upon the seizure and destruction of enemy aircraft, and that "whenever a departure from these principles is alleged to be necessary, its cogency must be proved by reference either to express agreement or to the peculiar conditions of aerial warfare." Oppenheim-Lauterpacht, *op. cit.*, p. 520. No doubt this opinion may be considered as justified—in theory at least. Yet it would serve little purpose to ignore the obstacles encountered in applying the general principles of the law of war to aerial warfare. In the case of aerial bombardment these difficulties have long been painfully apparent (see pp. 146–9). If they are less apparent with respect to seizure and destruction of enemy aircraft this may be attributed largely to the peripheral importance of this problem alongside the momentous issues posed by aerial bombardment. The dearth of actual practice relating to seizure and destruction of enemy civil aircraft is a further reason for continued speculation that may prove to have little relevance to actual practice. The unfortunate truth is that in the absence of customary or conventional rules effectively regulating the conduct of aerial warfare in some detail, the invocation of general principles has a distinctly limited utility, particularly when these general principles are themselves subject to varying interpretations (see pp. 46–50).

[44] Article 52 of the 1923 draft Rules, in following maritime practice, provided that enemy private aircraft "are liable to capture in all circumstances." Article 55 declared that the capture of aircraft or goods on board "shall be made the subject of prize proceedings, in order that any neutral claim may be duly heard and determined."—During World War II a number of belligerents—including Great Britain and the United States—amended their prize legislation so as to include aircraft and goods carried on board. (See S. W. D. Rowson, *op. cit.*, pp. 209–13 and A. W. Knauth, *op. cit.*, pp. 76–7.) The American Prize Act of June 24, 1941 (55 Stat. 261; 34 U. S. Code Sec. 1131) does not specify where aircraft may be captured, though the capturing

But belligerent practice has not yet given rise to any definite procedure governing the conduct of seizure in the case of enemy civil aircraft.[45]

No particular problem would appear to arise with respect to the destruction of enemy aircraft once seizure has been made and the captor has been able to remove passengers and crew to a place of safety. In these circumstances the capturing belligerent must be regarded as having at least the same discretion as he already possesses in destroying enemy merchant vessels. Of critical importance, however—and as yet far from resolved—is the question of the occasions in which enemy civil aircraft may be fired upon while still in flight. In principle, the rule granting non-combatants immunity from direct attack must be regarded as applicable to hostilities wherever conducted. There is no apparent reason why aerial warfare should be thought of as an exception, and—in fact—belligerents have never contended that in the air they may discard a distinction long operative in hostilities on land and at sea. At the same time, it has frequently been contended that given the special circumstances attending aerial hostilities the scope of the immunity from direct attack granted non-combatants necessarily must prove more restricted than elsewhere.[46]

In earlier pages attention has been directed to those acts which when performed by enemy merchant vessels serve to deprive the latter of immunity

---

agency appears to have been limited to the Navy. The British Prize Act of 1939, in extending prize law to aircraft, is quite clear that the capture of aircraft may occur even though the aircraft is over land.—Presumably, the rules governing the enemy character of vessels will apply by analogy to aircraft. On the question of belligerent aircraft in enemy territory at the outbreak of war, see p. 90. On the rules governing the use of medical aircraft and transports under the 1949 Convention on the Amelioration of the Condition of Wounded, Sick and Shipwrecked Members of the Armed Forces at Sea, see pp. 129–31. And, finally, on the application of prize law to neutral aircraft, see pp. 354–6.

45 No doubt it is true that as in the case of enemy vessels so in the case of enemy aircraft the act of seizure must consist in the assertion of effective control over the aircraft. Assuming that the place of encounter is over the high seas a belligerent may use any convenient method to signal to the enemy civil aircraft and to order her to proceed to one of the belligerent's landing fields (on the rarest of occasions landing at sea may even prove feasible). Failure to carry out such orders will constitute sufficient reason for employing forcible measures. But what course of action is permitted to a belligerent aircraft (or, for that matter, to a belligerent warship) against enemy civil aircraft that lack the fuel to carry out the belligerent's directions? The problem has no parallel in naval warfare. For suggestions on the conduct of visit, search and seizure of aircraft see *U.S. Naval War College, International Law Situations, 1938*, pp. 15–25.

46 The nature of these circumstances are sufficiently apparent and need not be examined once again in these pages. Spaight (*op. cit.*, pp. 398–9) points out that although the attack of civil aircraft results in a more serious danger to the individual occupants than does similar action when directed against merchant vessels, nevertheless, "the military necessity for warlike action that may involve loss of innocent life is greater in the former case, for the speed of an aircraft, its ability to elude siezure, and its capacity for damaging action (either by bomb-dropping or by observing important movements), render it a more dangerous potential enemy than a sea vessel; and there is always the possibility that an apparently non-military aircraft may be a combatant one disguised."

from attack.[47] There is little question but that the same acts if performed by enemy civil aircraft may result in a liability to attack. Thus any attempt by enemy civil aircraft to resist the orders given by belligerent aircraft, or to flee upon being duly summoned by a belligerent, will justify the use of force. Similarly, civil aircraft found flying under escort of enemy military aircraft may be fired upon. Liability to attack may also result from the carriage of armament.[48] Finally, if the civil aircraft of a belligerent are integrated in any way into the military effort of the state they need not be accorded immunity from attack on sight.[49]

F. THE TREATMENT OF ENEMY SUBJECTS

1. *Prisoners of War*

It has always been clear that the combatant personnel of belligerent warships, whether vessels of the line or auxiliaries, who fall into the hands of an enemy during the course of naval hostilities are to be accorded the status of prisoners of war. The same status has been held to attach to the non-combatant members of a belligerent's naval forces, unless granted special exemption, as well as to those persons who officially accompany the naval

---

[47] See pp. 56 ff.

[48] Quite apart from military consideration, which would clearly dictate attacking any enemy aircraft found to be bearing armament, there is no practice to which belligerents can turn to justify the "defensive" arming of civil aircraft. Any attempt to apply here the practices of naval warfare would not bear serious scrutiny, and belligerents have never suggested otherwise.

[49] In the circumstances enumerated above the liability of enemy civil aircraft to attack does not succeed in raising serious question. In warfare at sea it has always been true that the immunity from attack granted belligerent merchant vessels is dependent upon the abstention from all acts of force against a captor as well as upon the absence of any relationship to the military operations of a belligerent. The fulfillment of the same general conditions must be regarded as even more mandatory in the case of aerial warfare. It is beyond this point, however, that uncertainty persists. To what extent does the nature of aerial warfare, and the potential danger posed by enemy aircraft, permit the resort to measures that are yet to be accepted in naval warfare? (Of course, if the position is accepted that belligerents are now at liberty to attack enemy merchant vessels without warning, and to destroy them without first insuring the safety of passengers and crew, then no problem arises in the case of aerial warfare. What is permitted atainst merchant vessels is equally permitted—from this point of view—against civil aircraft.) In this respect, Spaight (*op. cit.*, pp. 400–2) suggests that belligerents may close limited aerial zones over the high seas to both enemy and neutral aircraft, and attack any aircraft thereafter entering these aerial enclosures. Nevertheless, he insists that the belligerent in establishing such a zone must be able to show "concrete grounds for his action, e. g., to operations actually in progress on the spot, or important concentrations therein for pending operations, to the constant patrolling of the zone by his aircraft in the search for enemy submarines, to the regular passing of transports over a line of communications, or to some other form of military activity which differentiates the area in question from the ordinary high sea." There can be little question but that as against belligerent civil aircraft the closure of such restricted aerial zones over the high seas—and their rigid enforcement— does not raise any substantial question. As to the operation of these zones with respect to neutral aircraft, see pp. 300–1.

forces without actually being members thereof.[50] In an even broader sense, the status of prisoners of war has been customarily conferred upon the personnel of all the public vessels of a belligerent.[51]

With respect to the officers and crew of a captured private enemy merchant ship, the traditional practice of belligerents prior to this century had generally been to make them prisoners of war.[52] But a quite different procedure was provided for in Hague Convention XI (1907). In the event of capturing an enemy merchant ship the parties to that Convention were obliged not to make prisoners of war those members of the crew who were nationals of a neutral state. The same rule applied in the case of the captain and officers, likewise nationals of a neutral state, if they promised formally in writing not to serve in an enemy ship for the duration of the war.[53] Nor were the captain, officers, and members of the crew who were nationals of the enemy state to be made prisoners of war, if they undertook, on the faith of a formal written promise, not to engage, while the hostilities lasted, in any service connected with the operations of the war.[54] In each instance a pledge was given, the captor was to notify the other belligerent, and the latter was forbidden knowingly to employ the said persons.[55] The preceding provisions were qualified, however, by the stipulation that they did not apply to ships "taking part in the hostilities,"[56] a phrase which was given from the very start the broadest possible interpretation.

In the light of belligerent practice during the two World Wars it is hardly useful to continue to accord any significance to these provisions of Hague XI, at least to the extent that they concern the status of enemy subjects

---

[50] See *Law of Naval Warfare*, Article 511a, which reflects the customary international law applicable to hostilities whether conducted on land, at sea or in the air. As between the parties to the 1949 Geneva Convention Relative to the Treatment of Prisoners of War, the categories of individuals entitled to that status are enumerated in Article 4. The other 1949 Geneva Conventions For the Protection of War Victims are: The Convention for the Amelioration of the Condition of the Wounded and Sick Armed Forces in the Field, the Convention For the Amelioration of the Condition of the Wounded, Sick and Shipwrecked Members of the Armed Forces at Sea, and the Convention Relative to the Protection of Civilian Persons in Time of War. For a detailed treatment of the Convention governing treatment of wounded, sick and shipwrecked at sea, see pp. 117–38. The United States ratified the four 1949 Geneva Conventions in August 1955.

[51] Even though not forming a part of the naval or military forces of a belligerent—e. g., customs and police vessels. Exemption must of course be made for the personnel attached to those public vessels granted special immunity from either attack or seizure.

[52] Article 11 of the U. S. Naval War Code of 1900 provided that: "The personnel of a merchant vessel of an enemy captured as a prize can be held, at the discretion of the captor, as witnesses, or as prisoners of war when by training or enrollment they are immediately available for the naval service of the enemy, or they may be released from detention or confined."

[53] Article 5.

[54] Article 6.

[55] Article 7.

[56] Article 8.

making up the crews of enemy merchant ships captured by a belligerent.[57] They clearly were not intended to apply to the personnel of publicly owned and controlled belligerent merchant vessels. It seems equally clear that they were never designed to apply to the officers and crews of enemy merchant vessels which, though privately owned, operate under the instructions of the state and—for all practical purposes—are integrated into the military effort at sea. Certainly they ought not to apply, and in fact have not been so interpreted as applying, to enemy merchant ships offering—or intending to offer—forcible resistance to capture. Such intent to offer forcible resistance, and thus to "take part in the hostilities," may not improperly be imputed to any enemy merchant ship bearing "defensive" armament.[58]

Hence, the present character of naval hostilities hardly permits the expectation that belligerents will give any greater effect in the future to these provisions of Hague XI than they have in the past. Instead, the expectation must be that enemy nationals making up the crews of belligerent merchantmen will be detained by the captor as prisoners of war, and as between the parties to the 1949 Geneva Convention Relative to the Treatment of Prisoners of War this is a status which—if detained—they are now entitled to receive.[59] Similarly, the officers and crews of enemy merchantmen who are nationals of a neutral state may also be detained as

[57] ". . . the provision that members of the crew who were enemy subjects might only be made prisoners if they refused to give parole was *ipso facto* modified by the practice followed during the First World War, according to which all enemy civilians of military age could be prevented from returning home, and could be interned. Accordingly, all the belligerents interned the enemy crews of captured enemy merchant-vessels." Oppenheim-Lauterpacht, *op. cit.*, p. 267. A similar practice obtained throughout the 1939 war, though the detention of enemy crew members of captured belligerent merchant vessels frequently resulted in their receiving the status of prisoners of war rather than that of interned enemy aliens. In the past the problem of the status to be accorded detained enemy merchant seamen has frequently been complicated by the fact that in some states the merchant marine may be taken over by the state, and the personnel may even be included within the armed forces. In this latter case the status of the individuals when captured is clear—i. e., they are entitled to the protection accorded prisoners of war. But in those states where the personnel of the merchant marine remained civilians the captor has been free to treat them simply as interned enemy aliens. Even further, the civilian personnel of the merchant marine have been frequently deprived of the protection accorded by Hague Convention X (1907) to the sick, wounded and shipwrecked at sea. As will presently be noted, the 1949 Geneva Conventions have altered this situation.

[58] None of the observations made in the text above are immediately apparent from the actual wording of Articles 5–8 of Hague XI, for these articles speak only of "enemy merchantships" and of the deprivation of the benefits contained therein when "taking part in the hostilities." Yet it seems clear that the Convention was to apply only to privately owned merchant ships of the enemy. Furthermore, belligerents have interpreted—and not unreasonably—any of the acts indicated above as indicative of taking part in the hostilities. See also, in this connection, pp. 57–70.

[59] Article 4A (5) of that Convention provides that among the categories of individuals entitled to receive the status of prisoners of war are: "Members of crews, including masters, pilots and apprentices, of the merchant marine and the crews of civil aircraft of the Parties to the conflict, who do not benefit by more favorable treatment under any other provisions of

prisoners of war if the vessel on which they are serving has taken any part in the hostilities prior to capture. But if the enemy merchantman has abstained from any participation in the hostilities prior to capture, and in particular has not attempted to offer any resistance to the captor, the officers and crew who are nationals of a neutral state normally are not to be made prisoners of war.[60]

The civilian passengers carried on board enemy merchant vessels may be composed of nationals of the enemy state as well as of neutral states. If they are nationals of the enemy state, and have refrained from any participation in the hostilities prior to the capture of the vessel, they are normally not to be made prisoners of war. However, as enemy nationals they are subject to detention by the belligerent into whose hands they fall; and under exceptional circumstances they may even be treated as prisoners of war.[61] On the other hand, the nationals of a neutral state on board cap-

---

international law."—The "other provisions of international law" is a reference to Articles 5–8 of Hague XI. In view of the doubtful validity today of the latter articles, at least as they apply to enemy nationals, it may be assumed that the status of prisoners of war will prevail with respect to enemy nationals making up the personnel of enemy merchant ships. It should also be pointed out that Article 4A (5) of the 1949 Convention on prisoners of war deals with the personnel of enemy civil aircraft in the same manner as with the crew of enemy merchant ships. Unless entitled to more favorable treatment under any other provisions of international law the crew of enemy civil aircraft are to be made prisoners of war. In this instance, however, the "other provisions of international law" are non-existent. For this reason it may be contended that, in principle, the rules governing the status and treatment of individuals taken from enemy merchant vessels apply, *mutatis mutandis*, to the personnel taken from the civil aircraft of an enemy (see *Law of Naval Warfare*, Article 512). At the same time, it may be noted that the 1923 Rules of Aerial Warfare (Article 36) would have granted belligerents substantially greater power over the crew and passengers of enemy civil aircraft than had theretofore been accorded in the case of enemy merchant vessels. Not only would these draft rules have permitted making prisoners of war of all enemy nationals composing the crew, but neutral nationals making up the crew of enemy civil aircraft would also be liable to detention as prisoners of war unless signing a written undertaking not to serve in any enemy aircraft while hostilities lasted. Passengers found to be of enemy nationality and fit for military service could be made prisoners of war. In addition, passengers found to be in the "service of the enemy" could be made prisoners of war, regardless of nationality. Finally, a belligerent could hold as prisoner of war any member of the crew of an enemy civil aircraft or any passenger whose service in a flight had been of special and active assistance to the enemy (and see generally, Spaight, *op. cit.*, pp. 411–4).

[60] In practice, belligerents have not detained—either as prisoners of war or as "civil prisoners"—nationals of neutral states serving as crew members on board enemy merchantmen, if not found to have participated in acts of hostilities against the captor. But it is fairly well established that release is dependent upon the abstention from committing hostile acts or from participating in such acts. On the other hand, it follows from Article 4A (5) of the 1949 Convention on prisoners of war that if the nationals of neutral states serving on board belligerent merchantmen are detained they are to receive the status of prisoners of war.

[61] E. g., if officials of the enemy state.—As between the parties to the 1949 Convention Relative to the Protection of Civilian Persons it would appear that such enemy nationals as are found on board captured enemy merchant vesesls as private passengers are entitled to the status of "protected persons." The first paragraph of Article 4 of the Convention on civilian

tured enemy merchant vessels as passengers are not to be made prisoners of war unless they have previously participated in acts of hostility against the captor. Nor are they to be detained by the captor any longer than proves necessary, the captor being under the obligation to release such nationals of neutral states as expeditiously as is possible.[62]

It has already been observed that neutral merchant vessels may acquire enemy character by undertaking to perform any one of several services on behalf of a belligerent. In the more serious forms of unneutral service, where the neutral vessel takes a direct part in the hostilities or acts in any manner as a naval auxiliary to an enemy's forces, it may be assimilated to an enemy warship and rendered liable to attack on sight. There can be little question that if the personnel of such vessels fall into the hands of the other belligerent they are subject to detention as prisoners of war.[63]

---

persons states: "Persons protected by the Convention are those who at a given moment and in any manner whatsoever, find themselves in case of a conflict or occupation in the hands of a Party to the conflict or Occupying Power of which they are not nationals." The same article goes on to declare that persons protected by the prisoners of war Convention or the Convention relating to the wounded, sick and shipwrecked at sea "shall not be considered as protected persons within the meaning of the present Convention."

[62] *Law of Naval Warfare*, Article 512. In addition to participation in acts of hostility committed against the captor prior to seizure, it seems reasonably clear that nationals of a neutral state on board a captured enemy merchant vessel as passengers may be made prisoners of war if found to be in the service of the enemy.

[63] It has occasionally been urged that the crews of neutral vessels taking a direct part in the hostilities may even be liable to punishment as war criminals. But this opinion would seem justified only where such vessels undertake offensive operations directly aimed against the warships or merchantmen of an enemy—and this will prove exceedingly rare. Hyde (*op. cit.*, p. 2066) distinguishes between neutral vessels "primarily devoted to the military service of a belligerent" and those neutral vessels taking part in hostilities but "not given over to a belligerent service." Whereas the crews of the former may be treated as prisoners of war Hyde would permit the crews of the latter to be dealt with "summarily"—presumably meaning as war criminals. The distinction is not easy to follow, since a vessel of neutral registry that takes part in the hostilities is always acting—in a broad sense—in the "military service of a belligerent"—unless, of course, it is undertaking purely private acts of depredation in the manner of a pirate vessel.—In any event, a distinction should be carefully drawn between neutral merchant vessels acquiring enemy character through acts of unneutral service, and whose crew members are liable to treatment as prisoners of war, and neutral vessels acquiring enemy character—whether by committing acts of unneutral service or other acts—but whose crew members are not subject to detention as prisoners of war. The acquisition of enemy character on the part of a neutral merchant vessel does not necessarily mean that the captor has a right to treat members of the crew bearing neutral nationality as prisoners of war. Indeed, it is only exceptionally that such treatment may prove warranted, i. e., when the neutral vessel has by its actions identified itself with the armed forces of a belligerent. Acts of unneutral service which do not result in such identification may nevertheless result in the neutral vessel acquiring enemy character and rendering it liable to capture. But a neutral vessel acting under belligerent orders or direction does not, for that reason alone, give the belligerent capturing it the right to make prisoners of war those members of the crew as are nationals of a neutral state. In short, the imputation of enemy character to neutral merchant vessels is not to be taken as an indication that the officers and crews of such vessels, when captured, may therefore be made prisoners of war.

There is surprisingly little guidance of a specific character for the treatment of prisoners of war while detained on board a belligerent warship. The customary rule that they must be treated in a humane manner fails to indicate with any precision the specific duties and rights of the captor. For those states that are parties to the 1949 Geneva Convention Relative to the Treatment of Prisoners of War it is apparent that the general obligations laid down for the protection of prisoners of war in Articles 12 through 16 must be complied with, at least to the degree that these obligations are relevant to the circumstances attending internment on board belligerent warships.[64] But these latter provisions are of a very general character and consequently leave unanswered many questions that may well arise in the course of operations at sea. Doubtless a belligerent must refrain either from imposing unnecessary hardships upon prisoners of war interned on board his warship or from subjecting prisoners to unnecessary danger. Nevertheless, the fulfillment of these obligations, given the facilities of warships and the circumstances characterizing naval operations, may present numerous difficulties.[65] Of course, once prisoners of war are landed they immediately become subject to the detailed provisions relating to prisoners of war as are set out in the relevant Geneva Convention of 1949.

---

[64] In general these Articles provide that prisoners of war are in the hands of the enemy power though not of the individuals or military units who have captured them, that they must be humanely treated, that no act must be taken against them which would cause death or seriously endanger their health, that they must not be made the object of measures of reprisal, that they are entitled to respect for their persons, honour, and sex, that they must be accorded proper maintenance and medical attention, and that they must be granted equality of treatment without any adverse distinction based on race, nationality, religious belief or political opinions.

[65] These difficulties are hardly met by the observation that "the propriety of exposing prisoners taken at sea to great personal danger or hardship would depend upon whether, under the particular circumstances, the captor had the right to deprive them of the safeguards of their own craft without substituting others of substantial value, a question of which the solution might hang upon the propriety of the measures by which capture was effected." Hyde, *op. cit.*, p. 2067. In the case of enemy warships that have been destroyed there is no question of the right of a belligerent to deprive enemy personnel "of the safeguards of their own craft without substituting others of substantial value." The question does arise, however, with respect to enemy merchant vessels. In a strict sense the obligation of the captor to place the crews of such vessels in a "place of safety" prior to destroying enemy prizes may be interpreted as forbidding destruction when the warship itself does not constitute a place of safety—due either to the operations upon which it is engaged or to the nature of the warship itself. Even so, this is surely a counsel of perfection and one which belligerents can hardly be expected to follow, even under far more ideal conditions than those presently characterizing naval warfare.—It is, in fact, hard to avoid the conclusion that what is "unnecessary" (hence forbidden) in the hardships or dangers imposed upon prisoners of war carried on board warships must largely be judged by the facilities of the particular warship and the military operations it may be required to complete prior to landing the prisoners of war. In a way, this is only to say that at sea the military necessities of the belligerent may take priority over the comfort and safety of prisoners of war. These remarks are themselves far too broad for the kind of guidance that may be considered useful, though more pointed observations on the duties of the captor at sea do not appear possible.

2. *Wounded, Sick and Shipwrecked* (The 1949 Geneva Convention For the Amelioration of the Condition of Wounded, Sick, and Shipwrecked Members of Armed Forces at Sea).

Prior to the conclusion in 1949 of the Geneva Convention for the Amelioration of the Condition of the Wounded, Sick and Shipwrecked Members of Armed Forces at Sea the rules relating to the protection of the sick and wounded at sea were contained in Hague Conventions III (1899) and X (1907).[66] On the whole, it was the latter Convention that was recognized by the belligerents as applicable in the two World Wars. However, dissatisfaction with a number of the provisions of Hague X, and an awareness of the necessity for its revison and expansion to account more satisfactorily for changing conditions, had been expressed even before the close of the 1914 war.[67] During the second World War this need for revising and expanding the provisions of Hague X became even more clearly apparent, despite the efforts already made by the belligerents to interpret and adapt the Convention to some of the novel circumstances characterizing modern naval warfare.

As between the states that are parties to the 1949 Convention, the latter replaces Hague Convention X.[68] Although a number of the provisions of the 1949 Convention closely adhere to the rules laid down in the preceding convention, many significant modifications have been made and entirely new provisions added which reflect recent experience. An analysis of the present legal regime governing the protection of the sick, wounded and shipwrecked at sea must properly concentrate upon these changes. At the same time, it would appear only reasonable—and realistic—to avoid treating the 1949 Convention quite apart from the experience of the two World

[66] The 1899 Convention represented the first successful adaptation to naval warfare of the principles of the 1864 Geneva Convention for the Relief of the Wounded and Sick of Armies in The Field. In 1906 the Convention of 1864, applicable to land warfare, was revised and, as a consequence, in the following year (1907) the 1899 Convention dealing with sea warfare was also revised to bring it again into accord with the more recent Convention on the sick and wounded in the field. As between the parties to the tenth Hague Convention of 1907, the latter served to replace the earlier convention concluded in 1899. But some states—e. g., Great Britain—remained formally bound by the earlier convention, though in practice it was accepted that the 1907 Convention was authoritative for the belligerents.

[67] In 1929 the 1906 Geneva Convention on the wounded and sick in the field was revised, but the revision of the 1907 Convention dealing with naval warfare never got beyond the stage of draft proposals by the time World War II broke out.

[68] Article 58 of the 1949 Convention declares that in relations between the High Contracting Parties "the present Convention replaces the Xth Hague Convention of October 18, 1907, for the adaptation to Maritime Warfare of the principles of the Geneva Convention of 1906. . ."—To date the most detailed analysis of the 1949 Geneva Convention for the Amelioration of the Condition of the Wounded, Sick and Shipwrecked Members of Armed Forces at Sea is that of Raoul Genet, "La Revision de la X Convention de La Haye Relative a la Guerre sur Mer," *Revue Internationale Francaise de Droit des Gens*, Vols. 18 (1949), pp. 30–40, 160–6, 19 (1950), pp. 46–60, 231–43, 20 (1951), pp. 32–7, 181–8, 332–40, 21 (1952), pp. 31–40.

Wars, and the extent to which belligerents have indicated that they are willing to subordinate possible military advantage to a humanitarian cause.[69]

a. The Wounded, Sick and Shipwrecked

One of the principal assumptions upon which Hague Convention X (1907) had been based was that only those combatants sick or wounded as a result of hostilities at sea need be protected.[70] On this assumption the chief function of hospital ships was to accompany the warships of belligerent fleets and to provide assistance at the scene of action to rescue survivors and to treat the wounded. In modern naval warfare this function—while not yet obsolescent—has become subordinated to the task of transporting casualties suffered as a result of operations on land.[71] It has therefore become increasingly important to redefine—and, in so doing, to broaden—the categories of sick and wounded combatant personnel entitled to receive the benefits conferred by convention upon the sick and wounded at sea. In addition, the attack and destruction of enemy merchant shipping no longer permits the sanguine assumption that the wounded and shipwrecked at sea will be confined to the combatant naval forces of belligerents.[72]

---

[69] "It is axiomatic," one writer has observed in a survey of hospital ships during World War II, "that in the present state of international law it is essential to preserve some balance between the humanitarian benefit to be gained by an alteration in the law and the military advantage thereby conferred on one of the belligerents: if this balance is seriously disturbed the other side will certainly seek and find a pretext for denunciation." J. C. Mossop, "Hospital Ships In the Second World War," B. Y. I. L., 24 (1947), p. 400. These words, written in the context of proposals for a new convention to replace Hague X, are relevant to a consideration of the 1949 Convention. Doubtless, the provisions of the 1949 Convention are binding upon the states that ratify it, whatever the military advantages that may be sacrificed by its observance, and Article 1 declares that: "The High Contracting Parties undertake to respect and to insure respect for the present Convention in all circumstances." Nevertheless, the clarity of the legal obligation not to depart from the Convention for reason of military advantage does not detract from the possibility—and that is all it can be regarded—that belligerents may be reluctant to meet certain duties laid down in the Convention when such duties press hard upon considerations of military advantage. The occasions when this may be so can be surmised only on the basis of known experience. Besides, a substantial number of the provisions themselves permit the operation of military necessity as a justification for departing from behavior that must otherwise be observed. Finally, it need hardly be pointed out that in the interpretation of the provisions of the 1949 Convention—a number of which are far from being as clear and specific as is to be desired in an international convention—belligerents will not be unmindful of their respective military requirements. The latter reason alone constitutes sufficient justification for bearing in mind the experience of the two World Wars in considering the 1949 Convention.

[70] See Mossop, *op. cit.*, pp. 398–400, for a lucid analysis of the outlook of the framers of Hague Conventions III (1899) and X (1907).

[71] A task in which the great majority of hospital ships were engaged in the two World Wars.

[72] The civilian at sea was altogether excluded from the benefits of Hague X, which applied only to "sailors and soldiers on board, when sick or wounded, as well as other persons officially attached to fleets or armies . . ."—It is of course true that even prior to the 1949 Convention belligerents had recognized the necessity of expanding the categories of sick and wounded

The 1949 Convention clearly abandons the assumption which underlay the earlier Convention and recognizes that the most important function of hospital ships will be the transport of casualties resulting from warfare on land. The individuals who are therefore entitled to receive the benefits of the new Convention include the following categories:[73] members of the armed forces of a Party to the conflict, as well as members of militias or volunteer corps forming part of such armed forces; members of other militias and members of other volunteer corps, including those of organized resistance movements which belong to a Party to the conflict and which comply with certain conditions;[74] members of regular armed forces who profess allegiance to a Government or an authority not recognized by the Detaining Power; persons who accompany the armed forces without actually being members thereof, provided they have received authorization from the armed forces which they accompany; and members of the crews of the merchant marine and the crews of civil aircraft of the Parties to the conflict who do not benefit by more favorable provisions of international law.[75]

So far as warfare at sea is concerned, the last of the above categories may be regarded as the most significant of the extensions made by the 1949 Convention. (However, it may be pointed out that during World War II the belligerents were already allowing the carriage of sick and wounded members of the merchant marine in hospital ships.) On the other hand, Article 13 of the 1949 Convention fails to include civilians among those entitled to receive the benefits of the Convention, though this omission is tempered by a later provision, Article 35, that hospital ships shall not be deprived of the protection due to them for the reason that the humanitarian

---

entitled to be carried on board hospital ships. Nevertheless, the evolution that accompanied—in this respect—the two World Wars still left unsettled many and controversial questions, even as regards individuals claiming to be assimilated to the armed forces of belligerents.

[73] Article 13. This article makes the same enumeration as is made in Article 4 (A) of the Prisoners of War Convention. Apart from the categories enumerated in Article 4 (B) of the Convention relating to prisoners of war, which are not relevant to the present analysis, it will be apparent that any individual entitled to the status of prisoner of war is entitled to receive the benefits of the Convention on the sick, wounded and shipwrecked. In a formal sense the converse appears equally true (since Article 16 provides that "the wounded, sick and shipwrecked of a belligerent who fall into enemy hands shall be prisoners of war"), though as will presently be seen the Convention seems to provide that persons other than those entitled to the status of prisoners of war may be accorded at least certain benefits granted the wounded and shipwrecked.

[74] These conditions are: that of being commanded by a person responsible for his subordinates; that of having a fixed distinctive sign recognizable at a distance; that of carrying arms openly; and that of conducting operations in accordance with the laws and customs of war.

[75] One further category not listed above includes individuals making up a so-called *levée en masse*. The naval equivalent of a *levée en masse* has been thus defined in the *Oxford Manual of Naval Warfare, 1913:* "The inhabitants of a territory which has not been occupied who, upon the approach of the enemy, spontaneously arm vessels to fight him, without having had time to convert them into war-ships . . . shall be considered as belligerents, if they act openly and if they respect the laws and usages of war."

activities of such vessels have been extended to the "care of wounded, sick or shipwrecked civilians." [76]

According to Article 12 the categories of individuals to whom the Convention is applicable "who are at sea and who are wounded, sick or shipwrecked, shall be respected and protected in all circumstances, it being understood that the term 'shipwreck' means shipwreck from any cause and includes forced landings at sea by or from aircraft." [77] The Parties to the conflict in whose power such persons may be are obliged to care for them and to treat them in a humane manner, without any adverse distinction founded on sex, race, nationality, religion, political opinions, or any other similar criteria.[78]

In a general sense, almost all of the detailed rules laid down in the 1949 Convention may be considered as the application of the general duty to respect and protect the wounded, sick or shipwrecked. Thus the rules relating to the respect and protection that must be accorded hospital ships (which make up the heart of the Convention) can have no other purpose

---

[76] Does this refer to civilians wounded, sick or shipwrecked because of action at sea, or to civilians wounded and sick from any cause, or to both? It is surely reasonable to assume that civilians—of whatever nationality—wounded, sick or shipwrecked as a result of naval action are entitled to receive the benefits of the humanitarian activities of hospital ships, even though this is not expressly provided for in the Convention. More debatable, however, is the presence on board hospital ships of sick or wounded enemy civilians that have been taken on in port. Mossop (*op. cit.*, p. 400) states that during World War II the protection of hospital ships was extended to the sick and wounded wives and dependents of members of the armed forces, and goes on to suggest that "it is essential as a matter of both logic and common humanity to extend the protection offered by hospital ships to sick and wounded civilians when the Convention is next revised." Yet it seems clear that the 1949 Convention has not been so extended, save perhaps through the backdoor of Article 35. And Article 35 is itself, in this respect, somewhat anomalous. For if civilians are not included within the categories entitled to receive the benefits of the Convention then what is the precise meaning of the stipulation that hospital ships carrying wounded, sick or shipwrecked civilians are not to be denied the protection normally due to them? May a belligerent at least object to such carriage, and ultimately take some sort of action if it nevertheless continues as a regular practice? This ambiguity and potential source of confusion with respect to a highly important matter must be regarded as a serious defect in the drafting of the 1949 Convention.

[77] But the passage cited above is preceded by the words "members of the armed forces and other persons mentioned in the following Article (i. e., Article 13)." Thus Article 12 does not formally extend the benefits of the Convention beyond those categories earlier enumerated. The fact that "shipwreck" is defined as meaning "shipwrecked from any cause" does not alter this situation, since whatever the cause it still applies only to the persons mentioned in Article 13. And here again the restrictiveness of the wording so far as wounded, sick or shipwrecked civilians are concerned must be noted.

[78] The care and humane treatment to be accorded the sick, wounded and shipwrecked is further elaborated in Article 12 as follows: "Any attempts upon their lives, or violence to their persons, shall be strictly prohibited; in particular, they shall not be murdered or exterminated, subjected to torture or to biological experiments; they shall not wilfully be left without medical assistance and care, nor shall conditions exposing them to contagion or infection be created. — Only urgent medical reasons will authorize priority in the order of treatment to be administered. — Women shall be treated with all consideration due to their sex."

than that of insuring the respect and protection of the wounded, sick or shipwrecked. Nevertheless, it is useful to distinguish—if only for reasons of convenience—between the rules directly applicable to, and enjoining the respect and protection of, the wounded, sick or shipwrecked, and the rules designed to accomplish this same end by enjoining the respect and protection of hospital ships, sick bays, medical transports and the religious, medical and hospital staffs of captured vessels. Within the former category may be placed the obligation of the parties to the 1949 Convention to take all possible measures after each engagement at sea—and without delay—"to search for and collect the shipwrecked, wounded and sick, to protect them against pillage and ill-treatment, to ensure their adequate care, and to search for the dead and prevent their being despoiled." [79] For this purpose the Parties to the conflict may appeal to the charity of commanders of neutral merchant vessels, yachts or other craft, to take on board and care for wounded, sick, or shipwrecked persons, and to collect the dead; and neutral vessels responding to this appeal shall enjoy special protection and facilities to carry out such assistance.[80]

The respect and protection owed to the wounded, sick or shipwrecked does not extend to immunity from capture, however. In the 1949 Convention, as in the earlier Convention (X) of 1907,[81] all warships of a belligerant have the right to demand that the wounded, sick or shipwrecked—regardless of nationality—on board hospital ships, as well as merchant vessels and other craft, shall be surrendered.[82] In the 1949 Convention, though, the belligerent right of removal has been qualified by the stipulation that removal is justified "provided that the wounded and sick are in a fit state to be moved and that the warship can provide adequate facilities for necessary medical treatment." [83] Apart from this, it should be made

[79] Article 18. On the above obligation, also see pp. 71–3. Article 19 details the procedure to be followed in establishing the identification—as soon as possible—of each shipwrecked, wounded, sick or dead person of the adverse Party. This information is to be recorded and forwarded to the information bureau described in Article 122 of the prisoners of war Convention. Article 20 contains further prescriptions regarding the handling of the dead and the conduct of burial at sea.

[80] Article 21. At the same time Article 21 goes on to provide that although neutral vessels may not be captured on account of such transport, "in the absence of any promise to the contrary, they shall remain liable to capture for any violations of neutrality they may have committed."

[81] Article 12.

[82] Article 14. It is of interest to observe that Article 14 speaks of the right of "all warships of a belligerent Party," whereas most of the other provisions of the Convention speak only of "Party to the conflict." Presumably the reason for the different wording of Article 14 is that the right of removal extends to neutral vessels as well (neutral warships and military aircraft, of course, being excluded) and that in order to interfere in such manner with neutral vessels a formal state of belligerency is required. But as between the "Parties to the conflict" this formal condition is not required for the operation of the Convention (see pp. 134–5).

[83] This qualification, it will be noted, does not extend to the shipwrecked. How effective the qualification contained in Article 14 will prove in practice is quite another question.

clear that the belligerent right of removal [84] applies to all hospital ships—whether belligerent or neutral—as well as to all other vessels and aircraft which may be carrying the sick, wounded or shipwrecked, the only exceptions being neutral warships and neutral military aircraft.

The wounded, sick and shipwrecked of a belligerent who fall into enemy hands shall be considered, in accordance with Article 16 of the 1949 Convention, "prisoners of war, and the provisions of international law concerning prisoners of war shall apply to them." [85] The captor may—according to circumstances—hold them, convey them to his own country, to a neutral port, or even to an enemy port. But if returned to their home country they may not serve for the duration of the war.

The disposition of the wounded, sick or shipwrecked who are landed in neutral territory either by neutral warships (and neutral military aircraft) or by belligerent warships—with the consent of the local authorities—is dealt with in Articles 15 and 17.[86] In both cases, the neutral state must insure, where so required by international law, that these persons take no

---

[84] The objection occasionally taken in the past to the belligerent right of removal has been based, in part, upon the contention that it is both unnecessary and inhumane. Belligerents apparently made no use of it during World War I, but in World War II the German hospital ships *Tübingen* and *Gradisca* were taken in to Allied ports, and the enemy individuals carried on board made prisoners of war. The vessels had earlier been permitted to pass through Allied lines in the Adriatic in order to take on sick and wounded in Salonica, the diversion taking place on the outward voyage. See Mossop (*op cit.*, p. 405), who, in relating this incident, declares that "a high percentage were only slightly wounded and the great majority were considered likely to be fit for active service within twelve months. This action brought forth no protest from the German Government, who considered it justified by the terms of the Convention." In the Pacific theatre no similar incidents appear to have occurred.—Objection to the belligerent right to remove the sick, wounded and shipwrecked from neutral vessels has been—in the past—merely one facet of the broader objection made against the removal at sea of any enemy persons from neutral vessels, a problem that is dealt with later (see pp. 325–9). It is sufficient to observe here that the belligerent right to remove the sick, wounded and shipwrecked from neutral vessels is firmly established in law.

[85] Following Article 14 of the 1907 Convention, Article 16 of the 1949 Convention is a further indication—if such were needed—that the intent was to make the categories of individuals to which the Convention shall apply identical with those individuals liable to treatment as prisoners of war. It is true that Article 16 is prefaced by the words "subject to the provisions of Article 12," but this seems only for the purpose—as Genet (*op. cit.*, 20 (1951), p. 185) points out—of defining with greater precision the extent of protection due the sick, wounded or shipwrecked who fall into the hands of an enemy. Yet it is difficult—for reasons already noted—to take Article 16 quite literally, since hospital ships may be carrying sick, wounded or shipwrecked who are not entitled to the status of prisoners of war, and a belligerent in receiving such enemy individuals need not—and perhaps even ought not—treat them as such.

[86] Articles 15 and 17, concerning the problem of neutral asylum to naval forces, may be cited in full:

"Article 15. If wounded, sick or shipwrecked persons are taken on board a neutral warship or a neutral military aircraft, it shall be ensured, where so required by international law, that they can take no further part in operations of war.

Article 17. Wounded, sick or shipwrecked persons who are landed in neutral ports with the consent of the local authorities, shall, failing arrangements to the contrary between the neutral

further part in operations of war. But the Convention does not provide for the disposition to be made of the wounded, sick or shipwrecked who are brought into neutral ports by neutral merchant ships. Nor does it provide for the disposal of shipwrecked members of armed forces who reach a neutral coast by their own efforts. This silence in the 1949 Convention may be taken as reinforcing the opinion—which is believed to be correct—that the neutral state is under no obligation to resort to internment in these two latter cases.[87]

b. Hospital Ships

The 1949 Convention permits the use of three types of hospital ships.

---

and the belligerent Powers, be so guarded by the neutral Power, where so required by international law, that the said persons cannot again take part in operations of war.

The costs of hospital accommodation and internment shall be borne by the Power on whom the wounded, sick, or shipwrecked persons depend."

In principle, Articles 15 and 17 follow Articles 13 and 15 of Hague X, save for the introduction of the phrase "where so required by international law." The meaning of the latter phrase is not free from a certain ambiguity, however. The traditional rules governing neutral asylum to naval forces are clear to the effect that the neutral state has a duty to intern combatant personnel that are either brought into neutral ports by its own warships or by the warships of a belligerent (the neutral so consenting). But Professor Kunz has suggested that in this phrase we see "the impact of changes in the law of neutrality, brought about by treaties such as the United Nations Charter." "The Geneva Conventions of August 12, 1949," in *Law and Politics in the World Community*, p. 290. If this suggestion is correct, then these traditional rules governing neutral asylum are subject in their operation to a significant qualification. Genet (*op. cit.*, 20 (1951), p. 184) interprets the phrase as resulting from the unresolved question as to whether or not the duty of internment should extend only to the sick, wounded or shipwrecked picked up by neutral warships on the *high seas*, though not within the *territorial waters* of the neutral state. In opposition to the view that the duty of internment applies wherever such persons are rescued by neutral warships, it has been held that once within neutral territorial waters the wounded or shipwrecked have escaped the risk of being taken by the enemy and hence if then taken on board neutral warships need not be interned. If this controversy is in fact the reason for inserting the phrase "where so required by international law' in Articles 15 and 17, all that can be said is that these articles have left the controversy where they found it.

[87] To this effect see, for example, Oppenheim-Lauterpacht (*op. cit.*, pp. 734–5), where the further case is included of belligerent vessels unlawfully attacked in neutral territorial waters, and the combatant personnel of these vessels reach the neutral shore. Also Higgins and Colombos, *op. cit.*, pp. 432–3, and J. A. C. Gutteridge, "The Geneva Conventions of 1949," *B. Y. I. L.*, 26 (1949), p. 309. It must be acknowledged, however, that on the basis of the two World Wars neutral states have demonstrated no unanimity with respect to the disposition of the two cases cited in the text above. Yet this very disparity of state practice would appear itself as a further indication that there is no recognized neutral *duty* of internment. And the fact that the 1949 Convention does not specifically provide for these cases—despite the questions raised since the conclusion of Hague X—only serves to add further support to this conclusion. Nor is it useful, in this respect, to examine Hague Convention XIII (1907), since this instrument also fails to provide any guidance to the cases under consideration. But it is essential to distinguish these cases from the situation in which a belligerent warship, carrying enemy wounded or shipwrecked aboard as prisoners of war, is interned by a neutral state for having failed to leave one of the latter's ports in due time. In this instance the internment of the officers and crew of the warship must be accompanied by the internment of the prisoners of war carried on board.

First and foremost are military hospital ships, defined as ships specially built or equipped by the Powers solely to assist, treat and transport the wounded, sick and shipwrecked. It is declared that military hospital vessels may "in no circumstances be attacked or captured, but shall at all times be respected and protected, on condition that their names and descriptions have been notified to the Parties to the conflict ten days before those ships are employed." [88] The notification must include the following characteristics: registered gross tonnage, the length from stem to stern, and the number of masts and funnels.[89] The same protection and exemption from capture is accorded to private enemy hospital ships—utilized by National Red Cross Societies, by officially recognized relief societies or by private persons—on condition that they have been given an official commission by the Party to the conflict on which they depend and have complied with the provisions concerning notification applicable to military hospital ships.[90] Finally, the protection and exemption granted to military hospital ships are likewise granted to private neutral hospital vessels—utilized by National Red Cross Societies, officially recognized relief societies, or private persons of neutral countries—on condition that they have placed themselves under the control of one of the Parties to the conflict, with the previous authorization of their own government, and have complied with the provisions concerning notification applicable to military hospital ships.[91]

Although the tenth Hague Convention permitted—at least by implication—the conversion of merchant vessels into hospital ships, it contained no provisions concerning the case in which a belligerent might reconvert a hospital ship, that had earlier been a merchant vessel, once again to its

[88] Article 22. The corresponding provision of Hague X, Article 1, merely required notification to the adverse Party before use. Genet (*op. cit.*, 21 (1952), p. 31) points out in criticism of Article 22 that with the speed of communications today, ships can be transformed into hospital vessels very quickly in order to carry out errands of mercy. The ten-day requirement may well mean that hospital ships converted and ready for use in a shorter period would have to suspend operations of a humanitarian character while waiting for a time limit to expire.—The respect and protection to be accorded hospital ships is extended, by Article 23, to shore establishments entitled to the protection of the Geneva Convention for Amelioration of the Condition of the Wounded and Sick in Armed Forces in the Field. Bombardment or attack from the sea against such establishments is prohibited.

[89] A new provision, designed to facilitate identification.

[90] Article 24 — which further declares that these ships must be provided with certificates from the responsible authorities, stating that the vessels have been under their control while fitting out and on departure.

[91] Article 25. With respect to the protection of sick bays Article 28 of the 1949 Convention states: "Should fighting occur on board a warship, the sick-bays shall be respected and spared as far as possible. Sick bays and their equipment shall remain subject to the laws of warfare, but may not be diverted from their purpose so long as they are required for the wounded and sick. Nevertheless, the commander into whose power they have fallen may, after insuring the proper care of the wounded and sick who are accommodated therein, apply them to other purposes in case of urgent military necessity."

original use. Nor did Hague X deal with the problem regarding the places where conversion of vessels into hospital ships might legitimately be accomplished. A still further question left open by the tenth Hague Convention related to the minimum tonnage that might be required of hospital ships. During the two World Wars each of these questions provided ground for controversy between the belligerents.[92] The 1949 Convention takes a long step forward in clarifying hitherto disputed issues. With respect to the tonnage required of hospital ships Article 26 of the Convention expressly extends protection to hospital ships "of any tonnage as well as to their lifeboats, wherever they are operating." Nevertheless, in order to insure the maximum comfort and security, the Parties to the conflict "shall endeavor to utilize, for the transport of wounded, sick and shipwrecked over long distance and on the high seas, only hospital ships of over 2000 tons gross." [93] Earlier controversy over the question of reconversion is resolved in Article 33 of the new Convention by the stipulation that merchant vessels "which have been transformed into hospital ships cannot be put to any other use throughout the duration of hostilities." [94] No indication is given, however, as to the possible restrictions upon the places where the conversion of vessels into hospital ships might legitimately be carried out. It would appear that, in principle, the latter question must be governed by the consideration that belligerents need not recognize such conversion when it has clearly been effected for the purpose

[92] See Mossop (*op. cit.*, pp. 403–4) for a consideration of these matters in World War II. Great Britain announced a lower limit of 3000 tons on hospital ships, though in practice it enforced—over German and Italian protests—a limit of 2000 tons. However, in the case of the 1500 ton German hospital ship *Freiburg* the British Government, after first seizing the vessel, released her on the apparent ground that she was a bona fide hospital ship. In fact, Hague X did not provide any lower limit, and the British position appears to have been very doubtful on this point. In the Pacific theatre no lower limit was placed on the tonnage required of hospital ships in order to enjoy protection. As will be noted shortly in the text above, the question as to where conversion might legitimately take place is really a part of the larger question concerning conversions that have been made merely to avoid capture. The British Prize Court has long held that conversion made merely to avoid capture may nevertheless result in the seizure of a hospital ship so converted and her condemnation as lawful prize. In this connection Mossop cites the cases of the *Ramb IV* and the *Rostock*. The former, an Italian merchant vessel converted into a hospital ship while lying blocked in Massawa, was seized by British forces and taken into an Allied port. Later, however, the conversion was recognized as having been genuine and not made simply to avoid capture. The seizure of the *Rostock*, a German warship hastily converted into a hospital ship, was clearly a different matter. Not only was the vessel converted while lying in the besieged port of Bordeaux, but when intercepted was found to be carrying codes and engaging in weather reporting—activities which deprived her of the right of continued protection.

[93] This provision is purely optional.

[94] The widsom of this provision has been questioned by Genet (*op. cit.*, 21 (1952), p. 38) as placing an undue restriction upon belligerents, who—instead—should be allowed to convert merchant vessels into hospital ships—and reconvert them back again—as the necessities of war may require. And Mossop (*op. cit.*, p. 404), looking at World War II experience, expresses the opinion that "a prohibition against denotification is of little practical value."

of avoiding capture.[95] If this position is correct the decisive consideration will concern the purpose of conversion rather than the place where conversion is actually carried out, though the place of conversion may frequently provide an important indication of purpose (e. g., if conversion is carried out in a besieged port).

By a novel provision in the 1949 Convention—Article 27—the respect and protection accorded to hospital ships is further extended—subject to the requirements of notification—to "small craft employed by the State or by the officially recognized lifeboat institutions for coastal rescue operations." But this extension of protection to coastal rescue craft is expressly subordinated to the "operational requirements" of the belligerents, a qualification that is not unlikely to limit severely the practical significance of the provision.[96]

It is not only at sea that hospital ships are granted exemption from capture. Article 29 of the 1949 Convention provides that exemption from capture shall be granted hospital ships caught in a port that has fallen into the hands of the enemy. "Any hospital ship in a port which falls into the hands of the enemy shall be authorized to leave the said port." [97]

The protection given hospital ships has always been dependent upon their not being used for any purpose other than to "afford relief and assistance to the wounded, sick and shipwrecked without distinction of nationality." [98] To undertake to use hospital ships for what is clearly a military purpose would obviously constitute a serious breach of faith on the part of a belligerent sanctioning such a practice.[99] Experience has shown, however, that the problem of defining those acts forbidden to hospital ships is not always an easy one. Not only is it difficult on occasion to determine the extent of the acts which, if performed, could be regarded as serving a

[95] Though even this principle—whose soundness ought not to be questioned—is not expressly enumerated in the 1949 Convention. In part, of course, it is met by the stipulation that hospital ships shall be "built or equipped . . specially and solely with a view to assisting the wounded, sick and shipwrecked."

[96] On the small craft used for air-sea rescue purposes by the German Government off the British coast in 1940, and the refusal of the British Government to extend immunity to these craft—as well as to ambulance aircraft—see Mossop, *op. cit.*, p. 403. The British argument that airmen shot down over the sea could not be considered as "shipwrecked" would no longer hold, since the 1949 Convention includes this newer category But the British refusal to assimilate light craft engaged in rescue operations to hospital ships—thereby granting them special protection—for fear of intelligence activities, would still be clearly permissible under Article 27 of the 1949 Convention.

[97] Article 29 has no counterpart in Hague X.—Article 32 of the 1949 Convention declares: "Vessels described in Articles 22, 24, 25 and 27 are not classed as warships as regards their stay in a neutral port." On the conditions governing the stay of belligerent warships in neutral ports, see pp. 240–5.

[98] Article 30.

[99] And Article 30 of the 1949 Convention obligates the contracting parties "not to use these vessels for any military purpose."

military purpose—hence forbidden; even more difficult may be the determination of acts which, though not supporting a military operation, are nevertheless forbidden to hospital ships. In an attempt to reduce future uncertainty in this regard Article 35 of the 1949 Convention lists certain conditions which shall *not* be considered as depriving hospital ships or sick bays of vessels of the protection due to them. These conditions are:

> (1) The fact that the crews of ships or sick bays are armed for the maintenance of order, for their own defense or that of the sick and wounded.
>
> (2) The presence on board of apparatus exclusively intended to facilitate navigation or communication.[1]
>
> (3) The discovery on board hospital ships or in sick bays of portable arms and ammunition taken from the wounded, sick and shipwrecked and not yet handed to the proper service.
>
> (4) The fact that the humanitarian activities of hospital ships and sick-bays of vessels or of the crews extend to the care of wounded, sick or shipwrecked civilians.
>
> (5) The transport of equipment and of personnel intended exclusively for medical duties, over and above normal requirements.[2]

Clearly, the presence on board hospital ships of any arms or communications apparatus in excess of that allowed above will give rise to suspicion of abuse. Furthermore, equipment of any kind, save that intended exclusively for medical duties, ought not to be carried, however innocent it may appear. Nor should hospital ships be used to carry convalescent personnel. And although hospital ships are not to be considered as deprived of protection because their humanitarian activities have been extended to wounded and sick civilians, it remains true that Article 35 does not contemplate such carriage as a regular practice. Finally, even though not being used for any military purpose, hospital ships must not act in such a manner as to hamper the movements of the combatants. It is probably due to the latter consideration that the removal of the wounded and sick by sea from a besieged or encircled area, and the passage of medical and religious personnel and equip-

[1] Paragraph 2 of Article 35 must be read with the second paragraph of Article 34, which declares that hospital ships "may not possess or use a secret code for their wireless or other means of communication."

[2] Both paragraphs 4 and 5 are novel, having no counterpart in Hague X. In practice, belligerents have permitted the carriage of medical and religious personnel as passengers, whether going to or from the forces in the field. So also in the case of medical supplies and equipment intended for armies in the field, the practice appears to have been to allow hospital ships to carry such supplies and equipment on their outward voyage. Article 35 now formally sanctions these activities.

ment to such an area, is made dependent upon the express agreement of the parties to the conflict.[3]

In order to ensure that hospital vessels and small craft are not being used improperly, as well as to guarantee that the movements of the combatants will not be hampered even by legitimate activities, the Parties to the conflict are given the right to control and search these vessels and small craft. Article 31 declares that the Parties to the conflict "can refuse assistance from these vessels, order them off, make them take a certain course, control the use of their wireless and other means of communication, and even detain them for a period not exceeding seven days from the time of interception, if the gravity of the circumstances so requires." A commissioner may be placed on board for a temporary period in order to see that the orders given hospital ships are carried out. Provision is also made in Article 31 for placing neutral observers on board hospital ships, and this may be done either unilaterally or by agreement between the Parties to the conflict.

It has always been true that if hospital ships are used to commit acts harmful to an enemy, and outside their humanitarian duties, the protection to which they are otherwise entitled ceases. Article 34 of the 1949 Convention reaffirms this rule, but at the same time provides that protection may cease "only after due warning has been given, naming in all appropriate cases a reasonable time limit, and after such warning has remained unheeded." The procedure thus laid down in Article 34 constitutes an innovation upon Hague Convention X (1907), which merely provided—without further qualification—that hospital ships were no longer entitled to protection if employed for the purpose of injuring the enemy.[4]

---

[3] Article 18, paragraph 2: "Whenever circumstances permit, the Parties to the conflict shall conclude local arrangements for the removal of the wounded and sick by sea from a besieged or encircled area and for the passage of medical and religious personnel and equipment on their way to that area." Mossop (*op. cit.*, pp. 405–6) relates two occasions during the 1939 war in which the German High Command sought to send a hospital ship through Allied patrol lines to a besieged port. In one of these instances the request was granted, though in the other it was denied for the reason that it would hamper the movements of the attacking forces.—No doubt belligerents will also be reluctant to grant removal of wounded and sick from a besieged area if the result will be to ease noticeably the burden of the defenders.

[4] Article 8.—The meaning of Article 34 is not altogether free from doubt, however. Presumably, neither attack nor capture is permitted under Article 34 without prior "due warning." In the case of a hospital ship found—after search—to be carrying signalling equipment in excess of a reasonable need Article 34 would prohibit seizure of the vessel—at least if the phrase "only after due warning has been given" is to be interpreted literally. If so, this clearly represents a change from previous practice, and—it is submitted—an undesirable change. On the other hand, the effect of Article 34 need not prove to be a substantial deterrent to a belligerent intent upon avoiding its obligations. Article 34 does not render any more difficult the manufacture of unfounded charges; and these charges apparently may be followed by the sternest of measures—including attack—provided only that a "reasonable time limit" is permitted in "appropriate" cases. Paradoxically, the effect of Article 34 could very well be to forbid the immediate seizure of hospital ships, even though found upon search to be performing acts harmful to an enemy, but at the same time to provide no insurance against unwarranted attacks upon hospital

c. Religious, Medical and Hospital Personnel

The religious, medical and hospital personnel of hospital ships and their crews must be respected and protected; they may not be captured during the time they are in the service of the hospital ship, whether or not there are wounded and sick on board.[5] If such personnel fall into the hands of the enemy they must be respected and protected, and the captor is to permit them to carry out their duties as long as is necessary for the care of the wounded and sick. They shall afterwards be sent back as soon as the commander-in-chief, under whose authority they are, considers it practicable; and on leaving the ship may take with them their personal property. However, should it prove necessary to retain some of these personnel owing to the medical or spiritual needs of prisoners of war, everything possible shall be done for their earliest possible landing.[6]

d. Medical Transports

Among the provisions of the 1949 Convention that have no counterpart in the earlier tenth Hague Convention of 1907 are those dealing with medical transports and medical aircraft. Ships may be chartered for the purpose of transporting equipment exclusively intended for the treatment of wounded and sick members of armed forces or for the prevention of disease, provided that the particulars regarding their voyage have been notified to the adverse Power and approved by the latter. In order to ensure that these ships are not being misused the adverse Party retains the right to board them, though not to capture them or seize their equipment. Further, through prior agreement, neutral observers may be placed on board such ships to verify the equipment carried.[7]

Medical aircraft are defined in Article 39 of the 1949 Convention as

---

ships by a belligerent that has been careful to observe the form of Article 34. Admittedly, these critical remarks would prove unjustified if, together with Article 34, adequate provision were made for an effective procedure whereby all charges of abuse could be made the subject of inquiry by an impartial third party. As will be seen (pp. 137–8), the 1949 Convention establishes a procedure of inquiry that may easily be frustrated by an unwilling belligerent.

It is difficult to ascertain, therefore, to what extent Article 34—and other relevant provisions of the 1949 Convention—will succeed in altering those practices built up during the two World Wars, and which have received the support of the majority of states. These practices may be summarized briefly. Save in the most exceptional of circumstances hospital ships suspected of abusing their privileged status were not to be attacked but rather to be visited and searched. If the result of visit and search was to confirm suspicions of abuse the vessel could be seized and taken into port for adjudication. Attack upon a hospital ship proved justified only if the attempt to visit and search was met by acts of forcible resistance *on the part of the hospital ship itself*.

[5] Article 36.

[6] Article 37.

[7] Article 38. A distinction must be drawn between the conditions governing the use of hospital ships in Articles 22, 24 and 25 of the Convention and the conditions governing the use of medical transports in Article 38. With respect to the use of the latter there must be in each instance a special agreement concluded between the Parties to the conflict, whereas no such agreement is required in the case of hospital ships.

"aircraft exclusively employed for the removal of the wounded, sick and shipwrecked, and for the transport of medical personnel and equipment." The strict conditions governing the use of medical aircraft are not to be confused, however, with the far more liberal provisions governing the use of hospital ships.[8] The former are to be respected, and not to be made the object of attack, "while flying at heights, at times and on routes specifically agreed upon between the Parties to the conflict concerned." In each instance, therefore, the use of medical aircraft is made dependent upon a prior agreement whose purpose is to ensure that the adverse Party may exercise close control over such aircraft.[9] This control is further ensured by requiring medical aircraft to be clearly marked with the distinctive emblem provided for in the Convention, together with their national colors, on their lower, upper and lateral surfaces. Additional markings may be made the subject of agreement. Special precaution is taken in Article 39 to prohibit flights of medical aircraft over enemy or enemy-occupied territory, unless otherwise agreed. Finally, medical aircraft are obliged to "obey every summons to alight on land or water,"[10] but in the event of alighting involuntarily on land or water in enemy-occupied territory, the wounded, sick and shipwrecked, as well as the crew of the aircraft—medical personnel excepted—are to be made prisoners of war.

The strict rule forbidding belligerent aircraft to fly over or land in neutral territory is mitigated in the special case of medical aircraft. Article 40 of the 1949 Convention permits the medical aircraft of the Parties to the conflict to fly over the territory of neutral Powers, land thereon in case of necessity, or use it as a port of call. But every flight over neutral terri-

---

[8] It is readily apparent from Article 39 that the inclusion of medical aircraft in the 1949 Convention was—at best—done only reluctantly To what extent belligerents will be able to utilize medical aircraft in future hostilities remains to be seen, though if Article 39 is any indication of future developments in this respect such use will certainly be very sparing.

[9] There is nothing in Article 39 or in the other provisions of the 1949 Convention which expressly prevents medical aircraft from being used to rescue the wounded and shipwrecked at sea—particularly such personnel as have been forced into the sea by or from aircraft. But it is quite clear that if medical aircraft are allowed to perform the function of so-called "seaplane ambulances" they are subject to the same strict conditions laid down for medical aircraft engaged in any other tasks. Hence, the recurrence of a controversy—between parties to the 1949 Convention—similar to the controversy that took place between Germany and Great Britain in 1940 regarding the use by Germany of seaplane ambulances to rescue German airmen shot down at sea, would still support the position taken by Great Britain. At that time the British Government insisted that the use of seaplane ambulances was subject to the prior approval and control of the adverse Power, an approval that was not given by Great Britain after it had been ascertained that some of these aircraft were being used for intelligence activities.

[10] The relevant paragraph of Article 39 reads: "Medical aircraft shall obey every summons to alight on land or water. In the event of having thus to alight, the aircraft with its occupants may continue its flight after examination, if any "—It is not unreasonable to assume that the power thus given belligerents to compel medical aircraft to alight is to be exercised with due discretion (e. g., having regard to the availability of safe landing facilities), though no such phrase is contained in Article 39.

tory must be preceded by notice given to the neutral state concerned, and every summons to alight, on land or water, must be obeyed. In addition, the immunity of medical aircraft from attack is guaranteed "only when flying on routes, at heights and at times specifically agreed upon between the Parties to the conflict and the neutral Power concerned.[11]

e. The Distinctive Emblem; The Problem of Identification

The distinctive emblem to be displayed on the flags, armlets and all equipment employed in the medical service is the red cross on a white ground. However, Article 41 of the 1949 Convention permits, in place of the red cross, the red crescent or the red lion and sun on a white ground, though only for those countries which already use these emblems. In the case of medical, religious and hospital personnel a water resistance armlet bearing the distinctive emblem is to be worn, and the armlet is to be issued and stamped by the competent military authority.[12] In addition, such personnel are to wear an identity disc and to carry a special identity card bearing the distinctive emblem and described in Article 42.[13]

The effectiveness of the protection from attack granted to hospital ships quite naturally depends very largely upon the ease with which belligerents can make the proper identification. In practice, the problem of insuring the proper identification of hospital vessels proved quite difficult during the 1939 war, and it is widely agreed that in the all too numerous cases of attacks made upon hospital ships the cause was nearly always attributable to a failure—particularly on the part of aircraft—to make the proper identification.[14] The 1949 Convention has sought to ensure that instances

[11] The second paragraph of Article 40 goes on to declare—though somewhat redundantly—that: "The neutral Powers may, however, place conditions or restrictions on the passage or landing of medical aircraft on their territory Such possible conditions or restrictions shall be applied equally to all Parties to the conflict."—Apparently these conditions or restrictions are of a special character and in addition to the restrictions governing routes, heights and times mentioned in paragraph 1 of Article 39. Finally, Article 40 provides that: "Unless otherwise agreed between the neutral Powers and the Parties to the conflict, the wounded, sick or shipwrecked who are disembarked with the consent of the local authorities on neutral territory by medical aircraft shall be detained by the neutral Power, where so required by international law, in such a manner that they cannot again take part in operations of war. The cost of their accommodation and internment shall be borne by the Power on which they depend."

[12] Article 42.

[13] The card is to be water resistant, of pocket size, and should bear—at the very least—the name, date of birth, rank and service number of the bearer, in what capacity he is entitled to receive protection, the bearer's photograph, fingerprints and stamp of the military authority. In no circumstances are personnel to be deprived of their insignia or identity cards or of the right to wear the armlet. In case of loss they shall be entitled to receive duplicates of the cards and to have the insignia replaced.

[14] Article 5 of Hague X provided that military hospital ships were to be distinguished by being painted white outside with a horizontal band of green about a metre and a half in breadth. Private (enemy or neutral) hospital ships were to be painted white outside with a horizontal band of red about a metre and a half in breadth. In addition, Hague X declared that in order to ensure by night freedom from interference, hospital ships must—with the belligerent's consent—take the necessary measures to render their special painting sufficiently plain. Mossop

of mistaken identification will be reduced to a minimum, and to this end prescribes—in Article 43—that hospital ships shall be distinctively marked as follows:

(a) All exterior surfaces shall be white.

(b) One or more dark red crosses, as large as possible, shall be painted and displayed on each side of the hull and on the horizontal surfaces, so placed as to afford the greatest possible visibility from the sea and from the air.[15]

Further provisions of Article 43 are directed toward providing more accurate identification of hospital ships, though apart from the specific provision regarding the use of flags on hospital vessels[16] they are stated in the most general terms. Thus it is declared that hospital ships "which may wish to ensure by night and in times of reduced visibility the protection to which they are entitled, must, subject to the assent of the Party to the conflict under whose power they are, take the necessary measures to render their painting and distinctive emblems sufficiently apparent."

(*op. cit.*, p. 401), points out that: "During the 1939 war additional markings on the sides, stern, and deck of hospital ships to aid identification by day, and illumination at night with a band of green lights on the sides and red crosses on the sides and deck picked out with red lamps, were adopted by common consent and provide a high degree of protection against underwater attack—although errors are not unknown in practice."—Spaight (*op. cit.*, pp. 490–1) writes that despite these efforts toward better identification the instances of air attacks on hospital ships were numerous—on both sides—and that the record of World War II is, in this respect, "not a happy one." But Spaight observes, as does Mossop, that in all probability these attacks from the air were accidental and not deliberate.

In World War I, however, German attacks upon Allied hospital ships were deliberate, though Germany defended these attacks by the claim that Allied hospital vessels were being used for military purposes (a charge denied by the British Government). An account of the World War I controversy is given in Hackworth, *op. cit.*, Vol. VI, pp. 460–3. Among the British vessels sunk by German submarines were the *Dover Castle* and the *Llandovery Castle*, and the sinkings provided the occasion for two of the well-known trials held after World War I before the Reichsgericht. In the one case the commander of the submarine which sank the *Dover Castle* was found not guilty because he had acted under superior orders. In the second trial the Reichsgericht found the accused guilty of a violation of the law of war in having fired upon the survivors of the torpedoed *Llandovery Castle* who had taken to the lifeboats.

[15] In this connection Article 44 declares that the distinguishing signs referred to in Article 3—and cited above—"can only be used, whether in time of peace or war, for indicating or protecting the ships therein mentioned, except as may be provided in any other international Convention or by agreement between all the Parties to the conflict concerned."

[16] "All hospital ships shall make themselves known by hoisting their national flag and further, if they belong to a neutral state, the flag of the Party to the conflict whose direction they have accepted. A white flag with a red cross shall be flown at the mainmast as high as possible." In case hospital ships are provisionally detained by an enemy they must haul down the flag of the Party to the conflict in whose service they are or whose direction they have accepted.—The identification system provided for hospital ships is, in general, applicable as well to the lifeboats of hospital ships, coastal lifeboats and all small craft used by the medical service.

And in an even more general way the Parties to the conflict are directed to endeavor at all times "to conclude mutual agreements in order to use the most modern methods available to facilitate the identification of hospital ships."

Despite the improved system of marking hospital ships, provided for in the 1949 Convention, and the exhortation made to facilitate further the proper identification of such vessels by the use of modern devices, it seems altogether likely that the difficulties attending identification in World War II will remain largely unsolved. It is only to be expected that belligerents will refrain from facilitating the identification of hospital ships if in so doing they run the risk of endangering the safety of their combatant forces. Illumination at night of hospital ships has proven feasible when such vessels travel alone upon the high seas. But belligerents have been understandably reluctant to illuminate these vessels when in port or when accompanying combatant forces at sea. In these latter situations hospital ships—though, of course, not liable to direct and deliberate attack—must accept the risk attendant upon their presence in the immediate area of legitimate military objectives.[17]

It may be, however, that through the use of modern devices belligerents will be able to resolve at least some of the past difficulties encountered in the identification of hospital ships. The suggestion has been made that radar could be effectively used to facilitate proper identification. But the ease with which this device, as well as others, could be misused by belligerents presents an obstacle to future developments along this line, particularly in a period that is not marked by a high degree of mutual trust between belligerents. At the very root of the problem, it would seem, is the difficulty of reconciling the belligerent practice of waging unrestricted warfare upon enemy merchant shipping with the precautions that are normally required if hospital ships are to be ensured against accidental attack as a result of faulty identification. In large measure, therefore, the problem of ensuring the proper identification of hospital ships must be

---

[17] To this extent it is hardly adequate that the 1949 Convention repeats in Article 30 the formula earlier used in Hague X that: "During and after an engagement, they (hospital ships) will act at their own risk." It is clear that hospital ships act at their own risk whenever they place themselves in the immediate vicinity of legitimate military objectives. For even though every effort must be made to avoid firing upon—or bombing—hospital ships, the presence of the latter cannot serve to exempt nearby military objectives from attack for fear that a hospital vessel might thereby suffer incidental injury. In this connection, however, it should be observed that there is no basis for the contention—put forward by Germany during the 1939 war—that hospital ships under convoy of belligerent warships surrender their right to claim exemption from direct attack. There is no provision either in the 1949 Convention or in Hague Convention X forbidding hospital ships from sailing under convoy Indeed, in accompanying fleet forces to the scene of an engagement in order to succor the wounded and shipwrecked—a task specifically conferred upon hospital ships—it is obvious that hospital vessels are—in a sense—sailing under convoy.

seen in the broader context of the present liability of belligerent merchant shipping to attack and destruction.[18]

f. Application and Enforcement

Each of the four 1949 Geneva Conventions For the Protection of the Victims of War contain a number of similar provisions relating to application and enforcement of all. However, the relevance of these provisions will necessarily depend largely upon the particular category of war victims under consideration. With respect to the wounded, sick and shipwrecked at sea, many of the general provisions found in the four Geneva Conventions have only a limited relevance and warrant no more than a brief summary.[19]

The 1949 Convention on the wounded, sick and shipwrecked at sea is applicable "to all cases of declared war or of any other armed conflict which may arise between two or more of the High Contracting Parties, even if the state of war is not recognized by one of them." [20] In the event that one of the Powers in conflict is not a party to the Convention, those Powers who are Parties shall nevertheless remain bound by it in their mutual relations. Moreover, those Powers already bound by the Convention shall be bound in relation to a Power not a Party, provided the latter accepts and applies the provisions of the Convention.[21] Special provision is also made—in Article 3—for the collection and care of the wounded, sick and shipwrecked during an armed conflict which is "not of an international character" (i. e., in a civil war and analogous situations); each Party to such conflicts being obligated to treat the sick, wounded and shipwrecked in a humane manner and without any adverse distinction

---

[18] See pp. 57–70. It need hardly be pointed out that the above remarks are not intended as a *justification* for the fact that hospital ships were frequently attacked during World War II. It is apparent, however, that a policy allowing unrestricted warfare against merchant ships by submarines and aircraft must—almost of necessity—render the hospital ship's position a far more hazardous one. And this is especially true when the weapons used to implement such a policy permit destruction at great distances.

[19] For a detailed analysis of these general provisions see, in particular, Paul de La Pradelle, *La Conférence Diplomatique Et Les Nouvelles Conventions de Genève du Août 1949* (1951).

[20] Article 2. The general significance of this provision has been noted elsewhere in the text (see pp. 23–4).

[21] The above provisions of Article 2 are completed by the further stipulation that the Convention applies "to all cases of partial or total occupation of the territory of a High Contracting Party even if the said occupation meets with no resistance."—Although the Convention normally comes into force for a Party six months after the instruments of ratification have been deposited, Article 61 declares that situations "provided for in Articles 2 and 3 shall give immediate effect to ratifications deposited and accessions notified by the Parties to the conflict before or after the beginning of hostilities or occupation."—Denunciation of the Convention shall take effect one year following notification, but a denunciation during a period of armed conflict shall not take effect until peace has been concluded and until operations connected with the release and repatriation of the persons protected by the Convention have been terminated (Article 62).

founded on race, colour, religion, sex, or any other similar criteria.[22]

The field of application of the 1949 Convention is limited by Article 4 to forces on board ship. Once forces are put ashore they immediately become subject to the provisions of the Convention for the Amelioration of the Condition of the Wounded and Sick in Armed Forces in the Field.[23]

The Convention takes precaution to ensure that the rights conferred upon protected persons shall not be adversely affected by special agreements Parties to the conflict may conclude in the course of hostilities.[24] Similar care is taken to emphasize that protected persons may "in no circumstances" renounce in part or in entirety the rights secured to them by the Convention.[25] Nor can this obligation imposed upon the parties to the Convention to respect the rights of the wounded, sick and shipwrecked be restricted by the operation of reprisals. For Article 47 of the Convention declares that: "Reprisals against the wounded, sick and shipwrecked persons, the personnel, the vessels or the equipment protected by the Convention are prohibited.[26]

The importance of the provisions in the Convention dealing with the Protecting Powers—neutral states whose duty it is to safeguard the interests of the Parties to the conflict—is limited. The difficulties involved in obtaining the presence of representatives of the Protecting Powers at the scene of operations—particularly at sea—are well known. Besides, Article 8 of the Convention directs such representatives of Protecting Powers to "take account of the imperative necessities of security of the

---

[22] Article 3 raises many novel problems which cannot be dealt with here. It is interesting to note, however, that this article seeks to obligate not only the present Parties to the Convention but also future rebel forces that may rise up within the territory of any of the Parties. There is no assurance, though, that such future forces will agree to consider themselves bound by the "fundamental" obligations laid down in Article 3. Nevertheless, Article 3 is—so far as the Parties to the Convention are concerned—unconditional and not dependent upon reciprocity of treatment on the part of unrecognized forces in a future civil war. However, once the rebellious forces are recognized by the parent state—and, perhaps, if not by the parent state then by third states—the conflict takes on an "international" character, and Article 2 applies. But once Article 2 applies the parent state is released from any of the obligations laid down by the Convention, if the newly recognized belligerent refuses to accept and apply the provisions thereof.

[23] And Article 5 declares that neutral Powers "shall apply by analogy the provisions of the present Convention to the wounded, sick and shipwrecked, and to members of the medical personnel and to chaplains . . . received or interned in their territory, as well as to dead persons found."

[24] Article 6.

[25] Article 7.

[26] A provision whose rigid observance may prove difficult with respect to an enemy who insistently refuses to adhere to the provisions of the Convention, and—in particular—resorts to inhumane measures in treating the wounded, sick or shipwrecked falling under its power.

State wherein they carry out their duties." [27] Nevertheless, provision is made for Protecting Powers, and in order to fulfill their tasks of safeguarding the interests of the Parties to the conflict these Powers may appoint delegates chosen from their diplomatic or consular staff, from amongst their own nationals or the nationals of other neutral Powers. The delegates so chosen are subject to the approval of the Power with which they are to carry out their duties, and once approved the task of the delegates is to be facilitated to the greatest extent possible.[28] One function of the Protecting Powers warrants special mention. Article 11 of the Convention provides that where they deem it advisable in the interest of protected persons, and particularly in cases of disagreement between the Parties to the conflict as to the application or interpretation of the Convention, the Protecting Powers shall lend their good offices with a view to settling the disagreements. For this purpose a Protecting Power may, either on its own initiative or at the invitation of one Party, propose a meeting of the representatives of the Parties to the conflict. The latter are bound to give effect to the proposals made to them for this purpose.

In general, the Parties to the Convention are obliged to ensure—through their Commanders-in-Chief—that the specific provisions of the Convention are properly executed and that unforeseen cases are provided for in conformity with the general principles laid down therein.[29] The text of the convention must be disseminated as widely as possible.[30] Of particular significance—not only for what they contain but also for their omissions—are the provisions dealing with the repression of abuses and infractions. The High Contracting Parties undertake, in Article 50, "to enact any legislation necessary to provide effective penal sanctions for persons committing, or ordering to be committed, any of the grave breaches of the present Convention . . ."—the latter being defined [31] as "wilful killing,

---

[27] And although Article 8 goes on to state that the activities of representatives of Protecting Powers "shall only be restricted as an exceptional and temporary measure when this is rendered necessary by imperative military necessities," it will be apparent that such "imperative military necessities" may prove to be of frequent occurrence in operations at sea.

[28] Article 9 provides that the provisions of the Convention "constitute no obstacle to the humanitarian activities which the International Committee of the Red Cross or any other impartial humanitarian organization may, subject to the consent of the Parties to the conflict concerned, undertake for the protection of wounded, sick and shipwrecked persons, medical personnel and chaplains, and for their relief." And Article 10 contains provisions which allow the Parties at any time to agree to entrust "to an organization which offers all guarantees of impartiality and efficacy the duties incumbent on the Protecting Powers by virtue of the present Convention." The organization referred to in Article 10 is not to be confused with the Red Cross or other humanitarian organizations already in existence. Instead, it refers to the possible future creation of an organization capable of taking over the functions of Protecting Powers in a war in which there may be no neutral states.

[29] Article 46.

[30] Article 48.

[31] Article 51.

torture or inhuman treatment, including biological experiments, wilfully causing great suffering or serious injury to body or health, and extensive destruction and appropriation of property, not justified by military necessity and carried out unlawfully and wantonly." The obligation is laid upon each contracting Party to search for persons alleged to have committed, or to have ordered to be committed, such grave breaches, and to bring them—regardless of nationality—before its own courts. As an alternative it may—though only if it so prefers—hand such persons over for trial to another contracting Party, provided the latter has made out a *prima facie* case. And apart from the acts held to constitute grave breaches of the Convention the Parties are further obliged to take whatever measures are necessary for the suppression of all acts contrary to the provisions of the Convention.[32]

Finally, attention may be directed to the inquiry procedure provided for in Article 53 of the Convention. Article 53 reads:

> At the request of a Party to the conflict, an inquiry shall be instituted, in a manner to be decided between the interested Parties, concerning any alleged violation of the Convention.
>
> If agreement has not been reached concerning the procedure for the inquiry, the Parties should agree on the choice of an umpire, who will decide upon the procedure to be followed.
>
> Once the violation has been established, the Parties to the conflict shall put an end to it and shall repress it with the least possible delay.

[32] Although the Convention does not so state, the "grave breaches" enumerated in Article 51 are certainly war crimes. It can hardly be said, however, that the procedure set out in the 1949 Convention for the punishment of grave breaches of the Convention constitutes a marked departure from traditional procedures. For all practical purposes Article 51 of the 1949 Convention obligates the contracting parties to do little more to repress abuses and infractions than did its predecessor—i. e., Hague X, in Article 21. This is all the more significant in view of the fact that the 1949 Convention was concluded during a period in which the establishment of new procedures to ensure individual responsibility for violations of international law through the creation of international criminal courts has been widely proclaimed as one of the essential tasks of the present international legal order. And the obvious reticence of the drafters of the 1949 Geneva Conventions even to use the term "war crimes," let alone to initiate a truly international procedure for the apprehension of war criminals, stands in clear contrast to many of the rather sweeping estimates of the significance to be attached to the recently concluded war crimes trials as well as to resolutions—without binding effect—made by the General Assembly of the United Nations concerning war crimes and individual responsibility for such crimes.

A further provision of the 1949 Convention—Article 52—states that: "No High Contracting Party shall be allowed to absolve itself or any other High Contracting Party of any liability incurred by itself or by any other High Contracting Party in respect of breaches referred to in the preceding Article (52)." The obligation imposed by this Article does not refer to the war but to the peace treaty concluded between Parties to the Convention (see Kunz, *op. cit.*, p. 286). The apparent intent is to prevent a victor from absolving himself of liability incurred for grave breaches of the Convention by means of a provision in the peace treaty he may impose upon the defeated state.

The inquiry procedure is optional, therefore, and dependent entirely upon the prior agreement of the Parties to a dispute. A similar procedure for investigating alleged violations was laid down in Article 30 of the 1929 Convention for the Amelioration of the Condition of Wounded and Sick of Armies in the Field, though this Article was never once used during World War II.[33]

G. RUSES IN NAVAL WARFARE

It has already been observed that one of the general principles of the law of war is the principle forbidding the resort to treacherous means, expedients or conduct in the waging of hostilities. Although belligerents are permitted to resort to ruses, or stratagems, in order to obtain an advantage over an enemy, acts of treachery are prohibited. Whereas both ruses as well as acts of treachery usually partake of the element of deception, the former are regarded as "measures for mystifying or misleading the enemy against which the enemy ought to take measures ot protect himself." [34] Acts of treachery, on the other hand, are held to consist of measures of deceit which involve a breach of faith with an enemy.

To the extent that the general principle forbidding the resort to treachery (and, conversely, permitting the resort to ruses) has been given express application in the form of specific rules of custom or convention no particular difficulty arises with respect to its interpretation.[35] Thus it is

[33] And doubt may be expressed over the future effectiveness of Article 53 of the 1949 Convention. Nor is this glaring defect of the 1949 Convention compensated for by the Resolution accompanying the Final Act of the Conference, which recommended that Parties unable to settle disputes by other means should endeavor to submit such disputes to the International Court of Justice.

[34] U. S. Army *Rules of Land Warfare*, paragraph 49. There is a certain terminological confusion with respect to the term "ruse" Many writers use the term to cover only those acts of deception permitted to belligerents. The term treachery—or perfidy—is then used to cover forbidden acts of deception. In the Hague Regulations (1907) Article 24 speaks of "ruses of war" as "permissible measures," and Article 23b forbids "treacherous" action. Not infrequently, however, the term "ruse" is used to cover both legitimate and illegitimate acts of deception; treachery then meaning an illegitimate ruse. In the text the former usage is adhered to.

[35] In the absence of specific rules considerable difficulty may arise. It has never been easy to establish general criteria that could be applied to all possible acts of deception in order to determine whether such acts may be regarded as permissible ruses or forbidden treachery. The difficulties involved are very similar to the difficulties involved in the attempted interpretation and application of the principle of humanity (see pp. 46–9). If it is stated that treachery consists of acts of bad faith which are forbidden by custom or convention, while ruses consist of acts permitted (at least negatively) by law, then this answer merely amounts to saying that deception expressly forbidden by law is treachery whereas acts of deception not expressly forbidden are ruses. This statement is quite true, but it is of little or no assistance as applied to novel acts of deception in order to determine whether such acts fall within the category of permissible ruses or within the category of treachery.

English and American writers generally follow Halleck, who distinguished between ruses and treachery by stating that "whenever a belligerent has expressly or tacitly engaged, and is,

clearly forbidden to use a flag of truce as a means of deceiving an enemy and in order to obtain an advantage over him. It is also forbidden to use the red cross, or other equivalent distinctive emblems, for any purpose other than those humanitarian purposes which such emblems are universally understood to signify. Hence in warfare at sea, hospital vessels and medical aircraft, as well as their personnel, which bear these distinctive emblems and enjoy the protection offered thereby, must not be used for any military purpose.[36] The same considerations apply to the attempted use for military purposes of cartel ships and any other vessels which—by special agreement between belligerents—have been accorded exemption from attack and capture.

The most important ruses employed in naval warfare relate to the measures belligerent warships may take in order to conceal their identity. Subject to those prohibitions indicated above, almost every conceivable form of disguise is permitted to belligerent warships. They may even take on the disguise of merchant vessels. In addition, they are permitted, according to custom, to disguise their true identity by the use of false colors, provided only that prior to the exercise of belligerent rights (attack, visit or search, seizure) they show their true colors.[37]

---

therefore, bound by a moral obligation, to speak the truth to an enemy, it is perfidy to betray his confidence, because it constitutes a breach of good faith " But when has a belligerent the obligation to speak the truth, particularly in an era (as both Stone (*op. cit.*, p. 561) and Spaight (*op. cit.*, p. 169) well point out) in which false communications and false reports have become standard practices? Spaight suggests that the preferable formula run as follows: "A procedure, emblem, or signal to which a recognized significance is attached by international law or custom, may not be diverted to another purpose prejudicial to its being respected when used for its original restrictive or humanitarian purpose." Apart from the fact that this formula does not seem to cover all possible acts of deception, it does not really solve the problem. The phrase "recognized significance" begs the decisive question. If "recognized significance" means "embodied in a rule of customary or conventional law" then Spaight's formula simply states that the law should be observed. To say, for example, that the red cross emblem should "not be diverted to another purpose" is merely to state what the law governing the use (and misuse) of this emblem already states.—Stone proposes that "the test (between ruses and treachery) on principle should be whether the deceit attacks the security of some interest or principle to which States generally, whether enemies or not, attach special importance. Thus, using civilians as a shield, or misuse of the flag of truce, undermines the principle of immunity of civilians, and that negotiations should be possible even between enemies. Of course, evaluations are here involved, which allow diversity of opinion even if such a test were accepted." There is much to be said for this proposal, despite the fact that it also raises some of the difficulties already referred to.

36 See pp. 126–8 for a discussion of the provisions which deal with the misuse of the red cross emblem in the 1949 Geneva Convention for the Amelioration of the Condition of the Wounded, Sick and Shipwrecked Members of Armed Forces at Sea.

37 See *Law of Naval Warfare*, Section 640a.—It is customary for writers to point out the well known case of the German cruiser *Emden* which, in 1914, "hiding her identity by rigging up a dummy fourth funnel and flying the Japanese flag, passed the guardship of the harbour of Penang in the Malay States, made no reply to its signals, came down at full speed on the Russian cruiser *Zemshug*, and then, after lowering the Japanese flag and hoisting the German flag, opened fire

Although the use of false colors (i. e., enemy or neutral) by belligerent warships is clearly permitted by custom—and was frequently resorted to during both World Wars—the practice has been the object of some criticism.[38] It has been claimed that whereas the use of enemy flags, uniforms and insignia is forbidden at all times in land warfare an analogous practice is permitted, in part at least, in naval warfare. In fact, however, the position with respect to the wearing of enemy uniforms and insignia in land warfare is—at present—unsettled.[39] Be that as it may, it does not appear entirely useful to compare, in this respect, land warfare to naval warfare. Even if it is assumed that in land warfare belligerent forces are permitted to wear enemy uniforms and insignia save when engaged in actual combat, this practice will involve only the combatants. In naval warfare the practice of permitting warships to disguise themselves as

---

and torpedoed her." Oppenheim-Lauterpacht, *op. cit.*, p. 510.—During World War II the Germans enjoyed a measurable degree of success through the skillful disguise they provided for their armed raiders. Roskill (*The War at Sea*, p. 277) describes this disguise as follows: "Their funnels and topmasts were telescopic, dummy funnels and derrick posts could be fitted; false bulwarks, false deck houses and dummy deck cargoes were other devices employed; and repainting was often carried out at sea to render valueless any reports of their colouring which the Admiralty might obtain and promulgate." The tactics of the armed raiders were to reveal their true identity only after having come within close enough range to overwhelm the victim (usually armed enemy merchant vessels) by surprise.—One of the most notable actions involving these armed raiders took place in November 1941 between the Australian cruiser *Sydney* and the German armed raider *Kormoran*. The disguised raider, when approached by the *Sydney*, identified herself as a Dutch merchant vessel. Before the *Sydney* could establish the truth or falsity of her claimed identity the *Kormoran* cast off her disguise and opened fire at a distance of 2,000 yards. As a result of the action the *Sydney* was destroyed with complete loss of officers and crew The incident is described by Roskill, pp. 547–9. Also Von Gosseln, "The Sinking of the *Sydney*," *U S. Naval Institute Proceedings*, 79 (1953), p. 25.

[38] For example, by H. A. Smith, *op. cit.*, pp. 91–3, and Erik Castren, *op. cit.*, pp. 264–6. Article 7 of the U. S. Naval War Code of 1900 declared that "the use of false colors in war is forbidden." Later discussions, however, indicated uncertainty over the desirability of this provision in the absence of international agreement. *U S. Naval War College, International Law Discussions, 1903*, pp. 37–42, also for the year 1906, pp. 7–20. Neither the 1917 nor the 1941 *Instructions* issued to the U. S. Navy contained a provision relating to the use of false colors by warships.

[39] Article 23f of the Hague Regulations merely forbids the "improper use" of the "military insignia and uniform of the enemy," leaving unsettled (at least by a literal interpretation) the question as to precisely what acts may constitute improper use. It has been contended that the wearing of enemy uniforms at any time is forbidden and that this was the true intent of Article 23f. Thus, one writer concludes, after a careful survey, that "international law, customary as well as conventional, forbids under all circumstances the use of enemy uniforms for purposes of deceiving the enemy " Valentine Jobst III, "Is the Wearing of the Enemy's Uniform a Violation of the Laws of War?," *A. J. I. L.*, 35 (1941), p. 441. Some writers contend, however, that this rule only extends to combat, and the U. S. Army *Rules of Land Warfare*, state in paragraph 54: "In practice it has been authorized to make use of national flags, insignia, and uniforms as a ruse. The foregoing rule (Article 23, paragraph (f) HR) does not prohibit such employment, but does prohibit their *improper use*. It is certainly forbidden to employ them during combat, but their use at other times is not forbidden."

merchant vessels has as one effect to render more difficult the retention of the distinction made between combatants and non-combatants. Experience has shown that it is futile to expect a belligerent to adhere to the traditional law when this can be done only under circumstances of great peril to the visiting warship.[40] Besides, the prohibition in land warfare against employing enemy uniforms and insignia in actual combat does serve to prevent further deception on the battlefield, and to insure that when engaged in combat belligerents will be able to distinguish friend from foe. In naval warfare it is difficult to see how the same purpose—or, for that matter, any purpose—is served by the rule requiring that a warship show its true colors prior to attack. The show of colors may be carried out almost simultaneously with the act of attack. But once the attack begins there is no longer any possibility to deceive. It is for this reason that the rule has been considered by some writers as arbitrary since it forbids certain acts of deception from the moment at which they cease to deceive.[41]

It is also true that the use of false colors may affect adversely the interests of neutral states. In the past the view has been that the use of neutral colors by belligerent warships was a matter primarily of concern to belligerents, neutral states having only an indirect interest. This view must assume, however, that belligerents will rigorously observe the traditional rules governing belligerent interference with neutral trade. But in a

40 "As things stand, the warship which honestly tries to conform to the traditional rules places herself in great peril. She may stop a vessel wearing some neutral flag and approach her in accordance with the prescribed routine. At any moment the other ship may hoist her true colours and discharge a heavy broadside upon the ship which is trying to obey the law." H. A. Smith, *op. cit.*, p. 92. Smith considers the rule permitting false colors to be an anachronism, a survival from the days of pirates and privateers. "In earlier times there were good reasons for the old rule, which often helped ships to make their escape from pirates or privateers. Pirates obeyed no law and privateers were often not much better. The outwitting of such enemies could call for no censure." There is, in addition, a considerable difference between the effectiveness of the ruse in modern combat, as distinguished from naval battles of earlier days. The speed and firepower of vessels allowed in earlier days time to establish identity and to provide for action in case of mistake. Today the loss of a few minutes, or even seconds, is likely to prove decisive, as the case of the *Sydney* seems to bear out.

41 W. E. Hall, *A Treatise On International Law* (5th ed., 1904), pp. 538–9. "A curious arbitrary rule affects one class of stratagems by forbidding certain permitted means of deception from the moment at which they cease to deceive. It is perfectly legitimate to use the distinctive emblems of an enemy in order to escape from him or to draw his forces into action; but it is held that soldiers clothed in the uniforms of this enemy must put on a conspicuous mark by which they can be recognized before attacking, and that a vessel using the enemy's flag must hoist its own flag before firing with shot or shell. The rule, disobedience to which is considered to entail grave dishonor, has been based on the statement that 'in actual battle, enemies are bound to combat loyally and are not free to ensure victory by putting on a mask of friendship.' In war upon land victory might be so insured, and the rule is consequently sensible; but at sea, and the position is spoken of generally with reference to maritime war, the mask of friendship no longer misleads when once fighting begins, and it is not easy to see why it is more disloyal to wear a disguise when it is absolutely useless, than when it serves its purpose."

period when belligerent claims of control over neutral trade are already extensive, the use of neutral colors by belligerent warships can serve only to provide belligerents with an additional reason for making still greater claims of control over neutral shipping.[42]

The criticisms raised against the ruse which permits the use of false colors is therefore not without substantial merit. Nevertheless, as matters now stand the law is reasonably clear, despite the fact that continuance of the practice forms a contributing cause in the increased liability of merchant vessels to attack. It is doubtful, however, that belligerent military aircraft are permitted to make use of similar ruses in operations at sea. Although there are no conventional rules regulating the marking of aircraft in time of war, the practice of belligerents during World Wars I and II would appear to indicate acceptance of a prohibition against the false marking of aircraft in order to deceive an enemy.[43]

---

[42] These neutral difficulties are considerably increased by the use of the neutral flag by belligerent merchant vessels in order to avoid capture or destruction. As between belligerents the practice of so disguising merchant vessels is not open to objection and probably should not be classified as a *ruse de guerre* in the strict sense. The neutral state may claim, however, that the practice represents the misuse of its flag and endangers its interests. When during World War I Great Britain ordered its merchant vessels to simulate neutral vessels as closely as possible, and to use the flags of neutral states, several neutrals protested. In particular, the United States declared that while the neutral flag could be used on occasion by belligerent merchant vessels in order to escape seizure by an enemy this did not mean that such vessels could make use of the neutral flag as a general practice or that the belligerent state could claim this as a right with respect to its merchant vessels. Great Britain did not accept the protest, maintaining that custom allowed belligerent merchant vessels to resort to such disguise. The British Government did state though that it had no intention of advising merchant shipping "to use foreign flags as general practice or to resort to them otherwise than for escaping capture or destruction." cited in Hackworth, *op. cit.*, Vol. VI, pp. 455–8. The concern of neutrals arose from a fear that the British action would serve to deprive neutral vessels of immunity from attack by German submarines. The British contention that belligerents were forbidden either to capture or to destroy a merchant vessel before ascertaining its nationality or character, and that hence neutral vessels were placed in no greater danger by the belligerent use of the neutral flag, was formally correct. Given the circumstances under which the conflict was being fought, however, the reply was no more than formal.

Section 14 of the U. S. Neutrality Act of November 4, 1939 provided.

"(a) It will be unlawful for any vessel belonging to or operating under the judrisiction of any foreign State to use the flag of the United States thereon, to make use of any distinctive signs or markings, indicating that the same is an American vessel.

(b) Any vessel violating the provisions of subsection (a) of this section shall be denied for a period of three months the right to enter the ports or territorial waters of the United States except in cases of force majeure." *U. S. Naval War College, International Law Situations, 1939*, p. 121.

[43] Spaight (*op. cit.*, pp. 169 ff.), in reviewing this practice, considers it as constitutive of a customary rule. Presumably this prohibition extends to aircraft which bear no markings. Stone (*op. cit.*, p. 612) states that: "Protests by each side against alleged false use in both World Wars, and the care taken to deny such charges, suggests an inchoate prohibition. But no details of any such prohibition have emerged, for instance, as to whether (as in naval warfare) false marks could be used while cruising, provided true colors are shown before opening fire."

H. BOMBARDMENT

In principle, bombardment may be undertaken either for the purpose of effecting the immediate entry and occupation of the area bombarded or for the purpose of attacking objectives the destruction of which would constitute a military advantage to the belligerent. Traditionally, the former purpose has been associated with the operations of forces on land, and in the circumstances of warfare that prevailed up to World War I the principal test for determining the legitimacy of land bombardment was whether or not the place attacked was "defended." [44] Perhaps the main circumstance that formerly characterized bombardment on land was the short range of artillery, which meant that a city or town being bombarded by land forces was within the combat zone. An "undefended" city or town was, in effect, one that was open to the immediate entry of and occupation by enemy forces, and because of its situation the further bombardment of such a place would merely cause unnecessary destruction of lives and property.[45]

In naval operations, however, the occupation of enemy coastal areas—even if only temporary in character—may prove exceptional. Instead of serving as a prelude to occupation the object of naval bombardment is frequently limited to that of denying an enemy the continued use of his military resources. For this reason the rules laid down in Hague Convention IX (1907), regulating bombardment in naval warfare, while forbidding the bombardment by naval forces of "undefended ports, towns, villages, dwellings, or buildings," [46] expressly exempted from this prohibition "military works, military or naval establishments, depots of arms or war material, workshops or plants which could be utilized for the needs of the hostile fleet or army, and ships of war in the harbor . . ." [47]

---

[44] Article 25 of the Land Warfare Regulations annexed to Hague Convention IV (1907) provided that the "attack or bombardment by whatever means, of towns, villages, dwellings or buildings which are undefended is prohibited."

[45] Thus John Westlake (*International Law*, (1907), part II, p. 77) wrote that the principle upon which Article 25 of Hague IV was based "is that a land force can occupy an undefended place and, if it must afterwards evacuate it, can destroy before doing so all that its military value to the enemy exposes to lawful destruction; therefore bombarding the place without or before occupying it would be wantonly to endanger both the lives of the population and the property not lawfully subject to destruction. The same reason will apply to the dealings of a fleet with the undefended coast town, unless it cannot spare the force or the time required for landing and occupying it, including re-embarkation if necessary· in that case only can the question of its right to bombard it arise."

[46] Article 1.

[47] Article 2. Furthermore, according to Article 2 the commander of a naval force could—as a rule—destroy such objectives in an "undefended" town or port only after the local authorities had been summoned to destroy them and had failed to do so. But this latter obligation was qualified by the further provision that "if military necessity demanding immediate action permits no delay, it is nevertheless understood that the prohibition to bombard the undefended

Hague Convention IX therefore expressly recognized the belligerent right to bombard certain "military objectives" even though located in or near an "undefended" enemy area. Nevertheless, this particular juxtaposition of the criterion of defense and the criterion of the military objective has been the source of some uncertainty and confusion in dealing with bombardment in naval warfare, and, it may be added, this confusion has carried over into aerial warfare as well. In naval warfare a town or port may be completely without defenses [48] though not open to entry by the naval forces of an enemy, for the reason that enemy naval forces may be incapable of occupying the undefended place. If enemy naval forces are not capable of occupation then bombardment is permitted, but only against military objectives. It is only if a town or port contains neither defenses nor other legitimate military objectives that bombardment is prohibited. Immunity from bombardment by naval forces need not result from the fact of being actually open to entry—in the sense that these forces are capable of effecting entry—but from the reason that the area contains no object that may lawfully be attacked. Of course, if an enemy place, though containing military objectives, can be entered and occupied by naval forces then further bombardment of these objectives is evidently superfluous and—if undertaken—would constitute a violation of the rule forbidding wanton destruction.[49]

---

town holds good . . ." Finally, a commander incurs no responsibility "for any unavoidable damage which may be caused by a bombardment under such circumstances."

Article 3, of negligible significance today, provided that an undefended town or port could nevertheless be bombarded if the local authorities declined to comply with the demand for requisitions "necessary for the immediate needs of the naval force before the place in question."

[48] Precisely when this will in fact be the case is a question over which there has been a good deal of controversy. It seems clear that the second paragraph of Article 1 of Hague IX, stating that a place "cannot be bombarded solely because automatic submarine contact mines are anchored off the harbor," is neither generally indicative of an answer to this question nor satisfactory in itself. For example, would fortifications placed on adjacent coasts be enough to turn a nearby town or port into a defended area in the sense of Hague IX?

[49] See *Law of Naval Warfare*, Article 621d.—It should be made clear, however, that the "incapacity" of a naval force to enter and occupy an undefended coastal town or port may be the result of the mission upon which it is engaged at the time. If the military mission upon which the naval force is engaged does not permit entry and occupation a coastal town or port containing military objectives may be bombarded *even though undefended*. Hence the phrase "can be entered and occupied"—and used in the text above—must be understood as implying not only the absence of any defense but also a compatibility between entrance and occupation and the military mission assigned to the naval force.—In aerial warfare a city or town located well behind the front lines, i. e., in the hinterland or well outside the zone of combat, is certainly not open to entry, even though not itself possessing any defenses. Terminology drawn from land warfare becomes very misleading here and it is best to omit altogether the term undefended town, as did Article 24 of the unratified 1923 Rules of Aerial Warfare. The criterion to be used in reference to cities or towns in rear areas is that of the military objective, and any defenses located within the city or town are simply considered as military objectives. Hence a town containing *neither defenses of its own nor any other military objectives* is immune from bombardment. Some confusion on this score arose during World War II, when claims for immunity from air

With respect to the military objectives that may be made the target of lawful attack according to Article 2 of Hague IX, it would appear that recent developments have rendered this list unduly restrictive, and it can no longer be accepted as exhaustive. It is clear, for example, that communication systems used for military purposes may be bombarded by naval forces, even though not included in the list given in Hague IX. The same may be said for other objectives that belligerents have now come to recognize as forming legitimate targets for attack.[50]

---

bombardment were made on behalf of "undefended" cities located, in many instances, at considerable distances behind the combat zone. Not being open to immediate entry and occupation they were not accorded exemption from aerial bombardment if containing military objectives. The fact that these cities did not possess defenses of their own, nor even attempt to intercept aerial attackers, was not held to be decisive. These cases are reviewed by R. Y. Jennings ("Open Towns," *B. Y. I. L.*, 22 (1945), pp. 258–64) who observes: "There is no virtue in mere lack of defense. Unless accompanied by its corollary of freedom of entry the exemption of the undefended town would lead to the absurd result that a belligerent could secure the immunity of his production centres and lines of communication from lawful bombardment simply by omitting to defend them, and could thus concentrate all his arms for attack" (pp. 260–1). It does appear, however, that on several occasions during World War II immunity was claimed on the basis that the belligerent putting forth the claim was allegedly prepared to deny himself the use of all military resources within the city This raises a different question. In principle, it would seem, as Jennings points out, "that a belligerent may claim exemption for a town if he voluntarily ceases to use its resources for military purposes . . ." Nevertheless, the experience of World War II is of little guidance on this point, and there are no instances where such a claim was conceded. Certainly, the practical difficulties in the way of insuring that an enemy would in fact forego use of the military resources of a city would be very great. Besides, there is the further objection that even if such abstinence could be insured there could be no guarantee that the agreement would not be broken off at any time with the result that the belligerent accorded immunity would be able to place in use those resources preserved intact. But the other belligerent would then be confronted with the task of destroying those resources at a time when, for various reasons, he might be unable to do so.—Finally, a careful distinction should be drawn—for the purposes of aerial bombardment—between bombardment in the zone where land operations are proceeding and bombardment carried out against cities in the rear areas. Within the combat zone aerial bombardment is restricted only by the rule forbidding wanton destruction—e. g., in attacking cities open to entry by the land forces. This follows for the reason that the zone of combat is regarded as constituting one vast military objective.

[50] Though Article 5 of Hague IX certainly remains valid and obligates the commander of naval forces undertaking the bombardment either of defended or undefended places to take "all necessary measures . . . to spare as far as possible buildings devoted to religion, to the arts and sciences, or to charitable purposes, historic monuments, hospitals, and places where the sick or wounded are collected, on condition that they are not used at the same time for military purposes." The inhabitants have the duty of indicating such places by visible signs consisting of large stiff rectangular panels divided diagonally into two coloured triangular portions, the upper portion black, the lower portion white. The provisions of Article 5 have been generally recognized as applicable to aerial warfare as well. See *Law of Naval Warfare*, Article 622, and notes thereto, for the relevant provisions of the 1949 Geneva Convention for the Amelioration of the Condition of the Wounded and Sick in Armed Forces in the Field which deal with the protection of medical establishments and units as well as with the establishment of hospital zones and localities. Special note should also be taken of the provisions of the 1949 Geneva Convention Relative to The Protection of Civilian Persons in Time of War dealing with

But where the limits of the legitimate "military objective"—against which bombardment is lawful—are to be drawn is a question to which no precise answer can presently be given. It need hardly be stated that the outstanding feature of warfare in the twentieth century is the constant expansion of the military objective. The effects of this expansion have not been without substantial effect in broadening the scope of action permitted to belligerent naval forces in attacking the cities, towns and ports of an enemy. It is in aerial warfare that the effects of this expansion have proven the most far reaching though, and given the importance of aircraft as a component part of the naval forces of belligerents the problem of aerial bombardment deserves at least brief comment.

The developments to date in aerial warfare provide an impressive illustration of the limited results that may follow from the attempt to apply directly to a novel form of warfare the general principles of the law of war, and particularly the principle requiring that a distinction be drawn between combatants and non-combatants. It has been asserted time and again on high authority that the minimum restrictions upon aerial bombardment are that non-combatants must not be made the object of direct attack, such attack being unrelated to a military objective, and that attack for the purpose of terrorizing the civilian population is forbidden.[51] Yet the

---

the establishment of hospital, safety and so-called neutralized zones. Thus Article 14 of this Convention provides for the conclusion of agreements between the Parties to a conflict establishing "hospital and safety zones and localities so organized as to protect from the effects of war, wounded, sick and aged persons, children under fifteen, expectant mothers and mothers of children under seven." And Article 15 provides for the establishment, again only by mutual agreement, of neutralized zones intended to shelter from the effects of war "(a) wounded and sick combatants or non-combatants; (b) civilian persons who take no part in hostilities, and who, while they reside in the zones, perform no work of a military character." These provisions are indicative of the state to which the practices of belligerents, and particularly the practices of aerial bombardment, have reduced the combatant-non-combatant distinction. It is significant to note that those civilian persons able to enjoy the protection of neutralized zones must perform no work of a "military character." Presumably this would include—though the phrase is far from clear—all those working in factories producing war materials, at the very least a large percentage of the population.

Finally, passing note should be taken of Article 6 of Hague IX requiring that, military exigencies permitting, the commander of attacking naval forces "before commencing the bombardment, must do his utmost to warn the authorities." And see *Law of Naval Warfare*, Article 623. In effect, warning is dependent upon the discretion of the commander of the attacking naval or aerial forces, though whenever possible it should be given.

[51] *Law of Naval Warfare*, Article 621 b, c.—Article 22 of the 1923 Rules of Aerial Warfare stated: "Aerial bombardment for the purpose of terrorizing the civilian population, of destroying or damaging private property not of military character, or of injuring non-combatants, is prohibited." The principles embodied in Article 22 were subsequently reaffirmed on several occasions prior to World War II by the League of Nations and other international bodies. Further, they were given prominent expression in the military manuals of many states. During World War II the belligerents never failed to render verbal service to these principles, if only by resolutely denying that aerial raids were taken against non-military objectives or in order to terrorize the civilian population.

practical significance of these restrictions in their application to aerial bombardment ought not to be overestimated, particularly by drawing misleading analogies with other forms of warfare. In bombardment by land or by naval forces it may still prove possible to determine with some degree of assurance when the civilian population deliberately has been made the object of direct attack, such attack being unrelated to a military objective. In aerial bombardment the difficulties involved in reaching a similar determination are obviously far greater; so much greater, in fact, that in the absence of specific rules commanding the general agreement of states, and providing for the detailed regulation of aerial bombardment, the mere attempt to apply directly the general principle distinguishing between combatants and non-combatants must prove in its effects far more apparent than real.[52]

It should be made clear, therefore, that the ominous threat posed by aerial warfare is not simply a result of the failure to agree upon what constitutes a military objective, against which bombardment is permitted,

[52] This would appear to be one reason for the significant absence of war crimes trials in which the accused were charged and convicted of terror bombing undertaken against the civilian population. And although one of the charges of war crimes listed in Article 6 of the Charter of the International Military Tribunal at Nuremberg was "the wanton destruction of cities, towns, or villages, or devastation not justified by military necessity", none of the accused was convicted of deliberately ordering the bombardment of civilian populations. In the Einsatzgruppen Trial there is an interesting passage in the Tribunal's judgment which reads as follows:

> "A city is bombed for tactical purposes; communications are to be destroyed, railroads wrecked, ammunition plants demolished, factories razed, all for the purpose of impeding the military. In these operations it inevitably happens that non-military persons are killed. This is an incident, a grave incident to be sure, but an unavoidable corollary of battle action. The civilians are not individualized. The bomb falls, it is aimed at the railroad yards, houses along the tracks are hit and many of their occupants killed. But that is entirely different, both in fact and in law from an armed force marching up to these same railroad tracks, entering those houses abutting thereon, dragging out the men, women, and children and shooting them. (*U. S. v. Otto Ohlendorf et al.*) *Trials of War Criminals* 4 (1949), p. 467.

No doubt there is a difference in law between the deliberate killing of the civilian population by forces on land and the incidental—though unavoidable—injury to the civilian population through aerial bombardment of military objectives. But this difference does not do away with the consideration that the danger to the non-combatant population may be, in fact, far greater as a result of the "unintentional" injury inflicted by aerial bombardment than intentional acts committed by land forces. More important, however, there remains unanswered the question as to the methods of determining in practice when the civilian population has been made the deliberate object of attack by aerial bombardment. It is precisely the difficulties involved in reaching such a determination that has led Lauterpacht to admit that the practical importance of the prohibition against resorting to the bombing of the civilian population for the "mere purpose of terrorization . . . is of limited value. In most cases centres of civilian population will in any case constitute centres of communication or contain or be located in the vicinity of some objectives which the attacking belligerent will claim to be of military importance. In these cases the terrorization of the civilian population, however real in intention and effect, can plausibly be represented as being incidental to attack upon military objectives." "The Revision of the Law of War," p. 368.

399334—57——11

though of course this failure is itself one of considerable moment. Even if it were possible to assume substantial agreement today upon this latter question there would remain the problem of determining the limits of the "incidental" or "indirect" injury that may be inflicted upon the civilian population in the course of attacking such objectives from the air.[53]

Here again, analogies drawn from land or naval warfare are frequently resorted to whose relevance can only prove—at best—extremely limited. It is quite true that the immunity of non-combatants from the injurious effects of bombardment by land or naval forces has never been considered absolute. In land warfare those measures permitted within the immediate zone of military operations may afford very little protection to the civilian population located therein. In naval warfare a commander need not abstain from the bombardment of "undefended" coastal areas even though "unavoidable damage" may be inflicted upon the lives and property of the civilian population located in the near vicinity of military objectives.[54]

[53] The solution to these problems put forward in Article 24 of the draft 1923 Rules of Aerial Warfare may be summarized. Bombardment undertaken outside the immediate neighborhood of the operations of land forces (i. e., combat zone) was considered as legitimate only when "directed exclusively" at the following objectives: military forces; military works; military establishments or depots; factories constituting important and well known centres engaged in the manufacture of arms, ammunition, or distinctively military supplies; lines of communication or transportation used for military purposes. In addition, Article 24 stipulated that where these objectives are so situated that they cannot be bombarded without the "indiscriminate bombardment of the civilian population" aircraft must abstain from attacking them. This prohibition against "indiscriminate bombardment" is not made dependent upon the intent of the attacker, but simply upon whether it is in fact possible in a specific instance to bombard military objectives without indiscriminately bombing the civilian population in the near vicinity. The point raised is an important one even today, since experience seems to indicate that although it is next to impossible to determine when the civilian population has been made the *deliberate* object of attack, unrelated to a military objective, it is by no means impossible to determine when the civilian population has been indiscriminately bombarded in the course of attacking military objectives. Indeed, it seems reasonably clear that the so-called target-area bombings of World War II entailed the indiscriminate bombardment of the civilian population, even though the primary purpose was to strike at an enemy's military resources. It is submitted that on this decisive point Spaight (*op. cit.*, pp. 259 ff.) is—at best—confusing. On the one hand, he endorses the legality of target-area bombing by declaring that: "If in no other way than by target-area bombing can a belligerent destroy his enemy's armament centres and interrupt his enemy's process of munitionment, then target-area bombing cannot be considered to offend against the principles of the international law of war . . . . Military effectiveness has been the test and by that test target-area bombing passes muster" (p. 271). On the other hand, Spaight insists that: "nothing that has happened in the second World War has shaken the legal objection to indiscriminate bombing. Against that kind of war-waging international law still sets its face" (p. 277). Presumably, this approval of target-area bombing and disapproval of indiscriminate bombing has as its basis the belief that the latter is unlawful because it is deliberately aimed against the civilian population. But this opinion is misplaced, since indiscriminate bombardment need not depend upon the element of intent. Nor is it easy, in this connection, to follow Spaight's stricture that: "while target-area bombing comes close to the border-line of permissibility, atom bombing definitely oversteps it" (p. 276). The latter need not prove any more indiscriminate in its effects than the former.

[54] Hague IX, Article 2.

Generally speaking, however, these examples—taken from the older forms of warfare—applied only to limited areas, and even then have been regarded as exceptional departures from the normal rule. But in aerial warfare the potential area of bombardment operations has no limitations save that of the ever expanding concept of the military objective, and what has formerly been an exceptional situation now threatens to become a normal condition. Given these circumstances the problem of determining the limits of the "incidental" injury that may be inflicted upon the civilian population in the course of attacking military objectives become crucial. The failure to provide a concrete solution to this problem may well mean that from a practical point of view the general prohibition against making non-combatants the direct object of attack will prove no more than nominal. At the present time though there is no indication that any solution holding the possibility of imposing detailed and effective restraints upon belligerents is in sight.[55]

[55] Of necessity, the above remarks cut short a rather complicated development. But the essential outlines of this development have been presented. They may be summarized by stating that so long as uncertainty exists both as to the nature of the military objective against which aerial bombardment is permitted and the limits of the indirect injury that may be inflicted upon the civilian population in attacking such objectives the reaffirmation of general principles must unfortunately prove largely illusory. Thus it is of little use to suggest that the limits of the indirect injury permitted against non-combatants may be determined by weighing the military advantage to be gained against the injury that will be caused to non-combatants. If the experience of World War II is at all indicative of how belligerents will carry out this vague procedure it is clear that the scales will be weighted heavily in favor of military advantage. In fact, it would seem that this path easily leads to the justification of indiscriminate bombardment and the consequent obliteration of the combatant—non-combatant distinction.—In a penetrating criticism of the problems raised by aerial bombardment in World War II, Professor Stone (*op. cit.*, p. 630) writes that the protection afforded civilians against deliberate attack through aerial bombardment "when such 'incidental' attack is clearly licensed, is verbal merely . . ." and that even more important than the "deceptive futility" of the general prohibition against the deliberate attack on civilians is "that by preserving the confusion of issues it prevents any real approach to agreed legal regulation." The confusion, according to Stone, lies in the failure to distinguish between the "quasi-combatant workforce and genuine civilians," and to recognize that belligerents "do regard the morale of the enemy's quasi-combatant workforce as a military objective." His proposal, therefore, is to effect a separation between these two categories of the civilian population, acknowledge the belligerent's right to strike at the quasi-combatant workforce, and set up effective safeguards for other civilians. The practical difficulties in the way of this proposal—already made prior to World War II—are admittedly enormous when applied to the entire populations of states. At the very least it would be essential to provide clear criteria for distinguishing between those individuals engaged in work of a "military character" and those not so engaged. As already noted, Article 15 of the 1949 Geneva Convention on the Protection of Civilian Persons makes this same distinction with respect to "neutralized zones," though offering no criteria for applying it in practice. Furthermore, even if such criteria could be provided the resulting dislocation involved in so separating belligerent populations would be staggering. Finally, the guarantee of effective observance would require both continuous inspection by neutral parties and a rather large degree of mutual trust as between the belligerents. Recent experience indicates, however, that there is small reason for believing that either of these conditions could be readily obtained.

V. ENFORCEMENT OF THE LAW OF NAVAL WARFARE

There are a number of means available to belligerents for inducing compliance with the rules governing war's conduct.[1] In the event of unlawful behavior on the part of an enemy remedial action may take the form of direct protest and demand for compensation as well as for the punishment of individual offenders. Assuming, however, that the unlawful behavior in question has either been directly instigated by order of the enemy government, or at least performed with its sufferance, other measures will generally prove necessary.[2] The injured belligerent may direct an appeal to neutral states, requesting the latter to intervene for the purpose of bringing pressure to bear upon the delinquent party.[3] And although neutral states have no duty to protest against the commission of illegitimate acts of warfare it has been frequently asserted that they have a right to do so.[4] Finally, the injured belligerent may resort to repressive measures—sanctions—in reaction to unlawful behavior on the part of an enemy, measures which take the form of reprisals or of punishing captured offenders as war criminals. It is to these two latter categories of measures that attention will be directed in the following pages.

---

[1] See *Law of Naval Warfare*, Section 300, for an enumeration of the types of remedial action an injured belligerent may resort to in the event of unlawful behavior on the part of an enemy

[2] It may be, of course, that the primary purpose of protesting the unlawful behavior is to influence world opinion against the offending belligerent. Protests may be communicated direct to the enemy state, through a protecting power, a humanitarian organization acting in the capacity of a protecting power, or any state not participating in the conflict.

[3] Neutral states may provide their good offices to the belligerents with a view to settling the controversy.

[4] "There can be no doubt that neutral States . . . may, either singly, or jointly and collectively, exercise intervention whenever illegitimate acts or omissions of warfare are committed (1) by belligerent Governments, or (2) by members of belligerent forces, if the Governments concerned do not punish the offenders and compensate the sufferers. . . . But although neutral States have without doubt a *right* to intervene, they have no duty to do so." Oppenheim-Lauterpacht, *op. cit.*, pp. 559–60.—Experience has shown that it is particularly in warfare at sea that neutral states have been vigilant to protest against unlawful belligerent behavior, even though such behavior may only directly concern for the moment the other belligerent. The reason for this is the intimate relationship between observance of belligerent rights and observance of neutral rights, violations of the former being either concomitant with or leading to violations of the latter. Needless to say, the effect of such neutral intervention will be directly proportional to the strength of the neutral states and the vigor with which protests are pressed.

A. REPRISALS

As between belligerents reprisals are acts, otherwise unlawful, which are exceptionally permitted to one belligerent as a reaction against illegal acts of warfare committed by an enemy.[5] It is generally acknowledged that

[5] See *Law of Naval Warfare*, Section 310a. In a recent survey of the problem of war reprisals the latter are defined as "otherwise illegitimate acts of warfare which under certain conditions may legally be used by a belligerent against the enemy in order to deter the enemy from a repetition of his prior illegal acts and thus to enforce compliance with the generally recognized rules of war." A. R. Albrecht, "War Reprisals in the War Crimes Trials and in the Geneva Conventions of 1949," *A. J. I. L.*, 49 (1953), p. 590.—It is preferable that a distinction be drawn between 'reprisals', in the strict sense of the term, and other 'collective measures' a belligerent may take, particularly against the population of an occupied territory. Whereas both types of measures involve the principle of collective responsibility, the basis for and consequences of these two types of measures differ. The legal basis for a reprisal—in the strict sense—must be an unlawful act ordered or authorized by the enemy government, or at least an unlawful act performed by the armed forces of an enemy which—though performed without higher authorization—is not met with measures of repression and (possibly) of compensation. Illegitimate acts of warfare may be performed by individuals—particularly by the enemy population in occupied territory—which cannot be attributed either directly or indirectly to the enemy state. As against these latter acts a belligerent appears to be permitted by customary law to take collective measures of repression, so-called "collective sanctions." In the war crimes trials held after World War II there does not appear to have been a case involving reprisals in the strict sense. Instead, the trials involving so-called "reprisals" dealt in reality with the measures of repression taken by Germany against civilian populations in occupied territories for allegedly illegitimate acts of warfare performed by individual members of the population. In two trials a distinction was drawn between reprisals—in the strict sense—and other collective measures of repression. In the *Trial of Hans Rauter* the Netherlands Special Court of Cassation declared that: "In the proper sense one can speak of reprisals only when a State resorts, by means of its organs, to measures at variance with International Law, on account of the fact that its *opponent*—in this case the State with which it is at war—had begun . . . to commit acts contrary to International Law . . ." *Law Reports* . . . 14 (1949), p. 132. In the second trial an Italian Military Tribunal at Rome stated that "the right to take reprisals arises only in consequence of an illegal act which can be attributed, directly or indirectly, to a State. On the other hand, if civilian citizens of the occupied State commit criminal acts within the occupied territory which harm the occupying state, and if the search for the culprits proves to be a matter of considerable difficulty, partly owing to the solidarity of the population, it is permissible to impose collective sanctions." *In re Kappler*, [1948], *Annual Digest and Reports of Public International Law Cases*, (1948), Case No. 151, p. 472. At the same time, most tribunals—particularly the American and British—insisted upon referring to the collective measures taken against civilian populations in occupied territories as "reprisals," thereby obscuring the fact that there are important differences between these measures and the measures belligerents may take against illegitimate acts of warfare performed by the armed forces of a state under the command or authorization of the government. There is no intention here of undertaking an analysis of these trials. It is sufficient only to state that despite a lack of uniformity in certain respects over the restrictions imposed upon a belligerent occupant in taking hostages and so-called "reprisal prisoners" (and even of executing them in the event of absolute necessity), there was a general consensus that such collective measures were—in principle—permitted, but that Article 50 of the 1907 Hague Regulations (IV) demanded, at the very least, that a clear connection be established between the victims of collective measures and the illegal actions which gave rise to these measures. See, for example, the Hostages Trial (*Trial of Wilhelm List and Others*) *Trials of War Criminals*, 11 (1950), pp. 1249–53 and the Einsatzgruppen

since the purpose of reprisals is to induce compliance with the laws of war reprisals should not be resorted to merely for revenge but only as a last resort in order to compel an enemy to desist from unlawful behavior. For this reason the injured belligerent should attempt, whenever possible, to obtain cessation of the illegal acts (and appropriate redress) through means other than reprisals. It is always preferable that if measures of reprisal are finally resorted to the order to employ them should emanate from the highest authority. However, in circumstances of urgent necessity it is conceded that subordinate military commanders may, on their own initiative, order appropriate reprisals. In all cases, reprisals must be terminated once they have achieved their objective, which is to induce a belligerent to desist from unlawful conduct and to comply with the rules regulating the conduct of war.[6]

According to customary law measures of reprisal may be directed generally against the persons and property of an enemy. There need be no connection between the individuals performing the unlawful acts which give rise to the right of reprisal and the individuals made the objects of retaliatory measures. In a word, the essential principle characterizing measures of reprisal is that of collective responsibility. However, as between the parties to the 1949 Geneva Conventions, the individuals (and their property) who may be made the objects of reprisals have been substantially restricted. For these Conventions prohibit the taking of reprisals against any of the several categories of individuals afforded the protection of the Conventions.[7] But apart from the prohibitions contained in the 1949 Geneva Conventions

---

Trial (*U. S. v. Otto Ohlendorf et al.*), *Trials of War Criminals*, 4 (1950), pp. 460 ff. It is, in fact, precisely this latter requirement that clearly illustrates the difference in the legal consequences attached to illegitimate acts of warfare which may be attributed directly or indirectly to the state, and the legal consequences attached to similar acts which cannot be so attributed. In the former cases the reactions are properly termed reprisals, and according to customary law reprisals may be directed against any or all of the population or property of the offending state. In the latter cases (of so called "reprisals," or, more accurately, "collective sanctions") the objects of repression are much more narrowly circumscribed by the customary law. The distinction was well summarized in the *Kappler* case, cited above, where it was declared that the legal consequence of reprisals is that "the injured state may effect any interest of the injuring state by means of reprisals." But the "collective santions" other than reprisals, "arises only if a strict connection, either in respect to the locality or in respect of the service or office, can be established between the authors of an attack and the civilian population" (pp. 474–9).

[6] See *Law of Naval Warfare*, Section 310b. It must be noted that a large measure of uncertainty characterizes many of the customary rules, summarized above, allegedly regulating the resort to reprisals. Thus it is by no means clear—at least not from belligerent practice—that reprisals may be resorted to only when other means prove to be of no avail. In recent maritime warfare belligerents have but rarely sought to take other remedial measures against allegedly unlawful behavior before resorting to reprisals. In many instances reprisals have been taken at the first possible opportunity, the belligerents seemingly welcoming the opportunity presented by an enemy's actions to escape from rules found to be unduly restrictive (see pp. 30–1, 188–90).

[7] See *Law of Naval Warfare*, Section 310e and notes thereto.

the only remaining restriction [8] laid upon belligerents is that forbidding retaliatory measures which are out of all proportion to the unlawful behavior forming the basis of the reprisals.[9]

B. PUNISHMENT OF WAR CRIMINALS

War crimes may be defined as acts which violate the rules regulating the conduct of war and which result in the liability to punishment of the perpetrators.[10] According to customary international law belligerents have

---

[8] At least this is the only remaining restriction laid upon belligerents in resorting to reprisal action directed exclusively against enemy persons and property. Quite different considerations arise in the case of inter-belligerent reprisals which affect neutral rights (see pp. 188–90, 254–8). The restrictions placed upon inter-belligerent reprisals adversely affecting neutral interests—assuming the legitimacy, in principle, of such measures—ought not to be confused with the restrictions operative solely as between belligerents.

[9] See *Law of Naval Warfare*, Section 310c—This latter restriction has never been easy to apply, if only for the reason that measures of reprisal need not consist of the same measures as the original illegality. Nor has it ever been entirely clear whether the "proportionality" required of reprisals must be judged by the character of the enemy's unlawful behavior or by the measures necessary to compel the enemy to desist from such behavior. In the main, the weight of authority has tended to emphasize the former as providing the proper criterion for judging the "proportionality of reprisals." Yet there is a good deal to be said for the latter criterion, since the real purpose of reprisals is to compel an enemy to desist from unlawful behavior. For a review of the principle reprisal measures taken by the naval belligerents in the two World Wars, see pp. 296–315.

Prior to 1914 there had been no significant attempt to resort to retaliatory measures in maritime warfare for over a century, and it is not surprising to find reprisals being dismissed in the years preceding World War I as "an almost wholly obsolete form of action." *U. S. Naval War College, International Law Discussions, 1903*, p. 43. It need hardly be pointed out that this opinion reflected the extremely favorable conditions attending the conduct of naval hostilities during the nineteenth century. These conditions did not obtain during the two World Wars, and as a consequence the belligerent resort to reprisals formed one of the regular features of naval hostilities. Elsewhere (see pp. 30–2) the question has been raised as to what extent the reprisal structure erected by the belligerents may be considered as having served a "legislative" function, i. e. of subverting the traditional law, rather than an enforcement function. Certainly this question admits of no easy and sweeping answer, and although it is quite clear that in numerous instances belligerent reprisals have succeeded in replacing traditional rules, in other instances the effect of reprisals upon the traditional law is still far from apparent. Even greater caution must be exercised in evaluating the effects of reprisal measures bearing adversely upon neutral rights (see pp. 193–5, 315–7).

[10] See *Law of Naval Warfare*, Section 320 for a definition and an enumeration of representative war crimes. Although, in the main, war crimes have reference to illegal acts of warfare committed by members of the armed forces of belligerents, it should be noted that war crimes may be committed by civilians as well. Generally speaking, the classification of an act as a war crime has been held to follow from the fact that the act performed has a direct relation to the conduct of war and, at the same time, is prohibited by the law of war. War crimes in the narrow and traditional sense, as defined above, are to be clearly distinguished from so called 'crimes against peace,' i. e., acts which consist in the planning, preparation, initiation or waging of an unlawful war. The distinction between 'crimes against peace' and war crimes in the narrow sense (as well as the distinction between 'crimes against humanity,' and war crimes) was initially set forth in Article 6 of the Charter of the International Military Tribunal at

the obligation to punish their own nationals found violating the law of war and the right—in principle—to punish captured enemy individuals who have committed similar acts.[11] Prior to World War II, however,

Nuremberg, and followed by the American military tribunals in the 'subsequent Nuremberg proceedings' as well as by the International Military Tribunal for the Far East (Tokyo Tribunal). In recent years the term war crimes has been used not infrequently to refer to 'crimes against peace' (and 'crimes against humanity') in addition to violations of the rules governing war's conduct. Unfortunately, one result of this usage has been to obscure the fact that there is no novelty attached either to the concept of war crimes—in the narrow sense—or to the punishment of individuals who violate the rules regulating the conduct of war. So far as war crimes in the traditional sense are concerned, the novelty of the post World War II period must rather be found in the number of enemy individuals charged with war crimes, in the vigor with which they were tried and punished, in the development of the rules governing the procedure of war crimes tribunals, and—very important—in the marked extension of the limits of individual responsibility for violations of the laws of war. A lucid review of state practice prior to World War II with respect to war crimes is given by Lord Wright, *History of The United Nations War Crimes Commission and the Development of the Law of War* (1948), pp. 40–86. The literature to which World War II developments have given rise is vast and—as might be expected—frequently controversial in character. Perhaps the most useful source for the decisions of war crimes tribunals in this later period is the *Law Reports of Trials of War Criminals*, consisting of 15 volumes, and selected and prepared by the United Nations War Crimes Commission over the years 1946–49. Volume 15 contains a systematic analysis and summary of the 89 representative decisions (which do not include, however, the trials of the major war criminals before the Nuremberg and Tokyo International Military Tribunals) reported in the first 14 volumes. In the period following the termination of hostilities in 1945 the United States alone conducted 956 war crimes trials involving over 3,000 defendants.

[11] Provided the most rudimentary requirements were fulfilled, the customary law traditionally permitted each belligerent to establish its own system of tribunals, to create its own procedure to govern the trial of war criminals, and to impose whatever penalties it deemed just upon individuals found to have committed war crimes. This was, at least, the situation that prevailed prior to World War II, belligerents having only the obligation—under international law—to refrain from imposing punishment upon captured members of an enemy's armed forces accused of war crimes without first granting the accused the benefit of a "trial." However, as a result of state practice during and following the second World War, and in consequence of obligations undertaken in the 1949 Geneva Convention Relative to the Treatment of Prisoners of War, the situation formerly prevailing with respect to the trial of captured enemy personnel accused of war crimes has been substantially altered. The cumulative effect of these recent developments has been to impose upon belligerents the obligation to accord the accused certain minimum requirements of a "fair trial." These procedural requirements of a fair trial were originally set forth in section IV of the Charter of the International Military Tribunal at Nuremberg and subsequently endorsed by other war crimes tribunals—national and international. They provide that the accused be informed of the charges made against him in a language he understands, that he have adequate time to prepare his defense, that he have aid of counsel, that he be permitted to attend trial and to give evidence, and that he have an interpreter if needed.—The 1949 Geneva Convention on prisoners of war provides—Article 102—that a prisoner of war "can be validly sentenced only if the sentence has been pronounced by the same courts according to the same procedure as in the case of members of the armed forces of the Detaining Power, and if, furthermore, the provisions of the present Chapter have been observed." The effect of this provision is to guarantee enemy prisoners on trial for war crimes the minimum requirements of a fair trial, summarized above. However, if a state goes beyond these minimum requirements for members of its own armed forces, then it must grant the same procedure to prisoners of war on trial for war crimes.—Finally, it may be noted that in reviewing

some doubt had existed as to whether or not a belligerent was entitled to exercise jurisdiction over individuals accused of war crimes when the acts in question were not performed either on the territory of the belligerent or against its nationals. But in the light of recent practice it now appears clear that the right of a belligerent to exercise such jurisdiction is limited neither to offenses having a particular geographical location nor to offenses committed against the nationals of the belligerent claiming jurisdiction.[12] In addition, there is no rule of customary law preventing a belligerent from trying and punishing war criminals during the period following the termination of active hostilities but prior to the conclusion of a peace treaty, though the past practice of states has not been to continue proceedings against individuals accused of war crimes once peace has been re-established.[13]

---

the nature of the penalties imposed upon war criminals by Allied courts and tribunals after World War II, one authoritative source has concluded that "despite the fact that international law has previously permitted the death sentence to be passed for any war crime, some kind of international practice is growing according to which Allied Courts, apart from avoiding inhumane punishment, have themselves attempted to make the punishment fit the crime; any habitual practice of this kind would tend in time to modify the general rule that any war crime is punishable by death." *Law Reports . . .* 15 (1949), p. 201.

[12] It is generally agreed that post World War II practice has firmly established the so-called principle of "universality of jurisdiction over war crimes," thereby permitting belligerents to exercise jurisdiction over individuals accused of war crimes without regard to the place where an offense was committed or to the nationality of the victims. In its most general form this principle might well be interpreted to permit neutral states to try and punish war criminals who fall under their control. But there is no record of neutral states making such an attempt, and the right of neutrals to do so remains doubtful.

[13] "We cannot say that there is no authority to convene a (military) commission after hostilities have ended to try violations of the Law of War committed before their cessation, at least until peace has been officially recognized by treaty or proclamation of the political branch of the Government. In fact, in most instances the practical administration of the system of military justice under the Law of War would fail if such authority were thought to end with the cessation of hostilities. For only after their cessation could the greater number of offenders and the principal ones be apprehended and subjected to trial." *In re Yamashita*, 327 U. S. 1 (1946). Of course, an armistice agreement terminating hostilities may itself make provision for the trial of war criminals. But if it does not belligerents may nevertheless prosecute those enemy individuals accused of war crimes who fall under their control. Following World War II the trial of German nationals accused of war crimes before Allied courts and tribunals was based not only upon the customary right of belligerents to try and punish violators in their tribunals but also upon the unconditional surrender of Germany and the assumption of supreme authority over Germany by the four occupant Powers (the United States, Great Britain, France and the Soviet Union). The legal basis for the trial of Japanese war criminals was expressly provided for in the armistice terms by which Japan unconditionally surrendered to the victorious United Nations. On the other hand, the effect of a peace treaty is to bring to a close the right to prosecute war criminals, unless the treaty of peace itself makes express provision to the contrary. Such provision was made after World War I in Articles 227 and 228 of the Treaty of Versailles. And in the 1947 peace treaties concluded between the Allied and Associated Powers and Bulgaria, Finland, Rumania, and Italy, provision was also made for the trial of persons accused of committing war crimes (as well as crimes against peace and crimes against humanity).

It is an interesting fact that among the war crimes trials held during and since the second World War only a relatively small number concerned violations of rules regulating the actual conduct of hostilities.[14] In part, this may be explained by a reluctance to try members of the armed forces of the defeated states for the violation of rules whose status is no longer a matter of certainty.[15] In part, the dearth of trials concerned with infractions of the rules regulating the actual conduct of hostilities may be attributed to the conviction that where both sides in a conflict openly departed from the established law, the requirements of justice forbade the prosecution of only those who happened to be on the defeated side.[16]

There is little question, however, but that the commission of certain acts during the course of hostilities at sea must continue to be regarded as resulting—in the absence of special reasons to the contrary—in the individual (criminal) responsibility of the perpetrators. The unnecessary use of force particularly as against the merchant vessels of an enemy, the denial of quarter at sea, the firing upon survivors of sunken ships, the failure to search out and make provision for the survivors of sunken vessels when military interests so permit, the deliberate attack upon hospital vessels or other vessels granted special immunity, and the misuse of the Red Cross emblem constitute a summary of only the more important acts the com-

---

[14] So far as naval hostilities are concerned, these reported trials have all been cited in a previous section dealing with the attack upon and destruction of enemy vessels (see pp. 70–3). There are no records at all of trials relating to illegitimate conduct in aerial warfare. *Law Reports* . . . 15 (1949), pp. 109–12. The great bulk of the war crimes trials dealt instead with offenses committed against prisoners of war and the civilian inhabitants of occupied territory.

[15] The American military tribunal in the I. G. Farben Trial took note of this point by stating that: "It must be admitted that there exist many areas of grave uncertainty concerning the laws and customs of war . . . Technical advancement in the weapons and tactics used in the actual waging of war may have been made obsolete, in some respects, or may have rendered inapplicable, some of the Hague Regulations having to do with the actual conduct of hostilities and what is considered legitimate warfare. But these uncertainties relate principally to military and naval operations proper and the manner in which they shall be conducted." (*Trial of Carl Krauch and Twenty Two Others*), *Law Reports* . . . 10 (1949), pp. 48–9.

[16] It was this consideration, among others, that the International Military Tribunal gave expression to in refusing to assess the sentence of Admiral Doenitz "on the ground of his breaches of the international law of submarine warfare." Elsewhere (see p. 302(n)) it is submitted that in so far as the "facts" upon which the Tribunal allegedley based this aspect of the judgment were held to justify refusal of sentence for the sinking without warning of *neutral* merchant vessels—serious objections must be raised. With respect to the facts held to justify refusal of sentence for the sinking without warning of *enemy* merchant vessels the matter is admittedly quite different (see pp. 67–9). There are no reported trials of naval personnel for the act of having attacked enemy merchant vessels without first attempting to seize such vessels and put passengers and crew in a place of safety before resorting to destruction. The argument that this failure to try individuals for the attack without warning of enemy merchant vessels points to the desuetude of the traditional rules—at least as these rules apply to submarine and aircraft—is difficult to accept, however.

mission of which may result in a liability to punishment upon capture by an enemy.[17]

Where individuals have been charged with the commission of war crimes the principal difficulty has been that of determining what recognition ought to be given the defense plea that the acts in question were performed either by order of the belligerent government or on the command of a superior.[18] Prior to World War II the attitude of states—and the opinions of writers on the law of war—had varied with respect to the treatment to be accorded the plea of superior orders, though a relatively strong case may be made on behalf of the assertion that illegitimate acts of warfare performed by direct order of the state were not considered to result in the individual responsibility of those performing such acts.[19]

A decided change from earlier opinion and practice occurred both during and after the 1939 war. While that conflict was still in progress several of the belligerents amended their military manuals to provide that a violation of the law of war is not deprived of its character of a war crime, and does not confer upon the actor immunity from punishment, simply for the reason that it was performed in response to the order of a belligerent government

17 And quite apart from the liability incurred as a result of misconduct during the course of naval hostilities there is—of course—a further liability for those acts involving the maltreatment of the sick, wounded and shipwrecked members of an emeny's armed forces carried on board belligerent warships (see pp. 135–7, for a discussion of liability resulting from "grave breaches" of the 1949 Geneva Convention on the treatment of the wounded, sick and shipwrecked).

18 The plea that illegitimate acts of war were perforned for reasons of military (or "operational") necessity has already been considered in another connection (see pp. 36–7).

19 The issues raised by the above statement are rather complicated, and their relevance to this study is distinctly limited—particularly in view of World War II practice. Nevertheless, some comment—however brief—is required. It will be noted, to begin with, that a distinction is drawn between illegitimate acts of warfare performed by order of the state and similar acts performed by command of a superior. It is very doubtful whether the plea of superior orders (i. e., whether or not the plea of superior orders should be accepted as a defense) has ever been directly or indirectly regulated by international law. Instead, the acceptance or rejection of this plea has been a matter left by international law to the discretion of the individual states. On the other hand, the fact that an illegitimate act of warfare was performed by order of the state (i. e., was an "act of state") was generally regarded as sufficient to divest the act of its character as a war crime (acts of espionage and war treason formed clear exceptions to the rule) according to international law. Against those acts which had the character of acts of state the injured state could take collective sanctions—i. e., reprisals—but international law was generally considered as excluding the individual (criminal) liability of the perpetrators. This followed from the rule of general international law which normally forbade one state from exercising jurisdiction in its courts over the acts of another state, i. e., from exercising jurisdiction over individuals performing acts possessing the character of acts of state. As will presently be noted, however, recent practice appears to have firmly established that the act of state doctrine is no longer applicable to acts having the character of violations of the law of war; the fact that an individual has performed an illegitimate act of warfare by order of the state does not deprive the act of its character as a war crime—though, of course, this circumstance may serve to mitigate punishment.

or a superior.[20] In the period following the termination of hostilities Allied courts and tribunals charged with the task of trying individuals accused of war crimes have uniformly endorsed this principle.[21]

At the same time, it has been the consensus of judicial opinion that in order to establish responsibility the person must know, or have reason to know, that the act he is ordered to perform is unlawful under international law.[22] Thus if the rule that allegedly has been violated is itself controversial or if—though of unquestioned validity—the rule has been departed from under the conviction that such departure forms a legitimate measure

---

[20] Both the American and British field manuals were altered in 1944. The 1944 change to the U. S. Army's *Rules of Land Warfare* (paragraph 345) provided, however, that if violations of the laws of war were performed by order of a belligerent government or a superior this fact could be "taken into consideration in determining culpability, either by way of defense or in mitigation of punishment." On the other hand, the British Manual of Military Law (paragraph 443) allowed the plea of superior orders to operate only as a factor in the mitigation of punishment, though liability was made dependent upon a knowledge that the act performed was clearly unlawful. Subsequently, Article 8 of the Charter of the International Military Tribunal declared that: "The fact that the defendant acted pursuant to order of his government or of a superior shall not free him from responsibility, but may be considered in mitigation of punishment if the Tribunal determines that justice so requires." A substantially similar provision formed a part of the Charter of the International Military Tribunal For the Far East and of the various United States theatre regulations governing the trial and punishment of individuals accused of war crimes.

[21] A summary of these decisions is given in *Law Reports* . . . 15 (1949), pp. 157–60.

[22] In the *Peleus Trial* (*Law Reports* . . . 1 (1947), pp. 1–21) the defendants, other than the captain (whose defense was "operational necessity," see p. 73(n)), pleaded the defense of superior orders. It was established during the course of the trial, held before a British Military Court sitting at Hamburg, that most of the accused had known that the captain's command to fire at helpless survivors struggling in the water—the war crime for which they were jointly charged—was not a lawful command. As against the defense argument that many rules of international law were vague and uncertain the Judge Advocate ruled "that if this were a case which involved the careful consideration of the question whether or not the command to fire at helpless survivors struggling in the water was lawful in International Law, the Court might well think that it would not be fair to hold any of the subordinates accused in this case responsible for what they were alleged to have done. In the present case, however, it must have been obvious to the most rudimentary intelligence that it was not a lawful command," (pp. 14–5). All of the accused were convicted by the Court.

The requirement of knowledge has been given prominence in recent formulations of the plea of superior orders in military manuals. See *Law of Naval Warfare*, Section 330b (1). And paragraph 509 of the recently revised U. S. Army *Rules of Land Warfare* declares:

"The fact that the law of war has been violated pursuant to an order of a superior authority, whether military or civil, does not deprive the act in question of its character of a war crime, nor does it constitute a defense in the trial of an accused individual, unless he did not know and could not reasonably have been expected to know that the act ordered was unlawful. In all cases where the order is held not to constitute a defense to an allegation of war crime, the fact that the individual was acting pursuant to orders may be considered in mitigation of punishment.

"In considering the question whether a superior order constitutes a valid defense, the court shall take into consideration the fact that obedience to lawful military orders is the duty of

of reprisal, either circumstance may prove sufficient to relieve the actor of responsibility[23] Furthermore, it would appear that if an individual though knowing that the act he has been ordered to perform is unlawful nevertheless has acted under duress this circumstance may be taken into consideration either by way of defense or in mitigation of punishment.[24]

What has been termed the "inverse case" [25] of superior orders concerns the scope of the responsibility commanding officers must bear for illegiti-

---

every member of the armed forces; that the latter cannot be expected, in conditions of war discipline, to weigh scrupulously the legal merits of the order received; that certain rules of warfare may be controversial; or that an act otherwise amounting to a war crime may be done in obedience to orders conceived as a measure of reprisal. At the same time it must be borne in mind that members of the Armed Forces are bound to obey only lawful orders."

[23] Apart from the more obvious objections that have been urged against the practice of holding individuals responsible for unlawful acts carried out in pursuance of an order by a superior authority, the two circumstances cited above have been singled out for special attention by critics. Yet a survey of the war crimes trials held after World War II indicates that the uncertainty of the law was seldom involved, the one major exception being the cases involving 'collective measures' taken against occupied populations. It may also be observed that in the few trials concerning violations of the rules regulating hostilities at sea there are no instances in which individuals were punished for the violation of controversial rules or for the violation of rules committed in the belief that such violations constituted instead legitimate measures of reprisal. Thus there was never any pretense to the effect that the so-called "Laconia Order" (see pp. 72–3) represented a legitimate reprisal measure.

[24] See *Law of Naval Warfare*, Section 330b (1), the last sentence of which corresponds to the statement made in the text above—and notes thereto.—One may be said to act under duress if the act is performed under an immediate threat—particularly a threat of physical coercion—in the event of noncompliance with the order. But the threat must be, in the words of one tribunal, "imminent, real and inevitable," it must pose a danger "both serious and irreparable." The Einsatzgruppen Case (*U. S. v. Otto Ohlendorf, et al.*) *Trial of War Criminals*, 4 (1950), p. 480. A review of the trials in which the plea of duress was considered does not reveal, however, any marked uniformity in the treatment of the plea. Courts differed over those precise circumstances that could be held to justify the plea of duress; and they also differed over whether duress, even when admitted in principle, could serve only in mitigation of punishment or as a complete defense against the charge of having committed a war crime. The decisions bearing upon the plea of duress have been summarized in the following manner:

"The general view seems . . . to be that duress may prove a defense if (a) the act charged was done to avoid an immediate danger both serious and irreparable; (b) there was no other adequate means of escape; (c) the remedy was disproportionate to the evil. According to the decision in the *Krupp Trial*, these tests are to be applied according to the facts as they were honestly believed to exist by the accused. Finally, if the facts do not warrant the successful pleading of duress as a defense, they may constitute an argument in mitigation of punishment." *Law Reports* . . . 15 (1949), p. 174.

[25] See Oppenheim-Lauterpacht (*op. cit.*, p. 572) where responsibility of the nature discussed above is said to arise "directly and undeniably, when the acts in question [i. e., unlawful acts of subordinates] have been committed in pursuance of an order of the commander concerned, or if he has culpably failed to take the necessary measures to prevent or suppress them. The failure to do so raises the presumption—which for the sake of the effectiveness of the law cannot be regarded as easily rebuttable—of authorization, encouragement, connivance, acquiescence, or subsequent ratification of the criminal acts."

mate acts of warfare performed by subordinates.[26] There is no question but that military commanders are liable for the unlawful acts they have ordered or authorized subordinates to perform. Equally well established is the responsibility of military commanders for the illegal acts of subordinates which the former had knowledge of but failed to take adequate measures to control. By the failure to suppress unlawful acts of subordinates as are known to military commanders, the presumption of acquiescence in these acts must arise. It is clear, therefore, that the responsibility of commanders can result solely from inaction, though here it is inaction based upon a knowledge that unlawful acts of subordinates have been committed. Finally, it would appear that the responsibility military commanders must bear for the acts of subordinates implies a further duty to take reasonable measures to insure that the latter will refrain from unlawful behavior, and, should unlawful behavior nevertheless occur, to discover and control the misconduct of subordinates. Where the failure to take precautionary or preventive measures is palpable and gross military commanders have been held liable for the unlawful behavior of subordinates even though without actual knowledge of such behavior.[27]

---

[26] The numerous cases that have come before war crimes tribunals involving the responsibility of military commanders for acts of subordinates are reviewed in *Law Reports* . . 15 (1949), pp. 65–78. See also *Law of Naval Warfare*, Section 330b (2) and notes thereto. Paragraph 501 of the U. S. Army *Rules of Land Warfare* reads:

"In some cases, military commanders may be responsible for war crimes committed by subordinate members of the armed forces, or other persons subject to their control. Thus, for instance, when troops commit massacres and atrocities against the civilian population of occupied territory or against prisoners of war, the responsibility may rest not only with the actual perpetrators but also with the commander. Such a responsibility arises directly when the acts in question have been committed in pursuance of an order of the commander concerned. The commander is also responsible if he has actual knowledge, or should have knowledge, through reports received by him or through other means, that troops or other persons subject to his control are about to commit or have committed a war crime and he fails to take the necessary and reasonable steps to ensure compliance with the law of war or to punish violators thereof."

[27] The statements made in the text above are believed to represent a reasonably accurate summary of the numerous—and occasionally conflicting—decisions relating to the scope of a commanding officer's responsibility for acts of subordinates. A review of these decisions indicates that perhaps the central issue giving rise to uncertainty—and controversy—has been the liability incurred by military commanders who are unaware of the offenses committed by subordinates but who have failed to take reasonable measures to prevent such offenses and—once committed—have made little effort to discover and control them. In this connection the *Trial of General Yamashita* (*Law Reports* 4 (1948), pp. 1–95) is instructive. Tried before an American Military Commission, General Yamashita was charged and convicted of failing "to discharge his duty as commander to control the operations of the members of his command, permitting them to commit brutal atrocities and other high crimes against people of the United States and of its allies and dependencies, particularly the Philippines . ." (3–4). Although the prosecution asserted that Yamashita must have known of, and permitted, the offenses committed by his troops, it was further insisted that he had—in any event—the duty to "discover and control" these offenses once they were committed, and failed to do so. A similar view was taken by the Commission in its findings. In its review of the case the Supreme

Court emphasized that a commanding officer, particularly in occupied territory, is responsible for the behavior of his troops. *In re Yamashita*, 326 U. S. 1 (1946). But the Court neither expressly accepted nor rejected the findings of the Military Commission that Yamashita, even in the absence of knowledge, had the duty to "discover and control" illegal acts of subordinates, and could be held liable for the failure to carry out this duty. Instead, the Court considered itself as bound by the finding of the Commission on the question of fact, namely, that Yamashita had known of the offenses being committed by his troops. In view of the state of disorganization and breakdown of communications in the Philippines at the time, this was a hotly disputed question—and one of the principal targets of critics of the trial. A further criticism was that even if Yamashita had known of the atrocities being committed by his troops he could not have brought a stop to this behavior since American military operations prevented him from exercising effective control over the members of his command.

In the German High Command Trial (*Trial of Wilhelm Von Leeb and Thirteen Others, Law Reports* . . . 12 (1949), pp. 71, 74–9, 105–12) the tribunal assumed, with respect to some of the accused, that actual knowledge was essential to establish responsibility for acts of subordinates. For other defendants, however, it was maintained that the accused "should have had knowledge" of the offenses, that they had a duty to find out that offenses were being committed and to stop them.—And in the Hostages Trial (*Trial of Wilhelm List and Others, Law Reports* . . . 8 (1949), p. 71) the tribunal declared that a Commanding General ". . . is charged with notice of occurrences taking place within that territory. He may require adequate reports of all occurrences that come within the scope of his power and, if such reports are incomplete or otherwise inadequate, he is obliged to require supplementary reports to apprise him of all pertinent facts. If he fails to require and obtain complete information, the dereliction of duty rests upon him and he is in no position to plead his own dereliction as a defense."

PART TWO

399334—57——12

VI. NEUTRALITY AND THE LEGAL POSITION OF WAR

A. THE TRADITIONAL RELATIONSHIP BETWEEN WAR AND NEUTRALITY

The changes that have marked the international order since the advent of the first World War undoubtedly have had a substantial effect upon the institution of neutrality. At the same time the task of evaluating this effect admits of no easy and wholly satisfactory solution. If anything, it seems reasonably clear that the present status of neutrality is, and will probably remain for some time to come, a matter over which considerable controversy and divergence of opinion can be expected.

In part, this uncertainty must be attributed to the changed position of war in international law. It has already been observed [1] that prior to World War I, at least, the act of resorting to war was considered as neither legal nor illegal but simply a fact, situation or event, occurring periodically in state relations. According to this interpretation states retained the liberty under customary international law to resort to war whenever they deemed such action to be expedient. It followed that the decision by third states to participate or to refrain from participating in war was, as the initial resort to war itself, "not a matter for International Law but for international politics." [2] Once war had broken out, third states, not immediately involved in the hostilities, were neither under a duty to participate nor to refrain from participating in the hostilities. Similarly, belligerents were at liberty to recognize or to refuse to recognize a status of non-participation on the part of third states.

Those states which refrained from participating in a war occupied a status of neutrality. The legal consequence of such non-participation, however, may be found in the fact that it served to bring into operation certain rules, rules presupposing an equality of legal status as between the belligerents with respect to the war itself, hence the duty of non-participants to fulfill their duties and to exercise their rights in an impartial manner toward belligerents. These rules—which may be termed the traditional law of neutrality—remained operative for the duration of a war or until such time as a neutral state abandoned its position of non-participation—either by attacking one of the belligerents or by being attacked by a belligerent.[3]

---

[1] See pp. 3–4.

[2] Oppenheim-Lauterpacht, *op. cit.*, p. 653.

[3] See pp. 196–202 for an analysis of the traditional concept of neutrality as well as of the problems relating to the commencement and termination of this legal status.

Given the obvious and close relationship between the position of war under customary international law and the traditional legal institution of neutrality, it must appear on first consideration that once the resort to war has been generally forbidden to states, neutrality—or, at the very least, the specific consequences attached to a status of non-participation in war by the traditional law—must be deprived of further legal justification.[4] This conclusion, that the foundations of the traditional system of neutrality have been overturned, appears particularly compelling to those who compare the obligations laid upon non-participants by the traditional system with the obligations incurred by member states within the system of collective security established by the Charter of the United Nations. Indeed, in view of recent developments many observers have ventured so far as to question the continued feasibility of referring to the traditional legal institution of neutrality at all save in the historical sense.

But although the nature of the relationship traditionally obtaining between war and neutrality seems clear enough, the precise changes effected in neutrality by the altered position of war are not as readily apparent as has been frequently assumed. In order to analyze these changes more carefully it is useful to consider the obligations imposed and the rights conferred at present upon third states during a war in which they are not immediately and directly involved as active participants. These obligations and rights may be considered both from the point of view of the General Treaty For The Renunciation of War (the so-called Pact of Paris or Kellogg-Briand Pact) and from the point of view of the Charter of the United Nations.

B. NEUTRALITY AND THE GENERAL TREATY FOR THE RENUNCIATION OF WAR

According to the provisions of the General Treaty For the Renunciation of War and, it may be assumed, according to present general international law,[5] the resort to war is permitted to states only in the following circum-

[4] ". . . the principle explanation and justification of the modern law of neutrality, conceived as an attitude of absolute impartiality, has now disappeared. That explanation consisted in the fact that, until the First World War, the right to wage war constituted an unlimited prerogative right of sovereign States; no neutral State, therefore, could arrogate to itself the right to pass judgment on the legality of a war and to shape its conduct accordingly. The question simply did not arise. In this respect the position has undergone a fundamental change. The unlimited right of war is no longer a prerogative of the sovereign State. International law now recognizes that a State may act unlawfully by the very act of declaring or going to war. It admits the distinction between wars which are lawful and those which are not. To that extent it has re-established the historic foundations of qualified—discriminatory and discriminating—neutrality." Lauterpacht, "The Limits of the Operation of the Law of War," p. 237.

[5] A note on terminology may be in order here. The term "general" international law refers to rules binding upon all states and is to be contrasted with "particular" international law, which refers to rules regulating the behavior only of certain states. Although it is possible that both general and particular international law can consist of rules that are either customary

stances: as a collective enforcement measure taken in accordance with the obligations incurred within a general system of collective security, as a measure of self-defense against a prior—and unlawful—resort to war, and as a measure of collective defense taken on behalf of a state waging a lawful war of self-defense.[6] Thus, apart from the obligations resulting from membership in the United Nations, states may now be considered as generally forbidden to resort to war except as a measure of individual or collective defense against a previous—and thereby unlawful—resort to war.[7]

What, then, are the possible effects upon the institution of neutrality brought about by this transformation in the legal position of war? It is clear, to begin with, that under the General Treaty For the Renunciation of

---

or conventional in origin, it is usual to associate general international law with rules of a customary origin and particular international law with rules of a conventional character. This practice is seldom misleading. There may be significant exceptions, however, especially with respect to conventional rules. Thus the almost universal adherence of states to the General Treaty for the Renunciation of War, and the absence of any time limit set upon the operation of its provisions, serve to give the rules contained therein a character closely akin to that of general international law. In view of this fact the question as to whether or not the position of war under *customary* international law has undergone change has been deprived, in large measure, of its former significance. In this connection, however, it is submitted that the correct view is that the legal position of war under customary law does not remain unaltered, and that customary international law may now be considered as restricting the liberty of states to resort to war in a manner substantially identical with the provisions contained in the General Treaty for the Renunciation of War. But this latter point need not be pressed.

6 The Preamble, in part, and the first two Articles of this Treaty, signed August 27, 1928, read as follows:

"Convinced that all changes in their relations with one another should be sought only by pacific means and be the result of a peaceful and orderly process, and that any signatory Power which shall hereafter seek to promote its national interests by resort to war shall be denied the benefits of this Treaty;

I The High Contracting Parties solemnly declare in the names of their respective peoples that they condemn recourse to war for the solution of international controversies, and renounce it as an instrument of national policy with one another.

II The High Contracting Parties agree that the settlement or solution of all disputes or conflicts, of whatever nature or of whatever origin they may be, which may arise among them, shall never be sought except by pacific means."

7 In Article I of the Pact of Paris war is renounced as "an instrument of national policy." However, it is clear that enforcement measures taken under then existing collective security arrangements (principally, measures taken under Article 16 of the Covenant of the League of Nations), and having the character of war, constituted a category of measures permitted by the Pact. It is equally clear that enforcement measures taken under Chapter VII of the United Nations Charter fall within this same permitted category.—The right of self-defense is a necessary consequence of the Pact and was so recognized by the contracting parties at the time of signature. The statement in the Pact's Preamble, that "any signatory Power which shall hereafter seek to promote its national interests by resort to war shall be denied the benefits furnished by this Treaty," has been interpreted as permitting other contracting parties the right to assist the state acting in self-defense. Thus in declaring war upon Germany in September 1939 Great Britain and France claimed to exercise a right conferred upon them by the Pact. In this latter respect the similarity between the General Treaty For The Renunciation of War and Article 51 of the United Nations Charter should be noted. (See pp. 177–9).

War there is neither an obligation on the part of third states to abandon a status of non-participation in a war unlawfully initiated nor an obligation to abandon any of the rights and duties attached to the status of non-participation by the traditional law of neutrality. To the extent that states have not incurred obligations in excess of those imposed by the Pact of Paris there seems little question but that non-participants in a war may continue to invoke the traditional law of neutrality.

At the same time, by resorting to war in violation of its obligations under the General Treaty For the Renunciation of War a state violates the rights of all other contracting Parties. The latter are thereby entitled not only to resort to war against the state so violating its obligations; they are also entitled to take measures of reprisal against the aggressor that may not involve active participation in hostilities but that may involve a departure from those duties otherwise imposed upon non-participants by the traditional law of neutrality.[8] Thus the measures of discrimination taken against Germany in 1940–41 by the United States, although the United States remained at the time a non-participant in the war, were partially justified as measures of reprisal permitted to this country in consequence of Germany's resort to war in alleged violation of the Pact of Paris.[9]

---

[8] Admittedly, the position taken above has not been accepted by many writers. The Pact of Paris does not expressly provide that contracting Parties may take discriminatory measures against a violator of its provisions. It has therefore been claimed that the only benefit furnished by the Treaty, which may be denied to states violating the Treaty's provisions, is the benefit of not being made the object of a resort to war by the other contracting Parties. However, states not participating in a war unlawfully initiated must observe a strict impartiality.—The opposing view, given expression in the text, has been formulated in the following manner: "The abrogation of the principle of impartiality is a legal effect which a multilateral treaty prohibiting the resort to war has under general international law. The right to take enforcement measures short of war as reprisals against a violator of the treaty is derived directly from general international law and exists even if not expressly stipulated by the treaty." Hans Kelsen, *Collective Security Under International Law* (*U. S. Naval War College, International Law Studies, 1954*), (1956), pp. 145–6.

Also the opinion of Oppenheim-Lauterpacht (*op. cit.*, pp. 644–5): "The guilty belligerent, by breaking the Treaty, violates the rights of all other signatories, who, by way of reprisals, may choose to subject him to measures of discrimination, for instance, either by actively prohibiting some or all exports into his territory or merely by submitting passively to otherwise unlawful measures on the part of the offending belligerent." And for an earlier opinion that parties to the Pact of Paris have the right to take discriminatory measures against a state resorting to war in violation of the Pact, see "Budapest Articles of Interpretation," International Law Association, *Report of the 38th Conference*, (1934). Nevertheless, a substantial number of writers have never shared this interpretation of the Pact.

[9] The Anglo-American Agreement of September 2, 1940, whereby the transfer of fifty destroyers to Great Britain was made in return for the right to lease naval and air bases, as well as the "Act to Promote the Defense of the United States" (Lend-Lease Act), by which Congress authorized the production and disposal of articles to "the government of any country whose defense the President deems vital to the defense of the United States," were partially justified as being measures of reprisal against Germany for the latter's resort to war in violation of the Pact of Paris. See *U. S. Naval War College, International Law Documents, 1940*, pp. 74–90, 150–200,

In view of the possibility that the Pact of Paris may be regarded as presently constituting general international law the right to discriminate against a state violating the Pact's provisions may appear to signify a fundamental change in the traditional legal institution of neutrality. In fact, however, the significance of this change ought not to be overestimated. In the absence of any further obligation to discriminate against an aggressor those states not immediately involved in war will continue to invoke the traditional law of neutrality—with its principle of strict impartiality—whenever they consider such action to be to their interests. The practice of states in the period that has elapsed since the conclusion of the General Treaty For The Renunciation of War furnishes impressive evidence in support of this observation.[10]

There is a further, and possibly more serious, objection to be considered in evaluating the contention that the General Treaty For The Renunciation of War has effected a basic change in the traditional institution of neutrality. The Pact of Paris provides for no objective authority competent to determine when a state has resorted to war in violation of the Pact's provisions. In the absence of a procedure making possible an authoritative and binding judgment that in a given instance a state has unlawfully resorted to war, each state must reach such determination independently.

---

and 132–7, for documents relating to the destroyer-base agreement and for text of the Lend-Lease Act.

In an address of March 27, 1941, before the Inter-American Bar Association the Attorney General of the United States declared:

"The Kellogg-Briand Pact of 1928, in which Germany, Italy, and Japan covenanted with us, as well as with other nations, to renounce war as an instrument of policy, made definite the outlawry of war and of necessity altered the dependent concept of neutral obligations . . . The Treaty for the Renunciation of War and the Argentine Anti-War Treaty deprived their signatories of the right of war as an instrument of national policy or aggression and rendered unlawful wars undertaken in violation of their provisions. In consequence, these treaties destroyed the historical and juridical foundations of the doctrine of neutrality conceived as an attitude of absolute impartiality in relation to aggressive wars. It did not impose upon the signatories *the duty* of discriminating against an aggressor, but it conferred upon them *the right* to act in that manner." *A. J. I. L.*, 35 (1941), pp. 353–4.

[10] In the period up to and including the second World War, the United States provided the only significant example of a neutral state attempting to justify discriminatory behavior toward a belligerent by reference to the Kellogg-Briand Pact. It is necessary to add, however, that the behavior of the United States in the period prior to 1940 would appear to deprive even this one example of much of its significance. In the neutrality legislation enacted during the period from 1934 through 1939 no recognition was given to the possible effects the Pact of Paris might have upon the rights of non-participants in an unlawful war. Instead, it was assumed that whatever the origin of the war the duties of non-participants under the traditional law—and particularly the duty to refrain from discriminatory behavior—continued unimpaired. It is also noteworthy that the resort to the Kellogg-Briand Pact as a justification for discriminatory measures against Germany never formed more than a partial justification for American policy. In large measure, this discriminatory behavior continued to receive justification by reference to arguments whose relevance could be assessed only in terms of the traditional law (see p. 198(n)).

The possibility—or, perhaps more accurately, the probability—must be envisaged that third states will differ in their respective judgments regarding the origin of a war. General international law may be interpreted as presently permitting states to discriminate against an aggressor, but it cannot prevent third states from reaching mutually contradictory decisions as to the identity of the aggressor.[11] The result must be wars in which both sides are made the objects of discriminatory measures. It was precisely this contingency—a product of the decentralization normally characteristic of the international legal order—that served historically as a partial justification, at least, for the traditional legal institution of neutrality with its principle of strict impartiality.[12]

Admittedly, this same argument may be used to call into question the practical utility of the change that has occurred in the legal position of war itself under general international law. For the mutually contradictory de-

---

[11] In this respect the Pact of Paris clearly did not improve upon the situation that has always characterized the application of customary international law. If anything, it provided a remarkable example of the futility of an international instrument which attempts to render the resort to war illegal except when taken as a measure of self-defense against an illegal resort to war, but takes no steps toward the solution of those problems which otherwise make the value of such attempts extremely limited. All the important weaknesses of international law are given express recognition in the Pact's provisions. Yet it attempted the solution of a problem the existence of which was largely the result of those very weaknesses it expressly recognized. Under the Pact each contracting party has the right to determine—for itself only—whether a resort to war constitutes a violation of the Treaty or a measure of self-defense permitted by the Treaty. It has been asserted that "elementary principles of interpretation preclude a construction which gives to a state resorting to an alleged war in self-defense the right of ultimate determination, with a legally conclusive effect, of the legality of such action." Oppenheim-Lauterpacht, *op. cit.*, pp. 187–8. This is correct, if by "the right of ultimate determination, with a legally conclusive effect" is meant the right to decide the legality of an action in a manner that other parties are bound to accept. It follows, then, that according to the Kellogg-Briand Pact, and according to general international law, the final—and authoritative—decision as to the character of a war allegedly waged in self-defense must depend upon an express agreement of the parties involved to submit disputed instances of self-defense to the decision of an organ endowed with the requisite competence. In particular, decisions made unilaterally by the victorious states following the conclusion of a war cannot be deemed to fulfill this requirement. And it is hardly necessary to point out that even if such authoritative decisions are finally rendered they do not resolve the difficulties of non-participants during the actual course of the war.

[12] Distinguish, however, between the foregoing criticism of the Pact of Paris and the opinion that since "each nation was to be the exclusive and unreviewable judge of the question whether its war was one of self-defense . . . the Kellogg Pact has no legal force whatever . . ." Edwin Borchard, "War, Neutrality and Non-Belligerency," *A. J. I. L.*, 35 (1941), p. 622. It is one thing to assert that the utility of an international treaty prohibiting—in principle—the resort to war will be severely limited if it leaves the interpretation and application of that instrument to each of the contracting parties, and quite another thing to state that this condition of decentralization serves to deprive the treaty of "legal force." The latter assertion is surely unwarranted, unless it be contended that most of the rules of international law—whose interpretation and application is normally a product of the same condition of complete decentralization—have no "legal force."

cisions non-participants must be expected to reach concerning the origin of war will necessarily lead to an equal lack of uniformity in the actual participation of third states in hostilities. Under these circumstances the former liberty to resort to war is likely to remain—in practice if not in law—the prerogative of each state. At the same time, however, the former duty of non-participants to observe the rules laid down by the traditional law of neutrality presumably would be abandoned. This rather paradoxical result can hardly be considered an improvement over the traditional law. Nevertheless, it may be said to follow from the attempt merely to place restrictions upon the liberty of states to resort to war while failing to provide a procedure whereby an authoritative determination can be made that in a given instance a state has resorted to war unlawfully. And it is for this reason that although the traditional law of neutrality grew out of, and received its principal justification from, the unlimited liberty of states to resort to war, a change in the legal position of war does not necessarily imply the desirability of modifying—let alone abolishing—the duties imposed and the rights conferred upon non-participants by this traditional law.[13]

C. NEUTRALITY UNDER THE CHARTER OF THE UNITED NATIONS

Under the collective security system established by the Charter of the United Nations, Member states no longer possess, in principle, the freedom either to refrain from actively participating in a war that has taken on the character of a United Nations enforcement action, or—should they not be called upon by the Security Council to take military measures—to observe the duty of impartiality as laid down by the traditional law.[14] This general observation must presuppose, of course, that the Security Council is able to exercise effectively those functions conferred upon it by the Charter. Even so, there is the possibility of distinguishing between several kinds of situations.

According to Article 39 of the Charter the Security Council shall decide, in the event it determines the existence of a threat to or breach of the peace, what measures shall be taken in order to maintain or restore international

[13] And it is presumably for the same reason that the *Harvard Draft Convention On Rights and Duties of States in Case of Aggression* (*op. cit.*, pp. 821 ff), while permitting third states to take discriminatory measures against an aggressor, nevertheless limited the applicability of the Draft Convention to "cases where a resort to armed force has been in violation of a legal obligation not to resort to such means and where such violation *has been duly determined by a procedure to which the law-breaking State has previously agreed*" (p. 825), [italics added].

[14] A substantial portion of the discussion immediately to follow in the text represents a reformulation of problems earlier examined in Chapter I (see pp. 13–20). Perhaps the best analysis to date of the possible effect that the United Nations Charter may have upon the traditional institution of neutrality is J. F. Lalive, "International Organization and Neutrality," *B. Y. I. L.*, 24 (1947), p. 80.

peace and security. These measures may consist of acts not involving (Article 41) or involving (Article 42) the use of armed force. In this connection, it is important to observe that the unlawful resort to armed force by a Member of the United Nations neither automatically involves other Member states in war with the delinquent state nor places upon Member states even the obligation to resort to war. The obligation to resort to measures involving the use of armed force follows only upon the requisite decision by the Security Council, and actual involvement in hostilities occurs only when the Member state has carried out the obligation imposed upon it by the Security Council.[15]

It is altogether possible, therefore, that in the event of an enforcement action ordered by the Security Council certain Member states may not be required to participate with their armed forces.[16] Article 48 of the Charter contemplates this possibility by providing that the "action required to carry out the decisions of the Security Council . . . shall be taken by all the Members of the United Nations or by some of them, as the Security Council may determine." Hence, the opinion that the *effective operation* by the Security Council of the powers granted it under the Charter precludes the possibility that Member states may retain a status of neutrality in a war

[15] Under the collective security system established by the Covenant of the League of Nations each Member state retained the right to determine for itself whether another Member state had resorted to war in violation of its obligations. The League Council could give its opinion as to whether a breach of the Covenant had occurred, but the Council's opinion was not binding upon Members. According to Article 16, paragraph 1, of the Covenant it was provided that: "Should any Member of the League resort to war in disregard of its covenants under Articles 12, 13 or 15, it shall *ipso facto* be deemed to have committed an act of war against all other Members of the League, which hereby undertake immediately to subject it to the severance of all trade or financial relations, the prohibition of all intercourse between their nationals and the nationals of the covenant-breaking State, and the prevention of all financial, commercial or personal intercourse between the nationals of the covenant-breaking State and the nationals of any other State, whether a Member of the League or not." This provision has been correctly described as a legal fiction "since the Members against which the delinquent Member did not resort to war are actually not in a state of war and are not obliged to resort to war against the delinquent state." Hans Kelsen, *Principles of International Law* (1952), p. 86. So long as each Member of the League did not itself decide that another Member had unlawfully resorted to war, the obligations imposed by Article 16 did not become operative. Even after having so decided there was no obligation to resort to war against the delinquent, although there was an obligation to take certain measures of discrimination, largely economic in character (and, according to paragraph 3 of Article 16, the further obligation to "take the necessary steps to afford passage through their territory to the forces of any of the Members of the League which are cooperating to protect the Covenants of the League.")

[16] It is also relevant to recall that the obligation of Member states to take measures of armed force provided for in Article 42 is probably dependent upon the conclusion of the special agreements provided for in Article 43. These agreements, to be concluded between the Security Council and Member states, are to regulate the conditions under which the armed forces and facilities of the Member states will be made available to the Council. However, in the absence of such agreements it is doubtful that the Security Council is competent to obligate Member states to take military measures against a state considered by the Council to have committed a threat to or breach of the peace.

that has the character of a United Nations enforcement action is correct only if neutrality is identified with the duties imposed upon non-participants by the traditional law, and particularly with the duty to observe a strict impartiality.

It is considered preferable, however, to identify neutrality simply with the status of non-participation in hostilities, and not with the specific consequences that are attached to the status of non-participation according to the traditional law.[17] If this concept of neutrality is accepted then it is clear that in an enforcement action taken by the United Nations that has the characteristics of war some Member states may remain neutral, in the sense that they are not required to participate in the hostilities. However, the consequences attached to such non-participation are not the consequences attached to the status of non-participation by the traditional law, for Member states are obligated by the Charter to assist the Organization by measures not involving the use of armed force and to refrain from rendering any assistance to state(s) against which enforcement action is taken.[18]

[17] See pp. 196–8. Though not accepted by perhaps the majority of writers, this identification of neutrality with non-participation in war need not pose any difficulty here. Whether accepted or not there is at least a clear distinction to be drawn between a status of non-participation in hostilities which does entail the duties imposed by the traditional law (particularly the duty to observe a strict impartiality toward the belligerents), and a status of non-participation which may impose a *duty* as well as confer a *right* upon a state to discriminate against the side that has unlawfully resorted to war. In the latter case the discriminatory measures taken by non-participants have their basis in norms constituting a general system of collective security. In the former case departure from the duties imposed upon non-participants by the traditional law has no apparent justification and gives rise to a belligerent right of reprisal.

[18] The discussion in the text necessarily assumes that in an enforcement action ordered by the Security Council Member states are obligated, even without specific direction by the Council, to depart from a position of strict impartiality and to discriminate against the delinquent state. In other terms, this assumption interprets Article 2, paragraph 5, as being automatic in its application to Member states. It is possible, though, to interpret Article 2, paragraph 5, as obligating states to take measures of discrimination only when so directed by the Security Council (this interpretation draws added weight if Article 2, paragraph 5, is considered together with Article 48). In the absence of such direction a Member state could then remain neutral *and observe a strict impartiality*. But there is little doubt that this latter interpretation is contrary to the principles upon which the collective security system established by the Charter is based. (Also see *Law of Naval Warfare*, Article 232.) At the same time, it would appear that in the light of recent developments a state may be accepted as a Member even though it is committed to a status of *permanent neutrality*, a status entailing not only the obligation to refrain from resorting to war against any state—save in self defense—but also the obligation to observe all the duties imposed upon non-participants by the traditional law. Thus in 1955 Austria was admitted as a Member state despite its announced intention to adopt a policy of permanent neutrality, and its request to all states to recognize this status. To date, Austria's request has been accorded recognition by a substantial number of states, including the permanent Members of the Security Council. On first consideration, the status of permanent neutrality appears clearly incompatible with membership in the United Nations (an opinion expressed by the framers of the Charter). Nevertheless, Professor Verdross, writing before Austria's admission into the United Nations, has declared that the Security Council "can decide freely

The position of a state that refrains from active participation in hostilities, but nevertheless resorts—in accordance with obligations undertaken within a system of collective security—to discriminatory measures against one side in a war, has frequently been termed "qualified" or "differential" neutrality.[19] During the League of Nations period a good deal of speculation was devoted to the possibility of states occupying a position of qualified neutrality, and was occasioned by the obligations imposed upon Member states by the Covenant of the League of Nations to take measures of discrimination—primarily economic in character—against another Member state that had unlawfully resorted to war. A similar problem arises with

---

which Members it wants to execute sanctions and compulsory measures and to what extent. The Security Council may therefore permanently relieve individual Members of these obligations by a resolution embodying a principle. Only the Security Council would be able to alter or annul such a resolution . . ." "Austria's Permanent Neutrality and the United Nations Organization," *A. J. I. L.*, 50 (1956), p. 66. In dealing with the same issue Professor Kunz has more recently stated that even if the Security Council does not adopt such a resolution "it seems that Austria's permanent neutrality is not endangered by its membership . . . For Austria's permanent neutrality has come into existence in international law by recognition on the part of the permanent members of the Security Council and many other states; recognition binds the recognizing states to respect permanent neutrality; this respect for permanent neutrality therefore obliges the members of the Security Council not to call on a permanently neutral state for participation in economic and military sanctions." "Austria's Permanent Neutrality," *A. J. I. L.*, 50 (1956), p. 424. It is clear, however, that the situation of Austria is exceptional, and does not detract from the statements made above concerning the obligation of other Member states to accord assistance to the Organization by virtue of Article 2, paragraph 5. Moreover, Austria's membership is not, as Kunz points out, "unconditional," since it does not entail all of the obligations normally imposed upon Members.

[19] The terminology employed by writers to describe the position of the discriminating non-participant is not always consistent, however, and this fact may account for some of the confusion that has accompanied discussions of "qualified" or "differential" neutrality. Some writers (e. g., Guggenheim, *Traité de Droit International Public*, Vol. II, pp. 496–500) use the term "qualified" neutrality to indicate the position of non-participants that assert a *right* (though not a *duty*) to assist the victim of an unlawful resort to war, primarily as a consequence of the Kellogg-Briand Pact, and thereby distinguish between the position of "qualified" neutrals and the position of non-participants under the Charter of the United Nations. Other writers (e. g., Verdross, *Völkerrecht*, pp. 424, 525–6) appear to use the terms "qualified" or "differential" neutrality to describe the position of non-participants that follow—for any reason—a policy of discrimination. In this sense, "differential" neutrality may refer to the position of Member states of the United Nations as well as to non-participants that remain bound by the rules of the traditional law.—It would appear desirable, however, to use the terms "qualified" or "differential" neutrality either to describe the position of states that have *both a right and a duty* to discriminate against an aggressor (e. g., the position of states Members of the United Nations) or to describe the position of non-participants having only a right of discriminating against a state unlawfully resorting to war (e. g., by virtue of the Kellogg-Briand Pact). In theory at least, it is true that there is a significant difference between these two types of "qualified" or "differential" neutrality. But if the duty to discriminate against an aggressor cannot be effectively implemented the difference between these two types is likely to prove—in practice—very small. On the other hand, the term "non-belligerent" may be reserved to describe the position of a non-participant that departs from the duties imposed upon the latter by the traditional law without having a right to do so (see pp. 191–3, 198–9).

respect to the position of Member states in an enforcement action undertaken by the United Nations.

To the extent that the idea of a qualified or differential neutrality has been based upon the contention that the impartiality required of non-participants by the traditional law refers only to military matters (thus permitting discriminatory acts with respect to non-military matters), it must be regarded as unfounded. In fact, it was hardly possible to reconcile the obligations assumed by Member states under the Covenant with the obligations imposed by the traditional law.[20] Member states could refrain from participating in a war against another Member state that had unlawfully resorted to war. They could not—consistently with their obligations under the Covenent—observe a strict impartiality. But under the Covenant all Member states expressly assumed the obligation to permit measures of discrimination to be taken against them in the event they resorted to war in violation of their obligations; for in this event they forfeited the rights formerly enjoyed by belligerents with respect to non-participants, though retaining all of the belligerent's duties. The same reasoning must also apply to United Nations enforcement actions. Of course, the real difficulty here is not primarily legal but political in character. Will the aggressor tolerate discriminatory measures on the part of non-participants? Experience to date has not yet furnished sufficient indication as to how meaningful, in practice, the position of a discriminating non-participant may be. If anything, it seems probable that this position—if seriously pursued—would necessarily prove difficult to maintain.[21]

The preceding remarks have dealt only with the effect the Charter of the United Nations may have upon neutrality so far as Member states are concerned, presupposing, of course, the effective operation by the Security

---

[20] This was illustrated in the case of Switzerland. In admitting Switzerland to the League the Council of the League declared that Switzerland had no obligation to undertake military measures against a violator or to permit the passage of troops through Swiss territory. Nevertheless, the obligation to take economic and financial sanctions against a Member state unlawfully resorting to war was retained. In order to reconcile this latter obligation with her traditional status of permanent neutrality the Swiss Government contended for some time—as did a number of Swiss writers—that a strict neutrality was compatible with an "economic partiality," that the impartiality demanded of neutrals by the traditional law referred only to the military, not to the economic sphere. This opinion was quickly abandoned, however, during the Italo-Ethiopian War, when economic sanctions were taken against Italy by League members. Shortly thereafter, in 1938, Switzerland declared it would no longer consider itself bound by the obligation to participate in sanctions of an economic character, thereby abandoning a position of "qualified" or "differential" neutrality.

[21] In the Italo-Ethiopian War of 1935–36, a limited application of the so-called "differential" neutrality provided for in Article 16 of the Covenant was attempted. Several Members applied discriminatory measures of an economic character against Italy, while maintaining that Italy should observe those duties toward the discriminating states imposed upon belligerents by the traditional law. But this case can hardly be considered as decisive in illustrating the political feasibility of a "qualified" or "differential" neutrality. By 1938 it was generally recognized that Article 16 was no longer obligatory for Member states of the League.

Council of the powers conferred upon it by the Charter. A further problem relates to the effect the Charter may have upon neutrality as far as non-Member states are concerned. The answer to this problem must depend largely upon whether or not the law of the United Nations may be considered as constituting general international law. Despite the claim in Article 2, paragraph 6, it is doubtful that the Charter can be considered as constituting general international law.[22] Accordingly, it is also doubtful that the Security Council possesses the competence to require that non-Member states, in a United Nations enforcement action, depart from a position of strict impartiality.[23]

---

[22] Article 2, paragraph 6 reads: "The Organization shall ensure that states which are not Members of the United Nations act in accordance with these Principles so far as may be necessary for the maintenance of international peace and security." Among writers, the majority seem to remain quite skeptical of the validity of Article 2, paragraph 6, so far as non-Members are concerned. Thus Lalive (*op. cit.*, p. 85) writes that there is "room for doubt whether the Charter can lawfully be invoked against a non-Member state," and Kelsen (*The Law of the United Nations*, p. 110) states that "from the point of view of existing international law, the attempt of the Charter to apply to states which are not contracting parties to it must be characterized as revolutionary." It has even been pointed out that it is not necessary to interpret Article 2, paragraph 6, as imposing obligations upon non-Members but only upon Members. "The Charter, in Article 2 (6), imposes upon the United Nations the obligation to ensure that non-Members act in accordance with its principles as far as may be necessary for the maintenance of international peace and security Non-Members are not bound by this provision and they may choose to react accordingly. But the fact makes no difference to the obligations of the Members . . . in all cases in which the Security Council has taken affirmative action under Articles 39, 41 and 42." Oppenheim-Lauterpacht, *op. cit.*, p. 652.

[23] Within the United Nations itself the problem of the status of non-Members during an enforcement action was discussed in connection with the Draft Declaration on the Rights and Duties of States, prepared by the International Law Commission in conformity with Resolution 178 (II) of the General Assembly, November 21, 1947 (*U. N. General Assembly, Official Records, 4th Sess. Supp. 10* (Doc. A/1925).)

Articles 9, 10 and 12 of the Draft Declaration state: "Article 9. Every state has the duty to refrain from resorting to war as an instrument of national policy, and to refrain from the threat or use of force against the territorial integrity or political independence of another state, or in any other manner inconsistent with international law and order.

"Article 10. Every state has the duty to refrain from giving assistance to any state which is acting in violation of Article 9, or against which the United Nations is taking preventive or enforcement action.

"Article 12. Every state has the right of individual or collective self-defense against armed attack."

The Draft Declaration does not itself constitute positive international law, and as an attempt even to formulate existing general international law it has been subject to much criticism. Even so, Article 10 of the Draft Declaration clearly does not attempt to endorse the claim made by Article 2, paragraph 6, of the Charter. "Every State," which includes non-Member states, is ***not*** under the obligation to discriminate against any state made the object of United Nations enforcement action, but is obligated only to refrain from giving assistance to states made the object of such action. To this extent the obligation laid down in Article 10 of the Draft upon non-Member states is no different from the obligation they would otherwise have according to the traditional law, requiring as it does that non-participants in a war refrain from discriminatory measures and observe an attitude of impartiality toward the belligerents.

The problem relating to the Charter's effect upon the status of non-Members in a United Nations enforcement action is likely to prove relatively unimportant in practice, however. Should the Security Council be able effectively to exercise those powers conferred upon it by the Charter non-Member states would, as one writer has observed, "be politically alive to the possible consequence of action in defiance of the United Nations." [24] It is the unlikelihood of such effective exercise of power by the Security Council that renders continued speculation over this problem of distinctly limited value.

More useful, therefore, is a consideration of the far more probable situation in which the Security Council will be unable either to order enforcement measures against a state that has unlawfully resorted to the use of armed force or even to determine the existence of a breach of the peace—as it was able to do at the time of the outbreak of hostilities in Korea.[25] In the event of Security Council inaction the position of Member states not immediately involved in hostilities will be substantially the same as the position of third states—not immediately involved in war—under general international law. Neither Article 51 of the Charter nor the General Assembly's resolution "Uniting for Peace" provide alternative methods whereby an authoritative and binding collective determination can be reached that a state has unlawfully resorted to the use of armed force.[26] It

[24] Philip C. Jessup, *A Modern Law of Nations*, p. 168. The above observation—to be sure—does not dispose of the strictly legal considerations.

[25] See pp. 16–8, where it has already been observed that the character of these Security Council resolutions renders doubtful the interpretation that the Korean action was a "United Nations' action" in the strict sense of that term. It is still more doubtful that Member states were under the obligation, imposed by Article 2, paragraph 5, to give the United Nations "every assistance in any action" the Organization takes in accordance with the Charter. For these reasons the contention that a strict impartiality in the Korean Conflict was legally excluded for Member states appears unacceptable. At the same time, the particular circumstances attending the Korean conflict, and especially the circumstance that the Security Council was able to determine the existence of a breach of the peace, does allow the interpretation that Member states were obligated to refrain from giving any assistance to the North Korean forces or to states acting in support of these forces.

In practice, questions concerning neutral-belligerent relations were never put to a real test in the Korean conflict, due to the geographical location as well as to the peculiar nature of the hostilities. But several Member states of the United Nations did maintain a position practically indistinguishable from that of non-participants under the traditional law. For a review of the Korean conflict and neutrality, see H. J. Taubenfeld, "International Actions and Neutrality," *A. J. I. L.*, 47 (1953), pp. 390–6.

[26] See pp. 18–20. In the first Report (1951) of the Collective Measures Committee (U. N. Doc. A/1891), established pursuant to the "Uniting For Peace" resolution, considerable emphasis was placed upon the desirability of obtaining universal support for the collective measures recommended in accordance with this Resolution. Thus one of the Reports "guiding principles of general application" was that: "All States should support the United Nations when it undertakes collective measures and participate to the fullest extent possible in carrying them out. . . ." Such recommendations as may be made to states, both Members and non-Members, in accordance with the "Uniting For Peace" resolution, cannot serve to create obligations, however.

is equally clear that apart from the powers granted the Security Council under Chapter VII, the collective security system established by the Charter provides no alternative method for obligating Member states either to take measures involving the use of armed force or to take measures of discrimination not involving the use of armed force against a state that is regarded as having violated its obligations under the Charter by resorting to war. Hence, in the event that the Security Council is unable to fulfill its functions Member states may, in the event of war, abstain from all participation in hostilities and observe a strict impartiality.[27]

It is quite true that under Article 51 the Charter does confer upon Members the right to assist any Member state that has been made the victim of an "armed attack," and this right is terminated only when the Security Council has taken "measures necessary to maintain international peace and security." Nor is there any reason for interpreting Article 51 as permitting only such assistance on behalf of the victim of an armed attack as involves the use of armed force. The "collective self-defense" allowed under Article 51 also permits measures of discrimination against an alleged aggressor that do not necessarily involve the discriminating states' active participation in hostilities.

Thus, according to the Charter, the right to participate in the collective defense of a state made the object of an unlawful resort to war may be considered to include the right to discriminate against the aggressor by measures falling short of active participation in hostilities. But the difficulties attending the exercise of this right to discriminate against an alleged aggressor are as readily apparent in relation to the Charter as they

[27] Nor can there be much doubt that—events permitting—a substantial number of Membe states would do just this. There is, in fact, little point in continuing to place undue emphasis upon the *possible* effects the collective security system established by the Charter may have upon neutrality. For that system has never functioned as originally intended, and it is at least highly unlikely that it will do so in the foreseeable future. It is almost equally unlikely that the modest experiment in "collective security" effected during the Korean hostilities will be repeated, dependent as it would have to be upon the same fortuitous circumstances which permitted the Security Council to take in June and July of 1950 a limited form of action. And even during the Korean conflict not only did a number of Member states consider themselves to occupy a position of "neutrality" in relation to the hostilities, but the armistice terminating the hostilities provided for a "commission of neutrals" to insure its observance (though, ironically, four of the five states composing this "commission of neutrals" were Member states of the United Nations). It is true that no state issued a formal declaration of neutrality during the Korean conflict or actually invoked the traditional law of neutrality. It is also true that the accuracy of the term "neutral" with respect to the states policing the Korean armistice may be easily challenged from a technical point of view. But it would be quite unwarranted to dismiss the overall significance of these, and other, recent developments, which indicate that neutrality—even the "old-style neutrality"—may have to be disinterred once again by those who had buried it in the hope that the principle of collective security had finally made this traditional institution obsolescent. Certainly, the framers of the 1949 Geneva Conventions on the Treatment of the Victims of War did not share this view, for these Conventions assign important functions to neutral states.

are when considered in relation to the General Treaty For the Renunciation of War. It may be assumed that under Article 51 of the Charter states will reach the same mutually contradictory decisions concerning the origin of a war with the result that both sides to a conflict will be made the objects of discriminatory measures.[28]

This undesirable situation will not be relieved by the transformation of the right of collective defense, granted under Article 51 of the Charter, into a duty. The conclusion of agreements implementing the right of collective defense may indeed severely limit the possibility of states retaining the right to refrain from participating in a war, or, if allowed to remain in a non-participant status, to observe an attitude of impartiality.[29] It

---

[28] More than one writer has accorded clear recognition to the undesirable consequences to which this situation would probably lead. Thus, Professor Jessup (*op. cit.*, p. 205) in considering the possibility of an outbreak of war unaccompanied by the binding decision of a competent "international authority" (in this case the United Nations Security Council) declares:

"If the legal position of non-participants in the conflict is to be regulated by some international agreement short of a return to the old status of war and neutrality, it would be disastrous to agree that every state may decide for itself which of the two contestants is in the right and may govern its conduct according to its own decision, even if it were agreed that they would not actually support one or the other side by force. . . . There is no alternative except to extend throughout the duration of the conflict the system of impartial blockade against both parties to the fighting."

The essence of this proposal is a mixture of both old and new. States are generally forbidden to resort to war. But if war should break out—and be unaccompanied by the binding decision of a competent "international authority"—third states are forbidden to participate, either for reasons formerly admitted by the traditional law or for reason of collective defense on behalf of the alleged victim. Nor are non-participants to be allowed to discriminate against an alleged aggressor. Instead, the position of third states is to resemble the position of non-participants under the traditional law, with the important exception that private neutral trade with the belligerents—allowed by the traditional law—is to be forbidden. The proposal recalls somewhat similar suggestions made in the period preceding World War II, to the effect that an enforced isolation of the belligerents would reduce the danger of conflict spreading and induce the belligerents to cease hostilities. Apart from its possible merits, and they are not inconsiderable, it should be observed that this proposal is at variance both with the General Treaty For the Renunciation of War and with Article 51 of the United Nations Charter.

[29] Here again, however, the compatibility of neutrality and collective defense agreements will depend, in practice, not only upon the nature of the obligations incurred but also upon the procedure that is provided for determining the existence of those circumstances (i. e., an "armed attack") serving to bring the obligations in question into operation. Thus, Article 5 of the North Atlantic Treaty, concluded at Washington, April 4, 1949, reads:

"The Parties agree that an armed attack against one or more of them in Europe or North America shall be considered an attack against them all; and consequently they agree that, if such an armed attack occurs, each of them, in exercise of the right of individual or collective self-defense recognized by Article 51 of the Charter of the United Nations, will assist the Party or Parties so attacked by taking forthwith, individually and in concert with other Parties, such action as it deems necessary, including the use of armed force, to restore and maintain the security of the North Atlantic area. Any such armed attack and all measures taken as a result thereof shall immediately be reported to the Security Council. Such measures shall be terminated when the Security Council has taken the measures necessary to restore and maintain international peace and security."

may also be that these agreements confer upon a central organ competence to determine when the duty of collective defense must be fulfilled, and even the extent of this duty. But such decisions are binding only upon the contracting parties to the agreement. It must be expected, therefore, that different decisions will be reached by those states parties to different—and, presumably, opposed—collective defense agreements. In this situation the resort by non-participants to measures of discrimination may only serve to provoke retaliatory measures on the part of the state against which they are taken. Nor will it normally prove possible during the course of a war to determine that acts of retaliation on the part of the alleged aggressor are without legal justification.

VII. NEUTRALITY AND THE TWO WORLD WARS

In the preceding chapter an attempt has been made to inquire into the possible effects upon the traditional institution of neutrality resulting from the changed position of war in international law. In general, it may be concluded that these effects, though certainly not without significance, have been limited in nature. Undoubtedly there is, in principle, a basic antagonism between the assumptions upon which a system of collective security must rest and neutrality. Nevertheless, the actual effects that a system of collective security may have upon neutrality—particularly in its traditional form—can only be judged by the extent of the obligations imposed upon member states, by the existence of a centralized—and operative—procedure for determining when these obligations must be fulfilled, and by the effectiveness of the machinery provided for ensuring that they are so fulfilled. It should be apparent that when judged by these criteria neutrality can hardly be regarded as constituting at present only a matter of historical interest.

In considering the present status of neutrality, it is of considerable importance, therefore, to distinguish between the effects upon neutrality resulting from the transformation in the legal position of war and those effects brought about by the two World Wars. Not infrequently writers fail to make this distinction clear, and—even worse—impute to the former what is clearly the consequence of the latter. This failure can only serve to breed confusion. In fact, however, the present decline of neutrality is the consequence primarily of the two World Wars and of the circumstances that have attended these conflicts.

A. BELLIGERENT ENCROACHMENT UPON TRADITIONAL NEUTRAL RIGHTS

It is fundamental that an equality—or an approximate equality—of neutral and belligerent rights must depend, in the first place, upon an equality of power. Where neutrals do not possess an equality of power with belligerents their interests, and hence their legal rights, will suffer accordingly. This has always been the case, even in the nineteenth century. The lesson taught by the Napoleonic Wars, which opened the nineteenth century, was—in this respect—quite clear, and the strong parallel between the practices of belligerents during the earlier wars and belligerent measures taken in World War I has not escaped the attention of writers.[1]

Historically, the major disputes between neutrals and belligerents have concerned the scope of the repressive measures permitted to belligerents against the trade of neutral subjects. It has long been customary to characterize the problems arising with respect to neutral commerce in terms of two conflicting rights: the right of the neutral state to insist upon continued freedom of commerce for its subjects despite the existence of war and the right of the belligerent to prevent neutral subjects from affording assistance to the military effort of an enemy. More accurate, perhaps, is the characterization of these problems in terms of conflicting interests rather than in terms of conflicting rights. Whereas the neutral's interest has been to suffer the least amount of belligerent interference in the trading activities of its subjects, the belligerent's interest has been to prevent neutrals from compensating for an enemy's weakness at sea. The reconciliation of these clearly diverse interests has never proven easy and, as the preamble to the Declaration of Paris stated a century ago, "has long been the subject of deplorable disputes . . . giving rise to differences of opinion between neutrals and belligerents which may occasion serious difficulties and even conflicts. . . ." The neutral claim—that hostilities should interfere as little as possible with neutral commerce—is not an unreasonable one. Still, the belligerent claim—that the neutral ought not to be allowed to compensate for an enemy's weakness—may be regarded as equally reasonable.

These initial observations may serve as a warning against the many attempts to find in the "general principles" alleged to govern neutral-belligerent relations at sea self-evident and fixed criteria from which precise limits upon belligerent freedom to interfere with neutral trade can be deduced. In an earlier period the assumption was common that these general principles "of necessity" dictated a minimum of belligerent interference with neutral trade. At present it is the contrary conviction that forms the basis of most inquiries into the issue of "neutral rights" at sea. Neither position appears well taken. It is quite true that the neutral state has the right to demand that no repressive measures be taken by a belligerent against *legitimate* neutral commerce with an enemy, and that this neutral right corresponds to a duty of abstention on the part of the belligerent. But it is hardly possible to deduce from this general principle the character of the neutral intercourse that must be regarded as legitimate and against which repressive measures by belligerents are forbidden. On the contrary, experience has shown that the practices establishing the respective rights and duties of belligerents and neutrals are not dependent upon logical de-

[1] See, for example, *Neutrality, Its History, Economics and Law* (4 vols); Vol. II, *The Napoleonic Period* (1936), by W. Alison Phillips and Arthur H. Reede; Vol. IV, *Today and Tomorrow* (1936), by Philip C. Jessup, pp. 58–85.

ductions drawn from general principles but upon the character of those concrete circumstances attending the conduct of warfare during a particular historical period.

During most of the nineteenth century a rough balance was struck between the conflicting claims of neutrals and belligerents, a balance duly reflected in the traditional law of neutrality. If anything, the traditional law inclined slightly in favor of neutral interests, and in doing so recorded the experience of the century which was one of limited warfare. Thus one of the principal assumptions underlying the traditional law, as H. A. Smith has observed, "is that the greater part of the world is at peace, that war is a temporary and local disturbance of the general order, and that the chief function of law is to keep the war from spreading, and to minimize its impact upon the normal life of the world." [2] It need hardly be pointed out that this assumption did not correspond—even remotely—to the conditions under which the two World Wars were fought, and the decline in this century of the traditional institution of neutrality may be attributed, in the first place, to the fact that this system was designed principally to regulate the behavior of belligerents and non-participants in local wars, not in global conflicts.

To the foregoing must be added the further consideration that the wars of the twentieth century have been conducted with an intensity unknown to the nineteenth century. It has become abundantly clear that if there is always a latent conflict between belligerent and neutral interests, even in a local war conducted with restraint and for limited purposes, the conflict between these interests in a major war that is total both in conduct and purpose becomes almost irreconcilable. On the one hand, a primary aim of the belligerents in recent warfare at sea has been the complete shutting off of enemy trade, the destruction or capture of all imports to and exports from enemy territory, without regard to whether this trade is carried in enemy or neutral bottoms.[3] On the other hand, the effect of the traditional law—if strictly adhered to—was to make it exceedingly difficult for the measures a belligerent could bring to bear at sea against an enemy's economy to play more than a limited role in the final decision of the war.[4] Given

---

[2] H. A. Smith, *op. cit.*, p. 75.

[3] And also without regard to whether such imports to and exports from enemy territory are immediately destined to or originating from neutral territory (see pp. 284–6).

[4] This antagonism in modern war between the restraints the traditional law imposes upon belligerents with respect to neutral trade and the importance of cutting off the enemy's sources of materials for waging war cannot be emphasized too strongly. And it is probably true that belligerent encroachment upon traditional neutral rights at sea must be attributed as much to this circumstance as to the relative strength of belligerent and neutral states. Even when confronted with considerable neutral strength—as belligerents were so confronted at least in the initial stages of both World Wars—belligerents were nevertheless willing to risk neutral ill will, and even possible neutral intervention, in order to deny an enemy the means for conducting war.

the transcendent importance of the economic factor in modern, and total, war the outcome—a steady belligerent encroachment upon traditional neutral rights—was hardly unexpected.[5]

In large measure, however, the marked predominance of belligerent interests that has so clearly characterized hostilities at sea since 1914 is the result of developments against which neutral protests have been—from a strictly legal point of view—all too frequently devoid of solid foundation. The nineteenth century balance between neutral and belligerent was reflected not only in law but also in the extra-legal restraints that had characterized belligerent behavior. Indeed, the importance of the restraints hitherto accepted by belligerents, even though not demanded by law, can only be fully appreciated with the advantage of hindsight. During the 1914 and 1939 wars many of the most effective measures taken by the Allied Powers against neutral trade consisted of so-called "interferences by sovereign right." In theory, the essential purpose of the varied belligerent measures falling within this category was to cut off trade with the enemy by threatening to deprive neutral traders and shippers of certain advantages hitherto enjoyed if found—or suspected of—aiding the enemy's cause. In practice, these measures went far toward reducing neutral trade to a position of near subservience to belligerent controls.[6]

Despite strong neutral protests, there were no established rules expressly forbidding belligerents to subject neutral commerce to strict control through the threat of interference by sovereign right.[7] For the most part, it would

---

[5] Though, of course, this is not to justify such belligerent encroachment upon traditional neutral rights. But it does go far in accounting for the persistence and intensity of belligerent efforts to restrain neutral commerce with an enemy. Of this, the history of American neutrality during World War I must provide the classic example.

[6] The continuation or withdrawal of these advantages depended almost entirely upon the discretion of the belligerent, hence the characterization of these belligerent measures as "interference by sovereign right." A survey of World War I practice in this respect has been made by Edgar Turlington (*The World Wa Period* (Vol. III, *Neutrality, Its History, Economics and Law* 1936) pp. 67–99), who observes that there was "no system of law which a neutral could invoke against the action of any or all of the belligerents in prohibiting the exportation of specified goods from their territory; in refusing bunker supplies or ship's stores to neutral vessels; in forbidding their nationals to have commercial or financial dealings with the enemy or with neutral nationals suspected of trading with the enemy; or in requisitioning, subject to compensation, ships within their ports. Against such action the neutrals had no defense except their economic and potential military strength" (p. 67). And Turlington has concluded that: "On the whole, it seems safe to say that belligerent interferences by sovereign right were far more prejudicial to the economic life of the neutrals in the World War than were all the other forms of belligerent interference" (p. 151). British practice in World War II, in which the experience of the previous conflict was utilized and developed still further, has been described in detail by W. N. Medlicott, *Civil History of The Second World War: The Economic Blockade* (1952), Vol. I. For further remarks on World War II practice, see pp. 280–2, 312–5.

[7] It may be contended—and neutrals occasionally have so contended—that belligerents are prohibited from interfering with legitimate neutral intercourse with an enemy even though the forms such interference might take are not expressly forbidden by law. Obviously this

appear, neutral protests failed to acknowledge that a significant area of neutral-belligerent relations depended upon the character of hostilities and the restraints belligerents would feel compelled to accept, not as a matter of strict law but for reasons of expediency. And this implied, in turn, that belligerent interferences with neutral trade by sovereign right could be contested on the political and economic levels though only with difficulty on a legal basis.

Admittedly quite different considerations were raised by belligerent measures that clearly could be interpreted as departures from the established law. Here, neutral protests against what were alleged to be belligerent violations of traditional neutral rights at sea required belligerent justification. In part, belligerents responded to neutral protests by maintaining that legally controverted measures taken against neutral trade merely represented a reasonable adaptation of the traditional law to the novel circumstances in which hostilities were being conducted. In part, belligerents sought to justify measures whose legality could not otherwise be seriously contended for by the claim that they formed legitimate measures of reprisal taken in response to the unlawful behavior of an enemy.

The belligerent contention that novel circumstances may serve to justify novel belligerent measures no doubt suffered from the obvious criticism that may always be made of this plea. Neutrals had little trouble, therefore, in pointing out to belligerents that once recognition is accorded to the plea of novel circumstances it may readily be used as an instrument for the subversion of all established law. Nor did the belligerents strengthen their position by claiming the right to invoke the doctrine of novel circumstances in their own case, and—from the neutral's point of view—for their own interests, though invariably rejecting the same plea when invoked by an enemy. Thus the unreserved British condemnation of the contention that allegedly novel circumstances could ever serve to release the submarine from any of the traditionally accepted rules was seldom viewed as hindering support for the contention that changed conditions justified the diversion of neutral vessels into port for visit and search.[8] Admittedly, cogent considerations could be—and were—offered after 1914 in support of the practice of diversion. Yet there is little doubt that this practice was not permitted by the law as it stood at the outbreak of hostilities in 1914.[9]

---

argument is not a particularly strong one. When seriously pressed by neutrals it has only succeeded in raising the broad question of the nature of the trade that might yet be regarded as legitimate, given the conditions in which the two World Wars were fought.

[8] The controversy over diversion formed only one among many novel measures taken by Great Britain, largely under the plea of novel circumstances. In part, the entire structure of the British "long-distance" blockade of Germany rested upon the argument that changed conditions required—and justified—alteration of the traditional rules governing blockade (see pp. 305–14).

[9] For a discussion of diversion of neutral vessels for visit and search from the point of view of the present law, see pp. 338–43.

It may, of course, be contended that novel practices are justified—even though constituting departures from established rules—if such practices do not prove destructive of the basic purposes of the law, but merely seek to adapt the latter to changing conditions. This argument takes on added force when it is once recognized that although the conditions attending naval warfare do change—and did change during World War I [10]—states have nearly always shown a pronounced reluctance to amend the law through express agreement in order that the rules defining the character and scope of belligerent restraints upon neutral commerce will bear a reasonable relation to altered conditions. Change, if it is to come at all, must come through what will necessarily appear as departures from established law. These departures are to be condemned—so the argument runs—only if they strike at the basic purposes of the law, as did the resort to unrestricted submarine warfare against neutral shipping. On the other hand, departures are not necessarily to be condemned if they conserve these basic purposes, as did the practice of requiring deviation for visit and search.

Even if it is assumed that this argument is well founded it remains true that the standard for judging belligerent behavior is no longer rigidly restricted to the rules of the positive law. Instead, belligerent behavior is to be judged—at least in part—by the degree to which it conforms to the law's essential purposes (to the "spirit of the law"). Unfortunately, however, whereas it may prove possible to reach a reasonably clear statement of the former it has always been next to impossible to state the latter with any degree of clarity. The traditional law regulating neutral-belligerent relations at sea can probably be understood only as the product of conflicting interests, informed—at best—by the spirit of compromise. And even if it were the case that the traditional law reflected some measure of identity of purpose as between neutral and belligerent, this was largely dissipated once hostilities broke out in 1914.[11]

---

[10] Though this view has not always been accepted by writers. In one of his best known essays, John Bassett Moore endeavored to dispel the "illusion of novelty" put forth by belligerents during the war of 1914–18. *International Law and Some Current Illusions* (1924), pp. 1–39 (the essay is of the same title). A similar theme was taken up some years later by Professor Jessup, and applied to belligerent attempts during World War I to justify encroachment upon neutral rights. *Op. cit.*, pp. 59–85. Professor Jessup, in emphasizing the marked similarity between belligerent arguments in the Napoleonic Wars and in World War I, observed that the contention of "novel circumstances" has always formed the stock-in-trade of belligerents anxious to provide a justification for unlawful measures taken against neutral commerce.—No doubt it is true that belligerents are often tempted to use the plea of novel conditions in order to rid themselves of irksome restraints. But this does not prove that the plea is necessarily a belligerent hoax. The fact is that the conditions attending World War I did represent many elements of novelty when contrasted with the preceding wars of the nineteenth century.

[11] In reviewing the difficulties confronting Great Britain in 1939, of reconciling her plans for the conduct of "economic warfare" with the traditional law, W. N. Medlicott (*op. cit.*, pp. 4–5) has declared that "legal definition lagged behind economic circumstance." Neverthe-

There is a further difficulty to note at this point. The immediately preceding remarks have assumed that the controverted measures taken by belligerents—apart from reprisals—were readily acknowledged to be departures from the strict letter of the law. Normally, however, the novel measures resorted to by belligerents have been viewed by the latter as adaptations to changed conditions permitted by, and taken within, the established legal framework of neutral-belligerent relations. Here again the belligerent's claim could not always be dismissed as a patent subterfuge for the justification of unlawful action. In retrospect, it is all too easy to fall into the error of exaggerating the degree to which the maritime powers of the world had by 1914 settled upon the limits of the belligerent right to interfere with neutral trade. In fact, many points of controversy had remained unresolved throughout the preceding century. A case in point was the all important question of trade in contraband, a question that had long provided the controversial core of neutral-belligerent relations.[12]

In the years preceding the outbreak of World War I an attempt was made to resolve these various points of controversy. The 1909 Declaration of London had laid down a fairly definitive code governing neutral-belligerent relations at sea. But the Declaration was never subsequently ratified by any of the signatory Powers, and although most of the belligerents announced their initial willingness in 1914 to adhere to the provisions of that instrument, subject to certain reservations, it was not long before the

---

less, he goes on to observe that: "The real difficulty lay in the fact that the 1914 war had created conditions for which the existing prize law was unprepared, and the point at issue between Great Britain and the neutrals was, or should have been, not whether the letter of the existing international law was being observed, but whether the new practices demanded by the changed conditions of economic warfare were in accordance with the spirit of international law as it concerned the relations of belligerents and neutrals. The inadequacy of the existing law becomes clear when it is remembered that in 1914, and indeed in 1939, there had been no generally ratified agreement [i. e., on the subject of neutral commerce] since the Declaration of Paris in 1856." But if Medlicott has reference to the nineteenth century "spirit of international law as it concerned the relations of belligerents and neutrals" it is very doubtful whether the "new practices demanded by the changed conditions of economic warfare" were in basic accord with this spirit. Of course, it may be argued instead that the decisive point was not the "spirit of international law" but rather the changed conditions which led belligerents to depart from this law—though the latter contention places the matter on a quite different basis. Medlicott has further observed that: "The whole approach to the problem of contraband at the Hague Conference was, indeed, governed by an assumption of fact which happened to be wrong, namely, that the control of contraband was powerless to accomplish its purpose and its only result was to harm neutral commerce." Yet, the "assumption of fact" referred to was based only in part upon technical considerations as to the capabilities of belligerents in interfering with neutral trade. In part, this "assumption of fact" had as its basis the expectation that for reasons of political expediency the traditional law would have to be observed—at least in broad outline.

[12] See pp. 263 ff.

Declaration was substantially abandoned by the belligerents.[13] During World War II the London Declaration ceased to have real significance as a standard for judging belligerent behavior.[14] In effect, then, many of the long-standing controversies over neutral rights at sea were never satisfactorily resolved. In both World Wars these controversies were to provide ample opportunity to belligerents for pursuing courses of action whose unlawful character could not be regarded as self-evident, despite neutral assertions to this effect.

To the difficulties resulting from the claim of changed conditions and the uncertainty characterizing a substantial portion of the traditional law must be added the seemingly insoluble problem of belligerent reprisals at sea. In the final analysis, a number of belligerent measures bearing upon neutral trade could scarcely be reconciled even with the most liberal interpretation of the traditional law. Belligerents therefore sought to justify these measures by the claim that they formed a necessary—and permitted—incidence of reprisal action taken in response to the unlawful behavior of an enemy. Elsewhere in this study the content of the belligerent reprisal measures during the two World Wars are reviewed and analyzed.[15] So also are the legal considerations—still largely obscure—raised by inter-bel-

---

[13] The declaration was formally abandoned by the Allied Powers on July 7, 1916. In a memorandum addressed to neutral governments it was stated that the Declaration of London "could not stand the strain imposed by the test of rapidly changing conditions and tendencies which could not have been foreseen" and that the Allies would thereafter "confine themselves simply to applying the historic and admitted rules of the law of nations."

Long before this formal action was taken the several reservations made to the Declaration by the Allied Powers, plus the operation of reprisal orders, had reduced its force to a vanishing point.

[14] An English writer has recently noted that: "The most striking difference between 1914 and 1939 is the complete absence of the Declaration as a factor of any importance in modern prize law. . . ." S. W. D. Rowson, "Prize Law During the Second World War," p. 170. This is perhaps something of an overstatement. The German Prize Law Code of September 1939 substantially followed the Declaration, and the prize codes of a number of other states also followed it in part. The attitude of the United States—as a neutral—with respect to the Declaration had certainly changed, however. Whereas in 1914 this country had urged all of the belligerents to accept the Declaration of London as an authoritative code of conduct, a similar request was not forwarded to belligerents in 1939. And whereas during the period 1914–17 the United States depended very largely in its controversies with belligerents upon the provisions of the Declaration, hardly a reference was made to this instrument in American notes addressed to belligerents during the 1939 war. Nevertheless, the 1909 Declaration of London continues to be of some importance in an inquiry into the law regulating belligerent interference with neutral commerce, if only for the reason that it is the best indication of what the major naval powers were prepared to accept in the period preceding World War I. And even though the claim made in the preamble of the Declaration—that the rules contained therein "correspond in substance with the generally recognized principles of international law"—was not altogether justified, it is true that in most respects the instrument was in accord with previous practice and custom.

[15] See pp. 296–315.

ligerent reprisals which adversely affect neutral rights.[16] Here, it is sufficient to sketch in broad outline the controversy thus raised between belligerent and neutral and to observe that whatever the strictly legal merits of this controversy the overall effect in practice of belligerent reprisal measures has been to subvert the traditional rules regulating the scope of the measures permitted to belligerents as against neutral commerce.

The right of a belligerent to take reprisal measures against an enemy that persists in unlawful behavior is unquestioned. However, in naval warfare the problem of reprisals is almost always complicated by the presence of neutrals. As might be expected, the position of neutral states consistently has been one of denying that reprisals between belligerents can serve to justify any infringement of neutral rights. Such infringement, it has been contended, can follow only from a failure on the part of the neutral state to fulfill its duties. Belligerents, while not denying that reprisals taken in response to an enemy's misconduct should avoid—as far as possible—affecting neutral rights, have nevertheless refused to concede that consideration for neutral rights constitutes an absolute restriction upon belligerent measures of retaliation. This conflict of opinion between neutral and belligerent has been complicated further by the fact that normally the unlawful acts imputed to a belligerent by an enemy have adversely affected neutral rights as well. In this situation the injured belligerent has contended that if a neutral state will not or cannot take the necessary steps to compel the lawbreaker to observe neutral rights it may not complain if the other belligerent, in the course of retaliating upon an enemy, resorts to similar restrictions upon neutral rights. And here again the reply of the neutral has been to reject the belligerent's contention that the latter's obligation to respect neutral rights is dependent upon the effectiveness of the measures taken by the neutral to secure belligerent respect for these rights.

It will be readily apparent that if the belligerent's point of view is accepted the practical effect is to charge the neutral with the task of insuring that belligerents behave in conformity with the established law. In a major war the burden that is thereby imposed upon neutrals will usually

[16] See pp. 252–8. In these later comments the attempt will be made to show that—contrary to the contentions of belligerents and the opinions of numerous writers—it is a misnomer to categorize many of the belligerent measures in question as reprisals. This follows, in part, for the reason that the mere inability of the neutral to resist effectively the unlawful acts by one belligerent against its trade—a frequent cause for so-called belligerent "reprisal" orders—is not a violation of a neutral's duties. Hence, even if the other belligerent is permitted—in principle—to restrict neutral trade in a similar manner, such measures are not to be interpreted as reprisals directed against the neutral. But neither may they be interpreted as reprisals against the enemy that has initially resorted to unlawful measures against neutral trade, since in taking these measures the enemy has violated no legal *right* of the other belligerent. For convenience, however, these—and other—considerations may be neglected here, and the usual terminology may be followed.

prove out of all proportion to their resources, a conclusion clearly borne out by the experience of the two World Wars. Add to this the consideration that belligerents have been in frequent disagreement in their understanding of the rules regulating the scope of belligerent obligations, both with respect to the enemy as well as to the neutral. Given the first opportunity, therefore, it has proven relatively easy for one belligerent to charge an enemy with the violation of neutral rights at sea and, in the absence of an immediate cessation of the allegedly unlawful action through vigorous neutral response, to consider itself entitled to take appropriate measures of its own against neutral trade. The neutral, caught up in the belligerents' controversy, has generally been made the common victim of the belligerent difference of opinion.[17]

Nor can the essential function served by belligerent "reprisals" be overlooked. Clearly, this function has not been to preserve the traditional rights of neutrals. On the contrary, the evident intent of the belligerents has been to use reprisals as an instrument for changing this aspect of the traditional law of neutrality, and it was primarily for this reason that reprisal measures became a permanent feature of naval hostilities in the 1914 and 1939 wars.[18] Where belligerents have differed has not been in their resolve to use reprisals as a means for shutting off all neutral trade with an enemy but rather in the distinctive methods they have followed in pursuing this aim; and it is no less an error to refuse to recognize the effects this common belligerent goal has had upon the rules regulating neutral trade than it is to dismiss as without legal significance the varying methods belligerents have pursued in attempting the economic isolation of an enemy.[19]

---

[17] It is equally evident, however, that if the neutral's position is endorsed the law-abiding belligerent is placed at a grave disadvantage. Nor can this disadvantage be characterized merely as one which would deprive the belligerent of striking at an offending enemy "through the side" of the neutral. It has already been noted that in many situations the unlawful acts of an enemy—affecting belligerent and neutral alike—can only be effectively countered by acts which equally bear upon both the offender and the neutral. Apart from strictly legal considerations, there is much to be said for both the positions of belligerents and neutral. And it is largely for this reason that the entire problem of reprisals at sea has appeared to many as an insoluble dilemma.

[18] It is this consideration, above all others, that has rendered belligerent reprisal measures subject to severe criticisms. The rapidity with which belligerents resorted to reprisal orders of indefinite duration allowed hardly any conclusion other than that they welcomed an enemy's violation—or alleged violation—of law in order to resort to reprisal measures. A revealing discussion of the function served by reprisals has been presented by Medlicott (*op. cit.*, pp. 112 ff.) in tracing the origins of the British Reprisals Order in Council of November 27, 1939, the purpose of which was to shut off all enemy exports (see p. 312).

[19] For those observers who insist upon viewing the experience of World Wars I and II as little more than one long demonstration of "belligerent lawlessness" at sea, the significance of the various means by which belligerents sought to alter traditional neutral rights is bound to prove very limited. Thus, Thomas Baty (*International Law in Twilight* (1954), p. 105) can

B. THE ABANDONMENT OF TRADITIONAL NEUTRALITY BY NON-PARTICIPANTS: THE EMERGENCE OF "NON-BELLIGERENCY"

The decline of neutrality cannot be attributed simply to the fact of belligerent encroachment upon traditional neutral rights. The neutral states as well have played an important role in effecting this decline. It is a commonplace that the neutrality of the nineteenth century was based very largely upon an attitude of indifference on the part of non-participants to the final outcome of a given conflict.[20] Yet, the conclusion frequently drawn today from this former indifference of non-participants—that the traditional institution of neutrality reflected the absence of solidarity and "community feeling" [21]—would appear to be almost the reverse of the

dismiss the question of belligerent methods by declaring that at present neutrals are "ground between the millstones of the navally strong and weak belligerents—between the perverted jurisprudence of the former and the explosives of the latter." Yet it is disturbing to find that writers who do not share this evaluation of the two World Wars nevertheless manifest on occasion a similar lack of sensitivity to the significance of—and differences between—belligerent methods.—No doubt it is true that the British "long-distance blockade" resembled the German unrestricted submarine warfare in the resolve to isolate the enemy economically. It is equally true that both systems represented departures, though in varying degree, from the letter of the traditional law. But the British system clearly did not resemble the German system in the methods pursued against neutral trade, and the differences in this respect as between the two systems must receive prominent emphasis. The law of neutrality at sea is, after all, largely a matter of method. Nor is it enough to say that had Germany possessed adequate surface naval power she would have pursued, in all probability, the same methods as Great Britain. This may well be granted, though the admission does not—and cannot—diminish the importance of the fact that different methods were in fact followed.

[20] It should perhaps be made clear that this attitude of indifference on the part of non-participants constituted a *political fact*, and ought not to be considered as descriptive of a *legal obligation* imposed upon neutrals by the traditional law. It has never been required of neutral states that they be "indifferent" to the outcome of a war. In later pages it will be noted that the duty to observe a strict impartiality toward the belligerents is not to be understood as obligating neutral states to entertain an attitude of indifference toward the participants and toward the ultimate outcome of hostilities (see pp. 204–5). At the same time, it would be futile to deny that—certain exceptional cases apart—an attitude of indifference on the part of non-participants did form an important part of the political sub-stratum upon which the traditional legal institution of neutrality—marked by the principle of strict impartiality—could develop and flourish. In this sense it is true that the traditional or classic neutrality of the nineteenth century was based upon an attitude of indifference on the part of non-participants, and that with the disappearance of this political fact in the twentieth century the traditional legal institution of neutrality has become increasingly difficult to maintain.

[21] See, for example, Quincy Wright, "The Present Status of Neutrality," *A. J. I. L.*, 34 (1940), pp. 407–15 and "Repeal of the Neutrality Act," *A. J. I. L.*, 36 (1942), pp. 15–24. And Lalive (*op. cit.*, p. 73) points out that neutrality is increasingly viewed as "an obstacle to solidarity, to international organization, and to the formation of a society founded on respect for, and enforcement of, law." Nevertheless, these views form a clear reversal of the convictions of an earlier period. Thomas Baty (*op. cit.*, pp. 107, 124) has noted that: "One of the most deeply seated convictions of the Victorian age was that belligerents must not be allowed to make their

truth. If anything, the strength of neutrality during the nineteenth century may be taken as an indication of solidarity, not its absence. Neutrality, it has been rightly observed, "is possible only when there is sufficient community of interest between the belligerents and between the belligerents and the neutrals to cause the latter not to care too greatly which side wins. Neutrality therefore depends upon the existence of enough community to make the outcome of a war not a matter of alarming concern to the way of life of non-participating States. Where the community schism runs deep, neutrality becomes more and more difficult to maintain."[22]

It is at least clear that given the circumstances in which the two World Wars were fought non-participants have been increasingly drawn to the pursuit of discriminatory policies and to the abandonment of the strict impartiality demanded by the traditional law.[23] Thus one of the marked developments of the second World War was the emergence of so-called "non-belligerency," a term used to indicate the position of states that refrained from active participation in hostilities while at the same time abandoning the duties heretofore imposed upon non-participants.[24] When judged by the standards established for non-participants by the traditional law of neutrality, the legal significance of "non-belligerency" does not permit of much doubt; insofar as it implied the abandonment by non-participants of the strict impartiality demanded by the traditional law it served to give rise to the belligerent right of reprisal.[25] When judged from a still broader

---

private quarrels an excuse for disturbing the rest of the world. War might not be obsolete, but the belligerent must not make himself a nuisance. . . . The outstanding feature of our day is that whilst in the nineteenth century belligerents were considered a public nuisance, it is now the neutral who is the nuisance." Certainly, the well-known opinion of John Westlake, written in the pre-World War I period, that "neutrality is not morally justifiable unless intervention in the war is unlikely to promote justice, or could do so only at a ruinous cost to the neutral" (*International Law*, Vol. II, p. 162) may hardly be said to have commanded widespread agreement.

[22] *U. S. Naval War College, International Law Situations, 1939*, p. 54.

[23] The short-lived policy of "renunciatory" neutrality pursued by the United States for a period preceding and following the outbreak of war in 1939 forms an exception which—in view of later events—only seems to throw in bolder relief the strength of the forces that have operated in the contrary direction. From a policy in which traditional neutral rights at sea were renounced in favor of a self-imposed isolation that went far beyond the requirements of existing law, the United States rapidly moved in 1940 to a policy of discrimination and to an open abandonment of neutral duties that finds few parallels in the modern history of neutrality. Elsewhere in this study the principal features of United States' neutrality legislation during this period are briefly reviewed (see, in particular, p. 210 (n)).

[24] For a discussion of the legal issues raised by "non-belligerency" in World War II, see pp. 197–9.

[25] Unless, of course, such departure from impartiality had as its basis a treaty permitting the taking of discriminatory measures against a state unlawfully resorting to war (see pp. 166 ff.).

perspective, however, so-called "non-belligerency" must be seen as a further manifestation of the recent decline of neutrality.[26]

C. CONCLUSIONS

In view of the experience of the two World Wars the suggestion has been made that in evaluating the prospects for observance of the traditional law regulating neutral-belligerent relations in future conflicts, it may be useful—as a practical measure—to distinguish between great and small wars.[27] In great wars, involving most of the major states and fought with the intensity that characterized the two World Wars, the expectation that belligerents will closely adhere to the traditional law in their behavior toward non-participants necessarily must prove remote. Nor is it to be expected that the non-participants in such wars will prove either able or willing to maintain a strict impartiality toward the belligerents. In a limited war, however, it is considered altogether possible that the belligerents may be required, of necessity, to refrain from subjecting non-participants to what has often resembled discretionary treatment. In turn, the non-participants may consider it in their interests to pursue a policy of strict impartiality.[28]

The evident merit of this suggestion is to be found in the clear recognition it accords to the importance of the relative strength of belligerents and neutrals in estimating the future effectiveness of a legal regime that has served to regulate neutral-belligerent relations on the basis of an approximate equality of rights. But even if the assumption of a return to limited war is granted it is by no means certain that many of the rules that have heretofore made up the traditional system will be given effective application. Although the contemporary decline of the traditional institution of neutrality must be attributed in large measure to an imbalance in the relative power of belligerents and neutrals it would surely be a serious error to

---

[26] Thus it is from this broader perspective that Julius Stone (*op. cit.*, p. 405) writes: "Can this American (as well as the Italian non-belligerency on the other side) be reduced merely to violation of the traditional rules of neutrality, which Germany and the Allies respectively were not prepared to treat as a *casus belli*? Only history can finally show whether these events can be dismissed as a series of mere neutral infractions of neutrality, tolerated by the injured belligerents."

[27] "It now seems reasonable to expect that practice in future may draw a distinction between great wars and small, or at least between general wars involving the greater part of the world and limited wars in which only two or not more than a few states are engaged. There are indeed some signs that this distinction is already beginning to be drawn." H. A. Smith, *op. cit.*, p. 75.

[28] It is, from this latter point of view, difficult to envisage two or three of the smaller states engaged in war successfully imposing "rationing" policies upon Great Britain (or, for that matter, upon any of the major powers). If anything, recent experience would appear to indicate that the principal difficulty would be to obtain the endorsement of a policy of strict impartiality on the part of the major non-participants.

neglect the importance of other factors which have contributed to the present situation. Perhaps the most significant among these other factors has been the gradual invalidation of an assumption fundamental to almost the whole of the traditional law of neutrality—that a clear distinction could be drawn between the public and private spheres and that the neutral state would not enter into economic activities long considered outside its proper functions. It is difficult to discern what possible effect—if indeed there would be any effect—limited wars could have upon this growing obsolescence of rules dependent for their operation upon the possibility of preserving a clear distinction between neutral state and neutral trader.[29]

In any event, it must be observed that whatever the merit of the above suggestion it can have only a limited relevance to an inquiry into the present status of the traditional law governing neutral-belligerent relations. An analysis that is to constitute something more than speculation over future possibilities must concentrate instead upon an evaluation of the actual materials at hand, that is upon an examination of the recent behavior of states in applying—or failing to apply—once valid rules. In a word, attention must be directed to the experience of the two World Wars, however difficult it may be to assess this experience in terms of its effect upon the traditional law.

In performing this task, considerations raised earlier concerning the relationship between the validity and the effectiveness of rules may be considered applicable.[30] Where, for example, belligerents have effectively asserted new forms of control over neutral trade on the high seas, and neutrals have acquiesced in such measures, the traditional law may well be regarded as modified. Less certain are those belligerent measures which, though perhaps effectively exercised, drew repeated protests from neutral states and which were largely justified by the belligerent claim to the right of reprisal against allegedly unlawful acts of an enemy. In these latter circumstances—and they formed the more numerous and more important

[29] See pp. 209–18 for a more detailed consideration of the present status of the distinction between neutral state and neutral trader, and the effect the dimming of this distinction has had upon the traditional law. It is only right to add that in making the suggestion that future practice may distinguish between great and small wars Smith draws careful attention to the profound changes that have occurred in the activities undertaken by the modern state and the impact of these changes upon the traditional law. Indeed, most recent writers have shown an acute awareness of the problem and of the difficulties it poses.

[30] See pp. 28–32.

controversies between neutral and belligerent—any conclusions drawn from recent conflicts must necessarily prove tentative.[31]

[31] It is only to be expected that in performing this task the opinions of writers will vary—at times considerably. For example, one well-qualified observer has recently stated: "It is now clear that in view of the events of the two World Wars, the Hague Conventions which regulate sea warfare have actually shared the fate of the Declaration of London. This is due as much to abuse on the part of the belligerents—particularly Germany—as to the inherent and inevitable weakness of a series of conventions whose intention was to protect the rights of neutrals rather than those of belligerents." S. W. D. Rowson, *op. cit.*, p. 170. While recognizing the necessary relationship that must obtain between the effectiveness and the binding quality of law this opinion is regarded as extreme. It hardly seems warranted to state that Hague XIII, Concerning the Rights and Duties of Neutral Powers in Maritime War, "has shared the fate of the Declaration of London." The Declaration of London, which sought to regulate the problem of neutral trade, was never ratified by the signatory states, formed from the start the object of endless controversy, and was openly abandoned by many of the belligerents in the opening stages of the first World War. With limited exceptions, the provisions of Hague XIII received, in both wars, the adherence of both neutrals and belligerents. It may also be noted that at the time of their conclusion the Hague Conventions regulating sea warfare—insofar as they departed from nineteenth century practice—were more commonly regarded as a concession to belligerent—rather than to neutral—pretensions.

VIII. RELATIONS BETWEEN NEUTRAL AND BELLIGERENT STATES IN NAVAL WARFARE

A. THE CONCEPT OF NEUTRALITY

Under general international law states that refrain from participating in war occupy a status of neutrality. As a consequence of such non-participation international law imposes duties and confers rights upon both neutral and belligerent, and the law of neutrality comprises the totality of the duties imposed and the rights conferred upon participants and non-participants. It is to be observed, then, that although neutrality may be defined simply as the status of non-participation in war, the legal significance of such non-participation must be seen in the fact that it brings into operation numerous rules whose purpose is the regulation of neutral-belligerent relations. Not infrequently, however, these rules—the consequence of non-participation—have been identified with neutrality itself. In particular, there has long been a widespread tendency to identify neutrality with the principle of impartiality.

In a sense, the identification of neutrality with the various duties imposed upon non-participants, and especially with the duty of impartiality, is readily understandable. The principle of impartiality stands at the very summit of the duties imposed upon non-participants. Nevertheless, it is submitted that this identification of neutrality with the duties imposed by general international law upon non-participants leads—both in theory and practice—to certain difficulties and ought to be avoided.[1] Instead, neu-

---

[1] In the preceding volume published in this series (Hans Kelsen, *Collective Security Under International Law*, pp. 141–4) the endeavor has been made to examine and to criticize the usual identification of neutrality with the consequences traditionally attached to the status of non-participation in hostilities. Professor Kelsen has observed that the earlier Hague Conventions use the term neutrality somewhat indiscriminately to mean, among other things, both a status of non-participation in war and an attitude of impartiality on the part of non-participants. It is further observed that writers, too, have been frequently indiscriminate in their use of the term. Professor Kelsen has concluded, correctly it is believed, that the way to avoid ambiguity and confusion "is to understand neutrality as nothing else but the status of a state which is not involved in a war between other states, and impartiality as the principle according to which a neutral state shall fulfill the obligations and exercise the rights, which a neutral state has under general international law, equally towards all other belligerents."

trality may be considered simply as the status of states which refrain from participation in hostilities. (Put in a slightly different manner, the only essential condition for neutral status is that of non-participation in hostilities.) It is—of course—quite true that as a result of non-participation in war general international law imposes certain duties and confers certain rights upon non-participants, and that these duties and rights make up what is commonly termed the traditional institution of neutrality. It is equally true that a neutral state must carry out its duties and enforce its rights in an impartial manner and that if the neutral state fails to do so the belligerent made the object of discriminatory measures is no longer bound to observe its duties toward the neutral. But so long as the neutral state refrains from participating in the hostilities, so long as it refrains from attacking one of the belligerents, and belligerents refrain from resorting to war against the neutral, a status of neutrality is preserved.[2]

These brief considerations would appear relevant in clarifying the legal position of states which refrain from active participation in a war though refusing to carry out the obligations imposed upon non-participants by general international law—and particularly the obligation to remain impartial toward the belligerents. In the absence of a treaty granting non-participants the right to discriminate against one of the belligerents, and obligating the belligerent to permit this discrimination, such departures as non-participants may take from duties otherwise imposed upon them clearly afford belligerents the right to take appropriate measures of reprisal. Thus in pursuing discriminatory measures against the Axis Powers in 1940–41 the United States departed from its duties as a neutral, and insofar as these measures could not be justified on the basis of the Kellogg-Briand Pact [3] they furnished the Axis Powers with sufficient

[2] See *Law of Naval Warfare*, Section 230. The objection may be made to the identification of neutrality with non-participation in war that it suffers from a lack of precision, that it fails to indicate what "non-participation" signifies in law. The history of "neutrality" indicates that the status of "non-participation" has been regarded as compatible with quite disparate forms of behavior on the part of non-participants. Thus during the seventeenth and eighteenth centuries the passage of troops of one belligerent through the territory of a non-participant was permitted. After the nineteenth century, however, this form of "benevolent" neutrality was clearly forbidden to non-participants.—But this objection is not compelling. If anything, it would appear to add further support to the view adopted here, since it only serves to emphasize that the one essential condition for neutrality has always been that of non-participation in hostilities. It is, of course, quite true that the consequences of non-participation have varied considerably, and that the non-participation of earlier times is something quite different from the consequences attached to non-participation by the traditional or classic rules of neutrality as they developed during the course of the nineteenth and early twentieth centuries. However, the identification of neutrality with non-participation in hostilities in no way denies this fact. Nor does it obscure in any way the consequences still attached to a status of non-participation according to general international law.

[3] See pp. 166–70.

reason for claiming the right to resort to reprisals.[4] But prior to its actual entrance into hostilities as an active participant the United States retained its status as a neutral state.

If the foregoing observations are accepted as correct then the legal significance of policies of "non-belligerency" becomes equally clear. It has already been observed that to the extent that this term has not been used merely as a synonym for the usual position occupied by non-participants it has served to indicate varying degrees of departure from the duties traditionally consequent upon a status of non-participation in war. And once again it is to be noted that in the absence of a treaty granting non-participants the right—and, perhaps, even the duty—to discriminate against a belligerent, the failure of a neutral to observe the duties imposed upon non-participants by the traditional law affords belligerents the right to take measures of reprisal against the neutral. By abandoning its duties the neutral thereby surrenders its right to demand from belligerents that behavior which it would otherwise be entitled to claim. At the same time, a neutral status is maintained so long as the "non-belligerent" refrains from actively participating in the hostilities, either through attacking one of the belligerents or through being attacked by a belligerent. In turn, this must imply that the traditional duties and rights attending a status of non-participation in hostilities continue to remain applicable. Nor does it appear that the events of World War II—a period during which a number

[4] There is no need to inquire here into the political motives a state may have in departing from the duties imposed upon it as a non-participant. In resorting to discriminatory measures a state may claim that its vital interests are threatened by the course a war is taking. In part, the justification for both the destroyer-base agreement with Great Britain and the Lend-Lease Act (see p. 207(n)) rested upon considerations that may be regarded as devoid of proper legal foundation. However, in testifying (January 16, 1941) before Congress on behalf of the then pending Lend-Lease Act, the Secretary of State declared that although the provisions of the proposed act would admittedly lead to violations of established rules of neutrality under "ordinary circumstances . . . we are not here dealing with an ordinary war situation. Rather we are confronted with a situation that is extraordinary in character." *U. S. Naval War College, International Law Documents, 1940*, p. 109. In reviewing these same acts Hyde (*op. cit.*, pp. 2234–7) also denies their character as violations of international law, contending that a neutral need not establish "that inherently illegal action has been directed against itself by the belligerent . . . before it can properly free itself from restrictions that normally rest upon it. . . ." Hyde draws a distinction between the "breach and the inapplicability of particular rules of neutrality," concluding that the acts in question fell within the latter category, their inapplicability following from the alleged right of a neutral to depart from neutral duties in order to preserve what it considers to be its vital interests.

It is extremely difficult to accept this argument. According to general international law, neutral departure from the duty of impartiality may be justified only as a reaction to the belligerent's violation of neutral rights. Even then, it seems correct to state that such measures of reprisal must be taken *against the offending belligerent* and not take the form of assistance furnished to the other belligerent. On the other hand, it is quite true that a neutral can disregard its duties as a non-participant if it considers its vital interests threatened—as the United States obviously did so feel in 1940–41. But in so doing the neutral forfeits the right to demand from the offended belligerent that behavior to which it would otherwise be entitled.

of non-participants declared themselves to occupy a status of "non-belligerency"—provide substantial reason for suggesting any contrary conclusions.[5]

B. THE COMMENCEMENT AND TERMINATION OF NEUTRALITY

Unlike the law governing the mutual behavior of combatants, a large part of which may be considered operative in any international armed conflict,[6] the rules regulating the behavior of neutrals and belligerents remain

[5] An excellent survey of World War II events in this regard is given by J. L. Kunz, "Neutrality and the European War 1939–1940," *Michigan Law Review*, 39 (1940–41), pp. 747–54. Italy, Turkey, Hungary and Spain—among other states—proclaimed a status of "non-belligerency." Professor Kunz has concluded that the latter "has no foundation in law, is exclusively a political creation. It appears in Protean forms: there are 'non-belligerents' who are practically neutral, and 'neutrals' who are 'non-belligerents', some states are 'non-belligerent' out of their own free will, others more or less by coercion. 'Non-belligerency' . . . is born out of the desire to intervene under the name of non-intervention, to be in the war and yet not to be at war. . . . While the 'non-belligerent' is fully aware that the disfavored belligerent has a right in law to resort to reprisals or to a declaration of war, it is believed that from reasons of political expediency he will not do so" (pp. 753–4). The majority of writers concur with this position. On the other hand, the assertion that the traditional law does not "recognize" or does not attach "legal consequences" to a position of "non-belligerency" may prove somewhat misleading. The traditional law clearly does recognize this position, and precisely for the reason that it does attach to it certain legal consequences (e. g., reprisals). In fact, it would seem that what writers actually have in mind when they declare that the traditional law does not recognize a condition of non-belligerency is that this law does not grant neutral states a *right* to depart from the duties otherwise imposed upon non-participants, a right in the sense that the injured belligerent is obliged to permit these acts and to refrain from taking reprisals. It is, for example, in this sense that Stone (*op. cit.*, p. 383) may be understood when he remarks that: "The traditional law of neutrality confronts third states with only two choices, either to join in the war or to observe the duties of impartiality."—Furthermore, it is precisely the case of so-called "non-belligerency" that provides a clear illustration of the utility of identifying neutrality merely as the status of non-participation in hostilities. For although the "non-belligerent" may discriminate openly against one of the belligerents (and thereby furnish the latter with adequate cause for taking reprisals), it nevertheless retains a neutral status so long as it does not enter into the hostilities. If, on the other hand, neutrality is identified with the duty of impartiality then the discriminating non-participant must be regarded as not only violating its duties under general international law but as no longer neutral. The latter conclusion is obviously unwarranted, and its basis may be attributed to the insistence upon identifying neutrality with the principle of impartiality —In this connection, however, it has been observed that: "The notion of neutrality as merely non-involvement in direct hostilities is inconsistent with the traditional concept, and if it should come to have this meaning, the concept would have been strikingly narrowed." Robert R. Wilson, "'Non-belligerency' in Relation to the Terminology of Neutrality," *A. J. I. L.*, 35 (1941), pp. 122–3. But the "notion of neutrality as mere non-involvement in hostilities" is not inconsistent with the traditional concept. The inconsistency is rather between the duties attached by the traditional law to a status of non-involvement in hostilities and the legally untenable contention that so-called "non-belligerents" possess the *right* to depart from these duties, while remaining non-participants. This is indeed the crux of the matter, and the events of World War II can hardly be considered as detracting from this conclusion.

[6] See pp. 23–5.

strictly dependent for their operation upon the existence of a state of war. It may be, however, that states engaged in armed conflict are unwilling to issue a declaration of war or even to acknowledge the existence of a state of war.[7] In such situations it would appear that the decision as to whether or not to recognize the existence of a state of war, and thereby to bring into force the law of neutrality, must rest principally with third states. The attitude of the parties engaged in armed conflict need not prove decisive for third states, the latter being at liberty either to accept the position of the contestants (i. e., the position that war does not exist) or to reject this position and to invoke the law of neutrality.[8]

Although it is customary for belligerents to notify third states of the outbreak of hostilities[9] the latter cannot rely on the absence of such notification as a justification for the non-performance of neutral duties if it is estab-

---

[7] Thus both parties to the Sino-Japanese conflict of 1937 refused to acknowledge the existence of a state of war—though the Assembly of the League of Nations later found that Japan had "resorted to war" in violation of her obligations under the Kellogg-Briand Pact.

[8] This, at least, would seem to be the only feasible solution to the difficult situation that may arise in cases of undeclared hostilities. In practice, however, third states are likely to take the position of the contestants at face value, since the rules of neutrality invariably operate to restrict the behavior of non-participants—particularly with respect to trade. It is only to be expected that third parties will normally desire to avoid bringing these restrictions into effect. Distinguish, though, between the operation of the law of neutrality as determined by international law and the operation of municipal neutrality laws. The latter may be applied to situations other than war in the sense of international law. Thus Section 1 (c) of the Neutrality Act of May 1, 1937, declared that: "Whenever the President shall find that a state of civil strife exists in a foreign State and that such civil strife is of a magnitude or is being conducted under such conditions that the export of arms, ammunition, or implements of war from the United States to such foreign State would threaten or endanger the peace of the United States, the President shall proclaim such fact, and it shall thereafter be unlawful to export, or attempt to export, or cause to be exported, arms, ammunition, or implements of war from any place in the United States to such foreign State, or to any neutral State for transshipment to, or for the use of, such foreign State." For text, see *U. S. Naval War College, International Law Situations, 1939*, pp. 101 ff.

It should be observed that operation of the international law of neutrality presupposes, and is dependent upon, the recognition of insurgents in a civil war as belligerents. Prior to such recognition—whether by the parent state or by third states—there can be no condition of belligerency, hence no neutrality in the sense of international law. Although third states may grant any kind of material assistance to the parent government fighting insurrectionists, aid to the latter amounts to intervention in the internal affairs of the parent state and is forbidden. Of course, once the parent state recognizes the insurgents as belligerents, or once third states so recognize the insurgents independent from any act of recognition by the parent state, the civil war is transformed into an international war, and the rules of neutrality come into force. For a survey of the problems arising in this regard, see H. Lauterpacht, *Recognition in International Law* (1947), Part III. And for U. S. practice, Hyde, *op. cit.*, pp. 2330–5.

[9] According to Article 2 of Hague III (1907), Relative to the Opening of Hostilities, a state of war "must be notified to the neutral Powers without delay, and shall not take effect in regard to them until after the receipt of a notification, which may even be given by telegraph. Neutral Powers, nevertheless, cannot plead the absence of notification if it is established beyond doubt that they were in fact aware of the state of war."

lished that knowledge of the commencement of war in fact existed. Third states, in turn, are not required to issue special declarations proclaiming their intention to refrain from participating in the war and to observe the duties of a neutral state.

In practice, however, third states generally do issue, upon the outbreak of war, neutrality declarations or proclamations that are directed not only to their own officials and subjects but also to the belligerents. International law in laying down the scope of a neutral's duties and rights leaves to the neutral state the task of fulfilling these duties and of exercising these rights. Within the limits prescribed by international law the neutral state may act at its discretion. It must regulate, in various ways, the behavior of individuals located within neutral jurisdiction. It must decide, within the limits imposed by international law, upon the use it is to allow belligerents of its waters and ports. Thus the neutral state may choose to allow the use of its waters and ports up to the limits prescribed by international law; but it may choose to place severe restrictions upon the entrance and stay of belligerent warships. Still further, the neutral state may desire to place restrictions upon the activities of its subjects—particularly with respect to trading with belligerents—in excess of any requirements laid upon the neutral state by international law.[10] Neutrality declarations form a practical necessity, therefore, not only for the information of the officials and the subjects of the neutral state but for the information of belligerents as well.[11]

---

[10] As did the United States in its Neutrality Acts of 1935, 1937 and 1939 (see p. 210(n)).

[11] It is for the reasons discussed above that the preamble to Hague Convention XIII (1907) declares that "it is desirable that the powers should issue detailed enactments to regulate the results of the attitude of neutrality when adopted by them." An invaluable collection of neutrality legislation and declarations has been compiled by F. Deak and P. C. Jessup, *A Collection of Neutrality Laws, Regulations and Treaties of Various Countries* (1939), 2 vols. (Neutrality declarations issued by third states upon the outbreak of World War II are contained in a loose-leaf supplement.)

In 1939, upon the commencement of hostilities in Europe, the majority of non-participating states did issue neutrality declarations. For a general survey of World War II practice in this regard, see J. L. Kunz, *op. cit.*, pp. 729–32. Hyde (*op. cit.*, pp. 2316–7) has described United States practice in the following general terms: "Upon the outbreak of war, the executive issues a so-called neutrality proclamation addressed primarily to persons 'residing or being within the territory or jurisdiction of the United States.' By this means he endeavors to minimize the danger of the commission of acts which, unless retarded, may either expose the Government to the charge of neglect of its acknowledged duties as a neutral, or render their performance more burdensome. To that end the proclamation calls attention (a) to the several acts which the local statutory law prohibits; (b) to the decision of the executive as to the extent and nature of the privileges to be accorded belligerent ships of war within American waters; and (c) to the requirements of the law of nations as well as of the statutes and treaties of the United States, that no person within its territory and jurisdiction 'shall take part, directly or indirectly in the war. The individuals concerned are enjoined, moreover, to commit therein no act contrary to the law whether national or international. A warning is appended as to the impropriety of certain unneutral services on the high seas, and of the risks and penalties to be anticipated in case of capture. American citizens and others claiming the protection of the

The termination of neutral status presents no special difficulty, being subject to essentially the same considerations as those determining the commencement of neutrality. Just as there is no duty imposed by customary international law upon third states to refrain from participating in a war that has once broken out, or for belligerents to respect a status of non-participation, so there is no duty either on the part of the neutral or on the part of the belligerent to refrain from resorting to war against one another at any time thereafter. It is one of the seeming paradoxes of the traditional law that it may be violated only by acts of neutral or belligerent which fall short of war, though not by the act of resorting to war itself.[12] And even though it may now be contended that a belligerent is no longer free to attack non-participants for whatever reasons it may deem desirable, in view of the changes—earlier discussed [13]—in the legal position of war, there is no doubt that if a non-participant has been so attacked the status of neutrality has come to an end.

C. THE NEUTRAL'S DUTY OF IMPARTIALITY

Among the duties imposed upon non-participants by the traditional system the duty of impartiality occupies a central position.[14] Despite its

Government, 'who may misconduct themselves in the premises,' are informed that they can in no wise obtain any protection from the United States 'against the consequences of their misconduct.'" Upon the outbreak of war in September, 1939, the President issued, on September 5, 1939, two proclamations of neutrality. The first, a "general neutrality proclamation," outlined those acts forbidden within the jurisdiction of the United States. The proclamation was based upon the rules and procedure of international law as well as upon domestic statutes in conformity with these rules. The second, a "special" neutrality proclamation, was based upon the Neutrality Act of May 1, 1937, later replaced by the Neutrality Act of November 4, 1939.

[12] For a clear presentation of this and related aspects of the traditional institution of neutrality see J. L. Kunz (*Kriegsrecht und Neutralitätsrecht*, pp. 214 ff.) who properly emphasizes that as there is no obligation under customary law to take up a neutral status at the commencement of war, so there is no obligation to remain neutral for the duration of war. The same lack of obligation applies, *mutatis mutandis*, in the relation of the belligerent to the neutral. Occasionally, however, writers have refused to draw these conclusions, despite the fact that they constitute the obvious consequences of the traditional status of war itself. Thus it has been stated that in a war in which the rules governing neutral-belligerent relations are being observed, a neutral ought not to abandon its status of non-participation "except for a reason not connected with the cause of the war in progress, nor ought a belligerent to draw the neutral into the war." To declare war "simply because it does not suit the belligerent any longer to recognize its [neutral's] impartial attitude, or because it does not suit the neutral to remain neutral any longer . . . *ipso facto* constitutes a violation of neutrality. . . ." Oppenheim-Luaterpacht, *op. cit.*, p. 671. But it is difficult to reconcile these and similar statements either with the traditional legal interpretation of war or with the traditional institution of neutrality.

[13] See pp. 3–4, 165 ff.

[14] Although the law of neutrality imposes duties and confers rights upon neutral and belligerent alike the focus of an inquiry into this law may perhaps best be centered around the duties of the neutral. In brief, four general duties are imposed upon neutral states: the duty to act impartially toward the belligerents; the duty to abstain from furnishing belligerents any

admitted importance, however, the principle of impartiality has been a frequent source of controversy and misunderstanding.[15] As a duty imposed upon neutral states by the positive law the principle of impartiality may be defined simply as obligating neutral states to fulfill their duties and to exercise their rights in an equal (i. e., impartial or non-discriminatory) manner toward all the belligerents.[16] Hence the principle of impartiality, as a principle of the positive law, does not determine the contents of the

material assistance for the prosecution of war; the duty to prevent the commission of hostile acts within neutral jurisdiction as well as to prevent the use of neutral jurisdiction as a base for belligerent operations; and, finally, the duty to acquiesce in certain repressive measures taken by belligerents against private neutral commerce on the high seas. Under these general duties—which establish correlative rights of belligerents—may be grouped almost all the specific obligations regulating the conduct of neutral states in naval warfare. The duties of a neutral state may also be classified—and frequently are so classified—as duties of abstention, prevention and acquiesence (or toleration). Duties of abstention refer to acts the neutral state itself must refrain from performing; duties of prevention refer to acts the commission of which within its jurisdiction the neutral is obligated to prevent; and, finally, duties of acquiescence have reference to neutral obligations to permit belligerent measures of repression against neutral subjects found rendering certain acts of assistance to an enemy.

It is also helpful to observe that the duties of a neutral correspond to the rights of a belligerent, and that the rights of a neutral correspond to the duties of a belligerent. The neutral's duty to observe a strict impartiality corresponds to the belligerent's right to demand impartiality on the part of the neutral. At the same time, the neutral has a right to demand that the belligerent will act toward it in such a manner as to respect its position of impartiality, and there is no question but that the belligerent is under a duty to do so. A similar analysis applies, for example, to the neutral's duty to prevent its waters and ports from being used as a base for belligerent operations. Here again, the belligerent though having a right to demand that neutrals not permit their waters and ports from being so used, also has a duty to respect these waters and ports. Conversely the neutral, though having a duty, also has a right to demand that its waters and ports not be used by belligerents as a base of operations.

15 In large measure, this controversy would appear to stem from a failure to distinguish with sufficient clarity between impartiality in the sense of a moral-political postulate and impartiality in the sense of a duty imposed upon neutral states by the positive law. Historically, the significance of the idea that neutrals should occupy a position of impartiality toward the belligerents has been considerable. Elsewhere (see pp. 191–2), emphasis has been placed upon the degree to which the attitude of impartiality—and even of indifference—toward the belligerents formed part of the political structure upon which the traditional law of neutrality depended for its effectiveness during the nineteenth century. At the same time, it is a mistake to believe that the rules regulating the status of non-participants represent the "logical" application of the conviction that neutrals ought to behave impartially. It is hardly possible to derive from this conviction—as a moral-political postulate—the specific rules of the positive law regulating the conduct of neutral states, if only for the reason that the law of neutrality is the product of other factors as well (not the least of which has been the perennial conflict of interest between neutral and belligerent, and the sheer necessity for reaching a compromise as between these conflicting interests).

16 The preamble to Hague Convention XIII (1907) declares that "it is, for neutral Powers, an admitted duty to apply these rules impartially to the several belligerents." And Article 9 of the same Convention reads: "A neutral Power must apply impartially to the two belligerents the conditions, restrictions or prohibitions made by it in regard to the admission into its ports, roadsteads, or territorial waters, of belligerent warships or of their prizes." A brief, though excellent, discussion of the neutral duty of impartiality is contained in *Harvard Research in*

duties imposed and the rights conferred upon neutrals.[17] The impartiality demanded by the traditional law of neutrality does not even relate directly to the contents of other neutral obligations and rights, but to the manner in which these obligations and rights shall be applied.

Nor does the neutral's duty of impartiality require that the measures a neutral must—or may—take bear with equal effect upon the belligerents. It is entirely possible—and in many instances almost inevitable—that the strict fulfillment by a neutral of its obligations will result in the greater discomfort and disadvantage of one side in a war. A belligerent has not, for this reason, legitimate cause for complaint.[18] Even more possible is the unequal effect upon belligerents that may result from the exercise of neutral rights. Thus a neutral state in the exercise of its right to place special restrictions upon the belligerents' use of its waters and ports is obligated only to see that the restrictions it imposes are applied impartially. The same may be said of the neutral state's privilege either to allow or to restrict, or to forbid entirely, the export trade carried on by its nationals with the belligerents. The fact that the exercise made of these neutral rights thereby places one of the belligerents at a disadvantage with respect to its opponent does not provide the disadvantaged belligerent with a lawful basis for claiming that it has been made the object of discriminatory measures.

Nor is it a violation of neutrality if, in the exercise of its rights, a neutral state actually intends to confer an advantage upon one side. As already observed, the traditional law of neutrality permits to neutrals a substantial measure of discretion in determining whether or not to exercise their

---

International Law, Draft Convention on Rights and Duties of Neutral States in Naval and Aerial War, *A. J. I. L.*, 22 (1939), *Supp.*, pp. 232–5. Article 4 of the Draft Convention reads: "A neutral state, in the exercise of its neutral rights and in the performance of its neutral duties, shall be impartial and shall refrain from discriminating between belligerents." And see *Law of Naval Warfare*, Article 240b.

[17] But see the statement in Oppenheim-Lauterpacht (*op. cit.*, p. 653): "Neutrality may be defined as the attitude of impartiality adopted by third States towards belligerents and recognized by belligerents, such attitude creating rights and duties between the impartial states and the belligerents." However, it is not the attitude of impartiality which "creates rights and duties." It is rather the status of non-participation in war which creates rights and duties, among which is the duty of impartiality.

[18] "Impartiality is one of the essential features of neutrality. But at the same time I must emphasize very strongly . . . the fact that the statement that neutrality demands impartiality means simply impartiality in the application of law; it rarely ever results in impartiality in operation. International law imposes certain obligations upon a neutral nation which it must perform with reference to each belligerent in a war; but international law does not impose any obligation on a neutral to see that the performance of these obligations should operate in the same manner on each belligerent. And, in fact, a neutral obligation rarely, if ever, operates in the same manner on each belligerent." Statement by Charles Warren to the U. S. Senate Committee on Foreign Relations, February 5, 1936, cited in Hackworth, *op. cit.*, Vol. VII, p. 377. For equally clear statements to the same effect, see Kunz, *op. cit.*, p. 217, and Verdross, *Völkerrecht*, p. 412.

rights.[19] Within this area of discretion neutral states necessarily will be guided by considerations of policy, and the latter may dictate an exercise of neutral rights the result of which is intended to benefit one side in the conflict. The frequent contention that such intent on the part of the neutral state is a violation of the neutral's duty of impartiality has no foundation, however. The so-called "attitude of impartiality" demanded of neutrals does not refer, in its strict legal meaning, to the *political motives* behind neutral behavior, but to that behavior itself. Hence, it may well be that in the exercise of its rights the neutral state both intends to confer and does in fact confer an advantage upon one side. In doing so it does not depart from the duty of impartiality so long as it refrains from discriminating against either belligerent in the actual application of those regulations it is at liberty to enact.[20]

---

[19] It is to be observed, however, that the principle of impartiality cannot be interpreted as restricting the operation of the *duties* otherwise imposed upon a neutral state. Thus a neutral state is obligated to abstain from supplying belligerents with war materials and to prevent the use of its territory as a base for the conduct of belligerent operations. The duties of abstention and of prevention are violated even though the neutral state may act impartially in supplying belligerents with war materials and in permitting the use of its territory as a base of operations. In brief, the discretion allowed to a neutral does not pertain to the fulfillment of duties—though the neutral may choose different ways in which to secure the fulfillment of its duties—but to the exercise of rights.

[20] It should also be apparent from these remarks that the impartiality required of a neutral state does not obligate the latter to look upon the conflict with "indifference." The neutral state may be—in spirit—wholly in sympathy with one side in the conflict, but as long as it *acts* in an impartial manner, in the sense described above, it fulfills its obligation.—The failure to distinguish clearly between the various *policies* open to a neutral and the *legal duties* imposed upon the latter characterized much of the debate over American neutrality during the years prior to this country's entrance into World War II. This confusion of policy considerations with legal principle was particularly apparent in the unfounded contention that the duty of impartiality required not only the avoidance of any intent to confer an advantage upon one side in the conflict (even though such advantage would be conferred as a result of the impartial application of neutral rights) but also the adoption of measures that would insure the belligerents a factual equality of treatment.

In this connection brief note should be taken of the possible bearing the principle of impartiality may have upon the neutral's attempt to alter its laws and regulations *during the course of a war.* When in November 1939 the United States modified certain features of its neutrality legislation the question arose as to the compatibility of such change with the duty of impartiality. One of the principal effects of the Neutrality Act of November 4, 1939, was to remove the earlier embargo placed on the sale to belligerents of arms, munitions and other implements of war. In taking this action the United States removed a restriction which, as a neutral, it need never have imposed. At the same time, the effect of the change—and, it was claimed, its intent—was to aid the Allies. It is at least doubtful, however, whether the legitimacy of such change as a neutral may make in its neutrality legislation during the course of a war can be determined by reference to the principle of impartiality. Instead, it would appear that attention must be directed toward establishing whether or not state practice does expressly limit the neutral in this respect, quite apart from the principle of impartiality. From this point of view the question is admittedly a close one, though there is much to be said for the position expressed in the preamble to Hague XIII (1907), to the effect that the neutrality regulations issued by a neutral "should not, in principle be altered, in the course of the war . . .

Finally, it must be emphasized that the duty of impartiality applies to the acts of the neutral state (i. e., to the acts of organs or officials of the neutral state) and not to the private acts of its subjects. Apart from certain limited exceptions,[21] the neutral state is under no obligation to prevent its subjects from giving material assistance to a belligerent, though it may forbid such behavior should it so desire. Clearer still is the absence of any duty imposed upon the neutral state to prevent its subjects from giving moral assistance to, or expressing sympathy for, one side in the conflict.[22]

D. THE NEUTRAL'S DUTY TO ABSTAIN FROM SUPPLYING BELLIGERENTS WITH GOODS AND SERVICES

Together with the duty of impartiality, and of equal importance, is the obligation laid upon neutrals by the traditional law to abstain from furnishing belligerents with certain goods or services.[23] In naval warfare a

except in a case where experience has shown the necessity for such change for the protection of the rights of that (neutral) power. . . ." Certainly the United States took this position during World War I in response to complaints by the Central Powers that this country ought to place an embargo on the exportation of war implements to the Allies. The difficulty is in ascertaining when a neutral does change its regulations ostensibly for the purpose of better safeguarding its rights or fulfilling its duties, since it is commonly acknowledged that here—at least—change is permitted.

[21] See pp. 227–31.

[22] For this reason the claim advanced by the Axis Powers during World War II, that neutral states were obligated to prevent private expressions of sympathy or support for one belligerent, was wholly devoid of support in law. Known variously as "total" or "ideological" neutrality the essential features of this doctrine, as expounded by its leading protagonists, was to extend the neutral's duties to the strict control of public opinion in time of war as well as in time of peace. In particular, the neutral state was considered as obligated to maintain a rigid control over the press and to insure its impartiality. See E. H. Bockhoff, "Ganze oder halbe Neutralität," in *Nationalsozialistische Monatshefte* (1938), pp. 910 ff. Although the doctrine had no basis in law, and was repudiated by a number of writers (e. g., Edward Hambro, "Ideologische Neutralität," *Zeitschrift für öffentliches Recht*, 19 (1939), pp. 502 ff. and J. L. Kunz, "Neutrality and The European War," pp. 744–7), a number of neutral states did impose restrictions upon the freedom of private expressions of sympathy for one side. Distinguish, however, between expressions of sympathy for a belligerent by the subjects of a neutral state and by the organs or officials of the neutral government. Occasionally it has been asserted that even the latter are compatible with a strict impartiality, though this is very doubtful. For United States practice in this respect, see Hackworth, *op. cit.*, Vol. VII, pp. 374–7.

[23] In formulating the neutral duty under immediate consideration it is tempting to give it a broader scope than indicated above by stating that the neutral state is obliged to abstain from furnishing *any form of assistance to belligerents as would aid the latter in the prosecution of war*. Many writers formulate the neutral's duty in this manner. Nevertheless, this manner of formulation is apt to prove somewhat misleading, particularly when applied to neutral duties in naval warfare, if only for the reason that the use belligerents may make of neutral ports and waters do constitute—save perhaps in the purely formal sense—a form of assistance to belligerents. It is, of course, always possible to assert that—by definition—a neutral state is forbidden to render any assistance to belligerents as would aid the latter in the prosecution of war; hence the example of the various uses belligerents may make of neutral waters and ports cannot constitute—again by definition—assistance to belligerents. But this is surely a fiction, which can hardly succeed in hiding the legal reality, and it would appear much more accurate merely to

neutral state violates this duty if it provides belligerents with warships, munitions, or war materials of any kind.[24] In this respect, Article 6 of Hague Convention XIII (1907) declares that the "supply, in any manner, directly or indirectly, by a neutral Power to a belligerent Power, of warships, ammunition, or war materials of any kind whatever, is forbidden." [25]

Where the neutral state directly acts to sell, lend or otherwise furnish a belligerent with "warships, munitions or war materials" the situation does not admit of doubt.[26] Nor is the unlawful behavior of the neutral state

state—as a general principle—that neutrals are required to abstain from rendering certain supplies or services to belligerents, whether directly or indirectly In this connection it is of interest to note that although Article 5 of the *Harvard Draft Convention on The Rights and Duties of Neutral States in Naval and Aerial War* (*op. cit.*, p. 235) declares that a neutral state "shall abstain from supplying to a belligerent assistance for the prosecution of the war," the comment to this Article emphasizes the "considerable difficulty in drafting an adequate article on this subject. It has been found impossible to draft an article which would describe fully all the types of aid which a State may not furnish to a belligerent. There may be at least indirect types of aid which are permissible. . . . Thus . . . a neutral State may afford to belligerent warships certain facilities in its ports . . ." (p. 237).

[24] And, of course, if it provides belligerents with loans or credits.

[25] The term "war materials" can hardly be interpreted other than in relation to the prevailing conception of contraband (see pp. 263–7). In a war in which the articles considered to constitute contraband have been greatly expanded, the goods a neutral state must abstain from furnishing belligerents will be correspondingly expanded.

[26] Thus when judged solely by the obligations imposed by Article 6 of Hague XIII, the transfer by the United States of over-age destroyers to Great Britain in 1940 was clearly a violation of neutral duties. The same must be said of the Act to Promote the Defense of the United States, approved March 11, 1941—the so-called Lend-Lease Act. See *U. S. Naval War College, International Law Documents, 1940*, pp. 74–91, 132–7. Section 3 of the Lend-Lease Act declared:

"(a) Notwithstanding the provisions of any other law, the President may, from time to time, when he deems it in the interest of national defense, authorize the Secretary of War, the Secretary of the Navy or the head of any other department or agency of the Government—

(1) To manufacture in arsenals, factories, and shipyards under their jurisdiction, or otherwise procure, to the extent to which funds are made available therefor, or contracts are authorized from time to time by the Congress, or both, any defense article for the government of any country whose defense the President deems vital to the defense of the United States. (2) To sell, transfer title to, exchange, lease, lend, or otherwise dispose of, to any such government any defense article (3) To test, inspect, prove, repair, outfit, recondition, or otherwise to place in good working order, to the extent to which funds are made available therefor, or contracts are authorized from time to time by the Congress, or both, any defense article for any such government, or to procure any or all such services by private contract. (4) To communicate to any such government any defense information, pertaining to any defense article furnished to such government under paragraph (2) of this subsection. (5) To release for export any defense article disposed of in any way under this subsection to any such government."

Section 2 of the Act provided that: "The term 'defense article' means (1) any weapon, munition, aircraft, vessel or boat; (2) any machinery, facility, tool, material, or supply necessary for the manufacture, production, processing, repair, servicing, or operation of any article described in this subsection; (3) Any component material or part of or equipment for any article described in this subsection; (4) Any agricultural, industrial or other commodity or article for defense."

But for a justification of the Lend-Lease Act and the destroyer-base agreement on grounds other than those under immediate consideration, see pp. 168–9, 198(n)).

altered in any way by the fact that the aid furnished by the neutral has as its basis a trade agreement concluded prior to the outbreak of war. On the other hand, the application of this neutral duty may not always be clear. Difficult considerations frequently arise, for example, in the attempt to determine if and when a neutral state has acted "indirectly" to supply a belligerent with the sinews of war. Thus a neutral state may follow a policy of encouraging the supply of war materials to a belligerent through private traders, while itself abstaining from any direct action.[27] In instances such as these it may not be immediately apparent that the neutral state has acted in violation of its obligations. In fact, the growth in the power of the state has given rise to considerable difficulties in practice, and these difficulties will be dealt with shortly. Here it is sufficient to emphasize only the strict abstention from supplying belligerents with war materials that is, in principle, required of neutral states.

This same duty of abstention serves to limit the behavior of the neutral state in other respects as well. As Hyde has observed, "the duty to abstain from giving aid is a broad one and covers a vast field of governmental activities;" for in addition to the prohibition against supplying belligerents with war materials of any kind the neutral is obligated, in general, "to abstain from placing its various governmental agencies at the disposal of a belligerent in such a way as to aid it directly or indirectly in the prosecution of the war." [28] Thus in naval warfare, the public vessels of a neutral state must refrain from rendering services of any kind to belligerent naval units at sea. They must not act as supply vessels or tenders to belligerent warships, they must not serve as transports for carrying members of a belligerent's armed forces, they must not communicate any information to belligerent warships which would assist the latter in operations against an enemy, and they must not interfere—in any manner—with the legitimate operations of belligerent warships.[29]

---

[27] During the first year of World War II the United States resorted to a policy of making war materials owned by this Government available to Great Britain and France through the intermediary of private firms. Old stocks of arms and ammunition were turned back by the War Department to private manufacturers who then sold them through the Allied Purchasing Agency to the British and French Governments. Similar "trade in" agreements were carried out with respect to aircraft. In examining these measures one observer has noted: "None of these transactions appear to have been carried on directly between the United States and belligerent countries or their respective agencies. Yet it is clear that the purpose of the United States Government . . . was to give all possible aid to Great Britain and France in the present war, and these transactions appear to have been carried out in pursuance of that purpose, and as a result of negotiation and concerted action." Lester H. Woolsey, "Government Traffic in Contraband," *A. J. I. L.*, 34 (1940), p. 500.

[28] Hyde, *op. cit.*, pp. 2230–1.

[29] There are certain acts of a humanitarian character, however, that neutral warships may perform and that are not regarded as aiding a belligerent. The warships of a neutral state may rescue ship-wrecked survivors from a belligerent warship, provided only that the neutral prevents the survivors from participating again in hostilities. (See pp. 122–3).

It is one of the principal characteristics of the traditional system of neutrality that whereas the neutral state is under the strict obligation to abstain from furnishing belligerents with certain goods and services it is normally under no obligation to prevent its subjects from undertaking to perform these same acts of assistance.[30] With respect to trade in war materials carried on by the subjects of a neutral state Article 7 of Hague Convention XIII provides that a "neutral Power is not bound to prevent the export or transit, for the use of either belligerent, of arms, ammunition, or, in general, of anything which can be of use to an army or fleet." Occasionally, it is true, belligerents have questioned this absence of obligation on the part of the neutral state, especially when the export of war materials by private individuals has served to confer—in fact—a decided advantage upon one side. Thus, during World War I the Central Powers complained to the United States that the volume of traffic in arms and munitions being exported from this country to the Allies had reached such large proportions, and conferred so decided an advantage upon one side, as to raise the question whether the continuance of this traffic could be regarded as compatible with the obligations imposed upon a neutral state—and particularly with the obligation to observe a strict impartiality toward the belligerents. In rejecting the suggestion that an embargo be placed upon the export of war materials the United States contended that a neutral state was neither under an obligation to prevent private individuals from supplying war materials to belligerents nor under a duty to ensure that the resources coming from neutral territory would not serve to confer a decided advantage upon one side. It is clear that in taking this position the United States had the support of the established law.[31] The proper recourse open to dis-

[30] There are, however, some significant exceptions to this distinction between the obligations imposed upon a neutral state with respect to its own acts and the absence of obligation with respect to similar acts when performed by subjects of the neutral state. A neutral state is not only obliged to abstain itself from performing such acts as may be regarded as serving to turn its territory into a base of operations for belligerents; it is also obliged to prevent the commission of acts by private individuals within its jurisdiction which may be considered as having a similar effect (see pp. 227–31). It is sufficient to observe here, though, that the traditional law does not regard the export of war materials—warships apart—from neutral territory, when undertaken by private individuals in the course of ordinary commercial transactions, as serving to turn such territory into a base of operations for belligerents.

[31] The relevant correspondence dealing with the incident in question is given in Hackworth, *op. cit.*, Vol. VII, pp. 617–21. There can be little doubt as to the correctness—in strict law—of the American position, a conclusion reached at the time by several writers in an exhaustive review of the matter in *A. J. I. L.*, 10 (1916). See W. C. Morey, "The Sale of Munitions of War," pp. 476 ff.; C. N. Gregory, "Neutrality and the Sale of Arms," pp. 543 ff.; and J. W. Garner, "The Sale and Exportation of Arms and Munitions of War to Belligerents," pp. 749 ff. At the same time, it was equally clear not only that the scale of the traffic in arms and munitions to the Allies represented an unprecedented event but that the traffic itself was very likely a decisive factor in staving off Allied defeat. See, generally, Alice M. Morrissey, *The American Defence of Neutral Rights 1914–1917* (1939). It is of interest to note that the position taken by the Central Powers did not rest directly upon an advocacy of a "principle of equalization" but

advantaged belligerents is to undertake repressive measures against the subjects of a neutral state engaged in furnishing assistance to an enemy, and the rules relating to contraband, blockade and unneutral service, as well as the rules governing visit, search and seizure, prescribe lawful means belligerents may use to accomplish this end. In turn, the neutral state must acquiesce in the repressive measures a belligerent is permitted by law to take at sea against the subjects of a neutral state engaged in assisting an enemy—whether by supplying him with war materials or by furnishing him with other forms of assistance.

But although a neutral state is under no obligation to do so it may place restrictions upon, or forbid entirely, both the export from and transit through its territory of war materials intended for belligerents. The conservation of resources or the more effective preservation of neutral status may further lead non-participants to extend restrictive measures to private trade in goods other than war materials, and to loans or credits as well.[32] Indeed, there is nothing to prevent a neutral state from undertaking to prevent all kinds of commercial intercourse between its subjects and belligerent states, and provided only that such restrictions are applied in an impartial manner the legislation enacted by neutral states to this purpose raises considerations of policy though not of law.[33]

---

upon the fact—noted in the Austro-Hungarian note of June 29, 1915—"that the economic life of the United States had been made serviceable to the greatest extent [to the Allies] by the creation of new and the enlargement of existing concerns for the manufacture and exportation of war requisites and thus, so to say, been militarized, if it be permitted to use here this much-misused word . . . in the concentration of so many forces to the one end . . . lies a *fait nouveau* which weakens reference to supposed precedents in other wars."

[32] In the past, a number of states when neutral have enacted such restrictions, and practice in this respect has been reviewed in *Harvard Draft Convention On The Rights and Duties of Neutral States in Naval and Aerial War*, *op. cit.*, pp. 281 ff.

[33] The neutrality legislation enacted by the Congress of the United States during the years 1935–39 undoubtedly represents the most significant recent example of a neutral state imposing restrictions upon its citizens respecting commercial intercourse with belligerents that were far in excess of the requirements laid down by international law. The Neutrality Act of May 1, 1937 declared in Section 1 that: "Whenever the President shall find that there exists a state of war between, or among, two or more sovereign states, the President shall proclaim such fact, and it shall thereafter be unlawful to export or attempt to export, or cause to be exported arms, ammunition, or implements of war from any place in the United States to any belligerent state named in such proclamation or to any neutral state for transshipment to, or for the use of, any such belligerent state." The 1937 Act provided further, in Section 2, that no other materials listed in a presidential proclamation could be exported to belligerent states save in foreign vessels and after American citizens had yielded all right, title or interest. Loans and credits to belligerent governments were forbidden. The 1937 Act also forbade United States citizens to travel on belligerent merchantmen or aircraft and prohibited the arming of American merchantmen. Upon the outbreak of war in September 1939, the embargo on arms, ammunition, and implements of war was put into effect by Presidential Proclamation of September 5, 1939 (Section 2 of the 1937 Act having lapsed May 1, 1939). On November 4, 1939 a new joint resolution of Congress was approved which repealed earlier legislation, and particularly the arms embargo.

It is evident that the basic distinction drawn by the traditional law between the obligations of abstention imposed upon a neutral state with respect to its own acts and the normal absence of obligation on the part of the neutral state to prevent its subjects from performing similar acts rests upon the possibility of maintaining a clear separation between the public activities of the neutral state and the private activities undertaken by subjects of the neutral state. Recent wars have made it abundantly clear, however, that the continued possibility of maintaining this separation in practice has become very difficult. The extent to which states now exercise either direct ownership or indirect control over economic activities formerly regarded as outside their proper sphere of activity may—and does—vary considerably. Nevertheless, this variation has been significantly narrowed in time of war. Where a neutral state does not nationalize its foreign trade, control over exports through a system of licensing and similar measures no longer allows such trade to be characterized as "private" in any but the most nominal sense of that term.

It is, in fact, hardly possible to reconcile the conditions that generally prevailed during the two World Wars with the conditions that are plainly assumed by the traditional law. The trading activities of neutral subjects were no longer determined by the decisions of private neutral traders, a fact that is readily apparent where the state has nationalized foreign trade. Yet it is only slightly less apparent where the neutral state exercises decisive control in determining the kinds and quantities of goods to be allowed for export, as well as the destination of such exports. During World War II, the practices initiated in an earlier war were once again adopted by neutral states, subject only to expansion and further refinement. Not only did most neutral states enact stringent export (and import) controls, many of them concluded formal trade agreements with belligerents whose purpose was to set limitations upon the quantity of goods neutrals

---

According to the Act of November 1939, it was made unlawful for American vessels to carry either passengers or articles to any belligerent state named in a presidential proclamation. Among other features, the Act required the complete transfer of title (the so-called "cash and carry" provision) to all goods prior to export. It also authorized the President to declare combat areas ('war zones') within which American citizens and American vessels could not enter except under specially prescribed regulations. Other provisions of earlier acts—e. g., the prohibitions against loans and credits, travel by American citizens on belligerent merchantmen, and arming of American merchantmen—were re-enacted. On November 17, 1941 sections 2 (governing commerce with belligerents), 3 (dealing with combat areas) and 6 (forbidding the arming of American merchantmen) were repealed by joint resolution of Congress.—For texts of relevant Acts, Presidential Proclamations and Regulations, see *U. S. Naval War College, International Law Situations, 1939*, pp. 101–54, and *International Law Documents, 1941*, pp. 46–9. For a review of questions arising over the application of the Act of November 4, 1939, see Hackworth, *op. cit.*, Vol. VII, pp. 643–8. A general survey of the neutrality legislation of the period is given by F. Deák, "The United States Neutrality Acts," *International Conciliation*, No. 358, March 1940.

would permit to be exported to states with which the belligerent party to the agreement was at war.[34]

Nor has the transformation in the economic functions undertaken by the state affected only the status and application of the rules governing neutral trade in war materials with belligerents. In naval warfare this transformation may also affect the rules governing the supply and repair of belligerent warships in neutral ports. Subject to certain restrictions [35] the traditional law permits belligerent warships to obtain supplies and repairs in neutral ports by recourse to the market. However, this law does not permit the neutral state, or its agencies, to provide warships with such supplies and repairs as the warship is otherwise permitted to obtain in neutral ports and the neutral state is not obligated to prevent.[36] But where fuel supplies and the facilities of ports are either owned or controlled by the neutral state a strict interpretation of neutral obligations would appear to forbid altogether the granting of fuel and repairs to belligerent warships.[37]

---

[34] Indeed, the regulation of so-called "private" neutral trade became almost exclusively a matter to be determined between the belligerent and the neutral state. Medlicott (*op. cit.*, pp. 139) has described in considerable detail the work of the British Ministry of Economic Warfare in concluding the "war trade agreements" with neutral states. "The basic aim of these complicated negotiations," Medlicott writes, "was to ensure that the neutrals would prohibit altogether the re-export to Germany of goods reaching them through the Allied controls, and would limit the sale to Germany of other goods to 'normal' pre-war figures. In return the British Government agreed in each case to facilitate the passage through the controls of goods covered by the agreements, and to refrain from demanding individual guarantees against re-exports" (p. 55). In the draft war-trade agreements instructions sent out in September 1939, to all British missions in neutral states it was stated that: "Its (i. e., the proposed war trade agreements) underlying principle is . . . that, in return for certain undertakings as to the limitation and control of . . . trade with the enemy, His Majesty's government will undertake to permit and so far as possible to facilitate the importation by . . . of commodities essential for her domestic consumption" (p. 664).

[35] See pp. 240–4.

[36] Thus the United States Neutrality (General) Proclamation of September 5, 1939 declared: "No agency of the United States Government shall, directly or indirectly, provide supplies nor effect repairs to a belligerent ship of war." This provision merely states the neutral's obligation under the traditional law.

[37] In the case of *The Attilio Regolo and Other Vessels* (*Annual Digest of Public International Law Cases* (1947), Case No. 137, pp. 319–24), an arbitration between the United States, Great Britain and Italy on the one hand and Spain on the other, the Arbitrator was called upon to decide whether "the provisions of Article 19 of the Hague Convention (XIII) of 1907 entail an obligation on the neutral State to give active assistance in ensuring supplies of fuel to belligerent warships anchored in its waters, or, on the other hand, does refueling represent a right of the said ships, their inability to exercise which in good time does not preclude a strict application of the twenty-four hours' rule." The Arbitrator held that Article 19 "does not lay on the neutral State any specific obligation to assist actively in providing supplies of fuel," but that fueling does represent a "right which the belligerent warship may exercise by recourse to the market." The Arbitrator went on to point out: "In no sense—grammatical, logical or juridical—does the Article (19 of Hague XIII) under examination lay on the neutral State the duty of actively assisting in making supplies available. Such duty, we may add, is inconsistent with

It may be that revision of the law of neutrality to permit neutral states themselves to supply fuel to belligerent warships or to grant the latter use of state-owned port facilities would raise no "insurmountable difficulty," that "it is probable that even without express revision the established law of neutrality could be applied by way of a reasonable interpretation of its basic provisions in the light of new conditions."[38] It can be contended that the principal consideration is that belligerent warships ought not to make use of neutral ports in excess of the restrictions laid down by Hague Convention XIII (1907), and this may be ensured regardless of the fact that the limited assistance made available to warships in neutral ports is obtained directly from the neutral state itself rather than by recourse to the market.[39]

Even so, the major problem remains, that is of applying to present conditions the rule forbidding neutral states to supply belligerents in any manner, directly or indirectly, with war materials. In those states where foreign trade has been nationalized it seems clear that if the traditional law retains its validity the supply of war materials of any kind must be considered as a departure from the duties imposed upon a neutral state.[40] Nor is this conclusion subject to qualification either by the claim that this situation was not contemplated when the traditional law was established[41]

---

the conceptions of the State, prevailing in 1907, as remote from pursuits of a commercial nature and as being exclusively a constitutional organism whose specific duty as a neutral, under the system we are now examining, was merely to exercise control and supervision in order to prevent belligerent warships received in its waters from using the latter as a base of operations and thus compromising the neutrality of the State granting them access."

[38] Lauterpacht, "The Problem of the Revision of the Law of War," p. 377.

[39] On the other hand, the dissatisfaction long felt in many quarters over the "limited assistance" neutrals may grant belligerent warships under Hague XIII is not likely to be attenuated by this possible revision of the law in order to permit the neutral state to supply fuel and carry out repairs. If anything, it would be increased—and not unreasonably so.

[40] ". . . a neutral state which permits its publicly-owned vessels to carry cargo which would be subject to confiscation if carried in a privately-owned vessel, or whose publicly-owned vessels are guilty of any form of conduct which would render them liable to condemnation if they were privately-owned vessels, would itself be guilty of disregarding *pro tanto* the law of neutrality. . . ." S. W. D. Rowson, *op. cit.*, p. 178. For further expressions to the same effect, see Lawrence Preuss, "Some Effects of Governmental Controls On Neutral Duties," *Proceedings*, American Society of International Law, 31 (1937), pp. 108–19, and *Harvard Draft Convention on Rights and Duties of Neutral States in Naval and Aerial War*, *op. cit.*, pp. 238–44. Nor is the conclusion stated above denied by those writers who nevertheless contend that retention of the traditional law serves to penalize states adopting socialist economies, e. g., W. Friedmann, "The Growth of State Control Over the Individual, and Its Effect Upon the Rules of International State Responsibility," *B. Y. I. L.*, 19 (1938), pp. 130 ff.

[41] This point has been frequently made by writers and is, in any event, not a matter of dispute. During World War II the application of the rule forbidding the supply of war materials by neutral states may be interpreted, in view of the extension of the notion of contraband, as forbidding almost all trade between the Soviet Union (while still a neutral) and belligerent states. That the Soviet Union did not adhere in its behavior to this prohibition is a matter of public record. It may be argued that this example of the Soviet Union during the years 1939–41 shows the futility of attempting to apply the traditional law to a major neutral state

(and, obviously, it was not) or by the attempt to differentiate between the "political" as opposed to the "commercial" character of the transactions carried out by the neutral state.[42]

No clear conclusion can be drawn, however, with respect to the possible liability of state-owned neutral vessels and cargoes to the law of prize. Although it has been contended that the "vessels (other than men-of-war) and cargoes of such States are subject to the ordinary incidents of the law of blockade and contraband and of other belligerent rights," [43] practice to date does not as yet afford sufficient grounds for endorsing this claim. It is by no means certain that belligerents have even a right to visit and search the publicly owned vessels of a neutral which are engaged in commercial activities, let alone the right to seize and to condemn such vessels and their cargo in accordance with the rules relating to contraband and blockade.[44]

---

that has completely collectivized its economy. Nevertheless, in the absence of wider agreement among states that this aspect of the traditional law should be abandoned, it can only be assumed that the rule forbidding neutral states to supply belligerents with war materials remains valid.

[42] It has been suggested that if "the *nature* of the deal, whether political or commercial, and not the fact of governmental ownership or control, is to be the test for determining legal responsibility, and if it is political favoritism and political assistance rather than governmental supervision as such which gives taint to the transaction, then what is to be looked for in this quest for a criterion as to private capacity is the amount or extent of political bias or influence manifest in any given arrangements between a belligerent government and a corporation or agency owned or controlled by a neutral state." *"Neutral Duties and State Control of Enterprise,"* *U. S. Naval War College, International Law Situations, 1939*, p. 10. It may be doubted whether this suggested differentiation between the "political" and the "economic" acts of the neutral state is at all feasible, dependent as it must be upon a "search into the motives and into the details of each particular act" (p. 11). In any event, it has no basis in the traditional law, which is not concerned with whether the act of supplying a belligerent state with assistance for the prosecution of war has an "economic" or "political" motivation. Finally, it may be observed that little support for this suggestion can be found by the appeal to the principle of impartiality, since the latter too is concerned with the acts of a neutral state, not with its motives.

[43] Oppenheim-Lauterpacht, *op. cit.*, p. 657.

[44] The actual practice of states during World War II is scarcely conclusive even as to the right of visit and search. A number of writers have made much over the alleged insistence on the part of Great Britain during the early stages of World War II to subject Soviet state-owned vessels engaged in commercial activities to the same measures of control which privately owned neutral vessels are liable. It is true that on several occasions British warships exercised visit and search over Soviet vessels. The British Government, however, made no clear reply to the protests of the Soviet Government that state-owned merchant ships were exempt from the operation of belligerent rights. The matter was never put to a test since the Soviet Government thereafter avoided areas in which their vessels would possibly be subject to the British contraband control system. The incidents are recounted in some detail by Medlicott, *op. cit.*, pp. 318–20.—There are, on the other hand, certain indications in prize rules and manuals of a tendency to assimilate neutral state-owned vessels engaged in commercial activities to the position of privately owned neutral vessels. See section 500b *Law of Naval Warfare.* Note should also be taken of the German Prize Law Code of 1939, which provided in Article 1:

Undue concentration upon the criterion of state-ownership, however, ought not to lead to a neglect of the far more difficult considerations involved in applying the traditional law to neutral trade which, though not state-owned, is state-controlled. A strict application of this law would appear equally to forbid neutral trade in war materials when such trade is controlled and directed by the neutral state.[45] And in view of the near universal practices of neutral states in recent wars there must remain, on this consideration, only a negligible amount of neutral trade whose character does not involve the responsibility of the neutral state.[46]

In an admirable analysis of the numerous problems imposed by the breakdown in practice of the neutral state-neutral trader distinction Julius Stone has proposed the following "two main lines of legal reform" available to states:

> One would assimilate the legal position of the trading State to the private trader, permitting the State to trade subject to belligerent controls of contraband, blockade and the like. The other would assimilate the private trader's legal position to that of the State, forbidding him and forbidding his State to permit him to engage in the affected trade. Neither line has any *a priori* validity. Which should be adopted is a matter of legislative policy. . . . Between the two alternatives offering, therefore, the Writer

"Prize Law covers the authority to visit and search enemy and neutral ships as well as to deal with these ships and goods carried on them according to the following provisions. Warships and other public vessels which are designed or used exclusively for purposes of public administration and not for trade purposes are not subject to prize law." To date, however, these and similar manifestations have yet to stand the test of practical application. And it is difficult to avoid the conclusion of Rowson (*op. cit.*, p. 177), who declares that with respect to the liability of neutral state-owned merchant vessels the law is still "in its infancy."

45 And without regard to whether such control is exercised through export controls and licensing measures or by the state's creation of trading organizations endowed with a "private character." The latter measure may furnish a means for permitting belligerents to exercise those controls that have long been exercised over private neutral traders, but it cannot do away with the fact that decisive control would still be exercised by the neutral state.

46 The decisive point, therefore, is no longer that undue concentration upon the criterion of state ownership leads to conclusions that discriminate against states resorting to nationalization. Instead, it is that concentration upon the sole factor of state ownership neglects the more important—since far more widespread—practices of state control which fall short of ownership, and that these practices of state control constitute the most significant factor in subverting the clear intent of the traditional law. This is the burden of the excellent remarks of Julius Stone (*op. cit.*, pp. 410–1) in criticism of the position that "it is impossible to maintain one set of rules for countries organized on the basis of private enterprise and another for countries where the production of and trade in certain articles is in the hands of the State." Oppenheim-Lauterpacht, *op. cit.*, pp. 657–8. Professor Stone's reply is that in view of the extensive controls over trade now exercised by nearly all neutral states the insistence upon looking only at the criterion of state ownership has precisely this result—to lead to two sets of rules.

> accepts the former, namely, that trading activity of neutral Governments with belligerents should be assimilated to private trading in both respects. First, that the duty of the neutral Government not to supply arms, munitions, or to grant loans should be abolished. Second, that the ships, and cargoes, and other instrumentalities of the neutral Government employed in such trade should be subject to the ordinary penalties for contraband carriage, blockade breach, and the like, and should not enjoy (while involved in such trade) the immunities ordinarily enjoyed by State owned ships and property.[47]

These suggestions for legal reform represent a clear attempt to close the ever widening gap that exists between the behavior prescribed by the traditional rules and the actual practices of neutral states in the two World Wars. Even further, they recognize that it is unrealistic to consider the conditions that have brought about the present decline of the neutral state—neutral trader distinction as merely transient phenomena. Nevertheless, the proposal that the position of the neutral state should now be assimilated, in matters of trade, to the position traditionally held by the private neutral trader is one involving substantial difficulty.[48]

It is of course true that neutral trade has always been a significant factor in warfare at sea, and belligerents have always sought to go as far as possible in cutting off this trade with the enemy. But it is hardly necessary to observe that the ever present belligerent desire to cut off neutral trade with an enemy is—for reasons already noted—far greater today than in an earlier period. In view of the increased importance of the economic arm in the conduct of modern war the proposal that the neutral state be assimilated in matters of trade to the position of the private neutral trader might well have the effect of conferring upon neutrals the legal possibility of exercising a decisive influence upon the outcome of a conflict.

Nor should it be overlooked that private neutral trade, being motivated by considerations of gain and not by political considerations, was generally

---

[47] Stone, *op. cit.*, pp. 412–3.

[48] It should be made clear that the above discussion is independent of, and does not prejudice, any duties and rights of nonparticipants resulting from the changed legal position of war (see pp. 165 ff). With respect to the Charter of the United Nations it will be readily apparent that the effective operation of the collective security system established by that instrument would render any further consideration of the present problem of little more than nominal value. And even if the Security Council cannot effectively exercise the functions conferred upon it by the Charter, it may nevertheless be contended that member states have a right to assist a state made the victim of an armed attack and a duty to refrain from assisting the attacker. From this point of view the proposal to abandon the neutral state's duties of abstention would not be in accord with the obligation to refrain from assisting an aggressor. On the other hand, the alternative proposal of placing an embargo upon all neutral trade (public and private) with belligerents would not be in accord with the presumed right of third states to assist the victim of an unlawful resort to war.

without organization and direction. In this sense it was politically indifferent, and this political indifference was not substantially affected by reason of the fact that the neutral state might take up and press the cause of the private trader against belligerents. All this must change once the state is openly allowed to take over the position occupied by the private trader. Presumably, the neutral state would be under no obligation to act impartially in supplying belligerents with war materials, and, in any event, it is difficult to see how the principle of impartiality could be applied effectively in this instance. The neutral state would be able to organize and direct its assistance in a manner that would have been impossible for private traders. It does not appear realistic to expect that the neutral state would determine its trading policy in a non-political vacuum. On the contrary, the expectation must be that political considerations will prevail over considerations of economic gain.

In a word, the proposal that the neutral state's position be assimilated to that of the private neutral trader would, if accepted, result in the neutral state's interference in the conduct of a war just short of active participation in hostilities. Given the transcendent importance of the economic factor it would normally prove to be only a very short step to such active participation.[49] If past experience is to prove of any value it would appear to indicate that if neutrality is to be preserved at all it will be done only under the condition that it does not serve to confer a substantial—let alone a decisive—advantage upon either belligerent. This consideration may imply the desirability of forbidding all neutral trade in war materials with belligerents. The neutral state–neutral trader distinction has always been something of an anomaly, understandable in the context of the particular historic conditions in which it arose. These conditions obtain today only to a very limited extent. With their disappearance the retention of the rules which developed out of them lose further justification. Yet in altering these rules the traditional system of neutrality would seem best preserved—assuming such preservation to be the central purpose of legal reform—not by suggesting that an otherwise anomalous practice now be transformed into an even more general situation, but rather by forbidding all neutral trade with belligerents. The economic hardships complete abstention might impose upon the economy of a neutral state could un-

[49] Of course, given a preponderance of belligerent power such trade would only rarely be tolerated. The proposal would work, if at all, only in a local war. Yet even here its results would probably prove undesirable, if it is assumed that the objective would be to keep the war from spreading. For the proposal under discussion would most likely have the contrary effect. Instead of isolating a conflict it would constitute an open invitation for other states to fish in troubled waters, thus running the risk of expanding the conflict. No doubt states have done just this, even under the rules laid down by the traditional law, and will continue to do so. But there seems little point in providing them with the legal justification for doing so.

doubtedly be considerable. They are certainly no greater, however, than the hardships imposed by participation in modern war.[50]

All this is mere speculation, though. From the point of view of the present law the traditional rules based upon the distinction drawn between neutral state and neutral trader remain valid, though marked by ever increasing difficulty in their application and—in all probability—a corresponding decline in their effectiveness.

E. RESTRICTIONS ON THE USE OF NEUTRAL PORTS AND TERRITORIAL WATERS;[51] NEUTRAL DUTIES OF PREVENTION

A neutral state is obliged not only to abstain itself from the performance of certain acts; it is further obliged to prevent the commission of certain

[50] Admittedly, the proposal to place upon non-participants the duty to prevent all commercial intercourse with belligerents is also beset with difficulty. On balance, however, these difficulties would appear less formidable than the difficulties attendant upon the suggested assimilation of the neutral state to the position heretofore held by the neutral trader. The argument that the complete severance of trade would extend considerably the neutral's preventive duties is quite true, though not a compelling objection. Indeed, given the pervasive controls already exercised by states—when neutral—over exports, the extension involved would affect the scope of the neutral's duty of abstention far more than creating new duties of prevention. Undoubtedly, the more serious objection is the economic hardship complete abstention might impose upon a neutral state's economy. Yet it hardly seems hazardous to surmise that economic considerations generally have been far less influential in shaping neutral policies than have been considerations of a distinctly political character, and this despite Professor Stone's (*op. cit.*, p. 413) somewhat extravagant assertion that it is "fantastic" to assume that non-participants would "commit economic self-immolation for the sake of the law of neutrality." On the contrary, it is submitted that recent experience points far more clearly to the lesson that states are willing to suffer economic hardships to preserve neutrality, *if the preservation of neutral status is considered to be politically desirable.* For precisely the same reasons—i. e., political—neutral states have intervened in recent hostilities by directing economic aid to the side with whose interests they have become identified.

It may be relevant to add that the foregoing remarks are not designed to suggest either the widsom or the folly—from a political standpoint—of self-imposed neutral policies of preventing all trade with belligerents. But it does seem clear that in the period accompanying and directly following the collapse of American neutrality during World War II many observers drew conclusions whose generality was hardly warranted by the special experience on which they were based. It is one thing to assert that in a major conflict the attempt on the part of a third state to isolate itself, when its vital interests are directly involved in the conflict, must be foredoomed to failure. It is quite another thing to insist that failure must attend any attempts to isolate the combatants in a limited war where the interests of third states may not be directly involved—or, at least, where the interests of third states in the outcome of a conflict is less than their desire to prevent the conflict from spreading. And it will be apparent that it is precisely in a limited war, where the possibilities for the preservation of neutral status will normally be most favorable, that the economic hardships suffered by the prohibition against trade with the combatants will be the least severe. All this may be viewed as pointing to the conclusion—by now, almost a truism—that neutrality will prove feasible only where war is limited in the number, and power, of the participants. Yet the decisive point is that it may prove feasible in just such situations, and hence suggestions for legal reform of the traditional system must concentrate—to be realistic—upon this possible contingency.

[51] See, generally, *Law of Naval Warfare*, section 440 and notes thereto.

acts by anyone within its jurisdiction. Those acts a neutral state is obligated to prevent may be performed either by belligerents or by private individuals. In naval warfare attention is directed to the acts a neutral must forbid in its ports and territorial waters. The most authoritative source for an inquiry into the rules restricting the use of neutral ports and territorial waters remains Hague Convention XIII (1907).[52]

In defining the scope of a neutral's duties with respect to its waters and ports Hague Convention XIII does not purport to indicate the acts a neutral state may forbid but the acts it must forbid. There is nothing to prevent a neutral from placing restrictions upon the use of its waters and ports which are in excess of the requirements laid down by international law, and in practice many states when neutral do exercise their right to impose restrictions beyond those required by law. In so doing the neutral state is only under the obligation to see that its regulations are applied impartially toward all belligerents.[53]

1. *Belligerent Acts of Hostility in Neutral Waters*

Article 2 of Hague Convention XIII declares that: "Any act of hostility, including capture and the exercise of the right of search, committed by belligerent war-ships in the territorial waters of a neutral Power, constitutes a violation of neutrality and is strictly forbidden." In principle, the rule enjoining belligerent respect for the inviolability of neutral waters appears quite plain. In practice, however, certain questions have arisen that concern the precise scope of the belligerent's duty of abstention.

It is clear, to begin with, that this belligerent duty toward the neutral state is not without limitation. A belligerent is not obligated to refrain *under all circumstances* from taking hostile measures against the naval forces of an enemy located in neutral waters. In the event that the forces of one belligerent violate neutral waters (or ports) and the neutral state willfully permits such violation it cannot complain if the other belligerent—as an extreme measure—attacks his enemy while still in the waters of the neutral state. The neutral state has not only the right to prevent the misuse of its waters and ports but also a duty to take adequate measures of prevention. This neutral duty is owed to the belligerent that has otherwise respected the rights of the neutral state and that will be placed at a disadvantage in

[52] Though never ratified by Great Britain (nor, for that matter, by Russia) and not technically binding in either World War, the provisions of Hague Convention XIII (1907), have nevertheless been considered—on the whole—as declaratory of the customary rules restricting belligerent use of neutral ports and waters. However, there are certain provisions of the Convention that have not received the acceptance of numerous naval powers, and these provisions will be noted in the following pages. It should also be observed that Hague XIII does not deal with the rules concerning belligerent rights with respect to neutral commerce at sea. Even in relation to neutral waters and ports the Convention is not to be considered as exhaustive, which is one reason for Article 1 obligating belligerents "to respect the sovereign rights of neutral Powers and to abstain, in neutral territory or neutral waters, from any act which would, if knowingly permitted, constitute a violation of neutrality."

[53] Hague XIII, Article 9.

war by the unlawful use made of neutral waters and ports by an enemy. In allowing the forces of one belligerent to misuse its waters and ports the neutral state thereby violates its duty toward the other belligerent, and the acts of hostility that the offended belligerent may take against the forces of his enemy in neutral waters may be interpreted as permitted measures of reprisal against the delinquent neutral.[54]

The scope of the belligerent's obligation to abstain from committing hostile acts in neutral waters must therefore depend, in large measure, upon the nature and scope of the neutral's obligation to prevent the unlawful use by belligerents of its waters and ports. In naval warfare the generally accepted standard the neutral is obliged to meet in fulfilling its duties—and certainly the standard imposed by Hague XIII—is that it use the "means at its disposal."[55] But the fact that a neutral fulfills its duty so long as it exercises such surveillance as the means at its disposal allow to prevent violations of its waters and ports need not mean, however, that the belligerent's obligation of abstention is unqualified by the effectiveness of the preventive measures taken by the neutral.

It is evident that in the event the neutral state cannot effectively enforce its rights against an offending belligerent the ensuing situation may lead to one of considerable difficulty. Belligerent warships may be threatened with attack by an enemy while in neutral waters, and the shore state may be unable to exercise adequate measures of prevention. The forces of a belligerent may persistently violate the waters of a neutral state to the grave disadvantage of an enemy that has heretofore respected neutral waters. In these, and other, circumstances the neutral state, while using the means at its disposal, may be wholly unable to enforce its rights effectively. Must the belligerent whose interests suffer as a result of an enemy's violation of neutral waters nevertheless abstain from taking hostile measures in neutral waters against his adversary?

---

[54] These are measures of reprisal against the neutral, not against the belligerent. In misusing neutral waters the belligerent has violated no right of its enemy.

[55] Article 25 of Hague XIII declares: "A neutral Power is bound to exercise such surveillance as the means at its disposal allow to prevent any violation of the provisions of the above Articles in its ports or roadsteads, or in its waters.—Article 26 of the 1928 Habana Convention on Maritime Neutrality provides a substantially similar formulation in stating: "Neutral States are bound to exert all the vigilance within their power in order to prevent in their ports or territorial waters any violation of the foregoing provisions."—In the *Harvard Draft Convention On the Rights and Duties of Neutral States in Naval and Aerial War* (*op. cit.*, p. 245) the same concept of the scope of the neutral's duty is expressed. Article 6 of the Draft Convention states: "A neutral state shall use the means at its disposal to prevent within its territory the commission of any act the toleration of which would constitute a non-fulfillment of its neutral duty; the use of force for this purpose shall not be regarded as an unfriendly act."

The comment to Article 6 declares that the article expresses "the general standard by which a neutral State's fulfillment of its neutral duties is to be measured. A neutral state is not an insurer of the fulfillment of its neutral duties. It is obligated merely to use the 'means at its disposal' to secure the fulfillment of its duties" (p. 247).

It can hardly be said that the dilemma posed by the situation of the weak neutral has been clearly and satisfactorily resolved even today.[56] The relatively few incidents that appear to have a bearing upon this problem are not entirely free from ambiguity, and their significance as possible precedents ought not to be overestimated.[57] Despite this dearth of precedents it is the opinion of a number of publicists that if the neutral state is

---

[56] Equally difficult considerations arise as a result of a neutral's inability to prevent a belligerent from shutting off the neutral state's legitimate intercourse—particularly trade—with an enemy (see pp. 252–8).

[57] One such incident occurred during the Russo-Japanese War when a Russian destroyer, the *Peshitelni*, which had taken refuge in a Chinese port, was seized and towed off by Japanese warships. Japan, in justifying the action, maintained that the Chinese authorities had not taken the necessary measures toward disarming the vessel and ensuring that it would take no further part in the war. The incident is not entirely clear though, since at the time of the Japanese action the *Peshitelni* had ostensibly been interned (two days earlier), and there were Chinese naval vessels in the port (Chifu) that could have ensured effective internment. In part, it seems that the Japanese action was taken as a result of previous incidents in which Chinese waters had been violated by Russian naval forces and China either would not or could not resist these transgressions.

The most frequently cited incident arising out of World War I is the case of the *Dresden*. The incident is summarized in the following passage:

"On March 9, 1915 the German cruiser *Dresden* arrived in Cumberland Bay in the Chilean Juan Fernandez Islands, cast anchor, and asked permission to remain eight days to repair her engines. The maritime governor of the port refused to grant the request, considering it unfounded, and ordered the vessel to leave within 24 hours or be subject to internment. At the end of the period he notified the captain of the vessel that the penalty of internment had been incurred. On March 14 a British naval squadron arrived and opened fire on the *Dresden* while she lay at anchor some 500 meters from shore. The *Dresden* raised a flag of truce and sent an officer to inform the British squadron that she was in neutral waters. The British squadron ordered the *Dresden* to surrender or be destroyed; the captain of the *Dresden* thereupon blew up his own ship, and the crew made their way ashore." Hackworth, *op. cit.*, Vol. VII, p. 370. The Chilean government protested the action of the British squadron, maintaining that the internment of the *Dresden* was as effective as the circumstances would permit, and contended that, in any event, the British naval squadron could have prevented, by close watch, the possibility of the *Dresden* escaping to sea and once again attacking British commerce. In its reply the British Government stated that it was prepared to offer a "full and ample apology" to the Chilean Government for the action. It added, however, that if the Chilean authorities could not prevent the *Dresden* from abusing Chilean waters and properly intern her, these circumstances would "explain the action taken by the British ship." It is difficult to determine, therefore, whether the offer of an apology by Great Britain was intended as an unqualified apology for the action of the British squadron or whether it was offered because the British Government was not certain that under the circumstances the Chilean authorities might have been able to take the measures necessary to intern the *Dresden*.

The incident of the *Altmark* (see pp. 236–9) during World War II, though also frequently cited by writers, is of doubtful relevance. In the *Altmark* incident there appeared little doubt that Norway had the "means at its disposal" to enforce its neutrality. Nor did the British Government attempt to justify the measures of hostility it finally resorted to within Norwegian waters on the grounds that Norway was unable to enforce her rights. On the contrary, the British contention was that Norway had the means but was unwilling to use these means. The British action, if justifiable, must be interpreted then as a reprisal against Norway for the

unable to enforce its rights against one belligerent making unlawful use of its waters the other belligerent may—as an extreme measure—resort to hostile action against the forces of its enemy, though in neutral waters.[58] If this opinion is correct, as it is believed to be, then a belligerent's duty to abstain from committing acts of hostility in neutral waters must be limited not only by the willingness but also by the ability of the neutral to enforce its rights effectively.[59] At the same time, there is general agreement that where a neutral state is employing the means at its disposal (though ineffectively) to prevent belligerent violations of its waters, a belligerent ought not to take hostile measures against an enemy making unlawful use of these waters except when so required for reasons of self-preservation or—

---

latter's failure to observe her duties toward Great Britain. Interestingly enough, however, most of the writers approving the British action in the *Altmark* incident refer to the measure as one of "self help" rather than of reprisal.

More relevant in this connection is the British and French resort to the mining of Norwegian territorial waters in April 1940, on the eve of the German invasion of Norway. On this occasion the British and French Governments, alleging the persistent abuse by Germany of Norwegian territorial waters, declared that: "Whatever may be the actual policy which the Norwegian Government, by German threats and pressures, are compelled to follow, the Allied Governments can no longer afford to acquiesce in the present state of affairs by which Germany obtains resources vital to her prosecution of the war, and obtains from Norway facilities which place the Allies at a dangerous disadvantage . . ." cited in Hackworth, *op. cit.*, Vol. VII, p. 148. The implication was clear that the mining of Norwegian waters was a measure of "self help" justified in view of Norway's inability to prevent German misuse of her waters.

[58] Thus Hyde (*op. cit.*, pp. 2337–8) has stated that the "obligation resting upon the belligerent with respect to the neutral is not of unlimited scope. Circumstances may arise when the belligerent is excused from disregarding the prohibition. If a neutral possesses neither the power nor disposition to check warlike activities within its own domain, the belligerent that in consequence is injured or threatened with immediate injury would appear to be free from the normal obligation to refrain from the commission of hostile acts therein. In naval warfare such a situation may arise through the presence of vessels of war of opposing belligerents simultaneously in the same neutral port or roadstead." Also Oppenheim-Lauterpacht, *op. cit.*, p. 695n. Smith (*op. cit.*, p. 148) states that in naval, as in land, warfare the neutral "must be both willing and able to assert his exclusive sovereign rights over the area concerned." But see Kunz (*Kriegsrecht und Neutralitätsrecht*, p. 240), who asserts that the belligerent right of "self help" against the forces of an enemy violating neutral rights does not extend to the exercise of hostile acts within neutral waters.—It is interesting to note that in land warfare the standards applied to neutral and belligerent conduct have not been quite the same as in naval warfare. Although the territory of neutral powers is, according to Article 1 of Hague Convention V (1907), inviolable, the scope of the neutral's duty is not limited merely to using the "means at its disposal." And paragraph 520 of the U. S. Army *Rules of Land Warfare* states the rule applicable to land warfare in declaring that: "Should the neutral state be unable, or fail for any reason, to prevent violations of its neutrality by the troops of one belligerent entering or passing through its territory, the other belligerent may be justified in attacking the enemy forces on this territory." With respect to aerial warfare, Spaight (*op. cit.*, p. 434) asserts the legality of belligerent attack upon the aerial forces of an enemy making unlawful use of neutral jurisdiction. However, the precedents he is able to cite from World War II practice in support of this opinion are rather slight.

[59] See *Law of Naval Warfare*, Article 441.

though this is still a matter of some dispute—in order to prevent an enemy from gaining a material advantage in the conduct of war.[60]

It may appear incongruous to maintain, on the one hand, that the neutral state is bound only to use the means at its disposal to prevent belligerent transgressions of its ports and waters, while asserting, on the other hand, that should the means available to a neutral prove ineffective a belligerent is not forbidden under the circumstances referred to above from attacking an enemy that is misusing these waters. In part, however, this apparent incongruity stems from the characterization of the measures a belligerent is not forbidden to exercising in neutral waters as measures of reprisal. This characterization is mistaken, since the neutral, in using the means at its disposal, has fulfilled its duty. But although the neutral state has not violated its duty it is equally true that the belligerent, in taking hostile measures, has not violated the rights of the neutral. The seeming incongruity involved in this situation is resolved then simply by interpreting the scope of the belligerent's duty to abstain from committing hostile

[60] It is still the opinion of perhaps the majority of writers that the only exception ought to be self preservation—interpreted in the most narrow sense. If this is true then belligerent forces may resort to hostile measures in neutral waters only when in imminent peril from the forces of an enemy, and the appeal to local protection is either precluded by the known weakness of the neutral or is simply not feasible in view of the imminence of the peril. Thus, Stone (*op. cit.*, p. 401) observes that "where appeal for local protection is feasible, the aggrieved State's vessel would seem not to be entitled to defend or help itself in neutral territory or waters. If appeal to local protection was impossible or pointless, the attacked vessel's right of self-defense is more arguable; it does not seem likely that it could extend beyond what its own self-preservation or escape from peril required."—It is, of course, clear that where local protection is available—i. e., where the neutral is able to enforce its rights—measures of self help are not permissible. But then there is no problem. In practice, though, there is always the difficulty that the neutral state will later contend that it would have taken the necessary preventive measures and that the belligerent's action was hasty and unjustified. There is no easy answer to this difficulty, and each case must be judged by the attendant circumstances. But this does not alter the essential principle, which is that if such "local protection" is not available a belligerent may resort to hostile measures of self help in neutral waters. More important is the claim that hostile measures must be limited to cases of self-preservation—interpreted narrowly. Yet it should be apparent that belligerent misuse of neutral waters may thereby confer important advantages upon the lawbreaker, even though considerations of self-preservation—in the most immediate and narrow interpretation of that term—are not involved. To limit the belligerent whose interests suffer as a result of these unlawful activities merely to urging the weak neutral to use more effective measures of prevention, when it is evident such measures are not available to the neutral, would appear neither a reasonable nor a very realistic solution. No doubt the real danger attendant upon the position taken here is that the belligerent may use any alleged violation of neutral waters by an enemy—no matter how minor—and against which the neutral has not taken effective preventive measures, as an excuse for resorting to hostile acts within these same waters. Undoubtedly this danger exists, despite any attempt to restrict belligerents by laying down what can only be—at best—rather broad criteria. The only real alternative, however, is to prohibit all hostile belligerent measures in neutral jurisdiction despite neutral ineffectiveness in preventing the unlawful acts of an enemy. And it should be pointed out that even to restrict belligerents to the taking of hostile measures only for reasons of "immediate self-preservation" leaves the door more than slightly ajar to the above danger.

acts against enemy forces within neutral waters as limited, in principle, by the effectiveness with which the neutral state can enforce its rights.

One further problem warrants brief consideration here, and it concerns the geographical area within which the belligerent duty to abstain from hostile measures is applicable. In the preceding discussion the assumption has been that the belligerent's obligation extends only to the territorial waters of a neutral. Article 2 of Hague XIII expressly refers to the "territorial waters of a neutral Power" as the area within which hostile belligerent measures are forbidden, and the weight of customary practice also supports the same restriction of the area within which the belligerent duty applies.[61]

Nevertheless, neutral states have frequently expressed dissatisfaction in the past over the conduct of belligerent operations in waters contiguous to their territorial seas, either for the reason that such operations unduly interfered with legitimate neutral trade or because belligerent operations were alleged to constitute a danger to the security of the shore state.[62] During the first World War this neutral concern found occasional expression,[63] though there were no instances in which neutral states attempted, as a matter of legal right, to restrict belligerent operations in waters

[61] It will be apparent, therefore, that the area within which belligerents may conduct their naval operations may vary, depending upon the extent of the territorial waters claimed by neutral states and recognized by the belligerents. In the past, neutrals occasionally have sought to extend the limits of their territorial waters for the special purposes of neutrality. Although such extensions generally have been of modest nature belligerents have been very slow to accord them recognition.

[62] For a review of neutral practice in this respect, and belligerent responses, see *U. S. Naval War College, International Law Situations, 1928*, pp. 1–37. Also *Harvard Draft Convention on Rights and Duties of Neutral States in Naval and Aerial War, op. cit.*, pp. 343–53. Articles 18 and 19 of the Draft Convention state:

"Article 18. A belligerent shall not engage in hostile operations on, under or over the high seas so near to the territory of a neutral state as to endanger life or property therein.

Article 19. A belligerent shall not permit its warships or military aircraft to hover off the coasts of a neutral State in such manner as to harass the commerce or industry of that State."

In the commentary to these articles it is declared that, although sound in principle, there is little express authority for them.

[63] The best known instance occurred in 1915–16 and was occasioned over the United States' protest to Great Britain that the latter's practice of belligerent cruisers "patrolling American coasts in close proximity to the territorial waters of the United States and making the neighborhood a station for their observations is . . . vexatious and discourteous to the United States." The British Government replied that it was "unaware of the existence of any rules or principles of international law which render belligerent operations which are legitimate in one part of the high seas, illegitimate in another." In answering the British statement it was noted that: "The grounds for the objection of belligerent vessels of war cruising in close proximity to American ports are based, not upon the illegality of such action, but upon the irritation which it naturally causes to a neutral country." *Harvard Draft Convention on the Rights and Duties of Neutral States in Naval and Aerial War, op. cit.*, pp. 350–2. As a result of the exchange the British Government did accede, in part, to the expressed wishes of the United States, though as a matter of comity not of legal right.

contiguous to neutral territorial seas. Soon after the outbreak of hostilities in 1939 such an attempt was made, however. On October 3, 1939, the Governments of the American Republics meeting at Panama adopted a declaration whose principal provision read:

> As a measure of continental self-protection, the American Republics, so long as they maintain their neutrality, are as of inherent right entitled to have those waters adjacent to the American continent, which they regard as of primary concern and direct utility in their relations, free from the commission of any hostile act by any non-American belligerent nation, whether such hostile act be attempted or made from land, sea or air.[64]

The Declaration of Panama was without precedent in the recent history of neutral-belligerent relations. The "zone of security" established by the Declaration extended, in many places, as far as three hundred miles to sea. The Declaration was never accorded recognition by the belligerents whose behavior it was intended to regulate. Indeed, the various responses of the major belligerents to the Declaration were uniform in contending that it had no strict foundation in law, that it sought to infringe upon the established rights of belligerents, and that it therefore required—to achieve any legal standing—the acquiescence of the interested belligerents.[65] Such acquiescence was not forthcoming.

Although largely without results in regulating belligerent behavior the Declaration of Panama did serve to focus attention upon the possibility that the belligerent's duty to refrain from committing acts of hostility in neutral territorial waters might be extended, in time, to include a limited zone adjacent to the territorial seas. In principle, such an extension does not appear unreasonable. The security needs of states are no less during a period of war in which they are not active participants than they are in time of peace—if anything, they are considerably greater in time of war. The principle of a state's right to exercise a limited jurisdicton in waters contiguous to territorial seas is now recognized in time of peace. It may

[64] The text of the Declaration of Panama, as well as relevant diplomatic correspondence, together with an analysis of the legal standing of the Declaration may be found in *U. S. Naval War College, International Law Situations, 1939*, pp. 61–80. Strictly speaking, the Declaration did not insist upon the legal rights of the neutral states, referring rather to "inherent right," "self protection," "fundamental interests of the American States."

[65] The belligerents' reaction to the Declaration was made clear in their replies to the protest made by the American Republics on December 23, 1939. The immediate occasion for the protest was the action between the German vessel *Graf Spee* and British naval vessels off the coast of Uruguay on December 13, 1939. The Naval War College concluded, in its analysis of the legal status of the Declaration, that it did not form "a part of international law. Neutral jurisdiction for defense purposes over a part of the ocean extending 300 miles from the coast is without precedent and has not been generally accepted. There is agreement upon the principle but not upon its application to such a tremendously wide belt. Great Britain, France, and Germany were acting within their legal rights when they refused to recognize the binding nature of the Panama Declaration" (p. 80).

be expected to obtain similar recognition during a period of hostilities.[66] If so, this will require the neutral state to take on an added burden, for it can hardly be expected that belligerents will be willing to extend the area in which they must refrain from hostile operations if neutral states are unable to exercise an effective control over these waters.

2. *Neutral Ports and Waters As a Base of Operations*

Although the principle that a neutral state ought to prevent the belligerent use of its territory, waters and ports as a "base of operations" received universal acceptance during the course of the nineteenth century, the interpretation and application of this principle has nevertheless been marked by a substantial measure of controversy and uncertainty.[67] Not infrequently attempts have been made to draw specific consequences from the rule forbidding the use of neutral jurisdiction as a base of operations that have found recognition neither in the customary practices of states nor in the rules embodied in international conventions. This has been particularly true of numerous endeavors to determine the precise scope of the neutral's duties of prevention, and the belligerent's duties of abstention, in naval warfare.

It may well be that in the "light of logic" a neutral state ought to prevent the commission of any act within its domain—whether performed by belligerent forces or by private individuals—that may constitute a "direct source of augmentation of belligerent military or naval strength." [68] In fact, however, the interpretations states have given in naval warfare to the phrase "base of operations" have not been governed by the canons of logic but by the various and conflicting policies of states, by the peculiarities of historical development, and by the circumstances attending naval—as distinguished from land and now aerial—warfare.

Nor can it be asserted that Hague Convention XIII has succeeded in resolving the many difficulties involved in applying to naval warfare the general principle under consideration. Although Article 5 of this Convention obligates belligerents to refrain from using "neutral ports and waters as a base of naval operations against their adversaries," it is only the erection of "wireless telegraphy stations or any apparatus for the pur-

---

[66] See *Law of Naval Warfare*, Article 413d, and notes thereto.

[67] In *U. S. Naval War College, International Law Situations, 1932* (pp. 1–26), a useful historical review is made of the varying interpretations given to the term "base of operations" in naval warfare, and particularly the differences between the traditional American view, emphasizing the amount of supplies and repairs allowed in neutral ports, and the traditional British view, stressing the frequency and duration of belligerent stays.

[68] The phrases are Hyde's (*op. cit.*, p. 2249), who writes "that the term 'base of operations' fails to indicate with precision the character or scope of the preventive obligation which is generally acknowledged to rest upon the neutral; for as yet there seems to be no common disposition to impose upon such a State an endeavor to prevent its domain from becoming in numerous situations what, in the light of logic, must cause or permit it to be in fact a direct source of augmentation of belligerent military or naval strength."

pose of communicating with the belligerent forces on land or sea" that is specifically defined as falling within this general prohibition. There are, of course, a large number of further provisions of Hague XIII that may be regarded properly as applications of the general prohibition contained in Article 5. But the Convention is not exhaustive in enumerating the acts a neutral state is obligated to prevent (and a belligerent is obligated to abstain from committing), and the commission of which would serve to turn the neutral's waters and ports into a base of naval operations. For this reason alone, it has not wholly succeeded in removing a measure of the uncertainty still encountered in any endeavor to elaborate upon the consequences following from the prohibition against the use of neutral jurisdiction as a base of operations for belligerent forces.[69]

The duty imposed upon a neutral state not to permit its territory, ports and waters to be used as a base of operations requires the neutral to prevent the commission of certain acts, whether performed by belligerent forces located temporarily within neutral jurisdiction or by private individuals. The scope of the neutral's duties of prevention with respect to acts of belligerent forces within its jurisdiction will be considered in later pages. Here it is desirable to examine the restraints a neutral state must impose upon the acts of private individuals.

It has been pointed out [70] that although a neutral state must abstain both from the supply of war materials to belligerents as well as from the performance of certain services that would serve to aid belligerents in the prosecution of war it is normally under no obligation to prevent its subjects from undertaking similar acts of assistance to belligerents. The neutral state is therefore under no duty to prevent its subjects from trading in war materials with belligerents; and in carrying on such trade it is immaterial whether war materials are exported to belligerent ports in neutral bottoms or are carried away from neutral ports by belligerent merchant vessels.

There are, however, certain exceptions to this distinction between the obligations of abstention imposed upon a neutral state with respect to its own actions and the absence of any obligation to prevent similar acts when performed by private individuals within neutral jurisdiction. One such exception may be seen in Article 8 of Hague XIII, which reads:

> A neutral Government is bound to employ the means at its disposal to prevent the fitting out or arming of any vessel within its

[69] In addition, the more detailed provisions of Hague XIII are not always free from ambiguity. It is customary for writers to assume that in the event of doubt as to the meaning of these more detailed provisions such doubt must be resolved—whenever possible—by reference to Article 5. Although the Convention does not expressly establish this procedure, and does not specifically create any hierarchy among its various norms, the assumption that ambiguous provisions may be interpreted by reference to Article 5 is not unreasonable. But even if it is assumed that this procedure is justified the result may be only to return to the general prohibition whose interpretation and application created so much uncertainty in the first place.

[70] See pp. 209 ff.

399334—57——16

jurisdiction which it has reason to believe is intended to cruise, or engage in hostile operations, against a Power with which that Government is at peace. It is also bound to display the same vigilance to prevent the departure from its jurisdiction of any vessel intended to cruise, or engage in hostile operations, which had been adapted entirely or partly within the said jurisdiction for use in war.[71]

In explanation of the above rule it has been stated that a vessel "intended for operations of war is so complete a weapon of war, its departure may so nearly amount to the use of neutral territory as a base of operations, and its activities may be of such decisive influence, that it has now come to be regarded as not unreasonable to require a neutral government to take upon itself the comparatively simply duty of preventing such a vessel from leaving its jurisdiction".[72] It is tempting to find in this explanation a still more general basis for distinguishing between those acts of private individuals a neutral state is obligated to prevent within its jurisdiction and those acts the commission of which does not involve the neutral's responsi-

[71] Article 8 of Hague XIII is derived from the so-called "Three Rules of Washington", which grew out of the *Alabama* controversy between Great Britain and the United States at the time of the American Civil War. By the Treaty of Washington, May 8, 1871 the parties to the controversy agreed upon the settlement of their differences by arbitration, and further agreed that the arbitrators would be bound by the three rules. The first rule is practically identical with Article 8 of Hague XIII, except that it obligated neutral governments to use "due diligence" to prevent the measures now prohibited by Article 8, whereas Article 8 uses the phrase "means at its disposal."

[72] J. A. Hall, *The Law of Naval Warfare* (1921), p. 150.—The applicability to aircraft of the obligations embodied in Article 8 of Hague XIII is still unsettled. According to Article 46 of the unratified 1923 Rules of Aerial Warfare, a neutral government must use the means at its disposal:

"1. To prevent the departure from its jurisdiction of an aircraft in a condition to make a hostile attack against a belligerent Power, or carrying or accompanied by appliances or materials the mounting or utilization of which would enable it to make a hostile attack, if there is reason to believe that such aircraft is destined for use against a belligerent Power.

"2. To prevent the departure of an aircraft the crew of which includes any member of the combatant forces of a belligerent Power.

"3. To prevent work upon an aircraft designed to prepare it to depart in contravention of the purposes of this Article."

The necessity of an "Alabama" rule for aircraft is evident, and in view of the greater adaptability of aircraft for hostile operations such a rule should be—if anything—more strict than the present obligations imposed upon neutrals with respect to warships. Nevertheless, no clear rule with respect to aircraft has yet emerged, although there can be little question that a neutral state in allowing aircraft to leave its jurisdiction in a *condition to make a hostile attack* against a belligerent would thereby become liable to the charge that its territory had been used as a belligerent base of operations. See Spaight, *op. cit.*, pp. 474–7. Beyond this, however, the obligations of the neutral state—even after World War II—remain undefined. It is relevant, in this connection, to quote common Article 15 (paragraph 2) of the 1938 Neutrality Regulations of the Northern European Neutrals: "Any aircraft in a condition to commit an attack against a belligerent, or which carries apparatus or material the mounting or utilization of which would permit it to commit an attack, is forbidden to leave . . . territory if there is

bility. The former may be considered to consist in acts which *directly* assist or strengthen a belligerent's military and naval forces; the latter consisting only in the *indirect* strengthening of the belligerent's general capacity to wage war. To a substantial degree this distinction can be considered as well-founded in the traditional law.[73] In certain respects, however, its applicability must remain doubtful. It is, for example, not even entirely applicable with respect to the neutral's obligation in Article 8 of Hague XIII, for Article 8 has been interpreted by states to imply not only the duty of a neutral to prevent the departure of vessels intended for immediate delivery at sea to a belligerent, there to be used for hostile operations, but also to imply the duty of a neutral state to prevent the departure from its jurisdiction of said vessels even though they are first to be delivered to a belligerent port in a manner similar to any other commercial transaction. Whereas the private delivery of other kinds of war materials from a neutral state to a belligerent port does not involve the responsibility of the neutral state, the same cannot be said of the delivery to belligerent ports of a vessel intended to engage in hostile belligerent operations and which has been adapted—in whole or in part—within neutral jurisdiction for warlike use.[74]

---

reason to presume that it is destined to be employed against a belligerent Power. It is likewise forbidden to perform work on an aircraft in order to prepare its departure for the above-mentioned purpose." *A. J. I. L.*, 32 (1938), *Supp.* pp. 141 ff.—It should perhaps be made clear that the remarks in this note do not have reference to the quite different question concerning the entry into, or subsequent departure from, neutral territory of belligerent military aircraft (see pp. 251–2).

[73] Though it certainly does not invalidate the excellent criticism of Hyde (*op. cit.*, p. 2297), to wit: "The exportation of war material from neutral territory constitutes usually the general strengthening of the sinews of the belligerent behind the transaction, rather than the proximate cause of the augmentation of a unit of military power. Neutral territory is, nevertheless, utilized as a base of belligerent supply as certainly as if a particular force such as a fleet were the direct recipient of aid. To limit, therefore, the duty of the neutral to the case where its territory affords aid to, or is creative of, a unit of military or naval strength capable of engaging in immediate hostile operations, is to raise an artificial distinction which is hardly responsive to principle or to existing conditions of warfare."—Yet despite the admitted 'artificiality' of the distinction it remains one of the principal bases of the traditional law.

[74] It is occasionally contended that a distinction must still be drawn between selling armed vessels to belligerents and building them to belligerent order; that whereas the neutral state is not obligated to prevent the sale of such vessels when having the character of an ordinary commercial transaction, it is forbidden to allow building to the order of a belligerent. Thus: "An armed ship, being contraband of war, is in no wise different from other kinds of contraband, provided that she is not manned in a neutral port, so that she can commit hostilities at once after having reached the open sea. A subject of a neutral who builds an armed ship, or arms a merchantman, not to the order of a belligerent, but intending to sell her to a belligerent, does not differ from a manufacturer of arms who intends to sell them to a belligerent. There is nothing to prevent a neutral from allowing his subjects to sell armed vessels, and to deliver them to belligerents, either in a neutral port or in a belligerent port . . . On the other hand, if a subject of a neutral builds armed ships *to the order of a belligerent*, he prepares the means of naval operations, since the ships, on sailing outside the neutral territorial waters and taking in

In those instances where warships are built to the order of a belligerent, or are otherwise intended for belligerent use, the neutral's duty is clear. Equally clear is the neutral's obligation to prevent the conversion of belligerent merchant vessels into warships while in neutral ports. Difficulties may arise, however, in the event that belligerent merchant vessels take on arms and war supplies for the purpose of conversion to warships once on the high seas. Although the scope of the neutral's duty in this latter instance is not entirely clear, it would seem that the neutral is obliged to exercise the means at his disposal in order to prevent belligerent merchant vessels suspected of intended conversion from receiving any war materials while in neutral ports. Similar care must be exercised by the neutral with respect to armed belligerent merchant vessels, if suspected of not having used such armament solely for defensive purposes. Indeed, the far-reaching transformation in the position now occupied by merchant vessels in relation to a belligerent's military effort at sea—a transformation the consequences of which are still far from being generally recognized—necessitates the re-examination of the status to be accorded these vessels while in neutral waters and ports. The contention that this transformation no longer justifies the differentiation in treatment formerly drawn between the warships and merchant vessels of a belligerent must be given serious consideration. If this contention is well founded, and it will be examined in a further section,[75] then the duties of a neutral state will be increased considerably. It is at least clear that in relation to belligerent merchant vessels the neutral's duties of prevention under Articles 5 and 8 of Hague XIII have become increasingly wider in scope as a result of the recent practices of belligerents.

In this connection, brief consideration may be given to one further category of acts the commission of which by private individuals may serve to turn neutral waters and ports into a base of operations. Although the neutral state is under no obligation to prevent the departure of merchant vessels carrying contraband of war to the ports of a belligerent, is it obliged

---

a crew and ammunition, can at once commit hostilities." Oppenheim-Lauterpacht, *op. cit.*, p. 713. The distinction drawn by Oppenheim was relied upon in the opinion (dated August 27, 1940) of the Attorney General of the United States on the legality—under international law—of the exchange of over-age American destroyers for the lease of British naval and air bases. For text of opinion, see *A. J. I. L.*, 34 (1940), pp. 728–35. There can be little doubt, however, that the distinction in question has almost no foundation in the practice of states. See, for example, the criticism of Herbert W. Briggs, who points out that "the practice of states . . . has overwhelmingly rejected Oppenheim's distinction since 1871, and the United States Government is on record as never having accepted it." "Neglected Aspects of the Destroyer Deal," *A. J. I. L.*, 34 (1940), p. 587. It may be noted further that even if the distinction made by Oppenheim could be accepted it would not have justified the destroyer-base agreement, since the distinction refers only to the actions of neutral subjects, not to acts of the neutral state. The latter is clearly forbidden by Article 6 of Hague XIII from engaging in such transactions.

[75] See pp. 247–51.

to prevent the departure of merchant vessels carrying war materials intended for direct delivery to a belligerent's naval forces at sea? It should be made clear that the question raised does not refer to vessels bearing the formal status of auxiliary warships, or to vessels which—though not possessing this status—nevertheless act in the direct and continuous employ of a belligerent fleet. With respect to either of these categories of vessels there is no question, since a neutral state certainly must treat them in the same manner as belligerent warships.[76] Under consideration here are rather vessels—whether neutral or belligerent—not in the direct and continuous employ of a belligerent fleet but which the neutral state has reason to believe intend to deliver certain war materials to belligerent warships.

No doubt as judged by the "standards of logic" the neutral's duty is clear. To forbid belligerent warships from obtaining armaments and other supplies of war in neutral ports, while at the same time allowing neutral and belligerent merchant vessels to provide belligerent forces at sea with these materials, would not unreasonably appear to be a patent evasion of the principle forming the basis of the neutral's duty to prevent its waters and ports from becoming a base of operations. Nonetheless the matter remains unsettled in law, and it is not possible to define with certainty the scope of the neutral's duty of prevention. In practice, however, an increasing number of states when neutral do prohibit the departure of any merchant vessel from their ports when there is reason to believe that the supplies carried are destined for direct delivery to a belligerent fleet.[77] But whether this practice may be declared sufficient to constitute a custom presently binding upon neutral states must remain doubtful.[78]

a. The Passage of Belligerent Warships and Prizes Through Neutral Territorial Waters

The problem of belligerent *passage through* neutral waters must be dis-

---

[76] See pp. 39–40.

[77] During both World Wars most neutral states prohibited this practice.—The United States Neutrality Regulations of September 5, 1939 prohibited, in paragraph 12, the "dispatching from the United States, or any place subject to the jurisdiction thereof, any vessel, domestic or foreign, which is about to carry to a warship, tender, or supply ship of a belligerent any fuel, arms, ammunition, men, supplies, dispatches, or information shipped or received on board within the jurisdiction of the United States." In the Neutrality Act of November 4, 1939 (section 10) the President was given still broader powers to prevent the departure of vessels from American ports whenever reasonable cause existed for believing that such vessels intended to supply belligerent warships with fuel, arms or ammunition.—Common Article 14 of the 1938 Neutrality Regulations of the Northern European Neutrals provided that: "Vessels or aircraft obviously navigating with a view to supplying the combatant forces of the belligerents with fuel or other provisions are prohibited to take on supplies in ports . . . or anchorages exceeding in quantity that necessary for their own needs." *A. J. I. L.*, 32 (1938), *Supp.*, pp. 141 ff. And to the same effect, Article 5 of the Recommendation (February 2, 1940) of the Inter-American Neutrality Committee, *A. J. I. L.*, 34 (1940), *Supp.* p. 80.

[78] The opinions of writers are neither consistent nor altogether clear on this point, though the majority are reticent to assert that the practice referred to above may be considered as now possessing a customary character.

tinguished from the case of belligerent *entry and stay* in neutral waters and ports. Article 10 of Hague Convention XIII provides that the "neutrality of a power is not affected by the mere passage through its territorial waters of war-ships or prizes belonging to belligerents," and this conventional rule finds general support in customary international law as well.[79] In permitting neutral states to allow the mere passage of belligerent warships and prizes through their waters Article 10 does not thereby determine what a neutral state may forbid to belligerents. Since a neutral's rights are, in this respect, no less in time of war than in time of peace it may place severe restrictions upon—and probably forbid altogether—the passage of belligerent warships and prizes through its waters, or at least through those waters that do not connect two parts of the high seas and are not used as a highway for international navigation.[80] In imposing restrictions upon the

[79] See *Law of Naval Warfare*, Article 443.

[80] See *Law of Naval Warfare*, Article 412 (and notes thereto), where it is pointed out that extension of the right of innocent passage in time of peace to warships remains an unsettled matter. It would appear that the practice of states does indicate a general reluctance to recognize a clear right of innocent passage as extending to warships, although it is true that under normal circumstances the denial of passage to foreign warships frequently has been regarded as an unfriendly act. Recently, the International Law Commission, in its final Report on the Law of the Sea, adopted at its Eighth Session (see *U N. General Assembly, Official Records, 11th Sess. Supp. No. 9* (Doc. A/3159)), dealt with the scope of the right of innocent passage in time of peace. Article 24 of the Report declares that the coastal state "may make the passage of warships through the territorial sea subject to previous authorization or notification. Normally it shall grant innocent passage subject to the observance of the provisions of Articles 17 and 18." And paragraph 1 of Article 17 states that the coastal state "may take the necessary steps in its territorial sea to protect itself against any act prejudicial to its security or to such other of its interests as it is authorized to protect under the present rules and other rules of international law." According to Article 25 a warship failing to comply with the regulations of the coastal state concerning passage through the territorial sea may be ordered to leave such waters.

It should be fairly apparent that the argument directed against conceding any right of passage through territorial waters to foreign warships is much stronger in time of war than during a period of peace. The interest of a neutral state in preventing belligerent use of its waters as a base of operations, and in preserving a strict impartiality, may well appear to dictate a policy of prohibiting altogether the lateral passage of belligerent warships through its territorial waters. As presently noted in the text, the passage of belligerent warships through neutral waters is—in any event—an anomoly which finds no parallel in land or aerial warfare. Although it has been justified by pointing out that the interests of a strict neutrality must be qualified in this instance by the character of the sea as a highway for international navigation the argument is not impressive. There has long been a conviction that neutrals ought to have a right to deny passage altogether to warships, and this view was given expression at the Hague Conference of 1907. At that Conference, however, a number of states—and particularly Great Britain—insisted upon a right of innocent passage for warships. Article 10 of Hague XIII formed a compromise between these conflicting views. During World War I the Netherlands adopted the rule that—save in distress—belligerent warships were forbidden either to enter or to stay in Netherlands territorial waters, though this denial of passage was later justified against Germany by the argument that Netherlands waters did not constitute a normal route for the navigation of German warships. Hence, the possible significance of

passage of warships through its waters the neutral state is only required to act impartially toward all belligerents.

Although Article 10 permits neutrals to allow belligerent warships "mere passage" through their waters it leaves unanswered several questions. May the neutral state grant anything more than "mere passage," or does Article 10—without expressly so stating—indicate the scope of the neutral's duty with respect to belligerent passage through its territorial waters? In addition, if Article 10 states the scope of the neutral's duty—which is to prevent belligerent transit through its territorial waters other then for the purpose of "mere passage"—then what is the meaning of the "mere passage" a neutral may permit? Finally, and in close connection with the preceding question, is there any time limit imposed upon belligerent passage through neutral waters?

There would appear to be general agreement that Article 10 does define the scope of the neutral's preventive obligation. There is less agreement, however, upon the precise nature of the neutral's obligation to prevent belligerent transit through its waters other than for purposes of "mere

---

the Netherlands action is not altogether clear. Nevertheless, it is believed that a neutral state would not violate international law if it did forbid passage—however innocent—through its territorial sea to the warships of belligerents (the same position is taken in the *Harvard Draft Convention on the Rights and Duties of Neutral States in Naval and Aerial War, op. cit.*, pp. 422–4).

One clear exception to the position advanced above may be seen in the case of straits connecting two parts of the high seas and used as a highway for international navigation; here the belligerent would appear to have a right to claim innocent passage for its warships and prizes. In the case of canals that are regulated by international agreement passage is governed by the terms of the agreement. In either case, however, passage is subject to the right of the neutral littoral state to take reasonable measures to secure the protection of the waterway and to insure the integrity of its neutral status. According to treaty, when the United States is neutral the Panama Canal shall be free and open, on terms of entire equality, to the vessels of commerce and of war of all nations observing the rules laid down in the Hay-Pauncefote Treaty concluded November 18, 1901 between the United States and Great Britain. On September 5, 1939 two Executive Orders were proclaimed setting forth the regulations governing neutrality in the Canal Zone and the passage of warships through the Panama Canal. For texts of orders, *U. S. Naval War College, International Law Situation, 1939*, pp. 139–43. Among other things these Orders restricted belligerent passage or stay in the waters of the Canal Zone to twenty-four hours (with certain exceptions) in addition to the time required to transit the Canal, limited the number of warships of one belligerent permitted at any one time in either port or waters to three, restricted the total number of warships of all belligerents allowed at any one time in the Canal and the waters of the Canal Zone to six, and prohibited warships from effecting repairs and obtaining fuel and provisions except under written authorization from Canal authorities. Finally, a belligerent warship was permitted to pass through the Canal "only after her commanding officer has given written assurance to the authorities of the Panama Canal that the rules, regulations, and treaties of the United States will be faithfully observed."—A detailed survey of the practice of states with respect to the passage of belligerent warships through international waterways, when the littoral or riparian state is neutral, may be found in R. R. Baxter, "Passage of Ships Through International Waterways in Time of War," *B. Y. I. L.*, 31 (1954), pp. 192–202.

passage."[81] It has been contended that the passage a neutral may permit belligerents must be considered, both by custom as well as by convention, together with, and restricted by, the neutral obligation to prevent its waters from being used as a belligerent base of naval operations; that in terms of Hague XIII Article 10 must be read along with Article 5 of the Convention. According to this interpretation the "mere passage" a neutral may permit belligerent warships must be of an innocent nature, in the sense that it is strictly incidental to the normal requirements of navigation and not intended in any way to turn neutral waters into a base of operations. Thus the circuitous and prolonged passage through neutral territorial waters for the ostensible purpose of avoiding combat with an enemy has been held to fall within the prohibition—contained in Article 5—against using neutral waters as a base of operations, and for this reason cannot be considered as constituting "mere passage" allowed in Article 10.[82]

In principle, this argument would appear well founded and reasonable. The practice of permitting belligerent warships (and prizes) to use neutral territorial waters for passage is, in any event, an anomaly which finds no parallel either in land or in aerial warfare.[83] Recent experience indicates that if belligerent passage through neutral waters is to be tolerated at all it must be kept within the narrowest of limits. At the same time, it must be pointed out that even if it is assumed that—from the point of view of Hague XIII—Article 10 is to be interpreted by reference to Article 5 (i. e., "mere passage" must not be so used as to turn neutral waters into a "base

[81] There is no doubt at all, however, that the passage allowed a belligerent warship through neutral waters does not permit taking on provisions or making repairs. But a neutral state may allow, according to Article 11 of Hague XIII, the use of neutral pilots by belligerent warships.

[82] "While according to customary International Law and to Hague Convention XIII the neutral State is entitled to permit the passage of men-of-war through its territorial waters, the nature and duration of such passage are governed by the overriding principle that neutral territorial waters must not be permitted to become a basis for warlike activities of either belligerent. The prolonged use of neutral territorial waters by belligerent men-of-war or their auxiliaries for passage not dictated by normal requirements of navigation and intended, *inter alia*, as a means of escaping capture by superior enemy forces must, therefore, be deemed to constitute an illicit use of neutral territory which the neutral State is by International Law bound to prevent by the means at his disposal or which, in exceptional cases, the other belligerent is entitled to resist or remedy by way of self-help." Oppenheim-Lauterpacht, *op. cit.*, pp. 694–5. A substantially similar view has been taken by the majority of British writers. For the position of the British Government in the *Altmark* incident, see pp. 237–8.

[83] See, for example, the observations of Hyde (*op. cit.*, p. 2312), who considers the present use belligerents may make of neutral waters as "grotesque and unrealistic," and also suggests that "passage of belligerent vessels of war through neutral waters should, by general agreement, be greatly restricted, if not entirely forbidden." Also B. M. Telders, "L'Incident De L'Altmark," *Revue Générale De Droit International Public*, 68 (1941–45), p. 100, who suggests that the moral of the *Altmark* incident, considered below, is to support the belief that the prohibition of entry to belligerent warships into neutral waters—save in case of distress—is the best means of insuring the neutrality of non-participants.

of operations"), this will result only in raising the question—the answer to which is hardly self-evident—as to when belligerent transit through neutral waters does clearly cease to be "mere passage" and constitutes instead the use of such waters as a base of operations. Apart from the express prohibition already contained in Hague XIII, the nature of the acts that may be regarded, when performed by belligerent warships, as turning neutral waters into a base of operations has admittedly long been a matter of controversy and uncertainty. If the answer to this question may not be found in the provisions of Hague XIII, it is still less probable that it will be found in the customary law; for it is the latter that has always provided so much uncertainty as to the specific meaning to be accorded the phrase "base of operations." The interpretation is not altogether excluded, therefore, that passage through neutral territorial waters, although undertaken in order to avoid an enemy, "does not diminish the privilege of using the territorial waters for transit." [84]

Whether or not any time limit is imposed upon the "mere passage" neutrals may permit to belligerent warships forms a related, though some-

[84] Edwin Borchard, "Was Norway Delinquent in the Case of the Altmark," *A. J. I. L.*, 34 (1940), p. 294. Other writers share this opinion; e. g., Erik Castren (*op. cit.*, p. 515) asserts that: "Warships entering neutral waters in order to escape from the enemy may also pass through them." This position hardly seems sustainable, however, if passage through neutral waters also involves following a circuitous route having no reasonable relation to normal requirements of navigation. But the matter may not always be so clear-cut. What if belligerent passage through neutral waters does conform to ordinary navigational requirements? May it nevertheless be regarded as exceeding "mere passage" if it serves either to confer a direct military advantage upon a belligerent or to result in endangering the peace and security of the neutral state? Belligerent passage through neutral waters always forms a part of naval operations and therefore can always be interpreted as conferring some sort of advantage upon the belligerent which makes use of neutral territorial waters. It may prove next to impossible to determine whether or not passage does serve in a concrete instance to confer a direct military advantage (or, put in other terms, whether or not passage serves to turn neutral waters into a base of operations). This is particularly so when passage conforms to ordinary navigational requirements. Of course, it may be argued—as a number of writers have so argued—that the legitimacy of passage is determined not only by the specific use to which neutral waters may be put but also by the degree to which passage—whatever its actual purpose—may endanger the peace and security of the neutral state. This latter criterion is a significant one and ought not to be confused with the base of operations criterion. Although the use of neutral waters as a base of operations necessarily endangers the peace and security of the neutral the converse proposition is not always the case. The peace and security of the neutral state may be endangered by belligerent passage, but such passage clearly need not constitute the use of neutral waters as a base of operations. From this point of view, passage is no longer "innocent" (and hence no longer "mere passage") if it is likely to result in tempting an enemy to take hostile measures in neutral waters. One obvious difficulty here, however, is that the determination of the "innocence" of passage may thereby be left in practice to the initiative of the belligerents, since the latter have only to react adversely to an enemy's passage through neutral waters and the consequence will be to endanger the peace and security of the neutral state.—Admittedly, the preceding remarks raise difficult—and as yet unsettled—questions. Nor is it likely that these questions will ever be resolved satisfactorily short of clear change in a rule that has long been an anachronism in the law of neutrality.

what subsidiary, question. In terms of Hague XIII this latter question concerns the relation of Article 10 to Article 12. Article 12 states:

> In the absence of special provisions to the contrary in the legislation of the neutral Power, belligerent ships of war are forbidden to remain in the ports, roadsteads or territorial waters of the said Power for more than twenty-four hours, except in cases covered by the present Convention.

The problem is essentially that of determining whether or not Article 10 is one of the "cases covered." Either interpretation is possible, and it would therefore appear that the matter of determining the time limit to be allowed for passage through neutral waters must be left to the decision of the neutral state concerned. In general, the practice of neutral states has been to limit belligerent passage to a period not exceeding twenty-four hours.[85] But it should be emphasized that whatever length of period the neutral state may establish for the passage of belligerent warships through its waters this cannot affect the nature of the passage allowed. If belligerent passage has a character other than that of "mere passage," provided for in Article 10, it is forbidden for any period of time. On the other hand, it is not unreasonable to contend that the length of the period of passage—i. e., a prolonged use of neutral waters—is itself one indication of the purposes for which transit is made.

The difficulties involved in interpreting the scope of the neutral's duty in regulating belligerent transit through its territorial waters were strikingly illustrated during the second World War in the *Altmark* incident. On February 14, 1940, the German naval auxiliary vessel *Altmark* entered Norwegian territorial waters on a return trip from the South Atlantic to Germany. The vessel carried almost three hundred captured British seamen on board, a fact which, in itself, had only a limited relevance to the principal legal issues involved. The German auxiliary was granted permission by the Norwegian authorities to navigate through the latter's territorial waters. At the same time the Norwegian authorities refused the request made by the commander of British naval forces in the area that the *Altmark* be searched in order to determine whether she carried British prisoners. On February 16, 1940, after the *Altmark* had passed through approximately four hundred miles of Norwegian waters, a British

[85] See p. 241 (n). In the regulations of many neutral states no attempt has been made to distinguish clearly between the time allowed for passage through neutral waters and the period governing entry and stay in neutral waters and ports. Thus the United States Neutrality Regulations of September 5, 1939 declared: "If any ship of war of a belligerent shall, after the time this notification takes effect, be found in, or shall enter any port, harbor, roadstead, or waters subject to the jurisdiction of the United States, such vessel shall not be permitted to remain in such port, harbor, roadstead, or waters more than twenty-four hours, except in case of stress of weather, or for delay in receiving supplies or repairs, or when detained by the United States . . ." The preceding regulation was interpreted, however, as applying both to passage through territorial waters as well as to stay in port.

destroyer entered these waters and forcibly released the prisoners held on board the German vessel. No attempt was made by the British destroyer carrying out the action either to capture or to sink the *Altmark*.[86]

In justification of the British action in the *Altmark* case it has been urged that Norway failed to comply with the obligations of neutrality by not conducting a proper investigation into the nature and object of the *Altmark's* voyage and of the use to which she was putting Norwegian territorial waters.[87] Still further, it has been argued that, in taking an extremely

---

[86] A brief summary of the *Altmark* incident, and part of the diplomatic correspondence provoked by the incident, are given in Hackworth, *op. cit.*, Vol. VII, pp. 568–75. The texts of the notes exchanged between Great Britain and Norway during the period extending from February 17, 1940 to March 15, 1940 were published in 1950 by Great Britain (Norway No. 1 (1950), Cmd. 8012). In an abundant literature the clearest, and most detailed, exposition of the legal issues raised by the case—though reflecting the British position—has been given by C. H. M. Waldock, "The Release of the Altmark's Prisoners," *B. Y. I. L.*, 24 (1947), pp. 216–38. Upon entering Norwegian waters the *Altmark* was hailed by a Norwegian naval vessel which confined itself to an examination of the *Altmark's* papers. Although a number of writers have concentrated upon the question of the precise status of the vessel there was no disagreement between Great Britain and Norway on this point. The *Altmark* was a German naval auxiliary, listed as such by Germany, and entitled to be treated in a manner similar to any other warship. Prior to her return voyage from the South Atlantic she had operated with the *Graf Spee*, and indeed the British prisoners she carried on board were taken from ships sunk by the *Graf Spee*. Nor could there by any question about the plainly circuitous nature of the *Altmark's* voyage, since during the course of her initial examination the captain had stated that the *Altmark* was on her way from Port Arthur, Texas, to Germany. On the second day of passage another Norwegian naval vessel sought to inspect the *Altmark* but the request was refused. In response to questions put to him the captain of the *Altmark* denied carrying any nationals of another belligerent. When asked why the *Altmark* had earlier violated Norwegian neutrality regulations by making use of her wireless the captain responded that he was unaware of any prohibition against such use. During the greater part of her passage through Norwegian waters the *Altmark* was escorted by Norwegian naval vessels.

[87] The precise nature of this particular argument should be thoroughly understood. Initially, much was made of the fact that the *Altmark* was carrying prisoners of war, and in its earlier notes and public statements the British Government weakened its position considerably not only by its almost exclusive concentration upon this aspect but also by giving the impression of contending that the passage of a belligerent warship through neutral waters was unlawful if the warship carried prisoners of war. However, a belligerent may enter neutral waters and ports even though carrying prisoners of war on board and this fact in itself does not legally alter the position of the vessel or the obligations of the neutral. Provided that the *Altmark's* passage through Norwegian waters was in accordance with international law and Norway's neutrality regulations there was no duty on Norway's part to object to the transport of prisoners through her waters. The duty to release prisoners of war held on board a warship follows only upon the act of interning the warship for violation of neutral waters. (It is also possible that, exceptionally, the release of prisoners may occur in other circumstances. Thus the Uruguayan Government released the prisoners held by the *Graf Spee*, as a condition for granting the *Graf Spee* a seventy-two hour stay in Montevideo for the purpose of making repairs to damage incurred in battle. But it would be premature to draw any conclusions from this one incident.) Hence Norway's duty to release the British seamen held on board the *Altmark* would arise only as a result of interning the vessel for unlawful use of Norwegian waters.

The decisive point, therefore, concerned the nature of the *Altmark's* passage—i. e., its legality

circuitous route which involved making prolonged use of Norwegian waters for the evident purpose of avoiding capture by British forces, the *Altmark's* passage went far beyond the "mere passage" a neutral state may grant belligerent warships under Article 10 of Hague XIII. Given these circumstances, the passage of the German auxiliary vessel amounted to the use of Norwegian waters as a "base of operations," within the meaning of Article 5 of the same convention. Hence, Norway had the duty either to intern the vessel and to release the prisoners, or, at the very least, to order the *Altmark* out of Norwegian waters.[87a]

---

or illegality—and the later British note of March 15, 1940 properly emphasized this point. At the same time, the note of March 15th insisted that a neutral was obliged to take those measures necessary to insure that belligerent warships do not make improper use of its waters. The final British position concentrated then upon two principal legal arguments. The first concerned what may be termed the extent of the investigative measures a neutral must take to ensure the integrity of its waters, whereas the second dealt with the problem of what actually constitutes belligerent misuse of these waters under the guise of "mere passage." Great Britain contended that the Norwegian Government in allowing its attempts at further investigation of the *Altmark* to be frustrated had violated its neutral obligations, that the refusal by the captain of the *Altmark* to permit the search of his vessel obligated Norway to order the *Altmark* out of Norwegian waters. Search of the *Altmark* would have revealed the presence of prisoners, and although the transport of prisoners through neutral waters is not in itself unlawful *their transport under these particular circumstances* would have enabled Norway to judge the true nature and purpose of the voyage—hence its unlawful character. Instead, the British note pointed out, Norway contented itself not only with making a very inadequate investigation but even went out of its way to facilitate the *Altmark's* voyage.

The *Altmark* incident thus raised the general question as to what measures—if indeed any—of an investigative character a neutral is bound to take with respect to belligerent warships entering its waters. More specifically, does a neutral have a duty—as well as a right—to search a warship in circumstances raising reasonable doubt as to the legitimacy of the use to which neutral waters may be put. In the *Altmark* case Norway insisted that the peacetime immunity accorded foreign warships was equally applicable in time of war and that the *Altmark* was merely exercising this right of immunity when she turned down the Norwegian request to search the vessel. This position is hardly conducive to an effective neutrality, however, which would rather appear to require that an exception be made to the normal immunity granted foreign warships. Certainly there is much to be said for the view "that a neutral state which has bona fide reasons for questioning a particular use of its waters by a belligerent warship has both the right and the duty to investigate the ship's activities, even to the extent of a reasonable inspection of the ship itself." Waldock, *op. cit.*, p. 221.

87a Professor Waldock's (*op. cit.*, p. 235) conclusions are as follows:

"(a) Norway's view that passage is covered only by Article 10 and is not touched by the 24 hours' rule of Article 12 ought not to be accepted. Norway was therefore in default in permitting the *Altmark's* passage to exceed 24 hours.

"(b) The Altmark's circuitous passage to escape attack was not 'mere passage' within the meaning of Article 10, but a use of Norwegian waters for defensive naval operations contrary to Article 5. Norway was therefore in default in allowing such passage at all.

"(c) Even if a breach of Article 5 is not regarded as conclusively established under the existing rules of international law, the *Altmark's* use of Norwegian waters was undeniably for refuge as well as for passage. In these circumstances it was inadmissible for Norway to regard the *Altmark's* passage as 'mere passage' within the meaning of Article 10, and accordingly

Whether the hostile action taken by Great Britain within Norwegian waters was justified, even under the assumption that Norway was clearly derelict in her neutral duties, may receive separate consideration.[88] Here it is relevant only to observe that the contention that the *Altmark's* use of neutral waters did not constitute "mere passage," but rather the use of neutral waters as a base of operations, was not without substantial foundation. In retrospect, the *Altmark* case serves to emphasize once again that a belligerent will not readily accede to his enemy's use of neutral waters for purposes other than those strictly incidental to the normal requirements of navigation. And although the matter cannot be regarded as conclusively settled it is probable that the present scope of the neutral's duty is such that it must prevent passage through its waters by belligerent warships when such passage has as its purpose the use of these waters as a refuge from enemy forces.

Norway ought at least to have limited her use of Norwegian waters to 24 hours under Article 12."

The difficulty with Professor Waldock's last point (c) is that it simply assumes that belligerent passage cannot constitute the "mere passage" permitted under Article 10 if it is motivated by reason of seeking refuge. Yet it is just this point that—however reasonable—cannot be regarded as self-evident. Nor is the first stated conclusion (a) compelling, since the relation between Articles 10 and 12 allows either interpretation—as already noted—thus leaving it to the neutral to regulate the time limit allowed for passage through its waters. Waldock further argues that: "Norway, in its Neutrality Regulations, including that concerning the 24 hours' rule, made no distinction between entry for passage and entry for other purposes, but the evidence seems to point to the conclusion that Norway intended this provision not to apply to passage—as was shown in the *City of Flint* incident." (On the *City of Flint*, see p. 246 (n)). These points are believed to be somewhat peripheral, however. The central legal issue raised by the *Altmark* incident, and which forms Professor Waldock's second conclusion, is clear: are belligerent warships permitted—for any period of time—to use neutral waters for circuitous passage in order to escape from enemy forces? The argument Professor Waldock offers in support of a negative reply to this decisive question is not easy to refute.

In Great Britain's note of March 15, 1940 the British Government reiterated its belief that "mere passage" must be interpreted to mean "innocent passage," and the latter was defined as "passage through such territorial waters as would form part of a ship's normal course from the point of her departure to her destination, and in particular through such territorial waters as form part of straits which provide access from one area of the sea to another." On the relation between Articles 10 and 12 the note went on to declare that: "His Majesty's Government regard the question of passage through territorial waters as governed by Article 10 of the Convention [Hague XIII] and not by Article 12, and, in their view, the time limit of passage is not the fixed one of 24 hours prescribed by the latter Article but that which results from the very nature of 'innocent passage' . . . but Article 12 is at any rate a refutation of the contention that no time limit exists if the ship does not enter a port or anchorage, and the existence of this general prohibition, applicable to both ports and territorial waters, reinforces the view which His Majesty's Government hold as to the nature of the passage which is permitted by Article 10.

[88] See p. 262 (n).

b. Belligerent Stay in Neutral Ports and Waters

(i) Warships

It has been observed that a neutral state may prohibit altogether the passage of belligerent warships through its territorial waters. In like manner a neutral may place restrictions upon the entry and stay of belligerent warships in its waters, ports or roadsteads in excess of the obligations imposed by international law, and even forbid altogether such entry and stay.[89] It is generally recognized, however, that international practice requires that exception be made in the neutrality regulations of states to permit the entry of belligerent warships in distress. Entry in distress may result from weather or sea conditions, but it may also result from damage incurred in battle. Even pursuit by the enemy appears to give belligerent warships a right of entry. But this right of entry in distress cannot be held to prejudice the measures a neutral state may take once admission into its waters and ports has been granted. The belligerent has no right to repair the damage he has suffered, to take on needed supplies, or to depart freely. And in the event entry has been sought as a result of battle damage or of active pursuit by enemy forces a neutral state that has otherwise forbidden belligerent entrance into its waters or ports may properly intern the vessel, together with its officers and crew.[90]

So far as the scope of neutral duties is concerned Hague XIII is not entirely clear as to those circumstances—if any—in which a neutral must forbid entry and stay to belligerent warships. Article 12 merely refers to the time limits placed upon warships which "remain in" the ports, roadsteads and territorial waters of neutrals. Article 14 refers to the prolongation of neutral stay in beligerent ports "on account of damage or stress of

---

[89] The right of neutral states to exclude belligerent warships from their waters and ports is now generally recognized, though previously subject to some doubt. During the first World War the Netherlands' Government did in fact resort to a policy of complete exclusion, exception being made only for entry in distress and for vessels employed exclusively for humanitarian and scientific purposes. In *Harvard Draft Convention on the Rights and Duties of Neutral States in Naval and Aerial War* (*op. cit.*, pp. 425 ff.), the past practice of states is reviewed. Article 26 of the Draft Convention states:

"A neutral state may exclude from its territory belligerent warships other than:

(a) Warships entering in distress; and

(b) Warships employed exclusively in scientific or humanitarian missions."

There do not appear to have been any instances during World War II in which neutrals resorted to a policy of complete exclusion.

In addition, neutrals may—without resorting to complete exclusion—place special restrictions upon certain categories of belligerent warships. During both World Wars a number of neutral states—including the United States—prohibited the entry of belligerent submarines into their ports or waters, exception being made for distress or *force majeure* (in which cases the submarine was required to navigate on the surface).

[90] See *U. S. Naval War College, International Law Situations, 1939*, pp. 43–4. A general review of the problem of asylum in neutral ports is given in *U S. Naval War College, International Law Situations, 1935*, pp. 42–53.

weather.[91] Neither these nor any other provisions of Hague XIII place restrictions upon the possible reasons for permitting entry and stay in neutral ports. Presumably, then, the neutral state may permit belligerent entry and stay, without liability to immediate internment, even though it is clear that this may well serve to provide a warship with a place of refuge from enemy forces. The practice of neutral states during the two World Wars leaves little doubt as to this conclusion.[92]

Although there is some question as to the applicability of the twenty-four hour rule to belligerent passage through neutral waters there is no question as to the application of this rule to entry and stay. Unless the neutral state expressly provides to the contrary the period of stay in neutral ports is limited to twenty-four hours.[93] At the same time, Article 12 of Hague XIII provides for certain exceptions to the normal twenty-four hours' limit on the period of stay, apart from exceptions that may be

---

[91] Article 14 reads: "A belligerent ship of war must not prolong its stay in a neutral port beyond the period legally allowed except on account of damage or stress of weather. It must depart as soon as the cause of the delay is at an end.

"The regulations as to the limitation of the length of time which such vessels may remain in neutral ports, roadsteads, or waters, do not apply to ships of war devoted exclusively to religious, scientific, or philanthropic purposes."

[92] It may appear inconsistent to refuse a belligerent warship passage through neutral waters, when such passage is used in order to escape from an enemy, and yet to allow a belligerent warship to stay in neutral ports for precisely the same reason. In part, this may be explained by the fact that belligerent warships staying in neutral ports can be subjected to far more effective surveillance and control by neutral authorities than would normally prove possible with vessels passing through the neutral's territorial waters. In any event, whereas Article 10 of Hague XIII does expressly restrict passage through neutral waters to "mere passage," no specific restrictions are placed upon the possible reasons for belligerent entry and stay in neutral ports. And it is clear that the practice of states does not yet permit the assertion that the belligerent's use of neutral ports as a temporary refuge imposes upon the neutral a duty to intern the vessel and its crew. During World War II the *Graf Spee* incident (see p. 245 (n)) and analogous cases served to emphasize this point.

[93] Smith (*op. cit.*, p. 154) states that: "The 'twenty-four hours rule' has now been so widely adopted in practice that it may be taken as almost equivalent to a general rule. In its normal application it means that the warship must leave the neutral port within twenty-four hours of receiving notice from the neutral authority, and it is the duty of the neutral to give this notice as soon as possible."—No instances are known of neutral states granting a normal stay in excess of twenty-four hours during World War II. The General Declaration of Neutrality of the American Republics, October 3, 1939, stated on this point that the signatories: "May determine, with regard to belligerent warships, that not more than three at a time be admitted in their ports or waters and in any case they shall not be allowed to remain for more than twenty-four hours. Vessels engaged exclusively in scientific, religious or philanthropic missions may be exempted from this provision, as well as those which arrive in distress." text in *A. J. I. L.*, 34 (1940), *Supp.*, p. 10. The twenty-four hour rule is equally applicable to belligerent warships in neutral ports or roadsteads at the outbreak of hostilities. Article 13 of Hague Convention XIII declares: "If a Power which has been informed of the outbreak of hostilities learns that a belligerent ship of war is in one of its ports or roadsteads, or in its territorial waters it must notify the said ship to depart within twenty-four hours or within the time prescribed by the local regulations."

specifically provided for in the legislation of the neutral state. In the first place, the twenty-four hours' rule does not apply to belligerent warships devoted exclusively to humanitarian (e. g., hospital and relief vessels), scientific, or religious purposes.[94] In addition, a belligerent warship may have its stay in neutral ports prolonged—according to Article 14 of Hague XIII—"on account of damage or stress of weather." Still further, the requirement laid down in Article 16, that a minimum period of twenty-four hours must elapse "before the departure of the ship belonging to one belligerent and the departure of the ship belonging to the other," may also lead to extension of stay in excess of the normal period.[95] Finally, a belligerent warship unable to take on the fuel otherwise permitted to it in a neutral's port may be permitted by the neutral state to extend its normal period of stay by an additional twenty-four hours.[96]

In the event a belligerent warship either enters a neutral port in violation of the neutral state's regulations or does not leave a port where it is no longer entitled to remain, the neutral state is obliged to intern the vessel, together with its officers and crew, for the remainder of the war. This duty is a strict one, and the neutral must ensure that the measures it takes are adequate to prevent the vessel and its personnel from leaving neutral territory.[97]

Once admitted to neutral ports or roadsteads belligerent warships are forbidden—according to Article 5—to commit any acts that might serve to turn neutral ports into a base of operations, and it is both the right as well as the duty of neutral states to prevent such acts. It is for this reason that neutral states must not allow belligerent warships that have once entered their territorial waters to communicate in any manner with bellig-

---

[94] Article 14.

[95] Articles 15 and 16.

[96] Article 19.

[97] Article 24 outlines the neutral's duties in this respect and may be cited in full:

"If, notwithstanding the notification of the neutral authorities, a belligerent ship of war does not leave a port where it is not entitled to remain, the neutral Power is entitled to take such measures as it considers necessary to render the ship incapable of taking the sea during the war, and the commanding officer of the ship must facilitate the execution of such measures.

When a belligerent ship is detained by a neutral Power, the officers and crew are likewise detained.

The officers and crew thus detained may be left in the ship or kept either in another ship or on land, and may be subjected to the measures of restriction which it may appear necessary to impose upon them. A sufficient number of men for looking after the vessel must, however, always be left on board.

The officers may be left at liberty on giving their word not to quit the neutral territory without permission."

Although Article 24 only speaks of a neutral being "entitled" to intern, the neutral state—as emphasized above—is also under the duty to do so. On the disposition to be made of prisoners of war carried on board an interned warship, see p. 123 (n).

erent forces at sea.[98] It is for the same reason that Article 18 of Hague XIII forbids belligerent warships to use "neutral ports, roadsteads, or territorial waters for replenishing or increasing their supplies of war material or their armament, or for completing their crews."

More difficult, however, are those questions concerning the supplies of food and fuel belligerent warships may obtain, and the repairs that may be undertaken, in neutral ports. It may appear that the logical consequence of forbidding belligerent warships to use neutral waters and ports as a base of operations must be to prohibit such vessels from obtaining within neutral waters and ports any supplies or repairs. This has not been the case. In principle, the right of a neutral state to allow belligerent warships to take on provisions and fuel, as well as to undertake repairs, is firmly established in the traditional law, despite the apparent inconsistency between this freedom and the prohibition against allowing belligerents to use neutral waters or ports as a base for conducting hostile operations. In question is only the extent of the neutral's right to grant supplies, fuel and repairs (or, conversely, the scope of the neutral's duty).

A review of neutral practice indicates no uniformity with respect to the amount of supplies and fuel that may be allowed belligerent warships in neutral ports. In practice, therefore, the matter of determining the conditions for replenishment and refueling belligerent warships would appear to rest largely within the discretion of the neutral state—a situation that can hardly be regarded as satisfactory.[99]

[98] The neutral practice of placing the most severe restrictions upon the use of radio and other communications by belligerent warships within neutral waters and ports became almost universal in World War II.

The United States Neutrality Regulations of September 5, 1939 declared that: "All belligerent vessels shall refrain from use of their radio and signal apparatus while in the harbors, ports, roadsteads, or waters subject to the jurisdiction of the United States, except for calls of distress and communications connected with safe navigation or arrangements for the arrival of the vessel within, or departure from, such harbors, ports, roadsteads, or waters, or passage through such waters; provided that such communications will not be of direct material aid to the belligerent in the conduct of military operations against an opposing belligerent. The radio of belligerent merchant vessels may be sealed by the authorities of the United States, and such seals shall not be broken within the jurisdiction of the United States except by proper authority of the United States."—Substantially similar provisions were laid down in Article 12 of the common neutrality regulations of the Northern European Neutrals. *A. J. I. L.*, 32 (1938) *Supp.* pp. 141 ff.

[99] Article 19 of Hague XIII provides, in part, that: "Belligerent ships of war cannot revictual in neutral ports or roadsteads except to complete their normal peace supply. Similarly these vessels can take only sufficient fuel to enable them to reach the nearest port of their own country. They may, on the other hand, take the fuel necessary to fill up their bunkers properly so called, when in neutral countries which have adopted this method of determining the amount of fuel to be supplied." But neither Article 19 nor—for that matter—Article 20 ("Belligerent ships of war which have taken fuel in a port of a neutral Power can not within the succeeding three months replenish their supply in a port of the same Power") can be considered conclusive statements of the present law.—Article 10 of the 1928 Habana Convention on Maritime Neu-

Equally unsettled is the question of the repairs a neutral may permit belligerent warships to make while in its ports. Article 17 of Hague Convention XIII merely states that belligerents "can carry out only such repairs as are absolutely necessary to render them seaworthy, and cannot add in any manner whatsoever to their fighting force. The neutral authorities shall decide what repairs are necessary and these must be carried out with the least possible delay." No distinction is made between the *causes* of damage for which repairs are made absolutely necessary. It is altogether possible, then, to interpret Article 17 as permitting a neutral to allow belligerent warships to make repairs which result from damage incurred in battle. A warship does not necessarily add to its "fighting force" any more by repairing damage due to enemy fire than by repairing damage due to the sea. Nor does Article 14 clarify the matter in any real way, since in allowing a belligerent warship to extend its stay in port "on account of damage" no specification is made as to the causes of damage. Hence, taking Articles 17 and 14 together it is entirely plausible to interpret Hague XIII as permitting the repair of battle damage in neutral ports, and as further permitting belligerent warships to remain in neutral ports for a period in excess of twenty-four hours in order to effect such repairs.

In practice, the tendency of many states when neutral has clearly been toward restricting the repairs belligerents may make in their ports and of forbidding altogether the repair of damage that has been incurred in battle.[1] But it is more than doubtful that the law presently forbids the

---

trality allows the neutral to establish the conditions for replenishing and refueling, and in the absence of neutral regulations permits belligerent warships to "supply themselves in the manner prescribed for provisioning in time of peace."—The actual practice of states has been less diverse than might be anticipated. During World War II many of the neutrals—including the United States, the Northern European Neutrals and a number of the Latin American countries—allowed replenishing supplies of food to that of peacetime standards and refuelling in quantities sufficient only to carry the vessel to the nearest port of her own country (or, in certain cases, to the nearest port of an ally).

[1] Article 9 of the 1928 Habana Convention on Maritime Neutrality provided that:

"Damaged belligerent ships shall not be permitted to make repairs in neutral ports beyond those that are essential to the continuance of the voyage and which in no degree constitute an increase in its military strength.

Damages which are found to have been produced by the enemy's fire shall in no case be repaired.

The neutral state shall ascertain the nature of the repairs to be made and will see that they are made as rapidly as possible."

The United States Neutrality Regulations of September 5, 1939 declared, with respect to repairs: "No ship of war of a belligerent shall be permitted, while in any port, harbor, roadstead, or waters subject to the jurisdiction of the United States, to make repairs beyond those that are essential to render the vessel seaworthy and which in no degree constitute an increase in her military strength. Repairs shall be made without delay. Damages which are found to have been produced by the enemy's fire shall in no case be repaired." Similarly, the neutrality regulations of the Northern European Neutrals during World War II prohibited the repair of damage incurred in battle.

repair of battle damage in neutral ports, and, in fact, some states when neutral still allow such repairs.[2] Here again the only conclusion possible is that, as matters now stand, the scope of the neutral's duties are only vaguely defined. In permitting belligerent warships to repair damage incurred at sea the neutral state retains a large measure of discretion, despite the injunction to permit only such repairs as are absolutely necessary to render belligerent warships seaworthy.[3]

(ii) Prizes

The entry and stay of prizes in neutral ports are dealt with in Articles 21, 22, and 23 of Hague Convention XIII. In many respects, the position of belligerent prizes in neutral ports is similar to that of belligerent warships. Nevertheless, there remain certain differences that require brief consideration.

---

[2] As illustrated by the incident involving the German battleship *Admiral Graf Spee*. See Hackworth, *op. cit.*, Vol. VII, pp. 450–1. On December 13, 1939, the *Graf Spee* entered the Uruguayan port of Montevideo, following an engagement with British naval forces. A request was made to the Uruguayan authorities to permit the *Graf Spee* to remain fifteen days in port in order to repair damages suffered in battle and to restore the vessel's navigability. The Uruguayan authorities granted a seventy-two hour period of stay. Shortly before the expiration of this period the *Graf Spee* left Montevideo and was destroyed by its own crew in the Rio de la Plata. The British Government, while not insisting that Article 17 of Hague XIII clearly prohibited the repair of battle damage, did point to the widespread practice of states when neutral in forbidding the repair of battle damage in their ports. In accordance with this practice it was suggested that the *Graf Spee's* period of stay be limited to twenty-four hours. Uruguay maintained, however, that the scope of the neutral's duty required it only to prevent those repairs that would serve to augment the fighting force of a vessel but not repairs necessary for safety of navigation.—The incident is noteworthy as an example of the extent to which belligerents seemingly can make use of neutral ports without violating the prohibition against using neutral territory as a base of naval operations.

[3] "May one say that a neutral state may sanction such repairs as they are needed to make a vessel seaworthy, but not such further repairs as may be needed to make her 'fightworthy'." Oppenheim-Lauterpacht, *op. cit.*, p. 709. Kunz (*op. cit.*, pp. 249–54) would go further still and apply the distinction between "seaworthiness" and "fightworthiness" to food and fuel as well as to repairs. It is evident, however, that in a great number of cases to make a vessel seaworthy is, in effect, to make her fightworthy. And Hyde (*op. cit.*, p. 2269) correctly observes that: "In a strict sense, any repairs productive of seaworthiness, irrespective of the cause of damage, necessarily increase the fighting force of the recipient if it is otherwise capable of engaging in hostilities." Articles 34 and 36 of the *Harvard Draft Convention on the Rights and Duties of Neutral States in Naval and Aerial War* (*op. cit.*, pp. 462 ff.), are indicative of the dissatisfaction felt with respect to the present rules governing refuelling and the making of repairs in neutral ports. Whereas Article 34 stipulates that "a condition of distress which is the result of enemy action may not be remedied and if the vessel is unable to leave it shall be interned," Article 36 declares that the neutral state shall not allow belligerent warships (other than vessels devoted exclusively to scientific or humanitarian purposes) "to take on any supply of fuel or otherwise to augment its fighting strength." Neither draft article can be said to be declaratory of existing law, though they are, as the commentary points out, "expressive of a view, which has been reflected in some international practice, that any aid afforded to belligerent warships in neutral ports does in reality compromise the neutrality of the State" (p. 477).

Article 21 declares that a prize may be brought into a neutral port "only on account of unseaworthiness, stress of weather, or want of fuel or provisions," and that it must leave "as soon as the circumstances which justified its entry are at an end." In enumerating the possible reasons for the entry of prizes into neutral ports Article 21 is—if anything—more restrictive than the provisions dealing with the reasons for entry of belligerent warships.[4] And if a prize is brought into a neutral port for reasons other than those described above it is the duty of the neutral state—according to Article 22—to release the prize, together with its officers and crew, and to intern the prize crew.[5] The same duty falls upon the neutral state in the event that a prize will not leave a neutral port once the circumstances which justified its entry are at an end.

So much is clear. The difficulty is created by Article 23 in that it allows a neutral state to permit belligerents to send prizes to a neutral's ports "there to be sequestrated pending the decision of a prize court." It is evident that this provision, if widely accepted by neutral states, would serve to restrict the effectiveness of Articles 21 and 22 and would provide a neutral state permitting sequestration in its ports with an important opportunity for assisting the naval operations of belligerents. Article 23 has never been accepted by several of the major naval powers, however, and during the two World Wars practically all neutral states did in fact forbid belligerents from laying up prizes in their ports pending the decisions of prize courts.[6] At the same time, it cannot as yet be said that the practice

---

[4] Thus Article 21, taken by itself, excludes the use by prizes of neutral ports as a temporary refuge from a pursuing enemy, although such use is not prohibited to warships. In fact, whereas belligerent warships may enter neutral ports for any number of reasons, without becoming liable to internment, prizes are limited to those reasons specified in Article 21 (excepting, for the moment, Article 23).

[5] Thus when on November 4, 1939 the Norwegian Government released the American merchant vessel *City of Flint*, together with its officers and crew, and interned the German prize crew, it clearly acted in accordance with Articles 21 and 22 of Hague XIII. The entry of the *City of Flint* into Haugesund on November 3, 1939 was not justified by reason of any of the circumstances laid down in Article 21. During the previous month the vessel had put into the Norwegian port of Tromsoe for fresh water and had been allowed to depart after having taken on needed supplies. The *City of Flint* had then proceeded to the Russian port of Murmansk where Soviet authorities after having first interned the German prize crew and informed the American captain of the *City of Flint* that he might at once take the vessel out, later reversed this decision and placed the German prize crew again in charge. Although the episode at Murmansk remained obscure it is evident that the Germans had no valid reason for putting into the port and that the Russian authorities were thereby derelict in their neutral duties in not releasing the vessel and its crew, and interning the German prize crew. The incident, together with diplomatic correspondence, is summarized in Hackworth, *op. cit.*, Vol. VII, pp. 482–8. Other accounts are given in Hyde, *op. cit.*, pp. 2277–82 and *U. S. Naval War College, International Law Situations, 1939*, pp. 24–8.

[6] The United States, Great Britain and Japan refused to accept Article 23 of Hague XIII. During World War I the position of the United States was made clear in the well-known case

of permitting sequestration of prizes in neutral ports is forbidden to neutral states, either through the invalidation of Article 23 or through the emergence of a contrary practice that may be considered sufficient to constitute a rule of customary international law.[7]

(iii) Armed Belligerent Merchant Vessels

Discussion over the status of armed belligerent merchantmen in neutral ports has frequently suffered from the failure to distinguish sufficiently between the scope of a neutral state's duties and the extent of its rights. Whereas there is legitimate room for inquiry into the present scope of the neutral's duty in receiving armed belligerent merchant vessels into its waters and ports, there ought to be little doubt as to the scope of a neutral's rights. It is apparent that with respect to the merchant vessels of other states the rights of a neutral can be no less than they are in time of peace. Apart from the duty to accord to the merchant vessels of all states freedom of innocent passage through its territorial waters there is no further duty of a state to allow merchant vessels into its ports. So long as it acts impartially a neutral may place special restrictions upon the entry and stay of armed belligerent merchantmen or even close its ports entirely to the latter.[8] The difficulty, of course, concerns the scope of the neutral's duties. The obligations imposed upon neutral states by Hague Convention XIII

of the British steamship *Appam*.—In the United States Neutrality Proclamation of September 5, 1939, Articles 21 and 22 of Hague XIII are repeated almost verbatim.

[7] Thus while Article 29 of the *Harvard Draft Convention on the Rights and Duties of Neutral States in Naval and Aerial War* (*op. cit.*, p. 446) states that: "A neutral state shall either exclude prizes from its territory or admit them on the same conditions on which it admits belligerent warships," the commentary to this article observes: ". . . Article 23 (Hague XIII) has not been widely adopted in practice and strong objections have been raised against it. On the other hand, it could not be said that a neutral state would violate international law if it acted upon the basis of Article 23. In this unsatisfactory state of the law, it seems permissible to suggest a new rule for adoption . . ." (p. 448). Most writers, however critical of Article 23, refrain from stating that a neutral state would violate its duties were it to permit the sequestration of prizes in its ports.

[8] During the first World War the Government of the Netherlands did in fact choose to close its ports to all armed belligerent merchant vessels. In a note of April 7, 1915 the Netherlands Government stated that vessels provided with armament and capable of committing acts of war would be assimilated to warships and thereafter forbidden to enter the ports and territorial waters of the Netherlands. In reply, the British Government took the position that British merchant vessels were armed solely for purposes of self-defense, that the law of nations permitted this measure, and that the British vessels so armed could not be regarded as assimilated to the status of warships. Even assuming the validity of these contentions it is difficult to see how they can limit the right of a neutral state to exclude armed belligerent merchant vessels from its ports. This last point was emphasized by the Netherlands Government in a note of August 15, 1917, in which it was declared that: "The law of nations does not prescribe for neutrals the duty either of admitting armed belligerent merchant vessels within their jurisdiction, or of refusing them entry. It leaves them to determine for themselves their line of conduct on this point." cited in Hackworth, *op. cit.*, Vol. VII, p. 498.—The only possible objection a belligerent could legitimately raise would be over the neutral's denial of innocent passage through its territorial waters to armed belligerent merchant vessels.

expressly refer only to the entry and stay of "belligerent men-of-war" (and prizes) in neutral waters and ports. According to the traditional law the restrictions applicable to warships when in neutral jurisdiction are not applicable to belligerent merchant vessels, privately owned and engaged in trade. The latter enjoy, in principle, the same treatment in neutral ports as the merchant vessels of other neutral states.

At the same time, there has been little disposition to deny that the restrictions a neutral state must apply to warships in its ports and waters apply equally to belligerent vessels which, though not qualifying as warships in the formal sense and therefore not competent to exercise belligerent rights at sea,[9] directly assist a belligerent's naval operations. Thus a belligerent merchant vessel serving in the employ and acting under the direction of belligerent warships must be treated by neutral states in a manner similar to belligerent warships.[10] The reason for this similarity

---

[9] See pp. 38–40.

[10] The vessels referred to in the text are not "auxiliary warships" in the strict sense of that term, that is they are not commissioned naval vessels, commanded by commissioned naval officers and flying the naval ensign. With respect to the latter there is no doubt that they are warships within the meaning of Hague Convention XIII, even though they merely perform auxiliary services to fighting vessels (i. e., supply tenders, colliers, transports). In question here is the status of vessels that perform the same auxiliary services to warships though not formally incorporated into the naval forces of a belligerent. In British practice these vessels are known as "fleet auxiliaries;" they do not fly the flag of a warship nor are they competent to exercise belligerent rights at sea. Nevertheless, with respect to neutrals they are in the same position as warships.

When the United States has been neutral, merchant vessels serving as auxiliaries to warships have been subject to the same restrictions as warships. Thus on November 8, 1914 the German steamship *Locksun* was interned at Honolulu for not having conformed to the rules governing warships. The *Locksun* served as a supply ship for the German warship *Geier*. The details of the incident are given in Hackworth, *op. cit.*, Vol. VII, pp. 506–8. The United States neutrality regulations of September 5, 1939 provided that: "The provisions of this proclamation pertaining to ships of war shall apply equally to any vessel operating under public control for hostile or military purposes."

During World War II the incident involving the German merchant vessel *Tacoma* provided a further illustration of the treatment accorded by neutrals to merchant vessels serving, in effect, as a naval auxiliary to a belligerent's forces. The *Tacoma* was found to be acting in the capacity of an auxiliary to the German battleship *Graf Spee*. For this reason the Uruguayan Government gave the *Tacoma*, upon putting into Montevideo on December 30, 1939, twenty-four hours within which to depart or suffer internment. On January 1, 1940 the vessel was interned.—In the General Declaration of Neutrality of the American Republics, approved October 3, 1939, it was declared that the American Republics "may submit belligerent merchant vessels, as well as their passengers, documents and cargo, to inspection in their own ports; the respective consular agent shall certify as to the ports of call and destination as well as to the fact that the voyage is undertaken solely for purposes of commercial interchange. They may also supply fuel to such vessels in amounts sufficient for the voyage to a port of supply and call in another American Republic, except in the case of a direct voyage to another continent, in which circumstances they may supply the necessary amount of fuel. Should it be proven that these vessels have supplied belligerent warships with fuel, they shall be considered as auxiliary transports." *A. J. I. L.*, 34 (1940), *Supp*, p. 11.

in treatment may be attributed to the obligation imposed upon the neutral state to prevent its waters and ports from becoming a belligerent base of operations; an obligation that would be seriously restricted if the latter were free to permit merchant vessels serving as auxiliaries to warships to make unlimited use of neutral ports.

These observations would appear to bear directly upon the scope of the neutral's duties with respect to armed belligerent merchant vessels. The fact that such vessels do not possess the status of warships need not prove decisive in determining the treatment they must receive while in neutral waters and ports. It is rather the use to which the vessel's armament has been, or clearly will be, put that must form the guiding consideration. If such use is for offensive purposes the neutral state is obliged to assimilate armed belligerent merchant vessels to the position of warships. To act otherwise would result in turning neutral jurisdiction into a base for the belligerent's naval operations.[11]

It is in the application of this principle to armed merchant vessels that difficulties have arisen. The belligerent state that has armed its merchant vessels will naturally insist—as did Great Britain in both World Wars—that such armament is only intended for defensive purposes, and will rely upon the long established practice under which defensively armed merchantmen have enjoyed the same treatment while in neutral ports as given to other merchant vessels. The neutral state, on the other hand, must run the risk of being charged with unneutral conduct if it is established that the armed merchant vessels it has received in its ports, and treated as ordinary merchant vessels, have in fact been used for offensive operations at sea.[12] Neutral states have not been insensitive to the liability they may thereby incur, and the attempt has therefore been made to establish criteria that would enable the neutral state to determine—in the absence of other-

[11] In the course of the prolonged diplomatic exchange between the United States and Great Britain during the years 1914–16 the principle enunciated above was not subject to dispute. In a lengthy memorandum of March 25, 1916 the Department of State declared, in part, that: "Merchantmen of belligerent nationality, armed only for the purposes of protection against the enemy, are entitled to enter and leave neutral ports without hindrance in the course of legitimate trade. Armed merchantmen of belligerent nationality, under a commission or orders of their government to use, under penalty, their armament for aggressive purposes, or merchantmen which, without such commission or orders, have used their armaments for aggressive purposes, are not entitled to the same hospitality in neutral ports as peaceable armed merchantmen." cited in Hackworth, *op. cit.*, Vol. VII, p. 495.

[12] It has been stated that neutral states "are under no imperative necessity to ascertain, at their peril, the nature and purpose of the armaments of the merchant vessel. There seems therefore to be no valid reason, dictated by International Law, for departing from the established practice under which defensively armed merchantmen may be admitted to neutral ports on the same conditions as other merchant-vessels so long as there is no conclusive proof that the particular vessel has used her armaments for the purposes of attack." Oppenheim-Lauterpacht, *op. cit.*, p. 712. It is difficult to share this view regarding the scope of the neutral's duties. On the contrary, the neutral state would appear to be under the obligation to take active measures to ascertain the nature and purpose of such armament.

wise conclusive evidence—the offensive or defensive nature of the armament carried by belligerent merchant vessels.[13] In practice, however, it has proven next to impossible to establish objective criteria enabling neutral states to draw a rational distinction between armament used solely for defensive rather than for offensive purposes.

It is submitted that a proper perspective of the problems involved in dealing with the status of armed belligerent merchantmen in neutral ports and waters cannot be gained without adequate recognition of the circumstances that have so radically altered the position traditionally occupied by belligerent merchant vessels. The nature of this transformation has already been indicated.[14] Here it is sufficient to obesrve that the extent to which the merchant vessels of belligerents were integrated into the military effort during World War II left little doubt as to the purposes for which armament would be used. There is, therefore, a distinct air of unreality in the continued attempts to analyze the position of armed belligerent merchantmen in neutral ports and waters by the assumption of conditions which have not obtained since the outbreak of World War I. In an earlier period there was legitimate reason to inquire into the nature of the armament carried by a belligerent merchant vessel. During the nineteenth century such armament—if carried—would generally have been purchased at the expense of the owner of the vessel, manned by members of his crew, and used at his discretion. At present the armament of merchant vessels is supplied by the state, manned by naval gun crews, and used in accordance with a plan established by the military authorities of the state. Hence, even if it is assumed that the armament of belligerent merchant vessels is used solely for defensive purposes—and on this point there is abundant

[13] It would serve little purpose to review the many attempts made to reach such determination, in the absence of direct evidence in support of the offensive nature of a vessel's armament. During the initial stages of World War I the attempt was made to make *motive* the test, but it soon became apparent that this test posed insurmountable difficulties in practice. The attempt was therefore made to overcome these difficulties by setting out certain objective criteria which would enable the neutral to establish the "defensive" or "offensive" nature of the armament (e. g., number and size of guns, where mounted, how manned, and amount of ammunition). When the first World War came to a close the problem had not yet been resolved satisfactorily, and with the outbreak of war in 1939 it was once again taken up. Many neutral states, while assimilating "offensively" armed belligerent merchantment to the position of warships, gave no indication of the means to be used in determining the offensive purpose of armament. Thus the neutrality regulations of the Northern European Neutrals merely provided, in common Article 3, that: "Access to . . . ports or to . . . territorial waters is likewise prohibited to armed merchant ships of the belligerents, if the armament is destined to ends other than their own defense." *A. J. I. L.*, 32 (1938), *Supp*, p. 143.—In the General Declaration of Neutrality of the American Republics, October 3, 1939, the latter agreed not to "assimilate to warships belligerent armed merchant vessels if they do not carry more than four six-inch guns mounted on the stern, and their lateral decks are not reinforced, and if, in the judgment of the local authorities there do not exist circumstances which reveal that the merchant vessels can be used for offensive purposes." *A. J. I. L.*, 34 (1940), *Supp.*, pp. 11–12.

[14] See pp. 57–70.

evidence to the contrary [15]—the fact remains that such use forms a definite part of the military operations of the belligerent. For this reason alone the continued relevance of attempts to determine the defensive character of armament must be seriously questioned. Despite these considerations, neutral states continue to base their treatment of armed belligerent merchant vessels upon standards that have little or no application to the circumstances under which modern naval warfare is conducted.[16]

3. *Restrictions On the Use of Neutral Air Space*

The numerous difficulties attending the determination of the extent to which belligerent warships may make use of neutral jurisdiction find little parallel in aerial warfare. The practices of states during World Wars I and II may be regarded as having firmly established both the right as well as the duty of the neutral state to forbid the entrance of belligerent military aircraft into its air space.[17] In consequence, the neutral state is obliged to use the means at its disposal to prevent the entry of belligerent military aircraft, to compel such aircraft to alight should they once succeed in unlawfully penetrating neutral air space, and, once compelled to land, to intern the aircraft together with its crew.[18]

There are, however, certain peripheral questions that have yet to be clearly and definitely resolved. One of these questions relates to the status of belligerent military aircraft in neutral territory at the time of the outbreak of hostilities. It has been suggested that in this instance a brief period of grace—usually twelve hours—should be granted such aircraft, during which period they may be permitted to leave neutral jurisdiction.[19] This suggestion follows a parallel rule applied to belligerent warships in neutral ports, the latter being accorded a twenty-four hour period in which

---

[15] See pp. 57–70.

[16] Here again, the gap between the assumptions underlying the traditional law and the conditions characteristic of modern naval warfare will serve only to defeat the purposes of the traditional law. Nevertheless, it cannot be said that the few attempts to rectify this situation have had any considerable effect. Although Article 12 of the 1928 Habana Convention on Maritime Neutrality declared that where "the sojourn, supplying, and provisioning of belligerent ships in the ports and jurisdictional waters of neutrals are concerned, the provisions relative to ships of war shall apply equally to armed merchantmen," this provision was not accepted by the United States. Nor did it receive the acceptance of an appreciable number of other American states.—On the outbreak of war in 1939 the *Harvard Draft Convention on Rights and Duties of Neutral States in Naval and Aerial War* (*op. cit.*, pp. 435–47) suggested that: "A neutral State shall either exclude belligerent armed merchant vessels from its territory or admit such vessels on the same conditions on which it admits belligerent warships." The arguments presented therein on behalf of this recommendation are believed to be sound. During World War II, however, the general practice of neutrals was—if anything—toward a relaxation in the attitude previously manifested toward armed belligerent merchant vessels.

[17] See, generally, Spaight, *op. cit.*, pp. 420 ff.

[18] *Law of Naval Warfare*, Article 444 a, b.

[19] *Harvard Draft Convention on Rights and Duties of Neutral States in Naval and Aerial War*, *op. cit.*, p. 764, Article 94 and comment.

to leave these ports and neutral territorial waters. On the other hand, it has been argued that the neutral state ought immediately to intern all belligerent military aircraft found within its jurisdiction at the outbreak of war.[20] It does not appear possible to endorse either position at the present time, though it is probably safe to assert that a neutral may (even if not strictly obliged to) resort to immediate internment.

A further question concerns the entry in distress of belligerent military aircraft. Does the duty of a neutral to prevent belligerent military aircraft from entering its jurisdiction extend to such aircraft as are in evident distress? Here again, no categorical answer as to the scope of the neutral's duty seems possible, although it is doubtful that a neutral state violates any duty in permitting entry in distress. The neutral state is bound, of course, to intern the aircraft and its crew. Thus the matter of entry in distress in aerial warfare must be clearly distinguished from entry in distress in naval warfare. Whereas belligerent warships in distress enjoy a right of entry into neutral waters and ports, the entry of belligerent aircraft within neutral jurisdiction, even though in distress, is—at best—a matter within the neutral's discretion.[21] In addition, whereas in naval warfare the neutral state may or may not intern the belligerent vessel and crew seeking entry in distress, in aerial warfare the neutral must intern the aircraft together with its crew.[22]

F. BELLIGERENT INTERFERENCE WITH PRIVATE NEUTRAL TRADE; NEUTRAL DUTIES OF ACQUIESCENCE

It has been observed earlier that whereas the neutral state is obliged to abstain from furnishing belligerents with a wide range of goods and services

[20] Although the 1923 Hague Rules of Aerial Warfare contain no specific provision on this point, the report of the Commission of Jurists notes—in connection with Article 42—that the "obligation to intern covers also aircraft which were within the neutral jurisdiction at the outbreak of hostilities." *U. S. Naval War College, International Law Documents, 1924*, p. 130.

[21] Spaight (*op. cit.*, p. 436) is of the opinion that the "highest that one can put the neutral obligation is that asylum should be granted in all cases of evident distress, so far as the circumstances allow this obvious concession to humanitarian claims to be made. The neutral authorities remain bound, of course, to apprehend and intern the aircraft and its crew in such cases, as well as in those of error on the part of the airmen, loss of way, or miscalculation of the exact boundary line."—During World War II there were several reported incidents of neutral states employing measures of force to drive away belligerent military aircraft seeking entry into neutral jurisdiction for reasons of distress.

[22] To the above stated rules two exceptions may be noted. Aircraft attached to a warship may enter neutral waters and ports so long as such aircraft are, and remain, in physical contact with the warship. In this circumstance aircraft are considered merely as items in the equipment of the vessel, and the only question is whether the vessel itself has lawfully entered neutral jurisdiction. Finally, Article 40 of the 1949 Geneva Convention for the Amelioration of the Condition of the Wounded, Sick and Shipwrecked Members of Armed Forces at Sea provides that, subject to such regulations and restrictions as the neutral may see fit to apply equally to all belligerents, the medical aircraft of belligerents may pass over, or land in, neutral territory (see pp. 129–31).

it is normally under no obligation to prevent its subjects from undertaking these same activities. Belligerents are permitted, however, to take certain measures to prevent the subjects of a neutral state from rendering various forms of assistance to an enemy. The neutral state, in turn, is obliged to acquiesce in the exercise by belligerents of repressive measures international law permits the latter to take against neutral merchantmen engaged in the carriage of contraband, breach—or attempted breach—of blockade, or the performance of unneutral service.[23]

[23] It remains a matter of some controversy among writers as to the proper characterization of the acts falling under the categories enumerated above. The weight of opinion in the past has been that acts constituting contraband carriage and blockade breach ought not to be regarded as unlawful under international law but only—if at all—under national law. In large measure, this opinion has been influenced by the consideration that international law does not obligate neutral states to forbid their subjects from engaging in the above mentioned activities (although a neutral state may forbid these activities on the part of its subjects). From this point of view, the repressive measures international law permits belligerents to take against neutral nationals undertaking carriage of contraband is a right corresponding to the neutral state's duty of acquiescence. But the belligerent cannot complain to the neutral state for having failed to prevent the acts in question. On the other hand, the individuals who carry contraband or undertake to break blockade are held to act at their peril; they perform a "risky" act, though one allegedly not forbidden by international law, and if caught must take the consequences of being deprived of their property (cargo or ship, or both).

The alternate view, in holding that carriage of contraband and breach of blockade are acts forbidden by international law, declares that it is by no means necessary that international law obligate the neutral state to prevent the commission of these acts in order that they may be considered unlawful. Thus a neutral national engaged in carriage of contraband may act in accordance with the law of his state, which need not and does not prohibit the act, and yet perform an act forbidden by international law. (In the same sense the act of piracy may be considered as forbidden by international law, though no state is obligated either to prohibit this act in its municipal law or to prevent its subjects from committing acts of piracy.) The neutral state need not, and is not, obligated to prevent all acts of its subjects which belligerents are entitled to repress (or, from this alternate point of view, to punish). Instead, it is bound only to prevent part of them, whereas the prevention and repression of other acts are left to the belligerents.

Although the theoretical implications of this controversy are not without a substantial measure of interest, the practical significance of whether or not contraband carriage, blockade breach and unneutral service are considered as acts forbidden by international law is negligible. From both points of view the nature and extent of the measures a belligerent is permitted to take against neutral commerce remain the same. It may be observed, however, that international law unquestionably does establish the latitude permitted belligerents in controlling the trading activities of neutrals. Similarly, international law determines—though within varying limits—the consequences belligerents may attach to these activities. It is true that these consequences are realized only by virtue of judgments rendered by national prize courts, judgments whose immediate basis must be found in municipal law. Nevertheless, in this instance the judgment of a national prize court may properly be regarded as the application of international as well as national law. Indeed, states are clearly under the obligation to insure that the substantive law applied by their prize courts conforms with international law. Hence, the application of international law is carried out through its prior transformation into national law, a transformation that ought not to be obscured for the reason that prize courts derive their immediate power from national law and are bound to apply this law even if occasionally inconsistent with international law.

So long as a belligerent confines the measures it takes against the trade of neutral subjects to the limits clearly allowed by international law there will be little occasion for controversy. Normally, the relationship involved will primarily concern the belligerent and private neutral traders. When, however, the neutral state considers a belligerent to have acted in excess of the limits prescribed by international law, when the neutral state considers a belligerent as endeavoring either to suppress legitimate neutral trade or to prevent illegitimate neutral trade though by means of otherwise unlawful measures, the matter then directly involves the duties and rights of belligerent and neutral states. This is so for the reason that it is a duty of belligerents to abstain from interfering with neutral commerce which international law does not regard as of such a character to justify belligerent measures of suppression, and a right of neutral states to demand that belligerents refrain from interfering with the legitimate commerce of their subjects. In addition, even with respect to neutral trade belligerents are permitted—in principle—to suppress, neutral states have a right to insist that belligerents employ only those measures of suppression as are sanctioned by law.

At the same time, the belligerents' duty to abstain from the suppression of legitimate neutral commerce is not without limitation. The neutral state is bound not only to acquiesce in certain permitted forms of belligerent interference with private neutral trade; it is also obliged to employ the means at its disposal to prevent belligerent encroachment upon established neutral rights at sea. Should the neutral state either openly permit or tacitly acquiesce in the unlawful interference with its trade by one belligerent it cannot complain if the other belligerent—thereby placed at a grave disadvantage—resorts to otherwise unlawful measures against neutral trade by way of reprisal against the neutral. On this point at least there would appear to be widespread agreement.

But beyond this point the greatest uncertainty—and controversy—exists even today with respect to the precise scope of the belligerent's duty to abstain from interfering with legitimate neutral commerce. In general, belligerents have sought to qualify their obligation by contending that the restriction of neutral rights may prove justified either as a necessary incidence to retalitory measures taken in response to the unlawful behavior of an enemy (and even though such behavior has been directed, in the main, only against the retaliating belligerent) or as a result of the ineffectiveness of neutral efforts to prevent continued belligerent encroachment upon the former's rights.

It should be apparent that the position of the neutral is strongest in insisting that inter-belligerent reprisals—in the strict sense—cannot of themselves provide injured belligerents with a legitimate basis for restricting neutral rights. The neutral state, it has been asserted, cannot be held responsible in any way for unlawful belligerent measures that are directed exclusively—or even principally—against an enemy. Nor is this conclusion modified, from the neutral's point of view, by virtue of the fact that a belligerent may be able to bring the greatest pressure to bear upon an offending enemy through measures taken against neutral commerce.[24]

Even if accepted, however, the neutral's position with respect to the legitimacy of inter-belligerent reprisals which adversely affect neutral rights may prove of no more than limited importance. In practice, belligerents have had a much stronger basis upon which to limit the scope of their obligations toward the commerce of neutrals. Since the unlawful conduct of a belligerent in warfare at sea will seldom be directed solely against an enemy, but will bear upon neutral commerce as well, the injured belligerent has insisted that his continued respect for neutral rights is dependent upon the effectiveness of neutral efforts in preventing the further occurrence of the unlawful measures imputed to an enemy.[25]

[24] Hyde (*op. cit.*, p. 2345) gives expression to the position summarized above by stating that: "It is a sound proposition that the illegal conduct of its enemy in prosecuting a war does not excuse a response by the offended belligerent which, insofar as it returns like for like, or otherwise marks a departure from the requirements of the law, involves an impairment of obligations normally due to unoffending and non-participating powers." A similar view may be found in the *Harvard Draft Convention on Rights and Duties of Neutral States in Naval and Aerial War* (*op. cit.*, pp. 392–419), where the conflicting—and frequently obscure—attitude of neutrals and belligerents is given careful and illuminating historical review. Article 23 of the Draft Convention declares: "A belligerent is not relieved of its duty to respect the rights of a neutral State as provided in this Convention, even when engaged in acts of reprisal or retaliation for illegal acts of its enemy." Certainly in the past this has always represented the position of the United States when neutral. Thus the British Reprisals Order of Nobember 27, 1939 (see p. 312) brought forth the following statement by the American Government: "Whatever may be said for or against measures directed by one belligerent against another, they may not rightfully be carried to the point of enlarging the rights of a belligerent over neutral vessels and their cargoes, or of otherwise penalizing neutral states or their nationals in connection with their legitimate activities." cited in Hackworth, *op. cit.*, Vol. VII, p. 145.

[25] In both World Wars this provided perhaps the principal belligerent argument in justification of otherwise unlawful restrictions upon neutral trade. During World War I the British Prize Court gave expression to, and endorsed, the argument in a number of significant decisions. In *The Stigstad* [1918]—(5 *Lloyds Prize Cases*, p. 393) the Judicial Committee of the Privy Council, speaking through Lord Sumner, upheld the Reprisals Order of March 11, 1915, and expressly rejected the contention that a neutral "too pacific or too impotent to resent the aggressions and lawlessness of one belligerent, can require the other to refrain from his most effective or his only defense against it, by the assertion of an absolute inviolability for his own neutral trade, which would thereby become engaged in a passive complicity with the original offender." And in a note of April 24, 1916, replying to a United States protest against the Reprisal Order of March 11 as being "without precedent in modern warfare," the British Government observed that if one belligerent "is allowed to make an attack upon the other regardless of neutral rights, his opponent must be allowed similar latitude in prosecuting the struggle, nor should he in that case be limited to the adoption of measures precisely identical with those of his oponent." cited in Hackworth, *op. cit.*, Vol. VII, p. 144. A substantially similar argument has been urged by most British writers dealing with this same question. Thus: "The rule that belligerents must not interfere with the legitimate commerce of neutrals presupposes that both belligerents will carry it out, and that neutrals will prevent both of them from violating it. If, on the contrary, neutrals acquiesce in or are unable to prevent the violation of this rule by

In certain respects, a parallel situation to that under present consideration has already been dealt with in connection with the consequences arising from the neutral's inability to prevent misuse of neutral jurisdiction.[26] It was there observed that although a neutral state fulfills its duty if it employs the means at its disposal to prevent belligerent violation of its waters and ports, in the event these efforts prove ineffective the belligerent that has heretofore respected neutral jurisdiction—and whose interests would suffer from an enemy's unlawful acts—is not forbidden from resorting to hostile measures against its adversary even though within neutral jurisdiction. However, these hostile measures, exceptionally permitted to a belligerent, are not to be interpreted either as reprisals against the neutral state or as reprisals against the belligerent that has misused neutral jurisdiction. The former interpretation is unacceptable for the reason that the neutral state, by employing the means at its disposal, has fulfilled its duty. The latter interpretation is misplaced for the reason that in misusing neutral jurisdiction a belligerent commits no wrong against an enemy, and the latter is certainly not permitted to justify hostile measures taken in neutral waters by contending that he is assisting in the enforcement of the neutral's rights. Instead, it was submitted that the correct interpretation is simply that the scope of the belligerent's obligation to refrain from taking hostile measures within neutral jurisdiction is limited by the ability of the neutral effectively to enforce its rights.

If the same general analysis is applied to the problem of neutral commerce—and it is difficult to see how such application may be avoided—it may be stated that a neutral state fulfills its duty when it employs the means at its disposal to prevent unlawful belligerent interference with the trade of its subjects. Nevertheless, if one belligerent persists in unlawfully interfering with a neutral's trade, and the efforts of the latter prove clearly ineffective in terminating these illegal measures, the other belligerent thereby placed at a disadvantage is no longer obliged to refrain from taking what would otherwise prove to be unlawful measures of interference with the neutral's trade.[27] Admittedly, the central issue

one belligerent to the vital disadvantage of the other belligerent, the latter cannot be expected to suffer this without redress, and must be excused if, in retaliating upon the enemy, he also violates the rule." Oppenheim-Lauterpacht, *op. cit.*, p. 679. Also see A. P. Higgins, "Retalitation in Naval Warfare," *B. Y. I. L.*, 8 (1927), pp. 129–46; H. A. Smith, *op. cit.*, p. 145; and Higgins and Colombos, *op. cit.*, pp. 565–7. It should be added that Germany and France placed equal reliance upon this same argument in resorting to "reprisal" measures affecting neutral commerce.

[26] See pp. 220–6.

[27] The position taken in the text above is still far from being shared by many writers, however. It should be carefully noted that, as stated in the text, this position amounts neither to an endorsement of the contention that inter-belligerent reprisals—in the strict sense—may operate to restrict neutral rights nor to an approval of the assertion that belligerents may take *reprisal measures* against neutrals for the reason the latter are incapable of effectively enforcing their rights. What is asserted is simply that the scope of the belligerent's obligation toward the neutral is limited by the ability of the neutral to compel the observance of its rights. Hence

involved here ought not to be obscured by the belligerent habit of characterizing these measures restricting neutral trade as "reprisals," ostensibly directed against an enemy. In violating the neutral's rights a belligerent does not, for that reason alone, violate an enemy's rights as well. Belligerents placed at a disadvantage by the unlawful measures of an enemy that are directed against neutral trade have almost invariably taken this position, though the claim has no substantial justification in law. What can be claimed, and all that can be claimed, is that the scope of the obligation imposed upon a belligerent to respect neutral rights at sea is limited—in principle—not only by the neutral's willingness to enforce its rights but by its effectiveness in doing so.[28]

At the same time, it must be conceded that in fact, if not in law, it may prove seriously misleading to attempt to draw too close a parallel between the hostile measures exceptionally permitted belligerents within neutral jurisdiction and the measures exceptionally permitted to belligerents against neutral trade. The former clearly must be limited to the forces of an enemy; they may be taken only for an expressly defined purpose, and once this purpose has been attained the hostile measures must cease. It is difficult to discern similar limitations on the measures taken by belligerents against neutral trade, owing to the neutral's inability to enforce its rights effectively. In character and duration these measures have been held to be subject—at best—only to the vague criteria that they conform to the "requirements of humanity" and do not impose an "unreasonable" hardship—in the light of relevant circumstances—upon the neutral. And whether or not belligerent measures restrictive of neutral trade do conform

---

it is no answer to the dilemma raised by the weak neutral to declare, as does article 24 of the *Harvard Draft Convention on the Rights and Duties of Neutral States in Naval and Aerial War* (*op. cit.*, p. 419) that: "A belligerent may not resort to acts of reprisal or retaliation against a neutral State except for illegal acts of the latter, and a State is not to be charged with failure to perform its duties as a neutral State because it has not succeeded in inducing a belligerent to respect its rights as a neutral State."

28 These remarks may serve to clarify a measure of the ambiguity—and confusion—that has so often characterized the problem of belligerent "reprisals" at sea. In part, this ambiguity may be attributed to the belligerent insistence upon identifying *interest* with *legal right*. Undoubtedly the belligerent has a strong interest in preserving his trade with neutral states. Nevertheless, the measures his enemy may take to shut off this trade constitute—on the whole—a violation of the belligerent's rights only to the extent that the latter's merchant vessels are rendered liable to hazards clearly forbidden by law. To the extent that unlawful measures are directed against neutral shipping it is the right of the neutral state—not of the belligerent—that has been violated. The belligerent possesses neither a right to demand that an enemy refrain from unlawful measures against neutral commerce nor a right to assist a neutral in the latter's efforts to resist an enemy's depredations at sea. In practice, it seems clear that most belligerent "reprisal" measures have actually been a compound of measures directed against an enemy for conduct directly injurious to the belligerent and measures restrictive of neutral rights. Whereas the former may be considered as reprisals in the strict sense the latter may not (unless, of course, the neutral has acted in league with the enemy).

to these criteria is a matter the belligerent has generally insisted upon having the sole right to determine.[29]

It is perhaps for these reasons, and in view of the evident use (or, perhaps, misuse) by belligerents of "reprisals" at sea as an instrument for subverting the traditional law, that many writers continue to express serious opposition to the position—endorsed above—that one belligerent may resort to measures restrictive of neutral rights when the neutral proves unable to prevent the transgressions of another belligerent. It seems clear, though, that this opposition may lead to even greater difficulties in practice. Nor does this opposition, quite apart from practical considerations, appear sound in principle. Despite the hazards admittedly implicit in limiting the scope of the belligerent's obligation to the effectiveness of neutral measures of prevention, there is room for insisting that belligerents may not regard themselves at liberty to resort to *any* measures against the trade of neutrals that are too weak—or too unwilling—to enforce their rights effectively.[30]

G. VIOLATIONS OF NEUTRALITY

1. *Violations of Neutrality as Distinguished From Termination of Neutral Status*

On frequent occasions violations of neutrality have been confused with the termination of neutral status. It would appear that the principal reason for this confusion may be traced to the tendency to identify neutrality with the obligations imposed upon a non-participant by the traditional law. If neutrality is to be identified with the obligations imposed upon a state

[29] The position taken in British prize proceedings whose basis rested upon "reprisal orders' issued by the executive, and bearing upon neutral rights, was laid down in *The Zamora* [1916]—(4 *Lloyds Prize Cases*, p. 97), where the Judicial Committee of the Privy Council declared that while bound to accept the Executive's statement of the facts alleged in justification of reprisal orders the prize court's function is to determine whether or not the order in question is reasonable in the hardships it imposes upon neutrals. In neither World War were the reprisal orders issued by the Executive found "unreasonable," and in the 1939 war neutral claimants do not appear to have taken the trouble even to have questioned their illegality in prize court proceedings. In this connection Stone's (*op. cit.*, p. 367) comments deserve attention. "This check," he writes of the British system, "has an obvious ambiguity. Is the 'reasonableness' of the inconvenience to be measured against the enormity of the enemy's illegality, against what is necessary to make retaliation effective, or some other test, or against all together? In any case, the neutral's position is unenviably weak. The supposed proportionality of retaliation to the original wrong is itself hardly measurable; a hardly measurable relation to this hardly measurable proportionality is not a promising basis for a cause of action." Even so, the protection offered by the British system was superior to the practice of most other belligerents. In the case of German, Italian and French prize courts the validity of retaliatory orders affecting neutrals does not appear to have been subject to any check, however imperfect, the courts considering themselves bound completely by the action of the executive. See Colombos, *A Treatise on The Law of Prize*, pp. 272–3, 276–7.

[30] For further reflections on this and related points, see pp. 296–315, where belligerent "reprisal" measures during the two World Wars are examined in some detail.

that does not participate in war—and particularly with the obligation of impartiality—then it seems only logical to consider that a state in abandoning these obligations thereby abandons the status of neutrality. In the present study, however, the usual identification of neutrality with the duties imposed upon a neutral state has not been followed.[31] Instead, the status of neutrality has been conceived as the non-participation of a state in hostilities. If this latter conception of neutrality is followed the confusion attendant upon the identification of violations of neutrality with the termination of neutral status becomes clear.

A state may abstain from active participation in a war while at the same time abandoning many of the duties imposed upon non-participants by the law of neutrality. In abandoning its duties the neutral state thereby surrenders its right to demand from belligerents that behavior it would otherwise be entitled to claim. The offended belligerent may demand appropriate measures of redress and—should it so desire—resort to reprisals against the offending neutral. But as long as the belligerent refrains from attacking the neutral, and the neutral refrains from directly joining in the hostilities by attacking one of the belligerents, a status of neutrality is maintained.

2. *Rights and Duties of Neutral States In the Event of Belligerent Violation of Neutral Rights*

It is one of the peculiarities of the neutral-belligerent relationship that a belligerent violation of neutrality serves to give rise to a right as well as to a duty of the injured neutral state. With respect to the offending belligerent a neutral state has the right to take those measures necesssary to bring about the immediate cessation of the unlawful acts and to demand such action on the part of the offending belligerent as may be required to repair the wrong that has been done. If the offending forces of a belligerent are within neutral jurisdiction the neutral state may even resort to forceful means in order to compel a belligerent to desist from the commission of hostile, or otherwise unlawful, acts. Thus the neutral state has the right to take measures necessary to effect the release of ships that have been captured by a belligerent within neutral waters. Forcible measures may also be taken, if necessary, against belligerent warships otherwise failing to conform to the regulations governing passage through neutral waters as well as entry and stay in neutral ports. If, on the other hand, the offending belligerent forces are no longer within neutral jurisdiction the neutral state may insist upon the performance of certain measures of reparation. Prizes that have been seized by a belligerent in neutral waters must be restored upon the demand of the neutral state. Nor is it excluded that if the demand for adequate measures of reparation—material or moral [32]—remains

[31] See pp. 196–9.

[32] E. g., an apology on the part of a belligerent for the hostile acts its forces may have committed within neutral waters.

399334—57——18

unsatisfied the aggrieved neutral may resort to other, and more stringent, measures.[33]

With respect to the belligerent that has otherwise respected the neutral's rights, the situation is somewhat more complicated. It has already been observed that the traditional law imposes upon neutral states the duty to employ the means at their disposal in order to prevent the violation by belligerents of their ports or waters.[34] However, this duty relates to the prevention of unlawful acts, not—at least not directly—to the measures a neutral must take against a belligerent for unlawful acts already committed.[35] In Hague XIII there is, apart from Articles 3[36] and 24,[37] no clear guidance as to the measures a neutral state must take—if indeed any—against a belligerent that has misused neutral ports and waters. It has been contended, therefore, that it is doubtful whether international law "imposes upon a neutral a duty to resort to retaliatory acts in response to the illegal conduct of a belligerent. It is not even clear that a neutral is under a duty to protest against illegal belligerent conduct."[38]

Whatever merit the above opinion might once have enjoyed it would

---

[33] Though it is very difficult to define, in a satisfactory manner, the nature and limits of the measures available to neutrals. Certainly, the neutral state may seek to exclude altogether the warships of the offending belligerent from entry and stay in its waters and ports. There are also instances of neutral states placing embargoes upon the export of munitions and other implements of war to an offending belligerent. Whether or not an aggrieved neutral may—as a measure of retaliation—directly assist the other party to the conflict is not altogether clear, though it would appear that the answer to this question must be negative.

[34] See p. 220.

[35] The strict wording of Article 25, Hague XIII, only obligates the neutral states "to exercise such surveillance as the means at its disposal allow to prevent any violation" of its waters or ports.

[36] Article 3 states: "When a ship has been captured in the territorial waters of a neutral Power, this Power must, if the prize is still within its jurisdiction, employ the means at its disposal to release the prize with its officers and crew, and to intern the prize crew.

If the prize is not within the jurisdiction of the neutral Power, the captor Government, on the deamnd of that Power must liberate the prize with its officers and crew."

Article 3, paragraph 2—on a strict interpretation—only implies the right, not the duty, of the neutral state to demand liberation of a prize taken within its waters but no longer within neutral jurisdiction. The United States adhered to Article 3 with the understanding that this particular provision implies a duty on the part of the neutral state, not merely a right. In practice, neutral states have demanded the restoration of neutral prizes seized within their waters, and failure to do so would no doubt be regarded by the belligerent whose vessel was seized as a dereliction on the part of the neutral state. It should be observed, however, that the restoration of such vessels by a belligerent is made to the neutral state, not to the owner of the vessel.

[37] In strict wording, however, Article 24 speaks only of the measures a neutral state "is entitled to take" against belligerent warships which do not leave a port where they are no longer entitled to remain, but not of measures of internment the neutral *must* take. Here again, practice has established these measures as constituting not only neutral rights but neutral duties as well.

[38] *Harvard Draft Convention on Rights and Duties of Neutral States in Naval and Aerial War, op. cit.*, p. 334.

appear that the present practice of states no longer allows the conclusion that a neutral's duty is fulfilled merely in taking such measures as the means at its disposal allow to prevent belligerent violation of its rights. On the contrary, it would appear that the same standard that is applied to judging the adequacy of a neutral's preventive measures must also apply to judging the adequacy of a neutral's measures to secure the vindication of rights that have once been violated. In failing to use the means at its disposal to secure this vindication the neutral state may be regarded as having acquiesced in the violation of its rights and thereby furnished assistance to one side in the conflict.[89]

3. *Belligerent Rights In the Event of Neutral Failure to Fulfill Obligations of Neutrality*

Whereas a belligerent violation of neutrality gives rise to both a right and a duty of the neutral state, a violation of neutrality on the part of the neutral state merely gives rise to a right of the injured belligerent. The decision as to whether to exercise this right or to acquiesce in a neutral's violation of its duties is one that remains at the discretion of the belligerent. In this respect the position of the injured belligerent differs from that of the injured neutral.

The remedies available to an aggrieved belligerent as a consequence of the neutral's failure to fulfill its obligations range from the demand for moral or material reparation to the taking of retaliatory measures. In general, the procedure required of belligerents prior to the taking of reprisals against an offending neutral does not differ substantially from the procedure laid down by general international law for the resort to reprisals in time of peace. In addition to the requirement that the commission of an act contrary to international law must precede a measure of reprisal, the latter is normally justified only when a demand for adequate redress has proven unavailing. It is difficult though to view this latter criterion as a rigid requirement to be fulfilled on every occasion prior to the taking of

[89] Note, for example, the view in Oppenheim-Lauterpacht (*op. cit.*, p. 754): ". . . in case he [i. e., the neutral] could not prevent and repulse a violation of his neutrality, the same duty of impartiality obliges him to exact due reparation from the offender; for otherwise he would favour the one party to the detriment of the other. If a neutral neglects this obligation, he himself thereby commits a violation of neutrality, for which he may be made responsible by a belligerent who has suffered through the violation of neutrality committed by the other belligerent and acquiesced in by him." No doubt serious difficulties may arise—and have arisen in the past—in judging whether or not a neutral state has used the means at its disposal in exacting due reparation from an offender. These difficulties are no greater, however, than those encountered in determining whether or not the neutral employed the means at its disposal to prevent the commission of the unlawful acts. Distinguish, however, between the inability of a neutral either to prevent violations of its rights or to exact due reparation, though using the means at its disposal, and the failure of the neutral state to employ such means. Whereas the latter may properly constitute a violation of neutrality on the part of the neutral the former does not, despite the fact that in both cases the belligerent suffering from his enemy's unlawful measures may be released from his obligations toward the neutral.

reprisals. Exceptionally, the circumstances attending a neutral's failure to fulfill its obligations may be of such a nature that the injury thereby inflicted upon a belligerent can never be made the subject of adequate redress. In these circumstances, it is submitted, the belligerent does not act unlawfully even though he immediately resorts to retaliatory measures. Finally, it is generally recognized that there must be at least a rough proportionality between the reprisal and the offense that has given rise to the reprisal.[40]

[40] When judged by the above criteria it is believed that there are strong grounds for supporting the action finally taken by Great Britain in the *Altmark* incident (see pp. 236–9). The Norwegian Government clearly possessed the means either to intern the German auxiliary or to require its abandonment of Norwegian territorial waters. Provided, then, that the *Altmark's* passage through Norwegian waters constituted the use of these waters as a "base of operations," and it is difficult to refute the soundness of this position, the refusal of the Norwegian Government to follow either of the courses of action indicated above may be regarded as a departure from neutral duties. The precipitate character of the British action, in forcibly removing the British prisoners held on board the *Altmark*, while the vessel remained in Norwegian waters, has been defended by Waldock (*op. cit.*, pp. 235–6) in the following terms: "A breach of the rules of maritime neutrality in favour of one belligerent commonly threatens the security if not the existence of the other belligerent. The breach is thus seldom really capable of being remedied in full by subsequent payment of compensation. Nothing but the immediate cessation of the breach will suffice. Accordingly, where material prejudice to a belligerent's interests will result from its continuance, the principle of self-preservation would appear fully to justify intervention in neutral waters." In the light of the relevant circumstances in the *Altmark* incident there is certainly much to be said for this view, though it seems preferable—for reasons already indicated—frankly to characterize the British action as a reprisal measure directed against Norway for the latter's refusal to carry out neutral obligations.

IX. CONTRABAND

A. CONCEPTION OF CONTRABAND

The foundation of the law of contraband must be found in the belligerent claim to prevent an enemy from receiving such goods as will enable him the more effectively to wage war. The law of contraband therefore deals with the extent to which this belligerent claim has been accorded legal recognition. Here, as elsewhere, it will be useful to begin the discussion with a brief statement of the basic features of this law as they appeared in the period preceding the outbreak of World War I.

Purpose and destination have always formed the distinguishing criteria of contraband. With respect to the first of these criteria the traditional law effected a threefold division: articles used primarily (i. e., specialized) for war, articles equally susceptible of use for warlike or for peaceful purposes, and articles either not susceptible of use in war or—though of such possible use—granted exemption on humanitarian grounds. The first category could be seized if found destined to territory belonging to or occupied by an enemy, or the armed forces of an enemy, the nature of the goods making their use for hostile purposes a near certainty once they had entered the belligerent's jurisdiction. The second category, known as conditional contraband, could be seized only if found to be destined for delivery to an enemy government or to its armed forces, thus resolving the uncertainty as to the purpose for which the goods would be used. The third category, known as free goods, were exempt from seizure without consideration of their destination.[1]

The foregoing may be taken to represent the basic framework of the traditional law of contraband, and in a sense it is true that this framework remains valid even today.[2] Susceptibility of use in war and hostile destination still form the essential conditions that must be present if goods are to be seized as contraband of war. It is a different matter, however, to inquire

[1] It is also desirable to note that the law of contraband applies to neutral owned goods shipped aboard either a neutral or an enemy vessel as well as to enemy owned goods shipped aboard a neutral vessel. This for the reason that according to Article 2 of the Declaration of Paris the neutral flag covers enemy goods, with the exception of contraband, and—according to Article 3—neutral goods under an enemy flag are not liable to seizure, contraband excepted. In practice, however, the prevention of contraband carriage is concerned primarily with neutral commerce. This is particularly true in view of recent developments which have rendered Articles 2 and 3 of the Declaration of Paris almost inoperative.

[2] *Law of Naval Warfare*, Article 631a.

how meaningful it may be to assert that the traditional basis of the law of contraband remains unchanged in view of belligerent practices during the two World Wars. For these practices have succeeded in effecting a radical transformation even while retaining the traditional forms. Whereas in an earlier era the law of contraband tended to represent a compromise between the conflicting claims of neutral and belligerent, recent practice represents the successful realization of the belligerent aim of preventing almost any type of goods from reaching an enemy. In this process the traditional distinction between absolute and conditional contraband, though formally retained, has become a distinction without a difference. The category of free goods, also retained in form, has shrunk to a vanishing point. In both global conflicts the major disputes between neutral and belligerent centered primarily upon the specific methods adopted by belligerents in pursuing the avowed goal of seizing or destroying practically the whole of an enemy's imports. But the legitimacy of this goal became a subordinate question even during World War I, and in the second World War neutral protests against the all-inclusive character of belligerent contraband lists assumed an almost perfunctory character.[3]

In so reducing the area of freedom formerly enjoyed by neutrals, belligerents received a substantial measure of support from the very uncertainty marking nineteenth century practice. The law of contraband had always provided the controversial core of neutral-belligerent relations, and a number of disputed issues had never been clearly resolved. Once hostilities broke out in 1914 ample opportunity was therefore provided belligerents to pursue courses of action whose unlawful character could hardly be regarded as self-evident, despite neutral, and enemy, assertions to this effect.

This opportunity afforded belligerents can be attributed in part to the absence of any clear restraint upon the admitted right of a state to draw up contraband lists once it became involved in war.[4] The position of belliger-

[3] Thus several neutral states protested against the British contraband list issued in September 1939, though the protests were neither energetically pressed nor seriously received. On October 3, 1939 the Foreign Ministers of the American Republics resolved: "To register its opposition to the placing of foodstuffs and clothing intended for civilian populations, not destined directly or indirectly for the use of a belligerent government or its armed forces, on lists of contraband." *A. J. I. L.*, 34 (1940), *Supp.*, p. 14.

[4] Apart, of course, from those limitations imposed by treaty. During the 18th and 19th centuries a number of bilateral treaties were concluded defining the articles to be considered contraband in the event of a war in which one of the parties to the treaty was a participant. But the significance of these treaties is now almost entirely historical. At present, the only conventional restrictions of a multilateral character imposed upon belligerents in drawing up contraband lists are those contained in the 1949 Geneva Convention Relative to the Protection of Civilian Persons in Time of War. Article 23 of this Convention obligates the contracting parties to "allow the free passage of all consignments of medical and hospital stores and objects necessary for religious worship intended only for civilians of another High Contracting Party, even if the latter is its adversary. It shall likewise permit the free passage of all consignments of essential foodstuffs, clothing and tonics intended for children under fifteen, expectant mothers and maternity cases." But this obligation of belligerents is subject to the conditions that the

ents has been not merely to contend that the precise nature of contraband lists is necessarily dependent upon the concrete circumstances of the war—which is true enough—but that the significance of these circumstances, and hence the particular items to be classified as contraband, must be left to the determination of the belligerents [5]—an altogether different and frequently controverted claim. The latter contention must imply that the only limitations placed upon the belligerent's discretion in devising his contraband lists are those imposed by the general rules defining the nature of contraband goods. On the other hand, states not involved in hostilities have sought to place more precise restrictions upon the discretion claimed by belligerents. At the very least, neutrals have maintained that belligerents cannot act in complete disregard of neutral opinion when devising contraband lists.

In Articles 22 through 29 of the unratified Declaration of London the attempt was made to compromise the issue by listing articles that might "without notice" be regarded as absolute contraband and to which further articles "exclusively used for war" could be added by means of a notified declaration addressed to other states. Similar provision was made for articles that could be treated without notice as conditional contraband and to which further articles and materials "susceptible of use in war as well as

---

party allowing for the free passage of these goods has no "serious reasons for fearing: (a) that the consignments may be diverted from their destination, (b) that the control may not be effective, or (c) that a definite advantage may accrue to the military efforts or economy of the enemy through the substitution of the . . . consignments for goods which would otherwise be provided or produced by the enemy or through the release of such material, services or faculties as would otherwise be required for the production of such goods." Article 59 of the same convention provides for the passage of certain goods (e. g., foodstuffs, medical supplies and clothing) to occupied territory "if the whole or part of the population of an occupied territory is inadequately supplied." Nevertheless, the state granting such passage shall have the right "to search the consignments, to regulate their passage according to prescribed times and routes, and to be reasonably satisfied through the Protecting Power that these consignments are to be used for the relief of the needy population and are not to be used for the benefit of the Occupying Power."—These provisions may be regarded as a striking illustration of the extent to which states have granted recognition—in a humanitarian convention—to the virtual absence of restraints upon the belligerent freedom to deprive an enemy of all goods, even those expressly designed to serve humanitarian purposes. For the discretion given to belligerents in Articles 23 and 59 is of such a character as to nullify, for practical purposes, the obligations ostensibly undertaken in these provisions.

Finally, note should be taken of the customary practice of permitting free passage of articles serving exclusively to aid the sick and wounded of the enemy. See Article 631c (2), *Law of Naval Warfare*. Also exempt from seizure, by custom, are articles intended exclusively for the use of the crew and passengers of a vessel.

[5] Thus the British Government, in replying on November 20, 1939 to earlier protests made by the Netherlands' Government against the former's contraband lists, took the usual belligerent position in declaring that: "It is the undoubted right in international law of a belligerent Power to declare what articles it will consider as contraband, within the general definition of contraband as being any article of use for the prosecution of war." cited in Hackworth, Vol. VII, *op. cit.*, p. 26.

for purposes of peace" could be added by proper notification. Finally, the Declaration contained a list of articles and materials "not to be declared contraband of war."

It would serve little purpose to retrace here the steps by which these provisions, though provisionally adopted by the belligerents in 1914, were abandoned. Within a brief period of time most of the items listed by the Declaration of London as free had been shifted to the category of conditional contraband, and a large number of articles originally listed as conditional contraband were moved to the category of absolute contraband. In each instance belligerent justification for expanding contraband lists followed a uniform pattern. The novel circumstances in which hostilities were being conducted were alleged to have resulted in rendering almost all goods susceptible of use in war. In addition, these same circumstances were held to have resolved the otherwise ambiguous character of numerous articles formerly considered as conditional contraband; the use of these articles for warlike purposes now being considered so probable as to justify their reclassification within the category of absolute contraband.[6]

By the end of World War I it was no longer expedient to list each separate item declared to constitute either absolute or conditional contraband. Instead, the new belligerent procedure—introduced in the 1917 *Instructions For the Navy of the United States Governing Maritime Warfare*—was to list only a few broad categories within which particular items were considered to

[6] In this manner the "nature" of absolute contraband underwent a subtle transformation. It can be argued that the description given absolute contraband always varied to some extent. Nevertheless, the traditional meaning—according to even the most liberal interpretation—was a strict one. Absolute contraband consisted of goods "specialized for war," or, in the words of Article 34 of the U. S. Naval War Code of 1900, of goods "primarily and ordinarily used for military purposes in time of war." Belligerents were not justified, however, in listing items as absolute contraband simply because there was a probability—even a certainty—that a part of these goods would be used for warlike purposes. It was precisely this latter consideration that formed the justification for conditional contraband; the ambiguity attached to the latter being removed when it was once established that they were destined to the armed forces of the enemy. Yet, belligerent practice during the two World Wars was not only to do away with the distinction between absolute and conditional contraband by giving to both a common destination (a point to be dealt with shortly) but also by alleging that a large portion of the goods in question (e. g., fuel and lubricants) would be used for warlike purposes. This latter claim may be readily admitted; a portion of almost any type of goods will be consumed by the military effort. The same was also true of an earlier era, however, though it did not serve to classify goods as absolute contraband. The point of all this is not, as has been suggested, "that while such articles may be of ambiguous use, abstractly speaking, in a particular stage of a particular war and as against a particular enemy there may be no ambiguity whatsoever about the use to which they will be put if they reach that enemy." Stone, *op. cit.*, p. 481. On the contrary, even in "total war" an appreciable uncertainty remains over the use to which a *particular shipment* of goods may be put. What is not uncertain is that a part of the total quantity of shipments will most assuredly be used for warlike purposes; and it has been on this basis that belligerents have declared such goods to be absolute contraband. But on this reasoning it is difficult to see the logic in placing fuel on the list of absolute contraband and food on the conditional list, though belligerents did just this even in World War II.

fall. Upon the outbreak of war in 1939 this procedure was adopted by several of the major belligerents, although some states retained the former practice of publishing detailed lists. In either case, the central feature common to the belligerent contraband lists was their all embracing character.[7]

B. CARRIAGE OF CONTRABAND: THE PROBLEM OF DESTINATION

Carriage of contraband occurs only when goods whose nature renders them of use in war are found to have a hostile destination. It has earlier been observed that according to the traditional law the hostile destination required of goods before they could be seized and condemned as contraband of war turned upon the nature of the goods. In the case of goods used primarily for war (absolute contraband) the territory belonging to or occupied by an enemy, or the armed forces of an enemy, formed the required

[7] The contraband list proclaimed by Great Britain in September 1939, and adopted by Canada, New Zealand, Australia and France, was closely patterned after the list contained in Article 24 of the U. S. Navy's 1917 *Instructions*. The British list read as follows:

"Schedule I.

Absolute Contraband

(a) All kinds of arms, ammunition, explosives, chemicals, or appliances suitable for use in chemical warfare and machines for their manufacture or repair; component parts thereof; articles necessary or convenient for their use; materials or ingredients used in their manufacture; articles necessary or convenient for the production or use of such materials or ingredients.

(b) Fuel of all kinds; all contrivances for, or means of, transportation on land, in the water or air, and machines used in their manufacture or repair; component parts thereof, instruments, articles, or animals necessary or convenient for their use; materials or ingredients used in their manufacture; articles necessary or convenient for the production or use of such materials or ingredients.

(c) All means of communication, tools, implements, instruments, equipments, maps, pictures, papers and other articles, machines, or documents necessary or convenient for carrying on hostile operation; articles necessary or convenient for their manufacture or use.

(d) Coin, bullion, currency, evidences of debt; also metal, materials, dies, plates, machinery, or other articles necessary or convenient for their manufacture.

Schedule II.

Conditional Contraband

(e) All kinds of food, foodstuffs, feed, forage, and clothing and articles and materials used in their production." *U. S. Naval War College, International Law Documents, 1944–45*, pp. 91–92.

Article 22 of the German Prize Law Code of August 28, 1939, declared as absolute contraband "all articles and materials which: 1. Directly serve the land, naval or air armament and 2. Are consigned to the enemy territory or the armed forces." This was soon changed, however, by an absolute contraband list that closely paralleled the Allied list. On September 12, 1939, the German Government declared "foodstuffs (including live animals) beverages and tobacco and the like, fodder and clothing; articles and materials used for their preparation or manufacture" to be conditional contraband. — In effect, the major belligerents therefore had a common contraband list.

destination.[8] Goods possessing an ambiguous nature (conditional contraband) required a destination to the government authorities or to the armed forces of an enemy state.[9]

It is clear that this differentiation in destination must depend, in turn, upon the assumption that belligerents will be able and willing to make a reasonable clear distinction between the combatant forces and the civilian population of an enemy. Once the latter distinction is discarded it is no longer meaningful to distinguish between absolute and conditional contraband, since the destination required of all goods susceptible of use in war will then be assimilated to the destination formerly reserved only for absolute contraband. It was precisely this development that marked belligerent practice almost from the initial stages of World War I. The belligerents contended that given the circumstances it was no longer possible

[8] And Article 31 of the Declaration of London reflected the customary law in stating that the proof required for establishing hostile destination in the case of absolute contraband is complete "(1) when the goods are documented to be discharged in a port of the enemy, or to be delivered to his armed forces," and "(2) when the vessel is to call at enemy ports only, or when she is to touch at a port of the enemy or to join his armed forces, before arriving at the neutral port for which the goods are documented." According to Article 32 the ship's papers were to be considered conclusive unless the vessel was found to have deviated from her route and unable to account properly for such deviation. But ship's papers have never been regarded as conclusive if facts establish their contents to be false.

[9] But pre-World War I practice had never clearly resolved the controversy over the presumptions open to belligerents with respect to the destination required for conditional contraband. The importance of this matter is clear, since once a presumption of enemy destination has been made the claimant has the burden of establishing innocent destination before a prize court in order to obtain restitution of goods seized. British practice in the 19th century distinguished between goods destined to an enemy port used primarily for commercial purposes and goods destined to enemy ports serving the armed forces. In the latter instance enemy destination was presumed for goods consisting of conditional contraband. However, Article 34 of the Declaration of London stated that, with respect to conditional contraband, enemy destination is presumed "if the consignment is addressed to enemy authorities, or to a merchant, established in the enemy country, and when it is well known that this merchant supplies articles and materials of this kind to the enemy," or, if goods are "destined to a fortified place of the enemy, or to another place serving as a base for the armed forces of the enemy." These presumptions of enemy destination could be rebutted, but then the burden of proof would fall upon the neutral claimant. There is no question but that as judged by 19th century practice Article 34 represented a considerable concession to belligerent claims and prepared the way for the later practices of belligerents in World War I. Writing shortly before the outbreak of World War I, John Bassett Moore prophetically observed of this provision that: "These grounds of inference are so vague and general that they would seem to justify in almost any case the presumption that the cargo, if bound to an enemy port, was 'destined for the use of the enemy forces or of a government department of the enemy state.' Any merchant established in the enemy country, who deals in the things described, will sell them to the government; and if it becomes public that he does so it will be 'well known' that he supplies them. Again, practically every important port is a 'fortified place;' and yet the existence of fortifications would usually bear no relation whatever to the eventual use of provisions and various other articles mentioned. Nor can it be denied that, with well kept highways, almost any place may serve as a 'base' for supplying the armed forces of an enemy." *The Collected Papers of John Bassett Moore*, (1944) Vol. VI, p. 57 (address on "Contraband of War, February 2, 1912).

to distinguish with sufficient clarity between goods destined for the use of the armed forces and goods intended for civilian consumption. These circumstances were alleged to be the large proportion of the enemy population taking an active part in the military effort and the strict control exercised over all enemy imports through policies of requisition and rationing. The same circumstances appeared in a still more pronounced form in World War II, and belligerents responded by once again making enemy territory the requisite hostile destination for seizure and subsequent condemnation of all goods deemed susceptible of being put to a warlike use.[10]

The major problem remains, however, since it is still necessary for a belligerent to establish an enemy destination in order to condemn goods as contraband of war. In the simplest case involving the direct carriage of contraband, where the vessel is encountered carrying goods susceptible of use in war and documented to be discharged in an enemy port, no difficulty will normally arise.[11] But experience has shown that under modern conditions the direct carriage of contraband is likely to prove the exception rather than the rule. In the case of a belligerent adjoined by neutral states, as was Germany in both World Wars, the carriage of contraband will almost invariably be indirect, through the ports of adjacent neutrals, and the belligerent's problem of contraband control will center very largely upon the extent of the right to intercept goods documented to neutral ports though having—or suspected of having—an ultimate enemy destination.

[10] The major steps in this development—facilitated by Article 34 of the Declaration of London—may be briefly traced. By 1915 Germany had declared that almost every major port in the British Isles was either a "fortified place" or a base for serving the armed forces. The effect of this action was to abandon the distinction between absolute and conditional contraband, even while claiming— as Germany did so claim—to have upheld it. British practice followed along similar lines, and in April 1916 the British Government openly abandoned the attempt to distinguish between the destinations formerly required of conditional and absolute contraband. But this distinction had already been abandoned by the British Prize Court. Thus in *The Kim and Other Vessels* [1915] it was declared, in condemning foodstuffs held to be destined to Germany, that: "Apart altogether from the special adaptability of these cargoes for the armed forces, and the highly probable inference that they were destined for the forces, even assuming that they were indiscriminately distributed between the military and civilian population, a very large proportion would necessarily be used by the military forces. *3 Lloyds Prize Cases*, p. 367.

In World War II the issue was never in any doubt, given the total character of each belligerent's war effort. Thus in *The Alwaki and Other Vessels* [1940], the British Prize Court declared, in condemning foodstuffs held to be destined to Germany, that "there is the clearest possible evidence of German decrees which, to put it quite shortly, impose Government control on all these articles and prescribe that they are automatically seized at the moment of crossing the frontier or, to put it more accurately, at the moment of coming into the customs house." *Annual Digest and Reports of Public International Law Cases* (1938–40), Case No. 223, p. 586.

[11] Nor will any difficulty normally arise even when cargo is found to be documented to a neutral port, if the vessel is to touch at an enemy port on its way to the neutral port or if the vessel is encountered having deviated from the route indicated on the ship's papers. In either case the goods on board may be presumed to have an enemy destination; the destination of the goods being assimilated to the least favorable destination of the vessel.

Over the basic principle governing such cases involving the indirect carriage of contraband—and most appropriately termed the principle of ultimate enemy destination—there can no longer be any real doubt.[12] Goods documented to neutral ports and consigned to persons in neutral territory are nevertheless liable to seizure at any time after leaving their port of origin if it can be shown that the ostensible neutral destination serves only as an intermediate point for further transit—whether by land, sea or air—to an enemy.[13]

At the same time, the specific consequences following upon the application of this principle to the carriage of contraband have not only been extremely far-reaching in practice but have provoked controversies between neutral and belligerent that are still far from being satisfactorily resolved. Nor are the reasons that have led to these controversies—in which neutrals have alleged unwarranted interference with their legitimate

---

[12] The neutral trader's purpose in making such circuitous voyages is clear. Since goods destined for use in neutral territory are exempt from belligerent interference, the risks incurred in undertaking to trade in contraband would be considerably reduced provided only that cargo could enjoy exemption from seizure simply because documented to a neutral port. If the contraband goods are to be carried from the neutral port to an enemy destination by sea, whether in the same vessel (continuous voyage) or after being reshipped in another vessel (continuous transport), the period of liability to seizure would then be reduced to the latter leg of the voyage. If, on the other hand, the goods are to be transported to an enemy, after reaching a neutral port, by land or by inland waterway (continuous transport), no risk would be run at all.

The application to contraband of the principle of continuous voyage, or transport, was first undertaken by American prize courts during the period of the Civil War. However, these decisions were confined to the condemnation of goods consisting of absolute contraband. At the time, the majority of writers—and states—strongly condemned the decisions. But Great Britain, whose trade was the most directly affected, did not protest. In 1900, during the Boer War, the British sought to apply the principle—as a belligerent—against German merchant vessels and met with strong German protests. The matter remained unsettled down to the outbreak of World War I, despite the well known compromise attempted in the Declaration of London to apply the principle of ultimate enemy destination to absolute contraband (Article 30) though not to conditional contraband (Article 35). Great Britain abandoned the compromise almost directly upon the initiation of hostilities, and in taking this action was followed by her Allies. In British prize law rejection of the compromise sought by the Declaration of London came in *The Kim and Other Vessels* [1915], 3 *Lloyds Prize Cases*, pp. 355–9. In April 1915 Germany also abandoned Article 35 of the Declaration of London, though treating her action as a retaliatory measure taken against the unlawful action of the Allies. Paragraphs 69 and 70 of the U. S. Navy's 1917 *Instructions* expressly endorsed the application of the principle of ultimate enemy destination to both absolute and conditional contraband. A detailed treatment of the historical development of the principle of continuous voyage through World War I may be found in H. W. Briggs, *The Doctrine of Continuous Voyage* (1926).

In World War II continued controversy over the application of the principle of ultimate enemy destination to conditional contraband almost disappeared. However, Article 24 of the German Prize Law Code of August 28, 1939 did declare that conditional contraband is not liable to capture if discharged in a neutral port "on condition of reciprocal procedure on the part of the enemy." The "reciprocal procedure" not being forthcoming Germany abandoned this provision.

[13] See *Law of Naval Warfare*, Article 631c.

trade—hard to trace. It cannot be emphasized too strongly that the traditional system regulating trade in contraband had been based largely upon the assumption that the destination of a cargo would generally be the same as that of the vessel in which it was carried. This assumption goes far in explaining the traditional methods of contraband control as well as the procedure of prize courts. Visit and search at sea—the principal method of contraband control—was confined to an examination of the ship's papers and the interrogation of crew members. If the result of visit and search indicated an enemy destination, or a reasonable suspicion of enemy destination, the vessel and goods could be seized and placed in prize. Before the belligerent's prize court the normal procedure had been to restrict the evidence that could be brought forward in the first hearing to that provided by the vessel herself. The introduction of extrinsic evidence by the captor was generally permitted only if the preliminary hearing did not establish with sufficient clarity a proper case either for condemnation or for restitution. Hence, the primary burden was placed upon the captor to justify his act of seizure, and in this task the evidence he could generally bring forth was of a limited nature.[14]

It need hardly be pointed out that this system would seriously limit—if not frustrate altogether—any benefits to be derived from applying to contraband the principle of ultimate enemy destination, particularly in view of the present complexity of commercial transactions. In the case of vessels destined to a neutral port adjacent to enemy territory, carrying goods documented to the neutral port and consigned to persons in neutral territory, the ship's papers will generally reveal nothing concerning the ultimate destination of the cargo.[15] The information required to establish enemy destination will almost always be of a very complex character and can be gathered—if at all—only through the vast intelligence facilities at the disposal of belligerent governments. In these circumstances interception at sea can no longer possess its former significance. Instead of ascertaining through visit and search whether sufficient cause for seizure exists the normal procedure has been to intercept neutral vessels and to divert

---

[14] This, at least, had been the Anglo-American practice until it was abandoned by Great Britain in the prize rules issued by the British Government shortly before the outbreak of war in 1914. Formally, it still represents the procedure in American prize courts, as Hyde (*op. cit.*, pp. 2378–82) points out, though American courts have been inactive in prize proceedings since the Spanish-American War.

[15] "Modern facilities of communication, as well as the modern system of company organization and finance, have made it possible to conceal the truth of any commercial transaction under a thick coat of legal camouflage, and a boarding officer would merely be wasting his time if he tried to determine the real destination of a cargo from an examination of the manifest and the bills of lading." H. A. Smith, *op. cit.*, p. 124. Of course, the falsification or forgery of papers has always been practiced. However, as Smith observes, the difference between former days and the present period "is that modern commerce and finance have now made it possible completely to conceal the truth without recourse to such crude methods as forgery."

them to a contraband control base.[16] Here, during the period of detention, information may be collected that will lead either to the release of the vessel and goods or to their seizure as prize.[17]

In the latter eventuality the procedure followed in both World Wars has been for the captor to initiate proceedings in prize by introducing any evidence that may serve to justify seizure and—possibly—condemnation. If the evidence introduced is regarded as sufficient to create a reasonable suspicion of ultimate enemy destination the claimant, in order to avoid condemnation, must refute the presumption of enemy destination thus held to arise by a positive showing that the cargo has a genuine neutral destination. Provided, then, that the belligerent can establish circumstances creating a reasonable suspicion of enemy destination the burden of proving an innocent destination is thrown upon the neutral claimant.[18]

In this connection the belligerent's task has been facilitated still further by the creation of a detailed set of presumptions governing hostile destination. Thus a presumption of enemy destination has been held to arise where goods are consigned "to order," or if the ships papers do not indicate the real consignee of the goods, or if goods are merely consigned to a dealer or agent and the ultimate buyer is unknown, or if the parties engaged in the transaction—though known—have or are suspected of having enemy

---

16 At least this has been the normal procedure followed in the absence of the vessel's cargo being covered by a navicert (see pp. 281–2).

17 The measures by which belligerents, and principally Great Britain, sought to mitigate the inconvenience thereby caused to neutral shippers through forced diversion and detention in contraband control bases will be considered in later pages. The legality of diversion for search (and even for visit) is now generally accepted, though when initiated in World War I it could not be said to have had legal sanction (see pp. 338–43). Nor should the primary purpose of compulsory deviation be obscured by belligerent claims—although in part justified—that the dangers attending visit and search at sea, as well as the increased size of vessels, required the adaptation of traditional methods to these novel circumstances. For the practice of compulsory deviation was essentially a result of the belligerent need to detain a vessel for a period of time sufficient either to work up an adequate case for seizure in prize or to establish the innocent destination of the cargo.

18 In British prize law this principle was clearly laid down in World War I in *The Louisiana and Other Ships* [1918], 5 *Lloyds Prize Cases*, p. 252. During World War II the Judicial Committee of the Privy Council reaffirmed the principle in the following terms: ". . . the captor must show that the case is one involving reasonable suspicion. If they do so, and if no claim is made, or if the claim fails, the court will in due course condemn the property as prize, but on the side of the claimants positive proof to the satisfaction of the court is exacted. . . The contrast between the two sides is sometimes explained as depending on the onus of proof. In a sense that may be a true description, but more exactly the difference depends on what is the case of either side. The captor has to maintain his seizure by showing the case of reasonable suspicion in order to justify what he did. The claimant has to establish by evidence of fact his affirmative case, which he can do in any case like this by showing the precise character of the adventure and showing that the ostensible destination is the real destination." *The Monte Contes* [1943], *Annual Digest and Reports of Public International Law Cases* (1943–45), Case No. 196, pp. 544–5.

connections.[19] In any of the foregoing circumstances the inference of an ultimate enemy destination has been strong and could be displaced only by a positive showing that the goods in question had an innocent destination.[20]

Nor has it been considered sufficient to establish that neither the shipper nor the nominal consignee intended to supply an enemy with contraband of war. In applying the principle of ultimate enemy destination it is not the intention of the neutral claimant in whose possession the goods are at the time of seizure that has been decisive but rather the intention of those who have—or will have—control over the ultimate destination of the goods.[21] And so long as an ultimate enemy destination is held to exist at the time of seizure, condemnation has been considered justified.[22] This has also implied the abandonment of restraints that formerly resulted from considering the act of contraband carriage as necessarily constituting a single commercial transaction. In considering the question of final destination as decisive goods have been condemned that were intended to pass through a number of intermediate transactions in a neutral state before reaching an enemy. It may be, for example, that goods are immediately destined to a neutral country to be there transformed from raw materials into manufactured articles, then to be re-exported to an enemy. In these circum-

---

19 In World War I Great Britain, by a series of Orders in Council, established a number of such presumptions relating to enemy destination. The most comprehensive of these Orders in Council, that of July 7, 1916, declared that: "The hostile destination required for the condemnation of contraband articles shall be presumed to exist, until the contrary is shown, if the goods are consigned to or for an enemy authority, or an agent of the enemy State, or to or for a person in a territory belonging to or occupied by the enemy, or to or for a person who, during the present hostilities, has forwarded contraband goods to an enemy authority, or an agent of the enemy State, or to or for a person in territory belonging to or occupied by the enemy, or if the goods are consigned to 'order', or if the ship's papers do not show who is the real consignee of the goods." *U. S. Naval War College, International Law Documents, 1944–45*, p. 49 (and see pp. 42–69 for a general review of enemy destination in World War I). The Prize Court in Great Britain has added to these presumptions, and an illuminating survey may be found in Colombos, *op. cit.*, pp. 198 ff.

20 Of course, the captor may still fail to establish a case sufficiently strong to warrant condemnation by a prize court. But so long as "reasonable suspicion" can be shown to have existed at the time of seizure the belligerent cannot be held liable for losses incurred as a result of seizure. Nor is it actually necessary, from the belligerent's point of view, to obtain condemnation. It is sufficient merely to obtain possession of the goods and thus to deprive the enemy of their use. This may be accomplished, for example, either by the sale of the goods or by their requisition during the period they are being held in prize. For a further discussion of these—and related—points, see p. 346(n).

21 "When an exporter ships goods under such conditions that he does not retain control of their disposal at the port of delivery, and the control, but for their interception and seizure, would have passed into the hands of some other persons, who had the intention either to sell them to an enemy government or to send them to an enemy base of supply, then the doctrine of continuous voyage becomes applicable, and the goods on capture are liable to condemnation as contraband." *The Norne and Other Vessels* [1921], 9 *Lloyds Prize Cases*, p. 427.

22 Though, of course, account has been taken of events occurring after seizure.

stances British prize law has not considered such goods as having been legitimately incorporated into the "common stock" of the neutral country, but ultimately intended for an enemy, hence liable to seizure and condemnation.[23]

Finally, a presumption of enemy destination has been held to arise where goods being imported into a neutral country are found to be in appreciable excess of the state's normal import requirements. It is this presumption that has provided the most striking, and certainly the most controverted, development in the expansion of belligerent claims to control neutral trade in contraband. In effect, the belligerent has sought by this method to ration the imports of neutral states. Whereas the presumptions of enemy destination described above still attempt to preserve a connection—however tenuous—with the traditional system, the presumption that has as its basis the fact that a neutral state has exceeded its normal import requirements would appear to have abandoned this attempt altogether. Up to this point the application of the principle of ultimate enemy destination remains based upon the assumption that whatever may transpire between the initial shipment of goods and their final destination the events that must be inquired into form a single chain of occurrences—though not necessarily a single commercial transaction—dealing with a particular shipment of goods. Admittedly this sequence of events has become very complex, and the possibility of establishing—or even inferring—a discernible connection has correspondingly declined. For this reason the number of circumstances held to create a presumption of enemy destination has increased. Nevertheless, these presumptions do relate to a particular shipment of goods.[24]

In this final presumption, though, based as it is upon the fact of excessive

---

[23] Thus in one instance it was declared that "the notion that leather, imported to a neutral country (Sweden) for the express purpose of being at once turned into boots for the enemy forces, becomes incorporated in the common stock of the neutral country, is illusory. Instances can be given and multiplied which appear to reduce to an absurdity the argument that if work is done in the neutral country upon goods which are intended ultimately for the enemy, that circumstance of necessity puts an end to their contraband character, and prevents their being confiscable according to the doctrine of continuous voyage." *The Balto* [1917], 6 *Lloyds Prize Cases*, p. 148.—Less certain—though apparently not from the viewpoint of British practice—is the application of the principle of ultimate enemy destination to the practice of "substitution," i. e., of condemning goods destined to a neutral country which—though consumed therein—have the effect of releasing a similar quantity of goods to an enemy. The problem comes very close to the issues involved in "rationing," and may be distinguished from the latter insofar as it is established that the same party receiving a particular shipment of goods was directly responsible for releasing a like quantity of the same goods to an enemy. Hence, it is not any *general relationship* between the import of goods into a neutral country in substitution for the release of similar goods to an enemy that here provides a basis for applying the principle of ultimate enemy destination; it is rather the specific relationship between the import and export—in the form of substitution—of goods.

[24] And the "highly probable destination" that has been held to follow if these presumptions are not clearly disproved, and which is sufficient to warrant condemnation, is a probability relating to a particular quantity of goods and based upon the facts attending its shipment.

neutral imports, attention is no longer directed to an enquiry into tracing a particular shipment of goods from its point of origin to its final destination. Instead, attention is directed to quantitative considerations, or, more precisely, to a comparison between what is regarded as a neutral country's normal import requirements for a given commodity and the amount of goods actually being imported. Once it has been determined that the latter exceeds normal requirements a strong presumption has arisen that the surplus goods are either themselves ultimately destined to an enemy or that their importation into the neutral country would serve to release a like quantity of similar goods. In a word, the presumption is in the nature of a statistical probability, drawn from a detailed analysis of a neutral state's trading pattern and applied to a particular shipment of goods.[25] And although there are apparently no cases in which prize courts have condemned goods solely on the basis of a "statistical presumption," it is nevertheless certain that such presumption has formed an important, and perhaps even the decisive, consideration in a number of instances. It is clear that prize courts (e. g., in Great Britain) have considered statistical presumptions as providing sufficient basis for seizure and for throwing upon the owner the burden of establishing that effective steps had been taken to insure that goods entering a neutral port would never reach an enemy destination.[26]

[25] It is scarcely possible to discuss in any detail the many problems—legal and political—arising in connection with presumptions having a statistical probability as their basis. In a noteworthy discussion of so-called "rationing" policies (as well as other methods of contraband control), Sir G. G. Fitzmaurice ("Some Aspects of Modern Contraband Control and the Law of Prize," *B. Y. I. L.*, 22 (1945), pp. 89–95) has indicated some of the difficulties involved in fixing—whether through agreement with the neutral country or through belligerent imposition—the neutral's "reasonable domestic needs, having regard to all the circumstances, including manufacture for export to innocent destinations." In wartime "all sorts of factors may operate to justify a neutral in importing *more* than its normal peace-time requirements of a given commodity." Yet it does not appear to carry matters very far by saying of these difficulties that they involve "the question whether some revision of the concept of what constitutes enemy destination is not called for under modern conditions." Given the transformation that has already been effected by belligerent application of the principle of ultimate enemy destination the only "revision" left to belligerents is to consider neutral territory—as such—to be assimilated to the concept of enemy destination—in brief, to cut off all neutral trade on the theory that some part of this trade might eventually find its way to an enemy.

[26] "It appears to be settled . . . that an adequate 'statistical' case will *per se* (i. e., even in the absence of any suspicion attaching to the consignment on grounds specially connected with it as such) justify seizure and place upon the owner the burden of proving innocence, so that no damages can be recovered against the Crown in respect of the seizure. On the other hand, no case has as yet occurred where goods have been *condemned* on statistical evidence alone." Fitzmaurice, *op. cit.*, p. 91. Generally speaking, it has been considered desirable, for obvious reasons, to base condemnation on other grounds as well, and not upon a statistical probability alone. Besides, from a practical point of view, it may be quite sufficient only that seizure can be justified, for—as earlier noted—once goods have been seized the liklihood of their ever leaving the captors jurisdiction is small.

C. CONSEQUENCES OF CARRIAGE OF CONTRABAND

Neutral merchant vessels engaged in the carriage of contraband, or reasonably suspected of being so engaged, are liable to seizure.[27] This liability begins from the time the vessel leaves a neutral port with the contraband and terminates only upon completion of the voyage.[28]

In considering the further consequences attached to the carriage of contraband a distinction must normally be made between the vessel and the contraband cargo. With respect to the contraband goods there is no question but that they are always subject to condemnation. Also subject to condemnation, according to the practice of some states, are the non-contraband goods that bear a common ownership with the noxious cargo.[29]

Less settled are the rules governing the fate of the vessel seized while engaged in the carriage of contraband.[30] Whereas some states have traditionally placed primary emphasis upon the element of knowledge on the part of the owner (or master) of the vessel,[31] other states have stressed the

---

[27] Even if carrying no contraband goods the neutral vessel may nevertheless be liable to seizure if she is herself considered to be contraband. In both World Wars vessels (and aircraft) were placed in the category of absolute contraband.—For a further discussion of visit and search as well as the varying circumstances under which seizure at sea is justified, see pp. 332 ff.

[28] See *Law of Naval Warfare*, Article 631d. Note should also be taken of the British and American practice of holding that seizure of the vessel is permitted even on her return voyage if it is found that the carriage of contraband goods was accomplished by means of fraud, e. g., by false or simulated papers. In this instance condemnation of the vessel will also follow.

[29] This according to the so-called doctrine of infection which, as Colombos (*op. cit.*, p. 222) points out, "concerns strictly the ownership of the goods, and it is 'common' ownership which leads to the confiscation of the innocent cargo. Condemnation is an incident of the owner's position. It is not an incident of the quality or nature of the goods." The Declaration of London endorsed the principle of infection, and Article 42 declared that: "Goods which belong to the owner of the contraband and are on board the same vessel are liable to condemnation." Great Britain has always followed this rule, as has the United States, and despite the traditional opposition of continental countries a number of these states have, in recent years, included the principle in their prize codes. In practice, however, the doctrine of infection can have only a limited significance today in view of developments in the conception of contraband.

[30] The loss of freight and other expenses now appears to constitute the minimum common penalty imposed upon a vessel seized for carriage of contraband. It is beyond this point that diversity may be found.

[31] This has been the position of Great Britain and—in large measure—of the United States. Thus Oppenheim-Lauterpacht (*op. cit.*, p. 826): "Great Britain and the United States of America confiscated the vessel when the owner of the contraband was also the owner of the vessel; they also confiscated such part of the innocent cargo as belonged to the owner of the contraband goods; they, lastly, confiscated the vessel, although her owner was not the owner of the contraband, if the vessel sailed with false papers for the purpose of carrying contraband, or if the vessel was by a treaty with her flag State under an obligation not to carry the goods concerned to the enemy and the owner knew that his vessel was carrying contraband." Yet even where the owner has knowledge of the carriage of contraband Anglo-American practice has generally required such contraband to form a substantial proportion of the whole cargo; hence the element of proportionality is not altogether excluded.

proportion of contraband carried by the vessel.[32] The Declaration of London reflected the latter practice in stating that a vessel carrying contraband "may be condemned if the contraband, reckoned either by value, weight, volume, or freight, forms more than half the cargo;" [33] and although this rule has not yet been endorsed by the prize codes of all states it may be regarded as having succeeded in obtaining widespread acceptance.[34]

---

[32] Though continental European countries have required that the contraband form a certain percentage of the cargo—whether by volume, weight or value—the proportion required has varied from one-fourth to three-quarters, and in certain states the element of knowledge—through presumption, at least—formed an additional requirement.

[33] Article 40. But Hyde (*op. cit.*, p. 2161) observes that this rule should not "be deemed necessarily to forbid condemnation of the ship if the owner thereof has knowledge that goods constituting a substantial part of the cargo are contraband. Nor should he be permitted to profit from lack of such knowledge if he has chartered the vessel on a time charter to one who is notorious in supplying contraband to a belligerent, if at the time of capture the vessel was being employed as a vehicle of transportation on such a mission."

[34] British prize law still insists upon condemnation of the vessel being dependent upon the element of knowledge, despite the fact that the Order in Council of July 7, 1916 declared Article 40 of the Declaration of London as applicable against all vessels seized for carriage of contraband. In practice, this continued insistance upon the complicity of the owner is qualified in its effects by requiring the latter to take reasonable precautions to insure that his vessel is not used for the carriage of contraband. And Colombos (*op. cit.*, p. 225) points out that: "No immunity is, of course, available to a shipowner who charters his vessel and does not concern himself with the cargo. A neutral shipowner must see to it that his vessel is not used for the purpose of conveying contraband goods to one of the belligerents. Feigned or deliberate ignorance on his part does not afford any protection." One important reason for presuming knowledge will be the proportion of the cargo carried that consists of contraband. Hence the rule enunciated in the Declaration of London (which is also based, in a sense, upon a presumption of knowledge on the part of the owner) and the position still maintained in British prize law will frequently lead to similar results. Such divergence as will occur follows from those cases where, on the one hand, contraband is carried without the knowledge and against the will of the owner, and, on the other hand, where carriage of contraband is accomplished by means of fraud in which the owner either actively participates or has an interest. Regardless of the proportion of the cargo that is contraband, in the former instance the vessel is not condemned, whereas in the latter instance it will always be condemned (even if seized on its return voyage after having disposed of the contraband goods).

Finally, brief mention should be made of the circumstance in which a vessel is encountered carrying contraband, though unaware of the outbreak of war or of contraband declarations applicable to the cargo. On this point, Article 43 of the Declaration of London has been generally accepted. Article 43 states:

"If a vessel is encountered at sea making a voyage in ignorance of the hostilities or of the declaration of contraband affecting her cargo; the contraband is not to be condemned except with indemnity; the vessel herself and the remainder of the cargo are exempt from condemnation and from the expenses referred to in Article 41. The case is the same if the master after becoming aware of the opening of hostilities, or of the declaration of contraband, has not yet been able to discharge the contraband.

A vessel is deemed to be aware of the state of war, or of the declaration of contraband, if she left a neutral port after there had been made in sufficient time the notification of the opening of hostilities, or of the declaration of contraband, to the power to which such port belongs. A

D. CONCLUSIONS

As between the belligerents it is doubtful whether any of the developments occurring in the law of contraband since 1914 can be regarded as unlawful, even as judged solely by the standards of the traditional law. It is true that occasionally the argument has been pressed that a belligerent in endeavoring to seize all goods destined to an enemy state, including goods intended for consumption by the civilian population, thereby violates the principle requiring a distinction to be drawn between the treatment of combatants and non-combatants.[35] However, to the extent that the distinction in question has served to restrict inter-belligerent behavior in warfare at sea such restriction has sought primarily to prohibit belligerents from endangering the lives of enemy non-combatants by making them the objects of direct attack.[36] On the other hand, in exercising his undoubted right to seize and to confiscate enemy private property found at sea a belligerent is not considered to violate the combatant-non-combatant distinction. Nor is this distinction violated by exercise of the belligerent right to blockade the ports and even the entire coast of an enemy; though it is clear that the effects of blockade weigh as heavily upon non-combatants as upon combatants. These measures have long formed an accepted part of the law governing naval hostilities. They are believed to provide a clear answer to the contention that a belligerent violates any obligation toward an enemy in shutting off imports intended for consumption by the civil population.[37]

As between belligerent and neutral the matter is admittedly altogether different, and no doubt it is from the neutral that the challenge to belligerent practices must come—if at all. In considering the validity of neutral claims, however, it will be useful not only to refrain from finding in the traditional law of contraband general principles where none have existed but also to abstain from imputing a degree of certainty—and precision—to

---

vessel is also deemed to be aware of a state of war if she left an enemy port after the opening of hostilities."

Article 43 does not prevent *seizure*, however, where vessels are encountered carrying contraband of war. The ultimate disposition of the vessels and goods—in accordance with Article 43—falls upon the prize courts.

[35] "While the exigencies of belligerency must primarily control the definition of contraband, and therefore to a great extent settle the list of contraband merchandise, there is a point at which accepted law offers a barrier to further dictation on their part. Except to the limited degree which has been indicated in treating of belligerent rights, acts of war cannot be directed against the non-combatant population of an enemy state. Hence seizure of articles of commerce becomes illegitimate so soon as it ceases to aim at enfeebling the naval and military resources of the country and puts immediate pressure upon the civil population." E. W. Hall, *A Treatise On International Law*, p. 656.

[36] The status of these restrictions has been examined elsewhere (see pp. 56–70) and bears no direct relation to the contention under present consideration.

[37] Assuming, of course, that a reasonably clear distinction can even be drawn between the combatant and the civilian enemy population.

such principles as have existed. The law of contraband has not been the product of any overarching principle, save perhaps the principle of compromise. For this reason it must prove as mistaken to consider the development of this law—whether past or present—from the viewpoint of the neutral's interests as to consider it from the viewpoint of the belligerent's interests. Still further, such general principles as did undoubtedly form a part of this law were frequently marked by controversy, both as to their content and their manner of application. Thus there has never been clear agreement over the discretion allowed a belligerent in determining the character and extent of his contraband lists. Nor has there ever been any marked consensus upon the limits, if any, to the belligerent's right of determining the procedural rules that are to govern the conduct of its prize courts, even though these rules are frequently as important in controlling neutral trade as the substantive rules of prize.[38]

At the very least, this uncertainty has made it difficult for neutrals to challenge the belligerent contention that the traditional law of contraband provides a broad framework within which specific measures taken by belligerents may vary as the circumstances of war vary. In particular, these circumstances have been held to determine both the scope of articles regarded as susceptible of use in war and the possibility of applying the traditional distinction between absolute and conditional contraband.[39]

The real difficulty though in any attempt to assess the present status of the law of contraband must be found in the principle—or, more precisely, in the manner of applying the principle—of ultimate enemy destination. As to the validity of the principle itself there can no longer be any real doubt;

[38] As might be expected belligerents have usually contended—as did Great Britain in World War I—that changes in prize court procedure form a matter of national—not international—law, and therefore fall within the discretion of the belligerent. The contention has been just as frequently denied by neutral states, though generally without success. Whatever the merits of the controversy it is clear that many changes considered by belligerents as merely procedural in character have had a pronounced bearing upon the effectiveness of substantive rules of prize (admittedly a matter of international concern). If the decision to apply the principle of ultimate enemy destination to contraband represents a change in the substantive law—which it clearly does—then the effective application of this principle has been made possible largely through changes of an allegedly procedural character. Thus the various rules—discussed in preceding pages—establishing presumptions of enemy destination have often been described as of a procedural nature, though it is certain that the effect of these presumptions in facilitating the control of neutral commerce can hardly be exaggerated. And if the Declaration of London is to be regarded as generally reflecting the traditional position in this matter it would appear that the creation of rules in which a presumption of enemy destination can be held to arise (even though rebuttable) is not a matter within the sole discretion of belligerents.

[39] And although it is true that the actual practices of belligerents during the two World Wars reduced the traditional framework to an empty shell, this fact probably cannot serve to refute the formal argument that the traditional framework nevertheless retains its validity and would once again be applicable, circumstances permitting. It is, of course, another matter to ask how relevant this formal argument may be in view of the conditions that presently attend war's conduct.

goods ultimately destined for an enemy cannot escape seizure and condemnation merely because their immediate destination is to neutral territory. At the same time, experience has clearly shown that this principle cannot be given effective application by belligerents short of the resort to measures whose validity have been—and still are—seriously questioned. The resulting situation is therefore not without an element of paradox, since acquiescence in the principle of ultimate enemy destination has nevertheless been accompanied by controversy over measures designed to make the principle effective. These measures extend from the initial acts of interception and detention in a belligerent's contraband control base—while information is being gathered concerning the nature and destination of the cargo—to the final act of condemnation by means of a procedure that is admittedly based largely upon conjecture and the "probability" of enemy destination.[40] Yet it is not difficult to see that the retention of traditional methods in modern conditions would make nonsense of the principle of ultimate enemy destination. The belligerent has been confronted with the choice of either permitting goods to enter neutral ports, part of which are certainly destined to find their way into enemy hands, or to impose rigid controls upon such commerce at the risk of interfering on occasion with what is undeniably legitimate neutral trade.

In practice, this dilemma has been partially resolved (though only partially) by the introduction of measures designed to reduce the inconvenience otherwise caused to neutrals engaged in lawful trade, while at the same time insuring that an enemy is prevented from obtaining any supplies useful in the prosecution of war. Thus agreements have been concluded between the belligerent [41] and associations of merchants in neutral states, whereby the latter have guaranteed that goods consigned to them would not reach an enemy. In turn, the belligerent has undertaken to refrain from interfering (save in exceptional circumstances) with such goods on their way to a neutral destination.[42]

Perhaps the most notable method—developed principally by Great Britain—for the regulation of trade between neutral states has been the so-

[40] Thus the presumption of enemy destination that has as its basis a statistical probability may appear as far removed from any reasonable method to render effective the principle of ultimate enemy destination as it is possible to take. In fact, it is not, for it merely represents the final step in a process that has departed in ever increasing degree from a procedure demanding proof as to the destination of contraband goods to one based upon conjecture and the mere probability of enemy destination.

[41] Here again it has been primarily British practice that forms the basis for discussion.

[42] These agreements were first initiated by Great Britain in 1915 with the Netherlands Overseas Trust. Thereafter merchant associations in other neutral states entered into similar agreements. In 1939 the practice was revived. It should be noted that these agreements did not preclude the inspection and acceptance of particular shipments through the use of the navicert system, discussed below. Nor did it prevent later seizure of cargoes in circumstances indicating an enemy destination.

called "navicert" system.[43] By submitting his cargo to investigation prior to sailing a neutral shipper might obtain a certificate, or navicert, from the belligerent's representative in the port of origin, stating that the cargo inspected was of an innocent nature. In the absence of any later circumstances that might raise independent cause for suspicion, a vessel carrying a fully navicerted cargo could expect to pass through the certifying belligerent's contraband controls with a minimum of delay.[44] The system provided obvious benefits to both parties. To the neutral shipper it provided a means of avoiding the losses incurred through detention and delay at a belligerent contraband control base. To the belligerent the system provided a method for avoiding friction with neutrals, while reducing the burden placed on naval patrols and the work done at contraband control bases.

Prior to July 31, 1940,[45] the navicert was a facility voluntarily provided by the belligerent to neutral shippers, and one which the latter were under no legal compulsion to accept. The neutral shipper in refusing to make use of this facility was not, for that reason, subject either to seizure or to any other *legal liability* that a belligerent could not in any event already impose.[46] For this reason it has been argued that there is no legal basis for alleging that neutrals were compelled to obtain navicerts. This being so, it must remain entirely within the belligerent's discretion in deciding

[43] Developed in World War I (the best account of the earlier system being H. Ritchie's, *The Navicert System During The World War* (1938)) the navicert system was again introduced by Great Britain in December 1939. For a brief though excellent account of World War II practice, see Malcolm Moos, "The Navicert In World War II," *A. J. I. L.*, 38 (1944), pp. 115–9.

[44] The full benefits of the system could be realized only if the vessel carried no unnavicerted cargo at all; otherwise navicerted cargo would normally be subject to delay while inquiries were being made into the unnavicerted cargo. And Medlicott (*op. cit.*, pp. 96–7) points out that during the first year of the 1939 war: "There was also the 'Ship Navicert', for which the master of a ship or his agent could apply when the whole cargo of the ship was covered by navicerts, and which was intended to minimize further the formalities of visit and search. Ships so covered could normally count on the formalities of visit and search being reduced to a minimum, and they were in fact usually given clearance at sea by a naval patrol. There was thus an important difference between a ship sailing with fully-navicerted cargo, and a ship sailing under cover of a ship navicert. In the latter case, the ship was not normally subject to any delay or inspection beyond that necessary for her identification; in the former case, the ship would, where possible, be cleared at sea without diversion to a control base, but only if the weather permitted boarding and if the ship were found to be carrying no mails or passengers."

[45] See pp. 313–5 for the Order in Council of July 31, 1940, which introduced substantial change in the navicert system.

[46] This, at least, was the belligerent's (Great Britain) argument, though the legal controls it assumes a belligerent already possesses were precisely the measures that neutrals—particularly in World War I—objected to as being in excess of normal belligerent competence. As seen from the neutral's point of view, then, the navicert system frequently was interpreted as imposing an unlawful constraint upon neutral shippers. In British prize law there are no decisions dealing with the navicert system until after the Order in Council of July 31, 1940 came into effect. As this order placed the system on a different basis the relevance of these decisions to the "voluntary" system is limited.

whether to grant or to refuse navicerts to individual neutral shippers.[47]

From the viewpoint of a strictly legal analysis this position would appear sound, although in practice the neutral shipper was under constraint to obtain a navicert, since the consequences following upon a refusal to do so were serious.[48] Even so, this system of "voluntary" controls exercised by a belligerent raises legal problems both for the neutral state that permits a belligerent to inspect cargoes within its territory [49] and—much more important—for the neutral trader who "voluntarily" submits to the system. The other belligerent may well consider such cooperation with an enemy's contraband control system as an act of unneutral service on the part of the neutral shipper, thereby making the vessel and cargo liable to seizure and condemnation.[50] At any rate, the voluntary system of navicerting neutral goods—with the other features attending its operation—ultimately proved insufficient to achieve the purpose of shutting off all overseas imports to Germany. Within less than a year after the outbreak of war in 1939 Great Britain had adopted a far more comprehensive system of controlling neutral trade, and a system that could no longer be termed voluntary in almost any sense of the term. The nature of that system will be dealt with in the following chapter on blockade.

[47] The above position is forcefully presented by Fitzmaurice (*op. cit.*, pp. 83–85), who also observes: "Naturally, the navicert system is capable of grave abuse at the hands of an unscrupulous belligerent, as for instance if navicerts were refused arbitrarily or capriciously or allocated with a view to the belligerents own commercial advantage, or as a means of bringing political pressure to bear. It would seem, however, that such abuses would be of a political and not a legal character, that they could be made the subject of diplomatic complaint on general and political grounds by the neutral government concerned, but that it would be difficult to allege a breach of any rule of international law."

[48] In addition to detention in a belligerent contraband control base, these consequences frequently included a denial to the shipper of belligerent controlled facilities.

[49] Occasionally neutral states have forbidden the operation of the navicert system within their territory. On the whole, British writers assert that the operation of the system in neutral territory should not be construed as a violation of neutrality, e. g., Oppenheim-Lauterpacht, *op. cit.*, p. 855n. (3). Neither in World War I nor in World War II did the United States—while a neutral—ever officially recognize the navicert system, though American shippers were permitted—and frequently encouraged—to cooperate with this system of licensing neutral trade. And for the view that a neutral state in permitting the operation of the navicert system within its territory violates basic obligations of neutrality, namely the obligations to abstain from giving material support to either belligerent and to treat the belligerents impartially, see V. Bruns, "Der britische Wirtschaftskrieg und das geltende Seekriegsrecht," *Zeitschrift für ausländisches öffentliches Recht und Völkerrecht*, 10 (1940), pp. 101–2. Certainly, there is much to be said for the opinion that in permitting the operation of the navicert system within its territory a neutral provides the belligerent important assistance in the conduct of war.

[50] See pp. 322–3, for a more detailed discussion of this point.

X. BLOCKADE

A. CONCEPT OF BLOCKADE

Whereas the law of contraband regulates the extent to which a belligerent can prevent an enemy from receiving goods useful in the conduct of war, the law of blockade deals with the belligerent right—and limits thereto—to prevent the vessels (and aircraft) of all states from entering and leaving either the whole or a part of an enemy's coast.[1]

In its origin,[2] blockade was conceived as a measure analogous to that of siege in land warfare, and the attempt to bar the sea approaches to an enemy port was considered legitimate only when carried out in conjunction with military operations on land. Even when dissociated from siege by land blockade remained a measure designed to reduce certain ports of an enemy into submission through "investment by sea." In the pursuit of this objective a belligerent was considered as justified in prohibiting all neutral intercourse with the besieged or blocked up port. However, during the course of the nineteenth century the practice arose of using a blockade principally to cut off an enemy's sea-borne trade, and thereby to deprive him of the resources for waging war, rather than simply to force

[1] *Law of Naval Warfare*, Article 632a.—This, at least, represents the traditional concept of blockade, though it must be added that in the light of recent developments—to be reviewed shortly—blockade is now frequently considered to relate as well to the belligerent right to prevent the cargoes of vessels and aircraft from reaching the blockaded area whatever the route and method of conveyance. On the issues to which this extended concept of blockade gives rise, see pp. 310–12, 316–17.—In the following pages attention will be directed to the problem of blockades by sea. The extension of blockades to include the air space over the high seas remains a development for the future. It is next to impossible to declare with any degree of assurance what procedures may govern blockade by air. Certainly, there are grave difficulties in assuming that the practices of naval blockade can be applied readily, by analogy, to aerial blockades.

[2] "In its origin," implying when once conceived as a distinct and separate measure of naval warfare. Prior to such emergence it was, as Jessup and Déak point out, "closely tied up with contraband. The common root from which both doctrines sprang is the total prohibition of commerce with an enemy. This type of belligerent pretension was much in vogue from very early times, still flourishing in the early seventeenth century, and has reappeared in various guises at intervals ever since. In the face of neutral protests, and the growing strength of the law of neutral rights in general, the belligerents receded from their insistence on total prohibitions by two types of compromise or concession, one geographical and the other categorical; geographically, the ban, instead of extending to the entire country of the enemy, was confined to certain ports which were besieged or blocked up; categorically, the ban was limited to certain categories of goods such as arms and munitions which came to be known as contraband of war." *The Origins* (Vol. I, *Neutrality, Its History, Economics and Law*, 1935), p. 104.

him to abandon further military resistance in a limited area. At the time, opposition to the developing practice of so-called "commercial" blockades was considerable, and even today it has not entirely disappeared. The basis for opposition can be attributed largely to the conviction that in this development the original purpose—and hence the justification—of blockade had been abandoned; that from a military measure designed to permit belligerents to conduct effective siege by sea, unimpeded by neutral efforts to relieve an enemy made the object of attack, blockade had become a measure whose significance was economic rather than military. As such it was questioned, if only from the conviction that an enemy's economy could not of itself form a legitimate military objective, particularly if this implied striking at an opponent primarily through action immediately directed against neutral trade.[3]

Nevertheless, the attitude and practice of states during the half century preceding World War I provided little support for this opinion. The 1856 Declaration of Paris had laid down the principle that blockades, in order to be binding, must be effectively maintained, but beyond this had furnished no indication that commercial blockades were forbidden. Nor did the provisions of the 1909 Declaration of London, dealing with blockade, contain any stipulation that could be interpreted as limiting this belligerent measure to any well-defined purpose. If anything, the period under review indicated acceptance of the notion that blockade could serve purposes other than the narrowly construed military operation that had provided its earlier justification.

Since 1914 the controversy over the legitimate purposes of a blockade has lost its former significance. In both World Wars the belligerents considered the economy of an enemy not only a legitimate, but a principal, military objective. "Economic warfare," in the words of the British

[3] Thus John Westlake in an essay written during the period of the American Civil War, declared that "commercial blockades ought to be abolished from motives both of justice and policy." The burden of the argument ran as follows: "A neutral cannot be touched by a belligerent unless he has in some way identified himself with the enemy. Actual mixing in the hostilities is such an identification, and to relieve a place which is the actual object of attack at the time, whether such attack be conducted only by sea, or by land also, is actually to mix in the hostilities; therefore blockade in the case of siege is justifiable. To ship a cargo to or from a country with which the shipper is at peace, that cargo being neither contraband nor destined for the supply of a besieged place, is neither an actual mixing in the hostilities, nor in any way an identification of the shipper with the enemy; therefore blockade except in the case of siege is unjustifiable." *The Collected Papers of John Westlake On Public International Law*, pp. 342–3. Westlake quoted with approval the opinion expressed by the American Secretary of State Cass, in 1859, that the "blockade of a coast, or of commercial positions along it, without any regard to ulterior military operations, and with the real design of carrying on a war against trade, and from its very nature against the trade of peaceful and friendly powers, instead of a war against armed men, is a proceeding which is difficult to reconcile with reason or with the opinions of modern times." Within four years the American Government was to declare one of the most important "commercial blockades" of the nineteenth century.

Ministry of Economic Warfare, "is a military operation, comparable to the operation of the three Services in that its object is the defeat of the enemy, and complementary to them in that its function is to deprive the enemy of the material means of resistance."[4] In warfare at sea the pursuit of this objective has led to a determined effort on the part of each belligerent to achieve the complete economic isolation of an opponent; to prevent any imports to or exports from the territory of an enemy. Not infrequently the term blockade has been used to indicate this belligerent effort.

This use of the term blockade to comprehend the most varied of belligerent measures designed to cut off the whole of an enemy's sea-borne trade undoubtedly has served to introduce an element of ambiguity. In part, so-called "measures of blockade" came to include those developments in the law of contraband that have already received consideration. In part, however, they referred to actions whose justification was alleged to rest upon the right of reprisal, and it is this latter category of measures that will form one of the principal concerns of the present chapter. Admittedly, these belligerent reprisal measures bear—at best—only a faint resemblance to the blockades envisaged by the traditional law. Nor did they conform to the customary rules governing blockade, though the degree to which the respective belligerents departed from the customary law varied considerably. Nevertheless, it is abundantly clear that these measures of reprisal were intended, in almost every instance, to achieve the purpose of blockade as presently conceived. At the same time, the frequency of belligerent reprisal measures stands in marked contrast to the disuse into which the traditional blockade, conducted in accordance with the customary rules governing blockade, has fallen.[5]

The explanation of this seemingly anomolous situation is as easy to discern as a satisfactory solution is difficult to reach. It is by now a commonplace that the customary rules regulating blockades have been found by belligerents to be unduly restrictive—or, more accurately, almost impossible of application—under modern conditions. The customary law in force at the outbreak of World War I was at once the product of, and designed to regulate, "in-shore" or "close" blockades—i. e., blockades maintained by a line of vessels stationed in the immediate vicinity of the blockaded coast. But developments in the weapons of war have made the close blockade a feasible operation today only in the most exceptional of circum-

---

[4] Cited in Medlicott, *op. cit.*, p. 17.

[5] During World War I several blockades were imposed which did conform to the customary rules, but they were all of distinctly limited importance. These blockades, and the prize decisions to which they gave rise, are reviewed by Garner, *Prize Law During The World War*, pp. 621–30. During World War II the Russian declaration of a blockade of the Finnish coast, proclaimed in January 1940, furnishes perhaps the only known instance of what was alleged to be a blockade in the traditional sense. However, the Soviet Union denied being at war with Finland, and the latter asserted that the alleged blockade was completely ineffective.

stances. The difficulty, however, has not been that the customary law forbade so-called "long-distance" blockades, as such, but that it required the latter to conform to rules established for close blockades. And this proved to be an impossible task.

To the foregoing must be added the further consideration that the very intensity of the belligerent's desire to effect the complete economic isolation of an enemy has been a factor of importance in preventing the adaptation of the law governing blockade to changed conditions. For this intense desire to cut off the whole of an enemy's sea-borne trade is itself one of the changed conditions, along with the changes that have occurred in the means for conducting naval hostilities; and it has meant that belligerents have been more than content to rest their so-called "blockade" measures upon the right of retaliation rather than to insist that this branch of the law—as all others—cannot be frozen into a mold no longer suitable to modern conditions No doubt it is true that neutral intransigence to change has contributed to the belligerent decision to take retaliatory measures rather than to argue on behalf of the legitimacy of altering the established law. It is equally true, however, that belligerents have not been unwilling—on the whole—to avoid posing a clear and direct challenge to the continued validity of the customary rules governing the operation of blockade, and this unwillingness may be attributed largely to the recognition that reprisal measures provided the opportunity of pleading for greater freedom of action than could reasonably be justified on any other grounds.[6]

[6] In a word, reprisal action furnished the pretext for belligerents to claim the right to do what they wanted—which in both World Wars was nothing less than the complete stoppage of enemy trade with the least possible commitment of surface naval forces—whereas the claim that the customary rules were obsolescent under modern conditions probably would have led—at best—only to modifications of the traditional law. This is apparent in the case of Germany, whose methods of "blockading" Great Britain necessitated not only the abandonment of the rules heretofore governing blockade but, in addition, the abandonment of the most fundamental rules applicable to any form of belligerent interference with neutral trade. On the other hand, the case of Great Britain is more complex. It will presently be submitted that at least a very large part of the British reprisals system in both World Wars may well be regarded as a reasonable adaptation of the customary law to changed conditions. At least this is considered true with respect to the reprisal Orders in Council of March 11, 1915 and November 27, 1939 (see pp. 305–6, 312), and during World War I Great Britain herself so argued (see pp. 308–10). On the whole, however, Great Britain sought the method of reprisals and avoided contending for clear legal change. Nor does it appear sufficient to explain this behavior by a fear that the British Prize Court would have refused to justify action on any other grounds. Instead, British reluctance to seek the path of legal change may also be attributed to a desire to retain an undefined—and undefinable—freedom of action, a desire admirably served by the doctrine of reprisals. In this connection, however, it has been observed that: "Both for political and for legal reasons it is unfortunate that so important a part of British economic warfare should have so unstable a foundation as the doctrine of retaliation. Politically it implies uncertainty, prior to the event, whether the regulations will be introduced." S. W. D. Rowson, "Modern Blockade: Some Legal Aspects," *B. Y. I. L.*, 23 (1946), p. 351. But this "instability" has its virtues (from the belligerents point of view), not the least of which is the retention of a "free hand." This is true not only for future conflicts in which Great Britain may again find herself a bellig-

The net result has been a growing tension between the customary law and belligerent practice. But to what extent recent belligerent practice, though assuming the form of reprisals, may now be regarded as having succeeded in replacing the traditional law assuredly remains an unsettled issue. Before turning to this issue it will be useful both to restate in summary manner the customary law governing blockade and to review the various recent measures taken by belligerents which served the purposes of blockade, though departing from the rules traditionally governing its form and operation.

B. THE CUSTOMARY RULES GOVERNING BLOCKADE

1. *Establishment and Notification.*

The formal requirements of a blockade concern the manner by which it must be established and its existence made known. The authority to establish a blockade rests solely with the belligerent government. For this reason a declaration of blockade will generally be made direct by the blockading state, though it may be made by the naval commander instituting the blockade, who thereby acts on behalf of his government. In either case the necessity for a declaration containing the date a blockade will begin, and its geographical limits, is clear. Equally settled is the requirement that a belligerent must grant a certain period of grace to neutral vessels in order that the latter may be able to leave ports included within the blockaded area.[7]

---

erent (and in a position approximately the same as in the two World Wars). It is equally true for future conflicts in which Great Britain may occupy the position of a non-participant. In the latter instance, the admittedly vague and controversial character of "reprisal" measures bearing upon neutral rights at sea would leave Great Britain free to deny the legitimacy of measures analogous to those she herself has resorted to in two wars.

[7] *Law of Naval Warfare*, Article 632b.—The length of the period of grace granted neutral vessels to leave the blockaded area is dependent—in principle—upon the discretion of the state establishing the blockade. The only clear requirement is that allowance must be made for such departure.—Distinguish blockades as a regular measure of naval warfare between belligerents from so-called "pacific blockades," as well as from the act of a parent state in closing its ports during a period of insurrection or "insurgency." The legality of "pacific blockades" is very doubtful today in view of the obligations imposed upon states Members of the United Nations. In any event, "pacific blockades" are not belligerent measures, but actions directed by one state against another with which it is at peace. While involving the ships of the state being "blockaded," the vessels of third states cannot be interfered with. At least this has always been the position taken by the United States. More disputed is the right of a parent government to close waters and ports to the vessels of third states when such waters and ports are held by insurgent forces. Although the legal position here is far from clear, it does seem settled that acts of closure cannot be made effective by measures which extend beyond territorial waters. In the absence of a recognized condition of belligerency neither the parent government nor insurgents can exercise belligerent rights against the vessels of third states on the high seas. On the other hand, it is generally recognized that: "Within territorial waters both parties may prevent supplies from reaching their opponent. This right of barring access gives no authority to seize or destroy foreign ships." *U S. Naval War College, International Law Situations, 1938,*

Since knowledge of the existence of a blockade is deemed essential to the offenses of breach and attempted breach of blockade, it is customary that neutral governments be notified by the blockading state of the establishment of a blockade and that the local authorities within the blockaded area receive similar notification from the commander of the blockading forces.[8] But although neutral vessels are certainly entitled to notification of a blockade before they can be made prize for its attempted breach, it is doubtful whether formal notification is required by law. Thus according to Anglo-American practice the precise character such notification may take is not considered material.[9]

2. *Effectiveness*

Once a blockade has been properly declared and its existence made known it must satisfy three conditions in order to be considered binding: it must be effectively maintained, it must not bar access to neutral ports and coasts, and finally, it must be applied impartially. Each of these customary requirements require further elaboration.

The obvious intent of the requirement of effectiveness is to prevent belligerent resort to so-called "paper" blockades, that is, to the practice of declaring blockades when the naval power available is utterly inadequate to the task of enforcement. On the other hand, a blockade is effectively maintained when all—or nearly all—of the vessels attempting to enter or to depart from a blockaded area are prevented from so doing by the blockading force. Between these two situations doubt may well arise as to whether in a concrete instance a blockade has succeeded in meeting the test of effectiveness, and it would appear that the most satisfactory formula is that the degree of effectiveness required must be such as to render ingress to or egress from the blockaded area dangerous—hence seizure for breach of blockade probable.[10]

---

pp. 92–3. An excellent review and analysis of this question is given in H. W. Briggs, *The Law of Nations* (2nd ed., 1953), pp. 1000–4. A recent example of the attempted closure of ports during a period of civil war occurred in June 1949, when the Chinese Nationalist Government sought to close certain waters and ports held by the Communists. The incident is reviewed by L. H. Woolsey, "Closure of Ports by the Chinese Nationalist Government," *A. J. I. L.*, 44 (1950), pp. 350–6.

[8] *Law of Naval Warfare*, Article 632c. Any change in the conditions of a blockade—e. g., an extension of its geographical limits—will require fresh notification.

[9] Notification may therefore be actual, as by a vessel of the blockading forces, or constructive, as by proclamation, or by belligerent notice, or a matter of common notoriety. However, Articles 11 and 16 of the Declaration of London accepted the practice of the continental European states by requiring that a declaration of blockade be formally notified to neutral governments as well as to the local authorities of the blockaded area. Given the present state of communications the matter of notification no longer constitutes the problem it once did (see pp. 292–3).

[10] *Law of Naval Warfare*, Article 632d. Uncertainty over the application of the rule regarding effectiveness is of long standing. The 1856 Declaration of Paris, in laying down the requirement of effectiveness, defined an effective blockade as one "maintained by a force sufficient really to prevent access to the coast of the enemy." Article 2 of the Declaration of London repeated this formula and added—in Article 3—that the question whether a blockade is effec-

It is implicit in the customary rule of effectiveness, but should be given special emphasis in view of more recent developments,[11] that the means a belligerent may use in maintaining a blockade are not unlimited. More specifically, the effectiveness required of valid blockades cannot be secured by means violative of other firmly established rules. The element of danger associated with an effective blockade is therefore to be understood in terms of a liability to seizure and eventual condemnation, though not in terms of a liability to destruction upon entrance into the forbidden area.[12] But there is nothing in the traditional law preventing the use either of submarines or of aircraft in maintaining a naval blockade, so long as their employment does not thereby result in a violation of the rules applicable to surface vessels.[13]

3. *Area of Blockade*

It is a settled rule of the customary law governing blockade that a blockading force must not bar access to neutral ports and coasts.[14] As

tive is a question of fact." The formula "sufficient really to prevent access to the enemy coast" has never been regarded as very satisfactory, if for no other reason than that a literal interpretation might appear to require the prevention of any vessel from breaching a blockade—certainly no requirement of law. Nor is the question whether or not a blockade is properly effective merely a "question of fact." As Stone (*op. cit.*, pp. 495–6) well points out: "The degree of effectiveness reached in a particular case is a question of fact; but whether that degree satisfies the legal standard is a question of law." Inevitably, this question of law is one in which a substantial measure of discretion may be exercised, thus raising the possibility of controversy between neutral and belligerent. The formulation contained in Article 632d, *Law of Naval Warfare*, follows the wording of previous instructions to the U. S. Navy, and is in accord with the opinion expressed by the Supreme Court in the *The Olinde Rodriquez* (1899), 174 U. S. 510. In this respect there is a close correspondence between the traditional American and British views on the rule of effectiveness.

[11] See pp. 296–305.

[12] Unless, of course, the vessel attempting to breach blockade either persistently refuses to stop upon being duly summoned by a surface warship or offers active resistance to visit and search.

[13] In any event, at least one belligerent warship would be required to carry out the functions of visit, search and seizure. Beyond this minimum the number of surface vessels will vary according to circumstances, and one of these circumstances may be the degree of support a surface force receives from submarines and aircraft, particularly the latter. The problems arising from the use of mines as an instrument of blockade may be deferred for discussion in relation to more recent developments (see pp. 303–5). Here it may be observed, however, that it is very doubtful that the traditional law could be considered as having sanctioned the use of mines, even as an auxiliary means for enforcing a blockade. See, for example, *U. S. Naval War College, International Law Topics, 1905*, pp. 152–3. Finally, it should be observed in passing that the effectiveness of a naval blockade is not endangered by virtue of the fact that a belligerent does not render passage in the air over the blockaded area dangerous. At the same time, it is true that a blockade "maintained by surface vessels only without means of preventing or rendering dangerous the passage of aircraft . . . would be a 'paper blockade' insofar as such craft were concerned even though proclaimed to include these." *U. S. Naval War College, International Law Situations, 1935*, p. 89.

[14] *Law of Naval Warfare*, Article 632c. Restrictions upon the belligerent extension of a blockade to certain rivers, straits and canals constitute the more detailed application of this general principle. For a discussion of these restrictions, see Oppenheim-Lauterpacht, *op. cit.*, pp. 771–5.

applied to "close" or "in-shore" blockades the intent of the rule is to prevent a belligerent from deploying a blockading force in such a manner as to require vessels destined to neutral ports to pass through the line of blockade, thereupon being seized and condemned for breach of blockade. The extent to which the rule operated in the past to restrict belligerent behavior depended largely upon the circumstances of geography. Normally, however, the danger of barring access to neutral territory was reduced to a minimum in the case of close blockades. Conversely, it has been generally contended—though the accuracy of this contention must be closely examined—that the possibility of conforming to the rule in question necessarily decreases the farther a blockading force is stationed from an enemy coast.

Even prior to World War I the military feasibility of a close blockade was seriously questioned. As already noted, the traditional law did not require close blockade, and opposition to the "long distance" blockade maintained by Great Britain during the first World War merely for the reason that the blockading force was stationed at a considerable distance from the enemy's coast was scarcely decisive. Indeed, as a neutral the United States had conceded in the early stages of that conflict that "the form of 'close' blockade with its cordon of ships in the immediate offing of the blockaded ports is no longer practicable in the face of an enemy possessing the means and opportunity to make an effective defense by the use of submarines, mines and aircraft . . ." [15] Nor was it disputed that the necessities imposed by geography might even render imperative that a blockading cordon be drawn across the sea approaches common to both neutral and enemy ports. But if that contingency arose, it was declared that a blockading belligerent would nevertheless remain obliged "to comply with the well-recognized and reasonable prohibition of international law against the blockading of neutral ports, by according free admission and exit to all lawful traffic with neutral ports through the blockading cordon. This traffic would, of course, include all outward-bound traffic from the neutral country and all inward-bound traffic to the neutral country except contraband in transit to the enemy.[16]

What clearly emerges from the above statement is the contention that whatever the ultimate destination or origin of goods carried by a neutral vessel, seizure of the latter for breach of blockade (though not, of course, for carriage of contraband) is justified only if the vessel itself is bound to or

[15] The statements quoted in the text above form a part of the correspondence between the United States and Great Britain, and were occasioned by the British Order in Council of March 11, 1915. For a further discussion of this correspondence, together with references, see pp. 308–10.

[16] To which was added the further observation that: "Such procedure need not conflict in any respect with the rights of the belligerent maintaining the blockade since the right would remain with the blockading vessels to visit and search all ships either on entering or leaving the neutral territory which they were in fact, but not of right, investing."

from a blockaded port.[17] There can be little question that, in principle, this position formed an accurate statement of the customary law as it stood at the outbreak of war in 1914.

4. *Application of Blockade*

The third substantive principle governing the operation of a blockade is that it must be applied impartially to the vessels of all states—including the vessels of the blockading belligerent.[18] The purpose of this rule is to prevent a blockading belligerent from taking advantage of his position in order to discriminate in the treatment accorded to different countries. Thus a belligerent would violate the principle of impartiality if he allowed the vessels of certain states to pass through the blockaded area while excluding the vessels of other states. However, impartiality in the treatment of the vessels of all states refers only to the standard of behavior demanded of the blockading belligerent within the area that is being blockaded. More precisely, the rule applies only with respect to the vessels of all states attempting either to enter or to depart from the blockaded ports or coast by sea.[19] There is no requirement that a blockade must bear with equal severity upon the trade of neutral states. It may be that despite the blockade some neutrals will be able to continue to trade with blockaded ports by means of inland waterways. It may also be that by choosing to blockade only some of the ports of an enemy, while leaving others open, a blockade will bear more heavily upon the trade of one neutral than of another. In either case the neutral whose trade suffers as a result will have no ground for complaining that the blockading belligerent has failed to conform to the principle of impartiality.

Nor is the obligation of impartiality violated if the commander of a blockading force allows neutral warships to enter and subsequently to depart from a blockaded port. But it is within the discretion of the commander of the blockading force to decide whether or not he will permit such entrance and departure, and under what conditions permission will be granted.[20] Finally, merchant vessels in evident distress may be permitted to enter and subsequently to leave a blockaded port.[21] Whether such permission may be demanded as a matter of right is unsettled though.

---

17 Though it should be made clear that by 1914 there was ample authority for seizing a vessel immediately bound for a neutral port if it could be clearly established that after touching at the neutral port the vessel intended to go on to a blockaded port. (See pp. 293–5).

18 *Law of Naval Warfare*, Article 632f. Article 5 of the Declaration of London stated that: "A blockade must be applied impartially to the ships of all nations."

19 And it should be added that impartiality is quite compatible with a blockade that merely forbids the ingress of vessels or, conversely, the egress. There is no requirement that a belligerent forbid both ingress to and egress from the blockaded area. He may choose the one, or the other, or—as will generally be the case—both. Whatever his choice the blockade once established must then be applied impartially.

20 *Law of Naval Warfare*, Article 632h (1).

21 *Law of Naval Warfare*, Article 632h (2).

In any event, a vessel accorded the privilege of entry and departure must neither receive nor discharge any cargo in the blockaded port.[22]

5. *Termination of Blockade*

A blockade may be terminated, or raised, at any time by declaration of the blockading state, or by the commander of the blockading forces acting on behalf of his government. It is customary on such occasions for the blockading state to notify all neutral governments. Apart from formal notice neutral states may regard a blockade as raised once it is no longer maintained with the minimum degree of effectiveness required by law. For reasons already pointed out, the question as to when a blockade is no longer effective can hardly be regarded as self-evident, and on this question the opinion of neutral states may therefore meet with resistance on the part of a belligerent that has sought to establish—and claims to have established—an effective blockade. At the very least, however, it is clear that if a blockading force is driven off by an enemy the blockade has come to an end. Still further, in the event a blockading force leaves the area for reasons unconnected with the blockade the latter must be regarded as suspended.[23]

6. *Breach of Blockade*

It has already been observed that knowledge of the existence of a blockade forms an essential condition for the offenses of breach and attempted breach of blockade. At one time this requirement gave rise to a marked diversity in state practice, since the slowness of communications frequently made it difficult to determine whether or not a vessel (i. e., the owner or master) had the requisite knowledge. Today, however, the problem has lost much of its former importance, due to the rapidity with which a blockade's existence may be made known. There is at present general agreement that knowledge may be presumed in all instances where a vessel has sailed from the port of a neutral state whose government has already

---

[22] Article 7 of the Declaration of London provided that: "In circumstances of distress, acknowledged by an authority of the blockading forces, a neutral vessel may enter a place under blockade and subsequently leave it, provided that she has neither discharged nor shipped any cargo there." And as Higgins and Colombos (*op. cit.*, p. 546) observe: "In every case, the exemption based on distress must be one of uncontrollable necessity, which admits of no compromise, and cannot be resisted."

[23] Article 30 of the 1941 *U. S. Navy Instructions* declared that: "If the blockading vessels be driven away by stress of weather and return thereafter without delay to their station, the continuity of the blockade is not thereby broken. The blockade ceases to be effective if the blockading vessels are driven away by the enemy or if they voluntarily leave their stations, except for a reason connected with the blockade; as, for instance, the chase of a blockade runner." The factor of weather is no longer likely to play any role in the task of maintaining a blockade. More important, the entire problem of determining when a blockade has ceased to be effective can no longer be regarded merely by reference to the conditions characterizing close blockades. The "stations" for future blockading forces are likely to cover vast areas of the high seas, and it will prove as difficult to determine when vessels have "left their stations" as it will be to judge when they have been "driven away" by an enemy.

received notification of the blockade. And even in the absence of such formal notification a presumption of knowledge will arise—at least according to American and British practice—if the existence of the blockade is nevertheless considered to be a matter of common notoriety.[24]

Breach of blockade therefore occurs—according to the customary law—when a vessel knowing, or presumed to know, of a blockade passes through the forbidden area. In addition, according to the traditional view of the United States and Great Britain the liability to seizure of a blockade runner extended throughout the duration of her voyage. Hence if a vessel sailed from her home port with the clear intent to evade the blockade, liability to seizure (for attempted breach of blockade) began from the time the vessel first appeared on the open seas. Conversely, if a vessel once succeeded in breaking out of a blockaded port, liability to seizure continued until completion of the voyage.[25]

On the other hand, the position taken by a number of European states [26]

---

[24] With respect to breach of blockade by ingress Article 15 of the Declaration of London provided that: "Failing proof to the contrary, knowledge of the blockade is presumed if the vessel left a neutral port subsequently to the notification of the blockade made in sufficient time to the Power to which such port belongs." Article 16 went on to state that if a vessel did not know or could not be presumed to know of the blockade "notification must be made to the vessel itself by an officer of one of the ships of the blockading force." In effect, these provisions narrowed considerably the differences formerly existing between Anglo-American and continental practices, since notice by direct warning was restricted—by Article 16—to relatively infrequent cases.

With respect to breach of blockade by egress Article 16 went on to declare that: "A neutral vessel which leaves a blockaded port must be allowed to pass free if, through the negligence of the officer commanding the blockading force, no declaration has been notified to the local authorities, or, if, in the declaration, as notified, no delay has been indicated." But this provision was at variance with American and British practice, which always presumed knowledge on the part of vessels within blockaded ports.

[25] Thus paragraph 31 of the U. S. Navy's 1917 *Instructions* declared that the liability of a blockade runner to capture and condemnation "begins and terminates with her voyage. If there is good evidence that she sailed with intent to evade the blockade, she is liable to capture from the moment she appears upon the high seas. If a vessel has succeeded in escaping from a blockaded port, she is liable to capture at any time before she completes her voyage. But with the termination of the voyage the offense ends." Article 44 of the U. S. Naval War Code, 1900, made a substantially similar provision. The traditional British position has been summarized as follows: "Liability to capture, according to British practice, in the case of a ship which breaks out continues from the time of sailing until the whole voyage is completed, and is not discarded by touching at some intermediate port on the way to the final destination. Similarly in the case of breaking in the liability commences from the moment the vessel sails with the formed intention of breaking the blockade, and continues until the blockade has been raised or the intention has been clearly and voluntarily abandoned. But this change of intention must be complete. A ship is not permitted to proceed to a neighboring port with a view to making inquiries as to the chances of running in from there, and with the intention of taking those chances if they appear reasonable but abandoning the intention if force of circumstances and the vigilance of the blockading squadron make it inadvisable to persist. A ship must have a clear and innocent programme from the outset." J. A. Hall, *Law of Naval Warfare*, pp. 205–6.

[26] E. g., France, Italy, Germany and the Netherlands.

had been to insist that a vessel could be seized for blockade running only within the immediate area of operation of the blockading forces. Furthermore, liability to seizure followed—in this view—only from overt action on the part of a vessel to break through the lines of blockade.[27] In the 1909 Declaration of London the attempt was made to resolve these divergent views.[28] Accordingly, that instrument provided that the seizure of neutral vessels for violation of blockade could be undertaken "only within the radius of action of the ships of war assigned to maintain an effective blockade." [29] A further provision laid down that "whatever may be the ulterior destination of the vessel or of her cargo the evidence of violation of blockade is not sufficiently conclusive to authorize the seizure of the vessel if she is at the time bound toward an unblockaded port." [30]

It must be emphasized that in blockade it is the destination of the vessel—not of the cargo—that forms the decisive consideration. At least this was true prior to 1914. However, the Anglo-American view had been that liability for blockade running could not be avoided simply for the reason that a vessel intended to touch at an intermediate neutral port prior to making for a blockaded port. To this very limited extent the doctrine of continuous voyage may be said to have been applicable to the offense of attempting to break blockade, and for this reason Article 19 of the Declaration of London may not be regarded as providing an accurate statement of the position heretofore taken by the United States and Great Britain. But in providing that a vessel was not liable to seizure if encountered bound for a neutral port, simply because the cargo carried on board was ultimately

---

[27] The one exception being that seizure was considered permissible outside this area in the case of a blockade runner actively pursued by a vessel of the blockading forces.

[28] It is true that in practice these differences were not as great as might otherwise appear, and Higgins and Colombos (*op. cit.*, p. 552) point out that "there is no case in actual practice in which a vessel has been condemned for breach of blockade except when she was found actually close to or directly approaching the blockaded port." Nevertheless, there are a number of instances in which courts did give careful attention to the ultimate destination of vessels encountered some distance from the blockading forces, and even purportedly bound for neutral ports. Besides, this practice refers to close blockades. It is clear that in a long-distance blockade—considered as such—the standards regarding evidence of intention that were formerly applied to close blockades would necessarily present easy opportunity for evasion. Nor is it reasonable to expect belligerents to adhere to these former standards in operating long-distance blockades. In this respect belligerent practice in the two World Wars is likely to provide more accurate guidance for the future (see pp. 308–15).

[29] Article 17. This provision was viewed at the time as a compromise between the Anglo-American and the continental view, the term "area of operations" (*rayon d'action*) being regarded as a formula whose elasticity was sufficiently great to provide reasonable adaptation to the developing weapons of naval warfare. In reality, though, Article 17 left the old dispute very nearly where it found it, since the continental powers urged that the "area of operations" be rather strictly confined whereas the British and American delegations pressed for the right of the blockading belligerent to fix the radius of action, depending upon the circumstances governing each case.

[30] Article 19.

destined for the blockaded area, Article 19 did give expression to the consensus of the major naval powers. It is true that during the American Civil War there were several cases that could possibly be interpreted as extending liability to seizure for blockade breach to vessels sailing for neutral ports, with no ulterior destination, though carrying cargoes ultimately destined to pass through the blockade. But whatever the interpretation given these cases it is reasonably clear that prior to World War I they had not been considered either by the United States or by Great Britain—and certainly not by any other maritime powers—as having come to represent a part of the established law governing liability for breach of blockade.[31]

7. *Penalty for Breach of Blockade*

The penalty for breach—or attempted breach—of blockade is the confiscation of the vessel and cargo. As an exception, if the owners of (non-contraband) cargo can establish ignorance either of the existence of a blockade at the time they put their goods on board the blockade runner or of the intention of the vessel to violate the blockade such goods will not be condemned.[32]

---

[31] Nearly all of the Civil War cases were ambiguous in this respect since they also involved the carriage of contraband, and seizure (as well as condemnation) could have followed on this ground alone. It is Hyde's opinion (*op. cit.*, p. 2212) that "attentive examination of certain important American cases oftentimes regarded by the commentators as indicating an unfortunate invocation of the doctrine of continuous voyage to establish breach of blockade, reveals the fact that there were in almost every instance other grounds for decision. Hence numerous *dicta* in relation to blockade running lack the significance frequently attached to them." It should be added that these cases involved instances where either the ultimate destination of both vessel and cargo was the blockaded area or where the cargo alone was destined to pass through the lines of blockade (being carried on a different vessel). In the case of cargo destined for the blockaded area by a route other than by way of the forbidden passage there was a clear refusal to consider liability for breach of blockade as arising.

It is believed to be of some importance to emphasize the position held by the United States prior to 1914 with respect to the application of the doctrine of continuous voyage to blockade. In retrospect, a number of writers have ventured to attribute to this earlier position a character that would appear altogether unwarranted. Apart from a small number of rather obscure and controversial Civil War decisions, there is no indication that in the period prior to World War I the United States had ever endorsed the application of the principle of continuous voyage to blockade, save in the very restricted sense already referred to in the text. There is a considerable difference, however, between applying the principle of continuous voyage to a *vessel* and applying the same principle to *cargo carried by a vessel.* Whereas the former application had been clearly endorsed by this country the latter had not. Nor did any change occur in this respect in either the 1917 or the 1941 *Instructions*. But see *Law of Naval Warfare*, Article 632g (3), for a limited change from the earlier position in the light of belligerent practice during the two World Wars. And see pp. 305–17 for a discussion of recent belligerent practice and the problems to which this practice has given rise.

[32] Either possibility is highly unlikely. Besides, the exception does not apply to goods owned by those who also own the vessel, since in the latter instance the master of the vessel is considered to be the agent of the shipowners.

C. BELLIGERENT "BLOCKADE" MEASURES IN THE TWO WORLD WARS

1. *Claims to Restrict Neutral Navigation Through the Establishment of Special Zones*

The effective maintenance of a lawful blockade of any magnitude necessarily requires an appreciable commitment of surface naval forces.[33] Recent experience has indicated, however, that if belligerents are determined to isolate an enemy the temptation will prove strong to achieve the purposes of a blockade though without conforming to the established principles regulating this form of belligerent interference with neutral commerce. Since 1914 one of the principal devices for accomplishing the purposes of a blockade has been the establishment of special areas or zones, variously described,[34] within which belligerents have claimed the right either to restrict neutral freedom of navigation or to forbid such navigation altogether.

At the very least, the belligerent in proclaiming these special zones—which frequently covered vast tracts of the high seas—has assumed the competence to render the waters included therein dangerous to neutral shipping through the laying of mines. Neutral vessels have been warned

[33] This remains true even though the use of aircraft as an auxiliary arm of blockade may reduce considerably the need for surface vessels to patrol large areas—as in the case of blockades maintained at great distances from an enemy's coasts. For the necessity to effect lawful seizure of blockade runners remains.

[34] The varied terminology used in reference to these areas (e. g., "operational zones," "war zones," "barred areas," "military areas," "areas dangerous to shipping") forms a possible source of confusion. On the one hand, different terms have frequently been used to refer to areas in which substantially similar measures were employed. (E. g., the German distinction between *kriegsgebiet* and *sperrgebiet*, the former indicating a "military area" or "war zone" in which the use of arms is to be expected at any time and the latter signifying a "barred" or "forbidden" zone in which every merchant ship—enemy or neutral—may expect to be treated as an enemy warship. But from the point of view of the actual measures taken against neutral vessels the differentiation between *kriegsgebiet* and *sperrgebiet* (or *seesperre*) appears only to have resulted in a distinction without a difference). On the other hand, the same term has occasionally been used in reference to areas in which quite different measures were taken by belligerents. It remains true, however, that despite differences in the specific measures taken by belligerents within these zones the common intent has been to limit neutral freedom of navigation through the resort to methods that avoid the commitment of surface forces otherwise required in maintaining a lawful blockade (or, for that matter, in maintaining a system of contraband control conforming to the traditional law). This decisive point is clearly recognized by Stone (*op. cit.*, p. 572), who writes: "While its (i. e., "barred" or "war" zones) uses may vary, its function is essentially to reduce the belligerents required commitment of surface vessels in naval operations of economic warfare, whether defensive or offensive, and whether covering ports or coast line, or hundreds of miles therefrom. Such economies have been made possible by the invention of new methods and weapons such as submarines, contact mines, magnetic and acoustic mines, and radio-telegraphy. By such means, great areas of the high seas may be rendered so dangerous for navigation that they do not need surface patrols."

that if entering these areas the belligerent could not insure their safety—or accept responsibility in the event of their destruction by mines—unless the vessels folowed prescribed routes and submitted to certain further controls laid down by the belligerent.[35] The more extreme measures taken by belligerents sought to prohibit the entrance of neutral vessels into barred zones by threatening to deprive entering vessels of all safeguards normally accorded peaceful shipping. Thus the German war zone declarations of January 31, 1917 and August 17, 1940 stated that neutral vessels persisting in entering forbidden areas would thereby become liable to destruction at sight by submarines and aircraft.[36]

---

[35] Thus on November 3, 1914, Great Britain declared that the whole of the North Sea would thereafter be considered a "military area." The declaration went on to state that within this area "merchant shipping of all kinds, traders of all countries, fishing craft, and all other vessels, will be exposed to the gravest dangers from mines which it has been necessary to lay and from warships searching vigilantly by night and day for suspicious craft." *U. S. Naval War College, International Law Documents, 1943*, p. 52. The action was taken as a defensive "counter measure" against what was alleged to be the German policy of using merchant vessels (flying neutral flags) to lay mines indiscriminately on the high seas, and particularly along the ordinary trade routes, in violation of the provisions of Hague Convention VII (1907). In declaring the "military area" instructions were given to neutral vessels, intending to trade with Northern European and Dutch ports, to follow certain prescribed routes. Provided this was done, and other minor controls were adhered to, Great Britain accepted responsibility for insuring the safety of neutral traffic. One of the immediate effects of the measure was to bring neutral shipping using this area under the close scrutiny of the British contraband controls. The United States refrained from joining other neutrals in entering a strong protest against the measure, and upon entering the hostilities itself cooperated—in 1918—with the British in laying a mine field extending across the North Sea. See E. Turlington, *op. cit.*, pp. 36–48.

On the outbreak of war in September 1939, the British Government notified neutrals that mines were being laid in restricted areas off the British coast as well as in specified regions off the German coast. In December 1939, the Admiralty gave notice of its intention to lay extensive minefields in the North Sea off the east coast of England and Scotland. In April 1940, it was announced that minefields had been, or would be, laid in the North Sea from the proximity of the Dutch coast to the Norwegian coast, in the Skaggerak (except for a twenty mile wide channel), in the whole of the Kattegat, and in the Southern Baltic. Later, still further minefields were declared. Once again, Great Britain accepted the responsibility of providing for the safety of legitimate neutral shipping passing through some (though not all) of these mine fields. Neutral vessels found inside the areas were subject to removal by British warships and, if found making use of communication facilities contrary to zoning orders, even to seizure for unneutral service. Nor did Great Britain appear to have attempted to justify these measures as acts of a retaliatory character.

[36] The German declaration of February 4, 1915, in which the waters surrounding Great Britain and Ireland were proclaimed a "theatre of war," was not expressly intended—at least not on paper—to interdict neutral vessels. Instead, it was stated that enemy merchant vessels would be sunk without warning and neutral ships would navigate at their peril ". . . for even though the German naval forces have instructions to avoid violence to neutral ships in so far as they are recognizable, in view of the misuse of neutral flags ordered by the British Government and the contingencies of naval warfare their becoming victims of torpedoes directed against enemy ships cannot always be avoided. . . ." *U. S. Naval War College, International Law Documents, 1943*, p. 53. On the other hand, the declaration of January 31, 1917 broadened

It need hardly be pointed out that these belligerent measures cannot be regarded as conforming to the customary requirements laid down for lawful blockades. Even if completely effective in preventing all neutral traffic with an enemy, and this possibility can no longer be excluded,[87] the methods that have characterized war zone operations would not warrant serious consideration in this respect, for the degree of effective danger that is to attend the attempt to break blockade must be a lawful danger. There is no basis for the belief that the requirement of effectiveness, demanded of lawful blockades, can be met simply by using any means in order to render dangerous the passage of neutral vessels through areas of the high seas declared to be "blockaded." [88]

The foregoing considerations admittedly are not conclusive in judging whether the belligerent establishment of war zones may be regarded as legitimate methods of warfare at sea. The fact that they cannot be regarded as forming lawful measures of blockade does not prevent their possible justification on quite different grounds. In a sense it may even prove somewhat misleading to deal with these special zones in connection with the general problem of blockade, and the only reason for doing so—as already noted—is that they have been largely intended to accomplish the same purposes as blockade. Even so, the central question remains: Have belligerents any right either to restrict or to exclude altogether

---

considerably this earlier area (now termed a "war zone," and even a "blockade area") and extended the unrestricted submarine warfare to neutral vessels as well. In both declarations the measures were described as retaliatory, and a response to the allegedly unlawful behavior of the Allies.

In World War II the German Government announced, on August 17, 1940, a "total blockade" of Great Britain. Alleging that England had acted increasingly in violation of the rules regulating belligerent behavior at sea, thus justifying German retaliatory measures, the announcement concluded:

"Germany, having repeatedly warned these [neutral] States not to send their ships into the waters around the British Isles, has now again requested, in a note, these governments to forbid their ships from entering the Anglo-German war zones. It is in the interest of these States themselves to accede to this German request as soon as possible.

The Reich Government wishes to emphasize the following fact: The naval war in the waters around the British Isles is in full progress.

The whole area has been mined.

German planes attack every vessel. Any neutral ship which in the future enters these waters is liable to be destroyed." *U. S. Naval War College, International Law Documents, 1940*, pp. 46–50.

[87] Developments in submarines and aircraft alone make this possibility a very real one today.

[88] It is primarily for this reason that it has always been doubtful whether a belligerent is permitted to use mines as a supplementary means for enforcing an otherwise lawful blockade (and not so much for the reason, generally advanced, that Article 2 of Hague VII forbids the laying of automatic contact mines "off the coasts and ports of the enemy, with the sole object of interrupting commercial shipping"). By establishing a blockade a belligerent is not thereby granted the special license to subject neutral vessels and aircraft to grave hazards that are otherwise forbidden by law (see p. 289).

neutral vessels [39] from navigating within certain areas of the high seas by rendering these areas dangerous to shipping? [40] In addition, what is the extent of this belligerent right—assuming such right to exist—and the obligations that accompany its exercise?

It is reasonably well established, to begin with, that a belligerent is permitted to place restrictions upon, and even to forbid altogether, neutral navigation in two quite distinct—and limited—areas. In the first, the practice of states has sanctioned belligerent efforts to acquire a greater measure of security through according belligerents the right to exercise control over neutral vessels within a restricted area of the high seas adjacent

---

[39] It should be pointed out that in considering the legal issues raised by the belligerent establishment of war zones most writers have emphasized only the effect of such zones on neutral—though not enemy—merchant vessels, despite the fact that the zones have operated equally against both. Thus Stone (*op. cit.*, p. 572) writes that as "between the belligerents *inter se* this belligerent assertion of extended control raises no problems." In still another treatise it is observed that: "As between the belligerents only, provided that the war zone is enforced by the use of means, whether submarine contact mines, or surface or submarine craft, which comply with the laws of maritime warfare, both customary and conventional, there can be no doubt of the lawfulness of the practice." Oppenheim-Lauterpacht, *op. cit.*, p. 682. In reality, these statements, and particularly the latter, would appear an evasion of the issue. Insofar as operational zones "comply with the laws of maritime warfare" they are quite superfluous, at least if by this the traditional law is understood. Save as a measure of reprisal against an enemy, the mere fact that a belligerent has declared a war zone does not serve to confer upon him greater discretion in the measures taken against enemy merchant vessels. On the other hand, if it is assumed that as between belligerents the declaration of war zones "raises no problems," this can be so only for the reason that by such declaration the powers of a belligerent with respect to enemy merchant vessels are not substantially increased. This assumption, implying as it does a belligerent license to destroy enemy merchant vessels without first removing passengers and crew to a place of safety, cannot yet be accepted. But it is quite true that given the circumstances in which warfare at sea is now carried on (see pp. 67–70), as between belligerents the declaration of special zones in which merchant vessels are not accorded the immunities demanded by the traditional law may add very little to the measures a belligerent may in any event take against enemy shipping. And it is for this reason that the legal issues raised by war zones have related primarily to neutral shipping. However, should belligerents refrain in future hostilities from integrating their merchant vessels into the military effort at sea there would be no justification for the policy of destruction on sight. Nor, for that matter, would a belligerent be justified in introducing such a policy through the device of proclaiming war zones.

[40] To what extent the issues involved in the declaration of war zones at sea apply to aerial zones above the high seas—barred to neutral civil aircraft—is difficult to say. There would appear to be no difficulty in accepting the position taken by Spaight (*op. cit.*, pp. 400–1), that belligerents may forbid neutral aircraft from entering zones where military operations are in progress (a point that will be discussed shortly). But this claim is clearly a modest one, being limited to the immediate area of operations (naval or aerial). The real question, however, is not whether belligerent license in the air is as great as at sea, but whether it is greater—in view of the formative character of the law of aerial warfare. Nevertheless, it must be admitted that it is impossible to state with any real precision the present limits of the controls permitted to belligerents over neutral aircraft in the airspace above the high seas (and see pp. 354–6).

to territorial waters.[41] Within these waters belligerents may lay mine fields and take other measures designed to insure the defense of coastal regions. It does not appear possible at the present time, however, to state with any degree of precision either the extent these areas may take or the intensity of the controls that may be exercised within them. It does seem fairly clear that the general criteria to be used in judging the legitimacy of a particular defensive area must be the reasonableness of its extent, in terms of its essentially defensive function, as well as the ability of the belligerent to exercise a close and effective control over the area. But beyond this little more can be said.

Altogether different, yet equally well established in practice, is the right of a belligerent to control the movements of neutral vessels and aircraft within the immediate area of naval operations. If necessary, a belligerent commander can order such vessels and aircraft to depart from these areas. If allowed to remain within the vicinity where forces are operating they must obey such orders as are given to them (e. g., with respect to the use of radio), and any failure to do so—or to depart from the area when so ordered—will render offending vessels and aircraft liable to being fired upon or captured.[42] Nor can vessels complain if, while remaining within the near vicinity of belligerent operations, they are made subject to the incidental hazards invariably attending the conduct of such operations.

It should be emphasized, though, that the immediate area of naval operations refers to an area within which naval hostilities are taking place or within which belligerent forces are actually operating. As such it

---

[41] See pp. 224–6 for a discussion of similar measures undertaken by neutrals. In large measure, the considerations introduced in this previous discussion are equally applicable to belligerents. Apparently, the first instance of "defensive sea areas" proclaimed by a belligerent occurred during the Russo-Japanese War, when Japan proclaimed that within certain coastal zones neutral shipping would be subject to special restrictions. *U. S. Naval War College, International Law Topics, 1912*, p. 122. In both World Wars the United States, as a belligerent, established several "defensive sea areas" and "maritime control areas," which included territorial waters as well as a very limited area beyond these waters.

[42] *Law of Naval Warfare*, Articles 430b and 520a. Recognition of the right of belligerents to control the activities of neutral vessels and aircraft within the immediate vicinity of naval operations may be found in the naval manuals of a number of states. In Article 7 of the unratified Rules for the Control of Radio in Time of War, which formed Part I of the 1923 Rules drafted by the Commission of Jurists at the Hague, a belligerent commanding officer, considering the success of his operation to be prejudiced by the presence of vessels or aircraft equipped with radio installation, was authorized to order such vessels and aircraft to depart from the area or—if remaining—not to make use of their radio apparatus while within the vicinity of belligerent forces. Failure to conform with the orders given was held to result in liability to capture or to the risk of being fired upon. Finally, Article 30 of the 1923 Rules of Aerial Warfare declared that: "In case a belligerent commanding officer considers that the presence of aircraft is likely to prejudice the success of the operations in which he is engaged at the moment, he may prohibit the passing of neutral aircraft in the immediate vicinity of his forces or may oblige them to follow a particular route. A neutral aircraft which does not conform to such directions . . . may be fired upon."

must be clearly distinguished from those special areas or zones of indefinite extent not made the scene of naval hostilities and entrance into which is forbidden to neutral vessels for substantial periods of time. The claim to control neutral vessels and aircraft within the immediate vicinity of operating forces is essentially a limited and transient one and is based not only upon the right of a belligerent to insure the security of his forces but upon the right to attack and to defend himself without interference from neutrals.[43]

Neither of the preceding examples represent serious restrictions upon neutral freedom of navigation on the high seas. Both types of areas are related to belligerent requirements of a narrowly defensive character, and the controls belligerents may exercise within them are generally recognized as outweighing the limited inconvenience caused to neutrals. However, in the belligerent establishment of war zones there may be found a serious—and perhaps even a fatal—blow to the traditional law. This threat arises only in part from the fact that, in principle, war zones have had no clearly discernible limits, whether in their geographical extent or in their duration. Equally important is the central purpose they are designed to serve, which is to avoid committing large surface forces to the task of cutting off an enemy's sea borne commerce through adherence to methods sanctioned by the traditional law.

Nor may it be of more than limited relevance that the measures taken by belligerents in the establishment of war zones were based, at least in the 1914 war, almost entirely upon the right to retaliate against the allegedly unlawful behavior of an opponent. Even during the second World War belligerents retained in a number of instances the form of reprisals when establishing war zones, thereby acknowledging that the measures contemplated against neutral shipping were in normal circumstances without justification in law. Yet by the close of the 1939 war the persistent and widespread resort to war zones had undeniably served to raise the question whether the act of establishing such zones was any longer in need of the plea of reprisals,[44] a plea that had admittedly taken on a rather perfunctory

[43] It is only to be expected that belligerents will attempt—and have attempted—to assimilate the two types of areas into one category, the purpose being to justify war zones by an appeal to grounds properly reserved for immediate areas of naval operations. Occasionally, writers also fail to make the distinction emphasized above, with the result that the essential differences between these two areas are obscured.

[44] During the inter-war period a number of German writers had already concluded that the belligerent establishment of barred zones stood in no need of the special justification of reprisals. Instead, it was contended that neutral vessels must suffer the consequences (i. e., destruction) if they persist upon entering areas declared as forbidden or barred by the belligerent. The belligerent is obligated—from this point of view—only to make known to neutrals the exact position of the barred zone; having once proclaimed the extent of the zone and the measures to be taken therein against neutral vessels he is relieved of further responsibility (e. g., E. Schmitz, "Sperrgebiete im Seekrieg," *Zeitschrift für ausländisches öffentliches Recht und Völkerrecht*, 8 (1938), pp. 641–71. And for a more recent—and seemingly sympathetic—view by a

character and that on occasion was simply omitted altogether. And even if the latter question must still be answered affirmatively, the consideration remains that for all practical purposes there may be little difference between permitting war zones to be established only as retaliatory measures and according belligerents the competence to resort to these measures as a matter of legal right, quite apart from reprisal. In either event the consequences for neutral commerce may be very nearly the same, particularly if the resort to reprisals becomes—as it has become in recent naval hostilities—a permanent feature of warfare at sea.

Nevertheless, while a legal analysis cannot be unmindful of current—and persistent—realities it cannot make so easy an identification of legal right with belligerent practices Not only have the more extreme of these practices failed to receive the acquiescence of a majority of states, they have been made the object of general condemnation even when resorted to under the guise of reprisals Thus, it is at least clear that the measures Germany sought to take within war zones—against neutral vessels—have not received approval, whatever the justification urged on their behalf.[45]

Swiss writer, see H. E. Duttwyler, *Der Seekrieg und die Wirtschaftspolitik des Neutralen Staates* (1945), pp. 38–41). The novelty of this theory must be found in the contention that the principal requirement for almost any belligerent measure against neutral shipping—regardless of the degree to which such measure may depart from established law—is prior notice on the part of the belligerent. It need hardly be pointed out, however, that no legality attaches to a belligerent measure merely for the reason that neutrals have been given prior warning. Nor is there any merit in the equally novel argument that the effectiveness of the belligerent measures taken within barred zones provides a basis for asserting the lawful character of such measures.—Not infrequently, however, these arguments have been further obscured by identifying "barred zones" with what are in reality "immediate areas of operations," the apparent intent being to justify the attack upon neutral vessels that have allegedly interfered with "belligerent operations." The wholly unwarranted basis for this latter identification has been noted in the preceding discussion.

[45] As already noted, the essential feature of this practice has been the claim that the declaration of war zones provides a sufficient justification—particularly when taken as a reprisal—for barring all neutral shipping from a defined area, and for making neutral vessels entering the area after notification liable to destruction at sight by submarines or aircraft. In considering this practice the International Military Tribunal at Nuremberg declared:

". . . the proclamation of operational zones and the sinking of neutral merchant vessels which enter these zones presents a different question. This practice was employed in the war of 1914–18 by Germany and adopted in retaliation by Great Britain. The Washington Conference of 1922, the London Naval Agreement of 1930, and the protocol of 1936 were entered into with full knowledge that such zones had been employed in the first World War. Yet the protocol made no exception for operational zones. The order of Doenitz to sink neutral ships without warning when found within these zones was, therefore, in the opinion of the Tribunal, a violation of the protocol." For text of judgment, *U. S. Naval War College, International Law Documents, 1946–47*, p. 300.

Although the Tribunal did not expressly so state, the implication is reasonably clear that the sinking of neutral vessels within operational zones was not justified even as a measure of reprisal. Nevertheless, the Tribunal did not pronounce sentence on the accused (Admiral Doenitz) for his breaches of the international law governing the conduct of submarine warfare,

This same broad consensus appears lacking in the evaluation of belligerent claims to establish barred areas of indefinite extent on the open seas through the laying of mine fields. Indeed, the severe condemnation of war zones from which neutral shipping is barred under threat of destruction from submarines and aircraft has not infrequently been accompanied by the acquiescence to zones from which neutral shipping is barred by means almost equally destructive. In large measure, the source of this extraordinary position may be attributed to a convention—Hague Convention VIII (1907)—that has been described, and not inaccurately, as worthless.[46] Although the avowed purpose of Hague Convention VIII is to provide for the security of "peaceful shipping," the effect of that instrument has been to invite the abandonment by belligerents of any substantial restraints upon the use of mines. According to a literal reading of Article 2 a belligerent has only to proclaim that his "sole" intention is not to intercept peaceful shipping in order to lay automatic contact mines off the ports and coasts of an enemy. In addition, Article 3 allows the implication that, within the terms of the Convention, belligerents may sew anchored automatic contact mines anywhere upon the high seas. Nor is a belligerent even placed under a strict obligation to notify third states of the precise location and extent of mine fields once laid. Instead, the obligation is only "to notify the danger zones as soon as military exigencies permit." Hence the interpretation is allowed that it is only mine laying of an openly indiscriminate character that is prohibited—i. e., mines sewn without regard to any definite military operation save that of endangering all peaceful shipping, and without any reasonable assurance of control or surveillance.[47] The experience of World Wars I and II has shown that no appreciable amount of ingenuity is required

---

"in view of all the facts proved and in particular of an order of the British Admiralty announced on May 8, 1940, according to which all vessels should be sunk at sight in the Skaggerak, and the answers to interrogatories by Admiral Nimitz stating that unrestricted submarine warfare was carried on in the Pacific Ocean by the United States from the first day that Nation entered the war. . . ." It may be of some relevance to observe that the unrestricted warfare carried on in the Pacific Ocean by the United States was directed against Japanese merchant vessels, though not against neutral shipping (which was, by this time, almost non-existent). The British order in the Skaggerak, though certainly affecting neutral shipping, was given during the period following upon the German invasion of Norway. At that time the Skaggerak came very close to resembling an "immediate area of naval operations." For these reasons, it is difficult to see how the "facts" cited by the Tribunal could be considered as offsetting the measures taken by Germany within operational zones against neutral shipping.

[46] "As an instrument of control," H. A. Smith (*op. cit.*, p. 95) writes of Hague VIII, "the convention is quite worthless and does not merit detailed examination." In fact, it is somewhat worse than worthless in that it has provided belligerents with arguments that would otherwise find no justification. A useful review of the problem, as seen from the viewpoint of the customary law, is given in *U. S. Naval War College, International Law Topics, 1914*, pp. 100–38.

[47] See *Law of Naval Warfare*, Article 611, for the text of Hague VIII. According to Article 1 of the Convention the laying of unanchored automatic contact mines is forbidden except when so constructed as to become harmless one hour after the person laying them ceases to control them.

of a belligerent to reconcile almost any use of mines with the requirements laid down in these provisions.[48]

It may be suggested, however, that the provisions of Hague Convention VIII need not—and, indeed, should not—be considered as exhausting the scope of a belligerent's obligations. The general principle that the burden of proving the legitimacy of any particular form of interference with neutral vessels rests squarely upon the belligerent asserting it is as applicable—in the case of war zones—to the use of mines [49] as it is to the use of submarines.[50] There is no apparent reason for considering the one instrument less hazardous to neutral merchant vessels than the other. Nor is it easy to see why the destruction of neutral vessels through mines is somehow less violative of the rule forbidding the sinking of such vessels before first removing passengers and crew to a place of safety than is the same act of destruction when performed by submarines. Finally, if the mere act of declaring that within a certain area neutral vessels will thereafter be destroyed by submarines cannot serve to render such destruction lawful, how can a similar declaration notifying the extent of a minefield—entrance into which is accompanied by the risk of destruction—make the latter measure lawful? In either case neutral vessels may be confronted with the alternatives of avoiding the barred areas or entering it at the risk of destruction.[51]

[48] Thus in the initial stages of the 1939 war Great Britain charged that Germany—as in 1914—had violated the provisions of Hague VIII by the indiscriminate laying of mines along the paths of the principal trade routes, by failure to notify peaceful shipping of the precise extent of the minefields, and by laying mines off the English coasts for the sole purpose of interrupting neutral shipping. Germany denied these charges, asserting that the notification of minefields depended upon military considerations which Germany alone could judge and that the purpose of laying minefields off the English coasts was not for the "sole purpose of intercepting commercial shipping." See Hackworth, *op. cit.*, Vol. VI, pp. 509–12.

[49] A principle that appears equally applicable to the belligerent use of magnetic and acoustic mines (whether laid by surface vessels or aircraft), even though Hague VIII refers only to automatic contact mines.

[50] And this is particularly so when such belligerent claims to restrict neutral commerce as war zones represent are carried out by methods violative of other established rules of law.

[51] The above considerations may appear—when once they have been made—as almost self-evident. Yet it is surprising how frequently they have been neglected by writers who look upon the submarine with critical eyes, though viewing the use of mines with what approaches equanimity. And it is for this reason that some writers—particularly German publicists—have suggested that the belligerent measure of proclaiming barred areas, in which neutral vessels thereafter entering incur the risk of attack from submarine, does not essentially differ from the establishment of minefields from which neutral vessels are also barred. In considering the latter argument, Stone (*op. cit.*, p. 574) observes that: "Retaliation apart, the belligerent case may rest on the argument that neutrals cannot complain of the laying of individual mines of a lawful type, at particular places on the high seas, and that a 'barred zone' is after all merely a systematic disposition over a wide area of mines lawfully sown at each point within it. This argument on principle would, however, still afford no legal warrant for attaching any legal liabilities, such as liability to be sunk at sea, to the neutral's trespass into that zone." But this is surely an obscure position. A barred zone may be as much "enforced" by mines as by submarines, and in both instances there is an attempt to attach a "legal liability" in the event of forbidden entrance.

In brief, it is difficult to avoid the conclusion that there is no greater legitimacy attached to the use of mines as a means for establishing war zones on the high seas than there is in the use of other means (e. g., submarines) in order to realize the same purpose. Still further, it does not appear possible to assert that—apart from reprisal—belligerents have at present the right to restrict the movement of neutral vessels within vast tracts of the open seas merely by proclaiming that these areas have been rendered dangerous—in one form or another—to neutral shipping. Hence, despite bellgerent practices in two wars the establishment of war zones forms a lawful measure only when taken in response to the persistent misconduct of an enemy.[52] Even then, belligerents have not yet been conceded the right to bar altogether such areas to the use of innocent neutral traffic.[53] Instead, the right to restrict the freedom of movement of neutral vessels implies the belligerent obligation to indicate certain routes by which neutral traffic may pass through the declared war zones with a reasonable assurance of safety.[54]

2. *The Allied "Blockades" of Germany*

Although the practice of interdicting neutral intercourse with an enemy through the establishment of special areas or zones was not confined to any one belligerent it is properly associated—particularly in its more extreme manifestations—primarily with the German conduct of warfare at sea. Very different in character were the measures upon which Great Britain and her allies relied in both World Wars for effecting the economic isolation of Germany.[55]

What is frequently referred to as the British "long-distance blockade" of Germany in World War I rested largely upon two Orders in Council that were expressly justified as measures of retaliation. In the first of these orders, issued March 11, 1915, the declared intent was to prevent goods of

---

[52] Particularly enemy misconduct equally affecting belligerent and neutral rights at sea, but which neutral states are either unwilling or unable to prevent (see pp. 253–8).

[53] It was this feature—i. e., the attempt at total prohibition—that succeeded in arousing as much of the opposition to German was zones as the fact that these zones were partially enforced through the threat of destruction from submarines. On the other hand, the British war zone declarations were generally not total prohibitions, but the assertion of a right to control the movement of neutral traffic subject to the designation of lanes through which the mine fields could be passed in safety. The importance of this difference in the practice of the two states ought not to be underestimated.

[54] However, in reference to the British barred zones of World War II it has been stated that: "These developments tended in the direction of a successful assertion of the right of the belligerent to lay mine-fields on the high seas irrespective of reprisals but subject to the duty to insure the relative safety of neutral traffic." Oppenheim-Lauterpacht, *op. cit.*, p. 683n (1). In practice, the difference between this opinion and the opinion expressed in the text above is not likely to prove very great.

[55] Very different in character not merely for the reason that they were much more effective than the German war zone declarations in cutting off neutral commerce, but for the far more important reason that they were applied without unlawfully endangering neutral lives.

any kind from reaching or leaving Germany.[56] According to its terms no merchant vessel was to be permitted to proceed to or from Germany carrying goods destined to or laden in the ports of the enemy. Intercepted vessels were subject to compulsory deviation to a British or Allied port and required to discharge cargo having an enemy origin or destination. In addition, merchant vessels though proceeding to or from neutral ports could nevertheless be intercepted and required to discharge such goods as were found to be of enemy origin, ownership, or destination. The disposition finally made of goods discharged in British or Allied ports varied, but in all instances not involving contraband (which, of course, was in any event liable to condemnation) it fell short of confiscation. Nor was any penalty attached to a vessel in respect to the carriage of goods found—either upon calling voluntarily at an Allied port or upon being intercepted and escorted in to port—to be non-contraband in character. However, the severity of this earlier measure was increased by a later Order in Council of February 16, 1917, which, in addition to providing for the capture and condemnation of any vessel carrying goods with an enemy destination or of enemy origin, declared that any vessel "encountered at sea on her way to or from a port in any neutral country affording means of access to the enemy territory without calling at a port in British or Allied territory shall, until the contrary is established, be deemed to be carrying goods with an enemy destination, or of enemy origin, and shall be brought in for examination, and, if necessary, for adjudication before the Prize Court." [57] This presumption, which if not displaced resulted in condemnation of both vessel and cargo, could be avoided only by calling for examination at an appointed port. Even then, cargo found to be of enemy origin or destination was liable to condemnation.

As retaliatory measures taken in response to Germany's unlawful conduct of submarine warfare these two Orders need never have raised controversial questions relating to the scope of the belligerent right of blockade. Of course, the measures could be—and were—challenged by neutrals on the ground that reprisals taken by one belligerent against an enemy, for the alleged misconduct of the latter, could not be used as a basis for encroaching upon otherwise recognized neutral rights. In the absence of a lawful blockade it was therefore held that neutral vessels carrying non-contraband cargo—whether neutral or enemy owned—must be considered exempt from belligerent interference. Apart from the question of reprisals, the latter

---

[56] The German decree of February 4, 1915, proclaiming the waters around Great Britain a war zone in which enemy merchant vessels would be sunk without warning and neutral vessels would enter only at grave peril, provided the basis for this retaliatory order.

[57] Cited In Hackworth, *op. cit.*, Vol. VII, pp. 137–8. The justification given for the order of February 16, 1917 was declared to be the German war zone declaration of January 31, 1917, extending the area of previous war zones and applying measures of unrestricted submarine warfare to neutral vessels found within the prohibited zone.

contention was certainly supported by the traditional law.[58] But this admission cannot be considered as necessarily relevant in determining the legality of belligerent measures which—though departing from normal rules regulating the actions permitted against neutral commerce—are taken in response to enemy misconduct directed against both belligerent and neutral, and which neutral states are either unwilling or unable to prevent. Despite the admitted hazards and possible abuse implicit in these measures it has been earlier submitted that, in principle, their legitimacy may be upheld.[59]

On the other hand, it is a different question to ask whether the specific measures taken by Great Britain and her allies were justified by reason of the circumstances in which they were invoked and in view of the attendant hardships they imposed upon neutrals. The fact that before the British Prize Court the retaliatory measures taken during World War I were considered to be legitimate acts of reprisals,[60] and not imposing unreasonable hardships upon neutrals, cannot of itself be regarded as conclusively establishing the legality of the measures under international law. In general, the status of retaliatory measures bearing adversely upon the normally recognized rights of neutrals is necessarily one of uncertainty.[61]

[58] To this extent the reprisal measures went beyond the established law in the following respects. First, by ordering the detention—and finally the condemnation—of all goods having an enemy destination, even though not confiscable as contraband. In practice, the benefits received from this extension of belligerent right were not appreciable, considering the extent of belligerent contraband lists. Second, by ordering the detention—and finally the condemnation—of all goods having an enemy origin. Apart from reprisal, there was no other warrant for such action, since the seizure of goods carried on neutral vessels and bearing an enemy origin was justified only in case of blockade. Third, the condemnation of vessels—under the Order of February 16, 1917—for carrying goods of enemy destination or origin also went beyond the existing law, which provided for condemnation—in the absence of blockade—only in certain cases involving carriage of contraband (see pp. 276–7). Fourth, in laying down—again under the Order of February 16, 1917—that a vessel bound to or from a neutral port providing means of access to an enemy would be presumed to be carrying goods of enemy destination or origin if failing to call at a British or Allied port for inspection of the cargo. The effect of this presumption, even though rebuttable, was to permit the seizure of vessels merely for the failure to call at a British or Allied port, and to place the burden of establishing innocence of the cargo upon the neutral claimant. On the other hand, the compulsory diversion of neutral vessels to British or Allied ports for inspection of the cargo—allowed under the Order of March 11, 1915—may be considered independently from these issues (see pp. 338–44).

[59] See pp. 256–8.

[60] As a means of reprisal, the legitimacy of the Order in Council of March 11, 1915 was upheld in *The Stigstad* [1916], 5 *Lloyds Prize Cases*, p. 361; the Order of February 16, 1917 in *The Leonora and Other Vessels* [1919], 7 *Lloyds Prize Cases*, pp. 357–63.

[61] This is particularly so when the facts that are alleged to provide the basis for reprisal orders are themselves a matter of grave uncertainty. (And it should be noted once again that before the British Prize Court these facts are not made the subject of inquiry, the Court contenting itself to accept the statement of facts given by the Executive.) During World War I reprisal orders were based upon enemy acts that were, in turn, claimed to be retaliatory measures. Who initiated the endless series of reprisals by first resorting to unlawful behavior even now forms the subject of considerable controversy.

Probably for this reason Great Britain, though rejecting the neutral claim of immunity from the effects of belligerent "reprisal orders," was not unwilling to contend that in its operation at least the retaliatory system thus established did not depart from the essential principles demanded of a lawful blockade.

On this basis [62] the principal objections made by the United States against the British "long-distance blockade" were three in number.[63] The Order of March 11, 1915 was enforced largely by the presence of a British cruiser squadron in the North Atlantic, operating some 1000 miles from German ports. From this vantage point the British warships were in a position not only to intercept vessels bound to and from German ports by way of the principal Atlantic trade routes, but also to intercept vessels bound to and from northern European neutral ports that provided access to Germany. At the same time, trade between these neutral ports and Germany—being "inside" the "blockade"—remained open. In seizing vessels carrying goods suspected of having an ultimate enemy destination or origin, though bound at the time to or from a neutral port, it was contended that the so-called "blockade" measures thereby violated the principle requiring that blockades not bar access to neutral ports.[64] Still further, it was noted that since the measures in question did not have the effect of intercepting trade carried on directly between Scandinavian and German Baltic ports they did not bear with equal severity upon all neutrals and therefore lacked an impartial character. Finally, and in close connection with the preceding point, it was observed that in failing to close off trade between German and Scandinavian ports the "blockade" measures did not satisfy the requirement of effectiveness.

In reply to these objections the British Government asserted that while the measures taken ought not to be judged by strict reference to the letter of the rules applicable to blockade, they were in substantial conformity with the spirit of these rules and should be regarded as a reasonable adap-

[62] I. e., on the basis of whether the retaliatory measures in question conformed to the essential principles governing lawful blockade. Needless to say, there could be no question of the fulfillment of the formal requirements of blockade (declaration or notification).

[63] The immediate and following paragraphs consist of a brief summary of the American notes of March 30, 1915 and October 21, 1915, as well as the British notes of July 23, 1915 and April 24, 1916. Convenient texts may be found in *A. J. I. L.*, 9 (1915), *Spec. Supp.*, pp. 117, 157 and 10 (1916) *Spec. Supp.*, pp. 72, 134.—This controversy, it should be clearly understood, dealt only with the earlier order of March 11, 1915, and the measures taken by Great Britain to carry it out. By the time of the second—and more stringent—Order in Council of February 16, 1917 the United States was on the verge of becoming a participant in the conflict, and with its entrance into hostilities the mainstay of neutral resistance collapsed. Similarly, in World War II the British reprisal order of July 30, 1940 came at a time when neutral resistance, though still appreciable, had begun to diminish in strength. These facts should be kept in mind when considering the possible significance of the British retaliatory systems on future developments.

[64] Though no objection was made either to the long distances maintained between the "blockading" force and German ports or to the fact that the cruiser cordon was drawn across the sea approaches to neutral ports (see p. 290).

tation of the latter to the peculiar circumstances in which the "blockade" of Germany had to be conducted. The charge that neutral ports were being blockaded was therefore denied by the contention that a belligerent did not violate any "fundamental principle of international law by applying a blockade in such a way as to cut off the enemy's commerce with foreign countries through neutral ports if the circumstances render such an application of the principles of blockade the only means of making it effective." It was claimed that every effort was being made to distinguish between cargo consigned to neutral ports with a genuine neutral destination and goods ultimately destined to an enemy.[65] As against the charge that the "blockade" measures were partial in their application it was observed that "the passage of commerce to a blockaded area across a land frontier or across an inland sea has never been held to interfere with the effectiveness of the blockade. If the right to intercept commerce on its way to or from a belligerent country, even though it may enter that country through a neutral port, be granted, it is difficult to see why the interposition of a few miles of sea as well should make any difference. If the doctrine of continuous voyage may rightly be applied to goods going to Germany through Rotterdam, on what ground can it be contended that it is not equally applicable to goods with a similar destination passing through some Swedish port and across the Baltic or even through neutral waters only?" [66]

[65] To which the further argument was added that "we have tempered the severity with which our measures might press upon neutrals by not applying the rule which was invariable in the old form of blockade that ships and goods on their way to or from the blockaded area are liable to condemnation." This was quite true—at least until the Order of February 16, 1917—but could only serve to justify the measures in question as a legitimate reprisal (since not bearing too harshly upon neutrals), not as a legitimate blockade conducted in conformity with the customary law governing this belligerent measure. For that law, as earlier observed, permitted the seizure of vessels (and cargoes) only if the latter were found to be destined to a blockaded port—whether directly or after touching at an intermediate neutral port. The claim that vessels could be seized for blockade breach on the grounds that the cargo carried was ultimately destined to the blockaded area—the essence of the British position—simply could not be regarded as sanctioned by the customary law of blockade. Nor was this claim strengthened by the consideration that goods, upon reaching a neutral port, might be transshipped to another vessel and then pass through the forbidden area, since the decisive consideration was the ultimate destination of the vessel, not the cargo. That circumstances, as Great Britain pointed out, justified the extension of the concept of destination applicable in blockade to cargoes as well might be true (and, indeed, this position is subscribed to in the following pages). Nevertheless, this quite different consideration ought not to obscure the fact that the British position marked a departure from the strict letter of the traditional law.

[66] It is difficult to see the relevance of this reply to the charge of partiality, since instead of attempting to deal with this charge it makes the quite different point that the application of the doctrine of continuous voyage to blockade is justified. It was not disputed, however, that trade between Scandinavian and German ports was not being intercepted. Yet the order of March 11, 1915 purportedly applied to *all* neutral trade with *all* German ports. In this connection, Stone (*op. cit.*, pp. 502–3) declares—following a number of other writers—that the objection to the alleged partiality of the blockade was hardly critical, since "a blockade need not cover every approach to the blockaded port's coast. The fact that intra-Baltic traffic was beyond British reach seems to put the matter on no different basis; it was an objection to eco-

Finally, it was claimed that as measured by actual results the "blockade" was extremely effective.[67]

As judged by the accepted practice of states during the period prior to World War I there was indeed little basis for contending that the "long distance blockade" of Germany in World War I conformed to the essential principles governing the traditional blockade. Nevertheless, it is a curious fact that while allegedly novel circumstances have been generally considered as justifying far-reaching changes in the law of contraband, the circumstances that admittedly render a close blockade either impossible, or largely futile even if possible, have still to be generally accepted as sanctioning similar changes in the law governing blockade.[68] Acceptance of the principle of ultimate enemy destination with respect to contraband has been accompanied by a pronounced reluctance to apply the same principle to blockade. Yet if in the case of contraband neutral territory is no longer

---

nomic rather than naval effectiveness." But a blockade—at least according to the customary rules—*must cover all the sea approaches to the ports or coasts declared under blockade.* This the British "long-distance blockade" did not—and could not—do.

It should also be noted that the "impartiality" of the British "blockade" was open to question by reason of the large volume of British exports to Scandanavian and Netherlands ports. Although the United States did not press this point it did attach some significance to the fact that: "Great Britain exports and re-exports large quantities of merchandise to Norway, Sweden, Denmark, and Holland, whose ports, so far as American commerce is concerned, she regards as blockaded." Great Britain replied, in part, by pointing out that the volume of American exports to Northern Europe nevertheless showed a greater rate of increase than did British exports, and that American traders had made profits equal to or greater than the profits of British traders. This response was quite irrelevant from a legal point of view, since the traditional rules governing blockade required the blockading state to apply the blockade to its own trade as well as to the trade of neutrals. Of course, Great Britain could contend, and did contend, that British exports to neutral ports within the "blockaded" area were destined solely for neutral consumption, though there was at the time substantial question as to the validity of this contention. But even if true it did not do away with the charge that Great Britain was using the "blockade" in order to advance her commercial interests.

67 With respect to the sea approaches in the North Atlantic, through which lines of control could be drawn, this was true enough. A different conclusion must be reached with respect to intra-Baltic traffic. Trade between Germany and the Scandinavian countries did of course decline as the war progressed. But this was due largely to Allied rationing policies imposed upon neutral states, which form little or no relation to the issues at controversy

68 Nor is it altogether relevant to argue that whereas by 1914 ample precedent existed for applying the principle of ultimate destination to contraband carriage there was very little—if any—authority for its application to blockade. Indeed, this contrast is itself misleading, since the application of this principle to contraband clearly hung by a very slender reed up to 1914. Despite the decisions of American prize courts during the Civil War, opposition to acceptance of the principle of ultimate enemy destination in any form remained very strong. And quite apart from this hostility, it will hardly be argued that these earlier decisions sanctioned the remarkable application given the principle after 1914, in building up what amounted to a new law of contraband. Besides, if belligerent practice during the middle of the nineteenth century could introduce precedents of a far-reaching character why was the same attribute denied to belligerent practice a half century later? There is, in fact, no apparent reason for admitting legal change—in order to meet changed conditions—in the one case (contraband) and denying it in the other (blockade).

to be regarded as a safe emporium for goods whose ultimate destination is to an enemy it is difficult to understand the continued insistence upon just this point in the case of blockade.[69] The exercise of contraband controls, labelled as such, can surely prove quite as effective in barring access to neutral ports as a blockade in which the principle of ultimate enemy destination is considered applicable to the offense of blockade breach. Still further, the distinction between goods consigned to a neutral port, and having a genuinely neutral destination, and goods whose ultimate destination is to an enemy is just as possible (or perhaps more accurately: no more difficult) to make in the case of blockade as in the case of contraband.[70]

It is true that given the abandonment in recent hostilities of the distinction between absolute and conditional contraband, and the gradual dis-

---

[69] One of the best arguments to this effect remains J. W Garner's *International Law and the World War* (1920), Vol. II, pp. 327 ff. Also H. W Malkin, "Blockade in Modern Conditions," *B. Y I. L.*, (1922–23), pp. 87–98. And Hyde (*op. cit.*, p. 2199) writes that: "If the doctrine of continuous voyage may be fairly applied to a neutral ship ostensibly bound for a neutral port solely because of the fact that the vessel is ultimately bound for a blockaded enemy port, does it follow that non-contraband neutral cargoes may be likewise seized when bound for neutral ports, if further transportation by land or sea to the territory of the belligerent whose coast is blockaded is in reality sought to be effected? It is believed to be difficult to find a convincing negative answer, although it may be maintained with assurance that maritime states had not yielded so broad a right when World War I was initiated."—A limited concession to the application of the principle of ultimate enemy destination to blockade may be found in the position (which now enjoys a certain support from states, see p. 316) that the doctrine of continuous voyage may apply to blockade where both laps of the voyage are by sea and the goods (though not necessarily the vessel) are intended to reach the blockaded area by way of the forbidden route. But on this view goods intended, after reaching a neutral port, to be forwarded to the blockaded area by a route (land or inland waterway) that does not involve crossing the "lines of blockade" are exempt from seizure for blockade breach. The difficulty with this view is that while it does not follow the customary law, which fastened attention upon the final destination of the vessel and not of the goods, it fails to resolve the problem of destination given the conditions under which blockade normally must now be conducted. For it would fail to apply to goods destined to or originating from a blockaded area other than by way of the forbidden route. This in itself could render a blockade largely futile in modern conditions. Furthermore, in the case of blockades maintained at great distances from an enemy's coasts the blockade runner—in a sense—passes through the "lines" of the blockading forces on his way to a neutral port. Once in the neutral port the vessel might then sail for an enemy port without—in a strict sense—again passing through the forbidden area. These considerations suggest the difficulties involved in attempting to apply the traditional law in modern conditions. They also imply that a partial modification of the customary law governing destination in the case of blockade may prove to be no solution at all.

[70] Undoubtedly it is this consideration that has been a primary factor in the opposition to applying, in the case of blockade, the principle of ultimate enemy destination to cargoes as well as to vessels. In brief, the argument has been that once the destination of the ship is no longer conclusive in determining the destination of the cargo—as it is under the traditional rules governing breach of blockade—the way is opened to mere opinion and conjecture. In this process, it is contended, goods with a genuine neutral destination are seized and belligerents are left free to interfere with innocent neutral traffic. At the same time, it will hardly be denied that the conjecture that would admittedly accompany this application of the principle of ultimate enemy destination to blockade breach already characterizes the procedure

appearance of the category of free goods, the practical difference between contraband and blockade controls cannot be very great so far as enemy imports are concerned.[71] One important difference must necessarily remain, however, since seizure for carriage of contraband can apply only to goods having an enemy destination, whereas seizure for blockade breach may apply equally to exports from the blockaded area. Even so, the application of what has been termed the principle of ultimate enemy origin appears no less justified in the case of blockade than does the principle of ultimate enemy destination when applied to the carriage of contraband.[72]

In any event, World War II witnessed a repetition—though not without certain significant modifications—of the "blockade" measures adopted in the preceding conflict, and once again the legal basis for these measures was asserted to be the right of retaliation against the enemy's misconduct. Thus in response to what were alleged to be illegal German acts of submarine and mine warfare, an Order in Council of November 27, 1939 provided that any vessel sailing from a German port, or a port in territory under enemy occupation, after December 4, 1939 might be intercepted and required to discharge in a British or Allied port that part of its cargo as was laden in an enemy port. Vessels sailing from non-enemy ports and found to be carrying goods of enemy origin or ownership might also be required to discharge such goods in a British or Allied port. The disposition to be made of goods so discharged and placed in the custody of the marshal of the prize court varied, but—in principle—these goods could either be requisitioned by the government or sold under direction of the prize court with proceeds of the sale to be paid to the owners after the conclusion of peace under circumstances the court considered just.[73]

for determining destination in the case of contraband carriage. The unfortunate truth is that such conjecture is an inevitable result of the acceptance of the principle of ultimate enemy destination in any form. To say this, however, is not to justify the belligerent attempt to attach a legal liability to seizure of vessels and cargoes that have failed to obtain belligerent clearance prior to departure from neutral ports—a matter to be dealt with shortly

[71] Assuming, of course, that the principle of ultimate enemy destination is applicable to both.

[72] And experience indicates that there is less uncertainty—and less conjecture—involved in the attempt to determine the enemy origin of goods than in determining enemy destination.

[73] The text of the November 27th Order in Council, with later changes, is given in Hackworth, *op. cit.*, Vol. VII, pp. 138–40. (A French decree of November 28th substantially followed the British Order). A detailed account of the events leading up to the November 27th Order, as well as its operation, is given by Medlicott, *op. cit.*, pp. 112–24. Considerable neutral protest was raised against the measure, and numerous modifications were made to its operation. The measure was administered mainly by use of "certificates of origin and interest." These certificates, as Medlicott points out, "were issued in the form of a statement by the consular officer at the port of loading that he was satisfied that the merchandise in question had not been produced in enemy territory, and that no enemy person or firm, or firm on the Statutory list, had any interest in it. Separate certificates were required for each consignment, except in certain exceptional circumstances. . . ." Vessels outward bound from adjacent neutral ports were allowed to proceed if carrying cargoes covered by export passes. Vessels carrying cargoes not so covered were diverted to a contraband control base where a period of detention followed and inquiry was made into the origin and ownership of the goods.

The Order of November 27th served only as a prelude, however, to the later Order in Council of July 31, 1940. The relevant provisions of this later retaliatory Order read as follows.

> 2. Any vessel on her way to or from a port through which goods might reach or come from enemy territory or the enemy armed forces, not being provided with a Ship Navicert valid for the voyage on which she is engaged, shall, until the contrary is established, be deemed to be carrying contraband or goods of enemy origin or ownership, and shall be liable to seizure as Prize; provided that a vessel, other than a vessel which sailed from or has called at an enemy port, shall not be liable to seizure under the provisions of this Article unless she sailed from or could have called at a port at which she would, if duly qualified, have obtained a Ship Navicert.
>
> 3. (1) Goods consigned to any port or place from which they might reach enemy territory or the enemy armed forces, and not covered by a valid Cargo Navicert or, in the case of goods shipped from a British or Allied port, by a valid Export or Transshipment Licence, where such Licence is required, shall, until the contrary is established, be deemed to have an enemy destination.
>
> (2) Goods shipped from any port from which goods of enemy origin or ownership might have been shipped, and not covered by a valid Certificate of Origin and Interest, shall, until the contrary is established, be deemed to be of enemy origin or ownership.
>
> 4. Goods of enemy origin or ownership shall be liable to condemnation.
>
> 5. Any vessel seized under Article 2 hereof and carrying contraband or goods of enemy origin or ownership shall be liable to condemnation in respect of such carriage.[74]

---

[74] Statutory Rules and Orders, 1940, No. 1436. In the Preamble to the Order it was declared that "for the convenience of traders and for the avoidance of risks and delays inseparable from the diversion of ships into port in the exercise of belligerent rights against commerce at sea, a system has been instituted whereby passes can be obtained for approved cargoes and for ships which carry none but approved cargoes." Paragraph 1 of the Order contained the following definitions:

> "the term 'Cargo Navicert' means a pass issuable by the appropriate British or Allied authority in the neutral country of shipment in respect of goods consigned to any port or place from which they might reach the enemy, to the effect that, so far as is known at the date of issue, there is no objection to the consignment . . .
>
> "the term 'Certificate of Origin and Interest' means a pass issuable by the appropriate British or Allied authority in the neutral country
>
> "The term 'Ship Navicert' means a pass issuable to a vessel in respect of a given voyage by the appropriate British or Allied authority at all British, Allied or neutral ports, if that authority is satisfied that the vessel is duly qualified to receive it."

The principle, and novel, feature of the system of control thus introduced [75] may be found in the consequences attending the failure on the part of neutrals to obtain the belligerent's prior approval for voyages undertaken, and cargo shipped, to or from any port providing access to the enemy. By the terms of the Order liability to seizure was—in any event—justified when a vessel failed to carry a Ship Navicert or goods were not fully covered by Cargo Navicerts or Certificates of Origin and Interest. The presumptions held to arise as a result of such failure were sufficient—if not clearly rebutted—to warrant condemnation either of vessel or of cargo or of both. To these legal liabilities were added measures the exercise of which demanded no legal justification but whose effect in inducing neutral shipowners and traders to participate in the Allied control system was nevertheless very considerable. Thus the refusal on the part of neutral shipowners to undertake full compliance with Allied regulations entailed the deprivation of access to all British controlled facilities, e. g., bunkers, drydocking, repairing and insurance.[76]

[75] The background of the Order of July 31, 1940 deserves a few words. By July 1940, German conquests in Europe had rendered almost unworkable the system of contraband and enemy export controls heretofore exercised. Instead of patrolling only the supply routes leading to and from the principal ports of once adjacent neutrals, measures were now required to maintain close and direct control over practically the whole of the European coastline. To attempt this task through the use of naval patrols—which would continue to intercept neutral vessels—was evidently impossible in view of the coastline to be patrolled and the vessels of the Royal Navy available. Medlicott (*op. cit.*, pp. 416–7) has pointed out that even before the defeat of France "a complete naval blockade of German Europe was impossible . . . The result . . . was that a great extension of control at source . . became imperative. The naval blockade—the actual interception of blockade runners by ships of the Royal Navy—had, in other words, to be supplemented and, as far as possible, replaced by export control in all overseas territories from which these supplies could reach Europe." In brief, the former threat of interception and detention had to be replaced by other deterrents which would prove even more effective.

[76] A clear and detailed picture of the system of controls emerging from the Order of July 31, 1940 is given by Medlicott, *op. cit.*, pp. 422–62. In principle, this system rested upon three devices: compulsory navicerting, "ships warrants," and the rationing of neutrals. The nature of the first measure had already been indicated. "Ships warrants" were documents issued to each vessel whose owner agreed to comply with British regulations. In the absence of this document none of the British controlled facilities would be made available to the vessel. In addition, if even one vessel attempted to evade these regulations by carrying unnavicerted cargo all ships belonging to the same line might be denied a ship warrant. The rationing of neutrals implied the fixing of import quotas to be allowed neutral states, which were supposedly adequate for domestic consumption though not for re-export. The close interdependence of these three devices is made clear by Medlicott in the following passage: "The withholding of access to British-controlled facilities throughout the world supplied . . . an effective means of inducing neutral shipowners to compel traders to make the applications for navicerts which constituted the so-called compulsory system. It is also true that the compulsory navicert system was necessary to the success of the ship-warrant scheme. The scheme as a blockade weapon could be of full value only where there was machinery for the approval of cargoes and voyages, that is, where the navicert system was in operation. The success of the government's plans for the general control of neutral shipping in the interests of the Allies likewise depended to a considerable extent on the control of cargoes and the rationing of neutrals . . . as this would

In design, therefore, as in actual effect, the Order of July 31, 1940 imposed an almost complete control over neutral commerce, and did so by methods that bore little resemblance to the traditional law. Provided that neutrals submitted to this system of control, it is true that the Order made possible the avoidance of the risks and delays attendant upon the diversion of vessels into ports. This fact may be of relevance in judging the legitimacy of the Order as a measure of retaliation, but apart from retaliation the legal relevance of these "concessions" to neutral convenience must be doubted. Normally, a belligerent has no right to regulate neutral trade through the device of subjecting this trade to a legal liability to seizure merely for the reason that the neutral trader has not obtained the belligerent's prior approval.[77] Nor may neutrals safely expect that an enemy will fail to treat such compliance with one belligerent's regulations—even though made "compulsory"—as an act of unneutral service.[78]

D. CONCLUSIONS

The difficulties that frequently have been noted elsewhere in this study when attempting to evaluate the effect of recent belligerent practice upon the traditional law appear even more pronounced in the case of blockade.

enable the Ministry of Shipping to forecast accurately the amount of shipping required for the trade of a particular neutral. The rationing of the imports of adjacent neutrals was, in turn, almost indispensable as a basis for the compulsory navicert arrangements," (pp. 431–2). It may be noted that up to this point not only had navicerts been "voluntary" in character—insofar as their absence was no cause for seizure—but that neutral rationing had been attempted either by voluntary agreements (war trade agreements) with neutral states or by agreement with neutral shipping lines.

[77] In the case of the Order of July 31, 1940, the legal liability imposed was—as already noted—a liability to seizure and to eventual condemnation if the presumptions thus held to arise were not successfully rebutted. Sir G. G. Fitzmaurice (*op. cit.*, p. 87) points out that the Order "did not (and clearly could not), any more than was previously the case, *compel* shippers to take out navicerts as a precondition of effecting shipment. There was still no *legal* bar to shipment without a navicert . . . The real changes effected by it were, it would seem, that for the first time a legal *liability* to seizure was created, arising from the mere fact of the absence of a navicert, coupled with a legal presumption (unless and until rebutted) that unnavicerted goods had an enemy destination." But it is difficult to see why Fitzmaurice insists that shippers were not "compelled" to take out navicerts or why he cavils against describing the Order as establishing a "compulsory" navicert system. Admittedly, condemnation did not follow from the mere fact of the absence of a navicert, and in this particular sense the Order was not compulsory. But it is only in this sense true. From the point of view of subjecting unnavicerted vessels and cargoes to seizure—with a legal presumption of enemy destination—it certainly was compulsory. Besides, as a measure of reprisal the very purpose of the Order was, as Fitzmaurice himself points out, "to enlarge the normal legal powers of the Crown in the matter of effecting seizures and obtaining condemnations, for otherwise there would have been no point in it."—On the other hand, the opinion of S. W. D. Rowson, ("Prize Law During the Second World War," pp. 196–7), that the Order merely contains rules of a "procedural character" which are within the scope of a belligerent's normal legal powers, hardly seems acceptable.

[78] See pp. 322–3 for a brief comment on the navicert system—both in its voluntary and compulsory forms—in relation to unneutral service.

Undoubtedly, the principal reason for this added difficulty may be attributed to the almost uniform insistence of belligerents in justifying as reprisals measures designed to accomplish the purpose of blockade—as presently conceived—though without conforming to the traditional rules governing this belligerent measure.[79] In consequence, there is room for asserting that from the standpoint of a formal legal analysis it is unnecessary to go beyond an examination of the legitimacy of the measures reviewed in preceding pages, *as measures of reprisal;* that whatever judgment is made concerning the legitimacy of these measures, as measures of reprisal, it cannot affect the continued validity of the law governing blockade. If this position is adopted it would appear that the traditional law remains—on the whole—unchanged, with perhaps the one exception that breach of blockade may now be considered as extending to instances where either vessel or cargo is destined ultimately to a blockaded port (though immediately bound for a neutral port at the time of visit) by a route that requires passing through the blockaded area.[80]

At the same time, acceptance of this view entails at least the admission that in the circumstances characterizing recent naval hostilities the traditional blockade, and therefore a number of the rules governing its operation, have become largely irrelevant. If, however, recent belligerent practice is looked upon as a thinly veiled endeavor to replace the traditional law through the instrument of reprisals, and this would seem to represent the more realistic view, then the question of legal change must be squarely faced. It has already been pointed out that if the principle of ultimate

[79] In this connection note may be taken of the fact that, in contrast to World War I, there was no repeated attempt made by Great Britain in 1939 and 1940 to provide further justification for the reprisal measures taken against Germany by contending that the latter conformed, in substance at least if not in form, to the rules laid down for the traditional blockade. It would appear that one of the major reasons for this silence was the absence of firm protest against the British reprisal measures on the part of the United States.

[80] See *Law of Naval Warfare*, Article 632g (3). It will be apparent that the formulation presented above does not imply an unqualified application to blockade of the principle of ultimate enemy destination. On the contrary, it is only when vessel or cargo are destined to reach a blockaded port by way of the forbidden route that breach of blockade may arise. It would not apply, however, to goods ultimately destined to enemy territory under blockade if the goods are to reach their destination by a route that would not involve crossing the "lines of blockade." The difficulties that could easily arise in applying this qualified extension of the principle of ultimate enemy destination to blockade have already been noted (see p. 311 (n)). Nevertheless, it is not altogether clear that states have accepted even this limited change. Despite the assertion of Colombos (*op. cit.*, p. 256) and Stone (*op. cit.*, p. 498), that application of continuous voyage to blockade may now be considered an established principle of international law, there remains some question as to the general acceptance of this limited application of the principle with respect to cargoes, since the official position of a majority of naval powers has stopped short of a clear and unequivocal endorsement. Nor is it likely that there will be any attempt toward clarification, in view of recent developments in the law of contraband and the ready use that may be made of the instrument of reprisals in order to render enemy exports liable to seizure.

enemy destination is applicable to contraband there is no apparent reason for continuing to deny its unqualified application to blockade. On this basis, the further admission of the principle of ultimate enemy origin to blockade would appear as a necessary corollary.[81] Nevertheless, it would still remain necessary to insist that there is no warrant for asserting that other criteria used in determining the lawfulness of blockade measures have lost their validity. Blockades, in order to be binding, would still have to be effectively maintained, and the element of danger associated with an effective blockade would still have to be understood in terms of a liability to seizure—not to destruction upon entrance into the forbidden area.[82]

---

[81] The substance of this change, if endorsed, would involve the acceptance of the British reprisal measures of March 1915 and November 1939 (though not the measures of February 1917 and August 1940)—at least to the extent these measures implied the desirability of extending the principles of ultimate enemy destination and origin to blockades which are otherwise conducted in conformity with the traditional rules.

[82] Thus a belligerent could not argue that the necessity for patrolling vast areas of the high seas thereby excused him from meeting the traditional requirement of effectiveness. Nor could a belligerent—apart from reprisal—impose upon neutral vessels a liability to seizure and—possibly—to condemnation, unless neutral traders submitted to a system of control which thereby permitted the belligerent to ease his burden of assigning large surface forces to the task of intercepting blockade runners. The British reprisal Order of July 31, 1940 would still have to find its justification as a reprisal. Certainly, when judged by the traditional law it could have no other justification than as a reprisal.

XI. UNNEUTRAL SERVICE

Apart from the carriage of contraband and the breach of blockade the subjects of a neutral state may assist a belligerent in a number of ways. Almost all of these various acts of assistance may be considered as falling within the category of unneutral service. It must be stated at the outset that the present position of the law relating to unneutral service is one over which widespread dissatisfaction has been expressed, and rightly so. Difficulty has been experienced in defining the distinguishing features of unneutral service. Covering as it does a great variety of disparate acts the concept of unneutral service has come to signify little more than any service rendered by a neutral subject to a belligerent contrary to international law, excluding the acts of contraband carriage and blockade breach.[1]

The vagueness characterizing the concept of unneutral service therefore provides one reason for the divergencies that have often attended attempts to enumerate the specific acts making up this category. To the foregoing must be added the peculiarities that have marked the historical development of this area of the law. During the nineteenth century the efforts of states were directed primarily to the task of regulating contraband and blockade. The development of rules regulating the acts whereby neutrals rendered assistance to a belligerent, but which fell outside contraband and blockade, was sporadic and uneven. Unneutral service was conceived largely in terms of the carriage of certain persons and dispatches for a belligerent, and frequently treated as a situation analagous to the carriage of contraband. Little attention was given to other acts that might qualify as coming within this category. Nor does there appear to have been any serious attempt to distinguish more clearly between the various possible acts of unneutral service and to attach consequences to their commission commensurate with the precise nature and degree of assistance rendered a belligerent.

In the provisions of the 1909 Declaration of London relating to unneutral service the endeavor was made not only to provide a greater measure of uniformity in the practice of states than had previously existed, but also to enlarge upon those acts that could be regarded as constituting unneutral service. The Declaration sought further to distinguish between acts whose commission would result in the same treatment a neutral vessel

[1] This can hardly be regarded as a satisfactory definition, yet is perhaps the best that can be given. No doubt it is true that acts of unneutral service generally involve a closer relationship with, and a greater degree of control by, a belligerent than is the case in contraband carriage. But as will be presently noted, there are some acts of unneutral service that appear to require no more intense a relationship with a belligerent than is involved in the carriage of contraband.

would undergo when liable to condemnation on account of carrying contraband and acts whose commission would result in neutral vessels receiving the same treatment as that accorded enemy merchant vessels. But since the Declaration was never ratified its provisions relating to unneutral service have never been binding upon states. Even as a general indication of what the practice of states ought to be in this regard Articles 45–47 of the Declaration of London may no longer be considered as wholly satisfactory. The conditions in which naval hostilities are now conducted have been greatly transformed during the past half century. This transformation has undeniably affected the kinds of aid a neutral may render to a belligerent (thus extending the scope of unneutral service) as well as the severity of the measures a belligerent may take in preventing an enemy from receiving such assistance.

The resulting situation is, therefore, not essentially unlike the situation encountered in many other areas of the law relating to neutrality in naval warfare; no clear and continuous development can be traced from nineteenth century practice to the present. Nevertheless, it is apparent that the scope of unneutral service has expanded and that the consequences attached to the performance of acts coming within this category have—in certain instances at least—become more rigorous. In fact, the variety of acts included within the category of unneutral service prevents a useful discussion either of the general characteristics of acts of unneutral service or of the general liabilities attending the commission of these acts. As distinguished from contraband carriage and blockade breach, the consequences following upon the commission of acts of unneutral service may be almost as varied as the acts themselves.

A. ACTS OF UNNEUTRAL SERVICE RESULTING IN LIABILITY TO THE SAME TREATMENT AS ENEMY WARSHIPS

The most serious forms of unneutral service occur when neutral merchant vessels (or neutral private aircraft [2]) directly participate in the military operations of a belligerent, either by entering into the actual hostilities or by serving in any capacity as a naval or military auxiliary to

[2] In the discussion to follow it is assumed that the rules relating to unneutral service are, at the very least, equally applicable to neutral private aircraft. This is surely a conservative assumption, and it is altogether likely that as practice with respect to neutral aircraft develops the rules regulating the behavior of the latter will be much more severe. The 1923 Hague Rules of Aerial Warfare offer little guidance in this respect, providing only that "a neutral private aircraft is liable to capture if it is engaged in unneutral service" (Article 53 (c)). Certainly, the draft rules relating to the control of radio in time of war, and rendering an aircraft liable to be fired upon if found transmitting information for the immediate military use of an enemy, may be expected to be acted upon by a belligerent. Furthermore, neutral private aircraft found directly participating in hostilities or serving as an auxiliary to a belligerent's armed forces may be expected to receive similar treatment. But what of neutral private aircraft operating directly under the control or orders of a belligerent, even though not performing

belligerent forces (e. g., as colliers, troopships; laying of mines, reconnoitering). In performing these acts neutral merchant vessels (and aircraft) are considered to acquire an enemy character and must bear the same treatment accorded to enemy warships (and military aircraft). As such they are always liable to capture and—if necessary—to attack and destruction on sight.[3]

services related to military operations? And, finally, what of neutral aircraft known to be transporting enemy persons—particularly persons incorporated in the armed forces of an enemy—though not under the direct control or orders of an enemy? It would be futile to present an oversimplified analogy to the rules governing neutral merchant vessels. Where interception and seizure is rendered impossible, neutral private aircraft will run the strong risk of being shot down when known to be engaged in the above described acts. Nor is it clear that such action on the part of a belligerent would necessarily prove unlawful.

[3] *Law of Naval Warfare*, Article 501a: "Neutral merchant vessels and aircraft acquire enemy character and are liable to the same treatment as *enemy warships and military aircraft* when engaged in the following acts:

1. Taking a direct part in the hostilities on the side of an enemy;
2. Acting in any capacity as a naval or military auxiliary to an enemy's armed forces."

On the other hand, Article 46 of the Declaration of London stated: "A neutral vessel is liable to be condemned and, in a general way, is liable to the same treatment which she would undergo if she were a merchant vessel of the enemy·

(1) If she takes a direct part in the hostilities.
(2) If she is under the orders or control of an agent placed on board by the enemy Government.
(3) If she is chartered entire by the enemy Government.
(4) If she is at the time and exclusively either devoted to the transport of enemy troops or to the transmission of information in the interest of the enemy

"In the cases specified in the present Article, the goods belonging to the owner of the vessel are likewise liable to condemnation."

Neither paragraphs 2 nor 3 of Article 46 of necessity involve acts in direct support of a belligerent's military operations, but paragraphs 1 and 4 do clearly imply such support. In this latter respect, then, there is an evident divergence between Article 46 of the Declaration of London and Article 501a of the *Law of Naval Warfare* (as well as the position taken in the text above), the difference consisting in the more severe treatment permitted by the latter. There is strong support for the position that the acts in question should be regarded, when performed by neutral vessels, as resulting in the same treatment as enemy warships. Thus Articles 2 and 61 of the French Naval Instructions of 1934, and Articles 141, 179, and 180 of the Italian War Law of 1938, provide for either the attack upon or capture of neutral merchant vessels directly participating in hositlities. See also *Harvard Draft Convention on Rights and Duties of Neutral States in Naval and Aerial War*, *op. cit.*, pp. 653 ff. Article 65 of the Harvard Draft Convention, which is described in the commentary as correctly reflecting existing law, states that: "A belligerent may treat as an enemy warship: (a) A neutral vessel taking a direct part in hostilities on the side of the enemy; (b) a neutral vessel exclusively engaged at the time in the transportation of enemy troops." Articles 38–40 of the German Prize Law Code of September 1939 are, in this respect, somewhat equivocal, though the same inference may be drawn. And for a clear statement in support of the more severe treatment, see H. A. Smith, *op. cit.*, pp. 101, 105.—It is interesting to note that Article 16 of the U. S. Naval War Code of 1900 provided that: "Neutral vessels in the military or naval service of the enemy, or under the control of the enemy for military or naval purposes, are subject to capture or destruction." Whereas the 1917 and 1941 *Instructions* followed the Declaration of London, Article 501a of the *Law of Naval Warfare* signifies—in a sense—a return to this earlier and more severe position.

The general principle involved is reasonably clear, and no attempt need be made to enumerate all of the acts that may result in this assimilation to an enemy's armed forces. It is not the mere fact of assisting a belligerent that permits this severe treatment. Nor is it simply the consideration that the belligerent exercises a close control and direction over the neutral merchant vessel. The decisive consideration is rather that the services rendered are in direct support of the belligerent's military operations. It is this support, leading as it does to the identification of the neutral merchant vessel (or aircraft) with the belligerent's naval or military forces, that permits a treatment similar to that meted out to these forces.

These considerations would seem to have an even broader application. It may be recalled that in an earlier discussion[4] concerning the liability of enemy merchant vessels to attack it was concluded that the retention of immunities traditionally granted belligerent merchant vessels is dependent upon their not being integrated in any manner into the belligerents military effort at sea. Among the acts which may lead to such integration are sailing under convoy of belligerent warships or military aircraft and participation in the intelligence system of a belligerent's armed forces. There would appear to be no valid reason why neutral merchant vessels should escape treatment similar to that taken against belligerent merchant vessels, if found performing these same acts. It is true that the acts do not of necessity imply either direct participation in hostilities or serving as a naval or military auxiliary to a belligerent. Yet the relationship to the belligerent's military effort is sufficiently close to warrant the loss of the exemption from attack and destruction that must normally be accorded neutral merchant vessels.[5]

---

[4] See pp. 67–70.

[5] In the case of neutral vessels under convoy of belligerent warships the high degree of identification with the belligerent whose protection is sought is obvious. Although opinion has been unsettled in the past over the consequences to be attached to this act there is now a substantial consensus that the mere fact of enemy convoy is sufficient to assimilate a neutral vessel to the status of the belligerent warships providing protection. For a review of pre-World War II practice, see *Harvard Draft Convention on Rights and Duties of Neutral States in Naval and Aerial War*, *op. cit.*, pp. 674–80. A similar conclusion may be drawn with respect to neutral merchant vessels that deliberately reveal the position of the warships of one belligerent to an enemy. There is no reason why the neutral vessel that sends in position reports on belligerent warships should receive preferential treatment over enemy merchant vessels performing the same act, and the latter are, in this case, liable to attack (see pp. 67–8). In this respect, Article 6, paragraphs 1 and 2, of the unratified 1923 Hague Rules for the Control of Radio in Time of War provided:

> "The transmission by radio by a vessel or an aircraft, whether enemy or neutral, when on or over the high seas of military intelligence for the immediate use of a belligerent is to be deemed a hostile act and will render the vessel or aircraft liable to be fired upon.
>
> 2. A neutral vessel or neutral aircraft which transmits when on or over the high seas information destined for a belligerent concerning military operations or military forces shall be liable to capture. The Prize Court may condemn the vessel or aircraft if it considers that the circumstances justify condemnation."

H. A. Smith (*op. cit.*, p. 108) states of these provisions: "The wording is not quite so clear as

B. ACTS OF UNNEUTRAL SERVICE RESULTING IN LIABILITY TO THE SAME TREATMENT AS ENEMY MERCHANT VESSELS

Neutral merchant vessels (and aircraft) may be found operating directly under the control of a belligerent government, though not in support of the belligerent's military operations at sea. Thus a neutral vessel may be chartered entire to a belligerent government for the purpose of undertaking commercial voyages. If not chartered it may nevertheless be under the orders of an agent placed on board by the belligerent government. The precise form such control may take will vary, but in all instances where neutral merchant vessels are found to be operating directly under enemy control, orders, charter, employment, or direction, they may be considered as having thereby acquired enemy character and are liable to the same treatment normally accorded enemy merchant vessels.[6]

The reason for distinguishing between the present and the preceding category must be found in the nature of the service that is performed. In both categories there is a close identification with the belligerent on whose behalf the acts of unneutral service are performed, and it is this identification with—or control by—a belligerent that permits the imputation of enemy character to neutral merchant vessels. But in the former category the identification extends to the belligerent's armed forces and to his military operations at sea, whereas in the present category this is not the case. Although acquiring enemy character because operating directly under enemy orders or control, such neutral merchant vessels must not be attacked and destroyed at sight so long as they remain clear of all participation in, or direct support of, combat operations.

In this connection a problem of considerable importance arises as a result of the attempt by belligerents to institute a system of passes for neutral shipping. In principle, it is clear that such devices as the navicert and ships warrant are intended to establish an effective control over the activities of neutral merchant vessels. Neutral merchant vessels by submitting to such a system thereby ease the belligerent's task of patrolling the high seas in search either of contraband carriers or of blockade runners. It seems reasonably well-established that a neutral merchant vessel in accepting a safe-conduct pass from a belligerent subjects itself to the control of the latter and performs an act of unneutral service. The same conclusion would appear warranted in the case of a neutral vessel that cooperates with a belligerent by voluntarily applying for, and accepting, a navicert or

it might be, and Article 6 (1) should not be interpreted as meaning that a neutral vessel or aircraft not otherwise engaged in the enemy service may be sunk without warning merely because she makes a signal that warships are in the neighborhood. The use of force without warning can only be justified if there is a deliberate intention to transmit intelligence of military value to the enemy."

6 See *Law of Naval Warfare*, Article 501b.

ship's warrant.[7] If this reasoning is accepted then it must be further acknowledged that Germany would have been on solid ground in seizing and condemning neutral merchant vessels during both World Wars for the mere act of sailing with a navicert issued by the Allied authorities.[8]

---

[7] And as might be expected, a substantial number of German writers have taken the view—which is not easy to refute—that any neutral vessel submitting to the type of contraband controls established by Great Britain during the two World Wars commits an act of unneutral service. See, for example, Bruns, *op. cit.*, p. 85.

[8] The above conclusions are by no means generally accepted, however, and it must be admitted that the entire problem raised by navicerts is still a matter of doubt and uncertainty In both World Wars Germany threatened to treat neutral vessels participating in the Allied system of navicerts as acquiring enemy character by virtue of submitting to Allied control, though in practice the German conduct of unrestricted submarine warfare precluded any substantive development in German prize law with respect to the rules governing unneutral service. In one World War II decision, however, the German Supreme Prize Tribunal did consider the implications of the navicert system at some length. Thus in *The Ole Wegger and Other Vessels* [1942], a number of Norwegian whaling vessels were condemned which operated for the Norwegian Shipping and Trade Mission in London. The vessels were found to be under the control of the British Government, and thereby engaging in unneutral service in the sense of Article 38 (3) of the German Prize Law Code ("Aid to the enemy occurs if a vessel is chartered by the enemy government or is under its command or its control"). Part of the evidence accepted by the *Oberprisenhof* as proof that the vessels were under enemy control was the presence on board of ships' warrants issued by the British Ministry of War Transport, in accordance with the Order in Council of July 31, 1940. The following passages taken from the judgment deal with navicerts and ships' warrants respectively, and in view of their interest are quoted at some length:

> ". . . In examining the application for a navicert, the British authorities may obtain valuable information concerning the purpose and destination of the proposed voyage. This applies all the more in the case of a ship's navicert. It has practically the effect of a safe-conduct, which is intended to guide ships safely through the British contraband control. Moreover, the British authorities are thus enabled to extend the preliminary examination to the entire cargo of the ship. Any further examination on the high seas or in the port of control need therefore only ascertain whether the ship and its cargo are covered by the navicert. This means a considerable relief for the British naval forces, for the examining man-of-war is soon freed for other tasks . . .
>
> ". . . The control which is sought by the introduction of ships warrants . . . aims not at the prohibition of an individual voyage by means of military measures, but at the planned control of the entire maritime traffic of a shipowner by British authorities, with the intention thus to eliminate the application of military measures in the individual case, either entirely or in part . . . It is precisely a control of this kind, however, which is envisaged by Article 38 (3) of the German Prize Regulations. A vessel subject to this control thereby assists and facilitates the military and economic conduct of warfare of the enemy Government, and, subject to the special circumstances of the case, renders unneutral service." *Annual Digest and Reports of Public International Law Cases, 1943–45*, Case no. 193, pp. 532–7.

No clear indication was given as to the nature of the "special circumstances" referred to in the concluding sentence. It does appear though that the fact that navicerts or ships' warrants are made "compulsory" by one belligerent was not interpreted as necessarily depriving the other belligerent of the right to seize neutral merchant vessels (for hostile assistance) which complied with the system. And it may be noted that in response to action by the German Government during World War I (1918), whereby Swedish steamers carrying non-contraband cargoes to overseas countries were granted safe-conduct passes, the United States (Great Britain

C. ACTS OF UNNEUTRAL SERVICE RESULTING IN LIABILITY TO SEIZURE

A neutral merchant vessel may aid a belligerent by the performance of acts that result in no greater a degree of identification with the belligerent than is involved in the normal case of contraband carriage. It is therefore important to distinguish not only between the nature of the services performed on behalf of an enemy but also between the varying degrees of identification with an enemy that may be involved quite apart from the specific services. In undertaking to carry certain persons or dispatches for a belligerent a neutral vessel may be operating in the exclusive employment, or under the direct control, of the former. The enemy character thereby acquired by the vessel is the consequence of the intensity of the relationship maintained with the belligerent rather than of the actual services that are performed. On the other hand, the carriage of certain persons or dispatches may be undertaken in much the same manner as the carriage of contraband, that is without implying a direct control by—or a close relationship with—the belligerent. In the latter event the unneutral service thus rendered a belligerent results in a liability to seizure and to subsequent condemnation. Nevertheless, the vessel in performing these acts does not lose her neutral character, and the act of seizure therefore places a much more serious responsibility upon the captor than is normally incurred with respect to the seizure of enemy merchant vessels (or of neutral vessels that may be considered as having acquired enemy character).[9]

---

and France concurring) declared in a note to the European neutrals that "such control may operate to deprive vessels accepting the same of their neutral character, and the United States Government accordingly reserves the right to deal with any vessel which has subjected itself to enemy control as the circumstances in each case may warrant." cited in Hackworth, *op. cit.*, Vol. VII, pp. 106–7.—Rowson (*op. cit.*, pp. 197–8) expresses the opinion that "when navicerts are voluntary the degree of voluntary cooperation with a belligerent which is demanded of the neutral implies unneutral service on his part towards the other belligerent, to whom corresponding rights are automatically given. When navicerts are compulsory, the neutral had no choice and the opposing belligerent was not justified in drawing irrebuttable conclusions unfavorable to the neutral in respect of the carriage of goods covered by a navicert to neutral territory." On this reasoning the Order in Council of July 31, 1940 may be understood as reducing a neutral vessel's liability for unneutral service, since the neutral shipper had the choice either of complying with the system thus introduced or of risking seizure (with the presumption—rebuttable—of carrying goods with an enemy destination or origin). But Rowson's argument is open to serious question. Nor does it appear to have been accepted in the decision of the *Oberprisenhof*, quoted above. The truth of the matter is, it would seem, that neutral merchant vessels have been placed by belligerents in an unenviable position, since measures on the part of one belligerent compelling neutral vessels to comply with a system of contraband controls may nevertheless allow an enemy to seize vessels so complying on the basis that the latter have committed an act of unneutral service.

[9] See pp. 349–54 dealing with the destruction of neutral merchant vessels following their seizure.

1. *Carriage of Enemy Persons*

According to the customary law a belligerent was entitled to prevent neutral vessels from transporting persons actually incorporated in the armed forces of an enemy. On this point at least state practice during the nineteenth century was clear, and neutral vessels that knowingly transported military or naval personnel in the service of an enemy were liable to seizure and subsequent condemnation. Equally well settled was the rule that in the absence of a treaty a belligerent had no right to remove any enemy persons—including military or naval personnel—from a neutral vessel on the high seas without first seizing the offending vessel and placing her in prize.[10]

On many points, however, the practice of states was uncertain. The right of a belligerent to prevent the carriage of enemy persons other than those embodied in the armed forces of an enemy furnished an example. At least one state, Great Britain, claimed the right to seize neutral vessels if found carrying enemy agents sent out on public service of an enemy, at the public expense of an enemy.[11] Still further, it was not entirely clear

[10] The rule forbidding removal on the high seas was affirmed during the American Civil War in the case of the *Trent*. The *Trent*, a British mail steamer on her way from Havana to Nassau, was intercepted by the U. S. S. *San Jacinto* and compelled to surrender two Confederate commissioners sent out by the Confederate Government to represent the latter in France and Great Britain. Both the commissioners, Mason and Slidell, as well as their secretaries, were made prisoners of war. Great Britain immediately demanded their release, contending, in the first instance, that since the terminus of the voyage was neutral territory the persons seized could not be regarded as "contraband of war," and a neutral vessel carrying such persons could not be considered liable to seizure for contraband carriage. Later, Great Britain contended that a neutral vessel could not be prevented from carrying diplomatic agents sent out by a belligerent to represent it in a neutral state. The United States, although complying with the demand for release of the prisoners, maintained that the error on the part of the capturing officer consisted only in a failure to have seized the *Trent* and to have brought the vessel in for adjudication. For a brief account of the incident see Hyde, *op. cit.*, pp. 2165–7. No agreement was reached on the status of Mason and Slidell, but it would appear that if not diplomatic representatives in the strict sense (if only because the Confederacy had not been accorded recognition at the time by neutral states) they came very close to this status. In any event, this aspect of the incident does illustrate the rule—which remains valid today—that a neutral vessel carrying *bona fide* diplomatic representatives sent out by a belligerent to a neutral state, or returning from a neutral state, is not liable to seizure for such carriage. Nor can a belligerent intercept the vessel and remove the personnel. The incident of the *Trent* also illustrated the inapplicability of the law of contraband to cases involving the carriage of enemy persons. Having a neutral destination, Mason and Slidell were not "contraband." On the other hand, seizure of the vessel might have been based on the ground that they were public agents in the service of the enemy and sent out at the public expense of the enemy.

[11] Both the 1866 and 1888 editions of the British Manual of Naval Prize Law made provision to this effect. For a general review of the entire problem, see *U. S. Naval War College, International Law Situations, 1928*, pp. 74 ff. Very doubtful is the claim that prior to World War I a neutral vessel could be seized and condemned if found making a voyage with a view to transporting individuals (e. g., reservists), who though not incorporated at the time of seizure in the enemy's armed forces would become so upon reaching enemy territory. But Oppenheim-Lauterpacht (*op. cit.*, p. 833) and Stone (*op. cit.*, p. 514), among other writers, contend that

whether a vessel could be condemned for carrying persons in the armed forces of an enemy if both the owner and master of the vessel were found to be ignorant of this fact.[12]

But Article 45 of the Declaration of London stated with respect to the carriage of enemy persons that the liability of a neutral vessel to condemnation and, in general, to the same treatment accorded as for the carriage of contraband would arise in the following circumstances:

> (1) If she is making a voyage especially with a view to the transport of individual passengers who are embodied in the armed forces of the enemy . . .
>
> (2) If, with the knowledge of the owner, of the one who charters the vessel entire, or of the master, she is transporting a military detachment of the enemy, or one or more persons who, during the voyage, lend direct assistance to the enemy.[13]

Article 47 of the Declaration contained a provision, at the time altogether novel, which read as follows:

> Any individual embodied in the armed force of the enemy, and who is found on board a neutral merchant vessel, may be made a prisoner of war, even though there be no ground for the capture of the vessel.

It would prove difficult to state with any assurance the precise modifications the provisions of Article 45 would have made—if generally accepted—in the customary law, since in many respects the latter was far from clear. In general it may be said that Article 45 sought to restrict quite severely belligerent powers. In substance, the category of persons neutral vessels were forbidden to carry was limited to persons "embodied in the armed forces of an enemy," and even then condemnation could follow only if the vessel was either making a voyage "especially with a view to

---

the customary rules allowed seizure in this latter instance. No mention is made of the point in pre-World War I British prize manuals, nor is the matter dealt with in the 1900 U. S. Naval War Code. But there need hardly be any doubt over this point today. As will be noted presently, vessels making such voyages are liable to seizure and condemnation.

[12] Or if those in control of the neutral vessel were forcibly constrained to carry enemy military or naval personnel. In either case, however, the vessel could be seized on probable suspicion of acting in the service of the enemy. Failure to obtain subsequent condemnation of the vessel did not serve to prevent the captor from removing the noxious personnel—once in the captor's port—and making them prisoners of war.

[13] Article 45 went on to state that in the circumstances described—which included in paragraph 1 "the transmission of information in the interest of the enemy"—goods belonging to the owner of the vessel were likewise liable to condemnation. The concluding paragraph of Article 45 declared that the provisions of the Article "do not apply if when the vessel is encountered at sea she is unaware of the opening of hostilities, or if the master, after becoming aware of the hostilities, has not been able to disembark the passengers. The vessel is deemed to know of the state of war if she left an enemy port after the opening of hostilities, or a neutral port after there had been made in sufficient time a notification of the opening of hostilities to the Power to which such port belongs."

the transport of individual passengers" or knowingly transporting a "military detachment" of the enemy.[14] Article 47, however, went in the other direction of granting belligerents a power heretofore denied them by the customary law. Nevertheless, this power to remove persons from neutral vessels, even though "there be no ground for the capture of the vessel," extended only to individuals embodied in the armed forces of an enemy.[15] As it turned out this provision too was destined to give rise to later controversy between neutrals, who maintained Article 47 represented an unwarranted extension of the belligerent's right to interfere with neutral vessels, and the belligerents, who considered Article 47 as being far too restrictive in modern conditions.

Since 1914 state practice with respect to the carriage of enemy persons has therefore been very unsettled. At the beginning of the hostilities a number of the belligerents accepted Articles 45 and 47 of the Declaration of London, only to modify them—by way of extending belligerent powers of intercepting enemy persons—as the war progressed. The neutral states, as might be expected, fell back upon the strictest possible interpretation of belligerent powers. The result has been that the disputants have appealed, as the circumstances of their respective situations dictated, to the customary rules, to the provisions of the Declaration of London, and to the novel conditions alleged to justify departure from both the customary law and the Declaration of London.

Doubtless a belligerent must be accorded, at the very minimum, those powers provided for in Article 45 of the Declaration of London. Where a neutral vessel is encountered making a special voyage for the transport of members of an enemy's armed forces she may be seized and condemned. Nor does it appear useful any longer to question the belligerent right to seize neutral vessels specially undertaking to transport individuals who, upon reaching an enemy destination, will be incorporated into the enemy's armed forces. The same right of seizure may be considered applicable to neutral vessels found making a voyage for the purpose of conveying public agents of an enemy (though not *bona fide* diplomatic representatives of an enemy destined to or from a neutral state), regardless of whether such conveyance is to an enemy destination or to a neutral state, so long as the purpose is to promote the military operations of the enemy. Admittedly, neither of these latter grounds for seizure were recognized by the Declaration of London, and their support in the customary law is questionable. Yet it is clear that in each instance the neutral merchant vessel renders a distinct

[14] The additional category of "persons who, during the voyage, lend direct assistance to the enemy" is far from clear and never seems to have been satisfactorily explained.

[15] Thus, Article 47 compensated in part for the restrictions contained in Article 45. Belligerents could remove enemy military personnel from neutral vessels even though these personnel were traveling in a private capacity and at their own expense. Nor did it matter—according to Article 45—that the owner or master of the vessel possessed no knowledge of the status of the passengers carried.

and important service to an enemy, and one which belligerents can hardly be obliged to permit.

In practice, however, the core of neutral-belligerent controversy during the two World Wars has concerned the circumstances in which a belligerent is entitled to intercept a neutral merchant vessel at sea and, though not seizing the vessel, to remove certain categories of enemy persons found on board. It should be noted that there are two distinct, though related, questions involved here. The first is whether or not there is a belligerent right of removal at all, except after first seizing the vessel for due cause and sending her in for adjudication. And if there is a right of removal that may be exercised either in place of, or independently from, seizure, to what categories of enemy individuals does this right extend?

Despite neutral opposition during World War I to conceding any belligerent right to remove enemy persons from neutral merchant vessels at sea, it would now seem that—in principle—the practice of states may be regarded as having sanctioned this belligerent measure.[16] Nor does it appear that a

[16] The attitude of the United States in World War I, both as a neutral and later as a belligerent, is reviewed in Hackworth, *op. cit.*, Vol. VI, pp. 622–38, and *U. S. Naval War College, International Law Situations, 1928*, pp. 90 ff. In brief, the position of the United States was that there existed no legal right—apart from treaty—to remove any enemy person from a neutral vessel on the high seas without first seizing the vessel and placing it in prize. Seizure was considered justified only when exercised in order to prevent a neutral vessel from knowingly engaging in the transport of individuals actually incorporated in the armed forces of an enemy. Thus Article 45 of the Declaration of London was accepted whereas Article 47 was rejected, a position confirmed in paragraphs 36 and 89 of the 1917 *Instructions*. Yet in reviewing World War I practice, and its effects upon the law, the Naval War College concluded in 1928 that: "It is now generally admitted . . . that a belligerent should be permitted to remove enemy combatants from a neutral vessel and that it should not be longer necessary to bring such a vessel to port to render such action lawful" (p. 106). And the 1941 *Instructions* stipulated in paragraph 92 that: "Enemy nationals found on board neutral or enemy merchant vessels as passengers who are actually embodied in the military forces of the enemy, or in public service of the enemy, or who may be engaged in or suspected of service in the interests of the enemy, may be made prisoners of war." As will presently be seen, all of the belligerents during World War II asserted the right to remove enemy military personnel from neutral vessels, and—as distinguished from World War I—the disputes with neutrals no longer concerned the exercise of the right itself but the extent of the right. Thus in the case of the *Asama Maru*, which involved the removal by a British warship in January 1940 of twenty-one German nationals carried on board a Japanese steamship, the Japanese Government did not deny the right of a belligerent to remove enemy military personnel from a neutral vessel on the high seas. (Indeed, the Japanese Naval Regulations in World War I had expressly permitted the practice.) What the Japanese did deny was the right of a belligerent to remove enemy persons other than those incorporated in an enemy's armed forces. The incident of the *Asama Maru* is carefully reviewed by H. W. Briggs, "Removal of Enemy Persons From Neutral Vessels On The High Seas," *A. J. I. L.*, 34 (1940), pp. 249 ff. Professor Briggs concludes, however, that even by 1940 there existed "no legal right of removal of any enemy person from a neutral vessel on the high seas." Contrast this view with that expressed by Hyde (*op. cit.*, p. 2173): "It is believed that, at the present time, an enemy person whom a belligerent may lawfully intercept in transit, such as one embodied in an armed force and en route for a military service, may be justly removed from the neutral ship of which he is an occupant."

right of removal can be exercised by belligerents only as an alternative to the lawful seizure and condemnation of neutral merchant vessels. For the right of removal may be exercised even though no sufficient reason may exist for the seizure of a neutral vessel.[17]

The further problem of the categories of enemy persons that a belligerent may remove from neutral vessels remains unsettled. A strict interpretation of this belligerent right would probably admit—following Article 47 of the Declaration of London—the removal only of those persons actually embodied in the armed forces of an enemy and, perhaps, public agents sent out in the service of an enemy to perform missions directly related to the conduct of military operations. But belligerents have not demonstrated a readiness to adhere to this restrictive interpretation and have insisted upon including reservists, and even all able-bodied enemy nationals capable of rendering military service upon reaching their home country.[18] More recently it has been suggested that the belligerent right of removal should extend to any enemy individual returning to his own country who may prove of value to the war effort [19] (not merely the military effort in a narrow sense). And on the basis of this reasoning belligerents might easily assert a right of removal to include any enemy national sent out by his government to a neutral country, there to undertake services in support of the enemy's war effort.

[17] As, for example, when a neutral vessel engaged in a normal commercial voyage but is found carrying passengers who, though embodied in the armed forces of an enemy, are traveling in a private capacity at their own expense.

[18] The British view, expressed in a note to the Japanese Government during the *Asama Maru* incident, cited in Briggs (*op. cit.*, pp. 250–1) is that: ". . under modern conditions, where conscription laws impose a liability to military or naval service on all able-bodied males, it is obvious that a right to remove 'military persons' would be illusory if it did not cover individuals who, though not on the peace-time strength of their country's armed forces, are under a legal liability to serve and are actually on their way to take their place in the ranks. Such persons are precisely those who are likely to be found travelling on neutral ships in time of war . . ." The French Instructions of 1934, in Article 64, provided for the removal of enemy persons from neutral vessels—even where no cause existed for capturing the vessel—if making up a part of the armed forces, if en route to join these forces and, finally, if capable of military service (*aptes au service militaire*). On the other hand, the German Prize Law Code of 1939 provided, in Article 77, that enemy persons undertaking a voyage on neutral vessels in order to join the enemy armed forces could be made prisoners of war only after the vessel had been captued (presumably on any one of a number of grounds). It may also be noted that Article 38 (5) of the German Code declared that: "Aid to the enemy occurs if a vessel undertakes the voyage for the purpose of transmitting messages in the interests of the enemy or conveying members of the enemy forces or persons desirous of joining the enemy forces . " In effect, then, the Code did not appear to stipulate a right of removal independent of capture.

[19] In a current review of the problem the observation has been made that it "appears unlikely that the old rules concerning the removal of persons from neutral shipping can much longer survive, even extended to include reservists and that it would appear foolhardy for a nation to permit any person of value to an enemy's war effort—particularly scientists—to return to his own country." Cmdr. Joe Munster, U. S. Navy, "Removal of Persons from Neutral Shipping," *The Judge Advocate General Journal*, (October, 1952), p. 18.

Certainly these latter suggestions cannot be taken—and are not put forward—as indicative of present law, however prophetic they may be in pointing the way to future practice. But where the precise limits to the belligerent right of removal may now be placed is a matter upon which no final word can be given.[20]

2. *Carriage of Dispatches*

According to the customary practice of states the carriage of dispatches for a belligerent is treated on the same basis as the carriage of enemy persons. Neutral merchant vessels found carrying dispatches of a public nature for and in the service of a belligerent, and particularly dispatches concerning military operations, are liable to seizure and condemnation.[21] But one clear exception to this rule covers the official correspondence maintained between an enemy and a neutral state. Since a neutral state has the undoubted right to carry on official intercourse with the belligerents, such correspondence as it may send to, or receive from, belligerents is inviolable, and neutral merchant vessels conveying these dispatches must not, for that reason, be seized.[22] Furthermore, according to Hague Convention XI (1907) enemy dispatches in the form of ordinary postal correspondence are normally considered as inviolable, and a neutral merchant vessel carrying such dispatches among her postal correspondence is not, for that reason, liable to seizure.[23]

In view of the developments in the means of communication the carriage of dispatches now forms a subject of distinctly limited importance, but to the extent that it is still applicable to hostilities at sea the customary rules remain valid, though subject to the modifications already observed in examining the rules governing the carriage of enemy persons.[24] On the

[20] For one indication of the interpretation presently given to the belligerent right of removal see *Law of Naval Warfare*, Article 513.

[21] Such carriage may occur between two parts of an enemy's territory, between two enemy states, or between an enemy agent abroad in a neutral state and his government.

[22] Thus the correspondence between a neutral government and that government's representative in an enemy state must not be disturbed, even though it may contain information harmful to the interests of the other belligerent. The same immunity seems to extend to the carriage of dispatches between an enemy government and its diplomatic representatives in neutral states.

[23] But Article 2 of Hague Convention XI states that neutral mail ships are not exempt from the rules governing neutral merchant ships in general, and although they cannot be seized for carrying enemy dispatches among their regular postal correspondence, neutral mail ships may be seized for unneutral service. For a more general discussion on mail in time of war, see pp. 90–5.

[24] These changes will principally concern the belligerent right to remove disptaches from a neutral vessel without seizing the vessel as prize. The customary rule forbidding removal without seizure was equally applicable to enemy persons and dispatches. But the Declaration of London, while providing in Article 47 for the removal of enemy military personnel, even though no cause might exist for seizure of the neutral vessel, failed to refer to the removal of dispatches. Might, therefore, a belligerent remove from a neutral vessel dispatches intended for the enemy without seizing the vessel? Hyde (*op. cit.*, pp. 2173–4) and Oppenheim-Lauterpacht (*op. ct.*, p. 844), among others, answer this question affirmatively, and this position would appear to be sound.

whole, however, the "transmission of information in the interest of an enemy" [25] has now taken on new forms that bear only a faint resemblance to the more traditional act of carrying dispatches, and it may prove misleading to endeavor to fit these new forms into a legal framework designed to regulate quite different acts. The transmission by radio or wireless of information to an enemy concerning military operations at sea is hardly comparable—save perhaps in name—to the carriage of dispatches. The former acts will normally prove of much more serious moment to the immediate security of a belligerent's forces. And whereas such transmission of information assuredly gives rise to the belligerent right to seize the offending neutral merchant vessel, earlier pages have indicated that the preventive measures a belligerent may now resort to are considerably more severe in character.[26]

[25] The phrase is taken from Article 45 (1) of the Declaration of London, which provided, in this respect, for the seizure and condemnation of a vessel making a voyage "with a view to the transmission of information in the interest of the enemy."

[26] See pp. 319–21.

XII. VISIT, SEARCH, SEIZURE AND DESTRUCTION OF NEUTRAL VESSELS AND AIRCRAFT

A. VISIT AND SEARCH OF NEUTRAL VESSELS

Visit and search forms what has long been regarded as an ancillary right of belligerents, and serves the purpose of enabling the latter to determine the character of merchant vessels, the nature of their employment, and any other facts that may bear upon their relation to the war.[1] Generally speaking, the traditional justification urged on behalf of the belligerent right to visit and search neutral merchantmen remains unchanged today So long as neutral states are placed under no obligation to prevent their subjects from rendering certain forms of assistance to a belligerent they cannot complain if belligerents, in turn, make use of a procedure designed to prevent an enemy from receiving such assistance.

At the same time, the unquestioned right of belligerents to check the activities of neutral merchantmen through visit and search does not indicate with sufficient precision the scope of the measures belligerents may resort to in order to render their preventive efforts effective. It is only natural that belligerents have sought to interpret a right long accorded them by the customary law in a manner intended to achieve maximum effectiveness in preventing contraband carriage, blockade breach and the performance of unneutral services. Inevitably this has led to the belligerent plea that changed conditions necessitate alterations in a procedure that is no longer wholly applicable to these conditions. Equally natural, however, has been the reticence of neutrals to yield to novel procedures which—though perhaps justifiable from the viewpoint of the belligerent's

[1] See, generally, *Law of Naval Warfare*, Article 502. Article 31 of the U. S. Naval War Code of 1900 defined the traditional purpose of visit and search as follows: "The object of the visit or search of a vessel is: (1) to determine its nationality (2) to ascertain whether contraband of war is on board (3) to ascertain whether a breach of blockade is intended or has been committed (4) to ascertain whether the vessel is engaged in any capacity in the service of the enemy " The early history of visit and search is given detailed treatment in Jessup and Deák, *Neutrality:* Vol. I, *The Origins*, pp. 157 ff. A thorough survey of state practice through World War I may be found in A. P. Higgins, "Le droit de visite et de capture dans la guerre maritime," *Recueil Des Cours*, 11 (1926), pp. 70–166. World War II developments are briefly traced by S. W D. Rowson, *op. cit.*, pp. 202 ff., and the British system is described at length by Medlicott, *op. cit.*, pp. 70 ff. United States opinion and practice is reviewed in Hyde, *op. cit.*, pp. 1958 ff., and *U. S. Naval War College*, *International Law Situations, 1926*, pp. 43–73.

interests—clearly result in granting belligerents a far greater measure of control over neutral commerce than the traditional rules permitted. In consequence, both World Wars have witnessed a continuing controversy between neutrals and belligerents over the detailed interpretation and application of a right whose legitimacy—in principle—has long been sanctioned by international law.[2]

The visit and search of neutral merchantmen may be exercised anywhere outside of neutral jurisdiction [3] by the warships and military aircraft of a belligerent. Although the legitimacy of visit and search by military aircraft, and even by submarines as well, occasionally has been questioned by writers, it is clear that no valid objection can be posed to belligerent utilization of these instruments if they are otherwise used in conformity with the rules governing the conduct of surface warships. Controversy as to the use of aircraft and submarines in belligerent operations directed against neutral shipping has its real basis in the claim that the special characteristics of the latter may serve to justify departure from rules appli-

---

[2] Here again, as in the case of neutral-belligerent controversies over contraband and blockade, the nature of the difficulty is readily apparent. The belligerent has maintained that the detailed interpretation and application of a right (i. e., to visit and search neutral merchantmen) must be determined in the light of the general purpose the right is intended to serve (i. e., the prevention, through seizure, of contraband carriage, blockade breach). Hence if changed conditions—or at least what the belligerent alleges to be changed conditions—threaten to frustrate the effective exercise of an established right the detailed rules must be altered to meet these changed conditions, while still preserving the basic purpose. But the neutral has either denied the legitimacy of the plea of changed conditions or has disputed that the novel measures introduced by belligerents represent a reasonable interpretation of the essential purpose served by a right whose validity is not denied. In the light of earlier remarks it need hardly be stated that "in logic" there is no satisfactory way out of the situation, save by an examination of state practice and the possible efficacy of novel belligerent measures in altering traditional procedures.

[3] In practice this has meant the territorial waters of neutral states, though it has earlier been observed that there is a discernible tendency on the part of neutral states to extend the prohibition against the belligerent commission of hostile acts—including visit and search—to waters adjacent to the maritime territorial belt (see pp. 224–6). It may also be noted that the visit and search—as well as the seizure—of neutral merchantmen is permitted only during a period of belligerency, recognized as such by third states. The record of third states in denying this right either during a period of civil war (where the insurgents have not been yet accorded the status of belligerents) or in a situation of "armed conflict" (where the parties involved make no declaration of war and deny any intent to wage war) is reasonably consistent. Whether the right to visit and search—and seize—neutral merchantmen extends into the period following the conclusion of a general armistice, and prior to the formal termination of the war, is not entirely clear. Undoubtedly, as between the belligerents the exercise of the right of prize during this period may be regulated by the provisions of the armistice. But it is difficult to see how the latter agreement could affect in any way the rights and duties of neutrals. For an affirmative answer to this question, see Oppenheim-Lauterpacht (*op. cit.*, pp. 848–9): ". . . since an armistice does not bring war to an end, and since the exercise of the right of visitation is not an act of warfare, it may be exercised during the time of a partial or general armistice." It must be admitted, however, that actual practice in this regard is almost non-existent.

cable to surface warships, a claim that is more properly dealt with in a later connection.[4] Here it is necessary merely to emphasize that the subjects of the right of visit and search must be strictly limited to craft formally commissioned in the armed forces of a belligerent, and thereby generally permitted to exercise belligerent rights at sea.

The objects of the belligerent right of visit and search include all privately owned neutral vessels. It is equally settled that neutral warships, as well as other public vessels operating in the service of the neutral's armed forces, may not be made the objects of visit and search. Beyond this point, however, a measure of uncertainty prevails both as to the liability to visit and search of other publicly owned and operated neutral vessels and of privately owned neutral merchantmen sailing under convoy of neutral warships bearing the same nationality.[5] In either case, belligerent recognition of the neutral's claim to exemption from visit and search of necessity entails the latter's acceptance of full responsibility for insuring that the vessels so exempted will abstain from rendering any form of assistance to a belligerent.

Prior to World War I attention had been directed principally to the status of privately owned neutral merchantmen sailing under convoy of neutral warships. Despite persistent opposition on the part of Great Britain the opinion and practice of most states during the nineteenth century was to accord exemption from visit and search to convoyed vessels provided adequate assurance--based upon thorough examination—could be obtained from the commander of the convoy concerning the cargo carried by, and the innocent employment of, all vessels in the convoy.[6] This broad consensus of the so-called neutral "right of convoy" was accorded recognition in Articles 61 and 62 of the unratified 1909 Declaration of London, and, at the time, received even the approval of Great Britain.[7] However, in the

[4] See pp. 35-24. Thus the absence of any provision in the 1923 Rules of Aerial Warfare governing the visit and search of merchant vessels by aircraft was not due to an inability to agree upon the right, as such, when applied to aircraft, but upon the specific rules that were to govern the exercise of this right (see p. 342). In the case of submarines a similar distinction is relevant, though here Article 22 of the 1930 London Naval Treaty expressly regulated the matter by declaring that in their actions with respect to merchant vessels submarines must conform to the rules applicable to surface vessels.

[5] A clear distinction must be drawn between sailing under neutral convoy and sailing under belligerent convoy. It has already been observed (see pp. 321) that acceptance of the protection of belligerent warships renders neutral vessels liable either to attack or to seizure and subsequent condemnation.—It would also appear that neutral merchantmen under convoy of warships of another neutral have not been considered exempt from visit and search.

[6] See E. Gordon, *La Visite des Convoies Neutres* (1935).

[7] Articles 61 and 62 of the Declaration of London read:

"Neutral vessels under convoy of their national flag are exempt from search. The commander of a convoy gives, in writing, at the request of the commander of a belligerent ship of war, all information as to the character of the vessels and their cargoes, which could be obtained by visit and search.

If the commander of the belligerent ship of war has reason to suspect that the confidence

course of the 1914 war Great Britain reverted to her traditional position and insisted upon a right to exercise visit and search over neutral merchant vessels, even though the latter might be found sailing under convoy of warships of their own nationality. At the same time the vast majority of states have continued to endorse the practice which grants exemption to this category of vessels.[8]

In practice, the question of neutral convoys has decreased in importance, since neutral states have manifested little desire in recent naval hostilities to convoy their merchant vessels.[9] Much more important is the status of publicly owned and operated neutral vessels engaged in ordinary commercial activities. Liability of the latter to visit and search remains a matter that has yet to be clearly resolved by state practice, though it is true there

of the commander of the convoy has been abused, he communicates his suspicions to him. In such a case it is for the commander of the convoy alone to conduct an investigation. He must state the result of such investigation in a report, of which a copy is furnished to the officer of the ship of war. If, in the opinion of the commander of the convoy, the facts thus stated justify the capture of one or more vessels, the protection of the convoy must be withdrawn from such vessels."

Prior to the Declaration of London, Article 30 of the U. S. Naval War Code (1900) had provided that: "Convoys of neutral merchant vessels, under escort of vessels of war of their own State, are exempt from the right of search upon proper assurances, based on thorough examination, from the commander of the convoy." Later, the 1917 and 1941 *Instructions* substantially followed Articles 61 and 62 of the Declaration of London. And see *Law of Naval Warfare*, Article 502 as well as note 10 thereto.

[8] E. g., Article 110 of the 1934 French Naval Instructions, Articles 187 and 188 of the 1938 Italian Laws of War and Article 34 of the 1939 German Prize Law Code.—If the commander of a belligerent warship is dissatisfied with the assurances given him by the commander of the neutral convoy the proper action is to report the incident to his government. The latter may then complain to the neutral state and press for proper redress at the diplomatic level.

[9] There are only two or three instances of neutral convoy during World War I and apparently none at all in the 1939 war. See Hackworth, *op. cit.*, Vol. VII, pp. 208–12. See also Benjamin Akzin ("Neutral Convoys in Law and Practice," *Michigan Law Review*, 40 (1941), pp. 1–23), who attributes this atrophy of neutral convoys to the all inclusive character of modern contraband lists and the belligerent creation of so-called "blockade" zones covering vast areas of the high seas. Thus, in the case of apparently innocent goods having a neutral destination, application of the principle of ultimate enemy destination would give rise to uncertainty and controversy unless the neutral state were prepared to guarantee that the cargoes being convoyed were intended only for neutral consumption. Even then, the problem of barred zones would remain. Neutral convoys have never been permitted to pass through blockaded areas, and belligerents might well insist that in the case of barred zones or war zones—particularly when established as a measure of reprisal—neutral vessels could not be accorded passage under any circumstances. To these considerations must be added the unwillingness of neutrals to assign a substantial portion of their naval strength to the task of convoying merchant vessels. In this connection, mention may be made of the convoys undertaken by United States naval forces in the Atlantic during the final months prior to this country's entrance into hostilities in 1941. By this time the United States had openly abandoned any attempt to observe the duties laid upon neutrals by the traditional law. The American merchant vessels under convoy carried war materials to Great Britain, and, on occasion, these convoys also included British merchant vessels. Whatever the justification that may otherwise be urged on behalf of this abandonment of neutral duties (see pp. 167–8), it is clear that American policy during this period can have little relevance to the problem of neutral convoys in the sense indicated above.

is a growing opinion that these vessels ought to be assimilated—at least for the purpose of visit and search—to the status of privately owned merchant vessels.[10]

1. *The Traditional Procedure For Conducting Visit and Search*

Customary international law does not lay down detailed rules governing the mode of conducting visit and search and belligerents have always enjoyed a certain discretion in this regard. In general, however, a substantial measure of uniformity came to characterize the traditional practices of states, and this uniformity was reflected in the special instructions issued by maritime powers to their naval forces. Before calling upon a neutral merchantman to submit to visitation a belligerent warship is required to show its true colors. In addition, visitation must be preceded by a clear signal on the part of the warship that the merchant vessel is expected to stop and bring to. The notification of intention to visit may be accomplished by any of several means, e. g., by firing a blank charge, by international flag signal, or even by radio. Nor does international law prescribe the distance a belligerent warship must keep from the vessel being visited, which may vary according to the conditions of the sea, the size and character of the visiting warship, and many other factors.

If a neutral vessel complies with the summons the belligerent is forbidden to resort to forcible measures. However, if the neutral vessel takes to flight she may be pursued and brought to, even though this may require the resort to measures of force. In addition, a neutral vessel that responds to a belligerent summons to lie to by measures of forcible resistance may be made the object of a degree of force necessary to compel the neutral vessel to submit to visit and search.[11] Acts of forcible resistance on the part of a neutral vessel, justifying the employment of force by a belligerent warship,

[10] See p. 214 and note 44 thereto. The uncertainty that presently prevails over the status of publicly owned merchant vessels engaged in ordinary commercial undertakings can hardly be regarded with anything but dissatisfaction. Nevertheless, there is very little that may usefully be said on this subject other than to stress that it does remain unsettled in state practice and offers but one further example of the growing obsolescence of the traditional law and the unwillingness of states to agree upon changes in that law. Nor is the experience of World War II of material assistance in this respect, since the clearest lesson to be drawn from that experience is the reticence of belligerent and neutral to bring the question to a head. In principle, the belligerent claim to visit and search neutral public vessels other than those making up a part of the neutral's armed forces is only reasonable, for it is difficult to see any other method whereby the former could be assured that the neutral state was not undertaking to supply an enemy with war materials. It is beyond this point that the more serious question arises and that state practice to date provides almost no real guidance.

[11] A number of points arise in this connection which deserve at least cursory treatment. It is quite usual to encounter the opinion that although neutral vessels may attempt to evade visit and search (and possible seizure) through flight they may not offer forcible resistance to a summoning warship. The ostensible reason for this is that since belligerents have a ***right*** to visit and search neutral vessels the latter have a ***duty*** to submit to this procedure. On the other hand, a contrast is generally drawn between the position of neutral merchant vessels and of enemy merchant vessels. Since the latter are always liable to seizure and condemnation as

may take a variety of forms, e. g., the attempt to fire upon or to ram the summoning warship, the sending of position reports to an enemy warship, or even the attempt to scuttle the neutral vessel in order to prevent seizure.[12]

prize they may resist attempted visit and search (or seizure), though by doing so they incur the risk of being fired upon and possibly destroyed. But this manner of formulation may easily prove misleading. A merchant vessel (whether enemy or neutral) may be considered as having a *duty* to submit to visit and search (or, possibly, seizure) if the attempt either to evade or to resist permits belligerents to take measures *not otherwise permitted by law*. These measures may then be regarded as sanctions, imposed as a consequence of attempted evasion or resistance. In the case of enemy merchant vessels resistance to seizure permits the enemy to attack and even to destroy such vessels without insuring the prior safety of passengers and crew, a requirement otherwise demanded by the traditional law In the case of neutral merchant vessels the attempt to evade visit and search may lead not only to such forcible measures as are necessary to require submission, but to seizure and even to confiscation of vessel and cargo. At least this is true of the practice of many states, including the United States. Forcible resistance on the part of neutral merchant vessels must always lead to the risk of destruction, and once seized to condemnation of vessel and cargo. It has been contended by some writers that acts of forcible resistance to lawful visit and search may place the crew of a neutral merchant vessel in the position of *franc-tireurs* and allow a belligerent to treat them as war criminals. But there is little positive support in state practice for this opinion. In any event, it is clear that neutral merchant vessels neither have a right to evade nor a right to resist visit and search, though the sanctions attending the commission of these acts may vary.

[12] No question will arise with respect to the first of the examples cited above. It should be equally apparent that a neutral merchant vessel in sending position reports to enemy forces (on whose behalf it may be performing certain services) performs a serious act of resistance, entitling the summoning vessel to use any means at its disposal to stop. The last example—that of scuttling a neutral vessel—is somewhat questionable, since although scuttling is clearly an attempt to prevent or frustrate visit and search it hardly seems to constitute "forcible resistance" in the sense in which that term is normally used. It is of interest to note, however, that in a prize decision rendered during World War II the Supreme Court of Sierra Leone did decide that the attempted scuttling of a neutral (French) vessel constituted "forcible resistance" to visit and search, thereby justifying seizure and condemnation. *The Indo-Chinois* [1941], *Annual Digest and Reports of Public International Law Cases* (1941–42), Case No. 173, pp. 594–8. Distinguish, though, between "forcible resistance" on the part of neutral merchant vessels prior to visit and search and certain acts of resistance once the vessel has been brought to and visited (e. g., refusal to show papers or to unlock boxes). The latter may result in seizure and—perhaps—in subsequent condemnation, though there is no justification for the belligerent to resort to forcible measures. Finally, it is of importance to emphasize that a neutral vessel may not be considered as intending forcibly to resist visit and search simply for the reason that she is armed in order to defend herself against *unlawful attacks* on the part of a belligerent. The duty to submit to visit and search cannot be interpreted as forbidding the carrying of arms for use against a belligerent that persists in attacking neutral vessels without warning and in disregard of the safety of lives of passengers and crew In both World Wars the United States, while still a non-participant, placed naval armed guards on board American merchant ships, equipped them with guns and authorized the defensive use of armament against attack from German submarines. On both occasions, however, the arming of American merchant vessels came within a month of United States entrance into hostilities. This experience would appear to indicate that a belligerent intent upon waging unrestricted submarine and aerial warfare against both enemy and neutral shipping is not likely to be deterred by the neutral's policy of arming its merchant vessels. Still further, it seems clear that a neutral equally intent upon taking defensive measures against unlawful attacks made upon its merchant vessels will soon find itself an active participant in the hostilities.

Once a summoned vessel has been brought to the usual procedure is for the visiting warship to send a boat with an officer to conduct visit and search.[13] In a formal sense visitation is limited to an examination of the ship's papers, and the evidence furnished by papers against a vessel has always been regarded as justifying her immediate seizure.[14] It may happen, however, that although a ship's papers are seemingly in order the visiting officer nevertheless remains dissatisfied with the innocence of the vessel. It has always been true that regularity of papers and evidence of innocence of cargo or of destination are not necessarily conclusive, and if doubt persists a visiting officer may question the master and crew members and conduct a search of the vessel and cargo.[15] If the result of search does not dispel suspicion, and the visiting officer considers that reasonable cause for seizure exists, he may seize the vessel and send her into port. On the other hand, if the result of search and the interrogation of crew members satisfies the visiting officer of the innocence of vessel and cargo, the vessel may be released and allowed to continue on her voyage.

2. *Visit and Search Today: The Consequences of Diversion*

Normally, the traditional procedure of visit and search, as briefly outlined above, resulted in a minimum degree of interference and delay. The entire process—even if involving search—generally took no more than several hours. If the condition of the sea prevented visitation at the time of encounter the usual practice was for the belligerent warship to escort the neutral vessel to waters where visit was possible, and for this purpose belligerents could require a neutral vessel to undertake reasonable deviation from her normal course. Even so, deviation—however slight—was regarded as an unusual measure, justified only by exceptional circumstances.

It is equally necessary to emphasize that the result of visit and search, according to the traditional law, was either to release the neutral vessel or to seize (capture) her as prize. A belligerent was thus confronted with two

[13] Though the traditional practice of some states has been to require the master of the merchant vessel to bring his papers on board the visiting warship. Many writers still object to this practice of requiring a master to leave his ship.

[14] Thus if a ship's papers indicate carriage of contraband or the performance of any kind of unneutral service the vessel may at once be seized. Seizure is also justified if a vessel is found to be carrying double papers, or false papers—though instances involving such behavior are now rare. A clear deficiency of papers also may constitute sufficient cause for seizure, as well any attempt to spoil, deface, destroy, or conceal papers.

[15] In conducting search at sea the belligerent is obliged to prevent any damage to vessel or cargo. The master of the vessel is required to assist in the search and to open all holds, lockers and strongboxes. If he refuses to do so these spaces may not be forced open. But upon refusal to assist in the search the visiting officer is provided with sufficient cause for seizure of the vessel. It is also relevant to note that according to nineteenth century practice search consisted ordinarily in the "sampling" of the cargo and not in an intensive search of the entire cargo—even if this were possible. Upon completion of search everything removed must be replaced, and the officer conducting the search should enter the time, date and place of the visit and search in the ship's log.

clear alternatives. If he elected to seize the vessel and take her into port the action had to be justified before the prize court, and in order to escape claims for costs and damages arising from unlawful seizure the captor was obliged to show that the evidence found on board the seized vessel at the time of visit and search was of such a character as to furnish "probable cause" for capture.[16]

It was to this traditional procedure that the United States appealed as a neutral when it protested during World War I against the British practice of diverting neutral vessels into port for search.[17] There can be little doubt that the position taken at that time by the American government was in substantial accord with the then recognized practice of states.[18] Nevertheless, there can be even less doubt that given the conditions characterizing that conflict belligerent efforts to prevent contraband carriage would have been rendered largely futile if the traditional rules governing visit and search (and seizure) had been rigidly followed—a point Great Britain was not slow in making.[19]

In large measure, however, the principal causes that led to diversion were obscured through the belligerent contention that search in port was rendered essential by the increased size of merchant ships, which made concealed contraband difficult to detect at sea, and by the danger of attack from enemy warships, particularly submarines. Undoubtedly these were contributing

---

[16] For further remarks on the "probable cause" justifying capture or seizure, see pp. 271–2, 346 (n). Of course, condemnation before the prize court did not necessarily follow, but so long as a captor could show probable cause neutral claims to costs and damages were barred. Observe, also, that the traditional procedure required evidence justifying seizure to come from the vessel herself ("out of her own mouth") and not from external sources. Although British prize law never followed this procedure as rigidly as did the continental powers, it is not inaccurate to state that up to World War I the requirement was generally adhered to.

[17] Convenient texts of the detailed exchange of notes between Great Britain and the United States may be found in *A. J. I. L.*, 9 (1915), *Spec. Supp.*, pp. 55 ff. and 10 (1916), *Spec. Supp.*, pp. 73 ff. and 121. A summary of this exchange is given in Hackworth, *op. cit.*, Vol. VII, pp. 182 ff.

[18] The American position was succinctly stated in a note of November 7, 1914, in which it was observed that: ". . . the belligerent right of visit and search requires that the search should be made on the high seas at the time of the visit and that the conclusion of the search should rest upon the evidence found on the ship, and not upon circumstances ascertained from external sources. That evidence, in the view of this Government, should make out a *prima facie* case to justify the captor in taking the vessel into port. To take vessels into custody and send them into a port of the belligerent without *prima facie* evidence to impress the cargo with the character of absolute or conditional contraband, constitutes, in the opinion of the United States, a justifiable ground for complaint by a neutral government, and a basis for a legal claim for damages against the belligerent government which has detained the vessel for the purpose of inquiry through other channels as to the ultimate destination of the cargo, or as to the intended action of the government of the neutral country of destination."

[19] This formed the essential feature of the British argument in support of diversion—that in no other way could the right of search be exercised effectively, and that if diversion were abandoned then search itself might just as well be abandoned.

factors in prompting the belligerents to the practice of diversion. But the substantial and compelling reason for diversion was that little or no evidence to support a case for seizure—let alone for later condemnation—could be worked up by restricting attention to the ship's papers and to the nature of the cargo carried. In the vast majority of instances where vessels were encountered bound for a neutral port, and carrying cargo to be delivered to a neutral consignee, the ship's papers themselves furnished no real assurance of the ultimate destination of the cargo. Instead, the evidence necessary to justify seizure normally could come only from external sources. Not infrequently, this information was collected prior to the act of visit. More often, however, it could be gathered only after a vessel had been diverted to a belligerent contraband control base.[20]

In view of the experience of the two World Wars it does not appear very realistic to continue to question the legitimacy—in principle—of diverting neutral merchant vessels into port for search.[21] Indeed, by the time of the 1939 war nearly all the major naval powers recognized diversion as a lawful measure, at least where there was reason for believing [22] that a neutral vessel might be found liable to seizure, and if search at sea was considered either impossible or impracticable.[23]

The real difficulty, however, has been that of determining the limits to what may presently be regarded as the belligerent right of diversion. In theory, it is easy enough to insist that diversion must not be undertaken indiscriminately, in the hope that once a neutral vessel is in port further evidence of contraband carriage—or other unlawful acts—may be found

[20] In part, the passages in the text above form a restatement of observations made earlier in connection with the problem of establishing enemy destination in the case of contraband (see pp. 270 ff.). It can hardly be stressed too strongly that acceptance of the principle of ultimate enemy destination is at the root of the practice of diversion. Indeed, to insist upon rigid observance of the traditional procedure of visit and search, and the confining of evidence necessary to justify seizure to the vessel herself, would clearly have the effect of reducing the principle of ultimate enemy destination to a shadow, altogether devoid of real substance.

[21] Though, of course, it is quite possible to question the legitimacy of many of the specific measures resorted to by belligerents under the pretext of rendering diversion effective. But for a continued denial of the lawfulness of diversion, see *Harvard Draft Convention on Rights and Duties of Neutral States in Naval and Aerial War, op. cit.*, pp. 578–601. Also P. C. Jessup, "The Diversion of Merchantmen," *A. J. I. L.*, 34 (1940), pp. 312–5. And see the noncommital position of Hyde, *op. cit.*, pp. 1965–70. The majority of writers, however, now concede a belligerent right of diversion—at least in principle.

[22] Whether through evidence obtained as a result of visitation or obtained from external sources prior to visit.

[23] Thus—in addition to Great Britain—Articles 107–109 of the 1934 French Naval Instructions, Articles 60–63 of the 1939 German Prize Law Code, Article 182 of the 1938 Italian War Regulations and Article 120 of the Japanese Naval War Law (1942). Although the 1917 *Instructions* issued to United States naval forces made no allowance for diversion, the 1941 *Instructions* declared in paragraph 52, that "if for any reason . . search at sea is impracticable, the vessel may be escorted by the summoning vessel or by another vessel to the nearest port where search may conveniently be made." Finally, see *Law of Naval Warfare*, Article 502b (5).

and a case for seizure worked up that would satisfy a prize court.[24] In practice, this is very nearly the precise result to which diversion has led. Nor is this development—so clearly apparent during World War II [25]—any cause for surprise in view of the more profound causes that prompted belligerents to resort to diversion in the first place. In addition, it must probably be admitted that once diversion into port is granted it may be exercised in circumstances which justified search at sea according to the traditional law. But according to the traditional law the circumstances justifying search at sea—not to be confused with the circumstances justifying capture [26]—could be very slight. On this basis, the same slight reasons may serve to justify diversion into port for search. And if this is true then the difference between the indiscriminate diversion of merchant vessels and diversion in circumstances (usually derived from external sources) held to create sufficient reason to justify search is surely one bordering on sophistry.[27]

---

24 Even the majority of British writers—who have never looked askance at the practice of diversion—continue to insist upon this limitation as retaining at least a formal validity In 1927 the Naval War College concluded, after an extensive review of the problem, that diversion into port "presupposes a suspicion of liability to prize proceedings based on information in possession of the visiting vessel at the time. Suspicion that all vessels may be found liable is not sufficient ground for indiscriminately sending in of merchant vessels." *International Law Situations, 1927*, p. 71. But see the further remarks in the text above.

25 The British system has been extensively reviewed by Medlicott, *op. cit.*, pp. 70–105. At the outbreak of hostilities in September 1939, neutral vessels carrying goods to neutral ports adjacent to Germany were invited to call voluntarily at British contraband control bases for examination. Vessels attempting to avoid calling at these bases were liable to be compelled by naval patrols to undergo diversion. Within a very short time, as Medlicott notes, "all ships bound for adjacent neutral countries were sent in unless they had a naval clearance" (p. 71). Once in port the vast intelligence facilities at the disposal of the Ministry of Economic Warfare would go into operation, and a decision would be reached either to release the vessel and cargo or to seize the cargo—and perhaps the vessel as well—as prize. In November and December of 1939 the United States protested this forcible diversion of American vessels, particularly in view of the fact that contraband control bases were within "combat areas" defined by the President and into which American vessels were forbidden to sail by the Neutrality Act of 1939. However, the right of a belligerent to compel diversion in circumstances justifying suspicion was never clearly challenged. Instead, it was alleged that since American vessels were forbidden to sail within "combat areas" no reasonable suspicion of contraband carriage could arise thereby necessitating their diversion. Obviously this argument could easily be challenged, and was so challenged, on the ground that the cargoes carried to neutral ports might ultimately find their way to enemy territory. The real criticism that could be made of the British system of diversion—and which many neutrals did make during the early months of the war—was that it was obviously indiscriminate in character.

26 See p. 346 (n). As a matter of fact the circumstances now held to justify seizure are themselves very slight.

27 From the point of view of a strict legal analysis the considerations adduced above would appear very difficult to deny—once the bare right of diversion is conceded. And it is for these reasons that the scope of the belligerent right of diversion has proven so difficult to define. It is an interesting fact that in British prize law the question of diversion—as such—has never been adequately reviewed. In *The Zamora* [1916], the Judicial Committee of the Privy Council

Furthermore, once the right of diversion into port is granted the traditional procedure of visitation threatens to become little more than a formality devoid of any real meaning. Exceptionally, a formal visit may yet serve the purpose of bringing to light facts heretofore unknown to the visiting belligerent. Normally, however, the visiting belligerent will already possess that information he may obtain from an examination of the ship's papers, and he may even possess a good deal more. If so, he will gain nothing from visit, and if there is the slightest reason for believing that any of the vessel's cargo is ultimately destined to enemy territory he will almost certainly order her into port.[28] Under these circumstances continued insistence upon visitation prior to diversion can only serve the purpose of denying to aircraft the right to order the diversion of merchant vessels, owing to an inability to conduct visit. It is difficult to see the logic of this position, since the insuring of proper identification—without formal visit—and the communication of instructions to the master of a vessel can as readily be carried out by aircraft as by warships. In permitting military aircraft to order the diversion of merchant vessels, without undertaking prior visit, belligerents will not be conceded substantially greater control over neutral shipping than that which they already claim (and neutrals seem no longer seriously disposed to resist) on behalf of surface warships.[29]

---

merely held diversion to be a justifiable practice "because search at sea is impossible under the conditions of modern warfare," 4 *Lloyds Prize Cases*, p. 110. In *The Bernisse and The Elve* [1920]—(9 *Lloyds Prize Cases*, pp. 243 ff.), the Privy Council expressly refrained from reviewing the scope of the belligerent right of diversion, though the decision did make clear that under certain circumstances diversion could be held by the Prize Court as unjustified, and thereby giving rise to a liability of the Crown for costs and damages sustained by neutral claimants. More recently, in *The Mim* [1947] (*Annual Digest and Reports of Public International Law Cases* (1947), Case. No. 134, pp. 311–6), the British Prize Court held that "in the absence of reasonable suspicion the ship must be allowed to proceed. If she is detained, for example, by mistake . or if she is detained for some ulterior reason unconnected with search, the Crown cannot rely on the belligerent right of visit and search as an answer to the plaintiff's claim." At the same time, the clear implication of the decision in *The Mim* was not only that diversion could be ordered for the same reasons as would justify search at sea, but that very little reason was required to justify search. The same point was made by the Privy Council in *The Bernisse*.

[28] But writers remain—on the whole—reluctant to admit that recent developments have reduced the present significance of visit at sea almost to a vanishing point, and continue to insist upon formal boarding and visit as a requirement for diversion. Thus Erik Castren (*op. cit.*, pp. 357–8) expresses the rather anomalous view that "a merchant ship may not be diverted from its route except for good reasons. In practice this would mean that at least some kind of cursory visitation must be made at the actual place of meeting unless the merchant ship flies the flag of the enemy or the warship has ascertained its enemy character in some other way" But why does "cursory visitation" constitute a "good reason" for diversion unless good reasons are conceived in the retention of procedures that no longer serve a substantive purpose.

[29] It should be clear from the statements above, that there is no intent to argue on behalf of the desirability of two sets of rules for neutral shipping—one governing the action of warships and the other governing the action of aircraft. On the contrary, the rules governing warships are also applicable to aircraft. But the essential point is that the denial of the right

To date, it can hardly be said that the difficulties ensuing between neutral and belligerent as a consequence of diversion have been satisfactorily resolved. The belligerent's claim that the functions formerly served by the traditional procedure of visit and search at sea would be rendered almost wholly ineffective under modern conditions without a right to compel diversion has been met by the neutral's claim that the inconvenience and loss caused to legitimate neutral shipping through lengthy delay in contraband control bases represents an unreasonable—if not an unlawful—hardship.[30] It has already been noted [31] that in practice this conflict was partially resolved by the introduction of a system of passes which enabled neutral vessels—upon approval by the belligerent—to avoid diversion into port for search. Neutral vessels have also been able to avoid a period of delay in port by giving prior assurance to a belligerent that upon reaching a neutral destination the cargo would be held until the belligerent's representatives could examine and pass upon it.[32] But whatever the precise nature of the arrangement the essential purpose has been to shift the pro-

---

of diversion to aircraft, merely because the latter cannot conduct visit, makes very little sense when visit itself is a mere formality precedent to diversion, or—as the events of World War II indicate—simply omitted altogether by belligerent warships. It is true that the jurists which met at The Hague in 1923 were unable to agree upon whether aircraft should have a right to divert merchant vessels without prior visit or search or whether they should be required to board *sur place* before ordering diversion. The American delegation argued that although diversion might be "exceptionally" permitted to surface ships, "a similar concession to aircraft, with their limited means of boarding, would readily have the effect of converting the exception into the rule." General Report, Commission of Jurists on 1923 Rules of Aerial Warfare, *U. S. Naval War College, International Law Documents, 1924*, p. 138. But the present relevance of this argument must be questioned, since the exception has already been turned into the general rule in the case of surface ships. Nevertheless, most writers continue to insist that if aircraft cannot undertake the visit of neutral merchant vessels at the place of encounter they may not order their diversion. Even H. A. Smith (*op. cit.*, pp. 166–8), who points out that under modern conditions boarding has largely become "an idle formality," observes that unless an aircraft "is capable of alighting on the water, the visit must obviously be carried out by a warship, which must therefore be within reasonable distance of the ship visited." And this supposedly for the reason that "aircraft in flight can only assist naval forces in exercising the right of visit and search, a right which by its nature can only be exercised by ships of war."

30 It seems quite clear that the real bone of contention between Great Britain and neutral states during the fall of 1939 and the early months of 1940 did not primarily concern the legality as such of diversion, but rather the losses incurred by neutral traders through lengthy delays in contraband control bases. To alleviate this situation Great Britain sought to shorten the period in port and to bring into operation as quickly as possible the navicert system, whereby diversion into port might be avoided altogether.

31 See pp. 280–2.

32 Known variously as "black-diamond" and "hold-back" guarantees, Medlicott (*op. cit.*, p. 87) writes that the "essential feature of the 'hold-back' system was that in certain circumstances a ship might be allowed to proceed to a neutral destination after giving a guarantee not to deliver to the consignees any cargo which was still under consideration by the Contraband Committee, and to return to an Allied port any items of cargo which the committee had decided should be seized."

cedure of search from the high seas and belligerent ports to neutral territory, and has necessitated the voluntary cooperation both of neutral states and of private neutral traders. Quite apart from the tentative character of such arrangements, it is not easy to see how—from the viewpoint of the traditional law—either the neutral state or the neutral trader can acquiesce without raising serious questions. The neutral state in permitting a belligerent to inspect cargoes within its territory thereby renders a definite form of assistance to the belligerent. The neutral trader by actively participating in a system that eases the belligerent's task of contraband control risks the charge of performing an unneutral service.[33] Yet the alternative in both World Wars has been either enforced diversion, attended by costly delays, or belligerent "reprisal" measures, whose effect has been to render compulsory that action on the part of neutrals previously elicited on a voluntary basis.[34]

B. SEIZURE AND DESTRUCTION OF NEUTRAL VESSELS

It is of importance to distinguish as clearly as possible between the formal act of seizing or capturing [35] a neutral vessel and acts which, though apparently resembling seizure, nevertheless must receive a quite different interpretation. In particular, a clear distinction should be drawn between

---

[33] See pp. 322–3.

[34] See pp. 313–5. Small satisfaction can be derived in terminating a discussion of visit and search on so uncertain a note. Little more can be said, however, while remaining within the confines imposed by a legal analysis. It may be argued that even though a right of diversion must now be accorded belligerents the scope of this right remains unsettled. From this point of view, at least some of the belligerent measures taken in the two World Wars have yet to be recognized as the lawful consequences of the right of diversion. There is no real incompatibility between this position and the tentative conclusions that have been reached here. In either case, the precise limits of the right of diversion remain unsettled. Finally, it may be relevant to observe that the controversies attending recent developments in the belligerent right of visit and search will not be resolved short of a clear change in the largely obsolescent distinction between neutral state and neutral trader, and the imposition upon neutral states of the duty to insure that their subjects refrain from acts which they themselves have long been obligated to abstain from performing. And for the proposal that neutral states issue certificates covering cargoes carried on board ships of their nationality, see *Harvard Draft Convention on Rights and Duties of Neutral States in Naval and Aerial War*, *op. cit.*, pp. 487–530.

[35] Mention has already been made (see p. 105 (n)) of the possible ambiguity that may result from the indiscriminate use of the terms "capture" and "seizure" when applied to the act of asserting control over enemy vessels. In part, these earlier observations are also applicable to the present discussion. However, in the case of enemy vessels the need is to distinguish between those vessels (e. g., warships) which—in order that legal ownership may be transferred—do not require condemnation by a court of prize, and vessels (e. g., privately owned enemy merchant vessels) which require such condemnation before transfer of title can be effected. The same holds true with respect to enemy owned cargo found on board enemy vessels. In the case of neutral vessels the need is to distinguish between the act of taking control in order that a prize court may determine whether the vessel or cargo, or both, is liable to condemnation, and the act of taking control in order to determine through further search whether sufficient

the seizure of a neutral vessel and her detention by a belligerent in order hat search may be carried out in port. In either case the belligerent may exercise very nearly the same degree of control over the neutral vessel and subject her to similar measures of compulsion in the event his orders are not followed [36] In addition, the belligerent's prize courts may assert the right to entertain neutral claims entered against the captor for compulsory diversion and detention in port without sufficient cause in the same manner as they may entertain neutral claims for compensation as a result of unlawful seizure.[37]

In view of the apparent similarities between acts constituting seizure (or capture) and acts amounting to no more than diversion into port for search, it would appear that seizure must be distinguished primarily by the intent of the belligerent. Such intent may be manifested not only by the fact that the belligerent has succeeded in imposing his will upon the neutral vessel, thereby compelling her to abide by his orders, but also by the fact that he has done so because he is in possession of evidence which appears

---

cause exists to charge vessel or cargo as liable to condemnation before a court of prize. The terms "seizure" and "capture" may be—and are—applied to the former act, though it must be made clear that the control exercised is merely provisional until the prize court has finally adjudicated upon the seizure. Furthermore, in either case (i. e., whether seized (captured) or merely diverted into port for search) the vessel is "detained," though the legal significance of detention differs according to the intent of the belligerent.

[36] In seizing—or capturing—a neutral vessel the belligerent may place a prize crew on board, whereas in merely diverting the vessel into port for search he may place on board an "armed guard" to insure his orders are carried out. In both cases, however, the belligerent may simply order the neutral vessel to proceed into port under escort of a belligerent warship, or military aircraft. A neutral vessel under diversion that resists the orders given her by the escorting belligerent not only becomes immediately subject to seizure but to the use of forcible measures on the part of the belligerent.

[37] At least this seems to be the case in British prize law, though the practice in the prize courts of many continental countries has been to refuse to assert jurisdiction over, or take legal cognizance of, acts committed by the belligerent prior to formal seizure as prize (and particularly if such acts as diversion do not later result in a formal seizure or capture). A degree of uncertainty still prevails, however, as to the precise status in British prize law of a vessel that has been detained for search in port. Normally, the act of diversion must be interpreted simply as a prolongation of the act of visit and search; the diverted vessel is under detention in the same sense as a vessel being visited and searched at sea. In *The Netherlands American Steam Navigation Co. v. H. M. Procurator-General* [1926]—(1, Kings Bench, pp. 93–5; cited in Hackworth, Vol. VII, pp. 187–8), the Court of Appeal held that the placing of an armed guard on a neutral vessel and her compulsory diversion to a British port amounted to seizure, or capture, and thus gave the Prize Court authority to entertain a claim for compensation—whether on the ground that the compulsory diversion and detention was itself unjustified, or on the ground that the captor was negligent in insuring proper care of the vessel and cargo, or was unduly dilatory in carrying out the search. But in *The Mim* (cited above, p. 342 (n)) the Prize Court cast some doubt on the use of the term "seizure" (or capture) as applied to cases of diversion, and was content to declare that "the question is whether the act of the Crown was wrongful or not." The main point is that the British system does permit judicial review by the Prize Court of allegedly wrongful acts of the captor in cases of compulsory diversion, although it must be added that to date the "protection" thus afforded neutrals has proven to be largely of formal significance.

to him as probable cause for condemnation of vessel or cargo by a court of prize.[38]

At the same time, seizure need not lead to the condemnation of the vessel or of her cargo. The lawfulness of the act of seizure is not dependent upon later condemnation by a prize court. It may well be that the circumstances held to justify seizure will not be regarded by a prize court as sufficient to justify condemnation. It may even be that later information brought to the attention of a belligerent prompts him voluntarily to release a vessel that earlier had been seized as prize. Nevertheless, the captor may not be made liable to claims for costs and damages—as would follow upon an unlawful seizure—if he can establish that at the moment of seizure circumstances were such as to warrant suspicion of enemy character, whether of vessel or of cargo, or of the performance of acts held to constitute contraband carriage, blockade breach, or unneutral service.[39]

---

[38] As in the case of enemy merchant vessels (see pp. 103–4) so in the case of neutral vessels capture is, as Colombos (*op. cit.*, p. 305) points out, "the act whereby a belligerent warship compels a vessel to conform to her will." But a neutral vessel may be compelled to conform to the will of the captor for more purposes than one. Effective control takes on the meaning of a capture or seizure when the intent is to seek adjudication of vessel or cargo before a court of prize. See, in this respect, the remarks of Hyde, *op. cit.*, pp. 2021–3. It may also be noted that when a neutral vessel is undergoing diversion she may not be required to lower her flag, since she has not been captured. See *Law of Naval Warfare*, Article 502b (5). Seizure or capture does indicate that the vessel is for the time in the possession of the captor, and the latter may require the neutral vessel to lower her flag, or—if the neutral flag is flown as usual—the flag of the captor may be exhibited at the fore.

[39] See *Law of Naval Warfare*, Article 502b (7) and—for an enumeration of acts justifying seizure or capture of neutral vessels—Article 503d. Indeed, any of the various acts a neutral vessel may resort to in order to frustrate visit and search—reviewed in the preceding section of this chapter—give rise to a right of seizure. Of course, the real problem arises where the neutral vessel has not attempted to resist or frustrate the belligerent and where her papers (and cargo) do not indicate that she is evidently engaged in contraband carriage, blockade breach, or the performance of unneutral service. The Supreme Court of the United States (sitting in prize) has defined "probable cause"—sufficient to justify seizure—as existing "where there are circumstances sufficient to warrant suspicion, though it may turn out that the facts are not sufficient to justify condemnation. And whether they are or not can not be determined unless the customary proceedings of prize are instituted and enforced." *Olinde Rodriguez* [1899], 174 U. S. 510. But although "probable cause" depends upon the existence of circumstances deemed sufficient to "warrant suspicion," the question remains unanswered as to the nature and extent of the circumstances required in a given period to warrant suspicion—and hence to justify seizure. The practical importance of this question can hardly be overstated since a belligerent may well accomplish his purpose of cutting off all supplies to an enemy merely through seizure, and quite without the necessity of obtaining condemnation by a prize court. In this respect, the actual significance of seizure has undergone far-reaching change since the nineteenth century. During this earlier period the failure of a belligerent to obtain the condemnation of cargo seized as prize normally meant that the neutral owner was at liberty to re-ship his goods. This being so, the belligerent had no assurance that goods released by a prize court would not ultimately reach an enemy. Today, however, the belligerent need not suffer under any such apprehension, so long as he is able to justify his original act of seizure. One reason for this is the power of prize courts either directly to dispose of goods held in prize (e. g., because of perishability or

In seizing neutral vessels the belligerent incurs certain duties that have long enjoyed the sanction of state practice. Unless the neutral nationals serving as officers and crew of neutral vessels have taken a direct part in the hostilities they may not be treated as prisoners of war.[40] Nor is there any justification for placing the personnel of neutral prizes under any special restraint, unless this is shown to be necessary for the security of the prize crew. The captor may request the master and crew to assist him in navigating the prize into port, though he cannot compel them to render any assistance. And if not temporarily detained as witnesses in prize court proceedings the personnel of neutral prizes must be released at the earliest possible time by the belligerent undertaking capture.

The duties imposed upon the captor with respect to the seized neutral property follow largely from the fact that the seizure of neutral vessels and cargo does not serve to effect transfer of title in favor of the captor, but only places him in temporary possession of the property. The determination of title remains the sole responsibility of the prize court, which is charged

---

the shortage of storage space) or to authorize their requisition in response to a request by the executive that they are urgently needed for the national defense (see p. 348 (n)). In either event the neutral owner must receive compensation, but the belligerent has achieved his principal aim of preventing the goods from ever falling into enemy hands. Even if goods that have been lawfully seized are finally released—whether through failure by the belligerent to obtain condemnation or merely through the prize court ordering release with the executive's consent—the neutral owner may find himself unable to remove them from the belligerent's jurisdiction. Thus, in examining modern British practice of contraband control Fitzmaurice (*op. cit.*, p. 75) points out that: "The decision rendered in 1921 by the Judicial Committee of the Privy Council in the case of *The Falk* . . established the principle that an order for the release of goods seized in Prize only operates to place the owner of the goods in possession of them in this country and does not of itself entitle him to remove them from the realm. . . . In fact, the position which appears to result from this decision is that goods seized in Prize (as opposed to those merely detained pending investigation) are deemed to have actually entered the country and, on release from Prize, automatically fall under the general legislation governing the export or removal of goods from the country and can therefore only be exported or removed by complying with the requirements of this legislation." Fitzmaurice further observes that the drop in the activity of the Prize Court during the 1939 war was due to this "shift in emphasis as between the condemnation of goods and their initial seizure." Medlicott (*op. cit.*, p. 84), in surveying these same developments, declares that: "The practical effect of seizure in perhaps the majority of cases was . . . that, whether condemned or released, they would never reach the country to which they were originally destined." Even this cursory review should prove sufficient to indicate the importance of the nature and scope of the circumstances held to "warrant suspicion," and to justify seizure. If the consistent practice of belligerents during the two World Wars is to be regarded as law-making in character these circumstances are now such as almost to preclude successful neutral claims for damages arising from unlawful seizures—save in the most flagrant instances. Colombos (*op. cit.*, p. 309), writing of the 1914 and 1939 conflicts, states that: "The cases where a Prize Court has taken the view that no 'circumstances of suspicion' could be invoked by the captor in justification of the seizure are extremely few." And for a brief survey of the principal circumstances held to give rise to a presumption of contraband carriage, see pp. 272–5.

40 See *Law of Naval Warfare*, Article 513. As to the disposition of enemy nationals found on board neutral vessels, see pp. 325–30.

with the task of investigating the circumstances attending seizure and deciding whether or not there is sufficient cause for confiscating vessel or cargo—or both. In consequence of his purely provisional possession the captor must take reasonable measures to preserve the vessel (and cargo) intact and to take her into the nearest convenient port without undue delay, there to be turned over to the custody of officers of the prize court.[41]

---

[41] On the procedure to be followed by United States naval forces when sending neutral prizes in for adjudication, see the references given on p. 106 (n). A special problem arises should the captor desire to requisition seized neutral vessels or cargoes for his public use prior to final adjudication of the seizure by a court of prize. In British prize law the right of a belligerent to requisition vessels or goods in the custody of its prize court, pending adjudication, was upheld by the Judicial Committee of the Privy Council in *The Zamora* [1916]—(4 *Lloyds Prize Cases*, p. 108), though subject to the following limitations:

"First, the vessel or goods in question must be urgently required for use in connection with the defense of the realm, the prosecution of the war, or other matters involving national security Secondly, there must be a real question to be tried, so that it would be improper to order an immediate release. And, thirdly, the right must be enforced by application to the prize court, which must determine judicially whether, under the particular circumstances of the case, the right is exercisable."

Fitzmaurice (*op. cit.*, p. 81) observes that the justification for requisitioning is "(a) that it would be unreasonable that goods . . urgently required for national use, should have to be kept *in specie* to await the outcome of the proceedings, and (b) that the rights of the claimant are not prejudiced since, if an order for release is made in his favor, he will obtain, if not the goods themselves, their value." Since the word of the Crown is conclusive in testifying that the vessel or goods in question are urgently required, the function of the Prize Court—according to *The Zamora*—is to insure that there is a "real case for investigation and trial, and that the circumstances are not such as would justify the immediate release of the vessel or goods." Hence the purpose of requiring application to the Prize Court is to prevent the requisitioning of neutral vessels or goods simply for the reason that the Crown desires their use, but against which there is no real case. In this respect, British practice would appear to offer greater protection to neutrals than does the practice of other states. For while the right of a belligerent government to requisition seized neutral vessels and cargoes, pending adjudication, is now generally recognized, similar limitations upon its exercise are not imposed by the prize courts of other countries. The Prize Statutes of the United States have long permitted the requisition of seized vessels and goods, whether *before or after* such property comes into the custody of the prize courts (U. S. Code, Title 34, Sections 1140–41; also the 1942 Prize Act, 56 Stat. 746 (1942), which broadened the procedure whereby the United States can make immediate use of a captured vessel, without awaiting the institution of prize proceedings and without applying to the prize court for requisition). In all cases of requisitioning the government department for whose use the vessels or goods are taken "shall deposit the value thereof with the Treasurer of the United States or public depository nearest to the place of the session of the court, subject to the order of the court in the cause" (34 U. S. C. 1140). This procedure has always been regarded as of an exceptional nature, however, and to be resorted to only under compelling circumstances, since indemnification must follow if the prize court fails to condemn the neutral property converted to public use (see 1917 *Instructions*, paragraph 85; 1941 *Instructions*, paragraph 89; *Law of Naval Warfare*, Chapter 5, note 16).

The requisitioning of seized neutral vessels or goods brought into belligerent territory may be regarded as forming a special aspect of the more general right of belligerents to requisition any neutral property found within their jurisdiction. Normally, such property will be present *voluntarily* in belligerent territory, and the objections that are still occasionally voiced against the requisition of neutral prize, pending adjudication, arises mainly from the fact that this

As in the case of enemy prizes, however, occasions may frequently arise when the sending in of neutral prizes proves either impossible or highly inconvenient to the captor. Under these circumstances the customary practice of states has always drawn a distinction between the destruction of enemy prizes and the destruction of neutral prizes. Whereas belligerents admittedly enjoy a broad discretion in resorting to the destruction of enemy prizes the circumstances in which neutral prizes may be destroyed are considerably more restrictive. Indeed, during the nineteenth century there was substantial support for the position that if for any reason a captured neutral vessel could not be taken into port for adjudication the captor was obliged to release her, and that if instead he resorted to the destruction of a neutral prize the owners of the vessel and cargo were always entitled to receive full compensation.[42] This opinion still finds some support even today [43]

---

property has been *forcibly* brought into belligerent territory. With respect to neutral property voluntarily present (even though such presence is only temporary), requisition by the belligerent is frequently based upon a "right of angary," though it has been observed that "in reality little distinction is drawn in principle between the exercise of the power of eminent domain or expropriation for public use in time of peace, and requisitions in time of war, including requisitions of vessels or cargoes, in spite of this latter practice being sometimes based on a distinct 'right of angary'. In all these cases, the practice is based on the right of the sovereign to control property within his jurisdiction." *Harvard Draft Convention on Rights and Duties of Neutral States in Naval and Aerial War, op. cit.*, pp. 384–5. But see Lauterpacht, "Angary and Requisitions of Neutral Property" (*B. Y I. L.*, 27 (1950), pp. 455–9), who contends that "requisition" applies to neutral property "permanently and voluntarily residing" in belligerent territory—and requires only "reasonable compensation"—and that "angary" applies to neutral property brought to belligerent territory either "without the neutral's consent or . brought there for purely temporary purposes"—and requires "full compensation." And see, generally, C. L. Bullock, "Angary," *B. Y. I. L.*, (1922–23), pp. 99–129; J. E. Harley, "The Law of Angary," *A. J. I. L.*, 13 (1919), pp. 267–301; *U. S. Naval War College, International Law Situations, 1926*, pp. 65–87; Hackworth, *op. cit.*, Vol. VI, pp. 638–55; and Hyde, *op. cit.*, pp. 1760–9. On the requisitioning of Dutch merchant vessels by the United States and Great Britain in 1918, see G. G. Wilson, "Taking Over and Return of Dutch Vessels, 1918–1919," *A. J. I. L.*, 24 (1930), pp. 694–702.

[42] A review of nineteenth century practice and opinion is given in *Harvard Draft Convention on Rights and Duties of Neutral States in Naval and Aerial War, op. cit.*, pp. 559–75. The traditional British position, in particular, inclined very strongly toward release if neutral prizes could not be sent in, and compensation to the owners of vessel and cargo in the event of destruction. It has been pointed out on more than one occasion that the traditional British position was strongly influenced by the numerous bases maintained by Great Britain throughout the world. However that may be, even the British view seems to have allowed that in certain exceptional cases, involving unneutral service and blockade running, destruction might be permitted if absolutely necessary. No other major maritime power took so consistent and so strong a position against the destruction of neutral vessels.

[43] E. g. Colombos (*op. cit.*, p. 303) declares that: "The destruction of neutral ships must, as a rule, be altogether prohibited. If the captor is unable to bring a neutral vessel into port for adjudication, he must release her. Reasons of urgent military necessity or other exceptional circumstances are strictly excluded." Nevertheless, Colombos does make exception for unneutral service or blockade running.

It would be difficult to assert, however, that the traditional law prior to 1914 strictly forbade the destruction of neutral prizes. In fact, a number of maritime powers had never accepted the rule that would have denied to them, as belligerents, the right to destroy under any circumstances captured neutral vessels engaged in the supply of war material to an enemy.[44] In the provisions of the Declaration of London the attempt was made to clarify the problem and to resolve the diverse attitudes of states. Although declaring that—in principle—a captured neutral vessel was not to be destroyed by the captor, but instead must be taken into port for adjudication,[45] it was nevertheless provided that exceptionally a neutral prize—otherwise liable to condemnation—could be destroyed if taking her into port "would involve danger to the ship of war or to the success of the operation in which she is at the time engaged." [46] Before destroying the neutral prize all persons on board were to be removed to a place of safety and all ship's papers and other relevant documents were to be taken on board the belligerent warship.[47] If the captor who destroyed a neutral vessel could not establish to the satisfaction of a prize court that he acted only in the face of "exceptional necessity" the interested parties would be entitled to receive compensation, without regard to whether or not the capture itself was valid.[48] Finally, even though the captor might show that he resorted to the destruction of a captured neutral vessel only in the face of an exceptional necessity, the interested parties would remain entitled to compensation if

[44] It is true that prior to the Russo-Japanese War, at the beginning of this century, there had been very few incidents involving the destruction of neutral vessels. But during that conflict Russian naval forces did sink an appreciable number of neutral vessels. Despite British protests that the sinkings were unlawful the Russian Government refused to render any compensation to the owners of vessels her prize courts later found to have been liable to condemnation.

It is also relevant to note that Article 50 of the U. S. Naval War Code of 1900 declared:

"If there are controlling reasons why vessels that are properly captured may not be sent in for adjudication—such as unseaworthiness, the existence of infectious disease, or the lack of a prize crew—they may be appraised and sold, and if this can not be done, they may be destroyed. The imminent danger of recapture would justify destruction, if there should be no doubt that the vessel was a proper prize. But in all such cases all of the papers and other testimony should be sent to the prize court, in order that a decree may be duly entered."

A substantially similar order was given to American naval forces during the Spanish-American War. Yet in 1905 the Naval War College concluded—in a review of the question—"that if a seized neutral vessel cannot for any reason be brought into port for adjudication, it should be dismissed." *International Law Topics, 1905*, p. 62. In a still later study it was contended that although "the treatment of neutral vessels in time of war is not yet a fully settled question," nevertheless, "destruction, on account of military necessity, of a neutral vessel guilty only of the carriage of contraband entitles the owner to fullest compensation. Before destruction all persons and papers should be placed in safety" *International Law Situations, 1907*, pp. 107–8.

[45] Article 48.

[46] Article 49.

[47] Article 50. It is interesting to note that no further definition was given as to what would constitute "a place of safety"

[48] The "exceptional necessity" is a reference to the conditions earlier cited in Article 49.

it were subsequently shown that no adequate grounds existed for condemning the destroyed property.[49]

Although never ratified, these provisions of the Declaration of London indicate that in the years immediately prior to World War I most of the major maritime powers were willing to concede that under certain circumstances the destruction of captured neutral vessels—otherwise liable to condemnation—was not unlawful, and, if resorted to, ought not to give rise to an obligation of compensating the owners of the destroyed property. At the same time, the Declaration can hardly be regarded as clarifying the nature of the situations in which destruction was to be permitted. Instead, the formula provided was sufficiently vague to allow belligerents any number of possible interpretations, as the later events of World War I clearly demonstrated.[50]

---

[49] Article 52. The compensation Article 52 would have required was evidently intended to be applicable despite the fact that the captor could show "probable cause" for capture. The "validity" of the capture referred to the later condemnation by a prize court, and if such condemnation did not follow compensation had to be given. Article 53 declared that: "If neutral goods which were not liable to condemnation have been destroyed with the vessel, the owner of such goods is entitled to compensation." And Article 54 allowed the captor the right "to require the giving up of, or to proceed to destroy, goods liable to condemnation found on board a vessel which herself is not liable to condemnation, provided that the circumstances are such as, according to Article 49, justify the destruction of a vessel liable to condemnation."

[50] The possible interpretations of Article 49 of the Declaration of London offered belligerents a latitude in destroying captured neutral vessels that was not too dissimilar from the license granted in the destruction of enemy prizes (the only substantial check being the obligation to compensate if a prize court later found that adequate ground for condemnation did not exist). It may of course be argued that this possible latitude opened to belligerents was not the intent of the drafters. If so, the true intent was hardly realized in the wording of Article 49, since it would be difficult to find a much broader formula. Nor is this conclusion altered by the fact that Article 51 required destruction only "in the face of an exceptional necessity"—a phrase broadly synonymous with "military necessity." For these reasons, it is difficult to accept the opinion that according to Article 49 of the Declaration "a neutral prize might no longer be destroyed because the captor could not spare a prize crew, or because a port of a Prize Court was too far distant, or the like." Oppenheim-Lauterpacht, *op. cit.*, p. 864.

Although the Allied Powers refrained during World War I from pursuing a policy of destroying captured neutral vessels, it can not be maintained that this policy was expressive of established law. For a review of the relevant provisions of the German and Italian prize regulations during the two wars—which did permit destruction in a number of circumstances—see Hackworth, *op. cit.*, Vol. VII, pp. 256–8. Paragraph 96 of the 1917 *Instructions* issued to U. S. naval forces declared that unless a neutral prize had engaged in a form of unneutral service, which stamped it with enemy character, it "must not be destroyed by the capturing officer save in case of the greatest military emergency which would not justify him in releasing the vessel or sending it in for adjudication." A substantially similar provision was made in paragraph 101 of the 1941 *Instructions*. And see the review of practice and opinion presented in *U. S. Naval War College, International Law Documents, 1943* (pp. 38–50) where the conclusion is drawn that: "Although there has still been some discussion since the World War as to whether or not a neutral prize should be destroyed, practice and documents indicate that the destruction of neutral vessels and aircraft captured as prizes may be destroyed only if warranted by the extreme seriousness of the military situation and by the utter impracticability of bringing the prize in for adjudication. In the case of destruction, passengers (if possible, their personal effects also), the crew, and the craft's papers must be placed in safety."

As matters presently stand it does not appear possible to define with any real precision the circumstances in which neutral prizes lawfully may be destroyed.[51] Undoubtedly it remains true, however, that the destruction of neutral prizes involves a much more serious responsibility for a belligerent, as well as for a belligerent commander, than does the destruction of an enemy prize. If it is later found that either the vessel or the cargo was not liable to condemnation indemnification of the innocent property must be made. For this reason, among others, the destruction of neutral prizes ought to be avoided whenever possible.

If destruction is nevertheless resorted to the captor is obliged—prior to the act of destruction—to provide for the safety of passengers and crew, and to insure that all documents and papers relating to the neutral prize are removed and saved in order that a prize court may later adjudicate upon the validity of the capture. These duties of the captor have long formed a part of the customary law, though the latter was not entirely clear as to what could be reasonably interpreted as a place of safety for passengers and crew. This point was clarified in Article 22 of the London Naval Treaty of 1930,[52] and in the subsequent London Protocol of 1936, which, in reaffirming the customary law as valid for both surface vessels and submarines, declared that "the ships boats are not regarded as a place of safety unless the safety of the passengers and crew is assured, in the existing sea and weather conditions, by the proximity of land, or the presence of another vessel which is in a position to take them on board."

In an earlier chapter some of the measures resorted to by belligerents—and particularly by Germany—in the attempt to evade these restrictions have been reviewed and analyzed.[53] At that time it was submitted that despite the persistence of these belligerent measures during the two World Wars there is still no substantial warrant for asserting that the traditional law has lost its validity [54] If so, this must mean that apart from certain

[51] "Neutral prizes," let it be noted, and not neutral vessels undergoing detention for search in ports. Destruction of the latter, save in the case of forcible resistance, is in any event forbidden.

[52] See p. 63 for text of Article 22.

[53] See pp. 296–305.

[54] Although this conclusion may admittedly prove of little comfort in any future conflict attended by the conditions that characterized the two World Wars. Nevertheless, this consideration can not be regarded as sufficient reason for asserting that the rule forbidding the destruction of neutral vessels, without first resorting to seizure and removing passengers and crew to a place of safety, is no longer binding. Whatever the possible justification that may be urged on behalf of unrestricted submarine and aerial warfare against enemy merchant vessels (see pp. 67–70), there is no similar case to be made for the destruction of neutral vessels without complying with the obligation laid down by the traditional law, save perhaps the extravagant belligerent claim that the economic isolation of an enemy justifies the destruction of neutral shipping intended for the enemy, whatever the means employed. It is this latter point that Professor Stone (*op. cit.*, p. 604) places emphasis upon, when he observes—in a stimulating and perceptive analysis of recent developments—that "the traditional distinction, for purposes of

limited exceptions—persistent refusal to stop upon being duly summoned, any form of forcible resistance to visit and search, taking a direct part in the hostilities on the side of an enemy [55]—a belligerent may not proceed to the destruction of neutral vessels without having first captured them and removed passengers and crew, as well as ship's papers, to a place of safety [56] Nor does the inability of submarines or aircraft to comply with these obli-

---

the right of capture and destruction, between goods carried in enemy and neutral bottoms has only a faded meaning when the acknowledged objective is 'annihilation of the enemy commerce.' " But there are methods and methods for accomplishing this "acknowledged objective," in itself not unlawful. To argue, however, that this objective must determine the rules that are to regulate belligerent conduct toward neutral shipping is to reduce this law to a mere simulacrum. No doubt there is a very large grain of truth in Professor Stone's criticism that: "Anglo-American publicists have regarded air and submarine craft as interlopers in naval warfare, which must play the game according to surface rules, or not at all, with no ground of complaint if the rules forbid their effective use." At the same time, it is one thing to insist upon a rigid observance by submarines and aircraft of rules whose denial does not involve the taking of neutral lives (e. g., diversion prior to visitation), and quite another thing to insist upon submarines and aircraft observing rules whose denial does involve the taking of neutral lives. There is little warrant for the rather deceptive categorization of the latter as merely part of the "game according to surface rules."

[55] To the acts enumerated above may be added the special control a belligerent may exert within an immediate area of naval operations (see pp. 300–1). The failure of a neutral vessel to conform to the special regulations established by a belligerent within this restricted area, and even to avoid it altogether, may well give rise to a liability to being fired upon. But even in those circumstances where a belligerent is permitted to fire upon, and possibly to destroy, a neutral vessel, without first seizing her and removing passengers and crew to a place of safety, the obligation remains to take all possible measures to search for and to rescue survivors. Insofar as the so-called "Laconia Order" (see pp. 72–3) was intended to apply to ***both enemy and neutral merchant vessels*** its unlawful character is patent.

[56] See *Law of Naval Warfare*, Article 503c.—In this connection it may be relevant to cite a rather curious—and obscure—passage in the judgment of the International Military Tribunal dealing with Admiral Doenitz. After condemning the establishment of operational zones within which neutral vessels were sunk without warning by submarines, and declaring that the contents of the "Laconia Order" (see pp. 72–3) "were undoubtedly ambiguous and deserve the strongest censure," the Tribunal went on to declare:

"The evidence further shows that the rescue provisions were not carried out and that the defendant ordered that they should not be carried out. The argument of the defense is that the security of the submarine is, as the first rule of the sea, paramount to rescue and that the development of aircraft made rescue impossible. This may be so, but the protocol [i. e., the 1936 London Protocol] is explicit. If the commander cannot rescue, then under its terms he cannot sink a merchant vessel and should allow it to pass harmless before his periscope. These orders, then, prove Doenitz is guilty of a violation of the protocol." For text of judgment, *U S. Naval War College, International Law Documents, 1946–47*, pp. 300–1.

The statement is confusing in that it appears to imply that so long as the submarine can and will rescue survivors, neutral merchant vessels may be sunk without warning. But the rule to which the Tribunal had reference clearly obligates belligerents not to "sink or render incapable of navigation a merchant vessel without having first placed passengers, crew, and ship's papers in a place of safety " Thus, under the 1936 London Protocol the problem of rescue does not even arise, since belligerents are under the obligation ***to capture*** the neutral vessel before resorting to its destruction (exception being made for those circumstances enumerated above).

gations serve to confer upon them any right to depart from the rules heretofore applicable—and still applicable—to surface vessels.

C. VISIT, SEARCH, SEIZURE AND DESTRUCTION OF NEUTRAL AIRCRAFT

In preceding pages [57] attention has been directed to some of the difficulties involved in the assumption that the rules regulating seizure and destruction of enemy vessels may be applied by analogy to the treatment of enemy aircraft. Similar difficulties are apparent in the further assumption that the position of neutral aircraft may be assimilated to the position of neutral vessels, the rules applicable to the latter being considered as generally applicable to neutral aircraft.[58] Here again—as in the case of enemy aircraft—the practice of states through World War II is far too slight to provide sufficient basis for discerning the emergence of specific rules grounded in the behavior of belligerents and neutrals. In the absence of either conventional regulation or of state practice that may be regarded as constitutive of customary rules any discussion of the specific limits imposed upon belligerents in interfering with neutral aircraft necessarily must prove of limited utility. It is possible, however, to indicate in broad outline the nature and scope of the measures permitted to belligerents.[59]

Undoubtedly, the various forms of assistance neutral aircraft may render belligerents justifies the latter in claiming the right to check the activities of neutral civil aircraft encountered anywhere outside of neutral jurisdiction.[60] Nor has there been any disposition to question the right of belligerent military aircraft to require neutral civil aircraft to deviate from their

---

[57] See pp. 108–11.

[58] An assumption that formed the basis of the relevant provisions (Articles 49, 53–6) of the 1923 Rules of Aerial Warfare.

[59] In part, the measures permitted to belligerents against neutral aircraft engaged in certain forms of unneutral service have already been indicated (see pp. 319 ff.).

[60] As in the case of warfare at sea, visit and search of neutral aircraft must be limited to aircraft formally commissioned in the armed forces of a belligerent. Less certain are the objects of the belligerent right of visit and search. Although it is generally assumed that this right extends to aircraft owned by the state, but operated for commercial purposes, the matter has yet to be resolved in practice. Even less certain is the right of a belligerent to capture and condemn neutral state-owned commercial aircraft found engaged in assisting a belligerent. The 1923 Rules of Aerial Warfare assumed that the law of prize would apply not only to privately owned aircraft but to publicly owned aircraft other than military aircraft and aircraft employed for customs or police purposes. The same assumption is reflected in *Law of Naval Warfare*, Section 500b. On the other hand Rowson (*op. cit.*, pp. 211–2) points out that: "This assimilation of certain neutral public non-military aircraft to private aircraft . . . overlooks . . . that for a neutral state to permit its own commercial aircraft to engage in activities which would render them liable to condemnation if they were private property is a breach of neutrality against which a belligerent should be allowed to protect himself without reference to a prize court."

course to a suitable locality where visit and search may be carried out.[61] At the same time, there is little indication of the procedure that is to be followed in ordering the diversion of neutral aircraft or the measures available to a belligerent in the event a neutral aircraft is unable to undertake diversion.[62]

It is clear that the substantive grounds justifying the capture of neutral aircraft are at least as broad as the rules justifying the capture of neutral vessels.[63] Thus neutral aircraft engaged in the carriage of contraband, breach of blockade (extended to the air), or the performance of unneutral service may be seized as prize. In principle, the duties incurred by a belligerent in seizing neutral vessels would appear to be equally applicable when

[61] Article 50 of the 1923 draft Rules permitted diversion for visit and search "to a suitable locality reasonably accessible." Failure to obey such orders would expose an aircraft to the risk of being fired upon.

[62] Of course, if a neutral aircraft attempts to flee upon being summoned, or offers any form of resistance to a belligerent military aircraft, then the latter is entitled to resort to force and even—if necessary—to destroy the neutral aircraft. The critical—and as yet unanswered—question concerns the measures available to a belligerent if the neutral aircraft is unable to undertake diversion, e. g., because of want of sufficient fuel. Although this question was not specifically dealt with in the 1923 Rules of Aerial Warfare it is indirectly covered by the stipulation in Article 50 that neutral aircraft may be deviated only to a "suitable locality reasonably accessible." In the comment to Article 50 it is declared that: "It would be a hardship to the neutral if he was obliged to make a long journey for this purpose and the locality must, therefore, not only be suitable, but must be reasonably accessible—that is, reasonably convenient of access. A more precise definition than this can scarcely be given; what is reasonably convenient of access is a question of fact to be determined in each case in the light of the special circumstances which may be present. If no place can be found which is reasonably convenient of access, the aircraft should be allowed to continue its flight." General Report of The Commission of Jurists, cited in *U. S. Naval War College*, *International Law Documents*, 1924, p. 141. It is not difficult to conceive of circumstancefs in which the course of action advocated above would result in the belligerent surrenderin g—or practical purposes—his right to suppress neutral aircraft engaged in rendering assistance to an enemy. Nor is it to be expected that belligerents will readily acquiesce to this solution, particularly if future conflicts witness rapid developments in air transport.

[63] Indeed, this would appear as a very conservative assumption, and it is quite likely that future developments in this area of the law will see an extension (as compared with the maritime rules) of the grounds justifying capture. Even Article 53 of the 1923 Rules of Aerial Warfare, although applying to neutral aircraft the rules already applicable to neutral merchant vessels, went beyond the latter rules in certain respects. Thus "neutral private aircraft" were held liable to capture not only for the carriage of contraband, breach of blockade and the performance of unneutral service, but also if "armed in time of war when outside the jurisdiction of its own country," or if found bearing no external marks or using false marks. Violation of a belligerent's prohibition against entering an area of operations—as defined in Article 30—constituted a further ground for capture.—And see *Law of Naval Warfare*, Article 503d for an enumeration of acts held to create a liability to capture if performed either by neutral vessels or aircraft.—Distinguish, however, between acts of neutral aircraft resulting in a liability to capture and acts which result not only in a liability to capture but to the destruction—if necessary—of the aircraft prior to capture. Liability to destruction prior to capture may arise either from the attempt to evade or to resist the exercise of belligerent rights, or from the performance of several types of unneutral service.

399334—57——24

capturing neutral aircraft.[64] Unless the neutral nationals serving as crew members have taken a direct part in the hostilities against the captor (or are found to be serving in the enemy's employ) they may not be made prisoners of war. With respect to the seized aircraft and cargo the captor is placed only in temporary possession pending adjudication of the capture by a court of prize. In consequence of his provisional possession reasonable measures must be taken to preserve the seized property intact and to turn it over to the custody of the officers of the prize court without undue delay. Finally, it does not appear that a captor is under any greater restriction in resorting to the destruction of neutral aircraft seized as prize than he is in resorting to the destruction of captured neutral vessels.[65]

---

[64] See pp. 347–8.

[65] See pp. 349–53. Also *Law of NavalWarfare*, Article 503c.—It is of interest to note that Articles 58 and 59 of the 1923 Rules of Aerial Warfare, concerning the destruction of captured neutral aircraft, were—if anything—more strict than the corresponding provisions of the Declaration of London, dealing with the destruction of neutral vessels seized as prize. Article 58 would have permitted the destruction of neutral aircraft seized for unneutral service, or for having no marks or bearing false marks, only when sending the aircraft in "would be impossible or would imperil the safety of the belligerent aircraft or the success of the operations in which it is engaged." Apart from these cases destruction was held to be justified only in the "gravest military emergency, which would not justify the officer in command in releasing it or sending it in for adjudication." In any case—according to Article 59—all persons on board an aircraft were to first be removed to a place of safety and the aircraft's papers preserved. If the captor later failed to show sufficient cause for destruction the interested parties were to be entitled to compensation—even though the capture was held to be valid. Finally, if the capture was later held to be invalid, though the act of destruction held to have been justifiable, compensation would also follow.

APPENDIX:
LAW OF NAVAL WARFARE

CHAPTER 1

INTRODUCTION

100 SCOPE AND METHOD OF PRESENTATION OF LAW OF NAVAL WARFARE [1]

Law of Naval Warfare has been prepared as a reference covering international law affecting the conduct of the naval forces in armed conflict. Although primary emphasis is upon the rules concerned with the conduct of naval and aerial warfare, attention is also directed to certain principles and problems common to the whole of the law of war.

The method of presentation consists in the exposition and clarification of those substantive portions of international law relating to naval warfare. The *text* contains the law as currently interpreted. The *notes* at the end of each chapter are keyed to the text and are included to present material in clarification of the law and to illustrate examples of deviation from the law.

Appendixes are included for further reference in connection with the text and footnotes.

110 STATUS AND APPLICABILITY OF LAW OF NAVAL WARFARE

Although a publication of the Department of the Navy, the *Law of Naval Warfare* cannot be considered as a legislative enactment binding upon courts and tribunals applying the rules of war.[2]

The laws of naval warfare will be considered to be applicable in any of the following situations:

1. A war formally declared by the Congress of the United States, or
2. Any armed conflict in which the naval forces of the United States are engaged, and in which the President, or a responsible official so empowered by him, directs the application of the laws of war.[3]

NOTES FOR CHAPTER 1

[1] Many of the articles of *U. S. Navy Regulations* (1948) are concerned with international law and with international relations of the United States. Article 0505, Observance of International Law, is quoted herewith:

1. In the event of war between nations with which the United States is at peace, a commander shall observe, and require his command to observe, the principles of international law. He shall make every effort consistent with those principles to preserve and protect the lives and property of citizens of the United States wherever situated.

2. When the United States is at war, he shall observe, and require his command to observe, the principles of international law and the rules of humane warfare. He shall respect the

rights of neutrals as prescribed by international law and by pertinent provisions of treaties, and shall exact a like observance from neutrals.

The following Articles of *U. S. Navy Regulations* (1948) are concerned with international law and with international relations:

Article	*Title*
0505	Observance of International Law
0610	Relations With Diplomatic and Consular Representatives
0613	Violations of International Law and Treaties
0614	Use of Force Against a Friendly State
0615	Issue of Ultimatum
0616	Important Circumstances To Be Reported
0617	Requests for Services Through a Consular Representative
0618	Communications With Foreign Officials
0619	Absence of Diplomatic or Consular Representative
0620	Protection of Commerce of the United States
0621	Granting of Asylum
0622	Territorial Authority of Foreign Nations
0623	Dealing with Foreigners
0625 (2) (3)	Shore Patrol
0627	Medical or Dental Aid to Persons Not in the Navy
0629 (1)	Assistance and Repairs to Ships and Aircraft in Distress
0630	If Refused Assistance
0632	Libel Against a Foreign Vessel
0642	Exercise of Power of Consul
0647	Boarding Calls
0707	Prisoners of War
0730	Search Not Permitted
0731	Discharge or Desertion of Aliens
0732 (1)	Persons Found Under Incriminating Circumstances
0733	Rules for Visits
0758	Hospital Ship or Aircraft
0760	Leaving Foreign Port With Outstanding Financial Obligations
0764	Customs and Immigration Inspections
0765	Quarantine
0777	Marriages on Board
1214	Relations With Foreign Nations
1215	Foreign Religious Institutions
1267	Appointments in the Diplomatic or Consular Service
1355	Detail of Persons in Noncombatant Status
1606 (4) (5)	General Rules for Official Correspondence
2005	Hospital Ships and Aircraft
2102	Honors Restricted to Recognized Governments
2103	International Honors Modified by Agreement
2106 (2)	Procedure During Playing of National Anthems
2108 (3)	Salutes to the National Ensign
2117	Gun Salute to a Foreign Nation
2118	Returning Salute to the Nation Fired by Foreign Warship
2119	Gun Salutes to the Flag of a Foreign President, Sovereign, or Member of a Reigning Royal Family
2120	Gun Salutes When Several Heads of State are Present
2123	Gun Salutes to Foreign Flag Officers
2126	Inability To Render or Return a Gun Salute

Article	*Title*
2127	Returning Gun Salutes
2128 (1) (4) (7).	Restrictions on Gun Salutes
2133.	Passing Honors to Foreign Dignitaries and Warships
2135 (1).	Dispensing With Passing Honors
2141.	Table of Honors for Official Visits of Foreign Officials and Officers
2148	Official Visits With Foreign Officials and Officers
2167	Dipping the National Ensign
2180.	Display of Foreign National Ensign During Gun Salutes
2181	Display of National Ensigns of Two or More Nations
2182.	Choice of Foreign Flag or Ensign in Rendering Honors
2183 (3).	Dressing and Full-Dressing Ship
2188	Foreign Participation in United States National Anniversaries or Solemnities
2189.	Observance of Foreign Anniversaries and Solemnities
2196.	Burial in a Foreign Place
2198.	Death of Diplomatic, Consular, or Foreign Official

[2] In the course of the war crimes trials conducted after World War II the question of the status of such official publications as the British and United States military manuals arose on various occasions. Although the courts recognized these publications as "persuasive statements of the law" and noted that insofar as the provisions of military manuals are acted upon they mould state practice, itself a source of international law, it was nevertheless stated that since these publications were not legislative instruments they possessed no formal binding power. Hence, the provisions of military manuals which clearly attempted to interpret the existing law were accepted or rejected by the courts in accordance with their opinion of the accuracy with which the law was set forth.

[3] Thus, the laws of war may apply in the following situations, among others:

1. Declared wars between the United States and one or more states.
2. Armed conflict between the forces of the United States and the forces of one or more states.
3. The employment of naval forces of the United States pursuant to the decision or recommendation of an international organization, e. g., the United Nations.

In his message to the Congress on December 8, 1941, President Roosevelt declared that "hostilities exist" and asked the Congress to declare that since December 7, 1941, "a state of war has existed between the United States and the Japanese Empire." On December 11, 1941, following a declaration of war against the United States by Germany and Italy, the President requested Congress

> " . . . to recognize a state of war between the United States and Germany, and between the United States and Italy " *U. S. Naval War College, International Law Documents, 1941* (1942), pp. 70–3.

In general, it has been, and continues to be, the policy of the United States to apply the laws of warfare to those situations in which the armed forces of the United States are engaged in armed conflict regardless of whether or not such hostilities are designated as "war."

There is a growing tendency among states to apply the laws of war not only to that status formally designated as "war" under traditional international law, but also to other forms of international armed conflict. The 1949 Geneva Conventions for the Protection of the Victims of War are important indications of this trend. Article 2, paragraph 1, common to all four of these Conventions, states that the provisions of the Conventions

> " . . shall apply to all cases of declared war or of any other armed conflict which may arise between two or more of the High Contracting Parties, even if the state of war is not recognized by one of them."

In the Charter of the United Nations the term "war" does not even occur, save in the preamble. The Charter speaks of "the use of force," "armed attacks," "breach of the peace," "enforcement actions," etc., but not of "war." This should not be taken to imply that the laws of war are inapplicable in an enforcement action taken by states in accordance with the provisions of the Charter. In the Korean action—significantly called, using the terminology of the Charter, an "enforcement action" but not a "war"—the United States military commander of those forces acting on behalf of the United Nations specifically declared the 1949 Geneva Conventions applicable to the conduct of hostilities.

CHAPTER 2

THE GENERAL PRINCIPLES OF THE LAWS OF WAR

200 WAR AND LAW

Although the resort to war is generally prohibited by the Charter of the United Nations, it is exceptionally permitted as an enforcement measure taken by or on behalf of the United Nations and as a measure of individual or collective self-defense against an armed attack. However, the distinction must be made between the resort to war and the conduct of war. Whether the resort to war is lawful or unlawful the conduct of war is regulated by the system of rules known as the laws (or rules) of war. These rules regulate the conduct of war on land, at sea, and in the air. The laws of war are designed to control and mitigate the harmful effects of war by extending, during time of war, at least a minimum standard of protection to combatants and noncombatants and to all individuals who come under the control of the belligerents. These laws are also helpful in regulating the transition to peace at the conclusion of active hostilities.

The laws of war are effective to the extent that they are obeyed by the belligerents.[1]

210 THE SOURCES OF THE LAWS REGULATING WARFARE [2]

The principal sources of the laws of war are custom and treaties

211 CUSTOMARY LAW

Customary laws of war develop out of the usage or practice of states when such usage or practice attains a degree of regularity and is accompanied by the general conviction that behavior in conformity with this usage or practice is both obligatory and right.[3] In a period marked by frequent resort to armed conflict, customary law may develop within a short time.[4]

212 TREATIES

Treaties, or conventions as they are sometimes called, are international agreements between two or more states. Certain conventions represent a codification of the rules of war already established by custom. There are also conventions by which new laws of war are created. Both types of conventions have provided the more important developments in the rules of war.[5]

(Footnotes at end of chapter)

213 BINDING FORCE OF RULES REGULATING WARFARE

a. Customary rules of war are binding on all belligerents and under all conditions.[6] Special rules apply in cases of reprisals against a belligerent for illegitimate acts of warfare. (See Section 310.)

b. Rules Established By Treaties. Rules established through a convention (treaty) are usually binding only between parties which have ratified or adhered to, and have not thereafter denounced or withdrawn from, the convention. Furthermore, the rules established through a convention are binding only to the extent permitted by the terms of the convention or by the reservations, if any, that have accompanied the ratification of or adherence to the convention. However, even when the above requirements are not met, a convention may represent, or come to represent, a general consensus as to the established law. Hence, the widespread observance of these conventional rules frequently renders them enforceable as law regardless of ratification.[7] As occasions arise, it is the responsibility of higher authority to determine and instruct forces afloat as to which, if any, of these conventions are not legally binding between the United States and other states immediately concerned, and as to which, if any, are for that reason not to be observed or enforced for the time being.

220 THE BASIC PRINCIPLES OF THE LAWS OF WAR

Among the customary rules of warfare there are three rules frequently referred to as the "basic principles of the laws of war": military necessity, humanity, and chivalry.[8] These rules, or basic principles, are defined as follows:

a. Military Necessity. The principle of military necessity [9] permits a belligerent to apply only that degree and kind of regulated force, not otherwise prohibited by the laws of war,[10] required for the partial or complete submission of the enemy with the least possible expenditure of time, life, and physical resources.

b. Humanity. The principle of humanity prohibits the employment of any kind or degree of force not necessary for the purpose of the war, i. e., for the partial or complete submission of the enemy with the least possible expenditure of time, life, and physical resources.[11]

c. Chivalry. The principle of chivalry forbids the resort to dishonorable (treacherous) means, expedients, or conduct. (See Section 640.)

221 THE DISTINCTION BETWEEN COMBATANTS AND NONCOMBATANTS

a. Distinction. The traditional laws of war are based largely on the distinction made between combatants and concombatants. In accordance with this distinction, the population of a belligerent is divided into two general classes: the armed forces (combatants) and the civilian population (noncombatants).[12] Each class has specific duties and rights in time of war, and no person can belong to both classes at the same time.

b. Restriction of hostilities. Under customary international law individuals who do not form a part of the armed forces and who refrain from the commission of all acts of hostility must be safeguarded against injury not incidental to military operations directed against combatant forces and other military objectives.[13] In particular, it is forbidden to make concombatants the object of a *direct attack* by the armed forces of a belligerent, if such attack is unrelated to a military objective.[14] Attack for the sole purpose of terrorizing the civilian population is also forbidden.[15]

230 NEUTRALITY

a. Definition. Neutrality may be defined as the nonparticipation of a state in a war between other states. Such nonparticipation must in turn be recognized by the belligerents. In the absence of any treaty limiting the available scope of neutrality (see Article 232), whether or not a state chooses to refrain from participating in war is a policy decision. Similarly, recognition of such nonparticipation is also a policy decision.

b. Obligations and rights. Under general international law a neutral state has certain obligations and rights toward belligerents, and belligerents have corresponding rights and obligations toward a neutral (see Section 440). The principle of impartiality holds that a neutral state is required to fulfill its obligations and enforce its rights in an equal manner toward all belligerents. If a neutral state does not observe the principle of impartiality the belligerent injured by such nonobservance may consider itself to be bound no longer by its obligations toward the neutral.[16]

231 THE DETERMINATION OF NEUTRAL STATUS OF STATES

Although it is usual, on the outbreak of war, for nonparticipating states to issue proclamations of neutrality, a special declaration by nonparticipating states of their intention to adopt a neutral status is not required.[17] The status of neutrality is terminated only when a neutral state resorts to war against a belligerent or when a belligerent resorts to war against a neutral.[18]

232 NEUTRALITY UNDER THE CHARTER OF THE UNITED NATIONS

The Charter of the United Nations imposes upon the member states the obligations to settle their international disputes by peaceful means and to refrain from the threat or use of force in their international relations. The obligation to refrain from the threat or use of force is modified by the right of individual and collective self-defense to be exercised in case of an armed attack until the Security Council has taken the necessary measures to restore peace and by the obligation to carry out the decisions of the Security Council. In case of a threat to or breach of the peace, the Security Council is authorized to take enforcement action, involving or not involving the use of armed force, in order to maintain or restore peace. The member states are obligated to give the United Nations every assistance in any action it takes and to refrain from giving assistance to any state against which the United Nations is taking action. Consequently, the members of the United Nations may be obliged to give assistance with their armed forces to the United Nations in its enforcement actions, the fulfillment of which obligation is incompatible with the status of neutrality. On the other hand, member states may be obliged to give assistance to the United Nations in its enforcement actions only with measures not involving the use of armed force. In this case, they may remain neutral, since they are not obliged to participate in the hostilities, although they are obliged not to observe an attitude of impartiality toward the belligerents. These obligations of the member states, incompatible with the status of neutrality and with the principle of impartiality, come into existence only if the Security Council fulfills the functions delegated to it by the Charter. If the Security Council is unable to fulfill its assigned functions, the members may, in case of a war, remain neutral and observe an attitude of strict impartiality.[19]

233 NEUTRALITY UNDER REGIONAL AND COLLECTIVE SELF-DEFENSE ARRANGEMENTS

The right of individual and collective self-defense established by the Charter of the United Nations may be implemented by regional and collective self-defense arrangements. Under these arrangements the possibility of maintaining a status of neutrality and of observing an attitude of impartiality depends upon the extent to which the contracting parties are obliged to give assistance to the regional action, or in the case of collective self-defense, to the victim of an armed attack.[20]

240 THE LAWS OF LAND WARFARE

Naval forces operating on land will be governed by the laws and customs of war on land.[21]

250 THE LAWS OF AIR WARFARE

There is no comprehensive body of laws specially applicable to air warfare in the same sense that there is a comprehensive body of specialized laws relating only to sea warfare and a similar body of laws relating only to land warfare.[22] There are, however, certain customary and conventional rules of a general character underlying the conduct of war on land and at sea which must be considered equally binding in air warfare.[23] In addition, there are certain specialized laws of sea and land warfare which may be considered applicable to air warfare as well.[24]

This book applies to the whole of naval warfare and thereby includes naval air warfare. Appropriate note is taken throughout this book of the situations in which the specialized rules of naval warfare do not similarly regulate the conduct of naval air warfare. In the absence of these distinctions, operational naval commanders are to assume that the rules regulating warfare at sea are equally applicable to naval air warfare.

NOTES FOR CHAPTER 2

[1] This statement does not refer to occasional violations of the rules of warfare. Such occasional violations do not substantially affect the validity of the law. However, the continuous violation of certain rules of warfare is a different matter, especially when such violations are not answered by protests and reprisals on the part of the belligerent against whom they are taken. Hence, reference is made here to this question: When do rules of warfare, either customary or conventional, cease to be valid for the reason that over a period of time they are neither obeyed nor applied by belligerents?

The experience of World War II, and of the war crimes trials which followed, seems to indicate quite clearly that the present principal area of uncertainty in the rules of war is that relating to the permissible *methods and weapons* for the conduct of actual military operations against members of the armed forces and the civilians who suffer as a result of such operations.

[2] Section 210 is limited to a consideration of the international regulation of warfare, and does not cover national regulation by the United States, which is dealt with in the *Uniform Code of Military Justice* and *U. S. Navy Regulations.*

[3] It is necessary to distinguish clearly between the usages of warfare (manner of warfare) and the customs of warfare. The development from usage to custom is a decisive one since, in a strict sense, it is only after a usage or practice has developed into a custom—i. e. only after a certain behavior is generally considered as both obligatory and right—that we are entitled to speak of legal rules of warfare.

In recent years there has been a marked tendency to include among the sources of the rules of war certain principles of law adopted by many states in their domestic legislation. In the judgment rendered in The Hostages Case the United States Military Tribunal stated:

> "The tendency has been to apply the term "customs and practices accepted by civilized nations generally," as it is used in International Law, to the laws of war only But the principle has no such restricted meaning. It applies as well to fundamental principles of justice which have been accepted and adopted by civilized nations generally. In determining whether such a fundamental rule of justice is entitled to be declared a principle of international law, an examination of the municipal laws of states in the family of nations will reveal the answer. If it is found to have been accepted generally as a fundamental rule of justice by most nations in their municipal law, its declaration as a rule of international law would seem to be fully justified." (*United States v. List et al.*) *Trials of War Criminals*, Vol. XI (1950), p. 1235.

[4] It is frequently difficult to determine the point in time at which a usage of war has developed into a customary rule. In addition, it has been a characteristic feature of the customary law of war that there have been numerous controversies between states over the precise content of these rules once their existence as law has been definitely established. These difficulties, among others, have led in the past to increased effort toward the codification of the law of war through written conventions (treaties).

[5] The most recently concluded international conventions relating to the regulation of the conduct of warfare are the 1949 Geneva Conventions For the Protection of War Victims.

[6] See Note 10 below for a discussion of the effect of the principle of military necessity upon the binding force of customary laws of war.

[7] Numerous multilateral agreements contain a provision similar to that contained in Article 28 of Hague Convention No. XIII (1907); namely, that "The provisions of the present convention do not apply except to the contracting powers, and then only if all the belligerents are parties to the convention." The effects of this so called "general participation" clause have not been as far-reaching as might be supposed. In World Wars I and II belligerents frequently affirmed their intention to be bound by agreements containing the general participation clause regardless of whether or not the strict requirements of the clause were actually met. Furthermore, certain conventions have been generally regarded either as a codification of preexisting customary law or as having come to represent, through widespread observance, rules of law binding upon all

states. Both the International Military Tribunals at Nuremberg and For the Far East treated the general participation clause in Hague Convention No. IV (1907), Respecting the Laws and Customs of War on Land, as irrelevant. They also declared that the general principles laid down in the 1929 Geneva (Prisoners of War) Convention, which does not contain a general participation clause, were binding on signatories and non-signatories alike. Article 2, paragraph 3, of all four 1949 Geneva Conventions states:

> "Although one of the Powers in conflict may not be a party to the present Convention, the Powers who are parties thereto shall remain bound by it in their mutual relations. They shall furthermore be bound by the Convention in relation to the said Power, if the latter accepts and applies the provisions thereof."

8 The confusion surrounding the principles of military necessity and of humanity is due largely to the fact that they have been used in two distinctly different senses. There has been a failure to clarify these two meanings. They may be, and often are, referred to as principles or *ideals* which, though not possessing the status of law, have been significant in their influence upon the course of development of the law of war. On the other hand, the principles of military necessity and of humanity also form a part of the positive law of war. This is the second sense in which they may be used, and it is in this sense that these principles are referred to in Section 220.

9 An excellent definition of the principle of military necessity is found in the following quotation:

> "Military necessity has been invoked by the defendants as justifying the killing of innocent members of the population and the destruction of villages and towns in the occupied territory Military necessity permits a belligerent, subject to the laws of war, to apply any amount and kind of force to compel the complete submission of the enemy with the least possible expenditure of time, life and money In general, it sanctions measures by an occupant necessary to protect the safety of his forces and to facilitate the success of his operations. It permits the destruction of life of armed enemies and other persons whose destruction is incidentally unavoidable by the armed conflicts of the war; it allows the capturing of armed enemies and others of peculiar danger, but it does not permit the killing of innocent inhabitants for purposes of revenge or the satisfaction of a lust to kill. The destruction of property to be lawful must be imperatively demanded by the necessities of war. Destruction as an end in itself is a violation of international law There must be some reasonable connection between the destruction of property and the overcoming of the enemy forces. It is lawful to destroy railways, lines of communication, or any other property that might be utilized by the enemy Private homes and churches even may be destroyed if necessary for military operations. It does not admit the wanton devastation of a district or the willful infliction of suffering upon its inhabitants for the sake of suffering alone."

The Hostages Case (*United States v. List et al.*), *Trials of War Criminals*, Vol. XI (1950), p. 1253-4.

10 The customary rule of military necessity may be, and in many instances is, restricted in its application to the conduct of war by other customary or conventional rules. The opinion that all rules of war are subject to, and restricted by, the operation of the principle of military necessity has never been accepted by the majority of American and English authorities. Furthermore, this opinion has not been accepted by military tribunals. It has been held by military tribunals that the plea of military necessity cannot be considered as a defense for the violations of rules which lay down absolute prohibitions (e. g., the rule prohibiting the killing of prisoners of war) and which provide no exception for those circumstances constituting military necessity Thus, one United States Military Tribunal, in rejecting the argument that the rules of war are always subject to the operation of military necessity, stated:

> "It is an essence of war that one or the other side must lose and the experienced generals and statesmen knew this when they drafted the rules and customs of land warfare. In short these rules and customs of warfare are designed specifically for all phases of war. They

comprise the law for such emergency To claim that they can be wantonly—and at the sole discretion of any one belligerent—disregarded when he considers his own situation to be critical, means nothing more or less than to abrogate the laws and customs of war entirely " The Krupp Trial (*Trial of Alfred Felix Alwyn Krupp Von Bohlen und Halbach and Eleven Others*), *Law Reports of Trials of War Criminals*, Vol. X (1949), p. 139.

However, there are rules of customary and conventional law which normally prohibit certain acts but which exceptionally allow a belligerent to commit these normally prohibited acts in circumstances of military necessity In conventional rules the precise formulation given to this exception varies. Some rules contain the clause that they shall be observed "as far as military necessity (military interests) permits." Other rules permit acts normally forbidden if "required" or "demanded" by the necessities of war. Rules providing for the exceptional operation of military necessity require a careful consideration of the relevant circumstances to determine whether or not the performance of normally prohibited acts is rendered necessary in order to protect the safety of a belligerent's forces or to facilitate the success of its military operations.

[11] The opinion is occasionally expressed that these two principles, necessity and humanity, contradict one another in the sense that they serve opposed ends. This is not the case. In allowing only that use of force necessary for the purpose of war, the principle of necessity implies the principle of humanity which disallows any kind or degree of force not essential for the realization of this purpose; that is, force which needlessly or unnecessarily causes or aggravates both human suffering and physical destruction. Thus, the two principles may properly be described, not as opposing, but as complementing each other. The real difficulty arises, not from the actual meaning of the principles, but from their application in practice.

[12] The terms "civilian population" and "noncombatants" are used interchangeably in Article 221, and refer to those peaceful inhabitants of a state who neither are attached to, nor accompany, the armed forces.

It should be observed that the term "noncombatants" also has a more restricted meaning and refers to certain categories of individuals who are attached to or accompany the armed forces of a belligerent, e. g., hospital personnel, chaplains, correspondents, etc. The status of these noncombatant categories is dealt with in the detailed provisions of the 1949 Geneva Convention for the Protection of Victims of War.

[13] In land warfare the noncombatant population must not, as a rule, be deprived of their private property except with payment therefor when such property must be requisitioned because of military necessity. However, in naval warfare the private property of the enemy population, as a rule may be seized and condemned in a court of prize. There are certain minor exceptions to this general right of seizure of private property at sea, e. g., small coastal (not deep sea) fishing vessels may only be seized under conditions of military necessity.

[14] Recent developments in the methods and weapons of warfare have decidedly affected this once fundamental distinction between combatants and noncombatants. These developments have been summarized as follows: growth of the number of combatants; growth of numbers of noncombatants engaged in war preparations; the development of aerial warfare; economic measures; and the advent of totalitarian states. (Oppenheim-Lauterpacht, *International Law*, Vol. II (7th ed., 1952), pp. 207–8). To the foregoing should be added the development of guided missiles and atomic and thermonuclear weapons.

The restriction of hostilities to the armed forces of a belligerent is therefore now valid subject only to far-reaching qualifications, particularly with respect to the conduct of aerial warfare (see also paragraph 503b for changes in naval warfare which presently affect the distinction between combatants and noncombatants). It should be pointed out, however, that the partial breakdown of the distinction between combatants and noncombatants applies mainly to the actual conduct of hostilities. The distinction remains quite effective insofar as it applies not to the conduct of hostilities but to the treatment of the victims of war who fall under the control of an enemy belligerent. The Geneva Conventions of 1949 have further clarified this distinction as it applies to the victims of war in the conventions dealing with the treatment of prisoners of war and with the protection of civilian persons in time of war.

[15] It should be emphasized that despite recent developments in the conduct of warfare, discussed above, the prohibitions against subjecting noncombatants to direct attack unrelated to a military objective or of attacking them for the purpose of terrorization remain valid.

[16] A state may be neutral, insofar as it does not participate in hostilities, even though it may be not impartial. Whether or not the successful maintenance of a position of nonparticipation is possible, in the absence of complete impartiality, is quite another question.

[17] Article 2 of Hague Convention No. III (1907) Relative to the Opening of Hostilities obligates belligerents to inform neutrals of the existence of a state of war.

> "Article 2. The existence of a state of war must be notified to the neutral Powers without delay, and shall not take effect in regard to them until after the receipt of a notification, which may, however, be given by telegraph. Neutral Powers, nevertheless, cannot rely on the absence of notification if it is clearly established that they were in fact aware of the existence of a state of war."

The above Article is binding between a belligerent state which is a party to Hague Convention No. III (1907) and neutral states which also are parties to the Convention.

[18] When the United States is a belligerent, the designation of neutral status of third states will be promulgated by Department of the Navy directives.

[19] In the absence of a Security Council decision, states may discriminate, and even resort to war, against a state they deem guilty of an illegal armed attack. This follows from Article 51 of the Charter which stipulates the "right of individual or collective self-defense if an armed attack occurs against a Member of the United Nations . . ." (It should also be noted that under the resolution "Uniting For Peace" the General Assembly of the United Nations may, in the event of a breach of the peace, make "appropriate recommendations to members for collective measures, including . . . the use of armed force when necessary . . ." However, at present these recommendations of the General Assembly do not constitute legal obligations for the member states.) In sum, then, although members may discriminate against an aggressor, even in the absence of any action on the part of the Security Council, they do not have the duty to do so. In these circumstances neutrality and complete impartiality both remain distinct possibilities.

[20] The principal effect of regional and collective self-defense arrangements is to transform the *right* of the parties to assist that state suffering from an armed attack into a *duty* to assist a state attacked. This duty may assume various forms, ranging from economic assistance to the undertaking of measures of armed force on behalf of the state attacked. Article 2 of the Inter-American Treaty of Reciprocal Assistance and Article 5 of the North Atlantic Treaty both obligate the contracting states, including the United States, to consider an armed attack against any contracting party as an armed attack against all of the contracting parties and to take any and all such measures as each state may consider necessary to assist the state so attacked.

[21] A compilation of the rules of land warfare is contained in *Law of Land Warfare*, FM 27–10 (1956), issued by the Department of the Army, and in supplements thereto.

[22] The few provisions of the Hague Conventions of 1899 and 1907 pertaining to the conduct of aerial warfare are generally recognized as no longer valid. The Rules of Aerial Warfare of February 19, 1923, drafted by the Commission of Jurists at The Hague, were never ratified by any of the participating states.

[23] An example of a customary rule of war applicable to aerial warfare is the prohibition against "wanton destruction of cities, towns, or villages, or devastation not justified by military necessity" (See subparagraph 320b(6) and Article 621). Equally applicable is the customary rule forbidding the denial of quarter unless bad faith is suspected; though, given the peculiar conditions of aerial warfare, this rule is frequently difficult to carry out in practice. The relevant Geneva Conventions of 1949, governing the treatment of the sick and wounded and of prisoners of war, are conventional rules of a general character applicable to air warfare.

[24] Caution must be exercised in indiscriminately attempting to apply "by analogy" these specialized rules of land warfare to air warfare. The peculiar conditions of aerial warfare have occasioned practices unique to this form of warfare. Consequently, the attempt to apply "by analogy" the specialized rules of land and sea warfare to air warfare may lead frequently to a disregard of these practices and to this extent be quite misleading. For example, the distinctions made between legitimate ruses and forbidden perfidy are different in land and in naval warfare. Yet neither the distinctions made in land warfare nor the distinctions made in naval warfare have been in accordance with the practices of air warfare.

399334—57——25

CHAPTER 3

ENFORCEMENT OF THE LAWS OF WAR

300 MEANS OF ENFORCEMENT OF THE LAWS OF WAR

Various means are available to belligerents under international law for inducing the observance of legitimate warfare.

In the event of a clearly established violation of the laws of war, an injured belligerent may resort to remedial action of the following types: [1]

1. Publication of the facts with a view to influencing world opinion against an offending belligerent.
2. Protest and demand for punishment of individual offenders. Such protest and demand for punishment may be communicated directly to an offending belligerent or to the commander of the offending forces. On the other hand, an offended belligerent may choose to forward its complaints through a protecting power,[2] a humanitarian organization acting in the capacity of a protecting power,[3] or any state not participating in the armed conflict.
3. Demand for compensation from an offending belligerent.[4]
4. Reprisals.[5] (See Section 310.)
5. Trial and punishment of captured individual offenders for war crimes. (See Section 330.)

310 REPRISALS [6]

a. Character and purpose. Reprisals between belligerents are acts, otherwise illegal, which are exceptionally permitted to a belligerent as a reaction against illegal acts of warfare committed by an enemy. The illegal acts justifying reprisals between belligerents may be committed by order of a government, by order of military commanders, or by the armed forces of a belligerent acting without higher authorization. The purpose of reprisals is to induce compliance with the laws of war.

b. When employed.[7] Reprisals are never to be taken merely for revenge but only as a last resort to induce an enemy to desist from unlawful practices. Whenever possible, the injured belligerent first must attempt to obtain the cessation of the illegal acts through methods other than reprisal. Acts taken in reprisal should be brought to the attention of the enemy, and of neutrals, if necessary, in order to achieve maximum effectiveness. As a general rule reprisals should not be employed by subordinate commanders in the absence of direct orders of the highest military authority. The

(Footnotes at end of chapter)

latter should give such orders only after as careful an inquiry into the alleged offense as circumstances permit.[8]

If immediate action is demanded as a matter of military necessity, a subordinate commander may, on his own initiative, order appropriate reprisals, but only after as careful an inquiry into the alleged offense as circumstances permit. Hasty or ill-considered action may be found subsequently to have been unjustified and may subject the officer himself to punishment for violation of the laws of war. Reprisals must cease as soon as they have achieved their objective, which is to induce a belligerent to desist from illegal conduct and to comply with the laws of war.

c. Forms of reprisal. The acts resorted to by way of reprisal need not conform to those complained of by the injured belligerent, but should not be excessive or exceed the degree of violence committed by the offending belligerent.

d. Objects of reprisals. Subject to the prohibitions enumerated in paragraph (e) below, reprisals may lawfully be taken against enemy individuals (i. e., members of the armed forces and of the civilian population) and property.

e. Reprisals: against whom forbidden. Reprisals are forbidden against the following:

1. Prisoners of war.[9]

2. Wounded, sick, and shipwrecked persons, as the latter are defined in the 1949 Geneva Convention for the Amelioration of the Condition of the Wounded, Sick and Shipwrecked Members of Armed Forces at Sea; hospital ships and medical aircraft, and the personnel of such ships and aircraft, as are protected by the same Convention.[10]

3. Wounded and sick personnel in the field, as they are defined in the 1949 Geneva Convention for the Amelioration of the Condition of the Wounded and Sick in Armed Forces in the Field; the buildings, equipment, and personnel that are protected by the same Convention.[11]

4. Civilian persons and their property, as these persons and property are defined in the 1949 Geneva Convention Relative to the Protection of Civilian Persons in Time of War.[12]

320 WAR CRIMES UNDER INTERNATIONAL LAW [13]

a. Definition of war crimes. War crimes may be defined as those acts which violate the rules established by customary and conventional international law regulating the conduct of warfare. Acts constituting war crimes may be committed either by members of the armed forces of a belligerent or by individuals belonging to the civilian population.

b. Examples of war crimes. The following acts are representative war crimes:

1. Offenses against prisoners of war: killing without due cause; the infliction of ill-treatment and torture, denial of minimum conditions conducive to life and health; causing the performance of unhealthy,

dangerous, or otherwise prohibited labor; infringement of religious rights; and deprivation of the right of a fair and regular trial.

2. Offenses against civilian inhabitants of occupied territories: killing without due cause; infliction of ill-treatment and torture; subjection to illegal experiments; deportation; compelling forced labor; compelling entry into the armed forces of the occupant; denial of religious rights; denaturalization; infringement of property rights; and denial of a fair and regular trial.

3. Offenses against the sick and wounded: killing, wounding, or otherwise ill-treating members of armed forces in the field who are disabled by sickness or wounds or who have laid down arms and surrendered.

4. Offenses against the survivors of sunken ships: killing, wounding, or otherwise ill-treating the shipwrecked, wounded, or sick at sea; failure to search out and make provision for the safety of survivors of sunken ships when military interests so permit.

5. Plunder and pillage of public or private property.

6. Wanton destruction of cities, towns, or villages or devastation not justified by military necessity; aerial bombardment whose sole purpose is to attack and terrorize civilian population.

7. Deliberate attack upon hospital ships, medical establishments, or medical units.

8. Maltreatment of dead bodies.

9. Abuse of, or firing on, a flag of truce.

10. Misuse of the Red Cross emblem or a similar protective emblem.

11. Denial of quarter, unless bad faith is reasonably suspected.

12. Treacherous request for quarter.

13. Imposing punishment, without a fair trial, upon spies and other persons suspected of hostile acts.

14. Violations of surrender terms.

15. Other analogous acts violating the accepted rules regulating the conduct of warfare.

330 PUNISHMENT OF WAR CRIMES UNDER INTERNATIONAL LAW

a. General. Belligerent states have the obligation under customary international law to punish their own nationals who violate the laws of war and the right to punish enemy nationals, whether members of the armed forces or civilian persons, who fall under their control.

b. Special defenses to charges of war crimes under international law

(1) *Defense of Superior Orders*. The fact that a person acted pursuant to order of his government or of a superior does not relieve him from responsibility under international law but may be considered in mitigation of punishment.[14] To establish responsibility the person must know, or have reason to know, that an act he is ordered to perform is unlawful under

international law.[15] In addition, if an act, though known to the person to be unlawful at the time of commission, is performed under duress, this circumstance may be taken into consideration either by way of defense or in mitigation of punishment.[16]

(2) *Responsibility of Commanding Officers.* Commanding Officers are responsible for illegitimate acts of warfare performed by subordinates when such acts are committed by order, authorization, or acquiescence of a superior. The fact that a commanding officer did not order, authorize, or acquiesce in illegal acts of warfare committed by subordinates does not relieve him from responsibility, provided it is established that the superior failed to exercise his authority to prevent such acts and, in addition, did not take reasonable measures to discover and stop offenses already perpetrated.[17]

(3) *Acts Legal or Obligatory Under National Law.* The fact that national law does not prohibit an act which constitutes a war crime under international law does not relieve the person who committed the act from responsibility under international law. However, the fact that an act which constitutes a war crime under international law is made legal and even obligatory under national law may be considered in mitigation of punishment.

NOTES FOR CHAPTER 3

1 Commanders are not usually required to make the policy decision as to the appropriate use of one or more of the remedial actions set forth in the text, although there are exceptional situations in which even junior commanders may be required to decide upon the use of reprisals, or to make protests and demands addressed directly to the commander of offending forces. It is also apparent that a governmental decision cannot be made intelligently unless all officers upon whom the responsibility for decision rests understand the available remedial actions and report promptly to higher authority those circumstances which may justify their use.

2 A "protecting power" is a neutral state entrusted with the protection of certain legal interests of one belligerent—particularly the interests of the latter's nationals—which have come under the control of another belligerent.

3 The International Red Cross, for example, has performed the duties of a protecting power.

4 Article 3 of Hague Convention No. IV (1907), Respecting The Laws and Customs of War on Land states:

> "A belligerent party which violates the provisions of the said (Hague) Regulations shall, if the case demands, be liable to pay compensation. It shall be responsible for all acts committed by persons forming part of its armed forces."

It is now generally established that the principle laid down in Article 3 is applicable to the violation of any rule regulating the conduct of war and not merely to violations of the Hague Regulations.

5 Reprisals must be clearly distinguished from retortion. Retortion is retaliation for *legally permissible* acts of a state which are of a cruel, discourteous, unfair, harassing, or otherwise objectionable nature by acts of a similar kind, i. e., by acts that are legally permissible. Reprisal is distinguished from retortion in that a reprisal is a retaliation against an illegal act and has the legal character of an enforcement action which may involve the use of armed force.

6 Section 310 deals only with reprisals taken by one belligerent in retaliation for illegal acts of warfare performed by the armed forces of an enemy. Section 310 does not deal with the

collective measures an occupying power may take against the population of an occupied territory in retaliation for illegitimate acts of hostility committed by the civilian population. Although the collective measures taken by an occupying power against the population of an occupied territory are frequently referred to as reprisals, they should be clearly distinguished from reprisals between belligerents, dealt with in Section 310.

[7] In addition to the legal conditions which must be satisfied before a belligerent may resort to reprisals, there are various political factors which governments will usually consider before taking reprisals. The importance of any of these factors will obviously depend upon the degree and kind of armed conflict, the character of the enemy and its resources, and the importance of the states not participating in the hostilities. The political factors are as follows:

1. Reprisals may have an adverse influence on the attitudes of governments not participating in a war.
2. Reprisals may only strengthen enemy morale and underground resistance.
3. Reprisals may only lead to counter-reprisals by an enemy, in which case the enemy's ability to retaliate effectively is an important factor.
4. Reprisals may render enemy resources less able to contribute to the rehabilitation of an area after the cessation of hostilities.
5. The threat of reprisals may be more effective than their actual use.
6. Reprisals, to be effective, should be carried out speedily and should be kept under control. They may be ineffective if random, excessive, or prolonged.
7. In any event, the decision to employ reprisals will generally be reached as a matter of strategic policy. The immediate advantage sought must be weighed against the possible long-range military and political consequences.

[8] The principle that reprisals should be taken only as a last resort has been interpreted to mean that an injured belligerent should first attempt, where possible and appropriate, to exhaust other means of redress before resorting to reprisals. If protest by an injured belligerent leads to the cessation of the illegitimate acts and if appropriate redress is made to the injured belligerent, the right to reprisals ceases. However, this requirement and the requirement that a careful inquiry be made into the real occurrence of the alleged acts are subject to the important qualification that, in certain circumstances, an offended belligerent is justified in taking immediate reprisals against illegal acts of warfare, particularly in those situations where the safety of his armed forces would clearly be endangered by a continuance of the illegal acts. Where immediate action is demanded as a matter of military necessity, a subordinate commander may, on his own initiative, order appropriate reprisals.

[9] "Measures of reprisal against prisoners of war are forbidden."—Article 13 paragraph 3 of the 1949 Geneva Convention Relative to the Treatment of Prisoners of War. This provision of the 1949 Geneva Convention reproduces a similar provision of the 1929 Geneva Convention on Prisoners of War. War crimes tribunals have considered the rule forbidding reprisals against prisoners of war as a codification of existing customary law. Hence, this prohibition may be regarded as binding upon all States regardless of whether or not they are parties to the 1949 Convention. As to those individuals who may be considered as coming within the category of "prisoners of war," see Article 4 of the 1949 Geneva Convention Relative to the Treatment of Prisoners of War.

[10] Article 47 of the 1949 Geneva Convention for the Amelioration of the Condition of the Wounded, Sick and Shipwrecked Members of the Armed Forces at Sea reads: "Reprisals against the wounded, sick and shipwrecked persons, the personnel, the vessels or the equipment protected by the Convention are prohibited." The "wounded, sick and shipwrecked" persons protected by the Convention are defined in Article 13 thereof.

[11] Article 46 of the 1949 Geneva Convention for the Amelioration of the Condition of the Wounded and Sick in Armed Forces in the Field reads: "Reprisals against the wounded, sick, personnel, buildings or equipment protected by the Convention are prohibited." The "wounded and sick" persons protected by the Convention are defined in Article 13 thereof.

[12] Articles 33 and 34 of the 1949 Geneva Convention Relative to the Protection of Civilian Persons in Time of War state:

"Article 33. No protected person may be punished for an offense he or she has not personally committed. Collective penalties and likewise all measures of intimidation or of terrorism are prohibited. Pillage is prohibited.

Reprisals against protected persons and their property are prohibited.

Article 34. The taking of hostages is prohibited."

The persons "protected" by the Convention against the measures enumerated in Articles 33 and 34 are identified in Article 4 thereof as those individuals located in the territories of the parties to a conflict, or in occupied territories, who find themselves under the control of a belligerent of which they are not nationals. As outlined in Article 4, however, Articles 33 and 34 do not protect the nationals of a state not bound by the Convention, nor do they apply to nationals of neutral and cobelligerent states maintaining normal diplomatic representation with the belligerent state in whose control these nationals may find themselves.

[13] War crimes, as defined in Section 320 (that is, acts violating the rules regulating the conduct of war) must be distinguished from so-called "crimes against peace" and "crimes against humanity." This distinction may be seen from Article 6 of the Charter of the International Military Tribunal at Nuremberg, which defined the Tribunal's jurisdiction as follows:

"The following acts, or any one of them, are crimes coming within the jurisdiction of the Tribunal for which there shall be individual responsibility:

(a) Crimes against peace. Namely, planning, preparation, initiation, or waging of a war of aggression or a war in violation of international treaties, agreements, or assurances, or participation in a common plan or conspiracy for the accomplishment of any of the foregoing.

(b) War Crimes. Namely, violations of the laws or customs of war. Such violations shall include, but not be limited to, murder, ill treatment, or deportation to slave labor or for any other purpose of civilian population of or in occupied territory, murder or ill treatment of prisoners of war or persons on the high seas, killing of hostages, plunder of public or private property, wanton destruction of cities, towns, or villages, or devastation not justified by military necessity.

(c) Crimes against humanity. Namely, murder, extermination, enslavement, deportation and other inhumane acts committed against any civilian population before or during the war or persecution on political, racial, or religious grounds in execution of or in connection with any crime within the jurisdiction of the Tribunal, whether or not in violation of the domestic law of the country where perpetrated." *U. S. Naval War College, International Law Documents, 1944–45* (1946), p. 254.

Although the distinction between crimes against peace and war crimes is readily apparent, there is a certain difficulty in distinguishing war crimes from crimes against humanity. The precise scope of those acts included within the category of crimes against humanity is not entirely clear from the definition given in Article 6 of the Charter of the International Military Tribunal at Nuremberg. A survey of the judgments of the various tribunals which tried individuals for crimes against humanity may be summarized in the following manner:

1. Certain acts constitute both war crimes and crimes against humanity and may be tried under either charge.

2. Generally, crimes against humanity are offenses against the human rights of individuals, carried on in a widespread and systematic manner. Thus, isolated offenses have not been considered as crimes against humanity, and courts have usually insisted upon proof that the acts alleged to be crimes against humanity resulted from systematic governmental action.

3. The possible victims of crimes against humanity constitute a wider class than those who are capable of being made the objects of war crimes and may include the nationals of the enemy state committing the offense as well as stateless persons.

4. Acts constituting crimes against humanity must be committed in execution of, or in connection with, crimes against peace, or war crimes.

On November 21, 1947, the United Nations General Assembly adopted a Resolution (177 (II)) directing the International Law Commission of the United Nations to do the following:

"(a) Formulate the principles of international law recognized in the Charter of the Nurnberg Tribunal and in the judgment of the Tribunal, and

(b) Prepare a draft code of offenses against the peace and security of mankind . . ."

The text of the principles formulated by the United Nations International Law Commission, with a commentary, is to be found in the *Report of the International Law Commission, covering its Second Session, General Assembly Official Records: Fifth Session, Supp. No. 12 (A/1316), Pt. III*, pp. 11–4 (1950). The text of the principles as formulated by the International Law Commission reads as follows:

"Principle I. Any person who commits an act which constitutes a crime under international law is responsible therefor and liable to punishment.

Principle II. The fact that internal law does not impose a penalty for an act which constitutes a crime under international law does not relieve the person who committed the act from responsibility under international law.

Principle III. The fact that a person who committed an act which constitutes a crime under international law acted as Head of State or responsible Government Official does not relieve him from responsibility under international law.

Principle IV. The fact that a person acted pursuant to order of his Government or of a superior does not relieve him from responsibility under international law, provided a moral choice was in fact possible to him.

Principle V. Any person charged with a crime under international law has the right to a fair trial on the facts and law.

Principle VI. The crimes hereinafter set out are punishable as crimes under international law: *(Here follow substantially similar definitions of crimes against peace, war crimes, and crimes against humanity, as are given in Article 6 of the Charter of the International Military Tribunal at Nuremberg, quoted at the beginning of this Note.)*

Principle VII. Complicity in the commission of a crime against peace, a war crime, or a crime against humanity as set forth in Principle VI is a crime under international law."

[14] Article 8 of the Charter of the International Military Tribunal at Nuremberg stated:

"The fact that the defendant acted pursuant to order of his government or of a superior shall not free him from responsibility but may be considered in mitigation of punishment if the Tribunal determines that justice so requires." *U. S. Naval War College, International Law Documents, 1944–45*, (1946), p. 255.

[15] The following statement indicates those circumstances in which the plea of superior orders may serve as a defense:

"Undoubtedly, a Court confronted with the plea of superior orders adduced in justification of a war crime is bound to take into consideration the fact that obedience to military orders, not obviously unlawful, is the duty of every member of the armed forces and that the latter cannot, in conditions of war discipline, be expected to weigh scrupulously the legal merits of the order received; that rules of warfare are often controversial; and that an act otherwise amounting to a war crime may have been executed in obedience to orders conceived as a measure of reprisals. Such circumstances are probably in themselves sufficient to divest the act of the stigma of a war crime." Oppenheim-Lauterpacht, *International Law*, Vol. II (7th ed.; 1952), p. 569.

As to the general attitude taken by military tribunals toward the plea of superior orders, the following statement is representative:

"It cannot be questioned that acts done in time of war under the military authority of an enemy cannot involve any criminal liability on the part of officers or soldiers if the acts are not prohibited by the conventional or customary rules of war. Implicit obedience to orders of superior officers is almost indispensable to every military system. But this implies obedience to lawful orders only. If the act done pursuant to a superior's orders be murder, the production of the order will not make it any less so. It may mitigate but it cannot justify the crime. We are of the view, however, that if the illegality of the order was not known to the inferior, and he could not reasonably have been expected to know of its illegality, no wrongful intent necessary to the commission of a crime exists and the inferior will be protected. But the general rule is that members of the armed forces are bound to obey only the lawful orders of their commanding officers and they cannot escape criminal liability by obeying a command which violates international law and outrages fundamental concepts of justice."

The Hostages Case (*United States v. Wilhelm List et al.*), *Trials of War Criminals*, Vol. XI (1950), p. 1236.

[16] An individual may plead duress if he can establish that he acted only under pain of an immediate threat, e. g., the immediate threat of physical coercion, in the event of noncompliance with the order of a superior. In the judgment of one Tribunal it was declared that

"... there must be a showing of circumstances such that a reasonable man would apprehend that he was in such imminent physical peril as to deprive him of freedom to choose the right and refrain from the wrong." The High Command Case (*United States v. Wilhelm von Leeb et al.*), *Trials of War Criminals*, Vol. XI (1950), p. 509.

The International Military Tribunal at Nuremberg declared in its judgment that the test of responsibility for superior orders "is not the existence of the order, but whether moral choice was in fact possible." *U. S. Naval War College, International Law Documents, 1946–47* (1948), p. 260.

[17] Some military tribunals have held that, in suitable circumstances, the responsibility of commanding officers may be based upon the failure to acquire knowledge of the unlawful conduct of subordinates. In The Hostages Case the United States Military Tribunal stated:

"Want of knowledge of the contents of reports made him [i. e., to the commanding general] is not a defense. Reports to commanding generals are made for their special benefit. Any failure to acquaint themselves with the contents of such reports, or a failure to require additional reports where inadequacy appears on their face, constitutes a dereliction of duty which he cannot use in his own behalf." (*United States v. Wilhelm List et al.*), *Trials of War Criminals*, Vol. XI (1950), p. 1271.

The responsibility of commanding officers for unlawful conduct of subordinates has not applied to isolated offenses against the laws of war but only to offenses of considerable magnitude and duration. Even in the latter instances, the circumstances surrounding the commission of the unlawful acts have been given careful consideration.

"It is absurd ... to consider a commander a murderer or rapist because one of his soldiers commits a murder or a rape. Nevertheless, where murder and rape and vicious, revengeful actions are widespread offenses, and there is no effective attempt by a commander to discover and control the criminal acts, such a commander may be held responsible, even criminally liable, for the lawless acts of his troops, depending upon their nature and the circumstances surrounding them." (*Trial of General Tomoyuki Yamashita*), *Law Reports of Trials of War Criminals*, Vol. IV (1948), p. 35.

Thus the responsibility of a commanding officer may be based solely upon inaction. It is not essential to establish that a superior knew, or must be presumed to have known, of the offenses committed by his subordinates.

CHAPTER 4

AREAS OF OPERATIONS

400 SCOPE

This chapter describes the legal divisions of the sea and of the air space; the areas in which belligerent naval operations are permitted; and the restrictions upon belligerents in neutral jurisdiction.

410 THE LEGAL DIVISIONS OF THE SEA

In international law navigable waters are classified under three headings: from the land outward to the open sea there are first inland waters, then territorial sea (waters), and, finally, the high seas. This section describes the dividing lines distinguishing the different legal classifications of navigable waters and the character of the legal control (or jurisdiction) exercised in each classification by states in time of peace.[1]

411 INLAND WATERS

a. Geographic extent. Inland waters comprise all those waters which lie within the base line of the territorial sea (see paragraph 412a). They consist of landlocked waters, rivers (including their mouths), canals, waters in ports and harbors, and certain of a state's gulfs and bays.

b. Legal control. A state has the same exclusive legal control over its inland waters as it has over its territory.

412 TERRITORIAL SEA (WATERS)[2]

a. Geographic extent. The territorial sea consists of a belt of the sea extending outward from the base line for at least three nautical miles (see paragraph 413c). The base line of the territorial sea is normally a line which follows the low-water mark along a coast. However, where a coast is deeply indented or cut into, or where there are islands in the immediate vicinity of a coast, the base line may be independent of the low-water mark.[3]

b. Legal control. A state's legal control over the territorial sea [4] is the same generally as its legal control over its inland waters, but there is one important difference. According to a rule of customary international law every state has the right of innocent passage for its merchant vessels in time of peace [5] through the territorial sea of every other state subject only to those limitations discussed below. In exercising this right of innocent passage, foreign merchant vessels must comply with the local regulations

(Footnotes at end of chapter)

of the shore state. Whether or not this right of innocent passage in time of peace extends equally to the warships of foreign states remains an unsettled point. However, it is at least clear that a shore state may enact such regulations as it considers necessary to govern the passage of warships through its territorial sea and has the right to insist that foreign warships leave its territorial sea in case of noncompliance with such regulations.[6] In addition, the right of innocent passage in time of peace must be granted to all vessels, whether merchant vessels or warships, through those territorial waters of a state which connect two parts of the high seas and which are used as a highway for international navigation.[7]

For the purposes of security and defense, as well as for other purposes,[8] states may establish certain restrictions upon the right of innocent passage of foreign vessels through their territorial sea. Such restrictions upon the right of innocent passage are not prohibited by international law, provided they are reasonable and necessary to ensure the security and defense of the coastal state. These controls may be exercised either during periods of peace or during war.[9]

413 HIGH (OPEN) SEAS

a. Geographic extent. The high seas consist of all waters which lie to seaward of the outer limit of the territorial sea.[10]

b. Legal control. The important legal characteristic of the high seas is that they are not, in geographic whole or part, under the legal control of any state. The legal order of the high seas is international law rather than national law. The general rule of customary international law is that the vessels of all states are free to sail the high seas, subject in time of peace only to the limitations discussed in the following paragraphs.

c. Claims to territorial waters in excess of three nautical miles. The majority of states, including the United States and Great Britain, limit their territorial sea to three nautical miles. However, several states claim a belt of territorial sea in excess of three nautical miles.[11]

d. Special controls established beyond territorial sea. It is the practice of most states to exercise a limited jurisdiction over foreign vessels for certain defined purposes in waters contiguous to their territorial sea.[12] Among the purposes for which states claim to exercise a limited jurisdiction in these contiguous waters (or "contiguous zones" as they are often called) are those of security and defense. Although this practice is recognized, in principle, and admitted in the practice of states, international law does not determine the geographical limits of such areas (contiguous zones), or the degree of legal control a coastal state may exercise in them, beyond laying down the general requirement of reasonableness in relation to the needs of national security and defense.[13] These special controls established beyond a state's territorial sea may be exercised either during periods of peace or during war.[14]

420 THE LEGAL DIVISIONS OF THE AIR SPACE

In international law the air space is classified under two headings: air space over the land, inland waters and territorial sea of a state; and air space over the high seas and unoccupied territories (i. e., territories not subject to the sovereignty of any state).

421 LEGAL CONTROL OVER THE AIR SPACE

According to customary international law, each state has exclusive legal control (jurisdiction) in the air space above its territory, inland waters, and territorial sea. There is no freedom of flight over inland waters and territory; nor is there a right of innocent passage through the air space over the territorial sea analogous to the right of innocent passage through the territorial sea. In the absence of a convention (treaty) regulating the flight of foreign civil or military aircraft through its air space, each state has complete discretion in regulating or in prohibiting such flight.

The air space over the high seas and over unoccupied territories remains free to the aircraft of all states (see paragraph 422c).

422 SPECIAL SITUATIONS

a. Jurisdiction of states over aerial intruders. There are as yet no firmly established rules governing the treatment to be accorded to military aircraft forced by weather conditions or distress to enter the air space of a foreign state without having obtained prior permission. However, the recent practice of states indicates that such intruding military aircraft are considered subject to reasonable measures of control by the state whose air space they have entered. For example, it has been considered a reasonable measure of control to require intruding military aircraft to land at a local airfield. On the other hand, recent practice has indicated that a territorial state does not have the right to resort to measures of armed force which may involve the taking of human life where such aircraft indicate a willingness to submit to reasonable measures of control.

b. Claims to air space over territorial sea in excess of three nautical miles. Several states claim jurisdiction in the air space [15] above the territorial sea where this sea is claimed, in turn, to extend beyond three nautical miles (see paragraph 413c).

c. Establishment of identification zones in air space adjacent to territorial air space. International law does not prohibit states from establishing air identification zones in the air space adjacent to their territorial air space.[16]

430 THE AREAS OF NAVAL WARFARE

a. The general area of naval warfare. The general area within which the naval forces of belligerents are permitted to conduct operations includes: the high seas, the territorial sea and inland waters of belligerents, the territory of belligerents accessible to naval forces, and the air space over such waters and territory.

b. THE IMMEDIATE AREA OF NAVAL OPERATIONS.[17] Within the immediate area or vicinity of naval operations, a belligerent may establish special restrictions (see, for example, paragraph 500f) upon the activities of neutral vessels and aircraft and may prohibit altogether such vessels and aircraft from entering the area. Neutral vessels and aircraft which fail to comply with a belligerent's orders expose themselves to the risk of being fired upon. Such vessels and aircraft are also liable to capture (see subparagraph 503d (7)).

440 RESTRICTIONS UPON BELLIGERENTS IN NEUTRAL JURISDICTION

This section describes the rules restricting the use by belligerents of neutral waters, ports, and air space. These rules [18] establish correlative rights and obligations of neutrals and belligerents and presuppose a neutral's duty to exercise its rights and to fulfill its obligations in an impartial manner toward all belligerents.[19]

441 ACTS OF HOSTILITY [20]

As a general rule, all acts of hostility in neutral jurisdiction are forbidden. This includes both visit and search and capture or destruction. However, a belligerent is not forbidden to resort to acts of hostility in neutral jurisdiction against enemy troops, vessels, or aircraft making illegal use of neutral territory, waters, or air space, if a neutral state will not or cannot effectively enforce its rights against such offending belligerent forces.[21]

442 BASE OF OPERATIONS

Belligerents are forbidden to use neutral territory, territorial sea, or air space as a base for hostile operations.

443 NEUTRAL TERRITORIAL SEA AND PORTS

a. PASSAGE THROUGH TERRITORIAL SEA. A neutral state may allow the mere passage of warships, or prizes, of belligerents through its territorial sea.[22]

b. BELLIGERENT STAY IN NEUTRAL PORTS AND WATERS.

(1) *Twenty-Four-Hour Limit.* In the absence of special provisions to the contrary in the laws or regulations of a neutral state, belligerent warships are forbidden to remain in the territorial sea, ports, or roadsteads of a neutral for more than twenty-four hours. This restriction does not apply to belligerent vessels devoted exclusively to humanitarian, religious, or scientific purposes. In addition, belligerent warships may be permitted by a neutral to extend their stay in neutral ports on account of stress of weather or damage (see paragraph e below). It is the duty of a neutral state to intern a belligerent warship, together with officers and crew, that will not or cannot leave a neutral port where she is not entitled to remain.[23]

(2) *Limitations on Stay and Departure.* In the absence of special provisions to the contrary in the laws or regulations of a neutral state, no

more than three warships of a belligerent are allowed to be in the same port or roadstead of a neutral at any one time. When warships of opposing belligerents are present in a neutral port at the same time, at least twenty-four hours must elapse between the departure of the respective enemy vessels. The order of departure is determined by the order of arrival, unless the vessel which arrived first is granted an extension of the period of stay. A belligerent warship cannot leave a neutral port or roadstead less than twenty-four hours after the departure of an enemy merchant ship.[24]

c. War materials, armaments, and communications. Belligerent warships may not make use of neutral ports, roadsteads, or territorial waters to replenish or to increase their supplies of war materials or their armaments or to erect any apparatus for the purpose of communicating with belligerent forces on land or at sea.[25]

d. Food and fuel. Belligerent warships in neutral ports or roadsteads are not forbidden to supply themselves with food and fuel, although there is no unanimity on the amount of food and fuel that may be taken on. In practice, it has been left to a neutral state to determine the conditions for the replenishment and refueling of belligerent warships. A neutral state may extend the lawful period of stay to vessels being supplied with fuel by twenty-four hours.[26]

e. Repairs. In neutral ports and roadsteads belligerent warships may carry out only such repairs as are absolutely necessary to render them seaworthy, and may not add in any manner whatsoever to their fighting force. It is the duty of a neutral state to decide what repairs are necessary and to insist that these be carried out with the least possible delay.[27]

f. Prizes. A prize may be brought into a neutral port only because of unseaworthiness, stress of weather, or want of fuel or provisions. It must leave as soon as the circumstances which justified its entry are at an end.[28] It is the duty of a neutral state to release a prize, together with its officers and crew, and to intern the prize crew in the event that a prize is unlawfully brought into the neutral's port or, having entered lawfully, fails to depart as soon as the circumstances which justified its entry are at an end.[29]

444 NEUTRAL AIR SPACE[30]

a. Belligerent entrance forbidden. Belligerent military aircraft are forbidden to enter the air space of a neutral state or to land within neutral territory or neutral territorial waters.

b. Duties of neutral. A neutral state must prevent belligerent military aircraft from entering its air space; must compel such aircraft to alight once they have entered, and must intern an intruding belligerent military aircraft together with its crew.[31]

c. Belligerent medical aircraft. The medical aircraft of belligerents may fly over neutral territory; may land thereon in case of necessity; or may use neutral territory as a port of call, subject to such regulations as the neutral may see fit to apply equally to all belligerents.[32]

NOTES FOR CHAPTER 4

[1] These classifications are significant also as between belligerents and neutrals.

[2] Limits of the territorial sea as claimed by the various states were summarized by the International Law Commission of the United Nations in 1952. A study of current legislation, as collected by the Secretariat shows the following:

Argentine*	1 league
Security	4 leagues
Customs	4 leagues
Fishing	12 miles
Australia	3 miles
Belgium	3 miles
Customs	10 kilometres
Brazil*	3 miles
Fishing	12 miles
Bulgaria	12 miles
Canada	3 miles
Customs	3 leagues
Fishing	12 miles
Ceylon	3 miles
Customs	2 leagues
Sedentary fisheries.	
Chile*	50 kilometres (1948)
Security	100 kilometres
Customs	100 kilometres
China (Nationalist Government)	3 miles
Customs	12 miles
Columbia	6 miles (1930)
Fishing	12 miles
Pollution of the sea	12 miles
Customs	20 kilometres
Costa Rica*	
Fishing	12 miles
Pollution of the sea	3 miles
Cuba	6 miles
Customs	12 miles
Fishing	3 miles
Pollution of the sea	5 miles
Social welfare	3 miles
Security (maritime frontier)	3 miles
Denmark	1 ordinary league
Customs	1 nautical mile (4 kvartmil)
Fishing	3 miles
Greenland	3 miles
Dominican Republic	3 leagues
Ecuador	12 miles
Security	4 leagues
Customs	4 leagues
Neutrality	4 leagues
Fishing	12 miles

*States claiming rights over a continental shelf.

Egypt	6 miles
Security	12 miles
Navigation	12 miles
Health control	12 miles
Customs	12 miles
Fishing	3 miles
El Salvador*	200 miles
Security	4 leagues
Customs	4 leagues
Finland	4 miles
Customs	6 miles
France; Fishing	3 miles
Neutrality	6 miles
Customs	20 kilometres
Security	3–6 miles
Algeria; Fishing	3 miles
Indo-China; Fishing	20,000 metres
Morocco; Fishing	6 miles
Tunisia; Customs	20,000 metres
Germany	3 miles
Greece	6 miles
Neutrality	6 miles
Security	10 miles
Guatemala*	12 miles
Customs	2 leagues
Honduras*	12 kilometres
Iceland	4 miles
India	1 league
Indonesia	3 miles
Iran*	6 miles
Customs	12 miles
Security	12 miles
Ireland	In accordance with international law
Israel	3 miles
Italy	6 miles
Customs	12 miles
Security, merchant vessels	10 miles (in time of peace)
Security, warships	6 miles (in time of peace)
Security, warships and merchant vessels	12 miles (in time of war)
Neutrality	6 miles
Japan	3 miles
Neutrality	3 ri
Korea, South;* Fishing	50–60 miles
Lebanon; Fishing	6 miles
Customs	20 kilometres
Criminal law	20 kilometres
Liberia	1 league
Mexico*	9 miles (1945)
Fishing	20 kilometres
Customs	20 kilometres
Netherlands	3 miles

*States claiming rights over a continental shelf.

Nicaragua*	
Norway	1 ordinary marine league
Fishing	1 ordinary marine league (7,529 metres)
Neutrality	3 miles
Customs	10 miles
Pakistan*	
Panama*	
Peru*	3 miles
Poland; In 1932	3 miles
Defence	6 miles
Customs	6 miles
Portugal	6 miles
Customs	6 miles
Fishing (1917)	Reciprocity
Neutrality	6 miles
Romania	12 miles
Saudi Arabia*	6 miles
Security	12 miles
Customs	12 miles
Spain	6 miles
Customs	6 miles
Neutrality	3 miles
Fishing	6 miles
Spanish Morocco; Neutrality	3 miles
Sweden	4 miles
Neutrality	3 miles
Customs	4 miles
Fishing (in the frontier waters of Denmark and Sweden)	3 minutes of latitude
Syria; Fishing	6 miles
Customs	20 kilometres
Turkey	6 miles
Customs	4 miles
Union of South Africa	3 miles
Union of Soviet Socialist Republics	12 miles
United Kingdom	3 miles
United States of America*	3 miles
Customs	4 leagues
California	3 miles
Florida	3 leagues
Louisiana	27 miles
Oregon	1 league
Washington	1 league
Uruguay	5 miles
Fishing	3 kilometres
Venezuela	3 miles
Security	12 miles
Customs	12 miles
Protection of interests (1944)	12 miles
Neutrality	3 miles
Health control	12 miles

*States claiming rights over a continental shelf.

Yugoslavia.	6 miles
Customs.	6 miles
Fishing.	10 miles

Report on the Regime of the Territorial Sea, J. P. A. Francoise. International Law Commission, Fourth Session, *United Nations General Assembly*, A/CN.4/53 (4 April 1952), pp. 11–15.

[3] In the Anglo-Norwegian Fisheries Case the International Court of Justice declared:

"Where a coast is deeply indented and cut into . . . or where it is bordered by an archipelago . . . the base-line becomes independent of the low-water mark, and can only be determined by means of a geometric construction. In such circumstances the line of the low-water mark can no longer be put forward as a rule requiring the coast line to be followed in all its sinuosities . . ." *International Court of Justice. Reports of Judgments, Advisory Opinions and Orders* (1951), pp. 128–9.

The Court went on to state in its judgment that although there is no one method presently obligatory under international law for determining a base line, where such determination must be independent of the low-water mark, there are general criteria which states must follow whatever method they may use:

". . . while . . . a State must be allowed the latitude necessary in order to be able to adapt its delimitation to practical needs and local requirements, the drawing of base-lines must not depart to any appreciable extent from the general direction of the coast. Another fundamental consideration . . is the more or less close relationship existing between certain sea areas and the land formations which divide or surround them. The real question raised in the choice of base-lines is in effect whether certain sea areas lying within these lines are sufficiently closely linked to the land domain to be subject to the regime of internal waters. . . . Finally, there is one consideration not to be overlooked, the scope of which extends beyond purely geographical factors: that of certain economic interests peculiar to a region, the reality and importance of which are clearly evidenced by a long usage." (p. 133)

In practice, several states have made use of the "straight-base lines" method where circumstances have not permitted the determination of the base line by following the low-water mark along the coast. The International Court of Justice noted:

"This method consists of selecting appropriate points on the low-water mark and drawing straight lines between them. This has been done, not only in the case of well-defined bays, but also in cases of minor curvatures of the coast line where it was solely a question of giving a simpler form to the belt of territorial waters." (pp. 129–30)

On the other hand, the Court did not agree that international law set specific limits to the length of such straight base-lines. Although the practice of certain states has been to consider landlocked waters less than ten nautical miles wide at the openings (or which are at the first point across such openings ten miles wide) as inland waters, and to measure the base-line of the territorial sea from a straight line drawn across these openings, the Court pointed out that:

"the ten-mile rule has not acquired the authority of a general rule of international law.' (p. 131)

Finally, there is the exceptional category of waters generally described as "historic waters." The International Court of Justice defined "historic waters" as:

". . . waters which are treated as internal waters but which would not have that character were it not for the existence of an historic title." (p. 130)

Examples of bays which fall within this category of historic waters are: Chesapeake Bay in the United States, Conception Bay in Newfoundland, and the Bay of Chaleurs in Canada.

[4] For the legal status of the air space above the territorial sea, see Article 421.

[5] "The word 'innocent' (in the phrase 'innocent passage') is to be interpreted with reference to the interests of the shore state, and perhaps its meaning appears more clearly in its French equivalent *inoffensif*. The international right of passage in no way diminishes the inherent right of every state to take such measures in its own territory, whether land or water, as it

may judge to be necessary for the protection of its own interests, and a voyage ceases to be 'innocent' if its purpose involves any violation of those interest." H. A. Smith, *The Law and Custom of the Sea* (2nd ed., 1950), pp. 34–5.

[6] For example, almost all states require submarines to be navigated on the surface when passing through their territorial sea.

[7] In the Corfu Channel Case the International Court of Justice declared:

> "It is . . . generally recognized and in accordance with international custom that States in time of peace have a right to send their warships through straits used for international navigation between two parts of the high seas without the previous authorization of a coastal state, provided that the passage is *innocent*. Unless otherwise prescribed in an international convention, there is no right for a coastal state to prohibit such passage through straits in time of peace." *The Corfu Channel Case* (Merits), International Court of Justice, Judgment of April 9, 1949, *U. S. Naval War College, International Law Documents, 1948–49* (1950), p. 142.

The Court went on to state in its judgment that the decisive criterion was not to be found in the importance of the North Corfu Channel Strait for international navigation, but "rather its geographical situation as connecting two parts of the high seas and the fact of its being used for international navigation." It is of further interest to note that the Court emphasized that the right of innocent passage imposed an obligation on the coastal state not to allow its waters to be used in such a way as to impair this right of other states. The particular facts of the case were that British warships were damaged by mines anchored in Albanian territorial waters.

Neither paragraph 412b of this text nor the Corfu Channel Case, discussed above, deals with the right of innocent passage in time of peace or of war through those straits and artificial canals whose status is expressly governed by treaty (convention), e. g., the Bosporus and the Dardanelles, the Suez Canal, and the Panama Canal.

[8] Among these purposes are customs, sanitation, fisheries, and conservation of resources.

[9] In the practice of the United States, special control areas for the purpose of defense and limited to territorial waters, have usually been termed "defensive sea areas." The President has the legal authority (as cited in the Executive Order No. 10361, June 12, 1952, F. R.) to establish defensive sea areas by executive order either in time of peace or in time of war. However, the practice has been to establish defensive sea areas only in time of war or a declared national emergency. Executive orders establishing defensive sea areas are usually promulgated by the Department of the Navy through General Orders.

[10] The fact that a portion of the sea is surrounded by the land of a particular state does not deprive it of its status as high seas if it is navigable and navigably connected with the high seas. A portion of the sea which is connected with the oceans of the world through a navigable passage which is a part of the territorial or inland waters of a particular state is a part of the high seas provided that the salt water connection is navigably open to the vessels of all states for passage.

[11] See Note 2 above. Naval vessels should not be navigated in or near such claimed territorial waters without having obtained prior authorization from higher authority.

[12] Such purposes are, for example: customs, sanitation, fiscal, fisheries, and conservation of resources. For a discussion of measures a state may take in the air space contiguous to territorial air space, see paragraph 422c.

[13] "The law of nations recognizes the contiguous zone in principle, but fixes no bounds for it and does not specify in any comprehensive fashion as to type or kind. Each claim to a zone must be examined individually and it is a characteristic of these areas that their legal basis rests upon the attitude of foreign states in each case. Any new claim to jurisdiction over foreign ships beyond the customary marginal limits (i. e., of territorial waters) may meet with the objection of the foreign state or states affected. If the latter refuse to accord recognition, they may legally assert that the zone has no legal standing; if they give consent, either expressly or by failure, over a period of time, to make protest, the

special area may be said to have been accepted as internationally valid." *U. S. Naval War College, International Law Situations, 1939* (1940), pp. 61–2.

[14] Measures of protective jurisdiction referred to in paragraph 413d may be accompanied by a special proclamation defining the area of control and describing the types of controls to be exercised therein. During World War II the President, by virtue of his authority as President and as Commander in Chief of the Armed Forces, formally proclaimed and established seventeen "maritime control areas" some of which included both the territorial sea and areas of the high seas contiguous to the territorial sea. All of these maritime control areas were discontinued in 1945 and 1946. In addition, so-called "defensive sea areas", though usually limited in past practice to the territorial sea, occasionally have included areas of the high seas as well. The statute authorizing the President to establish defensive sea areas by executive order does not restrict these areas to the territorial sea. It should also be noted that the establishment of special control areas extending beyond the territorial sea, whether established as "defensive sea areas" or as "maritime control areas", has been restricted in practice to periods of war or of declared national emergency. On the other hand, in time of peace the United States has exercised, and continues to exercise, a limited jurisdiction over foreign vessels in waters contiguous to its territorial sea. This limited jurisdiction has been exercised without establishing special defensive sea areas, or maritime control areas, covering such waters.

[15] Naval aircraft should not be flown into or near such claimed air space without having obtained prior authorization from higher command.

[16] It is apparent that the potential threat to the security of states presented by aircraft is considerably greater than the potential threat presented by vessels. However, there has not yet emerged a recognized practice of "contiguous air space zones," analogous to contiguous zones established on the high seas (see paragraph 413d), enabling states to exercise certain *legal controls* over aircraft flying outside territorial air space. The present system of Air Defense Identification Zones (ADIZ) employed by the United States extends to the air space above the open sea, and is limited to the purpose of identifying aircraft.

[17] The belligerent establishment of an "immediate area of naval operations" should be clearly distinguished from the belligerent practice during World Wars I and II of establishing "operational (or war) zones." The immediate area of naval operations refers to an area within which naval hostilities are taking place or within which belligerent naval forces are operating at the time. Belligerent control over neutral vessels and aircraft within an immediate area of naval operations is based upon a belligerent's right to attack, his right to defend himself without suffering from neutral interference, and his right to insure the security of his forces.

Operational (or war) zones refer to areas of the high seas, of widely varying extent, which, for substantial periods of time, are barred altogether to neutral shipping or within which belligerents claim the right to exercise a degree of control over neutral vessels not otherwise permitted by the rules of naval warfare. In practice, belligerents have based the establishment of operational zones on the right of reprisal against alleged illegal behavior of an enemy.

[18] The rules restricting the belligerent use of neutral waters and ports are covered, for the most part, in Hague Convention No. XIII (1907) Concerning the Rights and Duties of Neutral States in Maritime War. Two important naval powers, Great Britain and the Soviet Union, have never ratified this Convention. Technically the Convention did not bind the naval belligerents either in World War I or II. Nevertheless, the provisions of the Convention have been considered by states as being, on the whole, in accord with the rules of customary international law governing neutral rights and duties in naval warfare. The U. S. War Department Manual, *Law of Land Warfare*, FM 27–10 (1956), contains a summary of neutral rights and duties in land warfare.

[19] The preamble to Hague Convention No. XIII (1907) speaks of the "admitted duty" of neutral states to apply the rules of the Convention "impartially to the several belligerents." Article 9 of the same Convention obligates a neutral state to apply impartially "the conditions, restrictions, or prohibitions made by it in regard to the admission into its ports, roadsteads, or territorial waters, of belligerent ships of war or of their prizes" (see Section 230). The duty

of a neutral state, under Hague Convention No. XIII (1907) and according to the customary rules of neutrality, to exercise its rights and to fulfill its duties impartially may be severely restricted, and even abolished, by a treaty establishing a system of collective security (see Article 232). The provisions of Section 440 herein do not prejudice this possibility and should not be so considered.

[20] Articles 441 and 442 herein formulate general customary rules applicable equally to the conduct of land, naval, and aerial warfare. As applied to naval warfare, these customary rules are codified in Articles 2 and 5 of Hague Convention No. XIII (1907).

[21] A neutral state has the right, as well as the duty, to prevent—even by force—the improper use of its territory, waters, or air space by belligerents. In relation to an offending belligerent, the exercise of such preventive measures must be considered a right of a neutral. However, in relation to other belligerents the exercise of such preventive measures must be considered a duty of a neutral. It is customary to state that a neutral's duty is only to use "the means at its disposal" to prevent a violation of its neutrality. Thus, Article 25 of Hague Convention No. XIII (1907) obligates a neutral "to exercise such surveillance as the means at its disposal allow to prevent any violation . . . in its ports or roadsteads or in its waters." Nevertheless, it is recognized that when the means at the disposal of a neutral are clearly inadequate to fulfill its neutral obligations a belligerent is not forbidden from taking, as an extreme measure, acts of hostility in neutral jurisdiction against an enemy making improper use of such jurisdiction.

[22] Hague Convention No. XIII (1907), Article 10. The phrase "mere passage", which occurs in Article 10 of Hague Convention No. XIII, should be interpreted by reference to Article 5 of the same Convention, which prohibits belligerents from using neutral waters as a base of operations. Thus, the "mere passage" that may be granted to belligerent warships through neutral territorial waters must be of an innocent nature, in the sense that it must be incidental to the normal requirements of navigation and not intended in any way to turn neutral waters into a base of operations. In particular, the prolonged use of neutral waters by a belligerent warship either for the purpose of avoiding combat with the enemy or for the purpose of evading capture, would appear to fall within the prohibition against using neutral waters as a base of operations.

A neutral state may place additional restrictions upon the passage of neutral warships through its territorial sea, or prohibit such passage altogether, though it is under no duty to do so. However, any restrictions must be applied impartially to all belligerents.

[23] Hague Convention No. XIII (1907), Articles 12, 13, 14, and 24. The recent practice of most neutral states has been to adopt the twenty-four hour limit as the normal period of stay granted to belligerent warships. Paragraph 443b has reference only to the stay of belligerent warships in neutral ports, roadsteads, or territorial sea—not to *passage* through neutral territorial sea. The question as to whether or not Article 12 of Hague Convention No. XIII (1907) limiting *stay* to a period of twenty-four hours applies equally to *passage* remains unsettled, although it would appear that if the Convention is interpreted as permitting passage through neutral waters in excess of twenty-four hours such passage could not be used for purposes other than those necessitated by the normal requirements of navigation.

A neutral state may forbid altogether the stay of belligerent warships in its ports and roadsteads, although according to international practice exception must be made to permit the entrance of vessels in distress. However, the right of entry in distress does not prejudice the measures a neutral may take after entry has been granted, as the following comment emphasizes:

> "Insofar as permission to *enter* is concerned, international law does not distinguish between the causes of the distress. Vessels damaged by enemy gunfire or pursued by enemy craft are granted asylum in a fashion no different from warships driven in by stress of weather. Once admitted in distress, a belligerent warship is subject to varying treatment depending upon the causes of the distress. What should be done *after* admission is therefore a separate problem from that of the original entry. Force majeure gives a *right of entry only*, but no necessary right to repair the damage, to replenish supplies, to depart freely, or to be immune from punish-

ment." *U. S. Naval War College, International Law Situations, 1939* (1940), pp. 43–4.

[24] Hague Convention No. XIII (1907) Articles 15 and 16.

[25] Hague Convention No. XIII (1907) Articles 18 and 5. During World War II practically all neutral states prohibited the employment by belligerents of radiotelegraph and radiotelephonic apparatus within their territorial sea.

[26] Articles 19 and 20 of Hague Convention No. XIII (1907) deal with the problem of supplies in neutral ports. Article 19 of the Convention limits warships to a "normal peace supply" of food and, in practice, this standard has been adhered to generally by neutral states. However, the same Article 19 also establishes two quite different standards for refueling. Vessels may take on sufficient fuel "to enable them to reach the nearest port of their own country," or they may "take the fuel necessary to fill up their bunkers properly so-called, when in neutral countries which have adopted this method of determining the amount of fuel to be supplied." The majority of neutral states appear to have used the former standard, although it is evident that, given the appropriate circumstances, either standard may easily permit warships to continue their operations against an enemy. Article 20 of Hague Convention No. XIII (1907) forbids warships to renew their supply of fuel in the ports of the same neutral state until a minimum period of three months has elapsed.

[27] Hague Convention No. XIII (1907), Article 17. Many states have interpreted a neutral's duty to include forbidding, under any circumstances, the repair of damage incurred in battle. Hence, a belligerent warship damaged by enemy fire that will not or cannot put to sea once her lawful period of stay has expired, must be interned. However, some states have not interpreted a neutral's duty to include forbidding the repair of damage produced by enemy fire. Article 17 would appear to allow either interpretation.

[28] Hague Convention No. XIII (1907), Articles 21 and 22. There is a difference of opinion as to whether or not prizes may be kept in neutral ports pending the decision of a prize court. Article 23 of Hague Convention No. XIII (1907) permits neutrals to allow prizes into their ports "when they are brought there to be sequestrated pending the decision of a prize court." The United States did not adhere to Article 23 and has maintained the contrary position. In 1916 the British steamship *Appam*, seized by a German raider, was taken into Hampton Roads under a prize crew. The U. S. Supreme Court restored the vessel to her owners and released the crew on the basis that the United States would not permit its ports to be used as harbors of safety in which prizes could be kept. *The Steamship Appam*, 243 U. S. 124 (1917).

[29] *The City of Flint* incident, which occurred during World War II, is described in the following comment:

> "On October 9th, 1939 the American merchant steamer *City of Flint* was visited and searched by a German cruiser at an estimated distance of 1,250 miles from New York. The *Flint*, carrying a mixed cargo destined for British ports, was seized by the German cruiser on grounds of contraband, and a German prize crew was placed on board. Between the 9th of October and the 4th of November 1939 the American ship was taken first to the Norwegian port of Tromsoe, then to the Russian city of Murmansk, and then after two days in the last-named port, back along the Norwegian coast as far as Haugesund where the Norwegian authorities on November 4th released the *Flint* on the grounds of the international law rules contained in articles XXI and XXII of Hague Convention XIII of 1907. Prizes may be taken to a neutral harbor only because of an 'inability to navigate, bad conditions at sea, or lack of anchors or supplies.' The entry of the *Flint* into Haugesund on November 3 was not justified by the existence of any one of these conditions. The original visit and search and seizure of the *Flint* by the German warship, the placing of the prize crew on board, and the conduct of that crew were apparently all in accord with law. The stay in the harbor of Murmansk, however, was of doubtful legality. No genuine distress or valid reason for refuge in a so-called neutral harbor is evident from the examination of the facts. Perhaps the Germans and the Russians hoped to invoke the provisions of Article XXIII of Hague Convention XIII which authorizes a neutral power to permit 'prizes to enter its ports and roadsteads * * * when they are brought there to be sequestrated pending the decision of a prize court.' This

article has never been accepted generally as a part of international law and was specifically rejected by the United States in ratifying the convention. The situation was complicated by the equivocal position of Soviet Russia which was not a neutral in the traditional sense, in the European war. Under strict rules of international law the U. S. S. R. was derelict in regard to its neutral duties and should not have permitted the *Flint* either to enter Murmansk or to find any sort of haven there." *U. S. Naval War College, International Law Situations, 1939* (1940), pp. 24-5.

[30] Paragraphs a and b of this article summarize the practices followed by almost all neutral states during World Wars I and II. These practices may now be considered as possessing the status of customary rules.

An exception to this prohibition arises in the case of aircraft aboard a belligerent vessel which enters neutral territorial waters. In this instance the aircraft are considered to be part of the vessel's equipment.

[31] Whether or not a neutral state is obligated to prevent the entry into its air space of belligerent military aircraft in distress remains an unsettled point. However, there is little doubt that, if belligerent aircraft should enter neutral air space, such aircraft must be compelled to alight and must be interned, together with their crews.

[32] Article 40 of the 1949 Geneva Convention for the Amelioration of the Condition of the Wounded, Sick and Shipwrecked Members of Armed Forces at Sea provides for the flight of belligerent military aircraft over neutral territory as well as for the right of neutrals to "place conditions or restrictions on the passage or landing of medical aircraft on their territory." Despite the rules stated in a and b of this article, it might be noted that armed military transport aircraft were permitted to enter and depart from some neutral states in World War II.

CHAPTER 5

VESSELS, AIRCRAFT, AND PERSONNEL AT SEA

500 VESSELS AND AIRCRAFT

This chapter describes the legal status or character of vessels, aircraft, and personnel in warfare at sea, and the action permitted against them under international law.

a. VESSELS AND AIRCRAFT.[2] The term "vessels and aircraft" as used herein includes all objects which are or may be used as a means of transportation by states on or under the sea or in the air above the sea and land.

b. MERCHANT VESSELS AND AIRCRAFT. The term "merchant vessels and aircraft" refers to all vessels and aircraft, whether privately or publicly owned or controlled, which are not in the warship or military aircraft category,[3] and which are solely engaged in ordinary commercial activities.[4]

c. WARSHIPS. The term "warships" includes all vessels commissioned as a part of the naval forces of a state and authorized to display the appropriate flag or pennant as evidence thereof. Such vessels must in addition be commanded by a member of the military forces of a state and must be manned by a crew subject to military discipline.

d. MILITARY AIRCRAFT. The term "military aircraft" includes all aircraft operated by commissioned units of the naval forces of a state and includes military aircraft operated by commissioned units or other component parts of the armed forces which are engaged in operations at sea. Such aircraft must bear the military markings of their state, must be commanded by a member of the military forces, and must be manned by a crew subject to military discipline.

e. BELLIGERENT RIGHTS. At sea, only warships and military aircraft may exercise belligerent rights.

501 ENEMY CHARACTER

All vessels operating under an enemy flag and all aircraft bearing enemy markings possess enemy character. However, the fact that a merchant vessel flies a neutral flag or that an aircraft bears neutral marking does not necessarily establish neutral character. Any merchant vessel or aircraft owned or controlled by or for an enemy state, enemy persons, or any enemy corporation possesses enemy character, regardless of whether or not such a vessel or aircraft operates under a neutral flag or bears neutral markings.[5]

a. Neutral merchant vessels and aircraft acquire enemy character [6] and

(Footnotes at end of chapter)

are liable to the same treatment as *enemy warships and military aircraft* (see paragraph 503a) when engaging in the following acts:

1. Taking a direct part in the hostilities on the side of an enemy;

2. Acting in any capacity as a naval or military auxiliary to an enemy's armed forces.

b. Neutral merchant vessels and aircraft acquire enemy character and are liable to the same treatment as *enemy merchant vessels and aircraft* (see paragraph 503b) when engaging in the following acts:

1. Operating directly under enemy control, orders, charter, employment, or direction;

2. Resisting an attempt to establish identity, including visit and search.[7]

502 VISIT AND SEARCH

a. Occasions for exercise. The belligerent right of visit and search may be exercised anywhere outside of neutral jurisdiction upon all merchant vessels and aircraft [8] in order to determine their character (enemy or neutral), the nature of their cargo, the manner of their employment, or other facts which bear on their relation to the war. Historically, visit and search was considered the only legally acceptable method for determining whether or not a merchant vessel was subject to capture. It is now recognized that changes in warfare have rendered this method either hazardous or impracticable in many situations. In the case of enemy merchant vessels and aircraft and neutral merchant vessels and aircraft acquiring enemy character as described in the preceding article, the belligerent right of capture (and, exceptionally, destruction as described in paragraph 503b) need not be preceded by visit and search, provided that a positive determination of status can be obtained by other methods.[9] Whether or not the right of visit and search may be exercised upon neutral merchant vessels under convoy of neutral warships of the same nationality remains an unsettled matter in state practice.[10]

b. Methods of visit and search of merchant vessels.[11] In the absence of special instructions [12] issued during a period of armed conflict, the following procedure should be carried out:

1. In general, the belligerent right of visit and search should be exercised with all possible tact and consideration.

2. Before summoning a vessel to lie to, a warship must hoist her own national flag. The summons should be made by firing a blank charge, by international flag signal, or by other recognized means. The summoned vessel if a neutral, is bound to stop, lie to, and display her colors; if an enemy vessel, she is not so bound and legally may even resist by force, but she thereby assumes all risks of resulting damage.[13]

3. If a summoned vessel takes to flight, she may be pursued and brought to, by forcible measures if necessary.

4. When a summoned vessel has been brought to, the warship should send a boat with an officer to conduct the visit and search. If practicable a second officer should accompany the officer charged with the examination. The arming of the officers and the boat's crew is left to the discretion of the commanding officer of the visiting vessel.

5. If visit and search at sea of a neutral merchant vessel is deemed hazardous or impracticable, the neutral vessel may be escorted by the summoning vessel or by another vessel or by aircraft to the nearest place where search may be made conveniently.[14] In this case the neutral vessel should not be required to lower her flag, since she has not been captured, but she must proceed according to orders of the escorting vessel or aircraft.[15] A neutral vessel disobeying a belligerent's orders may be captured and sent in for adjudication.

6. A boarding officer should first examine a ship's papers in order to determine her character, ports of departure and destination, nature of cargo and employment, and other facts deemed essential. The papers which are generally found on board a merchant vessel are:

(a) Certificate of registry of nationality
(b) Crew list
(c) Passenger list
(d) Log book
(e) Bill of health
(f) Clearance
(g) Charter party, if chartered
(h) Invoices or manifests of cargo
(i) Bills of lading
(j) A consular declaration certifying the innocence of the cargo may be included.

7. The evidence furnished by papers against a vessel may be taken as conclusive. However, regularity of papers and evidence of innocence of cargo or destination furnished by them are not necessarily conclusive, and if any doubt exists the personnel of the vessel should be questioned and a search made—if practicable—of the ship or cargo. There are many circumstances which may raise legitimate doubt or suspicion. For example, if a vessel has deviated far from her direct course, this, if not satisfactorily explained, is a suspicious circumstance warranting search, however favorable the character of the papers. If search, under suspicious circumstances, does not satisfy a boarding officer of the innocence of a vessel, the vessel should be captured and sent in for adjudication. Even though a prize court may later order the release of the vessel, the commander sending the vessel in for adjudication acted properly if the result of visit and search appeared to furnish probable cause for capture.

8. When sending in a captured vessel as prize, the detailed prize pro-

cedures contained in *Instructions for Prize Masters and Special Prize Commissioners* (NAVEXOS P-825) are to be followed.[16]

9. Unless military security prohibits, the boarding officer must record the facts concerning the visit and search in the log book of the vessel visited, including the date when and the position where the visit occurred. The entry in the log book should be authenticated by the signature and rank of the boarding officer. Neither the name of the visiting vessel nor the name and rank of her commanding officer should be disclosed.

503 CAPTURE AND DESTRUCTION [17]

a. Enemy warships and military aircraft

(1) *Destruction.* Enemy warships and military aircraft (including naval and military auxiliaries) may be attacked and destroyed outside neutral jurisdiction.[18]

(2) *Capture.* Enemy warships and military aircraft may be captured outside neutral jurisdiction. Prize procedure is not used for such captured vessels and aircraft because their ownership immediately vests in the captor's government by the fact of capture.

b. Enemy merchant vessels and aircraft

(1) *Capture.* Enemy merchant vessels and aircraft may be captured outside neutral jurisdiction.

(2) *Destruction of Enemy Prizes.* Enemy merchant vessels and aircraft which have been captured may, in case of military necessity, be destroyed by the capturing officer when they cannot be sent or escorted in for adjudication.[19] Should the necessity for the destruction of an enemy prize arise, it is the duty of the capturing officer to take all possible measures to provide for the safety of passengers and crew.[20] All documents and papers relating to an enemy prize should be saved.[21] If practicable, the personal effects of passengers should be saved. Every case of destruction of an enemy prize should be reported promptly to higher command.

(3) *Destruction of Enemy Merchant Vessels Prior to Capture.*[22] Enemy merchant vessels may be attacked and destroyed, either with or without prior warning, in any of the following circumstances:

1. Actively resisting visit and search or capture.
2. Refusing to stop upon being duly summoned.
3. Sailing under convoy of enemy warships or enemy military aircraft.
4. If armed, and there is reason to believe that such armament has been used, or is intended for use, offensively against an enemy.
5. If incorporated into, or assisting in any way, the intelligence system of an enemy's armed forces.
6. If acting in any capacity as a naval or military auxiliary to an enemy's armed forces.

c. ENEMY VESSELS AND AIRCRAFT EXEMPT FROM DESTRUCTION OR CAPTURE. The following enemy vessels and aircraft, when innocently employed, are exempt from destruction or capture:

1. Cartel vessels and aircraft, i. e. vessels and aircraft designated for and engaged in the exchange of prisoners.

2. Properly designated hospital ships, medical transports, and medical aircraft.[23]

3. Vessels charged with religious, scientific, or philanthropic missions.[24]

4. Vessels and aircraft guaranteed safe conduct by prior arrangement between the belligerents.

5. Vessels and aircraft exempt by proclamation, operation plan, order, or other directive.

6. Small coastal (not deep-sea) fishing vessels and small boats engaged in local coastal trade and not taking part in hostilities. Such vessels and boats are subject to the regulations of a belligerent naval commander operating in the area.[25]

d. NEUTRAL MERCHANT VESSELS AND AIRCRAFT are in general liable to capture if performing any of the following acts.

1. Carrying contraband (see paragraph 631d).

2. Breaking, or attempting to break, blockade (see paragraph 632g).

3. Carrying personnel in the military or public service of an enemy.[26]

4. Transmitting information in the interest of an enemy.

5. Avoiding an attempt to establish identity, including visit and search.

6. Presenting irregular or fraudulent papers; lacking necessary papers; destroying, defacing, or concealing papers.

7. Violating regulations established by a belligerent within the immediate area of naval operations (see paragraph 430b).

When sending in captured neutral merchant vessels or aircraft as prize, the detailed prize procedures contained in *Instructions for Prize Masters and Special Prize Commissioners* (NAVEXOS P-825) should be followed.

e. DESTRUCTION OF NEUTRAL PRIZES. Although the destruction of a neutral prize is not absolutely forbidden, it involves a much more serious responsibility than the destruction of an enemy prize.[27] A capturing officer, therefore, should never order such destruction without being entirely satisfied that the military reasons therefor justify it; i. e. under circumstances such that a prize can neither be sent in nor, in his opinion, properly be released.[28]

Should the necessity for the destruction of a neutral prize arise, it is the duty of the capturing officer to provide for the safety of the passengers and crew.[29] All documents and papers relating to a neutral prize should be saved.[30] If practicable, the personel effects of passengers should be saved.

Every case of destruction of neutral prize should be reported promptly to higher command.

510 PERSONNEL

The following articles define the legal status of personnel and set forth the action permitted against them under international law.

511 ENEMY WARSHIPS AND MILITARY AIRCRAFT

a. CAPTURED ENEMY PERSONNEL. The officers and crews of captured or destroyed enemy warships and military aircraft (including naval and military auxiliaries) should be made prisoners of war.[31] Persons authorized by a belligerent to accompany his armed forces, though without actually being members thereof, also should be made prisoners of war.[32] Religious, medical, and hospital personnel taken from enemy warships and military aircraft should not be considered prisoners of war, although they may be retained by the belligerent commander, under whose authority they are, to minister to the needs of prisoners of war.[33]

b. ENEMY WOUNDED AND DEAD. As far as military interests permit, after each engagement all possible measures should be taken without delay to search for and collect the shipwrecked, wounded, and sick; to protect them against pillage and ill-treatment; to ensure their adequate care; and to search for the dead and prevent their being despoiled.[34]

c. QUARTER. It is forbidden to refuse quarter to any enemy who has surrendered in good faith.[35] In particular, it is forbidden either to continue to attack enemy warships and military aircraft, which have clearly indicated a readiness to surrender [36] or to fire upon the survivors of such vessels and aircraft who no longer have the means to defend themselves.[37]

512 ENEMY MERCHANT VESSELS AND AIRCRAFT

The officers and crews of captured enemy merchant vessels and aircraft may be made prisoners of war.[38] Other enemy nationals on board captured enemy merchant vessels and aircraft as private passengers are subject to the discipline of a captor.[39] The officers and crew who are nationals of a neutral state normally are not made prisoners of war.[40] However, if they participate in any acts of resistance against a captor, they may be treated as prisoners of war. The nationals of a neutral state on board captured enemy merchant vessels and aircraft as private passengers should not be made prisoners of war.

If for any reason (see subparagraph 503b3) an enemy merchant vessel or aircraft is rendered liable to attack, either with or without prior warning, the belligerent obligations defined in paragraphs 511b and c apply.

513 NEUTRAL MERCHANT VESSELS AND AIRCRAFT

a. OFFICERS AND CREWS. The officers and crews of captured neutral merchant vessels and aircraft, who are nationals of a neutral state, should not be made prisoners of war.[41]

b. Enemy nationals. Enemy nationals found on board neutral merchant vessels and aircraft as passengers who are actually embodied in the military forces of an enemy, or who are en route to serve in an enemy's military forces, or who are employed in the public service of an enemy, or who may be engaged in or suspected of service in the interests of an enemy may be made prisoners of war.[42]

520 COMMUNICATIONS

a. Communications by neutral merchant vessels and aircraft. A neutral merchant vessel or aircraft which, when on or over the high seas, transmits information destined for a belligerent concerning military operations or military forces is liable to capture.

Within the immediate vicinity of his forces, a belligerent commanding officer may exercise control over the communications of any neutral merchant vessel or aircraft whose presence might otherwise endanger the success of his operations. Legitimate distress communications by neutral vessels and aircraft should be permitted if they do not prejudice the success of such operations. A neutral vessel or aircraft which does not conform to a belligerent's control exposes itself to the risk of being fired upon and renders itself liable to capture.

b. Submarine telegraph cables. Submarine telegraph cables between points in an enemy's territory, between points in the territories of enemies, between points in the territory of an enemy and neutral territory, or between points in occupied territory and neutral territory are subject to such treatment as the necessities of war may require. Submarine telegraph cables between two neutral territories should be held inviolable and free from interference.

NOTES FOR CHAPTER 5

[2] Although aircraft are included with vessels here, it must be made clear that there are certain differences between the established rules of naval warfare dealing with the treatment of vessels and the practices (whose legal character remains uncertain in many respects) that have developed with respect to the treatment of aircraft. The primary concern of Section 500 is with the treatment of vessels during warfare at sea. However, both in the text of Section 500 and in the notes to this section, attention will be directed to the similarities in, as well as the differences between, the treatment of vessels and the treatment of aircraft.

[3] The term "merchant vessels and aircraft" therefore includes state-owned vessels and aircraft engaged in carrying persons or goods for commercial purposes.

[4] There is some difficulty involved in determining the precise status of state-owned vessels whose purposes are other than commercial in nature (e. g., customs and police vessels) but which do not belong to the armed forces of a state. It is clear, however, that such public vessels are not competent to exercise belligerent rights at sea.

[5] A neutral state may grant a merchant vessel or aircraft the right to operate under its flag, even though the vessel or aircraft remains substantially owned or controlled by enemy interests. According to the international law of prize, such a vessel or aircraft nevertheless possesses enemy character, and may be treated as enemy by the concerned belligerent.

There is no settled practice among states regarding the conditions under which the transfer of enemy merchant vessels (and, presumably, aircraft) to a neutral flag legitimately may be made. Despite agreement that such transfers will not be recognized when fraudulently made for the purpose of evading belligerent capture, states differ in the specific conditions that they require to be met before such transfers can be considered as *bona fide*. However, it is generally recognized that, at the very least, all such transfers must result in the complete divestiture of enemy ownership and control. The problem of transfer is mainly the proper concern of prize courts rather than of an operating naval commander, and the latter is entitled to seize any vessel transferred from an enemy to a neutral flag when such transfer has been made either immediately prior to, or during, hostilities.

[6] With the exception of resistance to visit and search, the acts defined here (and in examples 3 and 4 of paragraph 503d) have been traditionally considered under the heading of "unneutral service." Although originally established for and applied to the conduct of neutral vessels, the rules regarding unneutral service have been considered generally applicable to neutral aircraft as well.

The term "unneutral service" does not refer to acts performed by, and attributable to, a neutral state; that is to say, acts, the performance of which would, if performed by a neutral state, constitute a violation of the neutral state's obligations. It does refer to certain acts which are forbidden to neutral vessels and aircraft (other than neutral warships and neutral military aircraft). Attempts to define the essential characteristics common to acts constituting unneutral service have not been very satisfactory. However, it is clear that the types of unneutral service a neutral merchant vessel or aircraft may perform are varied; hence, the specific penalties applicable for acts of unneutral service may vary. The services enumerated in paragraph 501a are of such a nature as to identify a neutral vessel or aircraft with the armed forces of the belligerent for whom these acts are performed, and, for this reason, such vessels or aircraft may be treated in the same manner as enemy warships or military aircraft. The services defined in paragraph 501b also identify neutral merchant vessels and aircraft performing them with the belligerent, but not with the belligerent's armed forces. Such vessels and aircraft are assimilated to the position of, and may be treated in the same manner as, enemy merchant vessels and aircraft. The acts of unneutral service cited in paragraph 503d (examples 3 and 4) imply neither a direct belligerent control over, nor a close belligerent relation with, neutral merchant vessels and aircraft. By custom, vessels performing these acts, though not acquiring enemy character, are liable to capture.

[7] There are a number of ways by which neutral merchant vessels may attempt to frustrate a belligerent in the lawful exercise of belligerent rights, particularly the belligerent right of visit and search. Resistance to visit and search is the most serious act of this group, and its performance by neutral merchant vessels results in enemy character. Other ways, less serious, which result in liability to capture when performed by neutral merchant vessels, are given in paragraph 503d (examples 5 and 6).

[8] There are no reported instances of visit and search *of aircraft by aircraft*. Although the right of visit and search of aircraft by aircraft is unquestioned, there are no established practices indicating the manner in which this belligerent right may be exercised. Under ordinary circumstances the visit and search of aircraft will prove feasible only by ordering aircraft to proceed under escort to the nearest convenient belligerent landing area. Paragraph 502b of he text is restricted to a consideration of the belligerent right of visit and search of *merchant vessels*. The problem of visit and search *of aircraft by aircraft* should not be confused with the quite different problem of visit and search *of merchant vessels by aircraft* (see subparagraph 502b(5) and Notes 14 and 15 below).

[9] The possible dangers attendant upon the attempt to visit and search enemy merchant vessels are readily apparent. Since enemy vessels, with the exception of those enemy vessels enumerated in paragraph 503c, are always liable to capture, the prior exercise of visit and search is not considered mandatory, *provided* that a positive determination of enemy status can be made by other methods. Similar considerations apply to neutral merchant vessels acquiring enemy character, though here even greater caution be exercised.

[10] There is no common agreement, hence there are no settled rules, among states on this

point. While some states have denied the right of belligerent warships to visit and search neutral merchant vessels under convoy of neutral warships of their own nationality other states have insisted that a belligerent does possess such a right. In the past, the United States has adhered to the former position and the earlier *1941 Instructions Governing Maritime and Aerial Warfare* (paragraphs 57, 58 and 59) contained the following provisions:

> "Neutral vessels under convoy of vessels of war of their own nationality are exempt from search. The commander of a convoy gives, in writing, at the request of the commander of a belligerent ship of war, all information as to the character of the vessels and of their cargoes which could be obtained by visit and search.
>
> If the commander of the United States vessel has reason to suspect that the commander of the convoy has been deceived regarding the innocent character of any of the vessels (and their cargoes or voyages) under his convoy shall impart his suspicions to the latter. In such a case it is to be expected that the commander of the convoy will undertake an examination to establish the facts. The commander of the convoy alone can conduct this investigation, the officers of the United States visiting vessel can take no part therein.
>
> The commander of the convoy may be expected to report the result of his investigation to the commander of the United States vessel. Should that result confirm the latter's suspicions, the former may further be expected to withdraw his protection from the suspected vessel; whereupon she shall be made a prize by the commander of the United States vessel."

The above-quoted provisions should serve as a guide for operating naval commanders in those situations in which commanders are without, and are unable to obtain, instructions from higher command. It should be emphasized that neutral merchant vessels under convoy of enemy warships acquire enemy character and are always liable to capture.

[11] See Note 8 above.

[12] The practice of issuing Navicerts resorted to by Great Britain in World Wars I and II and similar procedures are typical of such "special instructions." For the general consideration relating to Navicerts see Chapter 6, Note 23.

[13] On the other hand, a neutral merchant vessel is obligated not to resist the belligerent right of visit and search.

[14] The consistent practice of belligerents in World Wars I and II has firmly established the belligerent right of search in port. As to belligerent deviation of neutral merchant vessels before either visit or search, the following comment is instructive:

> "If deviation for search be conceded, there can in principle be no objection in proper cases to allowing the diversion to take place before visit, that is to say, without insisting upon a formal boarding of the suspected vessel. The purpose of visit is to ascertain whether there are any grounds for search and detention. Under modern conditions it will often happen that the evidence justifying detention is already in the hands of the belligerent government, having been obtained by . . . intelligence methods. If that be so, nothing that is likely to be found in the ship's papers will add to the available evidence, and the boarding in such case becomes an idle formality." H. A. Smith, *The Law and Custom of the Sea* (2nd ed., 1950), p. 168.

The question of deviation without prior visit or search is of particular relevance in the case of belligerent military aircraft. Although there is no question of the right of belligerent military aircraft to visit and search vessels at sea, it is apparent that this right can be exercised only infrequently. In those circumstances in which visit and search is impracticable (and particularly when information concerning a vessel is already held that, if verified by search, would justify her capture), a belligerent military aircraft may order a vessel to proceed under escort as directed.

[15] In its essential features, the practice of deviation (diversion) is merely a prolongation of the act of visit and search. A diverted vessel, while proceeding to port or any other convenient place, is under detention by a belligerent in the same sense as a vessel being visited and searched at sea. Hence, while vessels under diversion are subject to the control of escorting vessels or aircraft, they are not considered, or treated, as prizes.

[16] NAVEXOS P-825 (JAG) records the World War II amendments to the United States Prize Statutes and to the Federal District Court Rules relating to prize adjudication. Pages 1 through 10, and Forms 1 through 4 of that publication are of particular importance to commanding officers. The United States' statutes on prize, which apply to *captured vessels and aircraft*, are found in Title 34 of the United States Code, Chapter 20, Sections 1131–1167 (the applicable portions of which are quoted below).

Under ordinary circumstances, prizes should be sent promptly to a port within the jurisdiction of the United States for adjudication. In general, a prize master with a crew should be sent on board the prize for this purpose. If for any reason this is impracticable, a prize may be escorted into port by the capturing vessel, or by another vessel of war of the United States or a co-belligerent. The prize must obey the instructions of the escorting vessel, under pain of forcible measures.

The applicable provisions of the United States Code are as follows:

> "The commanding officer of any vessel making a capture shall secure the documents of the ship and cargo, including the log book, with all other documents, letters and other papers found on board, and make an inventory of the same and seal them up and send them, with the inventory, to the court in which proceedings are to be had, with a written statement that they are all the papers found and are in the condition in which they were found; or explaining the absence of any documents or papers or any change in their condition. He shall also send to such court, as witnesses, the master, one or more of the other officers, the supercargo, purser, or agent of the prize, and any person found on board whom he may suppose to be interested in, or to have knowledge respecting, the title, national character, or destination of the prize. He shall send the prize with the documents, papers, and witnesses, under charge of a competent prize master and prize crew, into port for adjudication, explaining the absence of any usual witnesses; and in the absence of instructions from superior authority as to the port to which it shall be sent, he shall select such port as he shall deem most convenient, in view of the interests of probable claimants. If the captured vessel, or any part of the captured property is not in condition to be sent in for adjudication, a survey shall be had thereon and an appraisement made by persons as competent and impartial as can be obtained, and their report shall be sent to the court in which proceedings are to be had; and such property, unless appropriated for the use of the Government, shall be sold by the authority of the commanding officer present, and the proceeds deposited with the Treasurer of the United States or public depository most accessible to such court and subject to its order in the cause." (34 U. S. C. 1133)
>
> "The prize master shall make his way diligently to the selected port and there immediately deliver to a prize commissioner the documents and papers, and the inventory thereof, and make affidavit that they are the same and are in the same condition as delivered to him, or explaining any absence or change of conditions therein, and that the prize property is in the same condition as delivered to him, or explaining any loss or damage thereto; and he shall further report to the district attorney and give to him all the information in his possession respecting the prize and her capture; and he shall deliver over the persons sent as witnesses to the custody of the marshal and shall retain the prize in his custody until it shall be taken therefrom by process of the prize court." (34 U. S. C. 1134)

If circumstances permit, it is preferable that the officer making the search should act as prize master. Section 1140, Title 34, of the United States Code defines the procedure to be followed when converting a prize, whether enemy or neutral, to public use. The code requires that, prior to any such conversion

> ". . . it (any captured vessel . . .) shall be surveyed, appraised, and inventoried by persons as competent and impartial as can be obtained, and the survey, appraisement, and inventory shall be sent to the court in which proceedings are to be had . . ." (34 U. S. C. 1140)

While any prize thus may be legally converted to immediate public use, and would be under compelling circumstances, it is inadvisable so to convert neutral property captured as prize, because indemnification will follow if the prize court fails to condemn the property. (See Note 19 below.)

[17] See Note 22 below.

[18] The prohibition against committing acts of hostility within neutral jurisdiction is subject to the provisions of Article 441.

[19] As against an enemy, title to captured enemy merchant vessels or aircraft vests in the captor's government by virtue of the fact of capture. However, claims may be made by neutrals, either with respect to the captured vessel or aircraft or with respect to the cargo (normally, non-contraband neutral cargo on board a captured enemy vessel is not liable to confiscation). For these reasons, it is always preferable that captured enemy prizes be sent in for adjudication, whenever possible.

[20] See Note 22 below.

[21] All the documents and papers of a prize, as required by United States Code, Title 34, Section 1133 (see Note 16 above), should be taken on board the capturing vessel of war and should be inventoried and sealed, in accordance with the procedure set forth in that section, for delivery to the prize court, with especial view to the protection of the interests of the owners of innocent neutral cargo on board, if such exists. A list of such documents and papers is furnished in subparagraph 502b (6).

[22] According to the customary and conventional law of naval warfare valid prior to World War II, a belligerent warship or military aircraft was forbidden to destroy an enemy merchant vessel or render her incapable of navigation without having first provided for the safety of passengers and crew; exception being made in the circumstances of persistent refusal to stop on being duly summoned or of active resistance to visit and search (or capture). Thus, Article 22 of the London Naval Treaty of 1930 stated:

> "(1) In their action with regard to merchant ships, submarines must conform to the rule of International Law to which surface vessels are subject.
>
> (2) In particular, except in the case of persistent refusal to stop on being duly summoned, or of active resistance to visit or search, a warship, whether surface vessel or submarine, may not sink or render incapable of navigation a merchant vessel without having first placed passengers, crew, and ship's papers in a place of safety. For this purpose the ship's boats are not regarded as a place of safety unless the safety of the passengers and crew is assured, in the existing sea and weather conditions, by the proximity of land, or the presence of another vessel which is in a position to take them on board."

Article 22 of the 1930 London Naval Treaty was incorporated *verbatim* into the London Protocol of 1936, to which almost all of the major belligerents of World War II expressly acceded. These rules, deemed declaratory of customary international law, have been interpreted as applicable to belligerent military aircraft in their action toward enemy merchant vessels. (On the other hand, it is difficult to estimate the extent to which the obligations embodied in the London Protocol of 1936 have been considered by belligerents as applicable, by analogy, to the treatment of nonmilitary enemy aircraft. The little experience to be gained in this respect from the practices of belligerents during World War II is not very instructive. At best, enemy nonmilitary aircraft received no better treatment than enemy merchant vessels. However, it may be stated that in addition to the difficulties of proper identification, the manifest difficulties of successfully exercising either visit and search or any similar type of effective control over aircraft forbid any easy application by analogy of the rules governing the treatment of merchant vessels to aircraft. Hence, in the absence of any clearly established practice to the contrary, it may be assumed that the obligations laid down in the London Protocol of 1936 have not been considered mandatory in the case of enemy aircraft.)

During World Wars I and II the belligerent practice of attacking and sinking enemy merchant vessels without warning (or only with the most peremptory warning), and without having first provided for the safety of passengers and crew, was widespread. It is true that in the early period of World War II, as in World War I, the belligerent claim to sink enemy merchant vessels, without warning and in violation of the obligations laid down in the London Protocol of 1936, was generally justified as a reprisal against illegal acts of an enemy.

In its judgment on Admiral Doenitz, the International Military Tribunal at Nuremberg acquitted the accused of the charge of waging unrestricted submarine warfare (i. e., sinking without warning) against British merchant vessels, for the following reasons:

"Shortly after the outbreak of war the British Admiralty . . . armed its merchant vessels, in many cases convoyed them with armed escort, gave orders to send position reports upon sighting submarines, thus integrating merchant vessels into the warning network of naval intelligence. On 1 October 1939, the British Admiralty announced that British merchant ships had been ordered to ram U-boats if possible." *U. S. Naval War College, International Law Documents, 1946–47* (1948), p. 299.

[23] Article 22 of the 1949 Geneva Convention for the Amelioration of the Condition of the Wounded, Sick and Shipwrecked Members of Armed Forces at Sea states:

"Military hospital ships, that is to say, ships built or equipped by the Powers specially and solely with a view to assisting the wounded, sick and shipwrecked, to treating them and to transporting them, may in no circumstances be attacked or captured, but shall at all times be respected and protected, on condition that their names and descriptions have been notified to the Parties to the conflict ten days before those ships are employed."

The proper marking for military hospital ships is described in Article 43 of this Convention. Further provisions of the Convention provide that enemy hospital ships must not "hamper the movement of the combatants" and that "during and after an engagement, they will act at their own risk" (Article 30). In order to insure that hospital ships are innocently employed, belligerents:

". . . shall have the right to control and search the vessels . . . They (belligerents) can refuse assistance from these vessels, order them off, make them take a certain course, control the use of their wireless and other means of communication, and even detain them for a period not exceeding seven days from the time of interception, if the gravity of the circumstances so require." (Article 31.)

Article 14 of this Convention gives to belligerents the right to demand that the wounded, sick and shipwrecked on board military hospital ships be surrendered "provided that the wounded and sick are in a fit state to be moved and that the warship can provide adequate facilities for necessary medical treatment."

On the whole, these provisions may be considered as declaratory of established rules of customary international law. On the other hand, the provisions of the same 1949 Geneva Convention for the Amelioration of the Condition of the Wounded, Sick and Shipwrecked Members of the Armed Forces at Sea on the subject of medical transports and medical aircraft are new, and go far toward resolving problems that the practices of belligerents hitherto had left unsettled. Article 38 states:

"Ships chartered for that purpose shall be authorized to transport equipment exclusively intended for the treatment of wounded and sick members of armed forces or for the prevention of disease, provided that the particulars regarding their voyage have been notified to the adverse Power and approved by the latter. The adverse Power shall preserve the right to board the carrier ships, but not to capture them or seize the equipment carried."

Article 39 states:

"Medical aircraft, that is to say, aircraft exclusively employed for the removal of the wounded, sick and shipwrecked, and for the transport of medical personnel and equipment, may not be the object of attack, but shall be respected by the Parties to the conflict, while flying at heights, at times and on routes specifically agreed upon between the Parties to the conflict concerned.

They shall be clearly marked with the distinctive emblem prescribed in Article 41, together with their national colors, on their lower, upper and lateral surfaces. They shall be provided with any other markings or means of identification which may be agreed upon between the Parties to the conflict upon the outbreak or during the course of hostilities.

Unless agreed otherwise, flights over enemy or enemy-occupied territory are prohibited.

Medical aircraft shall obey every summons to alight on land or water. In the event of having thus to alight, the aircraft with its occupants may continue its flight after examination, if any.

In the event of alighting involuntarily on land or water in enemy-occupied territory, the wounded, sick and shipwrecked, as well as the crew of the aircraft shall be prisoners of war. The medical personnel shall be treated according to Articles 36 and 37."

[24] Article 4 of Hague Convention No. XI (1907) states:

"Vessels charged with religious, scientific, or philanthropic missions are . . . exempt from capture."

[25] Article 3 of Hague Convention No. XI (1907) states:

"Boats used exclusively in the coast fishery or in local trade are exempt from capture, as well as their appliances, rigging, tackle, and cargo.

They cease to be exempt as soon as they take any part whatever in hostilities.

The Contracting Powers bind themselves not to take advantage of the harmless character of the said vessels in order to use them for military purposes while preserving their peaceful appearance."

It is necessary to emphasize that the immunity of small coastal fishing vessels and small boats depends entirely upon their "innocent employment". If found to be assisting a belligerent in any manner whatever (e. g., if incorporated within a belligerent's naval intelligence network) they may be captured or destroyed. Refusal to provide immediate identification upon demand is sufficient basis for the capture or destruction of such vessels and boats. See also Note 20 above and subparagraphs 632g (3) and (4).

[26] Normally, a neutral merchant vessel is not considered liable to capture for the acts enumerated in examples 3 and 4 of paragraph 503d if, when encountered at sea, she is unaware of the opening of hostilities, or if the master, after becoming aware of the opening of hostilities, has not been able to disembark those passengers who are in the military or public service of a belligerent. A vessel is deemed to know of the state of war if she left an enemy port after the opening of hostilities, or a neutral port after a notification of the opening of hostilities had been made in sufficient time to the Power to which the port belonged. However, it should be apparent that actual knowledge is often difficult or impossible to establish. Because of the existence of modern means of communication, a presumption of knowledge may be applied in all doubtful cases. The final determination of this question properly can be left to the prize court.

[27] By the fact of capture the title to a neutral merchant vessel or aircraft is held in trust by the government of the captor pending adjudication by a prize court. Innocent neutral cargo on board does not change title by reason of the capture. See also Article 633.

[28] It should be observed that paragraph 503e refers to the destruction of neutral merchant vessels whose capture for any of the acts enumerated in paragraph 503d has already been effected. Paragraph 503e does not refer to neutral merchant vessels merely under detention and directed into port for visit and search.

[29] See Note 22 above. The obligations laid down in the London Protocol of 1936, insofar as they apply to neutral merchant vessels and aircraft, remain valid; exception being made only for those neutral merchant vessels and aircraft performing any of the acts enumerated in paragraphs 501a and b, and paragraph 430b. In its judgment on Admiral Doenitz, the International Military Tribunal at Nuremberg found the accused guilty of violating the London Protocol of 1936 by proclaiming "operational zones" and sinking neutral merchant vessels entering these zones.

". . . the protocol made no exception for operational zones. The order of Doenitz to sink neutral ships without warning when found within these zones, was, therefore, in the opinion of the Tribunal, a violation of the protocol." *U. S. Naval War College, International Law Documents, 1946–1947* (1948), p. 300.

[30] See Note 16 above.

[81] The personnel of neutral merchant vessels and aircraft engaged in any of the acts enumerated in paragraph 501a also should be treated, when captured, as prisoners of war. *U. S. Navy Regulations* (1948), Article 0707, Prisoners of War, reads:

> "On taking or receiving prisoners of war, the commanding officer shall assure that such prisoners are treated with humanity; that their personal property is preserved and protected; that they are allowed the use of such of their effects as may be necessary for their health; that they are supplied with proper rations; that they are properly guarded and deprived of all means of escape and revolt. . . ."

Detailed provisions concerning the treatment to be accorded prisoners of war are contained in the 1949 Geneva Convention Relative to the Treatment of Prisoners of War.

[82] Article 4, paragraph A (4) of the 1949 Geneva Convention Relative to the Treatment of Prisoners of War states that the following persons are entitled to treatment as prisoners of war:

> "Persons who accompany the armed forces without actually being members thereof, such as civilian members of military aircraft crews, war correspondents, supply contractors, members of labor units or of services responsible for the welfare of the armed forces, provided that they have received authorization from the armed forces which they accompany, who shall provide them for that purpose with an identity card. . . ."

[83] Religious, medical and hospital personnel so retained are subject to the discipline imposed by the captor. The provisions of the 1949 Geneva Conventions governing the treatment of such personnel falling into the hands of the enemy are: Article 37 of the Convention for the Amelioration of the Condition of the Wounded, Sick and Shipwrecked Members of Armed Forces at Sea; Articles 28, 29, 30 and 31 of the Convention for the Amelioration of the Condition of the Wounded and Sick in Armed Forces in the Field; and Article 33 of the Convention Relative to the Treatment of Prisoners of War.

[84] The obligations defined in paragraph 511b may be considered as part of customary law. (See, in addition, Article 16 of Hague Convention No. X, 1907, and Article 18 of the 1949 Geneva Convention for the Amelioration of the Condition of the Wounded, Sick and Shipwrecked Members of Armed Forces at Sea.)

[85] Article 23 paragraphs c and d of the Regulations Respecting the Laws and Customs of War on Land, annexed to Hague Convention No. IV (1907), which are equally applicable to naval warfare, state that:

> ". . . it is especially forbidden— . . . c. To kill or wound an enemy who, having laid down his arms, or having no longer means of defense, has surrendered at discretion; d. To declare that no quarter will be given; . . ."

However, quarter can be refused when those who ask for it subsequently attempt to destroy those who have granted it.

[86] "As soon as an attacked or counter-attacked vessel hauls down her flag and, therefore, signals that she is ready to surrender, she must be given quarter and seized without further firing. To continue an attack although she is ready to surrender, and to sink the vessel and her crew, would constitute a violation of customary International Law, and would only, as an exception, be admissible in case of imperative necessity or of reprisals." Oppenheim-Lauterpacht, *International Law*, Vol. II (7th ed., 1952), p. 471.

In the trial of Helmuth Von Ruchteschell before a British Military Court, one of the war crimes charged to the accused was that he continued to fire upon enemy merchant vessels after the latter had indicated surrender. In the notes on the trial, the following comment occurs concerning surrender at sea:

> "The entire question . . . was: are there generally recognized ways of indicating surrender at sea other than hauling down a ship's flag? Two expert witnesses (a captain in the Royal Navy and a former vice-admiral in the German Navy) gave evidence, *inter alia*, on the customs in this regard of their respective services. The common denominator of their evidence could be thus stated: (1) the attacked ship must stop her engines; (2) if the attacker signals, the signal must be answered—if the wireless is out of action, it must be answered by a sig-

nalling pennant by day or by torch or flashlight by night; (3) the guns must not be manned, the crew should be amidships and taking to the lifeboats; (4) the white flag may be hoisted by day and by night, all the ship's lights should be put on." *Trial of Helmuth Von Rushteschell, Law Reports of Trials of War Criminals*, Vol. IX (1949), p. 89.

[37] It is useful to consider the prohibition against the firing at helpless survivors of enemy vessels together with the duty of a belligerent to take all possible measures, consistent with the security of its own forces, to rescue the survivors of enemy vessels after an engagement (see paragraph 511b). The duty to rescue survivors is subject to the qualification of operational necessity. On the other hand, the prohibition against firing at helpless survivors is not so qualified and is absolute.

[38] Article 6 of Hague Convention No. XI (1907) states:

> "The captain, officers, and members of the crew who are nationals of the enemy State, are not made prisoners of war, on condition that they undertake, on the faith of a formal written promise, not to engage, while hostilities last, in any service connected with the operations of the war."

However, the general practice of belligerents during World Wars I and II was to treat the officers and crews of all captured enemy merchant vessels as prisoners of war. Article 4, paragraph A (5) of the 1949 Geneva Convention Relative to the Treatment of Prisoners of War states that among those persons falling into the power of an enemy who are entitled to prisoner of war status are:

> "Members of crews, including masters, pilots and apprentices, of the merchant marine and the crews of civil aircraft of the Parties to the Conflict, who do not benefit by more favorable treatment under any other provisions of international law."

The "more favorable treatment" would appear to be a reference to Article 6 of Hague Convention No. XI (1907), quoted above, but since the present validity of Article 6 is doubtful, it can be assumed that the crews of captured merchant vessels (not merely "merchant marine" vessels) may be treated as prisoners of war.

[39] If necessary, enemy nationals found on board captured enemy merchant vessels may be treated as prisoners of war. Normally, however, enemy nationals who are merely private individuals are placed under detention and subjected to the discipline of the captor. Enemy nationals in the public service of an enemy state may be made prisoners of war.

[40] Article 5 of Hague Convention No. XI (1907) states:

> "When an enemy merchant ship is captured by a belligerent, such of its crew as are nationals of a neutral state are not made prisoners of war. The same rule applies in the case of the captain and officers likewise nationals of a neutral State, if they promise formally in writing not to serve in an enemy ship while the war lasts."

[41] This paragraph is applicable as well to the officers and crews, nationals of a neutral state, of captured neutral merchant vessels and aircraft which have acquired enemy character and which are liable to the same treatment as enemy merchant vessels and aircraft, as described in paragraph 501b. Hence, a distinction must be made between the treatment accorded to neutral merchant vessels acquiring enemy character, and the treatment accorded to the personnel of such vessels. There is a clear exception, however, in the case of personnel of neutral vessels and aircraft which take a direct part in the hostilities on the side of an enemy or which serve in any way as a naval or military auxiliary for an enemy. (See paragraph 501a and Notes 6 and 31 above.)

[42] The removal of any of the categories of enemy nationals enumerated in this article may be exercised by a belligerent even though no sufficient reason exists for the capture of a neutral merchant vessel or aircraft.

CHAPTER 6

LEGAL RESTRICTIONS UPON WEAPONS AND METHODS EMPLOYED IN NAVAL WARFARE

600 SCOPE

This chapter describes the legal limitations governing the employment of weapons and methods in naval warfare. The basic principles which apply in determining the legality of any weapon or method are stated in Section 220.[2] The rules governing the capture and destruction of vessels and aircraft are stated in Article 503.

610 WEAPONS

The following articles examine the rules of international law governing mines and torpedoes; chemicals, gases, and bacteria; and nuclear weapons.

611 MINES AND TORPEDOES

The only restrictions laid down by a convention governing the belligerent employment of mines and torpedoes are laid down in the Hague Convention No. VIII (1907). Articles 1 through 3 of this Convention read as follows:

> Article 1. It is forbidden:
>
> 1. To lay unanchored automatic contact mines, except when they are so constructed as to become harmless one hour at most after the person who laid them ceases to control them;
>
> 2. To lay anchored automatic contact mines which do not become harmless as soon as they have broken loose from their moorings;
>
> 3. To use torpedoes which do not become harmless when they have missed their mark.
>
> Article 2. It is forbidden to lay automatic contact mines off the coast and ports of the enemy, with the sole object of intercepting commercial shipping.
>
> Article 3. When anchored automatic contact mines are employed, every possible precaution must be taken for the security of peaceful shipping.
>
> The belligerents undertake to do their utmost to render these mines harmless within a limited time, and, should they cease to be under surveillance, to notify the danger zones as soon as military exigencies permit, by a notice addressed to ship-owners, which must also be communicated to the Governments through the diplomatic channel.[3]

(Footnotes at end of chapter)

612 CHEMICALS, GASES, AND BACTERIA

a. CHEMICALS. Weapons of chemical types which are at times asphyxiating in nature, such as white phosphorus, smoke, and flame throwers, may be employed.[4]

b. GASES AND BACTERIA. The United States is not a party to any treaty now in force that prohibits or restricts the use in warfare of poisonous or asphyxiating gases or of bacteriological weapons.[5] Although the use of such weapons frequently has been condemned by states, including the United States,[6] it remains doubtful that, in the absence of a specific restriction established by treaty, a state legally is prohibited at present from resorting to their use.[7] However, it is clear that the use of poisonous gas or bacteriological weapons may be considered justified against an enemy who first resorts to the use of these weapons.[8]

613 NUCLEAR WEAPONS

There is at present no rule of international law expressly prohibiting states from the use of nuclear weapons in warfare. In the absence of express prohibition, the use of such weapons against enemy combatants and other military objectives is permitted.[9]

620 BOMBARDMENT

The term bombardment as used herein includes both aerial and naval bombardment. This section is not concerned with the legal limitations on land bombardment by land forces.

621 GENERAL LIMITATIONS ON BOMBARDMENT

a. DESTRUCTION OF CITIES. The wanton destruction of cities, towns, or villages, or any devastation not justified by military necessity, is prohibited.[10]

b. NONCOMBATANTS. Belligerents are forbidden to make noncombatants the target of direct attack in the form of bombardment, such bombardment being unrealted to a military objective.[11] However, the presence of noncombatants in the vicinity of military objectives does not render such objectives immune from bombardment for the reason that it is impossible to bombard them without causing indirect injury to the lives and property of noncombatants. In attempting to bombard a military objective, commanders are not responsible for incidental damage done to objects in the vicinity which are not military objectives.

c. TERRORIZATION. Bombardment for the sole purpose of terrorizing the civilian population is prohibited.

d. UNDEFENDED CITIES. Belligerents are forbidden to bombard a city or town that is undefended and that is open to immediate entry by own or allied forces.[12]

622 SPECIFIC LIMITATIONS ON BOMBARDMENT

a. MEDICAL ESTABLISHMENTS AND UNITS, fixed or mobile, and vehicles of wounded and sick or of medical equipment may not be bombarded or attacked; however, belligerents must ensure that such medical establishments and units are, as far as possible, situated in such a manner that attacks against military objectives cannot imperil their safety. The protection afforded ceases if such establishments or units are used to commit harmful acts outside their humanitarian duties and when, after due warning has been given that the performance of harmful acts will remove protection, such warning has remained unheeded. The distinctive emblem—red cross, or red crescent, or the red lion and sun, on a white background—must be hoisted over medical establishments and units entitled to protection.[13]

b. SPECIAL HOSPITAL ZONES established by agreement among the belligerents are immune from bombardment provided that the conditions under which they are required to operate are continually observed.[14]

c. PROTECTED BUILDINGS. Buildings devoted to religion or to art or to charitable purposes, historic monuments, and the like should, as far as possible, be spared from bombardment on condition that they are not used at the same time for military purposes and are properly located (not near a military objective). It is the duty of inhabitants to indicate such places by distinctive and visible signs. This may be done by large, stiff, rectangular panels divided diagonally into two triangular portions—the upper portion black, the lower portion white. There is however no requirement to observe these signs or any others indicating inviolability of buildings that are known to be used for military purposes.[15]

623 WARNING BEFORE BOMBARDMENT

Where a military situation permits, commanders should make every attempt to give prior warning of their intention to bombard a place so that the civilian population in close proximity will have an opportunity to seek safety.[16]

630 MEASURES OF MARITIME WARFARE AGAINST TRADE

This section deals with the three principal measures of maritime warfare against trade: the control and capture of contraband, the imposition of blockade, and the capture or destruction of enemy property found at sea.[17]

631 CONTRABAND

a. CHARACTER. Contraband consists of all goods which are destined for an enemy and which may be susceptible of use in war. Contraband goods are divided into two categories: absolute and conditional. Absolute contraband consists of goods which are used primarily for war (or goods whose very character makes them destined to be used in war). Conditional contraband consists of goods which are equally susceptible of use either for peaceful or for warlike purposes.[18]

b. BELLIGERENT CONTRABAND DECLARATIONS. Upon the initiation of armed conflict, belligerents may declare contraband lists, setting forth therein the classification of articles to be regarded as contraband as well as the distinction to be made between goods considered as absolute contraband and goods considered as conditional contraband. The precise nature of a belligerent's contraband list may vary according to the particular circumstances of the armed conflict.[19]

c. CARRIAGE OF CONTRABAND

(1) *Absolute Contraband.* Goods consisting of absolute contraband are liable to capture if their destination is the territory belonging to or occupied by an enemy, or the armed forces of an enemy. It is immaterial whether the carriage of such goods is direct, or involves transshipment, or transport overland.[20] In the case of absolute contraband a destination of territory belonging to or occupied by an enemy, or the armed forces of an enemy, is presumed to exist in the following circumstances: when the transporting vessel is to call at an enemy port before arriving at a neutral port for which the goods are documented; when goods are documented to a neutral port serving as a port of transit to an enemy, even though the goods are consigned to a neutral; and when goods are consigned "to order," or to an unnamed consignee, but destined to a neutral state in the vicinity of enemy territory.[21]

(2) *Conditional Contraband.* Goods consisting of conditional contraband are liable to capture if destined for the use of an enemy government or its armed forces. It is immaterial whether the carriage of such goods is direct, or involves transshipment, or transport overland.[22]

d. LIABILITY TO CAPTURE. Vessels and aircraft carrying goods liable to capture as absolute or conditional contraband may be captured (see subparagraph 503d (1).[23] However, liability to capture for carriage of contraband ceases once a vessel or aircraft has deposited the contraband goods.[24]

e. EXCEPTIONS TO CONTRABAND. The following goods are exempt from capture as contraband:

1. Free articles, i. e., goods not susceptible of use in war.[25]
2. Articles intended exclusively for the treatment of wounded and sick members of the armed forces, and for the prevention of disease. The particulars concerning the carriage of such articles must be transmitted to the adverse state and approved by it.
3. Articles provided for by a convention (treaty) [26] or by special arrangement as between the belligerents.

632 BLOCKADE [27]

a. DEFINITION. A blockade is a belligerent operation intended to prevent vessels of all states from entering or leaving specified coastal areas which are under the sovereignty, under the occupation, or under the control of an enemy. Such areas may include ports and harbors, the entire coastline, or parts of it.[28] International law does not prohibit the extension of a blockade by sea to include the air space above those portions of the high seas in which the blockading forces are operating.[29]

b. ESTABLISHMENT. In order to be binding a blockade must be established by the belligerent government concerned.[30] A blockade may be declared either by the government of the blockading state or by the commander of the blockading force acting on behalf of his government. The declaration should include the date the blockade begins, the geographical limits of the blockade, and the period granted neutral vessels and aircraft to leave the blockaded area.[31]

c. Notification. It is customary for the blockade to be notified in a suitable manner to the governments of all states. The commander of the blockading force usually makes notification to local authorities in the blockaded area.[32]

d. Effectiveness. A blockade, in order to be binding, must be effective. This means that a blockade must be maintained by a force sufficient to render ingress and egress to or from the blockaded area dangerous.[33]

e. Limits of blockade. A blockade must not bar access to or departure from neutral ports or coasts.[34]

f. Application of blockade. A blockade must be applied equally (impartially) to the vessels and aircraft of all states.[35]

g. Breach of blockade

(1) *Knowledge of the existence of a blockade* is essential to the offenses of breach of blockade and attempted breach of blockade; presumed knowledge is sufficient.[36]

(2) *Breach of blockade* is the passage of a vessel or aircraft through the blockade.

(3) *Attempted breach of blockade* occurs from the time a vessel or aircraft leaves a port or air take-off point with the intent of evading the blockade. It is immaterial that the vessel or aircraft is at the time of visit bound to a neutral port or airfield, if its ultimate destination is the blockaded area, or if the goods found in its cargo are to be transshipped through the blockaded area. There is a presumption of attempted breach of blockade where vessels and aircraft are bound to a neutral port or airfield serving as a point of transit to the blockaded area.[37]

(4) *Capture.* Vessels and aircraft are liable to capture for breach of blockade and attempted breach of blockade (see subparagraph 503d2). The liability of a blockade runner to capture begins and terminates with her voyage or flight. If a vessel or aircraft has succeeded in escaping from a blockaded area, liability to capture continues until the completion of the voyage or flight.[38]

h. Special privileges

1. Neutral warships and neutral military aircraft have no positive right of entry to a blockaded area. However, they may be allowed to enter or leave a blockaded area as a matter of courtesy. Permission to visit a blockaded area is subject to any conditions, such as the length of stay, that the senior officer of the blockading force may deem necessary and expedient.

2. Neutral vessels and aircraft in urgent distress may be permitted to

enter a blockaded area, and subsequently to leave it, under conditions prescribed by the commander to the blockading force.

633 ENEMY PROPERTY

a. Enemy character of goods. The character of goods found on board a merchant vessel or aircraft is enemy if the commercial domicile of the owner is in territory belonging to or occupied by an enemy belligerent.[39] All goods found on board enemy vessels or aircraft are presumed to be of enemy character in the absence of proof of their neutral character.

b. Enemy goods in transit. Notwithstanding any transfer of title to enemy goods already at sea, these goods retain their enemy character.

c. Capture of enemy goods. Goods possessing enemy character may be captured. However, enemy goods, contraband excepted, found in neutral vessels or aircraft, normally are not liable to capture.[40]

640 STRATAGEMS AND TREACHERY [41]

a. Stratagems, or ruses of war, are legally permitted.[42] In particular, according to custom it is permissible for a belligerent warship to use false colors and to disguise her outward appearance in other ways in order to deceive an enemy, provided that prior to going into action such warship shows her true colors.[43]

b. Acts of treachery, whether used to kill, wound, or otherwise obtain an advantage over an enemy, are legally forbidden.[44]

641 IMPROPER USE OF DISTINCTIVE EMBLEMS

The use of the red cross and other equivalent distinctive emblems must be limited to the indication and protection of hospital ships and other authorized medical craft, medical aircraft, medical units and establishments, and medical personnel and materials. It is forbidden to use ships, aircraft and establishments protected by the distinctive emblem of the red cross or other equivalent distinctive emblems, for any military purpose.[45]

NOTES FOR CHAPTER 6

[2] Unless restricted by customary or conventional international law, belligerents legally are permitted to use any means in conducting hostilities. Article 22 of the Regulations annexed to Hague Convention No. IV (1907), Respecting the Laws and Customs of War on Land, states: "The right of belligerents to adopt means of injuring the enemy is not unlimited." This article, which refers to weapons and methods of warfare, is merely an affirmation that the means of warfare are restricted by rules of conventional (treaty) and customary international law. Although immediately directed to the conduct of land warfare, the principle embodied in Article 22 of the Hague Regulations is applicable equally to the conduct of naval warfare.

Article 23 (e) of the Regulations annexed to Hague Convention No. IV (1907) forbids belligerents: "To employ arms, projectiles, or material calculated to cause unnecessary suffering." This provision is the application to weapons of the general rule, or principle, of humanity which prohibits the employment of any kind or degree of force not necessary for the purpose of the war, i. e., for the partial or complete submission of the enemy with the least possible expenditure of time, life, and physical resources (see paragraph 220b).

However, the rule forbidding the use of weapons calculated to cause unnecessary suffering does not extend to the use of explosives contained in projectiles, mines, rockets, hand grenades, and the like, where a military purpose is apparent and suffering, though unavoidable, is incidental to the purpose of the war. The rule does apply to the use of irregular-shaped bullets, the use of projectiles filled with glass, the use of any substance on bullets that would tend unnecessarily to inflame a wound inflicted by them, and to the scoring of the surface or the filing off of the ends of the hard cases of bullets.

Finally, the principle of humanity places limitations upon the possible use to which weapons, otherwise lawful, may be put. Any weapon may serve an unlawful purpose, e. g., if used to cause unnecessary suffering or devastation not justified by military necessity. Hence, a distinction must be drawn between the legality of a weapon, irrespective of its possible use, and the legal limitations placed upon the possible use of any weapon.

[3] The qualifications contained in Articles 2 and 3 of Hague Convention No. VIII (1907) were sufficient to create, from the very start, serious doubt as to whether the spirit of this Convention as an instrument for providing for the security of peaceful shipping would ever in practice be observed. The experiences of World Wars I and II served to confirm the validity of these doubts. Still further, it is questionable whether or not these provisions (which apply specifically to torpedoes and to automatic, and anchored automatic, contact mines) can be considered as applicable to the newer types of mines (magnetic and acoustic) or to the use of aircraft for mine laying.

[4] It is equally permissible to use weapons employing fire, such as tracer ammunition, flame throwers and other incendiary instruments and projectiles.

[5] The most important of these treaties is the Protocol "for the prohibition of the use in war of asphyxiating, poisonous, or other gases, and of bacteriological methods of warfare" signed at Geneva 17 June 1925, on behalf of the United States and many other states. Although ratified or adhered to by a considerable number of the signatories, and now effective between them, the 1925 Protocol of Geneva was never ratified by the United States. The operative provisions of the Protocol obligate the contracting states not to use in war "asphyxiating, poisonous or other gases, and . . . all analogous liquids, materials, or devices" and to extend this prohibition "to the use of bacteriological methods of warfare." Great Britain, France, the Soviet Union, and a number of other states signed subject to the reservations that the Protocol was to be binding only with respect to those states which ratified it and would cease to be binding with respect to those ratifying states which, in time of war, failed to respect the prohibitions contained in the Protocol. It should be noted that the 1925 Protocol of Geneva forbids only the *use in warfare* of gases and bacteria, not the manufacture of such weapons.

[6] The United States has never used bacteriological weapons and has not used poisonous gases since World War I. During World War II President Roosevelt made the following statement in response to reports that one or more of the Axis Powers "were seriously contemplating use of poisonous or noxious gases or other inhumane devices of warfare":

> "Use of such weapons has been outlawed by the general opinion of civilized mankind. This country has not used them, and I hope that we never will be compelled to use them. I state categorically that we shall under no circumstances resort to the use of such weapons unless they are first used by our enemies." *U. S. Naval War College, International Law Documents, 1942* (1943), p. 85.

[7] Despite the frequent condemnation by states of poisonous gases and bacteriological weapons and the equally frequent claim that the use of such weapons must of necessity violate the prohibition against using weapons calculated to cause unnecessary suffering (see Note 2 above) it is difficult to hold that the use of these weapons is prohibited to all states according to customary international law. At the same time, it does seem correct to emphasize that to the extent that these weapons are used either directly upon the noncombatant population or in such circumstances as to cause unnecessary suffering their employment must be considered as unlawful.

[8] See Notes 5 and 6 above. Poisonous gases and bacteriological weapons may be used only if and when authorized by the President.

[9] The employment, however, of nuclear weapons is subject to the basic principles stated in Section 220 and Article 221. Also, see Articles 621 and 622, as well as Note 2 above. Nuclear weapons may be used by United States forces only if and when directed by the President.

[10] The general limitations on bombardment enumerated in paragraphs 621a and d are applications to bombardment of the basic principle of humanity (see paragraph 220b).

[11] The general limitations on bombardment enumerated in subparagraphs 621b and c are applications to bombardment of the customary rule distinguishing between combatants and noncombatants (see Article 221).

[12] Articles 1 and 2 of Hague Convention No. IX (1907) Respecting Bombardment by Naval Forces in Time of War states:

> "Article 1. The bombardment by naval forces of undefended ports, towns, villages, dwellings, or buildings is forbidden.
>
> A place cannot be bombarded solely because automatic submarine contact mines are anchored off the harbor.
>
> Article 2. Military works, military or naval establishments, depots of arms or war materiel, workshops or plants which could be utilized for the needs of the hostile fleet or army, and the ships of war in the harbour, are not, however, included in this prohibition. The commander of a naval force may destroy them with artillery, after a summons followed by a reasonable time of waiting, if all other means are impossible, and when the local authorities have not themselves destroyed them within the time fixed.
>
> He incurs no responsibility for any unavoidable damage which may be caused by a bombardment under such circumstances.
>
> If for military reasons immediate action is necessary, and no delay can be allowed the enemy, it is understood that the prohibition to bombard the undefended town holds good, as in the case given in paragraph 1, and that the commander shall take all due measures in order that the town may suffer as little harm as possible."

The provisions of Article 2 of Hague Convention No. IX (1907) are obviously inapplicable where the "undefended" locality is open to immediate entry by own or allied forces.

> "An open town properly so-called is one which is so completely undefended that the enemy may enter and take possession. Such a town is exempted from lawful bombardment, for in these circumstances bombardment would be contrary to the fundamental principle forbidding destruction superfluous to military requirements. This rule does not apply to a town behind the front line, for it cannot properly be said to be either open or undefended, and the enemy, being unable to take possession of its military resources, must be allowed to attempt their destruction by bombardment from the air. Such bombardment is, however (apart from the question of reprisals), strictly limited to military objectives. Therefore, a town without military objectives would be exempt." R. Y. Jennings, "Open Towns," Vol. XXII, *British Yearbook of International Law* (1945), pp. 263-4.

[13] See Articles 19 and 21 of the 1949 Geneva Convention for the Amelioration of the Condition of the Wounded and Sick. Articles 42, 43, and 44 of this Convention deal with the distinctive emblem over medical establishments and units entitled to protection.

> "Article 19. Fixed establishments and mobile medical units of the Medical Service may in no circumstances be attacked, but shall at all times be respected and protected by the Parties to the conflict. Should they fall into the hands of the adverse Party, their personnel shall be free to pursue their duties, as long as the capturing Power has not itself ensured the necessary care of the wounded and sick found in such establishments and units.
>
> The responsible authorities shall ensure that the said medical establishments and units are, as far as possible, situated in such a manner that attacks against military objectives cannot imperil their safety.
>
> Article 21. The protection to which fixed establishments and mobile medical units of the Medical Service are entitled shall not cease unless they are used to commit, outside their

humanitarian duties, acts harmful to the enemy. Protection may, however, cease only after a due warning has been given, naming, in all appropriate cases, a reasonable time limit, and after such warning has remained unheeded."

[14] Article 23 of the 1949 Geneva Convention for the Amelioration of the Condition of the Wounded and Sick in Armed Forces in the Field provides for the establishment through agreement of the Parties concerned of hospital zones and localities. A similar provision, though extended to include so-called "safety zones," is included in Article 14 of the 1949 Geneva Convention Relative to the Protection of Civilian Persons in Time of War. In the annex to each of these conventions, draft agreements relating to the establishment of these zones are provided.

[15] Article 5 of Hague Convention No. IX (1907) Respecting Bombardment by Naval Forces in Time of War states:

"Article 5. In bombardments by naval forces all the necessary measures must be taken by the commander to spare as far as possible sacred edifices, buildings used for artistic, scientific, or charitable purposes, historic monuments, hospitals, and places where the sick or wounded are collected, on the understanding that they are not used at the same time for military purposes.

It is the duty of the inhabitants to indicate such monuments, edifices, or places by visible signs, which shall consist of large stiff rectangular panels divided diagonally into two coloured triangular portions, the upper portion black, the lower portion white."

[16] Article 6 of Hague Convention No. IX (1907) Respecting Bombardment by Naval Forces in Time of War states:

"Article VI. If the military situation permits, the commander of the attacking naval force, before commencing the bombardment, must do his utmost to warn the authorities."

Article 27 of the regulations annexed to Hague Convention No. IV (1907) Respecting the Laws and Customs of War on Land states:

"Article XXVI. The officer in command of an attacking force must, before commencing the bombardment, except in cases of assault, do all in his power to warn the authorities."

[17] The principal aim of maritime warfare against trade is to *shut off* the trade of an enemy; that is, to prevent all imports to or exports from enemy territory by sea or by air over the sea, without regard to whether this trade is carried in enemy or neutral vessels or aircraft.

[18] "There are, in the first place, articles which by their very character are destined to be used in war. In this class are to be reckoned, not only arms and ammunition, but also such articles of ambiguous use as military stores, naval stores, and the like. These are termed *absolute contraband*. There are, secondly, articles which, by their very character, are not necessarily destined to be used in war, but which, under certain circumstances and conditions, can be of the greatest use to a belligerent for the continuance of the war. To this class belong, for instance, provisions, coal, gold, and silver. These articles are termed *conditional* or *relative contraband* . . . although belligerents must be free to take into consideration the circumstances of the particular war, as long as the distinction between absolute and conditional contraband is upheld it ought not to be left altogether to their discretion to declare any articles they like to be absolute contraband. The test to be applied is whether, in the special circumstances of a particular war, or considering the development of the means used in making war, the article concerned is by its character destined to be made use of for military, naval, or air-fleet purposes. If not, it ought to be declared absolute contraband. However, it may well happen that an article which is not by its very nature destined to be made use of in war, acquires this character in a particular war and under particular circumstances; and in such case it may be declared absolute contraband. Thus, for instance, foodstuffs cannot, as a rule, be declared absolute contraband; but if the enemy, for the purpose of securing sufficient (foodstuffs) for his military forces, takes possession of all the foodstuffs in the country, and puts the whole population on rations, foodstuffs acquire the character essential to articles of absolute contraband, and can therefore be declared to be such." Oppenheim-Lauterpacht, *International Law*, Vol. II (7th ed., 1952), pp. 801-3.

According to the traditional law, the specific meaning attached to the concept of "hostile (or enemy) destination" depends upon the nature or character of goods carried. Indeed, the real significance of the distinction made between absolute and conditional contraband becomes apparent only upon considering the destination required of either category in order to justify belligerent capture. In the case of absolute contraband, capture is justified if the goods are destined to territory belonging to or occupied by an enemy, or the armed forces of an enemy. The nature of absolute contraband makes it highly probable that a belligerent will appropriate such goods as long as they are anywhere within his jurisdiction. In the case of conditional contraband, capture is justified if the goods are destined for the use of an enemy government or its armed forces. The ambiguous character of conditional contraband is resolved when it is established that such goods are directly intended for military use by an enemy. Finally, goods which are not susceptible of use in war, i. e., so called "free goods," are not liable to capture by a belligerent.

[19] In view of the practices of belligerents during World Wars I and II it is difficult to estimate the extent to which the distinctions forming the basis of the traditional law of contraband, discussed in paragraph 631a and Note 18 above, still may be considered as valid. The categories of goods which are not susceptible of use in war are now extremely limited. During World Wars I and II, the practice of the belligerents was to treat as conditional contraband almost all goods which were formerly regarded as free. In addition, and much more important, the distinction between absolute and conditional contraband, although formally adhered to by most of the belligerents, came to have little, if any, real significance. The extensive control exercised by belligerents over all imports did not allow, in practice, a clear distinction to be made between goods destined to an enemy government, or its armed forces, and goods destined to the civilian population. The principal result of this extensive control exercised by belligerents over all imports was to consider goods as absolute contraband which had formerly been considered only as conditional contraband. The test of enemy destination, formerly applied only to a restricted number of articles constituting absolute contraband, came to be applied to all goods susceptible of use in war. Thus, one writer summarizes this experience of World Wars I and II as follows:

> "The distinction between absolute and conditional contraband dates from the time when armies were small, so that levies . . . did not cause a reorientation of the belligerent's national life. Major wars of the present century are waged by nations in arms, with mobilized manpower and pooled and rationed resources. Imports are controlled from the moment they land, even when they are not licensed and controlled in advance; and no clear distinction between destination of goods to military and to the civilian elements is maintainable. That distinction may still be important in localized conflicts; but its general importance is likely to become increasingly merely a *point de depart* for the drafting of more efficient belligerent regulations. By 1941 the British Crown was arguing before the prize court that it was not obliged to issue lists at all, and that, in relation to a totalitarian enemy, the line between absolute and conditional contraband was in any case indistinguishable." Julius Stone, *Legal Controls of International Conflict* (1954), pp. 481–2.

It is in any event clear that a belligerent has the right to draft its contraband regulations in accordance with the particular circumstances in which an armed conflict is being conducted.

[20] " 'Continuous voyage' is where in order to obtain immunity during a part of its voyage to the enemy port, the vessel breaks its journey at a neutral intermediate port, the contraband being ostensibly destined there. At the neutral port, for appearance's sake it may unload and reload the same contraband cargo, but in any case it then proceeds with the cargo on the shortened span of its journey to the enemy port. The *doctrine* of continuous voyage prescribes that such a vessel and its cargo are to be deemed to have an enemy destination (and, therefore, to be liable to seizure) from the time she leaves her home port. Similarly, 'continuous transports' is where the guilty cargo is unloaded at the neutral port, and is then carried further to the enemy port or destination by another vessel or vehicle. The corresponding *doctrine* of continuous transports applies with similar effect, rendering the cargo liable to seizure from the

time it leaves its home port." Julius Stone, *Legal Controls of International Conflict* (1954), p. 486.

The principles underlying the so-called doctrines of "continuous voyage" and "continuous transport" were applied by prize courts in both World Wars I and II.

[21] The circumstances creating a presumption of ultimate enemy destination enumerated in subparagraphs 631c 1 and 2 are of concern to operating naval commanders for the reason that circumstances held to create a presumption of enemy destination constitute sufficient cause for capture. Before a prize court each of these presumptions is rebuttable and whether or not a prize court will, in fact, condemn the captured cargo, and vessel (or aircraft), will depend upon a number of complex considerations with which an operating naval commander need not be concerned.

[22] See Note 20 above.

[23] There are a number of methods available to belligerents for the control of contraband trade, in addition to the belligerent right to capture vessels and aircraft found carrying contraband. In World Wars I and II the two major techniques of contraband control, used principally by Great Britain, were "navicerting" and "rationing."

> "The term *navicert* (or *letters of assurance*) is applied to documents issued by officials of a belligerent state, indicating that the cargo of a vessel sailing from a neutral port corresponds to the manifest. Its purpose is to serve as a 'sort of commercial passport,' to facilitate the passage of the vessel and avoid the necessity of search of the cargo by the belligerent, but it does not convey any guaranty that the vessel and cargo will be free from seizure or interference." Hackworth, *Digest of International Law*, Vol. 7 (1943), p. 212.

> ". . . it is clear that *in its origin* a navicert is simply a facility which the belligerent is not in any way obliged to afford and the grant or refusal of which in any given case he cannot be legally obliged to justify. Since the absence of a navicert is not in itself a ground for seizure or condemnation, and only entails the exercise of a contraband control which the belligerent in any case has an absolute legal right to exercise, the grant or refusal of any certificate on the basis of which the belligerent is prepared to forego or modify his strict rights, must legally be within his absolute discretion." G. G. Fitzmaurice, "Some Aspects of Modern Contraband Control and the Law of Prize," *British Yearbook of International Law*, Vol. 22 (1945), p. 84.

In practice a vessel covered by a navicert, in the absence of later suspicious circumstances, was normally considered free from capture. The important feature of the navicert system was that cargo examination was conducted in port before a voyage started.

The technique of contraband control termed "rationing" has been explained as follows:

> "The idea underlying this process (i. e., rationing) expressed in a non-legal manner, is that it is only by limiting neutrals who have land communications with enemy territory to their own strict necessities in the matter of overseas imports that it is possible to ensure that no substantial proportion of these will reach the enemy. Failing that, however innocent many shipments may appear, or indeed be in themselves at the time, it is certain that some considerable part of them, or of goods processed or manufactured from them, will find its way to the enemy. Put in legal terms, the foundation of a rationing system is that, where a neutral country is found to be importing greater quantities of any commodity on the contraband list than can be accounted for by its reasonable domestic needs, having regard to all the circumstances, including manufacture for export to innocent destination, a presumption arises that the surplus is going to the enemy." G. G. Fitzmaurice, "Some Aspects of Modern Contraband Control and The Law of Prize," *British Yearbook of International Law*, Vol. XXII (1945), p. 89.

A system of rationing may either be the subject of an agreement between a neutral state and a belligerent, or may be imposed on a neutral by a belligerent. In practice, rationing systems have been instituted through agreement between neutral and belligerent. Rationing agreements usually fix the annual amount of each rationed commodity to be imported and the specific procedure to be followed for licensing the agreed shipments. Shipments of commodities to a neutral state in excess of a quota agreed on by neutral and belligerent, or imposed by a bellig-

399334—57——28

erent on a neutral, have been considered as creating the presumption of ultimate enemy destination and hence as justifying capture. However, before a British prize court this presumption may be rebutted. In neither World War were goods condemned by prize courts on "statistical evidence" alone.

[24] As an exception, British and American practices have allowed for the capture of a vessel which has already deposited contraband goods, if such goods were carried under simulated or false papers.

[25] See Notes 18 and 19 above.

[26] The provisions of the 1949 Geneva Convention Relative to the Protection of Civilian Persons in Time of War, Articles 23 and 59, cover the types of articles contemplated in this paragraph.

[27] Article 632 refers to blockade as a normal measure of naval warfare between belligerents. A blockade, in the sense of this article, should not be confused with a so-called "pacific blockade."

[28] The traditional rules governing the operation of blockade in naval warfare are, for the most part, customary in character. They received their definitive form during the nineteenth century. Although the general principle underlying the law of blockade has been defined as the right of a belligerent possessing effective command of the sea

> ". . . to deprive his opponent of the use thereof for the purpose either of navigation by his own vessels or of conveying on neutral vessels such goods as are destined to or originate from him." (Oppenheim-Lauterpacht, *International Law*, Vol. II (7th ed., 1952), pp. 796–7.)

the traditional rules governing the operation of blockade tended in fact to represent a compromise between the above-mentioned claim by belligerents and the desire of neutral states to suffer the least possible interference in their trade with both belligerent and neutral states. The result of these conflicting claims was a system of rules designed to effect only a limited interference with neutral trade. In practice, these rules were at once the product of, and intended to regulate, inshore ("close-in") blockades; that is blockades maintained by a line of vessels stationed in the immediate vicinity of the blockaded coast.

Recent developments in the weapons for waging warfare at sea have now rendered the inshore blockade exceedingly difficult and unlikely, save in exceptional circumstances (e. g., local or limited war). In addition, the increasing importance of measures directed against an enemy's economy has led to a strong emphasis by belligerents upon the complete abolition of an enemy's seaborne trade, an aim which normally is not furthered substantially by the establishment of blockades in strict conformity with the traditional rules. Hence, during World Wars I and II several of the major belligerents resorted to methods which, though frequently referred to as measures of blockade, could not easily be reconciled with the traditional rules governing blockade. In particular, the so-called "long distance" blockades of Germany by Great Britain departed in a number of respects from these traditional rules. The British Government chose to base the legality of these so-called "long distance" blockades upon the belligerent right of retaliation against illegitimate acts of warfare rather than upon the right to establish blockade.

[29] However, the practical difficulties of visit and search of aircraft suspected of breach of blockade (e. g., the absence of suitable landing places under belligerent control, etc.) may preclude such extension by analogy. See Chapter 5, Note 16, for application of U. S. prize law to aircraft. The commander of blockading forces should request instructions from higher authority regarding enforcement procedures to be followed in the case of a blockade extended to include the air space.

[30] A blockade also may be ordered by the Security Council of the United Nations pursuant to Article 42 of the Charter which states:

> "Should the Security Council consider that measures provided for in Article 41 would be inadequate, or have proved to be inadequate, it may take such action by air, sea or land forces as may be necessary to maintain or restore international peace and security. Such action

may include demonstrations, blockade, and other other operations by air, sea or land forces of members of the United Nations."

It is not possible to say whether, or to what extent, a United Nations blockade would be governed by the traditional rules.

[31] A blockade shall not be established by naval forces of the United States unless directed by the President. Although it is the customary practice of states when declaring a blockade to specify a period during which neutral vessels (and aircraft) may leave the blockaded area, there is no uniformity with respect to the length of the period of grace. A belligerent declaring a blockade is free to fix such a period of grace as it may consider to be reasonable under the circumstances.

[32] Because the requirement of knowledge of the existence of a blockade is an essential element of the offenses of breach of blockade and attempted breach of blockade (see paragraph 632g), neutral vessels (and aircraft) are always entitled to notification. However, the specific form such notification may take is not material.

[33] The customary requirement that a blockade must be effective in order to be binding is intended to prevent a so-called "paper blockade"; that is, a declaration of a blockade by a belligerent that does not possess the power necessary to render the blockade effective. Originally intended to apply to the relatively restricted areas covered by (close-in) blockades, the requirement of effectiveness remains applicable to blockading forces that may operate at considerable distances from an enemy's coasts. In particular, a belligerent cannot argue that the necessity of patrolling large areas excuses it from the requirement of effectively maintaining the blockade.

The requirement of effectiveness does not preclude the temporary absence of the blockading force, if such absence is due to stress of weather or to some reason connected with the blockade, e. g., the chase of a blockade runner. Furthermore, a blockade ceases to be effective, and hence ceases to be binding, if the blockading force is driven away by the enemy, or if the blockading force leaves the blockaded area for reasons other than those stated above.

There is no requirement that a blockade must prevent access to every portion of an enemy's coast in order to be effective. Nor need a blockade cover every possible approach to the ports of the blockaded coast.

> "'Effective,' in short, comes to mean sufficient to render capture *probable* under ordinary weather or other similar conditions. But even on this view, due no doubt to the fact that the lines of controversy were set before the rise of steampower, mines, or submarines, aircraft and wireless communication, at least one man-o-war must be present. Aircraft and submarines, however, as well as mines, concrete blocks, or other sunken obstacles may be used as auxiliary to blockading surface vessel or vessels. How many surface vessels, with what speed and armament, are necessary, along with auxiliary means, and how close they must operate for effectiveness in view of the nature of the approaches to the blockaded port, are questions of nautical expertise in each case." Julius Stone, *Legal Controls of International Conflict* (1954), p. 496.

[34] The rule that a blockade must not bar access to neutral ports and coasts should be interpreted to mean that a blockade must not prevent trade and communication to or from neutral ports or coasts, provided that such trade and communication is neither destined to nor originates from the blockaded area (see subparagraph 632g (3)). It is a moot point to what extent conventions providing for free navigation on international rivers or through international canals have been respected by blockading states. The practice of states in this matter is far from clear (see paragraph 412b).

[35] The requirement that a belligerent must apply a blockade impartially to the vessels and aircraft of all states is intended to prevent measures of discrimination by the blockading belligerent in favor of or against the vessels and aircraft of particular states, including its own or allied vessels and aircraft.

[36] A presumption of knowledge should be held to exist once a blockade has been declared and notified.

[37] See Note 21 above.

[38] See subparagraphs 502b2 and 3 for acts which when performed by a blockade runner render her liable to forcible measures.

[39] "Under the Anglo-American practice the word 'enemy' in this connection (i. e., as used to determine the character of goods or property) has a special meaning . . . It does not connote either enemy nationality or enemy sympathy. The test is commercial residence or 'domicile,' which means that all those must be treated as enemies who carry on their business in the enemy country or in territory under enemy control. The reason for the rule is that the enemy economy is enriched by all trade that is carried on in his territory, and every profitable transaction increases his resources for waging war. Here, as elsewhere, the basic principle is that power at sea may lawfully be used to prevent any commerce which may assist the enemy in carrying on the war." H. A. Smith, *The Law and Custom of the Sea* (2nd ed., 1950), p. 128.

Although the enemy character of goods depends upon the enemy character of their owners, there are no universally accepted rules by which the enemy character of individuals may be determined. British and American practice has been to regard the commercial domicile of the owner as the criterion for determining enemy character, but many states have considered the nationality of the owner, irrespective of resident, to be the proper test for determining enemy character.

[40] Article 2 of the Declaration of Paris, 1856, generally considered as expressive of a rule of customary law, states: "The neutral flag covers enemy goods with the exception of contraband of war."

This exception to the seizure of enemy goods becomes less significant in the light of recent developments in the law of contraband and the law of blockade (see Articles 631 through 633).

[41] The following provisions of the Regulations Respecting the Laws and Customs of War on Land, annexed to Hague Convention No. IV (1907), are considered equally applicable to the conduct of naval warfare.

"Article 23, para. b. In addition to the prohibitions provided by special conventions, it is especially forbidden to kill or wound treacherously individuals belonging to the hostile nation or army.

"Article 24. Ruses of war and the employment of measures necessary for obtaining information about the enemy and the country are considered permissible."

[42] Legally permissible ruses include, but are not limited to, the following: surprises, feigned attacks; ambushes, retreats, or flights; simulation of quiet and inactivity, use of small units to simulate large units; transmittal of false or misleading messages or deception of the enemy by false instructions; utilization of the enemy's signals; deliberate planting of false information; and use of dummy ships, aircraft, airfields, and other installations.

[43] "The ruse which is of most practical importance in naval warfare is the use of the false flag. It now seems to be fairly well established by the custom of the sea that a ship is justified in wearing false colors for the purpose of deceiving the enemy, provided that she goes into action under her true colors. The celebrated German cruiser *Emden* made use of this stratagem in 1914 when she entered the harbour of Penang under Japanese colors, hoisted her proper ensign, and then torpedoed a Russian cruiser lying at anchor. It is equally permissible for a warship to disguise her outward appearance in other ways and even to pose as a merchant ship, provided that she hoists the naval ensign before opening fire. Merchant vessels themselves are also at liberty to deceive enemy cruisers in this way." H. A. Smith, *The Law and Custom of the Sea* (2nd ed., 1950), p. 91.

On the other hand, the attitude and practices of belligerents during World Wars I and II appear to indicate that belligerent military aircraft are not considered as permitted, by analogy with warships, to use false markings in order to deceive an enemy.

[44] It is, for example, an act of treachery to make improper use of a flag of truce.

[45] See Articles 30, 34, 35, 41, and 45 of the 1949 Geneva Convention For the Amelioration of the Condition of the Wounded, Sick and Shipwrecked Members of Armed Forces at Sea.

INDEX

A

C

D

E

F

G

H

I

J

K

L

M

N

O

P

Q

R

S

U

V

W

Y

Z

O

www.ingramcontent.com/pod-product-compliance
Lightning Source LLC
LaVergne TN
LVHW062108200926
848484LV00007B/1618